MEASUREMENT AND EVALUATION IN PSYCHOLOGY AND EDUCATION

MEASUREMENT AND EVALUATION IN PSYCHOLOGY AND EDUCATION

Second Edition

ROBERT L. THORNDIKE
Professor of Education
Teachers College, Columbia University

ELIZABETH HAGEN
Associate Professor of Education
Teachers College, Columbia University

New York · London, John Wiley & Sons, Inc.

SECOND EDITION
Third Printing, November, 1962

Library of Congress Catalog Card Number: 61-11494
Printed in the United States of America

Preface

The reception that this book received in its first edition has been sufficiently favorable, and the comments that have come back to us have been sufficiently kind, that we have tried to make this revision an evolution rather than a revolution.

We have, of course, tried to make adequate reference to major new tests that have appeared in the last six years—*Form L-M* of the *Stanford-Binet, WAIS, STEP,* and others. We have also tried to make some reference to significant recent research, where it fits the pattern of an introductory text.

Beyond that, we have redone a number of sections from the first edition—sections with which we or our users had been less than completely happy. Thus, the section on validity has been rather completely restructured to represent our current thinking. A fuller exposition has been developed on planning and blueprinting a test. We have dealt more fully with the practical mechanics of a testing program. We have reorganized and added to the material on aptitude-test batteries.

In two instances, we have changed the order of chapters into a sequence that seems to us more teachable. However, whenever information is presented in sequence, one feels the need for what is to come later while one is discussing what has come before. Some who have used the book in classes have told us that they teach the chapters in various sequences different from that which appears in the book, and, fortunately, this seems to lead to no insuperable problems.

We continue in the basic belief that it is as important for students to learn what tests will *not* do as to learn what they *will* do; as important to examine their own purposes and objectives for testing as to examine the tests. It is in the hope of developing more restrained, discriminating, and insightful testers that we offer this book to our colleagues and students.

ROBERT L. THORNDIKE
ELIZABETH HAGEN

New York, N. Y.
  April, 1961

Contents

Chapter 1

▼

Historical and Philosophical Orientation

HISTORICAL BACKGROUND

The roots of the measurement of man lie in antiquity. We must believe that even in prehistoric times Og, the cave man, made rudimentary appraisals of his fellows. He saw Zog go by, made some such judgment as "Big, strong, keep out of way," and acted upon it; or he came upon the campfire of Wog, observed "Small, weak, take dinner," and did so forthwith. But for much of recorded history, the appraisals that man has made of his fellows have been of this crude subjective type.

He who seeks imaginatively can find suggestions of more systematic and refined methods. Thus, the tournaments of the days of chivalry can be thought of as an effort to arrange men in an order from best to worst in feats of arms, and contests leading to the crowning of "champions" have always constituted a rough sort of measurement. Teachers have always catechized their pupils to appraise their degree of mastery of the tasks assigned them, evaluating them as best they could by their responses. But these approaches were more primitive than the sun dial and the ox cart. They are characteristic of the appraisal of man and his behavior up to the present century. Application of the quantitative methods of science to psychology and education is very new. In 1850 there was almost none of it; 1900 was still a pioneering period.

EARLY EDUCATIONAL TESTING

The appraisal of educational achievement in the United States before 1850 had relied very largely upon oral examination. The teacher or visiting examiner asked a question. The designated pupil undertook to answer it. The questioner arrived at an immediate subjective evaluation of the answer. There was uniformity neither in the questions asked different pupils nor in the evaluation of their replies. The method was burdensome and inefficient, since only one pupil could be tested at a time. It provided no comparability from pupil to pupil either in the task or in the evaluation of it.

During the latter half of the nineteenth century, oral examinations by boards of visitors were replaced by set written examinations as a basis for promotion or admission to an academy or college. Outside examination in turn yielded to evaluation by the classroom teacher. Whether carried out by an outside examiner or by a teacher, however, the technique was that of the essay examination, in which a pupil responded in his own words to a question set by the examiner.

The written examination had advantages over the oral examination of (1) presenting the same tasks to each member of the group and (2) letting each pupil work for the full examination period. However, though the task was made uniform, at least for the members of a given class, appraisal of each individual's response to the task remained highly subjective, depending upon the standards and prejudices of the particular scorer. As we shall see in Chapter 3, great variations were found in the *scoring* of a particular paper. Only since 1900 has there been any general development of objectively scored tests in which a pre-established key can be routinely and uniformly applied to the responses made by each pupil. Only since 1900 has the idea emerged of a general standard of performance for an age or grade, with which the performance by any class or any individual may be compared.

THE BEGINNINGS OF PSYCHOLOGICAL MEASUREMENT

Psychology in 1850 was still in large measure a part of philosophy. Courses dealing with man and his actions were presented under the title "Moral Philosophy," and discussed in an armchair fashion the nature of the Mind and the Soul. Psychology was almost entirely non-experimental, and the idea that one could measure in quantitative terms the speed of responding, the amount of forgetting, or the level of intelligence would have been received in most quarters with hostility or, more probably, ignored as not worthy of rebuttal. The nearest approaches to psychological measurement were a few scattered experiments by physicists and physiologists on the measurement of the ability to make sensory discriminations and the speed of simple elementary responses.

By 1900 psychology had felt the impact of the physical and biological sciences and was striving mightily to become a science itself. It was shaking off the ties that bound it to philosophy and forming new alliances with the biological sciences. It had adopted the experimental method and was measurement-conscious. The basic tool of experimentation is measurement, and psychology was expanding its measurement techniques in all directions. The record since 1900 is the record of the attempt to expand and adapt measurement techniques to cover all aspects of human behavior.

Three main streams combined to yield the vigorous measurement movement in psychology and its spread through education. Some of the flavor and some of the emphasis have come from each stream. These were (1) the physiological and experimental psychology that had its main growth in Germany in the nineteenth century, (2) Darwinian biology, and (3) the clinical concern for the maladjusted and underdeveloped individual.

BEGINNINGS OF EXPERIMENTAL PSYCHOLOGY

The modern scientific era was first ushered into the physical sciences in the seventeenth and eighteenth centuries. Scientific interest and method soon spread over to the biological sciences, and by the early nineteenth century experimental physiology was a center of active research interest in the experimental laboratories in Germany and other European countries. Experimental physiologists became interested in the operation of the senses, studying intensively seeing, hearing, and the other senses. Physiologists also became interested in measuring the speed of simple motor responses.

In 1879 the first laboratory for experimental psychology was established by Wilhelm Wundt at Leipzig. Early experimental psychologists were interested in many of the same measurements that had concerned the physiologists. These were measures of seeing, hearing, feeling, and speed of response. But gradually they extended their concern to more clearly psychological matters, such as measurement of perceptual span—the amount that the individual can "take in" at once, of rate of learning, of the timing of complex mental tasks, and so forth.

One area of particular interest for its contribution to the broad field of psychological and educational measurement was that known as *psychophysics*. The experimental psychologist was much interested in exploring the relationship between physical stimulus intensities, e.g., of light wave or of sound wave, and the experienced intensity of the resulting sensation. The designing of effective experimental procedures for studying these problems gave rise to a set of techniques that have proved adaptable to a wide range of problems of psychological measurement.

From experimental psychology came a legacy of respect for careful experimental method and precision of technique, a number of experimental designs, and statistical techniques that could be carried over to more general psychological and educational measurement problems.

EARLY STUDY OF INDIVIDUAL DIFFERENCES

A second stream contributing to psychological measurement was Darwinian biology. In 1859 Darwin brought out his *Origin of Species*. The basic concern in Darwin's work was with variation among the members of a species, that is, individual differences. Darwin's work was followed up in England and applied to distinctively human affairs, particularly by Sir Francis Galton. Whereas German psychology had focused on finding the general facts true of all people, Galton became interested primarily in the differences among people. Stimulated by Darwin to study the inheritance of traits, he gathered data both on physical and on psychological characteristics. The study of these individual differences required better statistical tools, and the British group, under the leadership of Karl Pearson, developed improved techniques for analyzing and describing the patterns of individual differences.

These, then, were the two main contributions of the British group to the growth of psychological measurement: a deep concern for studying the differences among people as interesting and significant facts and appropriate statistical techniques and tools for carrying out this study.

CLINICAL STUDY OF DEVIATES

During this same period, a third stream was gathering strength. This was concern for the individual who was not functioning successfully. Humanitarian concern for the insane, the feeble-minded, and the general misfit led in the nineteenth century to active research and investigation aimed toward understanding their condition and improving their lot. This clinical interest in the maladjusted individual was particularly strong in France, and it was here that it bore fruit for the field of measurement. As psychologists worked with these unfortunate deviates, the need became more and more apparent for some uniform way of expressing the degree of their defect, particularly in the mental sphere. It was in this context of concern for the child who was not getting along in school that Binet and his colleagues developed the series of intellectual tasks that ultimately grew into the whole array of measures of intelligence.

SYNTHESIS IN THE UNITED STATES

By the early years of the present century, all these streams of influence had made themselves felt in the United States. James McKeen Cattell had taken his graduate work in psychology in Germany with Wundt, where he had received a good grounding in quantitative and experimental psychology. But he had also been exposed to the work of Galton and had developed a lasting interest in individual differences and statistical method. When he returned to the United States, he began an investigation of individual differences in the simple sensory and motor performances that were being measured in German psychological laboratories. He studied the relationship between these performances and academic success.

E. L. Thorndike was a student of Cattell's just before the turn of the century and became a focal influence in the spread and development of standardized educational tests. Both his own work and that of a large group of students rapidly spread the gospel of objective measurement in education.

The work of Binet was eagerly seized upon in this country. His tests were translated and produced in several versions, of which by far the most influential became the *Stanford-Binet* first produced by Lewis Terman in 1916. The testing movement seemed especially suited to the temper of this country and took hold here with a vigor and enthusiasm unequaled elsewhere.

MEASUREMENT IN THE TWENTIETH CENTURY

The first 60 years of the twentieth century may conveniently be divided into four equal parts, so far as the recent history of psychological and educational measurement is concerned. We may designate the period from 1900 to 1915 the pioneering phase. This was the period of exploration and initial development of methods. It saw the emergence of the first Binet intelligence scales and their American revisions. Standardized achievement tests in different subjects began to appear, exemplified by Stone's arithmetic tests, Buckingham's spelling tests, and Trabue's language tests. Thorndike developed his first handwriting scale. Otis and others were initiating work on group tests of intelligence.

The next 15 years, 1915 to 1930, can perhaps be called the "boom" period in test development. The pioneers had shown the way, and in the hands of enthusiastic followers tests multiplied like rabbits. Standardized tests were developed for all the school skills and for the content areas of the school program. Achievement batteries made their appearance. Starting with *Army Alpha* of World War I, group intelligence tests were produced in great numbers. Also starting with a wartime product, the *Woodworth Personal Data Sheet,* a whole line of personality questionnaires and inventories came into being.

The rapid development of testing instruments and methods was pushed by a group of enthusiasts. They were converts who had "gotten the word." Their enthusiasm was contagious and extended not only to the production of tests but also to their use. Tests of intelligence and achievement were administered widely and somewhat indiscriminately. Test results were often accepted unhesitatingly and uncritically and served as the basis for a variety of unjustified judgments and actions with respect to individuals. In the expansive flood of enthusiasm for objective measurement, some enthusiasts were not inclined to be critical of their instruments or the interpretation of results from them. Many sins were committed in the name of measurement by uncritical test users.

After a while the pendulum began to swing back. More and more sharply voiced criticisms of tests and of the uses made of tests began to be heard. Heredity-environment discussions became acrimonious. The use of test scores as a basis for classroom grouping became the subject of bitter attack. Criticism was directed at specific tests in terms of their limited scope and their emphasis upon restricted and traditional objectives. It was also directed at the whole underlying philosophy of quantification and the use of numbers to express psychological qualities.

The critical attack had the healthy effect of forcing the test enthusiasts themselves to become more critical of their assumptions and procedures and to broaden their approach to the whole problem of psychological and educational appraisal. From about 1930 to 1945 may be considered a period of critical appraisal, of taking stock, of broadening techniques and delimiting interpretations. It was a period in which the center of attention shifted from "measuring" a limited range of academic skills to "evaluating" achievement of the whole range of educational objectives. It was a period in which the holistic, global projective methods of personality appraisal came to the fore.

It is difficult to view with any perspective at all events that have taken place within the last 15 years. History may eventually characterize the period quite differently than do we, standing so close to it. However, we will venture to predict that the period from 1945 to 1960 will be characterized as the period of test batteries and testing programs. Partly as a result of their successful use in World War II, integrated aptitude batteries for educational and personnel use have multiplied during this period. And the large-scale testing programs, such as those administered by the College Entrance Examination Board, though stemming from much earlier in the century, have expanded in size and multiplied in numbers at a striking rate. We have experienced a second boom period—not so much in test development and construction, as in test administration and use. The mid-twentieth century is a period in which standardized testing is a widely experienced and widely accepted phenomenon of our American culture.

Under these circumstances it is particularly important that construction, use, and interpretation of these instruments be well understood by teachers, guidance workers, and psychologists for whom they are daily tools of the trade. It is also important that the phenomenon of standardized testing be understood by the citizens who are exposed to it in their search for employment for themselves or education for their children. Therefore, let us try at this point to formulate a philosophy of measurement that will take into account the lessons of the last 60 years, and will serve to guide our attack on measurement problems and our use of measurement techniques in the years ahead.

PHILOSOPHICAL ORIENTATION

In education and in psychology we are concerned with human beings. Sometimes we are concerned with them as specific individuals, as when we want to know why Mary is having so much difficulty in learning to do long division. Sometimes we are concerned with them as specific groups of individuals, as when we inquire whether the children in class A can read as well as those in class B. Sometimes we are concerned with them as general representatives of mankind, as when we try to determine whether children with high verbal intelligence tend to show more or less signs of emotional disturbance than children of average intellectual ability.

KNOWLEDGE AS A GUIDE TO ACTION

In practically all of education and in much of psychology, our concern about individuals is to *do* something about them, individually or collectively. In so far as education is a science, it is an applied science, and in psychology, too, the applied aspects bulk large in the present scene. The educator or the practical psychologist is continually faced with the necessity of arriving at some decision as to a course of action. He must decide what to do about an individual or individuals, or he must help the person himself decide what to do. He must decide in which grade to place a child or what special instruction to provide for him. He must reach a diagnosis of a child with a reading disability, with a view to recommending treatment. He must recommend whether or not to employ a job applicant. He must help a student decide whether to plan for college and, if so, what sort of program to take and what type of job to aim for. The educator or psychologist wants each one of these decisions to be a sound and well-conceived one.

Our basic assumption is that *sound decisions arise out of relevant knowledge* of the individual or individuals. We assume that the more we know about a person that relates to our present decision, and the more accurately we know it, the more likely we are to arrive at a sound decision about him or a wise plan of action for him. By the same token, we assume that the more relevant and accurate information we can provide the individual about himself, the more likely he is to arrive at a sound decision on his own problem. It may be necessary for us to qualify this assumption as we proceed. There may be limits on the amount and kind of information that can be used in a particular situation. We shall indicate that knowledge in and of itself is not wisdom. But in its general form the assumption is basic not only to educational and psychological measurement but also to all science. We assume basically that knowledge is good, that knowledge is power, that knowledge is the basis for effective control of the problems that confront us from day to day. This is a basic tenet of our faith.

What does it mean to "know an individual"? Fundamentally, to know an individual means to be able to describe him accurately and fully. If we know John Jones well, we can describe not only how he looks—how tall he is and how heavy, the color of his hair and eyes, the birthmark under his chin. Much more importantly, we can describe what he can and will do—how he will dress, what he is likely to talk about, what he will be interested in, what types of tasks he can do and how well he can do them, how he will respond to the different stresses and strains of life. To know a person completely means to be able to describe him completely, to predict how he will behave in every possible situation. Obviously, we are far, far away from this objective, and we always will be. The function of educational and psychological measurement is to move us a little closer to it.

IMPORTANCE OF MEASURING THE RIGHT THING

The effectiveness of our description of any object or person depends upon two things. It depends (1) upon how wisely we have chosen the features to be described and (2) upon how truly and accurately we have managed to describe each one.

A description may fail to be useful for the need at hand because we choose irrelevant features to describe. Thus, in describing a painting we might report its height, its breadth, and its weight. We might report these with great precision. If our concern were to crate the picture for shipment, these might be just the items of information we would need. On the other hand, if our purpose was that of characterizing the painting as a work of art, our description would be worthless. The attributes of the picture we had described would be essentially irrelevant to its quality as a work of art.

Similarly, a description of a person may be of little value for our purposes if we choose the wrong things to describe. Thus, the Air Force in selecting pilots to fly jet fighters might get very accurate information on height, weight, years of education, size of vocabulary, and speed of reading for all its applicants. It would almost surely find, however, that none of these things helped at all in selecting the men who could successfully learn to fly the planes. Such factors as these are in large measure irrelevant to flying success, which appears to depend more on mechanical know-how and on motor coordination.

Again, a high school concerned about assessing the level of literary appreciation in its pupils might prepare a test inquiring exhaustively into the names of the characters and the details of the plot of Shakespeare's *Julius Caesar*. The worthlessness of this procedure may be less obvious, but is probably just as real as that proposed for the selection of pilots. This test seems useless for the task at hand, because detailed factual knowledge about an isolated literary work is no indicator of the quality of a pupil's literary appreciation. The test has asked the wrong kinds of questions. The evidence it provides is related to a faulty interpretation of the original question that was asked.

The first, and perhaps the most important, step in any project for educational or psychological measurement is defining just what it is that we wish to measure and determining what operations will serve to measure it. Educational objectives are likely to be incompletely formulated and expressed in vague terms. The concepts must be clarified and made more specific before we can make much progress toward sensible procedures of measurement. Until we can decide what is meant by "good citizenship" or what behaviors are exhibited by a person who shows "understanding of scientific method," we have little prospect of developing procedures to appraise either the one or the other.

THE NEED FOR PRECISION

Our description may be of limited value in the second place because the attributes we elect to describe are described inaccurately. Thus, if our description of the painting were expressed in terms of theme, composition, line and volume, and color values, it would certainly be a good deal more to the point as an appraisal of a work of art. But it would be much more wordy, more subjective, and less precise than our previous description of length, breadth, and weight. Different persons could be expected to differ markedly in the qualities they saw and the terms they used to describe them. This might be true to such an extent that a single individual's description would give us only a very rough, unclear, and undependable impression of the picture as a work of art.

As for the candidate for pilot training, we might get ratings from his friends on his speed of learning new coordinations, ability to pay attention to many things at once, and resistance to disturbance by emotional stress. We may hazard a guess that these ratings would again prove ineffective in predicting pilot success—not so much because the qualities themselves are unimportant, but because we are not skillful in observing such qualities in our fellows or in expressing our observations in exact quantitative form.

Our high school, concerned with literary appreciation, might ask each pupil to write a report on some book he had read recently, telling what he had liked about it, and why he had or had not thought it was a good book. Again, we may feel that such a report would provide information more related to appreciation than would a test of factual knowledge. But judging the quality of appreciation shown in a varied collection of compositions about an assortment of different books would be a very subjective enterprise, and the judgments would tend to be quite undependable. Each judge would have his own personal standards of what constituted good literary appreciation. He would make his judgments in terms of those personal standards. There would be little agreement from one judge to the next as to who had shown good appreciation and who had shown poor. Our appraisal would be unsatisfactory because it would be inaccurate.

DEGREES OF REFINEMENT IN MEASURING

There is enormous variation from one trait to another in the degree of refinement we have been able to achieve in describing it. At the crudest level, our appraisal may come to no more than a simple two-way classification. This may take the form present—absent: e.g.,

John lisps but Bill does not lisp; or the form trait—opposite: e.g., John runs fast but Bill runs slowly.

A somewhat more refined level of description is achieved when we characterize the trait by a set of adjectives which represent degrees of the trait: e.g., John runs fast, Joe goes like a streak, Jack runs fairly fast, Will goes like molasses in January. But the number of such qualitative descriptions is limited, and the meaning of such adjectives or similes is far from uniform from person to person.

A still further level of refinement in description is reached when we can arrange the members of a group in rank order with respect to an attribute and when we can locate any individual on such a rank order. Thus, we may say Joe runs the fastest, John runs faster than Jack, Jack runs faster than Will, and Will runs the slowest. Such a procedure of ranking could theoretically be extended to include all the children in a class, in a school, or even all the children in the whole country. Clearly, when we can appraise a trait well enough to produce such a ranking, a very great increase in the adequacy of our description has been achieved.

Finally, some attributes may be expressed in a quantitative statement of amount. Thus, we may be able to report that Joe ran 100 yards in 10 seconds, John in 14 seconds, Jack in 15 seconds, and Will in 17 seconds. This last is clearly the most precise type of statement of the essential facts and the one that makes us best able to decide upon appropriate action with regard to an individual, so far as that action depends upon speed of running 100 yards. It is certainly the type that the track coach would want to have before deciding whom to keep on the track team.

We have identified four points along a scale of quantification and precision of measurement.

1. *Either—Or.* A pupil is either a boy or a girl. A man is single, married, widowed, or divorced. A student is enrolled in the college preparatory, commercial, or general curriculum.

2. *Qualitatively Described Degrees.* Thus, a pupil may show "normal speech," "slight stuttering," "stammer," "marked stutter." Or the pupils in a class may be characterized as "quiet and relaxed," "slightly fidgety," or "tense and restless."

3. *Rank in a Group.* Thus, a series of graded tasks scored by uniform standards enables us to find who does best and who does worst on reading comprehension, arithmetic problems, or spelling. The rest of the group can be arranged in order from best to worst.

4. Amount, Expressed in Uniform Established Units. A boy weighs 56 pounds, is 45 inches tall, is 6½ years old.

This wide variation in the refinement of our appraisals must be frankly admitted. Some traits we may never be able to express more accurately than by a "very" and "not very" characterization. Our failure to have achieved greater refinement in measuring these traits is probably partly due to lack of clarity and sharpness in definition of the attribute that we propose to describe. When we characterize a person as sincere, cultured, socially adjusted, cooperative, a good citizen, our hearer may have only a very general idea of what we mean. (And, as a matter of fact, so may we.) In part our failure is certainly due to the limited ingenuity and skill we have shown to date in finding ways to represent degree or amount of the attribute with precision. It *may* sometimes be partly due to the essential nature of a particular attribute, which makes it fundamentally not expressible in quantitative form. There *may* be some things that, in their very nature, can never be quantified.

Certainly, our present ability truly to *measure* many of the attributes of persons that appear to be relevant and important for making decisions about them and planning actions with respect to them leaves much to be desired. However, while recognizing this fact we must also appreciate that enormous strides have been made since 1900 toward more objective and more accurate appraisals of human beings. The fact that we are limited in some directions does not lessen the value of increased precision wherever such increased precision has been achieved. While keeping a critical eye upon the limitations of measurement procedures, we should still use them for all they are worth in increasing the accuracy of our information about students, employees, or clients.

CRITICISMS OF PSYCHOLOGICAL AND EDUCATIONAL MEASUREMENT

Since about 1930, psychological and, particularly, educational measurement have come in for a good deal of criticism. The educational philosophers have been especially outspoken in expressing their dissatisfaction. In part, the criticisms have been directed at the basic logic of psychological measurement. These criticisms have been directed at the limitations we have just been discussing, as well as at some other problems concerning the equivalence of units and scores, which we shall consider briefly in a later chapter. In part, however, the criticisms have been directed at the effects that the measurement procedures have had upon school practice. The following types of criticisms have been made:

1. Standardized measurement procedures have been said to foster undemocratic practices and attitudes in the classroom. Forming homogeneous class groups on the basis of an intelligence or achievement test is a specific practice that has been the target of this criticism.

2. It has been contended that standardized tests have had the effect of freezing the curriculum and of preventing experiment and change, on the grounds that the commercial standardized test typically lagged behind the advance of educational thought and practice.

3. The limited scope of many standardized tests has been pointed out, and it has been indicated that they fail to appraise many of the changes in children that schools should be interested in producing.

4. The short-answer test items have been accused of producing undesirable study habits directed toward piecemeal memorization rather than understanding.

There has been at least a germ of truth in all these criticisms. Some of them we shall consider in more detail in later chapters. As the criticisms are examined, however, we find that they are not primarily criticisms of obtaining more information about the individual. They are criticisms either of (a) the incompleteness and imperfection of the information yielded by our measurement procedures or (b) the unwise things that we do with that information. It is as though we condemned the physicist because (a) he cannot yet control the weather, and (b) his knowledge has led to the construction of atom bombs which may destroy mankind. We must grant that our measurement procedures are not complete and our actions based on them are not always wise. But the remedy lies in developing better measurement procedures that will give us more complete and more accurate information about the individual. It lies in gaining better understanding of our measures—their strengths and their weaknesses—so that we may use them with more wisdom. It does *not* lie in getting less information.

It cannot be too much emphasized that measurement at best provides only information, not judgment. A test will yield only a score, not the conclusion to be drawn from that score. The information provided in a test score is not a substitute for insight. This information is the raw material with which insight must work, in the clinic, in the classroom, and in the research laboratory. Experience, training, and basic sagacity must provide the insight that will take a set of data about an individual or group, know how much faith to place in them and what meaning to give them, and draw from them a sound conclusion or plan for action.

Furthermore, it should be emphasized that the information that *any* measurement procedure gives is limited. It is limited by the nature of the measurement instrument itself. The typical intelligence test, for example, samples certain types of performances with abstract ideas expressed in symbolic form. It is not a measure of the general worth of the individual, of his ability to acquire mechanical skills or artistic techniques, or of his integrity and dependability as a member of society. The information is limited by the conditions under which the procedure is applied. Thus, an intelligence test given to an emotionally disturbed and resistant child may give a very inadequate picture of what that same child could do if the disturbing influences were removed and the resistance overcome. Learning to use measurement results wisely is in part learning what information a particular device does and does not provide and in part learning under what circumstances that information is likely to be trustworthy. Throughout this book there will be recurring attempts to guide that learning.

SUMMARY STATEMENT

We can summarize much of the foregoing discussion on a working philosophy of measurement in the following four points.

1. The process of measurement is secondary to that of defining objectives. The ends to be achieved must first be formulated clearly. Then measurement procedures can be sought as tools for appraising the extent to which those ends have been achieved.

2. Much of educational and psychological measurement is, and will probably remain, at a relatively low level of precision. We must recognize this fact, using the best procedures available to us, but always treating the resulting score as a tentative hypothesis rather than as an established conclusion.

3. The more elegant procedures of formal test and measurement must be supplemented by the cruder procedures of informal observation, anecdotal description, and rating if we are to obtain a description of the individual that is usefully complete and comprehensive.

4. No amount of ingenuity in developing improved procedures for measuring and appraising the individual will ever eliminate the need to *interpret* the results from those procedures. Measurement procedures are only tools. Insight and skill are required in the use of such

tools. The sharper and more varied the tools, the more skill it takes
to use them most effectively.

SUGGESTED ADDITIONAL READING

Boring, Edwin G., H. S. Langfeld, and H. P. Weld, *Foundations of psychology,* New York, Wiley, 1948, Chapter 18.

Cottle, William C. and N. M. Downie, *Procedures and preparation for counseling,* Englewood Cliffs, N. J., Prentice-Hall, 1960, pp. 158–162; 165–167; 174–175; 180–183.

Goodenough, Florence L., *Mental testing,* New York, Rinehart, 1949, pp. 3–96.

Harris, Chester W., Editor, *Encyclopedia of educational research,* 3rd ed., New York, Macmillan, 1960, pp. 807–816; 1502–1503.

Lorge, Irving, The fundamental nature of measurement, Chapter 14 in E. F. Lindquist, Editor, *Educational measurement,* Washington, D. C., American Council on Education, 1951.

Murphy, G., *An historical introduction to modern psychology,* rev. ed., New York, Harcourt, Brace, 1949, Chapters 6, 8, 11, 24, and 26.

Nunnaly, Jum C., *Tests and measurements,* New York, McGraw-Hill, 1959, Chapters 1 and 2.

Seward, Georgene S., and John P. Seward, *Current psychological issues,* New York, Holt, 1958, Chapter 11.

Wrightstone, J. Wayne, et al., Educational measurements, *Rev. educ. Res.,* **26,** 1956, 268–291.

Wrightstone, J. Wayne, Joseph Justman, and Irving Robbins, *Evaluation in modern education,* New York, American Book, 1956, Chapter 1.

QUESTIONS FOR DISCUSSION

1. The development of objective and standardized tests has proceeded faster and further in the United States than in any other country. What factors do you see as contributing to this?

2. Try to talk to a student from some foreign country and find out what examinations are like and how they are used in his country. What differences do you find, as compared with the United States? What are the advantages and disadvantages of each system?

3. In many graduate schools oral examinations are still used in examining candidates for higher degrees. What are the advantages and disadvantages of this type of examination?

4. From your reading or from your personal experience, give one or more concrete examples of the *misuse* or *misinterpretation* of the results from standardized tests.

5. How universally acceptable is the statement "knowledge is good" in the field of education and applied psychology? What objections would you have to this statement, or what limitations would you place upon it?

6. Give an illustration of a measuring procedure in education or psychology that would be of little or no value because it was not sufficiently precise; one that would be of no value because it was measuring the wrong thing.

7. Give two examples of educational or psychological measures to represent each of the following four points along the scale of quantification and precision of measurement: (a) either—or, (b) qualitatively described degrees, (c) rank in a group, (d) amount, expressed in uniform, established units.

8. Your textbook states that "to know an individual means to be able to describe him accurately and fully." What would be central in such a description for

a. A fourth-grade girl having difficulty with arithmetic.
b. An eighth-grade boy who has been picked up for throwing rocks through the school windows.
c. A recent high-school graduate who is being considered for a job as receptionist.

Chapter 2

▼

Overview of Measurement Methods

During the present century techniques for appraising the individual have been developed in great variety, and they have been applied to many aspects of his abilities and personality. Specific techniques will be discussed in detail in later chapters. The present chapter is devoted to a general overview, mapping out some of the main landmarks of the whole domain.

APPRAISAL BY TESTS VERSUS APPRAISAL BY OBSERVATION IN NATURAL SITUATIONS

Attempts to appraise and describe a person can be grouped into two main categories: those that depend upon setting up special test situations and those that depend upon observing behavior in the actual naturally occurring situations of life. The usual earmarks of a test are that (1) it occurs at a specified time and place, (2) it consists of a set of tasks uniform for each person tested, and (3) it is seen as a test situation by the person being appraised. By contrast, evaluation based upon the naturally occurring situations of life is likely to (1) extend over an indefinite period, (2) be based upon situations that vary from person to person, and (3) not be perceived as a test by the person being appraised. The distinction between test situations and natural life situations is not an entirely sharp and clear-cut one, and we will have occasion to consider some in-between cases. However, it is usually clear whether we are dealing with a test as such or with observations under the natural conditions of life.

In thinking about the evaluation and measurement of man, we are likely to think primarily of tests narrowly defined, a test of arithmetic, a test of scholastic aptitude, or a test of auditory acuity. But we must remember that many of the important appraisals we make of people have always been, and will continue to be, based on observations of them as they live from day to day.   Appraisals of the nursery-school child's insecurity in relation to other children, of the 10-year-old's cooperativeness, or of the junior executive's initiative will almost necessarily be based upon observations of him over a period of time as he functions in his natural social group.   Evaluations based on these observations have serious limitations.   We are likely to find little uniformity from person to person in either the situations observed or the standards of judgment of the observers.   But for some kinds of behavior we have no adequate tests to substitute for observations of natural situations—and very likely never will have.

Any complete picture of evaluation procedures must, therefore, pay attention both to test techniques and to devices for improving the observation of naturally occurring behavior.   We will tend to prefer test situations where suitable ones can be devised.   The examiner has more control over the situation, since he can present the same tasks or questions to everyone in the same way.   He can usually get more precise results from a test and results that depend less upon the particular person making the appraisal.   However, we must recognize that many significant aspects of individual behavior, by their very nature, defy reduction to a neat test.   These can be appraised validly only as the individual functions in a natural life situation.

Of course, not all tests are perfectly frank and aboveboard.   We shall have occasion to consider various types of test instruments in which the characteristics appraised are not those that the test seems to be getting at.   Outstanding in this group are the so-called *projective tests* discussed in Chapter 15.   What purports to be a test of "imagination" may in fact be directed at revealing anxieties, tensions, and inner emotional conflicts.   Or a test of arithmetic computation may be rigged to yield a measure of cheating.   But these are exceptions to the general rule that in a test the person knows that he is being tested and knows *what* is being tested.

TWO FORMS OF TESTS

Within a defined test setting we may again recognize an important distinction, which depends upon whether the examinee leaves a permanent record of his behavior or whether it must be observed "on the wing" as it takes place.   The first situation is represented by any test, such as one of reading comprehension, in which the examinee marks his answers on a paper.   The marks are then permanently recorded and can be scored at leisure.   The second type of test would be encountered in an appraisal of oral reading, for example, where errors are noted by the listener as they occur or the quality is judged by the listener as the reader speaks.

In this comparison, again, the advantages with respect to reliability and objectivity usually fall on the side of the test that gives a permanent record, the test with answers on an answer sheet or a definite product produced. It is hard to observe and record behavior accurately as it is taking place. Inaccuracies and biases tend to creep in. The observer is hurried; his attention lapses. Consequently, in developing testing devices the tendency has been to make them of the sort that leaves a permanent record.

But young children cannot read or write, and many others are handicapped in a test that requires them to do so. Again, some types of performances, such as speaking or singing, are not readily reduced to a usable permanent record. It is also true that sometimes we are interested not merely in *what* a person does but also in *how* he does it. If a child gets the right answer for 6×7, does he get it quickly or slowly? Surely or with fumbling? By automatic habituation of the correct answer or by counting up from 6×6? The process does not show in the written answer but can sometimes be observed if the child answers the problem orally or "thinks out loud."

There are test situations, therefore, in which we shall have to depend upon observations of the behavior as it takes place rather than upon scoring the written record. These test situations pose special problems. Observers must be taught what to look for. They must be taught what responses to record and how to record them. They must be trained in standards of judgment, so that the pronunciation that they accept as right, for example, will also be one accepted as right by other observers. It is for this type of test that special training of examiners is usually required.

EXTERNAL OBSERVERS VERSUS SELF-OBSERVATION

As we move out of a test setting into observation of the individual's behavior in the natural situations of life, two distinct options are again open to us. We may rely upon some outsider to observe the person's behavior, someone such as his teacher, his employer, a friend, or a member of his family. Or we can ask him to report on his *own* characteristics as *he* sees them. These provide two quite different views of the individual, the one from the outside, the other from the inside.

The outside view is filtered through the biases and limited contacts of a particular outsider. The teacher, for example, sees only one side of the youngster—the school side that is turned toward him. Furthermore, he sees it colored by his own prejudices and limitations. What he sees as "cooperation" may from another viewpoint appear to be docility; what he considers "insubordination" may appear to another to be independence.

The self-picture is limited by the reporter's lack of self-understanding and unwillingness to reveal himself to the watching world. We do not know ourselves perfectly. Some of our limitations, our petty meannesses and evasions, our weak and sensitive spots, we cannot face and admit even to ourselves. Still other shortcomings we recognize but are unwilling to acknowledge to an outsider.

Sometimes one set of limitations will seem more serious, sometimes the other. If a person is applying for a job he very much wants, we will probably feel that we can put more trust in the evaluations of outsiders than in his self-evaluation. He has too much at stake in the impression he makes. On the other hand, if he has come to us for help and guidance, his own more intimate self-picture may provide a better basis for counseling with him than will the impressions of an outsider. We shall need to become acquainted with evaluation instruments of both types.

PLANNED VERSUS RETROSPECTIVE OBSERVATION

When we rely upon observations, either by the subject himself or by others observing him from outside, we may call for new observations made specially for us, or we may fall back upon the informal and undirected observations that have occurred in the past. Suppose we are studying the individual's tendency to become angry. We might ask him to keep track of all the times he got mad during the following week, noting down the circumstances for each anger episode, i.e., when it occurred, what precipitated it, what he did, etc. This would be an example of planned self-observation. By contrast, a second possibility would be to give him a list of situations that tend to annoy or irritate people. We might then ask him to look into himself and judge how readily he had tended to get angry at people who push in front in line, at being called by the wrong name, at being called down for something he did, and so forth. The self-observations would now be retrospective. If an outsider—say, a teacher—were doing the job, he might be asked to note down times during a specified period when he saw the particular pupil push, hit, or talk sharply to another. Or he might be asked to think back over his contacts with the child and rate him on a scale ranging from "exceptionally calm and even-tempered" to "flares up and gets angry at the slightest provocation."

Again, there are advantages and disadvantages to both the planned and the retrospective type of observation. A major difficulty with systematic planned observations is that they are laborious and time-consuming. It takes a great deal of time and a high level of observer cooperation to get the necessary observations made. Partly because of this, the observations are likely to cover a limited time period and therefore to represent a rather meager sample of the individual's behavior. However, when observations are of actual current behavior, they tend to be more objective and less influenced by biases and the selective effects of memory than retrospective reports. The retrospective observations called for in self-report inventories and in rating scales have been widely used because of their administrative simplicity and because they summarize concisely the whole history of self-observation or contact with the person rated. But this type of summarizing judgment gives the biases of the respondent the fullest chance to express themselves.

OBSERVATION AND TEST COMBINED—THE SITUATIONAL TEST

As we noted earlier, some behavior in test situations leaves no record behind but must be observed as it occurs. Here we have something of a hybrid involving both observation and test. The observer notes the specific errors a child makes when he reads aloud or his hesitations and false starts in spelling a word. Sometimes the "test" may involve a much more complex and total situation and more subtle types of behavior. In many of these "tests," the person being observed may not realize what is being observed (or even that he is being observed). So, if we want to appraise the individual's tendency to get angry, we may put him in a standard anger-producing situation. For example, we may give him a job to do and two intentionally stupid assistants who keep making mistakes and getting in the way. In so far as we are able to present each subject with the same task, we have a test situation. But we must depend upon the observations and judgments of outsiders to evaluate his behavior.

These complexly structured lifelike situations, which strive for the uniformity of a test situation and yet for the naturalness of real-life events, may be called *situational tests*. They represent a compromise between the objectivity and standardization of the testing approach and the naturalness of a real-life situation. This approach presents interesting possibilities for getting at types of behavior that do not readily lend themselves to the conventional types of testing.

The practical problems faced in devising situational tests are very great. They call for elaborate staging if the naturalness of real life is to be preserved. In addition, the problems of obtaining satisfactory observations and adequate reports of them remain. For these reasons, situational tests have not been widely used. But they present an interesting type of tool, whose possibilities are only beginning to be explored.

FUNCTIONS FOR WHICH MEASUREMENT HAS BEEN UNDERTAKEN

Broadly speaking, psychologists and educators have been interested in measuring in two general areas, what a person *can* do and what he *will* do. Measures of the first sort are measures of *ability*. In our discussion we will divide ability measures into measures of *aptitude* and measures of *achievement*. Again, roughly speaking, an aptitude test undertakes to measure what a person *could learn* to do, whereas an achievement test measures what he *has learned* to do.

The distinction between aptitude tests and achievement tests is far from a clear one, because we often use what a person has learned as a cue to what he can learn. Thus, a measure of the amount of knowledge of mechanical devices a person has gained in the past may be one of the most accurate indicators of the amount of further knowledge of things mechanical he will acquire in the future. The clearest distinction between aptitude and achievement tests lies in the direction of our interest. In an aptitude test, our interest is to predict what the individual *can learn* or develop into in the future; in the achievement test our interest is in what he *has learned* in the past.

Measures of the second major category—of what the person *will* do—correspond to the area we may roughly label *personality* measurement. This is a somewhat broad and loose definition of personality. It is also a somewhat external one. That is, we have indicated a concern for what a person *does* rather than for how he feels or what his inner urges and conflicts are. We may be interested in those to a degree. But, so far as a testing or observational procedure is concerned, it is always based on what a person does—how he acts, what answers he marks, or what he says. His actions are the basic material that we study.

In the long run, his future actions are what we want to predict: whether he will graduate from college, whether he will continue in and apply himself to a clerical type of job, whether he will behave in a more socially acceptable fashion after a particular type of therapy. We may perhaps make these predictions more surely if we organize the test and observational appraisals around certain concepts of interests, needs, or conflicts.   But these terms describing the inner life of the individual represent inferences that we make as a way of structuring and organizing the observations of the individual's behavior. We cannot *see* a need for approval.   What we observe is that a child brings things into class, attempts to talk at all times, buys candy for other children, and tries to join any social group in the playground. We may *infer* a need for approval as an underlying factor related to the various behaviors.

When we try to measure what a person *will* do, as distinct from what he *can* do, we encounter some special problems.   These are primarily problems of intentional distortion of the test results.   In an ability test we want each individual to try hard and do the best he can.   But in personality measures, we do not want to know how cooperatively a person *can* behave or how energetic he *can* be.   We want to know to what degree he *typically* does show energy or behave in a cooperative manner.   In a limited test situation, where the nature of the test is clear to the examinee, everyone can put his best foot forward.   He can probably muster up all the virtues for a special occasion.   But will he in other situations?   It is this question, the question of the degree to which behavior in an identifiable test situation will represent behavior in real life, that pushes us into disguised tests and into observational evaluations of personality characteristics.

ASPECTS OF PERSONALITY

It will be convenient to use a number of terms to refer to certain fractions or aspects of personality that we may wish to evaluate. These terms and the meanings that attach to them are discussed briefly below.

Character.   Character traits are aspects of individual behavior to which a definite social value has been attached.   Honesty, cooperativeness, thrift, kindliness, and loyalty are all labels for social virtues. Educational and religious organizations have always been concerned with the inculcation of such virtues.   Based on this concern there have been developed a number of evaluation procedures that we shall refer to as measures of character.

Adjustment.   Educators and psychologists have long been concerned with the concept of adjustment.   The mental hygiene approach as applied both in and out of school has striven to develop "well-adjusted personalities." Maladjustment is recognized in individuals who fail to fit into the social group or who appear to live unhappy and unproductive lives. As with character, degree of adjustment represents a social judgment, and what is conceived to be well-adjusted behavior varies from one culture to another, depending upon what is normal for that culture. Normal behavior in our competitive, acquisitive society might seem pathological if transferred to a South Sea island. Adjustment will mean, then, behavior patterns that enable the person to get along in and be comfortable in his social setting—typically, the setting of middle-class, twentieth-century American-European culture. We shall encounter a group of instruments designed to evaluate deviations from this norm—the tendency to show maladjusted behavior or behavior typical of people who do not get on happily and successfully in our culture.

Temperament. From early days observers of human nature have noted conspicuous differences in energy level, prevailing mood, and general style of life. Literary men and men of science alike have proposed systems for classifying temperaments. Hippocrates, for example, proposed that men could be divided into the sanguine (energetic and cheerful), choleric (energetic and irascible), phlegmatic (sluggish and placid), and melancholic (sluggish and sad), and proposed physiological bases for these distinctions. There have been many other classifications before and since. Appraisals of such dimensions as these we shall speak of as measures of temperament.

Interest. The individual makes a variety of choices with respect to the activities in which he engages. He shows preferences for some, aversion to others. Appraising these tendencies to seek or avoid particular activities constitutes the domain of interest measurement.

Attitude. The individual responds with enthusiasm and aversion not only toward activities but also to social groups, social institutions, and the other aspects of his world. These reactions, with their various ramifications, constitute the individual's constellation of attitudes. Various devices have been developed for evaluating these prejudices pro and con, and these constitute the field of attitude measurement.

CONCLUDING STATEMENT

In summary, then, approaches to the measurement of the individual cover a great diversity both of methods and of content areas. Variations of method may be represented by the following outline:

I. *Test methods,* involving a defined task and testing period.
   A. Permanent record or product available for scoring or analysis.
   B. Process must be observed and evaluated as it occurs.

II. *Observational methods,* in which behavior is observed in the natural situations of life.
  A. *Self-observation,* in which the individual reports on his own reactions, as far as he is aware of them.
    1. Planned observations, planned in advance to cover a specified period.
    2. Retrospective observation, based on present memory and evaluation of past reactions.
  B. *Observation by an outsider,* in which relative, employer, teacher, etc., reports on the individual's reactions.
    1. Planned observations.
    2. Retrospective observations.
III. *Mixed methods,* characterized by some of the aspects of a test but also relying upon observation and evaluation of observed behavior.

Advantages and problems of these approaches have been sketched in but will need to be considered in more detail as specific methods are elaborated in later chapters.

Aspects of the individual for which evaluation procedures have been developed and in which we shall be interested include the following:

I. *Abilities,* evidences of what the individual *can* do if he tries.
  A. *Aptitudes,* performances serving as indicators of what he can learn to do.
  B. *Achievements,* performances used to show what he has already learned to do.
II. *Personality variables,* indications of what an individual *will* do, of how he will respond to the events and pressures of life.
  A. *Character,* certain qualities defined by society as estimable or the reverse.
  B. *Adjustment,* degree of ability to fit into and live happily in the culture in which one is placed.
  C. *Temperament,* qualities relating to energy level, mood, and style of life.
  D. *Interests,* activities that are sought or avoided.
  E. *Attitudes,* reactions for or against the people, the phenomena, and the concepts that make up society.

This analysis of aspects of the individual is neither complete nor detailed. However, it serves to indicate the range of measures with which we shall be concerned in the following chapters.

QUESTIONS FOR DISCUSSION

1. It would generally be agreed that personality measures are less satisfactory than measures of aptitude or achievement. What factors give rise to this?

2. How would you fit each of the following into the classification of measurement methods given in the chapter?

a. Anecdotal records kept by a teacher, describing behavior in his class-room.
b. An autobiography written by a pupil for a high-school counselor.
c. An individual intelligence test in which both questions and answers are given orally.
d. A Boy Scout's record of "good deeds," kept over a 2-week period and reported to his Scoutmaster.

3. Illustrate, from your reading or experience, each of the categories of measurement methods in the outline on pp. 24–25.

4. How would you fit each of the following into the outline of aspects of the individual to be evaluated, given on p. 25?

a. Observations of how well a high-school student gets along with adults.
b. A pupil's expression of his preferences for books in an annotated list of titles.
c. A kindergarten child's performance on a test of readiness to learn reading.
d. A pupil's performance on an English test, used to place him in the appropriate section.
e. Ratings of a pupil on his loyalty to his friends.

5. From your reading or personal experience, give an illustration of measurement procedures for each of the aspects of the individual identified in the outline on p. 25.

6. A class has just finished a unit on etiquette, and the teacher wishes to evaluate the effectiveness of the unit. Which of the methods outlined on pp. 24–25 might she use? What would be the advantages and limitations of each?

Chapter 3

▼

The Teacher's Own Tests

In this book dealing with educational and psychological measurement procedures, we have elected to start with a consideration of the teacher's own tests. We have done this for several reasons. In the first place, informal test making is an operation that is familiar to every teacher, and the outcomes of such test making are familiar to every student. In the second place, because the teacher-made test is so widely used and has such an important place in evaluating student achievement, it strongly influences students' views toward tests and test-taking specifically and toward education generally. In the third place, the techniques of testing available to every teacher form the backbone of standardized tests of achievement and of aptitude. Furthermore, the quality of the items on a standardized test and the adequacy of the coverage of a standardized test are judged by precisely the same standards that apply to teacher-made tests.

THE ROLE OF TEACHER-MADE TESTS

Evaluation of pupil progress is a major aspect of the teacher's job. A good picture of where the pupil is and of how he is progressing is fundamental to effective teaching by the teacher and to effective learning by the pupil. The evaluation * procedures the teacher uses with his group serve a number of functions. We will identify four, commenting briefly upon each of them. All the procedures the teacher develops for pupil evaluation may serve these functions, but we shall be concerned to point out how they may be served by the more formal evaluation instruments called tests.

* The term "evaluation" as we use it here is closely related to measurement. It is in some respects more inclusive, including informal and intuitive judgments of pupil progress. It also includes more definitely the aspect of valuing—of saying what is desirable and good. Good measurement techniques provide the solid foundation for sound evaluation, whether of a single pupil or of a total curriculum.

MOTIVATION

To some degree, varying from pupil to pupil and from class to class, tests determine when students study, what they study, and how they study. Tests that are well constructed and effectively used can motivate students to develop good study habits, to correct errors, and to direct their activities toward the achievement of desired goals. Tests that are poorly constructed or used punitively can just as effectively discourage the students or misdirect their learning. Testing procedures control the learning process to a greater degree, perhaps, than any other teaching device.

DIAGNOSIS AND INSTRUCTION

Testing serves to diagnose weaknesses and to provide practice for available knowledges and skills. The items on which an individual fails or on which many members of a class group fail can serve to identify points needing further study whenever the test task is sufficiently precise for the nature of the failure to be identified. The function of a test as a rehearsal of knowledge and a guide for further study has long been recognized.

DEFINING TEACHING OBJECTIVES

What a teacher emphasizes in his evaluation of pupils, and particularly in the more formal evaluation represented by tests, defines to his students what that teacher considers important. This definition is presented in a much more forceful way than any pretty speeches that the teacher may make. The teacher may avow, to his students or to his colleagues, that he considers the ability to apply facts to real situations and to understand basic principles to be much more important than just learning facts. But if his tests ask only for names, dates, places, and sentences from the book or his lectures, those will be his functional objectives, and those will be the things that his students will study—the docile ones who are influenced by him anyhow. We may know a teacher by the tests he makes. They tell what he is truly valuing in his pupils, even though he himself does not know it, and they influence profoundly what his students will learn.

DIFFERENTIATION AND CERTIFICATION OF PUPILS

The teacher inevitably has a responsibility for certifying pupils' accomplishments to higher levels of the educational enterprise and to the world outside the school. The testing procedures he uses help him to arrive at the judgment that is recorded in his mark, letter of recommendation, or other evidence of approbation or disapprobation.

In view of the many functions they serve and in view of the disservice that may be done the pupil from poorly conceived or executed evaluation instruments, it is important that the teacher's evaluation devices be well thought out and well made. To evaluate the range of outcomes in which a modern school is interested—understanding as well as knowledge, appreciation as well as skill, ability to apply as well as to reproduce, attitudes and interests as well as achievements— the teacher must call upon a variety of types of appraisal. He must profit from observation of classroom performance by recitation, by participation in informal discussions, by contribution to group enterprises. He must size up the student in conference, interview, and informal discussion. He may have occasion to rate the products produced in laboratory or shop and to appraise the quality of assignments carried out outside of school. He will also almost certainly make some use of class tests. Some of the objectives of his teaching can be measured efficiently, realistically, and completely by pencil-and-paper tests. Some can be measured only partially by such means. Some cannot be measured at all in this way. This chapter and the next are concerned primarily with those objectives that can be measured with tests and with the improvement of testing procedures to measure them. Some consideration will be given to observational procedures, ratings, and other types of appraisal devices in later chapters.

PLANNING THE TEST

The primary function of any evaluation procedure is to determine to what extent students have achieved the objectives of instruction. If a test is to serve this function effectively, it must be planned with that end in view. A test which "just growed" is unlikely to correspond very well to the teacher's stated objectives. This is particularly true in the case of objective tests, and it is here that careful planning is especially important. However, one should not overlook the importance of a good test plan even in the case of an essay test.

If the teacher just sits down and writes objective test items, the test is likely to be out of balance. It is easier to write simple factual items than it is to write items that call for understanding of generalizations or application of principles. It is easier to write items on some topics than on others. As a result, the teacher is likely to end up with an overload of items calling for simple information about the more testable topics. The same thing is true, to a degree, of essay tests. The outcomes measured by the test will then show a poor correspondence with those espoused by the teacher. What the pupils emphasize in their learning will soon follow what they find is emphasized in their tests, and the tests will fail to foster the learnings in which the instructor is most interested.

DEFINING OBJECTIVES

The thoughtful planning of a test involves several steps. The first and most important step is to define the objectives that are to be appraised. Before he can evaluate whether a student has achieved the objectives of instruction, a teacher must be able to state what the student was supposed to have achieved. Moreover, objectives that are to be evaluated must be stated in terms of pupil behavior. We must be able to specify the *processes* or *activities* that a student is expected to display if he has achieved the objectives. What do we expect him to know? What kinds of applications do we expect him to be able to make? How do we expect him to think or to solve problems? What actions on his part will show that he has acquired the attitudes that we are trying to inculcate? In other words what things must a student *do* to show that he has acquired the knowledge, understandings, skills, attitudes and appreciations that we say we have been trying to teach.

The failure to define objectives in terms of student behavior probably accounts for much of the inadequacy in evaluation of student progress in schools and also for the very poor quality of many classroom tests. Defining the objectives of instruction in terms of pupil behavior is not an easy task but it is necessary before a good test can be constructed or effective evaluation can be done.

The real work of defining objectives must usually be done by the teacher himself, perhaps assisted by his colleagues, and working from his textbook or course outline. In many schools the teacher has available a curriculum guide or course of study which does contain a set of objectives. But objectives listed in these sources tend to be too vague and global to be useful as a guide for evaluation. They need to be broken down into more specific components if they are to provide a sufficiently exact definition of just what the broad, global objectives mean.

Let us look at an actual example. In the section below are listed the objectives stated as the desired outcomes for an eighth-grade social-studies unit on the functioning of our national government.

Objectives of a Unit on How Our National Government Functions

1. Has a basic foundation of facts and information necessary to an understanding of the unit.
2. Understands why the Declaration of Independence was written.
3. Understands the ideas embodied in the Declaration of Independence.
4. Understands the Articles of Confederation.
5. Understands Articles I through VII of the Constitution.
6. Understands the Bill of Rights and other amendments to the Constitution.
7. Can use and interpret maps.
8. Can locate and interpret data.
9. Can do critical thinking.
10. Derives personal satisfaction from social studies reading.
11. Is able to plan, execute, and evaluate committee projects.
12. Uses parliamentary procedures.
13. Develops a love for and loyalty to the principles of the government of the United States.
14. Develops an abiding interest in civic affairs beyond the years of formal education.
15. Has an appreciation for the principles of a democracy which formed the basis of our government.

As stated, these objectives embody many of the faults typically found in the statements of objectives available to teachers in courses of study. Some of these may be pointed out and illustrated.

1. *The Objective Is One That Cannot Be Achieved, and Certainly Cannot Be Evaluated within the Unit.* Objective 14 refers to adult life, and not to anything that characterizes the pupil in the eighth grade. It is an expression of a pious and worthy hope, but of little help in guiding the teacher as to what he should do with a pupil or look for in him.

2. *The Objective Is Expressed in Terms of Unobservables.* Objectives 13 and 15 state worthwhile hopes, but provide no guidance to the teacher as to what the eighth grader is to *do* to show his love, loyalty, and appreciation. How does a student exhibit appreciation for the principles of democracy? Through giving lip service to the words and symbols? Through accepting individuals who differ from himself in various ways? Through participating in school government? Behaviorally, what do these objectives mean?

3. *The Objective Bears Little or No Relationship to the Content of the Unit.* Objective 7 is one that has little relationship to the unit being studied. There are certainly many better units in which to build up map-reading skills. Such skills play very minor roles, if any, in this particular content.

4. *The Statement of the Objective Implies a Process Quite Different from the One That Is Taught.* Objectives 2 through 6 start with the word "understand." But what does the word really mean in this context? Consider 2, for example. Further study of the curriculum guide brings out that the pupil is to "understand" that the Declaration of Independence was written to explain America's cause in the War of Independence. However, this point is specifically and explicitly made in the textbooks. A pupil could produce this statement on an examination on the basis of direct recall of what he had learned. No real understanding is called for. The same is true of objectives 3 through 6. These objectives should more appropriately begin with "knows," "can recall," or "can state," because these words more accurately reflect the process of reproducing from memory.

The term "appreciation" in objective 15 is also often used quite loosely. It is often used to refer to information about something, rather than an affective or aesthetic reaction to it. Thus, again, it may be more realistic to talk about knowledge of the principles, and perhaps ability to interpret or apply them, than about "appreciation" of them.

5. *The Objective May Be Inappropriate to the Level of Instruction.* To be realistic, we can expect eighth graders to achieve only a very limited understanding of this particular unit. The teacher should recognize this, and place "understanding" in a proper perspective both in the weight that is given to it and the level of sophistication that is expected.

The teacher *can* both develop and test for the level of understanding appropriate at a given grade level if he can identify the processes on the part of the student that represent understanding. The student can show understanding at different levels by (1) expressing concepts and principles in his own words, (2) pointing out similarities and differences not explicitly pointed out in class or text, (3) pointing out relationships, and (4) applying his information to situations about which he has not been taught.

We could point out other specific defects in the list of objectives as they are stated, but let us stop and see how the list might be revised so that the objectives would provide a better guide both for teaching and evaluation. For this purpose we want to separate the process from the content. A good guide for setting up objectives that relate to process rather than content is given by Bloom et al.[1] A revised set of process objectives for this unit is given below. When the word "knows" is used, it means the ability to reproduce, recall, recognize or define.

1. Knows terms and vocabulary.
2. Knows dates, events, persons, and places.
3. Knows generalizations, concepts, and principles.
4. Can trace the sequence of historical development (of our national form of government.)
5. Can express generalizations and concepts in his own words.
6. Can point out relationships, similarities, and differences.
7. Can apply generalizations and principles to particular concrete situations that are new to him.
8. Can use parliamentary procedures in committee or class meetings.
9. Can plan, execute, and evaluate committee projects.
10. Shows support either orally or in writing for governmental actions that follow the democratic principles on which the government is based.
11. Expresses concern either orally or in writing for an individual or group being deprived of the rights guaranteed by our constitution.

This set of objectives keeps the basic intent of the original set of objectives. For example, objectives 1 through 7 in the revised list include the intent of objectives 1 through 6, 8, 9, and 15 on the original list of objectives. Objectives 8 and 9 in the revised list parallel 11 and 12 on the original list. Objectives 10 and 11 on the revised list are redefinitions of 13 on the original list. Those objectives on the original list that were totally unrealistic or did not apply to the unit have been eliminated in the revised list.

OUTLINING CONTENT

The second step in planning for a test is to outline the content to be covered. The outline of content is important because the content is the actual vehicle through which the process objectives are to be achieved. An outline of content for our illustrative example follows.

Outline of Content of a Unit on How Our National Government Functions

I. The Foundations of Our Constitutional Government (Time allotment: 2 weeks)
   A. Early English documents—the Magna Charta, the Petition of Right, and the Bill of Rights
      1. Provisions of these documents
      2. Their influence on our heritage
   B. Mayflower Compact, Fundamental Orders of Connecticut, The New England Confederation, The Albany Plan
      1. Principles embodied in these documents
      2. Influences of these documents
   C. Representative Assemblies in the Colonies

    D. Declaration of Independence
       1. Events leading up to the drafting of the Declaration of Independence
       2. Drafting the document; ideas embodied in the declaration
         a. Principles of government the delegates believed in
         b. List of grievances against King George III
         c. A declaration of freedom
       3. Adoption of the Declaration of Independence on July 4, 1776
    E. The Articles of Confederation (1781–1789)
       1. Provisions
       2. Weaknesses
       3. Constitutional convention called by Congress in 1787
    F. The Constitutional Convention—1787
       1. Members
       2. Stated purpose
       3. Need for strong national government
       4. Disagreements solved by debate and compromise
       5. Contributions of influential men at the convention
       6. Ratification of the Constitution
II. Principles and Development of Our Constitutional Government (Time allotment: 4 to 6 weeks)
    A. Purpose as stated in the preamble
    B. Federalism versus Confederation
       1. Division of powers between central government and states
       2. Advantage of federalism
    C. Unitary and Federal Government
    D. Division of power in our federal system
       1. Reasons for separation of powers
       2. Division of powers in federal government
       3. Division of powers among local units
       4. Limitations placed on federal government
    E. The Three Branches and the System of Checks and Balances
       1. The executive, legislative, and judicial branches
       2. Meaning of checks and balances
    F. The Articles of the Constitution
       1. Provisions of the articles
    G. The development of the Constitution
       1. Elastic clause
       2. Changing the Constitution
         a. Amendments—process
         b. Statutes
         c. Court decisions
         d. Customs and usage
    H. The Bill of Rights

PREPARING THE TEST BLUEPRINT

The content outline and a statement of process objectives represent the two dimensions into which a test plan should be fitted. These two dimensions need to be put together to give a complete framework and to see which objectives relate especially to which segments of content. In planning for the *total* evaluation of a unit the teacher would be well advised to make a blueprint covering *all* objectives and add a column at the extreme right indicating the method or methods to be used in evaluating student progress toward achieving the objectives. However in making a blueprint for a *test,* only those objectives that can be measured either wholly or in part by a paper-and-pencil test should be included.

In the list of revised objectives, objectives 8 through 11 cannot be measured by a paper-and-pencil test. For example, objective 8, "Can use parliamentary procedures in committee or class meetings," can be evaluated only by putting the student in a somewhat formal meeting and observing whether he follows parliamentary procedures. On a paper-and-pencil test the teacher could determine whether a student *knows* parliamentary procedure but not whether he *uses* it. Since a student cannot use parliamentary procedure unless he knows it, such testing of knowledge is sometimes worthwhile, but the teacher should remember that in this unit the objective was stated in terms of using rather than of knowing. Observation of performance in assigned class groups and in informal school activities would seem promising approaches to evaluating objectives 9 through 11. The teacher should remember that no single test or evaluation medium can measure all the objectives that he is trying to achieve.

Figure 3.1 shows the process objectives in our revised list that can be measured by a paper-and-pencil test and their relation to the content of the unit. The objectives are listed in the left-hand column of the chart and the titles of the two major content areas are used to head the two right-hand columns. Each cell is then filled with notes suggesting terms, dates, events, generalizations, relationships, or applications that a teacher might consider important specific examples of that content and that process. For example, the upper left hand cell contains four terms—inalienable rights, tyranny, compromise, and confederation—that this teacher considered it important for students to know. The cell below that contains certain events, dates, and documents that this teacher considered important. The other cells have been filled in the same way in order to specify more precisely the content to be included and what the student is supposed to be able to do with that content.

The preparation of such a two-dimensional outline is undoubtedly an exacting and time-consuming task. The busy classroom teacher may often fall short of achieving such a complete analysis. There is no question, however, that attempting the analysis will go far toward clari-

Objectives:	I. The foundations of our Constitutional Government (30% of all items)	II. Principles and Development of our Constitutional Government (70% of all items)
1. Knows terms and vocabulary (10%)	1. Inalienable Rights 2. Tyranny 3. Compromise 4. Confederation (1 or 2 items)	Preamble Residual powers Legislative Sovereignty Executive Concurrent powers Judicial Check and balance system Federalism Unitary governments Suffrage Elastic clause (4 items)
2. Knows dates, events, persons and places (5%)	1. Articles of Confederation—1781 2. Magna Charta—1215 3. Bill of Rights—1689 4. Petition of Rights—1628 5. Declaration of Independence—1776 6. Setting of Constitutional Convention—Members, Agreements 7. Ordinance of 1787 (0-1 items)	Ratification of Constitution—1788 Federalist papers—Authorship and purposes (2 items)
3. Knows generalizations, concepts and principles (35%)	1. Provisions of Magna Charta, Bill of Rights, Petition of Right 2. Principles embodied in the Declaration of Independence 3. Weaknesses of Articles of Confederation 4. Provisions of Ordinance of 1787 (6 or 7 items)	1. Restrictions on the states and national government 2. Powers belonging only to the states 3. Powers belonging only to the national government 4. Powers shared by states and national government 5. Provisions of first III Articles 6. Changes and amendments to Constitution—how made 7. Provisions of Bill of Rights (14 or 15 items)
4. Can trace development of our national form of government (20%)	1. Identifies influences and trends that contributed to the establishment of representative assemblies in the colonies 2. Explains the development of representative government in the colonies between 1607 and 1776	1. Identifies events, forces and flaws that lead to separation of powers in federal government 2. Identifies forces that lead to amendments to the Constitution (8 or 9 items)

Objective	Topic I	Topic II
5. Can express generalizations and concepts in own words (10%)	3. Shows how the ordinance of 1787 affected the development of our country (3 or 4 items) 1. Equality of man 2. Governments derive their just powers from the consent of the governed 3. Explains why the articles of Confederation were not a complete failure (1 or 2 items)	1. Explains the meanings of the Amendments to the Constitution 2. Our Government as a democratic republic (4 items)
6. Can point out relationships, similarities, and differences (10%)	1. Relationship between national origins of the colonists and provisions of Mayflower Compact 2. Abuses set forth in declaration of Independence and whether these abuses are found in our country today (1 or 2 items)	1. Relationship between preamble of Constitution and the Articles of Confederation 2. Similarities and differences between national and local government 3. Similarities and differences between Virginia Plan and New Jersey Plan and the Constitution as it was adopted (4 items)
7. Can apply generalizations and principles to novel situations (10%)	1. Identifies advantages and disadvantages of confederate type organizations such as United Nations (1 or 2 items)	1. Points out differences to be expected between our government and a government organized on other principles 2. Identifies acts that violate the Bill of Rights and the right that is violated by each act. 3. Predicts probable outcomes if Constitution were not flexible 4. Explains the process by which Puerto Rico could be made a state 5. Identifies whether proposed laws are in conflict with the Constitution 6. Identifies errors in parliamentary procedure (4 items)

Total time for test — 50 minutes
Total number of items on test — 60 (Topic I — 18 items; Topic II — 42 items)

Fig. 3.1. Test blueprint for a unit on How Our National Government Functions.

fying the objectives of a particular unit and toward guiding not only the preparation of a sound test but also the teaching of the unit itself.

Once the basic outline has been prepared, the test maker must decide upon the relative emphasis to be given to the several content areas and process objectives. The number of questions that can be presented in a test is limited by the testing time available and by the ability and background of the students to be tested. Since time does not permit him to include everything, the test maker must select a sample of questions. The sample should truly represent the emphasis given in his teaching, both with respect to content and with respect to the process objectives. This can be done by having the proportion of questions in each content area correspond to the proportionate emphasis given to that topic, and the proportion of items calling for each process correspond to the importance the teacher considers that process to have in the learnings that the pupils are to achieve. The decisions made by the teacher in dividing up the questions on a test are necessarily subjective ones. The basic principle underlying these decisions is that the test should maintain the same balance in relative emphasis on both content and mental processes that the teacher has been trying to achieve through his instruction. This allocation of differing numbers of items to different topics and process objectives is one way of *weighting* these topics and objectives differentially in the test.

In the illustration of Figure 3.1, the test maker decided that about 30 per cent of the items should be on Topic I and 70 per cent on Topic II. This corresponds roughly to the allocation of teaching time to the two topics given on pp. 33–34, i.e., 2 weeks to Topic I and 4 to 6 weeks to Topic II. Time spent on the topic and space given to it in the textbook can help to guide the teacher's judgment of the basic importance of the topic and weight to be given it.

The test maker in Fig. 3.1 allocated 35 per cent of the total number of items to objective 3, 25 per cent to objective 4, 10 per cent each to objectives 1, 5, 6, and 7, and 5 per cent to objective 2. These reflect a judgment by this test maker that objective 3, knowledge of concepts, generalizations and principles, is clearly the most important objective of the unit, that objective 4, ability to trace sequences of historical events, is next most important, and that the others are of about equal, but lesser importance. Names and dates (objective 2) are relegated to a minor role. Note that here, as in the topical outline, 100 per cent has been distributed among the different categories.

The test maker must also decide now whether he will use essay test questions or short-answer, objective items, and if he decides on objective items he must decide which type or types he will use. The choice is governed, at least in part, by the objectives to be measured. The next section of this chapter will provide some discussion of the advantages and disadvantages of essay questions, in relation to the objective type of item. Different types of objective items will be described and compared in Chapter 4.

At about this point the total number of essay questions or objective test items must be decided upon. This is primarily a function of the time available for the test and the type of items being used. Different types of objective items differ in the time allotments they require, and, of course, an essay question demands a great deal more time than an objective item. It is almost impossible to state in general terms how much time should be allowed per item for objective items of a specific type. The appropriate time allowance is affected by a host of different factors. Among the most important are (1) the age of the pupils being tested, (2) the length and complexity of the item, (3) the type of objective being tested—knowledge of fact or concept versus application to new situation, (4) the amount of computation, if any, required by the item, and (5) the relative interest of the examiner in speed versus power—the amount the pupil can do with unlimited time.

In general, it seems undesirable to emphasize speed in an achievement test designed to measure one's range of information or ability to apply knowledge. Most teacher-made tests should be power tests; i.e., there should be enough time so that at least 80 per cent of the students can attempt to answer each item. As a teacher becomes familiar with the kinds of students he usually has in a class, he will be able to judge the number of items he can include in a given amount of testing time while still having a power test. As a rough rule of thumb, the typical student might require from 30 to 45 seconds to read and attempt to answer a simple factual type multiple-choice or true-false item, from 75 to 100 seconds to read and attempt a fairly complex item requiring problem-solving or some computation. If the test items are based on a reading passage, tabular material, map, or graph, time must be allowed for reading and examining the material.

Adequately to sample achievement in a large segment of work, i.e., the content of a whole semester, may require more items than can reasonably be included in a single-period test. The only satisfactory solution to this problem is to allow two or more periods for testing. If a single unit of sufficient length is unavailable or seems likely to go beyond the attention span of the group, the natural solution is to break the test up into two or more subtests that can be given on successive days.

Once the teacher has decided upon the total number of items to be included in the test, he should go back to the blueprint and determine how many items are needed for each cell. In the sample blueprint, Fig. 3.1, the total time available for testing was 50 minutes. The test maker decided to have a total of 60 questions on the test. Applying the percentages in the blueprint, approximately 18 questions should be on Topic I (30 per cent) and 42 questions should be on Topic II (70 per cent). The 18 questions on Topic I are distributed in the cells of that column according to the weights assigned to the objectives. To obtain the number of items for each cell, one multiplies the number of items for Topic I (18 items) by the percentage assigned to the objective in each row. For example, to determine the number of items for the first cell in Topic I, we multiply 18 by 0.1 (10 per cent) which gives 1.8 items. Since this product is between 1 and 2, we can note that we should have either one or two items covering this content and this objective. The other cells in the blueprint are filled in by the same process. It is probably desirable to indicate a range of frequency for each cell, as was done in our example, in order to provide flexibility if difficulty is encountered in writing acceptable items for certain cells. The frequencies are to be thought of as a guide and not as a strait jacket.

After all the items for the test have been constructed, the teacher should make a final check by sorting the items in piles to match the blueprint in order to make sure that the two agree.

The above discussion of allocation of items to topics and objectives applies primarily to objective tests made up of a large number of items. The same degree of analysis hardly applies to an essay examination, which will at best be composed of a relatively small number of items. But these few items should also be distributed over the content and the process objectives so that the test represents as well as possible the explicit goals of instruction.

A final decision that comes in as part of the preliminary planning concerns the desired difficulty of the test items. The decision depends in part upon the purpose of the test. When the test is to measure *mastery* of the basic essentials in an area, the questions should be limited to basic essentials. If the unit has been well taught, all the items may then turn out to be very easy for the group. When the purpose of the test is to *discriminate* levels of achievement of different members of a group, i.e., to serve as a basis for ranking or grading, some items should be very easy, most of them should be of moderate difficulty, and a few should be difficult enough to spread out the ablest members of the group.   Difficulty, in this context, is defined in terms of the percentage of examinees who get the item right.

Our test plan now consists of:

1. An outline of content and objectives.
2. Specific suggestions of what might be covered under each combination of content and objective.
3. An allocation of per cents of the total test by content area and by objective and an estimate of the total number of items.
4. Specifications for the spread of item difficulties.

The next task is to prepare the actual test items.   In the remainder of this chapter we will discuss the choice of item types and guides for improving the writing of essay questions.   In Chapter 4 we will discuss guides for improving objective-type items.

ADVANTAGES AND LIMITATIONS OF ESSAY AND OBJECTIVE TESTS

Teacher-made tests may be divided into two broad categories, essay or free-answer tests and objective tests.   One hears many arguments about whether essay tests or objective tests should be used in schools but these "either–or" arguments are pointless.   Neither the essay test nor the objective test is satisfactory as the sole type of test to measure academic achievement.   Each type has its own advantages and limitations and each has its place.   The problem is to use each type of test in those situations where its advantages are maximized and its weaknesses minimized.

THE ESSAY TEST

The essay test consists of such problems as:

Compare the organization and powers of the central government under the Articles of Confederation with the organization and powers of the central government under the Constitution.

Why did the merchants and business men particularly desire to have the Articles of Confederation changed?

The Fifth Amendment to the United States Constitution states that *no person shall be deprived of life, liberty, or property without due process of law*.   In your own words, explain what the underlined part of the statement means.

Why is the Magna Charta considered to be an important milestone in the establishment of a democratic government?

The essential characteristics of the task set by an essay test are that each student

1. Organizes his own answers, with a minimum of constraint.
2. Uses his own words (usually his own handwriting).
3. Answers a small number of questions.
4. Produces answers having all degrees of completeness and accuracy.

In these characteristics lie both the strengths and weaknesses of the essay examination. Let us consider each in turn.

The Student Organizes His Own Answers. Herein lies the distinctive advantage of the essay examination. It requires the student to produce, rather than merely to recognize, the answer. Thus, it minimizes the possibility of getting the answer by blind guessing or by using little cues to outguess the test maker. It can, if the questions are well prepared, bring out the examinee's ability to select important facts or ideas, relate them to one another, and organize them into a coherent whole. Emphasizing this integrative type of product, it elicits, so it is claimed, better study habits in those who are preparing for it.

The Answer Is in the Student's Words and Handwriting. At this point a premium is placed upon verbal fluency and skill of expression. The student who is able to write effectively will often get a higher grade than another student who clothes the same ideas in less attractive garb. Too often verbal fluency and aggressive salesmanship, bluffing, in short, pass for knowledge of the subject. In addition to skill in writing, quality of handwriting frequently influences the grade on an essay test. How often has a student been penalized because the instructor became irritated by poor handwriting, or could not be bothered to decipher obscure "hen tracks"? Effective written expression and good penmanship may be legitimate objectives of the educational enterprise, but they should be evaluated in their own right. They should not be allowed to contaminate our appraisal of a student's understanding of the causes of Hitler's rise to power or of Newton's laws of motion.

The Test is Limited to a Small Number of Questions. When the individual must organize and compose an answer of some length, as with questions like those on p. 41, the number of questions is inevitably limited. The time required to answer a single question makes it impossible to include more than five or ten questions in even a fairly lengthy test. This tends to result in what we might call a "lumpy" sampling of what the student knows. We sink four or five big shafts into the mine of knowledge that the student possesses. If these happen to hit pay dirt, the student does well; but if they hit the gaps in his knowledge, he does poorly. With this small number of samples, chance is likely to play a relatively large part. We may get a very unfair sample of a particular student's knowledge.

Of course, it is possible to ask free-response questions that call for quite short answers. We might ask: What qualifications does the Constitution set for United States Senators? This question requires only a list of qualifications or a sentence or two for a complete answer. Questions such as this are transitional between the essay and objective test. They can be numerous and can sample many items of knowledge or understanding. However, they sacrifice the main feature of the essay question—the requirement that the examinee put together an organized answer in which he relates, evaluates, and integrates a number of facts and ideas.

Answers Are of All Degrees of Correctness.   The bugaboo of the essay examination is the laborious and subjective operation of evaluating the answers. That it is laborious any teacher who has ever graded a set of essay papers for even a middle-sized class can testify. That the grading is subjective and relatively undependable has been shown by a number of separate studies.

Consider the following answers written by two eighth-grade students to the question "Compare the powers and organization of the central government under the Articles of Confederation with the powers and organization of our own central government today."

Student A

Our government today has a president, a house of representatives, and a senate. Each state has two senators but the number of representatives is different for each state. This is because of compramise at the Constitutional Convention. The Articles of Confederation had only a Congress and each state had delegates in it and had one vote. This Congress couldn't do much of anything because all the states had to say it was alright. Back then Congress couldn't make people obey the law and there wasn't no supreme court to make people obey the law. The Articles of Confederation let Congress declare war, make treaties, and borrow money and Congress can do these things today. But Congress then really didn't have any power, it had to ask the states for everything. Today Congress can tell the states what to do and tax people to raise money they don't have to ask the states to give them money. Once each state could print its own money if it wanted to but today only the U. S. Mint can make money.

Student B

There is a very unique difference between the Central Government under the Articles of Confederation and the National Government of today. The Confederation could not tax directly where as the National Government can. The government of today has three different bodies—Legislative, Judicial, and Executive branches. The Confederation had only one branch which had limited powers. The confederate government could not tax the states directly or an individual either. The government of today, however, has the power to tax anyone directly and if they don't respond, the government has the right to put this person in jail until they are willing to pay the taxes. The confederation government was not run nearly as efficiently as the government of today. While they could pass laws (providing most of the states voted with them) the confederate government could not enforce these laws, (something which the present day can and does do) they could only hope and urge the states to enforce the laws.

These two answers together with three other answers written by students in the same class were given to two groups of graduate students in courses in measurement or evaluation. Both groups of students were provided with a model answer to the question and given the following instructions:

Instructions: The essay question was a part of a social studies test consisting of fifty objective items and one essay question. The students were given 25 minutes to write their answers to the essay question. You have been given the answers written by five of the students. The class that these five students were in was a heterogeneous one. Twenty-five points is the maximum score for the question. Please grade each paper using the model answer provided. The grade is to reflect completeness and accuracy of the answer—not quality of English expression, spelling, or grammar.

Suppose that *you* grade these two answers in accordance with the instructions given above before you read any further. Record the scores that you would give the answers.

————————

Now look at Table 3.1, which shows the scores actually given to all five answers, including these two. Every one of the answers receives scores spreading over about 20 points of the possible range of 25. Any one of the papers might have gotten a score as high as 18; any one might have gotten a score as low as 5. The responses of students A and B were judged to be outstandingly good by some raters, poor by others. The inconsistency of the judgments is demonstrated most forcefully. A single rating of any one of these papers

Table 3.1.   Grades Given to Five Answers to Essay Question

Score	Student A	Student B	Student C	Student D	Student E
25	6	5	..	6	..
24	2	2	..	4	..
23	4	3	..	4	..
22	3	9	2	5	..
21	8	2	..	4	..
20	32	21	6	24	..
19	6	1	..	3	..
18	14	11	3	12	1
17	6	8	3	2	1
16	4	2	2	4	..
15	23	23	18	34	4
14	4	1	3	5	..
13	2	2	3	2	1
12	4	13	9	7	6
11	1	3	6	1	2
10	6	11	33	4	25
9	1	4	9	1	5
8	..	6	9	3	6
7	2	3	3	..	..
6	..	..	3	3	16
5	3	..	11	2	50
4	..	..	1	1	7
3	..	1	3	..	15
2	..	..	1	..	1
1	..	..	..	..	..
0	..	..	2	..	1

tells us very little about how that same paper will be rated by someone else. Why is this? What makes the appraisal of an essay response so undependable?

Let us admit to start with that the dice were somewhat loaded against the graders in this little experiment. Most of them were not social studies teachers, though the majority had had some teaching experience. (Previous experience has indicated that social studies teachers will show about as much variation.) Furthermore, they had not taught the class, and did not know anything about the general level of performance in this and similar groups.

One major reason for the wide range of scores found in Table 3.1 is that different raters maintained very different standards for rating *all* the papers. Different raters used quite different parts of the scale of scores. Though it was most common for a rater to spread his scores between about 5 and 20, a few awarded no grade higher than 10 to *any* of the answers while others assigned no grades below 15. These last two groups were operating in entirely different score ranges and showed no overlap. The best for one group was lower than the poorest for the other. Judges differed not only in the average level at which they rated the papers, but also in how much they spread out their scores. Some were very "conservative," bunching all their ratings close together, while others tended to spread them widely over the whole range. Such differences in grading standards are very real in actual school situations—as every student knows—and provide one main source for inconsistency in grading essay responses.

However, the judges were also not very consistent in the rank order in which they arranged the 5 papers. In Table 3.2 we have shown

Table 3.2. Rank Order Assigned to Each of Five Essay Questions

Rank	Student A	Student B	Student C	Student D	Student E
1	44	29	2	33	1
1.5	13	12	1	11	. .
2	28	23	8	31	1
2.5	12	10	5	17	. .
3	24	32	19	23	. .
3.5	1	6	9	5	3
4	3	16	55	9	11
4.5	3	1	18	1	20
5	1	1	13	. .	94

how often each paper was ranked first, how often second, and so on. (Tie ranks have been indicated as 1.5, 2.5, etc.) In this table we see that every one of the 5 answers was ranked first by somebody, and every answer was either last or tied for last. There is some consensus that student E wrote the poorest answer and student C the next poorest, but practically no agreement as to the relative standing of the other three. Students A, B or D could easily have been judged best of the group or only average. Thus, there is not only a marked difference in *absolute* standard from judge to judge, but also inconsistency in the *relative* judgment of one paper in comparison with the others.

Inconsistency in relative judgment is characteristic not only of different raters but also of the same rater at different times. Thus, when the evaluation class was asked to grade the papers a second time 3 weeks later (without advance notice that this was to be done), a third of the ratings differed from the original rating by 5 points or more (out of the possible range of 25 points). Only a third of the papers kept the same rank in the group of 5 on the second grading.

The results that we have presented illustrate the situation that commonly prevails in evaluating essay responses. The responses vary in many ways and by infinitely small degrees. Raters approach them with differing standards of severity and looking for different things. As a result the evaluation of these responses is generally highly subjective and quite unreliable. We shall consider later in the chapter what can be done to deal with these very real problems.

THE OBJECTIVE TEST

The objective test includes a variety of forms of test tasks having in common the characteristic that the correct answer, usually only one, is determined when the test item is written. The word "objective" in objective test refers only to the scoring of the answers; the choice of content and coverage of an objective test is probably as subjective as the choice of content and coverage of an essay test, and for some types of items there is subjective judgment involved in the original decision as to what is the correct answer. Common forms of objective test items are shown below.

True—False

T F̲   The Constitution states that United States Senators shall be elected for terms of 4 years.

Multiple Choice

A law passed by a legislature to punish a person without a court trial would be called
A. an ex post facto law.
B̲. a bill of attainder.
C. a writ of *habeas corpus*.
D. a warrant.

Completion

The right to vote is called   (suffrage) .

Matching

Column I—Documents		Column II—Dates
B	The Mayflower Compact	A. 1215
C	The Petition of Right	B. 1620
A	The Magna Charta	C. 1628
		D. 1689
		E. 1776

The essential features of a test made of objective items, as distinct from an essay test, are that the examinee

1. Operates within an almost completely structured task.
2. Selects one of a limited number of alternatives.
3. Responds to each of a large sample of items.
4. Receives a score for each answer according to a predetermined key.

Again, let us examine these characteristics to see the advantages and disadvantages of each. In large measure, they are the reverse of those discussed for essay examinations.

The Task Is Completely Structured. The examinee does not have a chance to organize and define the problem for himself. On the debit side, this means that a test of this sort is not useful for appraising skills of organizing and structuring ideas. On the credit side, we are more sure that each examinee is presented with the same problem. "Discuss the Articles of Confederation," can carry quite different meanings to different pupils.

The Examinee Selects from Among Given Alternatives. In most types of objective item, the possible alternatives are completely specified. (This is not the case with the completion type of item, and in that respect it is on the boundary line, approaching the short free-response type of question.) Where the alternatives are all provided, the student is only required to recognize the right answer, not to produce it by his own efforts. This has been criticized as representing a lower level of intellectual process, and one that is less true to life. How valid this criticism is probably depends upon how skillfully the objective items are written, and how much they manage to get away from the words of the text and simple memory of factual materials. When an objective test item presents a new problem that must be solved by recalling and applying facts or principles previously learned, this type of item can require just as active recall as any essay question.

Another outcome of the limited set of answer choices is that an examinee can be expected to get some answers right by guessing. This becomes a problem particularly for true-false questions in which there are only two choices. Tossing a coin would give 50 per cent right on the average, and people would get different scores to some extent because they were lucky or unlucky coin tossers. The problem of guessing is serious in a short test with few answer choices, but chance successes tend to even up in the long run if there are enough items, if enough time is given for everyone to complete the test, and if instructions about guessing can be made sufficiently definite so that all examinees will adopt the same policy.

The Sample of Items Is Large.   Since each item is brief, many items can be included.   These can be spread more evenly over the topics to be covered and a more representative sampling can be obtained.   This reduces the role of luck, of the individual just happening to have reviewed a particular topic.   As a consequence of the inclusion of many separate items, the score from a well-made objective test is likely to be more accurate than that from an essay test, so that two separate tests of an individual based on the same content areas will rank him in more nearly the same place in his group.

Each Item Has a Predetermined Key.   The key is established once and for all by the test maker at the time the test items are written.   This means that scoring the test is a routine clerical task and can be done by a person who knows nothing about the subject matter of the test or even by one of the electrical test-scoring machines on the market.   The saving in time to score the test is very substantial, but it must be remembered that much of that saving will have been used up in preparing the test.   Writing clear and unambiguous objective test items is a fairly demanding literary task.

The economy in time is less important than the uniformity in evaluating answers that results.   The score will be the same whoever scores the test, once the key has been agreed upon.   The score will be the same no matter who it was that chose the answers.   Teacher's pet or hellion, Spencerian specialist or scribbler, if they choose the same answer they get the same score.

SUMMARY COMPARISON

The issues we have been discussing are summarized in tabular form below.   In each case a plus sign is placed in the column of the test pattern that would be judged superior with respect to that factor.

Factor	Essay	Objective
Provides opportunity to test student's ability to select, organize, and integrate	+	
Requires student to produce answer and not just recognize it	+	
Is free from factors of skill in expression and penmanship		+
Is free from opportunities for bluffing		+
Is free from opportunities for guessing	+	
Provides an adequately representative sample of the topics covered		+
Can be prepared quickly	+	
Can be scored quickly		+
Can be scored routinely by a clerk		+
Can be scored with high consistency from scorer to scorer		+

The balance of importance between these factors will vary from situation to situation. It is clear that neither type has exclusive claim to all the advantages. In evaluating the work of his class, the teacher needs to use both kinds of testing procedures.

EFFECTIVE USE OF THE ESSAY EXAMINATION

Because of their advantages in evaluating abilities to organize an answer to a question, recall and select relevant information, and present it logically and effectively, essay examinations should continue to be used in the evaluation of student performance. If they are to be used, the teacher should have some guiding principles as to when to use them and what he can do to overcome their common weaknesses. These weaknesses are found partly in the format of the questions and partly in the process of evaluating the answers produced by the students.

WHEN TO USE ESSAY EXAMINATIONS

The factors that make it appropriate to use an essay examination are in part very immediate practical ones, in part more fundamental theoretical considerations.

Immediate Practical Considerations. The most obvious practical reason for using an essay examination is to save time. It takes a number of hours to prepare a good objective test. When the class group is small, there will be few papers to read and an essay examination may actually save time. Moreover, when time to prepare an examination is limited the teacher can substitute reading time *after* the examination for preparation time *before* the examination. Since many fewer essay questions than objective items are required for a given amount of testing time, the teacher may find it easier to construct a good essay test than a good objective test. However, it should be emphasized that making good tests of any kind requires considerable thought and effort on the part of the person writing the questions. A teacher cannot expect to produce good tests of any kind if he dashes off the questions a half-hour before the test is to be given.

A consideration that may be compelling in some cases is lack of reproduction facilities for running off copies of the test. Then a set of essay questions written on the blackboard is a practical solution. In such a situation it would probably be wise to use some short free-answer questions requiring only a few words or sentences for an answer as well as those in true essay form requiring extended answers. This will permit a wider and more adequate sample of the students' achievement. Another practical solution is to read objective questions to the class.   This procedure will work for rather alert students and for fairly simple items but it tends to be inefficient in requiring repetitions of the items and it requires a somewhat special ability to remember the total item well enough to indicate an answer.   With more complex items, the teacher will find that reading the items to the class becomes less satisfactory.

A third point that is sometimes made is that essay questions are less demanding upon the skill of the teacher.   It is probably true that ambiguities and poor expression are more apparent in an objective item, but confusion as to what is wanted in response to an essay question can also be substantial.   In many educational settings, the student must know the person who wrote the essay question in order to write an acceptable answer.   Many of the faults in writing objective items can be avoided once they have been pointed out, so that it seems more desirable to improve item-writing skills than to resort to essay questions as a defense.

More Basic Theoretical Issues.   The functions that can be appraised better by an essay question than by short-answer or objective questions are abilities to select, relate, and organize, to create essentially new patterns and to use language to express one's ideas.   For example, objective 5 on our blueprint on p. 33, "can express generalizations and concepts in his own words," can be measured only by an essay item since an objective item does not permit the student to use his own words.   There would be little justification for using essay items to evaluate objectives one through three on our blueprint since these objectives require the reproduction of factual information. The essay question is an inefficient way to measure factual information that could be more effectively and efficiently measured by a series of objective items.

Merely phrasing a question in the essay form does not automatically insure that the abilities to select and organize, to create new syntheses, to make new applications, or the other so-called higher mental abilities will be assessed.   Most of the essay tests given in elementary and secondary schools and colleges measure nothing more than the ability to reproduce facts.   In order to assess the abilities that are best measured by essay questions, the questions must be carefully phrased to require an application or creative synthesis of what has been taught. Thus, question *A* tests only information.

Question A

What rights are guaranteed to the people under the first amendment to the Constitution?

Question B

A newspaper, *The Evening Standard,* published a series of articles on the city government of Townsville. In one article, the reporter for the paper stated that the mayor of Townsville was incompetent and inefficient and did not spend enough time in his office to take care of city affairs. The mayor sued *The Evening Standard* in court for libel stating that the article made him look bad to the people of the city and reduced his effectiveness as mayor. What decision could be expected from the courts? Why?

Question *B,* by contrast, requires identification and selection of the proper items of information, and their application to the solution of a new problem. Question *B* seems more clearly appropriate for an essay examination.

In the early days of objective testing, some studies were carried out that showed that the prospect of an essay examination leads to study activities emphasizing the interrelationships of facts and principles in an area whereas the prospect of an objective examination leads to the memorizing of discrete details. There is little recent evidence on this point, and we wonder whether the relationship was a *necessary* one or merely a reflection of the low quality of the objective tests to which the groups had been exposed. This finding certainly points out a *potential* weakness of objective tests, and one escape from this weakness is to use essay tests. We suspect that study habits depend less upon the form of the test exercises than upon the type of objective that is emphasized—whether the items are objective or essay.

Variants on the Essay Examination. Values claimed for the essay examination are those of appraising ability to organize materials and to use language effectively to express the resulting organization. However, in the usual scheduled essay examinations these functions may become submerged because (1) differences in knowledge of the basic facts hide differences in ability to organize those facts and (2) time pressures hide the quality of the individuals' written expression.

Two variations may be considered that appear likely to bring out the factors in which we are particularly interested. One is to give an "open book" examination, in which every individual has access to any basic data present in his text, his notes, or other sources. Memory of facts is then reduced as a factor entering into individual performance, and ability to locate, select, and use the facts is brought to the fore.

The second variation is to give the problems as an out-of-class examination with unlimited time. This minimizes time pressure, and makes the test more nearly a pure power test—power both with respect to organizing ability and with respect to written expression. We do, of course, introduce a new problem, since we are less able to guarantee the integrity of the written material turned in. When the examination is used against rather than for the pupil, illicit help is likely to become a serious problem.

IMPROVING ESSAY TESTS

We have already pointed out in a previous section that essay tests can be improved by limiting their use to those objectives that are best measured by the essay format. There is not much that a teacher can do to overcome the weakness of essay tests that arises from the limited number of essay questions that can be presented to students in a given period of time except to give several essay tests during the school semester or year. A teacher can do much to overcome some of the other weaknesses of the essay test by (1) writing good essay questions, and (2) improving his methods of evaluating the answers. In the next section we will give some guides to writing better essay questions. Following that is a section suggesting ways to improve the scoring of answers to essay questions.

IMPROVING THE CONTENT OF AN ESSAY TEST

The following paragraphs present and discuss several suggestions for improving the questions that go into an essay test. These are not scientifically established principles, but they reflect the judgment of experienced test makers.

1. *Before starting to Write the Essay Question, Have in Mind Explicitly What Mental Processes of the Student You Want to Bring Out by the Question.* If you want to use the essay question to determine the extent to which a student can *use* his information, then the question must be phrased in such a way that the student must do such things as solve a problem that has not been directly taught, or point out relationships that have not been explicitly pointed out before.

2. *In General, Start Essay Questions with Such Phrases as "Compare," "Contrast," "Give the reasons for," "Present the arguments for and against," "Give original examples of," and "Explain how or why."* These words will help to present tasks requiring the student to select, organize, and apply his knowledge. Don't start essay questions with such words as "what," "who," "when," and "list." These words are likely to present tasks requiring only the reproduction of information.

3. *Write the Essay Question in Such a Way That the Task Is Clearly and Unambiguously Defined for Each Examinee.* A question such as "Discuss the factors and influences that led to the writing and adoption of our Constitution," is global, vague, and ambiguous. First, what does the teacher mean by the word "discuss"? Second, does the teacher want the student to start with the Magna Charta in 1215 or with the settlement of the colonies or with the end of the Revolutionary War? Third, does the teacher want the student to stop with the beginning of the Constitutional Convention in 1787 or with the ratification of the Constitution? Fourth, what does the teacher mean by "factors and influences?" The score that the student receives for his answer is likely to depend to a large extent on how lucky he is guessing what the teacher wanted.

A better way to phrase this question so that each examinee will interpret the question in the same way would be:

Explain how each of the following influenced the provisions written into our Constitution by the delegates to the Constitutional Convention.

    A. The Magna Charta, the Petition of Right, and the English Bill of Rights.
    B. The fear of tyranny or rule by one man or one group.
    C. The problems that arose in trying to operate under the provisions of the Article of Confederation.
    D. The fear of the small states that they would be controlled by the large states.
    E. Business rivalries between states.

The question as it has been rephrased guarantees a more common basis for response. In one sense it breaks the one question up into five. The analysis also makes clear that on the original question (and also the revised one) students will require a relatively long time to write an adequate answer.

4. *The Words "What do you think," "In your opinion," or "Write all you know about . . ." Almost Never Belong in an Essay Question to Measure Academic Achievement.* The use of these phrases is common on teacher-made essay tests. But when a teacher asks: "Why do you think that the Articles of Confederation provided a poor basis for the formation of our central government?," he is not really interested in the student's opinion. He actually wants to determine whether the student knows the fundamental weaknesses of the Articles of Confederation, as stated by the teacher or text. Therefore the question would be better if written: "Why did the Articles of Confederation prove to be unworkable as a framework for our national government?"

The only time when the use of "you," "in your opinion," or "do you think" is justified in an essay question (or any other type of test question) is when the purpose of the question is to obtain an expression of attitudes (which really cannot be graded) or to determine how good a logical defense a student can make of the position that he has taken. In the latter instance, the teacher should *not* be particularly interested in which position the student takes and should evaluate the answer given only on the basis of how well the student defends or supports his position.

5. *Be Sure That the Students Do Not Have Too Many or Too Lengthy Questions to Answer in the Time Available.* An essay test should not be a test of speed of writing. Good essay questions demand that the student consider the question, think about his answer, then write it. These processes take time and the younger the student or the more complex the question, the longer is the required time. In order to answer adequately the revised question on p. 54, the typical eighth grader would probably need from 45 to 60 minutes. In most essay tests given in the classroom, three to five such questions are given to be answered in a single classroom period. This practice may encourage both sloppy thinking and sloppy writing on the part of the student.

6. *Do Not Use Both Essay and Objective Questions in the Same Test when the Time for Testing is Limited.* Quite frequently teachers use both objective and essay questions on the same test. It is not unusual to see a teacher-made test consisting of thirty to fifty multiple-choice questions and one to three essay questions, all of which are to be answered in a 50-minute period. This practice is undesirable first because there is not enough time for the student to answer adequately all of the questions and second because there are very difficult problems in combining the scores on the two different kinds of items. (See Chapter 17.)

7. *Have Each Examinee Answer the Same Questions. Don't Offer a Choice of Questions to be Answered.* When an essay examination is being used to appraise achievement of the objectives of a common program of study, each examinee should be required to answer the same questions. Giving a choice of questions reduces the common base upon which different individuals may be compared. It adds one further source of variability to the subjectivity and inaccuracy that already exist. A choice of questions may have a public-relations value with the examinees, but it has no justification from the point of view of effective measurement.

A number of steps may be taken to mitigate the subjectivity and reduce some of the biases in evaluating the answers to an essay examination. These are mostly attempts to break up the process of evaluation into a series of more specific, fractionated judgments made upon a common base and applied to an anonymous product. Specific suggestions are outlined below.

1. *Decide in Advance What Factors Are to Be Measured. If More than One Distinct Quality Is to Be Appraised, Make Separate Evaluations of Each.* If facts are considered important, score for facts. If organization is important, give a rating upon organization. If mechanics of English, sentence structure, spelling, punctuation, etc., are considered a significant outcome, give a rating upon mechanics. However, do not contaminate the rating for knowledge or understanding with appraisal of mechanics. It is hard to isolate quality of organization from extent of factual information, but if the essay question is to serve its distinctive purpose an attempt should be made to do so.

2. *Prepare a Model Answer in Advance, Showing What Points Should Be Covered and How Many Credits Are to Be Allowed for Each.* This will provide a common frame of reference for evaluating each paper. After the preliminary model has been prepared, it should be checked against a sample of student responses to the question. The model and the scoring scheme should be modified in the light of these answers. They can now be used as the yardstick for assigning credits to each paper in turn.

3. *Read All Answers to One Question before Going on to the Next.* A more uniform standard can be maintained for a single question and for a short period of time. There is more chance to compare one person's answer with another's and thus to build up a "feel" for the answers. There is less contamination of judgment by what that same examinee had written on the previous question.

4. *Grade the Papers as Nearly Anonymously as Possible.* The less you know about *who* wrote an answer, the more objectively you can grade *what* was written.

5. *Greater Reliability Can Be Obtained by Averaging Independent Ratings.* If the importance of the test merits the expenditure of the extra effort, a more dependable appraisal can be obtained by having one or more additional raters each give an independent rating of the responses.

SUMMARY STATEMENT

Evaluation of pupil achievement is one of the teacher's important responsibilities. In view of the many functions that tests serve in motivating and directing learning, and in view of the disservice that may be done the pupil from poorly conceived or executed evaluation instruments, it is important that the teacher's evaluation devices be well thought out and well made. Both written tests and a variety of informal appraisals are needed to evaluate completely the objectives of the modern curriculum.

For any type of written test, it is desirable to have a definite plan in advance of preparing the test items. The development of such a plan requires an analysis of the outcomes one is trying to achieve in the teaching of a particular course or unit and of the significant segments of content through which those objectives are to be realized. A statement of objectives useful for guiding the construction of test items must be phrased in terms of pupil behaviors—specific things that the pupil is supposed to be able to do—rather than in broad generalizations. In addition, the plan should include the allocation of test items among the content areas and objectives, the types of items to be used, the total number of items in the test, and specifications for the spread of item difficulties.

Both essay and objective tests should be used to evaluate pupil achievement. The essay test is easier to prepare and has certain advantages in appraising ability to recall information, select relevant material, and organize it into an integrated answer. However, the objective test has marked advantages in freedom from such irrelevant factors as quality of handwriting or of English usage, in breadth of sampling of the desired outcomes of teaching, and in ease and objectivity of scoring.

Essay questions can be improved by phrasing the question so as to present a well-defined task to the student and by providing conditions for scoring that reduce as far as possible the subjectivity of grading.

REFERENCES

1. Bloom, Benjamin S., Max D. Engelhart, Edward J. Furst, Walker H. Hill, and David R. Krathwohl, *Taxonomy of educational objectives: the classification of educational goals: handbook I, cognitive domain,* New York and London, Longmans, Green, 1956.

SUGGESTED ADDITIONAL READING

Bloom, Benjamin S., Editor, *Taxonomy of educational objectives, Handbook I, Cognitive domain,* New York, Longmans, Green, 1956.

Dressel, Paul L., and Lewis B. Mayhew, *General education: explorations in evaluation,* Washington, D. C., American Council on Education, 1954, Chapters 3–8.

French, Will, *Behavioral goals of general education in high school,* New York, Russell Sage Foundation, 1957.

Harris, Chester W., Editor, *Encyclopedia of educational research,* 3rd ed., New York, Macmillan, 1960, pp. 650–657, 1506–1514.

Kearney, Nolan C., *Elementary school objectives,* New York, Russell Sage Foundation, 1953.

Lindquist, E. F., Preliminary considerations in objective test construction, Chapter 5 in E. F. Lindquist, Editor, *Educational measurement,* Washington, D. C., American Council on Education, 1951.

Odell, C. W., *How to improve classroom testing,* rev. ed., Dubuque, Iowa, William C. Brown, 1958, Chapters III, IV, V, and VI.

Smith, Eugene R., et al., *Appraising and recording student progress,* New York, Harper, 1942, Chapters 1 and 2.

Stalnaker, John M., The essay type of examination, Chapter 13 in E. F. Lindquist, Editor, *Educational measurement,* Washington, D. C., American Council on Education, 1951.

Thomas, R. Murray, *Judging student progress,* 2nd ed., New York, Longmans, Green, 1960, Chapter 2.

Vaughn, K. W., Planning the objective test, Chapter 6 in E. F. Lindquist, Editor, *Educational measurement,* Washington, D. C., American Council on Education, 1951.

QUESTIONS FOR DISCUSSION

1. Prepare a statement of the objectives for a course, or a unit within a course, that you are teaching or plan to teach.

2. Which of the objectives in 1 could be measured effectively by a written test? Which only partially or not at all. Why is a written test inadequate for these? How might these objectives best be appraised?

3. Based on the objectives identified in the first part of question 2 and a course outline, prepare a blueprint for a test to evaluate the unit or course.

4. In a junior high school, one teacher takes complete responsibility for preparing the common final examination for all the classes in general science. He makes the examination up without consulting the other teachers. What advantages and disadvantages do you see in this procedure?

5. It has been said that one of the goals of the music program in an elementary school is to "increase the sensitivity of pupils to music in its different forms." How could this goal be defined so that progress toward it could be measured?

6. Students are sometimes heard to remark: "You can't get a good mark on Miss X's tests unless you really know Miss X." What does this remark imply about Miss X's tests?

7. On p. 49 is a list of factors that have been presented as favoring either essay or objective tests. Do you agree with the classification given there? Which are the most important factors? What other points should be considered in deciding which type of test to use for the final examination in a particular course?

8. Criticize the following features of an essay test planned for a ninth-grade social studies class:

a. There will be 10 questions on the test.
b. Each student will answer any 5.
c. Each question will have a value of 20 points.
d. One point will be taken off for each misspelled word and each grammatical error.
e. A 5-point bonus will be given for neatness.
f. Time for the test will be 40 minutes.

9. Criticize and revise each of the following essay questions:

a. Discuss the increase in juvenile delinquency since World War II.
b. Discuss government support of farm prices.
c. Discuss the "cold war."

10. For what types of objectives would an open-book essay examination be appropriate? What would be the advantages and disadvantages of such an examination, as compared with the usual essay examination?

Chapter 4

▼

Preparing Objective Tests

INTRODUCTION

The objective type of test item was developed in order to overcome some of the disadvantages of the essay test discussed in Chapter 3. As we pointed out in that chapter, there is still a good deal of argument about the relative merits of the two types of test. Those who object to the objective type of test say that it emphasizes factual material, encourages piecemeal memorization of unimportant details, permits too much guessing of the correct answer, ignores the higher mental processes, neglects the more important educational objectives, and never gives the student any practice in writing. Except for the last objection, we have discussed the other criticisms in Chapter 3. As for the last objection, we might well raise the question as to whether the testing period is the place to give students practice in writing and whether the kind of writing practice provided by most essay tests encourages (or discourages) good writing.

As we have stated before, the question of which kind of test to use is not an either-or question. Both essay and objective tests can be used to advantage in the classroom. A poorly constructed test of either kind can inhibit or misdirect learning. The problem then is to construct good tests. In this chapter we will consider methods of improving and using the objective type of item and of analyzing and using the results of objective tests.

WRITING THE ITEMS FOR AN OBJECTIVE TEST

Writing good test items is an art. It is a little like writing a good sonnet and a little like baking a good cake. The operation is not quite so free and fanciful as writing the sonnet; it is not quite so standardized as baking the cake. It lies somewhere in between. So a discussion of item writing lies somewhere between the exhortation to the poet to go out and express himself and the precise recipes of a good cookbook. The point we wish to make is that there is no exact science of test construction. The guides and maxims that we shall offer are not tested out by controlled scientific experimentation. Rather, they represent a distillation of practical experience and professional judgment. As with the recipe in the cookbook, if carefully followed they yield a good product.

We shall first present some suggestions that apply to almost any type of objective item. Then we will consider specific item types, indicating some of the general virtues and limitations of that type of item and giving more specific suggestions for writing and editing. A number of the principles that we set forth will seem very obvious. However, experience in reviewing and editing items indicates that these most obvious faults are the ones that are most frequently committed by persons who try to prepare objective tests. Thus, it hardly seems necessary to insist that a multiple-choice item must have one and only one right answer, and yet items with no right answer or several occur again and again in tests that are carelessly prepared.

GENERAL MAXIMS FOR ITEM WRITING

1. *Keep the Reading Difficulty of Test Items Low* in relation to the group who are to take the test, unless the purpose is to measure verbal and reading abilities. Ordinarily you do not want language difficulties to interfere with a pupil's opportunity to show what he knows.

Example

Poor: What was the ostensible reason for requesting the states to designate one or more of their constituents as representatives to attend a general convention to meet in Philadelphia in 1787?

A. To draft a new Constitution.
B. To raise money to pay off Revolutionary War debts.
C. To settle commercial disputes among the states.
D. To revise the Articles of Confederation.

Better: When the states were asked to send representatives to a general convention to meet in Philadelphia in 1787, they were told that these representatives would be asked to

A. draft a new Constitution.
B. raise money to pay off Revolutionary War debts.
C. settle commercial disputes among the states.
D. revise the Articles of Confederation.

2. *Do Not Lift a Statement Verbatim from the Textbook.* This places a premium upon rote memory with a minimum of understanding. Also the statement may have little or no meaning when it is

removed from the context. A statement can at least be paraphrased. Better still, in many cases it may be possible to imbed the specific knowledge in an application.

Example

Poor. T F The House of Representatives shall be composed of members chosen every second year.

Better: T F A United States Representative elected for a full term of office to begin in 1961 would end his term in 1963.

3. *If an Item Is Based on Opinion or Authority, Indicate* Whose *Opinion or* What *Authority.* Ordinarily statements of a controversial nature do not make good items, but there are instances where knowing what some particular person thinks may be important for its own sake. The student should presumably be acquainted with the viewpoint of his textbook or instructor, but he should not be placed in the position of having to endorse it as indisputable fact.

Example

Poor: T F The Declaration of Independence influenced later political developments more than any other document.

Better: T F According to your textbook, the Declaration of Independence influenced later political developments more than any other document.

4. *In Planning a Set of Items for a Test, Take Care That One Item Does Not Provide Cues to the Answer of Another Item or Items.* The second item below gives cues to the first.

Example

1. Under the provisions of the Constitution, the judicial branch of our National Government is given the power to

   A. enforce the laws.
   B. interpret the laws.
   C. make the laws.
   D. repeal the laws.

2. The interpretation of laws by the judicial branch of our National Government has been one method used to

   A. keep the powers of government in the hands of the people.
   B. prevent a weak president from being dominated by a strong Congress.
   C. guarantee Constitutional rights to all citizens.
   D. keep the Constitution flexible enough to meet changing social, political, and economic conditions.

5. *Avoid the Use of Interlocking or Interdependent Items.* The answer to one item should not be required as a condition for solving the next item. This is the other side of the principle stated in 4 above. Every individual should have a fair chance at each item as it comes. Thus, in the example shown below, the person who does not know the answer to the first question is in a very weak position as far as attacking the second one is concerned.

Example

1. The name of the first written constitution in the American colonies was the   (Fundamental Orders of Connecticut)   .
2. This constitution was drafted in the year   (1639)   .

6. *In a Set of Items, Let the Occurrence of Correct Responses Follow Essentially a Random Pattern.* Avoid favoring certain responses, i.e., either true or false, or certain locations in a set of responses. Do not have the responses follow any systematic pattern.

7. *Avoid Trick and Catch Questions,* except in the rare case in which the test has a specific purpose of measuring ability to keep out of traps. Trick questions are likely to mislead the abler or better-informed student, who knows enough to be caught by the trap. If they do this, they defeat the basic purpose of the test, which is to identify levels of knowledge and understanding.

Example 1

Poor: T F The term of office for all senators is 6 years.
(The item is keyed true but the student who knows the most about government is likely to get it wrong because a senator who is elected or appointed to take the place of a senator who dies serves only the unexpired time. Also, among the first group of senators at the time the Constitution was adopted, some served only 2 years, some 4, and some 6.)
Better: T F The Constitution states that the term of office for senators shall be six years.

Example 2

Poor: T F On May 25, 1787, fifty-five delegates from twelve states met to revise the Articles of Confederation.
(This was keyed false because all fifty-five were not present on May 25. No revision is shown for this item because the idea being tested is considered so insignificant that it would be better not to use the item.)

8. *Try to Avoid Ambiguity of Statement and Meaning.* This is a general admonition, somewhat like "Sin no more," and it may be no

more effective.   However, it is certainly true that ambiguity of statement and meaning is the most pervasive fault in objective test items.
Many of the specific points already covered and many of those still to
be covered deal with specific aspects of the reduction of ambiguity.

Example

Poor: In the Constitution, the composition of Congress was established
in order to

A. maintain balance of power between the large and small states.
B. protect the interests of propertied classes.
C. get the delegates to accept and sign the Constitution.
D. provide for a stronger central government.

The keyed answer to the above question was A, but the examinee trying
to answer the item is faced with several problems.   First of all, what does
the writer of the item mean by "the composition of Congress?"   Does he
mean the division of Congress into two houses, the basis for determining
representation in Congress or the qualifications of the members of Congress?   Does the writer of the item want the student to give the immediate
reason for the compromise or the ultimate reason?   Actually the writer of
this item was trying to determine whether the student knew why the Constitution provided for a Congress made up of a House of Representatives
with proportional representation from each state and a senate with equal
representation from each state.

But even if the student guesses correctly what the item writer had in
mind when he wrote the item, he is likely to have difficulty with the answer
choices.

A case can be made for each of the answer choices being correct.   All
of the compromises at the Constitutional Convention had two aims: to
provide for a stronger central government and, at the same time, to draft
a document that the states would be willing to accept.   There is some truth
in choice B because the large states feared that the small states would pass
laws interfering with business and property.   Of all the answer choices,
the keyed answer A is probably the least correct since the purpose was not
to maintain exact balances of powers between large and small states but
to grant some concessions to each.

The item needs to be sharpened up in several respects.   The example
below would appear to test the same knowledge and to provide less occasion for misunderstanding of what the examiner was trying to say.

Better: At the Constitutional Convention, the delegates agreed to give
each state equal representation in the Senate and proportional representation in the House of Representatives in order to

A. satisfy the conflicting demands of the large and small states.
B. protect the rights of the sovereign states.
C. make the legislative branch of the central government the strongest.
D. keep the government in the hands of all the people.

9. *Beware of Items Dealing with Trivia.* An item on a test should appraise some important item of knowledge or some significant understanding. Avoid the type of item that could quite justifiably be answered, "Who cares?" Ask yourself in each case whether knowing or not knowing the answer would make a significant difference in the individual's competence in the area being appraised.

Example

Poor: A census every 10 years was provided for in the Constitution in Article I Section

A. 1
B. 2
C. 3
D. 4

Better: The reason the framers of the Constitution provided that a national census should be taken every 10 years was to

A. obtain information needed by Congress to carry out its duties.
B. determine how many Representatives each state should have.
C. determine how rapidly the country was growing.
D. obtain accurate information for use by government and industrial agencies.

TRUE-FALSE ITEMS

The true-false item has had a popularity in teacher-made objective tests far beyond that warranted by its essential nature. This has probably happened because bad true-false items can be written quickly and easily. To write good ones is quite a different matter.

Even when they are well written, true-false items are relatively restricted in the types of educational objective they can measure. They should be limited to statements that are unequivocally true or demonstrably false. For this reason, they are adapted to measuring relatively specific, isolated, and often trivial facts. They can also be used fairly well to test meanings and definitions of terms. But items testing genuine understandings, inferences, and applications are usually very hard to cast in true-false form. The true-false item is particularly open to attack as fostering piecemeal, fractionated, superficial learning and is probably responsible for many of the attacks upon the objective test. It is also in this form of test that the problem of guessing becomes most acute.

The commonest variety of true-false item presents a simple declarative statement, and requires of the examinee only that he indicate whether it is true or false.

Example

T <u>F</u> The Articles of Confederation provided for a strong central government.

Several variations have been introduced in an attempt to improve the item type.   One simple variation is to underline a part of the statement, viz., "strong" in the above example.   The instructions indicate that this is the key part of the statement and that it determines whether the statement is true or false.   That is, the correctness or appropriateness of the rest of the statement is guaranteed.   The examinee can focus his attention upon the more specific issue of whether the underlined part is compatible with the rest of the statement.   This seems to reduce guessing and make for more consistent measurement.

A further variation is to require the examinee to correct the item if it is false.   This works well if combined with the underlining described above but is likely to be confusing if no constraints are introduced in the situation.   Our example could be corrected by changing "Articles of Confederation" to "Constitution," by changing "strong" to "weak," or by changing "central" to "state."   Requiring that the item be corrected reduces guessing and provides some further cue to the individual's knowledge.

Generally, the true-false type of item tends to be most useful when it is based on some given stimulus material such as a chart, map, graph, table, or reading passage and when the student responds to the item only in terms of the given material.   This type of true-false item has been used effectively in testing ability to interpret data of different kinds.   However, in this case, the format is generally changed by requiring the student to answer in four or five categories such as definitely true, probably true, insufficient data to determine whether it is true or false, probably false, and definitely false.   In this format the item is more like a multiple-choice item than a true-false item.

CAUTIONS IN WRITING TRUE-FALSE ITEMS

1. *Be sure that the Item as Written Can Be Unequivocally Classified as Either True or False.*   One of the most common weaknesses in true-false items is that the person who knows the most about the content may find it difficult to judge whether the item is true or false. This is particularly likely to happen with items that were intended to be true statements.   The student who knows the most about the content can often think of a number of exceptions or reasons why the statement is not universally true.   Consider the following example.

Example

Poor: T̲ F   The presidential candidate who receives the majority of votes is elected President.

The item was keyed true but strictly speaking it is not true. The candidate must receive the majority of *electoral* votes but not necessarily the majority of the *popular* vote. It is the higher-achieving student who is likely to know about both the electoral votes and the popular vote and he is likely to mark the item false because it does not specify electoral votes. The item would be better if it were revised as follows:

Example

Better: T̲ F   The presidential candidate receiving a majority of the electoral votes is elected President.

2. *Beware of "Specific Determiners,"* words that give cues to the probable answer, such as all, never, usually, etc. Statements that contain "all," "always," "no," "never," and such all-inclusive terms represent such broad generalizations that they are likely to be false. Qualified statements involving such terms as "usually" or "sometimes" are likely to be true. The test-wise student knows this, and will use these cues, if he is given a chance, to get credit for knowledge he does not possess. "All" or "no" may sometimes be used to advantage in *true* statements, because in this case using the determiner as a cue will lead the examinee astray.

Example

Poor: T F̲   All sessions of Congress are called by the President.
Better: T̲ F   All persons elected to the House of Representatives must be at least 25 years old.

3. *Beware of Ambiguous and Indefinite Terms of Degree or Amount.* Expressions such as "frequently," "greatly," "to a considerable degree," and "in most cases" are not interpreted in the same way by everyone who reads them. Ask a class or other group what they think of when you say that something happens "frequently." Is it once a week or once an hour? Is it 90 per cent of the time or 50 per cent? The variation will be very great. (Ed.: How great is very great?) An item in which the answer depends on the interpretation of such terms as these is an unsatisfactory one.

Example

Poor: T F   The Supreme Court is frequently required to rule on the constitutionality of a law.
Better: T̲ F   The Supreme Court has the power to declare a law unconstitutional.

4. *Beware of Negative Statements and Particularly of Double Negatives.* The negative is likely to be overlooked in hurried reading of an item, and the double negative is hard to read and confusing.

Example

Poor: T F The Constitution does not provide that no state law can deny a citizen the right to vote.

Better: T F The Constitution grants to each state the right to make laws specifying the qualifications for voting in that state.

5. *Beware of Items that Include More than One Idea in the Statement, Especially If One Is True and the Other Is False.* This type of item borders on the category of trick items. It places a premium on care and alertness in reading. The reader must not restrict his attention to one idea to the exclusion of the other or he will be misled. The item tends to be a measure of reading skills rather than knowledge or understanding of subject content.

Examples

Poor: T F The President has the power to make treaties with foreign countries, but the Senate must approve them by a majority of votes.

Better: T F The Senate must approve a treaty with a foreign country by a majority of votes.

Poor: T F No person shall be elected to the office of president more than twice, but a person who has acted as president for 2 years or more shall be eligible for re-election for at least two full terms.

Better: T F A person who has acted as president for 2 or more years can be re-elected twice.

(In each of the poor items, the first statement is true and the second one is false.)

6. *Beware of Items Where the Correct Answer Depends upon One Insignificant Word, Phrase, or Letter.* Each test item should measure an important aspect of the student's achievement; therefore each true-false item should require the student to react to important ideas and should not require him to be a proofreader. Many teachers try to obtain a spread of scores on a test by introducing items that require the student to examine each word and each letter in the word in order to arrive at the correct answer. For example, the item, "Ulysses Sampson Grant was President of the United States from 1869 to 1877," appeared as a true-false item on a sixth-grade social studies test and was

keyed false because Grant's middle name was Simpson, not Sampson. Surely, knowing Grant's middle name is not a significant aspect of achievement in sixth-grade social studies; however, if it is, then the item should be written so that attention is drawn to the middle name of Grant; e.g., "T   F   Ulysses Grant's middle name was Sampson."

7. *Beware of Giving Cues to the Correct Answer by the Length of the Item.* There is a general tendency for true statements to be longer than false ones. This is a result of the necessity of including qualifications and limitations to make the statement true. The item writer must be aware of this trend and make a conscious effort to overcome it.

SHORT-ANSWER AND COMPLETION ITEMS

The short-answer and the completion item tend to be very nearly the same thing, differing only in the form in which the problem is presented. If it is presented as a question it is a short-answer item, whereas if it is presented as an incomplete statement it is a completion item.

Example

Short Answer: In what colony was the first representative assembly in America established?

Completion: The first representative assembly in America was established in the colony of   (Virginia)   .

Items of this type are well suited to testing knowledge of vocabulary, names or dates, identification of concepts, and ability to solve algebraic or numerical problems. Numerical problems that yield a specific numerical solution are "short answer" in their very nature. The measurement of more complex understandings and applications is difficult to accomplish with items of this type. Furthermore, evaluation of the varied responses that are given is likely to call for some skill and to introduce some subjectivity into the scoring procedure.

MAXIMS CONCERNING COMPLETION ITEMS

1. *Beware of Indefinite or "Open" Completion Items.* In the first example, on p. 70, there are many words or phrases that give factually correct and reasonably sensible completions to the statement, i.e., "arrested," "imprisoned," "acquitted," "critical of the government," "from New York," "a publisher." The problem needs to be more fully defined, as is done in the revised statement.

Example

Poor: The man whose case won freedom of the press for our country was   (Zenger) .

Better: The name of the man whose case won freedom of the press for our country was   (Zenger) .

2. *Omit Only Key Words.* Do not leave the verb out of a completion statement unless the purpose of the item is to measure knowledge of verb forms. The blank in a completion item should require the student to supply an important fact.

Example

Poor: The Constitutional Convention   (met)   in Philadelphia in 1787.

Better: The Constitutional Convention met in Philadelphia in the year   (1787) .

3. *Don't Leave Too Many Blanks in a Statement.* Overmutilation of a statement reduces the task of the examinee to a guessing game or an intelligence test.

Example

Poor: The   (Ordinance)   of   (1787)   provided for the   (admission)   of   (new states) .

Better: The procedure for admitting new states to the Union was first set forth by the   (Ordinance of 1787) .

4. *Blanks are Better Put Near the End of a Statement Rather Than at the Beginning.* This permits the problem to be stated before the blank is encountered.

Example

Poor: A(n)   (tariff)   is a tax on goods imported into a country.

Better: A tax levied on goods imported into a country is called a(n)   (tariff) .

5. *If the Problem Requires a Numerical Answer, Indicate the Units in Which It Is to Be Expressed.* This will simplify the problem of scoring and will remove one possibility of ambiguity in the examinee's response.

MULTIPLE-CHOICE ITEMS

The multiple-choice item is the most flexible and most effective of the objective item types. It is effective for measuring information, vocabulary, understandings, application of principles, or ability to interpret data. In fact, it can be used to test practically any educational objective that can be measured by a pencil-and-paper test except the ability to organize and present material. The versatility and effectiveness of the multiple-choice item is limited only by the ingenuity and talent of the item writer.

The multiple-choice item consists of two parts: the stem, which presents the problem, and the list of possible answers or options. The stem may be presented in the form of an incomplete statement or a question.

Example

Incomplete statement: If both the President and Vice-President died in office, the person who would act as President would be the

A. Majority Leader of the Senate.
B. President of the Senate.
C. Speaker of the House of Representatives.
D. Secretary of State.

Question: Who would act as President if both the President and Vice-President died in office?

A. The Majority Leader of the Senate.
B. The President of the Senate.
C. The Speaker of the House of Representatives.
D. The Secretary of State.

Inexperienced item writers usually find it easier to use the question form of stem than the incomplete sentence form. The use of the question forces the item writer to state the problem explicitly. It rules out certain types of faults that may creep into the incomplete statement, which we will consider presently. However, the incomplete statement is often more concise and pointed than the question, if it is skillfully used.

The number of options used in the multiple-choice question differs in different tests, and there is no real reason why it cannot vary for items in the same test. However, to reduce the guessing factor, it is preferable to have four or five options for each item. On the other hand, it seems more sensible to have only three good options for an item than to have five, two of which are so obviously wrong that no one ever chooses them.

The difficulty of a multiple-choice item will depend upon both the "closeness" of the options and the process called for in the item.

Consider the set of three items shown below, all relating to the First Amendment to the Constitution. We can predict with some confidence that version I will be passed by more pupils than will II, and II by more than III. The difference between I and II is in the closeness of the options—in I, the wrong choices fall completely outside the Bill of Rights, i.e., the first ten Amendments to the Constitution, while in II, each option refers to some one of these Amendments. The difference between II and III is primarily a matter of the intellectual process involved—II requires little more than remembering and recognizing the key concept involved in the different amendments, while III requires that the student identify that concept when it is embedded in a specific concrete situation.

Version I

The First Amendment to the Constitution is concerned with

A. powers of Congress.
B. the abolition of slavery.
C. freedom of speech, press, and religion.
D. the term of office of the President.

Version II

According to the First Amendment to the Constitution, the government is not permitted to

A. search a person's house without a warrant.
B. hold a person in jail for a long time without a trial.
C. make laws that interfere with freedom of speech or religion.
D. force a person to give evidence against himself.

Version III

Which of the following actions would violate the rights guaranteed to a person by the First Amendment to the Constitution?

A. An F.B.I. agent gets a tip that counterfeiters are operating in Mr. Jones' basement, so he breaks in the door to search the basement.
B. Mr. Smith is arrested and held in jail for three weeks but is not informed of the charges against him and is not allowed to see a lawyer.
C. Mr. Simpson is arrested for writing articles criticizing the government's defense policies.
D. Mr. Hoffman, who is on trial for conspiracy, is forced to take the witness stand and give evidence.

MAXIMS FOR MULTIPLE-CHOICE ITEMS

1. *The Stem of a Multiple-Choice Item Should Clearly Formulate a Problem.* All the options should be possible answers to a single problem that is raised by the stem. When the stem is phrased as a question, it is clear that a single problem has been raised, but this should be equally the case when the stem is in the form of an incomplete statement. Avoid items that are really a series of unrelated true-false items dealing with the same general topic.

Example

Poor: At the Constitutional Convention, the "great" compromise

A. gave small and large states equal representation in the Senate.
B. made slave holding legal.
C. was opposed by Washington.
D. gave the western lands claimed by the states to the federal govenment.

Better: At the Constitutional Convention, the "great" compromise between the large and small states was concerned with

A. representation in Congress.
B. importation of slaves.
C. the power to levy taxes.
D. commerce between states.

2. *Include as Much of the Item as Possible in the Stem.* In the interests of economy of space, economy of reading time, and clear statement of the problem, it is usually desirable to try to word and arrange the item so that the stem is relatively long and the several options relatively short. This cannot always be achieved but is an objective to be worked toward. This principle ties in with the one previously stated of formulating the problem fully in the stem.

Example

Poor: According to the Constitution, neither Congress nor the states can pass a law

A. that would require a citizen to be able to read and write before he could vote.
B. that would prevent a citizen from voting because he did not own property.
C. that would make it impossible for a citizen to vote because he had committed a crime.
D. that would deprive a citizen of the right to vote because he was of Chinese descent.

Better: According to the Constitution, neither Congress nor the states can pass a law that would deprive a citizen of his right to vote because he

A. could not read or write.
B. did not own property.
C. had committed a crime.
<u>D.</u> was of Chinese descent.

3. *Don't Load the Stem Down with Irrelevant Material.* In certain special cases, the purpose of an item may be to test the examinee's ability to identify and pick out the essential facts. In this case, it is appropriate to hide the crucial aspect of the problem in a set of details that are of no importance. Except for this case, however, the item should be written so as to make the nature of the problem posed as clear as possible. The less irrelevant reading the examinee has to do, the better.

Example

Poor: The framers of the Constitution faced many problems. The delegates to the Constitutional Convention represented states with different interests, and the delegates from the individual states wanted to see that their states' interests were protected. However, the delegates agreed that the Articles of Confederation needed to be changed in order to provide for

A. a President whom everyone could respect.
<u>B.</u> a stronger central government.
C. a better understanding between states.
D. a government for and by the people.

Better: The delegates to the Constitutional Convention agreed that the Articles of Confederation needed to be changed in order to provide for

A. a President whom everyone could respect.
B. a stronger central government.
<u>C.</u> a better understanding between states.
D. a government for and by the people.

4. *Be Sure that There Is One and Only One Correct or Clearly Best Answer.* It hardly seems necessary to specify that a multiple-choice item must have one and only one right answer, but in practice this is one of the most pervasive and insidious faults in item writing. Thus, in the following example, though choice A was probably designed to be the correct answer, there is a large element of correctness also in choices B and D. The item could be improved as shown in the revised form.

Example

Poor: The adoption of the Constitution was generally opposed by people who

A. owed money.
B. thought that most of the people were unfit to govern themselves.
C. owned businesses.
D. thought the states would be destroyed.

Better: The adoption of the Constitution was generally opposed by people who

A. owed money.
B. were engaged in commerce.
C. owned western land.
D. were engaged in manufacturing.

5. *Items Designed to Measure Understandings, Insights, or Ability to Apply Principles Should Be Presented in Novel Terms.* If the situations used to measure understandings follow very closely the examples used in text or class, the possibility of a correct answer being based on rote memory of what was read or heard is very real. The second and third variations of the example on p. 72 illustrate an attempt to move away from the form in which the concept was originally stated.

6. *Beware of Clang Associations.* If the stem and the keyed answer "sound alike," the examinee may get the question right just by using this superficial cue. However, superficial associations in the *wrong* answers represent one of the effective devices for attracting those who do not really know the fact or concept being tested. This last practice must be used with discretion, or one may prepare trick questions.

Example

Poor: A system of checks and balances was established by the Constitution in order to

A. balance majority power and minority rights.
B. appease the small states.
C. distribute powers between the central government and the state governments.
D. provide for flexibility in the central government.

Better: A system of checks and balances was established by the Constitution in order to

A. prevent one group or one person from seizing the power of government.
B. balance the powers of the small and large states.
C. distribute powers equally between the central government and the state governments.
D. provide for flexibility in the Constitution.

7. *Beware of Irrelevant Grammatical Cues.* Be sure that each option is a grammatically correct completion of the stem. Cues from the use of the indefinite article ("a" versus "an") in the stem, the number or tense of a verb, the use of the plural form of a noun or pronoun, etc., must be excluded.

Example

Poor: A power of the federal government that is suggested by the Constitution but is not directly stated in the Constitution is called an

A. concurrent power.
B. residual power.
C. implied power.
D. delegated power.

Better: A power of the federal government that is suggested by the Constitution but is not directly stated in the Constitution is called

A. an executive power.
B. a concurrent power.
C. an implied power.
D. a residual power.

(Note that one option was changed to provide for two options that used "an" since test-wise examinees sometimes use the one article that is different as a cue to the correct answer.)

8. *Beware of the Use of One Pair of Opposites as Options If One of the Pair is the Correct or Best Answer.* The directions for a multiple-choice test usually instruct the examinee to choose the one correct or best answer. If only one pair of opposites is used as options and one of the pair is the correct answer, the examinee is likely to limit his choice of answers to these two options because he thinks that both of them cannot be wrong. When this happens, the item is likely to operate as a two-choice item rather than as a four- or five-choice item, and the probability of guessing the correct answer is increased. It is better, if possible, to use two pairs of opposites or to eliminate the use of opposites.

Example

Poor: The chief objective of Daniel Shay's Rebellion was to force the state of Massachusetts to

A. grant ex-soldiers the right to vote.
B. issue paper currency.
C. withdraw paper currency.
D. stop slave trading.

Better: The chief objective of Daniel Shay's Rebellion was to force the state of Massachusetts to

A. grant ex-soldiers the right to vote.
B. issue paper currency.
C. pay ex-soldiers for their services in the Revolutionary War.
D. stop slave trading.

9. *Beware of the Use of "None of These," "None of the Above," "All of These," and "All of the Above" as Options.* Except for items requiring numerical computation the option "None of these" or "None of the above" usually fails to make any sense since it contradicts the stem or does not complete the stem grammatically. As a rule both options tend to be used as fillers, i.e., when the item writer cannot think of a fourth or fifth answer choice, he sticks in "None of these" or "All of these" usually as an incorrect answer.

The use of the option "All of these" as a correct answer in a four- or five-choice item generally makes an item less discriminating because if the examinee knows that at least two of the answer choices are correct he automatically gets the correct answer whether he knows anything about the other options or not.

If "None of these" or "All of these" is used as an answer choice, it should be used as frequently for the correct choice as are any of the other options.

Examples

Poor: The *Federalist Papers* were written by

A. Hamilton.
B. Jay.
C. Madison.
D. All of the above.

Better: The *Federalist Papers* were written by

A. Hamilton, Jay, and Madison.
B. Hamilton, Jefferson, and Madison.
C. Jefferson, Washington, and Franklin.
D. Washington, Franklin, and Jay.

Poor: Under the Articles of Confederation the national government obtained money to run the government by

A. putting a tax on imports.
B. printing additional paper currency.
C. borrowing money from foreign governments.
D. none of the above.

Better: Under the Articles of Confederation the national government obtained money to run the government by

A. putting a tax on imports.
B. printing additional paper currency.
C. borrowing money from foreign governments.
D. taxing property.

10. *Use the Negative Only Sparingly in the Stem of an Item.* It is usually desirable to emphasize the positive aspects of knowledge rather than the negative aspects of knowledge. However, there are times when it is important for the student to know the exception or to be able to detect errors. For these purposes a few items with the words "not" or "except" in the stem may be justified, particularly when over-inclusion is a common error for students. When a negative word is used in the stem of an item, it should be underlined and/or capitalized to call the student's attention to it.

Example

Poor: Which one of the following leaders of the Revolutionary War did not want the Articles of Confederation changed?

A. Benjamin Franklin
B. George Washington
C. Alexander Hamilton
D. Patrick Henry

(Note this is a poor use of the negative stem because it could be stated more effectively in positive form, "Which one of the following leaders of the Revolutionary War favored keeping the Articles of Confederation?")

Better: According to the Constitution, the President does NOT have the power to

A. declare war.
B. pardon a person convicted by a federal court.
C. call a special session of Congress.
D. nominate judges for the Supreme Court.

(Note this is a better use of the negative stem because (1) it requires the student to detect a common error made about the powers of the President; and (2) it would be difficult to get three good misleads if the item were stated in positive form. The stem of the item could not be stated "The Constitution forbids the President to ...." because the Constitution does not specifically forbid the President to declare war.)

THE MATCHING ITEM

The matching item is actually a special form of the multiple-choice item. The characteristic that distinguishes it from the ordinary multiple-choice item is that instead of a single problem or stem with a group of suggested answers, there are several problems whose answers must be drawn from a single list of possible answers.

The matching item has most frequently been used to measure factual information such as the meaning of words, dates of events, association of authors with titles of books or titles with plot or characters, names associated with particular events, or association of chemical symbols with names of chemicals. The matching item is a compact and efficient way of measuring this type of achievement.

Effective matching items may often be built by basing the set of items upon a graph, chart, map, diagram, or picture of equipment. Features of the figure may be labeled, and the examinee may be asked to match names, functions, etc., with the labels on the figure. This type of item is particularly useful in tests dealing with science or technology, e.g., identification of organs in an anatomy test.

However, there are many topics to which the matching item is not very well adapted. The items making up a set should bear some relationship to each other; that is, they should be homogeneous. In the case of many of the outcomes one would like to test, it is difficult to get enough homogeneous items to make up a set for a matching item.

Consider the example that appears below.

Instructions: Match the statements in Column I with those in Column II.

Column I	*Column II*
——— 1. First Ten Amendments	A. 1215
——— 2. We owe much of our democratic heritage to this country.	B. George Washington
	C. Authors of the *Federalist Papers*
——— 3. Date of the Magna Charta	
——— 4. Jay, Hamilton, and Madison	D. England
——— 5. Chairman of the Constitutional Convention	E. Bill of Rights

This example illustrates most of the common mistakes made in preparing matching items. First, the directions are vague because they do not specify either the basis for matching or how the examinee is to record his answers. Second, the statements in Column I have nothing in common except that all of them refer to materials usually included in an eighth-grade unit on the Constitution. Look at statement 3 in Column I which asks for the date of the Magna Charta. Column II includes only one date. Successful matching here requires no knowledge on the part of the student. Each item in the set can be matched in the same way, using only the most superficial cues. Third, note the number of answer choices provided in Column II to match with the five statements in Column I. If the instructions indicate that each answer is to be used only once, then the person who knows four of the answers automatically gets the fifth by elimination, and the person who knows three has a fifty-fifty chance on the last two.

MAXIMS ON MATCHING ITEMS

1. *When Writing Matching Items, the Items in a Set Should Be Homogeneous.* For example, they should all be names of persons, or all dates of events, or all provisions of different parts of the Constitution.

2. *The Number of Answer Choices Should Be Greater Than the Number of Problems Presented.* This holds except when each answer choice may be used more than once, as in variations that we shall consider presently.

3. *The Set of Items Should Be Relatively Short.* It is better to make several relatively short matching sets than one long one because (1) it is easier to keep the items in the set homogeneous and (2) it is easier for the student to find and record the answer.

4. *Response Options Should Be Arranged in a Logical Order, if One Exists.* Arranging names in alphabetical order or dates in chronological order reduces the clerical task for the examinee.

5. *The Directions Should Specify the Basis for Matching and Should Indicate Whether an Answer Choice May Be Used More Than Once.* These precautions will guarantee a more uniform task for all examinees.

A variation on the matching type of item which is sometimes effective is the classification type or master list. This pattern, illustrated on p. 81, presents an efficient means of exploring range of mastery of a concept or related set of concepts.

Another setting in which the master list variation of the classification type of item can often be used to advantage is that of testing knowledge of the general chronology or sequence of events. See Example II on p. 81.

There are a number of other varieties of objective test items that have been developed and used to some extent. The reader who is interested in a survey of these, together with a more extended discussion of teacher-made tests in general, is referred to the suggested additional readings at the end of the chapter.

Example I

Instructions: Below are given some happenings that could take place in a session of Congress. For each of these, you are to mark

A. if it is specifically permitted or required by the Constitution.
B. if it is specifically forbidden by the Constitution.
C. if it is implied by the Constitution but nothing is specifically stated about it.
D. if it has developed through custom and usage.

  (A)   1. At the opening session of Congress, the President delivers a "State of the Union Address."

  (C)   2. Congress passes a law raising minimum wages from $1.00 to $1.25.

  (B)   3. Congress passes a law requiring all children to attend school until they reach the age of 16.

  (D)   4. The President requests a senator from State X to suggest names of persons who would be satisfactory as collectors of customs.

               (and possibly others).

Example II

For each event on the left, pick the choice on the right that tells when the event took place.

Events	*Time Line*
(E) 1. Women were granted suf-frage.	A Declaration of Independence.
(D) 2. All persons born or naturalized in the U. S. were declared to be citizens.	B Adoption of the Constitution.
(A) 3. Zenger trial was held.	C
(B) 4. Plan for admitting new states was adopted.	Civil War.
(C) 5. Freedom of religion, speech, and press were guaranteed	D World War I.
(and possibly others).	E

TESTING FOR UNDERSTANDING

Since it is easier to construct questions testing factual knowledge than those that measure understanding, application of principles, and other meaningful outcomes of instruction, teacher-made tests, especially of the objective type, tend to emphasize facts. Teachers tend to assume that if a student knows the factual material, then he also understands that material. Although there is a positive relationship between factual knowledge and understanding, the relationship is not perfect. It is true that in order for the student to understand a principle, he must have the relevant facts and basic skills. But there is no assurance that mere possession of the facts means that the student really understands the material.

If students are to develop understandings, understandings must be taught and they must be evaluated. In the measurement of understanding, the situations or applications used in evaluation should be similar to, but not identical with, the examples used in class. If the same situations are used, the student may get the correct answer because he has memorized the example given in class, not because he understands the principle.

Objective test items do not divide up into two clearly distinct groups, those that measure factual knowledge and those that measure understanding, application, or interpretation. Many items involve understanding and application at various levels as well as the underlying factual knowledge. Thus, illustration III on p. 72 and the matching item on p. 81 both call for applications of knowledge to new situations. Multiple-choice items in particular readily lend themselves to testing the understanding and application of principles with novel material or in novel settings.

Another type of item is the interpretive type item. This type of item consists of an introductory selection of material, giving the necessary background and setting the problem, followed by a series of questions asking for interpretations of the material. The introductory material can be text, graphs, tables, maps, charts, or any similar material. It can be complete in itself, providing all the necessary information basic to the understanding, or it can be incomplete so that the student must know certain things in addition to those given.

The eighth-grade unit on the Constitution that we have used so far does not provide for good examples of the interpretative type of exercise. However, two examples of the interpretive test exercise that were constructed for a twelfth-grade unit on labor unions are given. The first is based on a graph showing certain data about union membership, strikes, and important social and economic events. In this item, the accuracy of the student's answer depends only upon his ability to understand the material as it is presented to him in graphic form.

The second example is based on a newspaper item, and the student is not given all the essential information but must know certain facts about the Taft-Hartley Act in order to answer the question.

Example I

The following statements refer to Fig. 4.1. Read each statement carefully. In front of each statement mark

A   if the statement is supported by the evidence in Fig. 4.1.
B   if the statement is contradicted by the evidence in Fig. 4.1.
C   if the statement is neither supported nor contradicted by the evidence in Fig. 4.1.

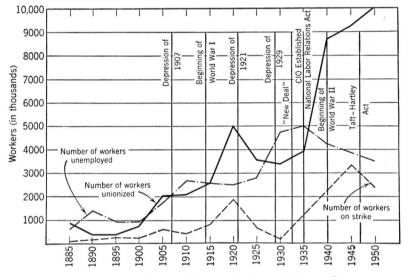

Fig. 4.1.   Factors relating to labor organization and labor conflict.

   (B)   1. Bad economic conditions tend to produce large numbers of strikes.
   (C)   2. The "New Deal" encouraged workers to join unions.
   (C)   3. The number of workers out on strike increases after a war.
   (B)   4. The passage of the Taft-Hartley Act caused a drop in union membership.
   (C)   5. By 1950, the majority of skilled and semiskilled workers in industry belonged to unions.
   (B)   6. As the number of unemployed workers increases, membership in unions increases.
   (C)   7. The large number of men on strike in 1945 caused the passage of the Taft-Hartley Act in 1947.

_(A)_   8. The period between 1920 and 1930 was marked by a steady decrease in union membership.

_(A)_   9. The establishment of the CIO was followed by an increase in union membership.

_(A)_ 10. The pattern of number of workers out on strike is similar to that of the number of workers belonging to unions.

Example II

Radio station WKRX uses only recorded music on its programs. A contract between the radio station and the musicians' union had required the station to hire a certain number of musicians, even though the musicians never played on any programs. When the contract ended, the radio station refused to renew it. Members of the musicians' union started to picket the radio station headquarters to force it to renew the contract. When the baseball season started, members of the union began to picket the local baseball park because the ball games of the local team were broadcast over station WKRX. The owners of the ball team and of the radio station took the case to court and asked the court to rule whether the picketing was legal.

What was the most probable ruling by the court?

A. Only the picket line at the baseball park was legal.
B. Only the picket line at the radio station was legal.
C. Both picket lines were legal.
D. Neither of the picket lines was legal.

From the statements below check all that support your answer.

_____   1. Workers cannot be prevented by management from using any peaceful method of protecting their jobs.

_____   2. The Taft-Hartley Act permits strikes when other means of settling disputes fail.

  X   3. Secondary boycotts are forbidden by the Taft-Hartley Act.

  X   4. "Featherbedding" practices by unions are forbidden under the Taft-Hartley Act.

_____   5. Since the picketing of the baseball park was against the radio station and not against the baseball team, the owners of the baseball team had no grounds for court action.

_____   6. Since baseball is a sport, not a business, a baseball park cannot be used to force the settlement of a dispute between labor and management.

_____   7. Strikes cannot be called against an employer who does not have a contract with a union.

The interpretive type of item provides an opportunity to ask meaningful questions about complex data in order to evaluate the student's ability to understand and interpret such materials.

However, this item type presents special problems. The introductory material must be carefully chosen to elicit the type of understanding that the teacher desires. Although a number of sources such as newspapers, magazines, or books can be used to furnish the introductory material, it usually has to be rewritten and adapted by the teacher to keep it at an appropriate reading level and to eliminate unnecessary parts. The success of this type of item is dependent to a large extent upon the adequacy of the introductory material.

Another disadvantage of the interpretive type of item is the reading load. Most of these items tend to be long, so that the evaluation of understanding will be contaminated by the reading level of the student.

A third disadvantage is the amount of space required to present the item and the amount of time required to answer it. With this type of item it is not possible to get as many different units of coverage as with the usual type of multiple-choice item.

For a more detailed discussion and for more examples of methods of measuring understanding in the different subject-matter fields, the reader is referred to the *Forty-Fifth Yearbook of the National Society for the Study of Education,* listed in the supplementary readings at the end of the chapter.

GETTING THE OBJECTIVE TEST READY FOR USE

So far we have considered the problems involved in improving the quality of the individual objective test items. Now we must give some thought to putting the items together into a test that is an effective whole. The quality of the total test will have been determined in large measure by the quality of our initial planning and by the skill with which we have written the separate test items. However, some further suggestions may help in achieving a sound and workmanlike product.

EXTRA ITEMS

When the items are originally written it will usually pay to write a surplus over the number that will finally be used. Items that seem masterworks in the first pride of authorship may show unsuspected flaws when coldly re-examined at a later date. Furthermore, some freedom for fitting the final test to the specifications of the blueprint is often helpful. A surplus of 20 or 30 per cent is none too much.

REVIEW AND EDITING

It is always sound policy, if time permits, to write the items early and put them aside for a while. When reread later, ambiguities will appear that were not seen at all when the item was first written. Even more helpful, if it is feasible, is to get another person who knows the subject matter to go over the items, keying them and criticizing them. This type of review will usually bring out a rather startling number of points of ambiguity or disagreement. Revision of the items in the light of such a critique or elimination of items that seem not to be salvageable will do much to avoid those debates with students and those ill-feelings that are an occasional feature of objective examinations.

FORM OF REPRODUCTION

Though it is possible to give objective examinations orally, it is far from satisfactory to do so. Oral administration is demanding upon students' concentration and introduces an element of speed pressure that is quite disturbing to some. One generally assumes that an objective test will be reproduced and that each pupil will have a copy. Gelatin duplicating processes are adequate for groups of moderate size, but most test makers will prefer to mimeograph the test if facilities for mimeographing are available. More important than the process is the quality of the work, both in organizing the layout of the test and in typing up the master copy.

ORDER AND GROUPING OF TEST ITEMS

After the items have been edited and those to be included in the test have finally been selected, they must be arranged in the order in which they are to appear in the test. There are three aspects that should be considered and reconciled as far as possible in deciding upon the arrangement and grouping of items.

1. Items in the same format (true-false, multiple-choice, etc.) should be grouped together, so that instructions for answering will carry throughout the set.

2. In general, an attempt should be made to progress from easy to more difficult items. This is especially important with younger children, who may become discouraged and quit if the early items are too difficult. It is also important if time is likely to be limited, so that some items will not be reached. These not-attempted items should be the more difficult ones that the examinee would not have been likely to answer correctly even if he had reached them.

3. Items dealing with similar content can well be grouped together. If this is done, it will help to reduce the feeling that the test is made up of unrelated bits and pieces. It will encourage a more integrated attack by the examinee.

DIRECTIONS

Clear instructions to the examinees are an important element in a well-constructed test. Examinees will usually know the purpose of a test, but if it is possible that they may not the purpose should be stated.   Complete instructions should be given as to how the pupil is to record his answers.   This is particularly important for novel or unusual item patterns.   The examinee should be given explicit information as to the scoring procedure that will be used, including the credit for each item or part and whether or not a correction will be made for guessing.   (See *Scoring,* p. 88.)

Sample sets of directions for matching items have been given on p. 81.

For a test made up of multiple-choice items that will not be corrected for guessing and for which separate answer sheets are used, one might use the following set of directions.

Directions:

Read each item and decide which choice *best* completes the statement or answers the question.

Mark your answers on the separate answer sheet.   Do *not* mark them on the test booklet.   Indicate your answer by blacking out on the answer sheet the letter corresponding to your choice.   That is, if you think that choice B is the best answer to item 1, black out the B in the row after No. 1 on your answer sheet.

Your score will be the number of right answers, so it will be to your advantage to answer every question, even if you are not sure of the right answer.

Be sure your name is on your answer sheet.

For a test made up of true-false questions in which answers are to be recorded on the test paper and the total score will be corrected for guessing, the following set of directions could be used.

Directions:

Read each of the following statements carefully.

If all or any part of the statement is false, circle the F in front of the statement.

If the statement is completely true, circle the T in front of the statement.

Your score will be the number of right answers minus the number of wrong answers, so *do not guess blindly.*   If you are not reasonably sure of an answer, omit the question.

Be sure your name is on your test.

LAYOUT OF ITEMS

The two points important to bear in mind when planning how the items and answers will be placed on the sheet are (1) clarity and convenience for the examinee and (2) convenience for the scorer.   In the interest of the person taking the test, items should not be crowded together too closely.   Multiple-choice items are easier to read if each response option is on a separate line.   Having part of an item on one

---

Course_____ Name_____

Exam_____ Date_____

Instructions: Read the directions on the test sheet carefully, and follow
them exactly. For each test item, mark your choice for the
correct answer by blocking out the letter which corresponds
to the best answer for the test item.

Item	Answer	Item	Answer	Item	Answer
1	A B C D E	26	A B C D E	51	A B C D E
2	A B C D E	27	A B C D E	52	A B C D E
3	A B C D E	28	A B C D E	53	A B C D E
4	A B C D E	29	A B C D E	54	A B C D E

Fig. 4.2. Part of a home-made answer sheet.

page and part on the next should be avoided if possible. If several
items all refer to a single diagram or chart, it is desirable that all of
them appear on the same page as the diagram or chart.

The arrangement of answers should be such as to facilitate scoring.
Even in the upper elementary school it is practical to put spaces for
all the answers in a column on one side of the page. A scoring key
can then be laid beside the answer column to speed up scoring. In
the junior high school and above, a simple separate answer sheet may
be used. Part of a home-made answer sheet which is adaptable for
both true-false and multiple-choice items is shown in Fig. 4.2.

In school-wide or city-wide testing projects, machine-scored answer
sheets of the type developed for standardized tests may be used, if facilities for machine scoring are available.

SCORING

Layout of answers to facilitate scoring has been discussed in the
previous paragraphs. A scoring stencil that can be placed alongside
the columns of answers or placed directly over a separate answer sheet
will make scoring go very quickly.

The test maker must decide how he is going to treat guessing in his
scoring procedure. As we have indicated, his decision should be
made known to the examinees. If time permits every student to at-

tempt every item, a score that is simply the number of right answers is quite satisfactory. In this case, examinees should be firmly instructed to guess, even if they have no idea of the answer. This procedure has sometimes been criticized as poor pedagogy, since it involves practice in errors. However, the student will think about each item anyhow. It seems doubtful that the final step of marking an answer, when one knows in one's own mind that one is just guessing, will have any very lasting impact on the impression one carries away from the test.

If the test is speeded, so that pupils will attempt different numbers of items, or if the test user wishes to discourage guessing on the part of examinees, a penalty should be applied for wrong answers. The usual correction formula, based on the assumption that the person who does not know the answer will make a random guess, is

$$\text{Score} = R - \frac{W}{n-1}$$

where R is the number of questions answered correctly;
W is the number of questions answered incorrectly;
n is the number of answer choices for an item.

For example, in a true-false test where there are only 2 possible answers, $n-1$ becomes $2-1$, or 1, and the correction for guessing is the number of right answers minus the number of wrong answers. Thus, if there were 75 true-false items on a test and a student got 48 right, got 20 wrong, and did not answer 7 of them, his score would be $48-20$ or 28. Note that omits do not count in this formula for guessing.

For a second example, suppose a student took a 60-item multiple-choice test in which each item had 5 possible answers. If he got 52 questions right and 8 wrong, his corrected score would be

$$52 - \frac{8}{5-1} \quad \text{or} \quad 52 - \frac{8}{4} = 50$$

ANALYZING AND USING THE RESULTS OF OBJECTIVE TESTS

Giving the test, scoring it, and recording a score for each pupil frequently ends the matter as far as the teacher is concerned. However, if the teacher drops the test at this point, he loses much of its value. An analysis of the responses the pupils made to the items can serve two important purposes. In the first place, the test results provide a diagnostic technique for studying the learnings of the class and the failures to learn and for guiding further teaching and study. In the second place, the responses of pupils to the separate items and a review of the items in the light of these responses provide a basis for preparing better tests another year.

The basic analysis that is needed is a tabulation of the responses that have been made to each item on the test. We need to know how many pupils got each item right, how many chose each of the possible wrong answers, and how many omitted the item. It helps our understanding of the item if we have this information for the upper and lower fractions of the group, and perhaps also for those in the middle. From this type of tabulation, we can answer such questions as the following for each item:

1. How hard is the item?
2. Does it distinguish between the better and poorer students?
3. Do all the options attract responses, or are there some that are so unattractive that they might as well not be included?

A simple form can be prepared for recording the responses to each item, like that shown in Fig. 4.3. This can be put on a separate card for each item, and then the information can be accumulated in a permanent item file. This form is planned for a multiple-choice item with as many as five choices but can be used for true-false items by using only the A and B columns.

Item: Which one of the following states was formed from the Northwest Territory?

      A. Indiana
      B. Iowa
      C. Montana
      D. Oregon

			Option			
	A	B	C	D	E	Omit
Upper 25%	10					
Middle 50%	17		1	2		
Lower 25%	5	1	1	3		

Fig. 4.3. Form for recording item-analysis data.

To illustrate the type of information that is provided by an item analysis, we present below certain items from a social studies test, together with the analysis of responses for each item. This test was given in 1960 to 100 high-school seniors who had had a course in current American problems. There were 95 items on the test. The highest score on the test was 85 and the lowest score was 14. The test papers were arranged in order of total score starting with the score of 85 and ending with the score of 14. The top 25 papers were selected to represent the upper group (score range 59 to 85) and the last 25 papers were selected to represent the lower group (score range 14 to 34). The count of responses is based on the 25 cases from the top and the 25 cases from the bottom of the group. The responses made to each item by each individual in the upper and lower groups were tallied to give the frequency of choosing each option. These frequencies are shown on the right. The correct option is underlined. Each item is followed by a brief discussion of the item data.

Item I

"Everyone's switching to Breath of Spring Cigarettes!" is an example of the propaganda technique called

	Upper	Lower
A. glittering generality.	0	2
B. bandwagon.	25	20
C. testimonial.	0	2
D. plain folk.	0	1
(Omit)	0	0

This is an easy item, since all 25 in the upper group and 20 in the lower group get it right. However, it does differentiate in the desired direction, since what errors there are fall in the lower group. The item is also good in that all of the wrong answer choices are functioning; i.e., each wrong answer has been chosen by one or more persons in the lower group. Two or three easy items like this would be good "ice-breakers" with which to start a test.

Item II

There were no federal income taxes before 1913 because prior to 1913

	Upper	Lower
A. the federal budget was balanced.	3	5
B. regular property taxes provided enough revenue to run the government.	9	15

C. a tax on income was unconstitutional.	13	0
D. the income of the average worker in the U. S. was too low to be taxed.	0	5
(Omit)	0	0

This was a difficult item but a very effective one. That it was difficult is shown by the fact that only 13 out of 50 got it right. That it was effective is shown by the fact that all 13 getting the item right were in the upper group. All of the wrong options attracted some choices in the lower group and all of the wrong options attracted more of the lower group than the higher group. Incidentally, an item such as this shows how faulty the idea of "blind guessing" often is when an item is effectively written. In this item, the majority of the lower group concentrated upon one particular wrong option that was particularly plausible and appealing.

Item III

Under the "corrupt practices act" the national committee of a political party would be permitted to accept a contribution of

	Upper	Lower
A. $10,000 from Mr. Jones.	15	4
B. $1,000 from the ABC Hat Corporation.	4	6
C. $5,000 from the National Association of Manufacturers.	2	8
D. $500 from union funds of a local labor union.	4	7
(Omit)	0	0

This item turned out poorly. Only 10 out of 50 got it right, and right answers were more frequent in the lower than in the upper group. As far as the test is concerned, it appears that this item would have to be either discarded or radically revised. If the group was supposed to have learned about the provisions of the "corrupt practices act," this shows clearly that the learning did not take place. In order to arrive at the correct answer to the item the student would have to know (1) the limit placed on contributions to the national committee of a political party, (2) who is forbidden to make contributions, and (3) what kind of organization the National Association of Manufacturers is. The teacher would have to discuss the item with the class to determine where the difficulty lies but one might guess that it is points 1 and 3 that are causing difficulty in the upper group.

Item IV

The term "easy money" as used in economics means

	Upper	Lower
A. the ability to borrow money at low interest rates.	21	17
B. dividends that are paid on common stocks.	0	0
C. money that is won in contests.	0	0
D. money paid for unemployment compensation.	4	8
(Omit)	0	0

This item shows some discrimination in the desired direction (21 versus 17), but the differentiation is not very sharp. The response pattern is one that is quite common. Only two of the four choices are functioning at all. Nobody selects either the B or C choices. If we wished to use this item again, we might try substituting "wages paid for easy work" for option B and "Money given to people on welfare" for option C. The repeat of the word "easy" in option B and the idea of getting money for not working in option C might make the item more difficult and more discriminating.

Item statistics such as these can be used not only for evaluating the items but to guide review and restudy of the material with a class. The items that prove difficult for the class as a whole provide leads for further exploration. Discussion of these items with the class should throw light on the nature of the misunderstanding. The misunderstanding may in some cases be cleared up by brief further discussion, although in some cases a fuller review of the topic may be indicated. It is desirable, if local policies permit, to let pupils have their answer sheets and a copy of the test and to make the answer key available to them, so that they can themselves use the test as a guide to review and clarification of the points they missed. An examination should teach as well as test.

SUMMARY STATEMENT

The deficiencies of essay examinations have led to the preparation of tests made up of objective short-answer questions. These questions may be prepared in true-false, completion, multiple-choice, matching, and many other forms. Experience of item writers has led to the formulation of a number of "do's" and "don't's" to guide the preparation of test items. These are considered in detail in this chapter.

Though there is an unfortunate tendency for writers of objective items to concentrate on factual information, ability to understand, interpret, and apply can also be tested by items that follow this format. For the measurement of understanding it is often desirable to describe a fairly complex problem situation or to present a fairly full set of data and to organize a set of related questions about the problem or data. Illustrations are provided.

It helps, in producing a good test, to prepare extra items and to have the items edited and screened before using. Items should be grouped so as to emphasize relationships and to provide a general progression from easy to more difficult. Answer sheets and scoring stencils facilitate scoring. The issue of correction for guessing should be resolved in advance, and examinees should be told what procedure will apply.

Test results can be analyzed with profit to guide (1) further teaching and review and (2) the construction of additional tests in later years.

SUGGESTED ADDITIONAL READING

Dressel, Paul L., and Lewis B. Mayhew, *Science reasoning and understanding,* Dubuque, Iowa, William C. Brown, 1954.

Ebel, Robert L., Writing the test item, Chapter 7 in E. F. Lindquist, Editor, *Educational measurement,* Washington, D. C., American Council on Education, 1951.

Gerberich, J. Raymond, *Specimen objective test items,* New York, Longmans, Green, 1956.

Micheels, William J., and M. Ray Karnes, *Measuring educational achievement,* New York, McGraw-Hill, 1950.

National Society for the Study of Education, *The measurement of understanding,* The Forty-Fifth Yearbook, Part I, Chicago, Illinois, University of Chicago Press, 1946.

Odell, C. W., *How to improve classroom testing,* rev. ed., Dubuque, Iowa, William C. Brown, 1958, chapters VII–XIII.

Traxler, Arthur E., Administering and scoring the objective test, Chapter 10 in E. F. Lindquist, Editor, *Educational measurement,* Washington, D. C., American Council on Education, 1951.

Wood, Dorothy Adkins, *Test construction, development and interpretation of achievement tests,* Columbus, Ohio, Charles E. Merrill, 1960.

QUESTIONS FOR DISCUSSION

1. A high-school principal has a system of using a different type of objective test item each month—one month it is true-false, the next month multiple-choice, the next month completion, and so on. Each teacher is expected to follow this uniform pattern. How would you evaluate this procedure? Why?

2. What steps can a teacher take to avoid ambiguous items on an objective test?

3. Under what conditions would it be important to correct scores on an objective test for guessing?

4. Collect some examples of poor items you have seen on tests. Indicate what is wrong with each item.

5. Construct four multiple-choice items designed to measure understanding or application in some subject area in which you are interested.

6. Prepare a short objective test for a small unit that you are teaching or plan to teach. Indicate the objectives that you are trying to evaluate with each item. (Use the blueprint from Question 3, p. 58 if one is available.)

7. What are the arguments for and against returning major examination papers to students?

8. A fourth-grade teacher has given a test in arithmetic. What analyses of the results could the teacher make that would help guide (a) future work for the class as a whole and (b) special assistance given to individual pupils?

9. A college teacher has given an objective test to a large class, scored the papers, and entered the scores in the class record book. What further steps might the teacher take before returning the papers to the students? Why?

Chapter 5

▼

Elementary Statistical Concepts

INTRODUCTION

In its various forms, measurement results in classification, rankings, or scores. Any attempt to describe, summarize, or compare results for individuals or for groups calls for numerical treatment. The branch of arithmetic and mathematics that deals with the analysis of sets of scores for groups of individuals is known as statistics. Every user of tests and measurement devices needs at least a consumer's understanding of the basic objectives and techniques of descriptive statistics. This is a book on measurement, not a statistics textbook. Discussion of statistics as such is limited to this one chapter. It cannot be expected that study of it will make the reader an accomplished statistician. This chapter points out to the novice some basic types of questions that the statistician tries to answer, and introduces him to the simplest tools used to answer them.

Suppose you have prepared tests in reading, arithmetic, and spelling and given them to the pupils in two sixth grades in your school. You have scored the papers and entered the names and scores on a record sheet for the two classes. Table 5.1 shows the way the record

Table 5.1. Record Sheet for Sixth Grades at School X

| | Test Scores | | |
Name	Reading	Arithmetic	Spelling
1. Carol A.	32	3	26
2. Mary B.	27	27	23
3. Ruby C.	31	9	29
4. Alice D.	36	18	27
5. Theresa E.	47	21	35
6. Ida F.	42	24	26
7. Vivian G.	22	4	17
8. Grace H.	50	42	32

Table 5.1. (*Continued*)

Name	Test Scores		
	Reading	Arithmetic	Spelling
9. Opal I.	20	18	11
10. Ursula J.	37	2	29
11. Beatrice K.	25	10	15
12. Karen L.	37	13	23
13. Susan M.	28	20	25
14. Jane N.	34	15	30
15. Dorothy O.	31	19	22
16. Frances P.	21	2	17
17. Elizabeth Q.	35	48	23
18. Pearl R.	59	41	33
19. Joan S.	44	41	29
20. Nancy T.	32	40	18
21. Judith U.	56	24	39
22. Edith V.	38	24	21
23. Louise W.	38	18	29
24. Helen X.	29	12	27
25. Martha Y.	24	26	22
26. Doris Z.	36	12	30
27. James A.	36	29	25
28. Albert B.	21	16	14
29. Donald C.	27	7	16
30. Peter D.	37	29	21
31. Samuel E.	46	36	32
32. George F.	33	10	27
33. Roger G.	17	14	17
34. Newton H.	35	18	29
35. Karl I.	30	12	19
36. Isidore J.	22	30	12
37. John K.	43	9	33
38. Benjamin L.	31	15	20
39. Theodore M.	50	38	30
40. Michael N.	34	20	20
41. Herman O.	30	15	19
42. Charles P.	52	39	36
43. Patrick Q.	40	33	26
44. William R.	42	6	32
45. Martin S.	17	26	11
46. Frank T.	32	20	18
47. Ralph U.	38	20	22
48. Thomas V.	29	29	24
49. Henry W.	36	25	27
50. Oscar X.	43	19	33
51. Edward Y.	27	19	24
52. Leonard Z.	39	19	25

sheet might look. Now, what sorts of questions might you ask these data? That is, to what questions might you ask the data to provide the answers? Before reading further, suppose you study the set of scores and jot down on a piece of scrap paper the questions that come to *your* mind in connection with these scores. See how many of the question types you can anticipate.

A first, rather general question you might ask is: What is the general pattern of the set of scores? How do they "run"? What do they "look like"? How can we picture the set of reading scores, for example, so that we can get an impression of the group as a whole? To answer this question we will need to consider simple ways of tabulating and graphing a set of scores.

A second type of question that will almost certainly arise is: What is this group like, on the average? Have they done as well on the test as other sixth-grade groups? Are they ready for the regular sixth-grade instruction and materials? What is the typical level of performance in the group? All these questions call for some single score to represent the group as a whole, some measure of the middle of the group. To answer this question we shall need to become acquainted with statistics developed to represent the average or typical score.

Third, in order to describe your group you might feel a need to describe the extent to which the scores spread out away from the average value. Are all the children in the group about the same, so that the same materials and procedures would be suitable for all? If not, how widely do they spread out on a given test? How does this group compare with other classes with respect to the *spread* of scores? This calls for a study of measures of variability.

Fourth, you might ask how a particular individual stands on some one test. Thus, you might want to know whether James A. had done well or poorly on the arithmetic test, and if you decided that his score was a good score you might want some way of saying just how good it was. You might ask whether James A. did better in reading or in arithmetic. To answer this question we need a common yardstick in terms of which to express performance in two quite different areas. Our need, then, is for some uniform way of expressing and interpreting the performance of an individual. How does he stand, relative to his group?

A fifth query is of this type: To what extent did those who excelled in reading also excel in arithmetic? To what extent do these two abilities go together in the same individuals? Is the individual who is superior in one likely also to be superior in the other? To measure this going-togetherness we shall need to become acquainted with measures of *correlation*.

The following sections of this chapter will be devoted to illustrating and discussing the routines that statistics has developed for answering these questions. There are many other questions that may arise with respect to a set of data. The most important ones concern the drawing of general conclusions from data on a limited group. Thus, one sample of fifty boys may have surpassed a sample of fifty girls from the same school on a history test. This is a *descriptive* fact true of these particular groups. We would like to know whether we can safely conclude that the *total population of boys* from which this sample was drawn would surpass the *total population of girls* on this same test. This is a problem of *inference*. Problems of statistical inference make up the bulk of advanced statistical work, but we cannot go into them here.

WAYS OF TABULATING AND PICTURING A SET OF SCORES

In Table 5.1 we showed a record sheet on which test scores for 52 sixth-grade pupils had been recorded. Let us look at the scores in the column headed Reading and consider how they could be rearranged so as to give us a clearer picture of how the pupils did on the reading test.

The simplest rearrangement would be merely to arrange them in order from highest to lowest. We would then have something that looked like this:

59	43	37	34	30	22
56	42	37	33	29	22
52	42	36	32	29	21
50	40	36	32	28	21
50	39	36	32	27	20
47	38	36	31	27	17
46	38	35	31	27	17
44	38	35	31	25	
43	37	34	30	24	

This arrangement gives a somewhat better picture of the way the scores fall. We can see the highest and lowest scores at a glance, i.e., 59 and 17. It is also easy to see that the middle person in the group falls somewhere in the mid-thirties. We can see by inspection that

roughly half the scores fall between 30 and 40. But this simple rearrangement of scores still has too much detail for us to see the general pattern clearly. It is also not a convenient form to use in computing. We need to condense it into a more compact form.

PREPARING A FREQUENCY DISTRIBUTION

A further step in organizing the scores for presentation is to prepare what is termed a *frequency distribution*. This is a table showing
how often each score occurred. Each score value is listed, and the
number of times it occurred is shown. A portion of the frequency
distribution for the reading scores is shown in Table 5.2. However,

Table 5.2. Frequency Distribution of Reading Scores

(Ungrouped Data)

Test Score	Frequency
59	1
58	0
57	0
56	1
55	0
54	0
53	0
52	1
51	0
50	2
.	.
.	.
.	.
20	1
19	0
18	0
17	2

Table 5.2 is still not a very good form for reporting our facts. The
table is too long and spread out. We have shown only part of it. The
whole table would take 43 lines. It would have a number of zero
entries. There would be marked ups and downs from one score to
the next.

In order to improve the form of presentation further, scores are
often *grouped* together into broader categories. In our example, we
will group together three adjacent scores, so that each grouping includes three points of score. When we do this, our set of scores is

represented as shown in Table 5.3. This provides a fairly compact
table showing how many scores there are in each group or *class interval*. Thus, we have eight scores in the interval 34–36. We do not
know how many of them are 34's, how many 35's, and how many 36's.
We have lost this information in the grouping. We assume that they
are evenly divided. In most cases, there is no reason to anticipate
that any one score will occur more often than any other and this assumption is a sound one, so the gains in compactness and convenience
of presentation more than make up for any slight inaccuracy introduced by this grouping.*

Table 5.3. Frequency Distribution of Reading Scores

(Grouped Data)

Score Interval	Tallies	Frequency
58–60	/	1
55–57	/	1
52–54	/	1
49–51	//	2
46–48	//	2
43–45	///	3
40–42	///	3
37–39	//////	7
34–36	////////	8
31–33	//////	7
28–30	/////	5
25–27	////	4
22–24	///	3
19–21	///	3
16–18	//	2

In a practical situation, we always face the problem of deciding how
broad the groupings should be, i.e., whether to group by 3's, 5's, 10's,
or some other grouping. The decision is a compromise between los-
ing detail from our data, on the one hand, and obtaining a convenient,
compact, and smooth representation of our results, on the other. A
broader interval loses more detail but condenses the data into a more
compact picture. A practical rule-of-thumb is to choose a class interval that will divide the total score range into roughly 15 groups.

* In some special types of social statistics, such as reports of income, certain
values are more likely than others, i.e., $2000, $3000, $5000, etc. Special pre-
cautions are necessary in grouping material of this type. In particular, one
should strive to get popular values near the *middle* of a class interval.

Thus, in our example the highest score was 59 and the lowest was 17. The range of scores is $59 - 17 = 42$. Dividing 42 by 15, we get 2.8. The nearest whole number is 3, and so we group our data by 3's. In addition to the "rule of 15," we also find that intervals of 5, 10, and multiples of 10 make convenient groupings. Since the purpose of grouping scores is to make a convenient representation, factors of convenience enter as a major consideration.

It should be noted that sometimes there is no need to group data into broader categories. If the original scores cover a range of no more than, say, 20 points, grouping may not be called for.

In practice, when we are tabulating a set of data, deciding on the size of the score interval is the *first* step. Next we set up the score intervals, as shown in the left-hand column of Table 5.3. Each individual is then represented by a tally mark, as shown in the middle column. (It is easier to keep track of the tallies if every fifth tally is a diagonal line across the preceding four.) The column headed Frequency is gotten by counting the number of tallies in each score interval.

GRAPHIC REPRESENTATION

It is often helpful to translate the facts of Table 5.3 into a pictorial representation. A common type of graphic representation, which is called a *histogram,* is shown in Fig. 5.1. This can be thought of, somewhat grimly, as "piling up the bodies." The score intervals

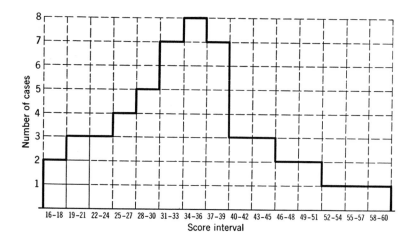

Fig. 5.1. Histogram of reading scores.

are shown along the horizontal base-line (abscissa). The vertical height of the pile (ordinate) represents the number of cases. The diagram indicates that there are two "bodies" piled up in the interval 16–18, three in the interval 19–21, and so forth. This figure gives a clear picture of how the cases pile up, with most of them in the 30's and a long low pile running up to the high scores.

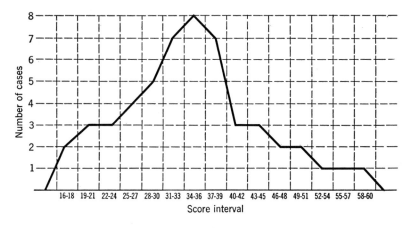

Fig. 5.2. Frequency polygon of reading scores.

Another way of picturing the same data is by preparing a *frequency polygon*. This is shown in Fig. 5.2. Here we have plotted a point at the mid-point of each of our score intervals. The height at which we have plotted the point corresponds to the number of cases, or frequency (f), in the interval. These points have been connected, and the jagged line provides a somewhat different picture of the same set of data illustrated in Fig. 5.1. Histogram and frequency polygon are essentially interchangeable ways of showing the same facts.

MEASURES OF CENTRAL TENDENCY

We often need a statistic to represent the typical, or average, or middle score of a group of scores. A very simple way of identifying the typical score is to pick out the score that occurs most frequently. This is called the *mode*. If we examine the array of scores on p. 99, we see that the score 36 occurs 4 times and is the mode for this set of data. We can also note another fact. The score values 38, 37, 32, 31, and 27 each occur 3 times. If there were 1 less 36 and 1 more 27, for example, the mode would shift by 9 points. The mode is sensitive to such minor changes in the data and is therefore a crude and not very useful indicator of the typical score. In Table 5.3, where we have the grouped frequency distribution, the *modal interval* is the interval 34–36. This is as closely as we can identify the mode for data presented in this way.

MEDIAN

A much more useful way of representing the typical or average score is to find the value on the score scale that separates the top half of the group from the bottom half. This is called the *median*. In our example, in which we have 52 cases, we want to separate the top 26 from the bottom 26 pupils. The required value can be estimated from the scores shown in Table 5.3. Starting with the lowest score, we count up until we have the necessary 26 cases. The "counting up" is best done in a systematic way, as shown in Table 5.4.

Table 5.4. Frequency Distribution and Cumulative Frequencies for Reading Scores

Score Interval	Frequency	Cumulative Frequency
58–60	1	52
55–57	1	51
52–54	1	50
49–51	2	49
46–48	2	47
43–45	3	45
40–42	3	42
37–39	7	39
34–36	8	32
31–33	7	24
28–30	5	17
25–27	4	12
22–24	3	8
19–21	3	5
16–18	2	2

Table 5.4 shows the cumulative frequencies as well as the frequency in each interval. Each entry in the column labeled Cumulative Frequency shows the total number having a score equal to or less than the highest score in that interval. That is, there are 5 cases scoring at or below 21, 8 scoring at or below 24, 12 scoring at or below 27, and so forth. As indicated, we wish to identify the point below which

50 per cent of the cases fall. Since 50 per cent of 52 = 26, we must identify the point below which 26 pupils fall.

We note that 24 individuals have scores of 33 or below. We need to include 2 more cases to obtain the required 26 cases. Note that in the next score interval (34–36) there are 8 individuals. We require only $\frac{2}{8}$ or $\frac{1}{4}$ of these individuals. Now how shall we think of these cases being spread out over the score interval 34–36? As we indicated on p. 101, a reasonable assumption is that they are spread out evenly over the interval. Then to include $\frac{1}{4}$ of the scores, we would then have to go $\frac{1}{4}$ of the way up from the bottom of the interval toward the top.

At this point we must define what we mean by a score of 34. In the first place, let us note that although test scores go by jumps of 1 unit, i.e., 34, 35, 36, we consider the underlying ability to have a continuous distribution taking all intermediate values. Thus, we do not get a score of 34.27, but this is only because our test does not register that precisely. Our definition will be that a score of 34 means closer to 34 than to either 33 or 35. That is, 34 will mean from $33\frac{1}{2}$ to $34\frac{1}{2}$. This definition is somewhat arbitrary but is rather generally accepted in statistics textbooks. Our class interval 34–36 is really to be thought of as extending from $33\frac{1}{2}$ to $36\frac{1}{2}$. Since we require $\frac{1}{4}$ of the cases in this interval, we have $\frac{1}{4}(36\frac{1}{2} - 33\frac{1}{2}) = \frac{1}{4} \times 3 = \frac{3}{4} = 0.75$. We must add 0.75 to the value $33\frac{1}{2}$, which is the borderline between the 2 intervals. The median for this set of scores is $33.5 + 0.75 = 34.25$.

To compute the median, then,

1. Calculate the number of cases that represent 50 per cent of the total group. In our example 50 per cent of 52 is 26.

2. Accumulate the scores up through each score interval. The cumulative frequencies, as shown in Table 5.4, are 2, 5, 8, 12, 17, etc.

3. Find the interval for which the cumulative frequency is just less than the required number of cases. In our example the cumulation through the 31–33 interval is 24.

4. Find the score distance to be added to the top of this interval, in order to include the required number of cases, by the following operation:

$$\left(\frac{\text{Number of additional cases required}}{\text{Number of cases in next interval}}\right)\left(\begin{array}{c}\text{Number of score} \\ \text{points in interval}\end{array}\right)$$

In our example this becomes $(\frac{2}{8})(3) = 0.75$.

5. Add this amount to the upper limit of the interval. We have for our data $33.5 + 0.75 = 34.25$. This score is the *median,* the score below which 50 per cent of the cases fall.

PERCENTILES

The same procedure may be used to find the score below which any other percentage of the group falls. These values are all called *percentiles.* The median is the 50th percentile, i.e., the score below which 50 per cent of individuals fall. If we want to find the 25th percentile, we must find the score below which 25 per cent of the cases fall. Twenty-five per cent of 52 is 13. Thirteen cases take us through the interval 25–27, and include 1 of the 5 cases in the 28–30 interval. So the 25th percentile is computed to be $27.5 + (\frac{1}{5})3 = 27.5 + 0.6 = 28.1$. Other percentiles can be found in the same way. Percentiles have many uses, especially in connection with test norms and the interpretation of scores.

ARITHMETIC MEAN

Another frequently used statistic for representing the middle of a group is the familiar "average" of everyday experience. Since the statistician speaks of all measures of central tendency as averages, he identifies this one as the *arithmetic mean.* This is simply the sum of a series of scores divided by the number of scores. Thus, the arithmetic mean of 4, 6, and 7 is

$$\frac{4 + 6 + 7}{3} = 5.67$$

In our example, we can add together the scores of all 52 individuals in our group. This gives us 1798. Dividing by 52, we get 34.58 for the "average" or arithmetic mean for this group.

Adding together all the scores and dividing by the number of cases is the straightforward way of computing the arithmetic mean. If the group is fairly small, and especially if an adding machine is available, it may be the best way. However, it can be rather laborious, especially with a large group. More efficient computing procedures are available, based on the frequency distribution given in Table 5.3. These calculations are based on a type of "trial balance." Picking a score interval that looks to be about in the middle of the group, we sum the plus and minus deviations from this starting place. An adjustment based on the excess of plus or minus deviations and applied

Table 5.5. Frequency Distribution of Reading Scores Showing Steps in Calculating Arithmetic Mean and Standard Deviation

Score Interval	Frequency f	x'	fx'	$f(x')^2$
58–60	1	8	8	64
55–57	1	7	7	49
52–54	1	6	6	36
49–51	2	5	10	50
46–48	2	4	8	32
43–45	3	3	9	27
40–42	3	2	6	12
37–39	7	1	7	7
			+61	
34–36	8	0	0	0
31–33	7	−1	−7	7
28–30	5	−2	−10	20
25–27	4	−3	−12	36
22–24	3	−4	−12	48
19–21	3	−5	−15	75
16–18	2	−6	−12	72
			−68	
Sum	52		−7	535

to this starting place gives the value for the mean. The application of this procedure to the reading test data is shown in Table 5.5, and the steps are outlined below.

1. Choose some interval for the arbitrary starting place or "origin." In this example the interval 34–36 has been chosen. Call this interval zero. (Note: Any interval can be chosen, and the final result will be the same. The particular interval chosen is purely a matter of convenience.)

2. Call the next higher interval +1, the one above that +2, etc.; call the next lower −1, the one below that −2, etc. These are shown in the column labeled x'. This column indicates the number of interval steps each interval is above or below our chosen starting point.

3. For each row, multiply the number of cases (frequency) by the number of steps (x') above or below the chosen origin. These products give the values in the column headed fx'. Note the minus signs in the lower half of the column. (Ignore the column headed $f(x')^2$ for now. It refers to a later topic.)

4. Sum the values in the fx' column, taking account of the plus and minus signs. (Mistakes will be avoided if the plus entries are summed separately, the minus entries summed, and then the two part sums combined to give the final total.)

5. Sum the frequencies in the column headed Frequency (or f) to give the total number of cases in the group. This is usually labeled N.

6. Divide the sum of the fx' values by N. Multiply by the number of score points in each interval. Add the result to the score corresponding to the mid-point of the zero interval. (Note that if the sum in step 4 is negative, adding it becomes in effect subtraction.)

These operations can be expressed by the following formula: *

$$\text{Mean} = \left(\frac{\text{Sum of } fx'}{N}\right) (\text{Interval}) + \text{Arbitrary origin}$$

In our illustration the values become

$$\text{Mean} = \left(\frac{-7}{52}\right)(3) + 35$$
$$= (-0.134)(3) + 35$$
$$= -0.40 + 35$$
$$= 34.60$$

Starting where we did, the minus deviations slightly overbalanced the plus ones. There was an excess of 7 on the minus side. Our starting point was a little too high. We had to shift it down $\frac{7}{52}$ of 1 interval or $\frac{7}{52} \times 3$ points of score to find a true balance point. Since the middle of our zero interval corresponded to a score of 35, we had to move down $\frac{21}{52}$ points below 35 to get the true balance point, the correct arithmetic mean.

The value 34.60 that we got in this way is almost the same as the 34.58 that resulted from adding all the scores together and dividing by the number of cases. The correspondence is usually not perfect, due to slight inaccuracies involved in grouping our scores into classes in the frequency distribution, but the values obtained by the two methods will always agree closely. It makes no difference which interval we use for our starting point. Barring mistakes in arithmetic, we will always get identically the same result.

The arithmetic mean and the median do not correspond exactly, but usually they will not differ greatly. In this example, the values are 34.60 and 34.25, respectively. The mean and median will differ substantially only when the set of scores is very "skewed," i.e., there is a piling up of scores at one end and a long tail at the other. Fig. 5.3 shows three distributions differing in amount and direction of

---

* A list of common statistical symbols and their meanings is given at the end of the chapter. Reference to these definitions may help in reading the remainder of the chapter.

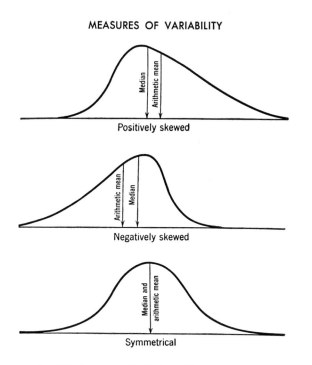

Fig. 5.3. Frequency distributions differing in skewness.

skewness. The top figure is positively skewed, i.e., has a tail running up into the high scores. We get a distribution like this for income in the United States, since there are many people with small and moderate incomes and only a few with very large incomes. The center figure is negatively skewed. A distribution like this would result if a class was given a very easy test, which resulted in a piling up of perfect and near-perfect scores. The bottom figure is symmetrical and is not skewed in either direction. Many physical and psychological variables give such a symmetrical distribution. In the many distributions that are approximately symmetrical either mean or median will serve equally well to represent the average of the group, but with skewed distributions the median generally seems preferable. It is less affected by a few cases out in the long tail.

MEASURES OF VARIABILITY

When describing a set of scores, it is often significant to report how *variable* the scores are, how much they spread out from high to low scores. For example, two groups of children, both with a median age of 10 years, would represent quite different educational situations if one had a spread of ages from 9 to 11 while the other ranged from 6 to 14. A measure of this spread is an important statistic for describing a group.

A very simple measure of variability is the *range* of scores in the group. This is simply the difference between the highest and the lowest score. In our reading test example it is $59 - 17 = 42$. However, the range depends only upon the 2 extreme cases in the total group. This makes it very undependable, since it can be changed a good bit by the addition or omission of a single extreme case.

SEMI-INTERQUARTILE RANGE

A better measure of variability is the range of scores that includes a specified part of the total group—usually the middle 50 per cent. The middle 50 per cent of the cases in a group are the cases lying between the 25th and 75th percentiles. We can compute these two percentiles, following the procedures outlined on pp. 105–106. For our example, the 25th percentile was computed to be 28.1. If we calculate the 75th percentile, we will find that it is 39.5. The distance between them is 11.4 points of score.

The 25th and 75th percentiles are called *quartiles,* since they cut off the bottom quarter and the top quarter of the group respectively. The score distance between them is called the *interquartile range.* A statistic that is often reported as a measure of variability is the *semi-interquartile range* (Q). This is half of the interquartile range. It is the average distance from the median to the 2 quartiles, i.e., it tells how far the quartile points lie from the median, on the average. In our example, the semi-interquartile range is

$$Q = \frac{39.5 - 28.1}{2} = 5.7$$

If the scores spread out twice as far, Q would be twice as great; if they spread out only half as far, Q would be half as large. Two distributions that have the same mean, same total number of cases, and same general form, and that differ only in that one has a variability twice as large as the other are shown in Fig. 5.4.

STANDARD DEVIATION

The semi-interquartile range belongs to the same family of statistics as the median. Its computation is based upon percentiles. There are also measures of variability that belong to the family of the arithmetic

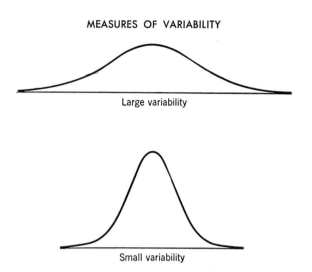

Fig. 5.4. Two distributions differing only in variability.

mean and are based upon score deviations. Suppose we had 4 scores which were 4, 5, 6, and 7 respectively. Adding these together and dividing by the number of scores we get

$$\frac{4 + 5 + 6 + 7}{4} = \frac{22}{4} = 5.5$$

This gives us the arithmetic mean. But now we ask how widely these scores spread out around that mean value. Suppose we find the difference between each score and the mean, i.e., we subtract 5.5 from each score. We then have -1.5, -0.5, 0.5, and 1.5. These represent *deviations* of the scores from the mean. The bigger the deviations, the more variable the set of scores. What we require is some type of average of these deviations to give us an over-all measure of variability.

If we simply sum the above 4 deviation values, we find that they add up to zero. This is necessarily so. We defined our arithmetic mean as the point around which the plus and minus deviations exactly balance. We shall have to do something else. The procedure that statisticians have devised for handling the plus and the minus signs is to square all the deviations. (A minus times a minus is a plus). An average of these squared deviations is obtained by summing them and dividing by the number of cases. To compensate for squaring the individual deviations, the square root of this average value is computed. The resulting statistic is called the *standard deviation* (*SD* or s).   It is the square root * of the average of the squared deviations from the mean.   For our little example of 4 cases, the calculations are as follows:

$$SD = \sqrt{\frac{(-1.5)^2 + (-0.5)^2 + (0.5)^2 + (1.5)^2}{4}}$$

$$= \sqrt{\frac{2.25 + 0.25 + 0.25 + 2.25}{4}} = \sqrt{\frac{5}{4}}$$

$$= \sqrt{1.25} = 1.12$$

STANDARD DEVIATION COMPUTED FROM FREQUENCY DISTRIBUTION

The standard deviation may also be computed from the grouped frequency distribution.   The necessary steps have been carried out in Table 5.5.   Take special note of the column headed $f(x')^2$.   Each entry in this column represents the number of cases (f) multiplied by the square of the deviation (x') of that score interval from the arbitrary origin.   The sum of the values in this column gives a sum of squared deviations, but these deviations are around our arbitrary origin and are expressed in interval units.   Several adjustments are necessary to express the deviations in *score* units and in terms of the *true* arithmetic mean.   The steps are outlined below.

1. Carry out the operations for computing the arithmetic mean, as described on pp. 106-108.
2. In addition, prepare the column headed $f(x')^2$.   Each entry in this column is the frequency (f) times the square of the deviation value (x').   However, this last column can be computed most simply by multiplying together the entries in the two preceding columns, i.e., x' times fx'.   Note that all the signs in this column are positive, since a minus times a minus gives a plus.

	In symbolism	*Illustrative example*
3. Get the sum of the $f(x')^2$ column. ("The sum of" will be indicated by Σ.)	$\Sigma f(x')^2$	535
4. Divide this sum by the number of cases.	$\dfrac{\Sigma f(x')^2}{N}$	$\dfrac{535}{52} = 10.288$
5. Divide the sum of the fx column by the number of cases.	$\dfrac{\Sigma fx'}{N}$	$\dfrac{-7}{52} = -0.135$

* The steps for computing the square root are shown in Appendix I.

	In symbolism	*Illustrative example*
6. Square the value obtained in 5 above.	$\left(\dfrac{\Sigma fx'}{N}\right)^2$	$\left(\dfrac{-7}{52}\right)^2 = (-0.135)^2$ $= 0.018$
7. Subtract the value in 6 from that in 4.	$\dfrac{\Sigma f(x')^2}{N} - \left(\dfrac{\Sigma fx'}{N}\right)^2$	$\dfrac{535}{52} - \left(\dfrac{-7}{52}\right)^2 = 10.288 - 0.018$ $= 10.270$
8. Take the square root of the value in 7.	$\sqrt{\dfrac{\Sigma f(x')^2}{N} - \left(\dfrac{\Sigma fx'}{N}\right)^2}$	$\sqrt{10.270} = 3.20$
9. Multiply by the number of score points in each class interval. (We call this width of interval i.)	$i\sqrt{\dfrac{\Sigma f(x')^2}{N} - \left(\dfrac{\Sigma fx'}{N}\right)^2}$	$3(3.20) = 9.60$

Presenting all the computations for our example in summary form, using the formula given in step 9 above, we have

$$SD = 3\sqrt{\frac{535}{52} - \left(\frac{-7}{52}\right)^2} = 9.60$$

INTERPRETING THE STANDARD DEVIATION

It is almost impossible to say in any simple terms what the standard deviation *is* or what it corresponds to in pictorial or geometric terms. Primarily, it is a statistic that characterizes a distribution of scores. It increases in direct proportion as the scores spread out more widely. The larger the standard deviation, the wider the spread of scores. A student sometimes asks: But what is a small standard deviation? What is a large one? There is really no answer to this question. Suppose that for some group the standard deviation of weights is 10. Is this large or small? It depends on whether we are talking about ounces, or pounds, or kilograms. It depends upon whether we are dealing with the weights of mice, or men, or mammoths. Large and small have only relative meaning—i.e., larger or smaller than that found for some other group or with some other test.

The standard deviation gets its most clear-cut meaning for one particular type of distribution of scores. This distribution is called the "normal" distribution. It is defined by a particular mathematical equation, but to the everyday user it is defined approximately by its pictorial qualities. The "normal" curve is a symmetrical curve having a bell-like shape. That is, most of the scores pile up in the middle score values; as one goes away from the middle in either direction the pile drops off, first slowly and then more rapidly, and the cases tail

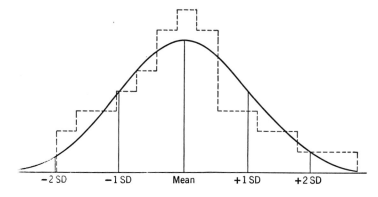

Fig. 5.5. Example of a normal curve (fitted to reading-test data).

out to relatively long tails on either end. An illustration of a typical normal curve is shown in Fig. 5.5. This curve is the normal curve that best fits the reading test data we have been using as an illustration. It has the same mean, standard deviation, and total area (number of cases) as the reading test data. The histogram of reading test scores appears in light dotted lines, so one can see how closely the curve fits the actual test scores.

For the normal curve, there is an exact mathematical relationship between the standard deviation and the proportion of cases. The same proportion of cases will always be found within the same standard deviation limits. This relationship is shown in Table 5.6. Thus, in *any* normal curve about two-thirds (68.2 per cent) of the cases will fall between $+1$ and -1 standard deviation from the mean. Approximately 95 per cent will fall between $+2$ and -2 standard

Table 5.6. Proportion of Cases Falling within Certain Specified Standard Deviation Limits for a Normal Distribution

Limits within Which Cases Lie	Per Cent of Cases
Between the mean and *either* $+1.0$ *SD* or -1.0 *SD*	34.1
Between the mean and *either* $+2.0$ *SD* or -2.0 *SD*	47.7
Between the mean and *either* $+3.0$ *SD* or -3.0 *SD*	49.9
Between $+1.0$ and -1.0 *SD*	68.2
Between $+2.0$ and -2.0 *SD*	95.4
Between $+3.0$ and -3.0 *SD*	99.8

deviations from the mean, and very nearly all the cases will fall between +3 and −3 standard deviations from the mean. An individual
who gets a score 1 standard deviation above the mean will surpass
84 per cent of the group, i.e., he will surpass the 50 per cent who fall
below the mean and the 34 per cent who fall between the mean and
+1 standard deviation.

This unvarying relationship of the standard deviation unit to the
arrangement of scores in the normal distribution gives the standard
deviation a type of *standard* meaning. It becomes a yardstick in
terms of which different groups may be compared or the status of a
given individual may be evaluated. Although the relationship of the
standard deviation unit to the score distribution does not hold *exactly*
in distributions other than the normal distribution, frequently the distribution of test scores or other measures approaches the normal curve
closely enough so that the standard deviation continues to have very
nearly the same meaning.

The meaning of being a given number of standard deviations above
or below the mean may be expressed in terms of the per cent of cases
in the group whom the individual surpasses. A number of values for
this relationship are given in Table 5.7. This table provides a basis
for interpreting any particular score. Consider the set of reading test
scores for which we computed the mean and standard deviation to be
34.6 and 9.6 respectively. Suppose a person had a score of 40. Since
the mean of the group is 34.6, he falls $40 - 34.6 = 5.4$ points above

Table 5.7. Per Cent of Group Falling below Selected Standard Deviation
Values for Normal Curve

Standard Deviation Value	Per Cent Having Scores below This Value
+3.0	99.9
+2.5	99.4
+2.0	97.7
+1.5	93.3
+1.0	84.1
+0.5	69.1
0.0	50.0
−0.5	30.9
−1.0	15.9
−1.5	6.7
−2.0	2.3
−2.5	0.6
−3.0	0.1

the mean of the group. The 5.4 points by which he surpasses the mean is equal to $5.4/9.6 = 0.56$ standard deviations. He is 0.56 standard deviations above the mean. We might expect him to surpass approximately 71 per cent of the cases in our group. (An actual count shows that this score is better than $39/52 = 75$ per cent of the scores in our set of data.) A score expressed in standard deviation units has much the same meaning from one set of scores to another, and these units are directly comparable from one measure to another.

In summary, the statistics most used for describing the variability of a set of scores are the semi-interquartile range and the standard deviation. The semi-interquartile range is based upon percentiles, i.e., the 25th and 75th percentiles, and is commonly used when the median is being used as a measure of the middle of the group. The standard deviation is a measure of variability that goes with the arithmetic mean. It is useful in the field of tests and measurements primarily as providing a standard unit of measure having comparable meaning from one test to another.

INTERPRETING THE SCORE OF AN INDIVIDUAL

The problems of interpreting the score for an individual will be treated more fully in Chapter 6, when we turn to test norms and units of measure. It will suffice now to indicate that the two sorts of measures we have just been considering, i.e., percentiles and standard deviation units, each give us a framework in which we can view the performance of a specific person. Thus, referring to the example we worked out, if a new boy in the class got a score of 40 on the reading test we could say either

a. That he surpassed 75 per cent of the group, i.e., that he fell at the 75th percentile, or

b. That he fell 0.56 standard deviations above the mean.

Either statement gives his score meaning in relation to his group; he is somewhat above average but not one of the best ones in the group. Since they are based on the same score, they are two ways of saying the same thing. Each has certain advantages, which we will examine more carefully in Chapter 6.

MEASURES OF RELATIONSHIP

We look now for a statistic to express the relationship between two sets of scores. Thus, in our illustration we have a reading score and an arithmetic score for each pupil. To what extent did those pupils who did well in arithmetic also do well on the reading test? In this case, we have two scores for each individual. We can picture these scores by a plot in two dimensions. This is shown in Fig. 5.6. The first person in our group, Carol A, had a score on the reading test of 32 and a score on the arithmetic test of 3. Her scores are represented by the X in Fig. 5.6, plotted at 32 on the vertical or reading scale and at 3 on the horizontal or arithmetic scale. There is a dot to represent each other child's scores.

If a child who does well in reading also does well in arithmetic, we will find his scores represented by a dot in the upper right hand part of our picture. A child who does poorly on both tests will fall at the lower left. Where good score on one test goes with poor score on the other, we will find the points falling in the other corners, i.e., upper left and lower right. Inspection of Fig. 5.6 will show some tendency for the scores to splatter out in the lower-left to upper-right direction, i.e., from low-low to high-high. But there are many exceptions. The relationship is far from perfect. It is a matter of degree. We need some type of statistical index to express this degree of relationship.

As an index of this degree of relationship, a statistic known as the

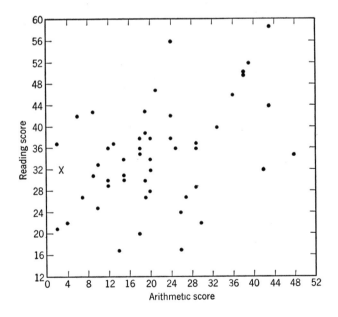

Fig. 5.6. Plot of reading versus arithmetic scores.

correlation coefficient can be computed. (The symbol *r* is used to designate this coefficient.)   This coefficient can take values ranging from +1 through zero to −1.   A correlation of +1 signifies that the person who had the highest score on one test also had the highest score on the other, the next highest on one was the next highest on the other, and so on, exactly in parallel through the whole group. A correlation of −1 means that the scores go in exactly the reverse direction, i.e., the person highest on one is lowest on the other, next highest on one is next lowest on the other, etc.   A zero correlation represents a complete lack of relationship.   In-between values of *r* represent tendencies for relationship to exist but with many discrepancies.

Figure 5.7 illustrates four different levels of relationship.   In box A the correlation is zero, and the points scatter out in a pattern that is just about round.   All combinations are found—high-high, low-low, high-low, and low-high.   Box B corresponds to a correlation of +.30.

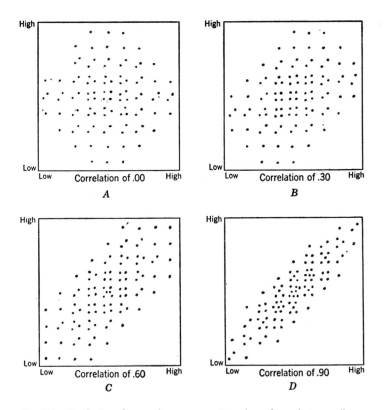

Fig. 5.7. Distribution of scores for representative values of correlation coefficient.

You can see a barely perceptible trend for the points to group in the low-low and high-high direction. The tendency is more marked in box C, which represents a correlation of +.60. In box D, which portrays a correlation of +.90, the trend is much more marked. But even with as high a correlation as this, the scores spread out quite a bit and do not follow an exact line from low-low to high-high. We may note in passing that the scores plotted in Fig. 5.6 correspond to a correlation coefficient of +.46. Procedures for computing the correlation coefficient are outlined in Appendix II for those readers who wish to carry out the calculations with a numerical example.

There are two important settings in which correlation coefficients will be encountered in connection with tests and measurements. The first situation is one in which we are trying to determine how precise and consistent a measurement procedure is. Thus, if we wanted to know how consistent a measure of speed we get from a 50-yard dash, we could have each child run the distance twice, perhaps on successive days. The correlation of his two scores would give us information on the precision or reliability of this measure of running speed. The second situation is one in which we are studying the relationship between two different measures, often in order to evaluate one as a predictor of the other. Thus, we might want to study a scholastic aptitude test as a predictor of college grades. The correlation of test with grades would give an indication of the test's usefulness as a predictor.

We face the problem, in each case, of evaluating the correlation we obtain. Suppose the two sets of 50-yard dash scores yield a correlation of .80. Is this satisfactory or not? Suppose the aptitude test correlates .60 with college grades. Shall we be pleased or discouraged?

The answer lies in part in the plots of Fig. 5.7. Clearly, the higher the correlation, the more closely one variable goes with the other. If we think of discrepancies away from the diagonal line from low-low to high-high as "errors," the errors become smaller as the correlation becomes larger. But, these discrepancies are still discouragingly large for even a rather substantial correlation coefficient, i.e., box C in Fig. 5.7. We must always be aware of these discrepancies and realize that with a correlation of .60, for example, between an aptitude test and school grades, there will be a number of children whose school performance differs a good deal from what we have predicted from the test.

However, everything is relative, and any given correlation coefficient must be interpreted in comparison to values that are commonly obtained. Table 5.8 contains a number of different correlations that have been reported for different types of variables. The nature of the scores being correlated is described and the coefficient reported. An examination of this table will provide some initial background for interpreting correlation coefficients. The coefficient will gradually take on added meaning as the reader encounters coefficients of different sizes in his reading about and work with tests.

Table 5.8. Correlation Coefficients for Selected Variables

Variable	Correlation Coefficient
Height of identical twins	.95
Intelligence of identical twins	.88
Height versus weight	.60
Intelligence of siblings	.53
Height of siblings	.50
Strength of grip and speed of running	.16
Height versus Binet IQ	.06
Height versus educational achievement	.01
Shape of head versus intelligence	.01
Height versus sociability	.00
No. of physical defects among boys versus school progress	−.29

SUMMARY STATEMENT

We opened this chapter by pointing out the various kinds of questions we might wish to answer by referring to a set of test scores. Let us look at these questions again and see what answers we have offered for them.

1. *How Do Our Scores "Run"; What Do They "Look Like"?* To answer this question, we can arrange our scores into a frequency distribution (Table 5.4) or plot them in a histogram (Fig. 5.1).

2. *What Score Is Typical of the Group; Represents the Middle of the Group?* To represent the middle of the group we may calculate the median—the 50th percentile (pp. 105–106), or the arithmetic mean—the common average (pp. 106–108).

3. *How Widely Spread Out Are the Scores; How Much Do They Scatter?* To represent the spread of scores statisticians have developed (1) the semi-interquartile range, half the distance between the 25th and 75th percentile (p. 110), and (2) the standard deviation

(pp. 111–113), a type of average of the deviations of the scores away from the average.

4. *How Are We to Determine What the Score of an Individual Means—Whether It Is High or Low?* Though this problem is left for fuller discussion in Chapter 6, we have seen that the individual score takes on meaning as it is translated into a percentile rank, the per cent of the group he beat, or into a standard score, how many standard deviations above or below the mean he fell (p. 116).

5. *To What Extent Do Two Sets of Scores Go Together; to What Extent Are the Same Individuals High or Low on Both?* A measure of relationship is given by the correlation coefficient, a numerical index of "going-togetherness" (pp. 116–120). This index is important as describing the precision or reliability of a test and as describing the accuracy with which a test score predicts some other factor, such as school grades or job success.

STATISTICAL SYMBOLS

The student who reads test manuals, books dealing with tests, or articles about testing in the educational journals will encounter a number of conventional symbols to refer to statistical concepts or operations. Some of the commonest are defined below. This table of definitions should help in reading later chapters of this book, as well as outside references.

Symbol	Definition
N	The total number of cases in the group.
f	Frequency. The number of cases with a specific score or in a particular class interval.
X	A raw score on some measure.
x	A deviation score, indicating how far the individual falls above or below the mean of the group.
x'	A deviation score from some arbitrary reference point, often expressed in interval units.
i	The number of points of score in one class interval.
$\overline{X}$ or M	The mean of the group.
Md	The median of the group.
Q_1	The lower quartile, the 25th percentile.
Q_3	The upper quartile, the 75th percentile.
Q	The semi-interquartile range. Half the difference between Q_3 and Q_1.
P	A percentile.
A subscript	Modifies a symbol and tells which specific individual or value is referred to, e.g., P_{10} is the 10th percentile, X_j is the raw score of person j.

Symbol	Definition
SD or s	Standard deviation of a set of scores.
σ	Standard deviation in the *population*, though sometimes used to refer to the particular sample.
p	Per cent of persons getting a test item correct.
q	Per cent of persons getting a test item wrong ($p + q = 100$).
r	A coefficient of correlation.
r_{11}	A reliability coefficient. The correlation between two equivalent test forms or two administrations of a test.
Σ	"Take the sum of."

SUGGESTED ADDITIONAL READING

Garrett, Henry E., *Elementary statistics,* New York, Longmans, Green, 1956.

Guilford, J. P., *Fundamental statistics in psychology and education,* 3rd ed., New York, McGraw-Hill, 1956.

Nelson, M. J., E. C. Denny, and A. P. Coladarci, *Statistics for teachers,* New York, Holt, 1956.

Walker, Helen M., and Joseph Lev, *Elementary statistical methods,* rev. ed., New York, Holt, 1958.

QUESTIONS FOR DISCUSSION

1. For each of the sets of scores indicated below, select what appears to you to be the most suitable class interval, and set up a form for tallying the scores:

Test	No. of Cases	Range of Scores
Arithmetic	84	8 to 53
Reading Comprehension	57	15 to 75
Interest Inventory	563	68 to 224

2. In each of the following distributions, indicate (a) the size of the class interval, (b) the mid-point of the intervals shown, and (c) the real limits of the intervals (i.e., the dividing lines between them).

(1)	(2)	(3)
4–7	17–19	50–59
8–11	20–22	60–69
12–15	23–25	70–79
.	.	.
.	.	.
.	.	.

3. Using the spelling scores given in Table 5.1 on p. 96, make a frequency distribution and a histogram. Compute the median and the upper and lower quartiles. Compute the arithmetic mean and standard deviation.

4. In the Bureau of Census reports the *median* is used in reporting average income. Why is it used, rather than the arithmetic mean?

5. A 50-item vocabulary test given to 150 pupils yielded scores ranging from 18 to 50. Ninety-seven fell between 40 and 50. What would this distribution of scores look like? What could you say about the suitability of the test for the group? What measure of central tendency would be most suitable? Why? What measure of variability would you probably use?

6. A high-school teacher gave two sections of a history class the same test. Results were as follows:

	Section A	Section B
Median	64.6	64.3
Mean	65.0	63.2
75th percentile	69.0	70.0
25th percentile	61.0	54.0
Standard deviation	6.0	10.5

From these data, what can you say about the two classes? What implications do the data have for teaching the two groups?

7. A test in social studies, given to 2500 tenth- and eleventh-grade students, had a mean of 52 and a standard deviation of 10.5. How many standard deviations above or below the mean would the following pupils fall?

Alice	48	Henry	60	John	31
Willard	56	Jane	36	Oscar	84

8. If the distribution in the previous example was approximately normal, about what per cent of the group would each of these pupils surpass?

9. Explain the meaning of each of the following correlation coefficients:

a. The correlation between scores on a reading test and on a group intelligence test is +.78.

b. Ratings of pupils on "good citizenship" and on "aggressiveness" show a correlation of −.56.

c. The correlation between height and score on an achievement test is .02.

Chapter 6

Norms and Units for Measurement

THE NATURE OF A SCORE

Johnny got a score of 15 on his spelling test. What does that mean, and how should we interpret it?

Actually, as it stands it has no meaning at all and is completely uninterpretable. At the most superficial level, we don't even know whether this represents a perfect score, i.e., 15 out of 15, or a very low per cent of the possible, i.e., 15 out of 50. But even supposing we do know that it is 15 out of 20, or 75 per cent, what then?

Look at Table 6.1. This shows two 20-word spelling tests. A score of 15 would have vastly different meaning if it were on test A than on test B. A person who got only 15 right on test A would not be outstanding in a second- or third-grade class. Try test B out on some friends or classmates. You will probably not find many of them who can spell 15 of these words correctly. When this test was given to a class of graduate students, only 22 per cent of them spelled 15 of the words correctly. A score of 15 on test B is a good score among graduate students of education.

As it stands, then, a score of 15 words right, or even of 75 per cent of the words right, can have no meaning or significance. It gets meaning only as we have some standard with which to compare it.

In the usual classroom test, the standard operates indirectly and imperfectly, partly through the teacher's choice of tasks to make up the test and partly through his standards for evaluating the responses. Thus, the teacher picks tasks to make up the test that he considers to be appropriate to represent the learnings of his group. No teacher in his right mind would give test A to a high-school group or test B to third graders. Where the responses vary in quality, as in essay examinations, the teacher sets a standard for grading that corresponds to what he considers it reasonable to expect from a group like his.

Table 6.1. Two 20-Word Spelling Tests

Test A	Test B
bar	baroque
cat	catarrh
form	formaldehyde
jar	jardiniere
nap	naphtha
dish	discernible
fat	fatiguing
sack	sacrilegious
rich	ricochet
sit	citrus
feet	feasible
act	accommodation
rate	inaugurate
inch	insignia
rent	deterrent
lip	eucalyptus
air	questionnaire
rim	rhythm
must	ignoramus
red	accrued

Quite different answers to the question "What were the causes of the War of 1812?" would be expected from a ninth grader and from a college history major.

However, the inner standard of the individual teacher is very subjective, inaccurate, and unstable. Furthermore, it provides no basis for comparing different classes or different areas of ability. We have no answers to such questions as: Are the children in school A better in reading than those in school B? Is Mary better in reading than in arithmetic? Is Johnny doing as well in algebra as we should expect? We need some broader, more uniform, objective and stable standard of reference if we are to interpret psychological and educational measurements.

Let us take a look at our tests A and B from another angle. Suppose, now, that we were to combine them into a single 40-word test and to give that test to 20 pupils in each grade from second through twelfth. What would we find? We would soon see that above the second or third grade almost everybody would get the first 20 words right. But until we got well up the grade ladder, children would get very few of the second set. It doesn't take much gain in spelling ability to improve from a score of 10 to one of 20 on this particular test, but to improve from 20 up to a score of 30 represents quite a respectable accomplishment. The two 10-point gains don't begin to be equal. The units on our scale of scores cannot be considered equal units, then. We have a rubber yardstick that has been stretched out at some points and squeezed in at others.

There is one further point that we should make about our spelling scores. Let us consider test B, since the point will be most clearly and obviously true in this case. A person who fails to get any of the items right on test B cannot be said to fall at an absolute zero of spelling ability. Actually, he may be able to spell hundreds, possibly thousands, of words. So a person who gets 10 words right on test B doesn't demonstrate twice as much spelling ability as a person who gets only 5 right. On this test, as in an iceberg, the great bulk of what we are examining lies below "sea level" and can't be seen. We cannot guarantee that even test A gets down to a true zero point. In fact, it would be hard to say what a real zero point is in spelling ability.

THE NEED FOR NORMS

We must look, then, for some better type of unit in which to express test results than a raw count of units of score or a crude percentage of the possible score. We would like the units to have these properties:

1. Uniform meaning from test to test, so that a basis of comparison is provided through which we may compare different tests—e.g., different reading tests, a reading test with an arithmetic test, or an achievement test with a scholastic aptitude test.

2. Units of uniform size, so that a gain of 10 points on one part of the scale signifies the same thing as a gain of 10 points on any other part of the scale.

3. A true zero point of "just none of" the quality in question, so that we can legitimately think of "twice as much as" or "two-thirds as much as."

The different types of norms that have been developed for tests represent marked progress toward the first two of the above objectives. The third can probably never be reached for the traits with which psychological and educational measurement is concerned. We can put five 1-pound prints of butter on one side of a pair of scales, and they will balance the contents of a 5-pound bag of flour poured into the other. "No weight" is *truly* "no weight," and units of weight can be added together. But we don't have that type of zero point or that way of adding together in the case of educational and psychological measurement. If you put together two morons, you will not get a genius, and a pair of bad spellers will not win a spelling bee.

Basically, a raw point score can be given meaning only by referring it to some type of group or groups. A score is not high or low, good or bad in any absolute sense; it is higher or lower, better or worse than other scores. There are two general ways in which we may relate a person's score to a more general framework. One way is to compare him with a graded series of groups and see which one he matches. Each group in the series usually represents a particular school grade or a particular chronological age. The other way is to find where, in a particular group, he falls in terms of the per cent of the group he surpasses or in terms of the group's mean and standard deviation. Thus, we find four main patterns for interpreting the score of an individual. These are shown schematically in Table 6.2. We shall consider each in turn, evaluating its advantages and disadvantages.

Table 6.2. Main Types of Norms for Educational and Psychological Tests

Type of Norm	Type of Comparison	Type of Group
Age norms	Individual matched to group he equals.	Successive age groups.
Grade norms	Same as above.	Successive grade groups.
Percentile norms	Per cent of group surpassed by individual.	Single age or grade group to which individual belongs.
Standard score norms	Number of standard deviations individual falls above or below average of group.	Same as above.

AGE NORMS

For any trait that shows a progressive change with age, we can prepare a set of age norms. The norm for any age, in this sense, is the average value of the trait for persons of that particular age. Let us take the example of height. If we get a representative sample of 8-year-old girls, measure the height of each, and get the average of those measures, we determine the norm for height for that age group. Note that in this case the norm is nothing more than the average value. It is not the ideal value. Nor is it the value to be expected of each person. It is simply the average value. It will pay to remember this in thinking about age and grade norms.

The average height can be determined in the same way for 9-year-olds, 10-year-olds, and each other age group. The values will fall on some such curve as that shown in Fig. 6.1. Points for the curve will ordinarily be computed only for full-year groups, but the curve is to be considered continuous. That is, we can estimate points in between the year groups by referring to the continuous curve. Thus, in Fig. 6.1 a height of 60 inches corresponds to (or is average for) the age 12, while 50 inches corresponds to about 7 years and 8 months.

We can refer any height measurement to this scale and find for what age it would be average. Each girl's height can be interpreted as being the average height for a girl of a particular age. Thus, the

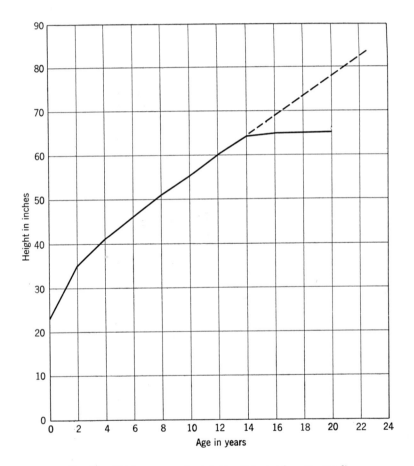

Fig. 6.1. Girls' age norms for height. (Adapted from Boynton.[1])

girl who has a height of 60 inches can be described as being as tall as the average girl of 12 years. If we also know how old the girl actually is, we can judge whether she is tall, average, or short for her age. Thus, if Mary is 55 inches tall and is only 8 years old, we know that she is tall for her age. Her height is average for a 10-year-old.

The age framework is a relatively simple and familiar one. "He is as big as a 12-year-old" is a common way of describing a youngster. For a trait that shows continuous and relatively steady growth over a period of years, the age framework is a convenient one. Its familiarity and convenience are its major advantages. Age norms have a number of disadvantages, and these we must now consider in more detail.

The big issue in using age norms is whether we can reasonably think of a year's growth as representing a standard and uniform unit. Is the growth from age 5 to age 6 equal to the growth from age 10 to age 11, and similarly for each age on our scale? As we push up the age scale, we soon reach a point where we see that the year's growth unit is clearly inappropriate. There comes a point, some time in the teens or early 20's, when growth in almost any trait that we can measure slows down and finally stops. In Fig. 6.1 the slowdown takes place quite abruptly after age 14. A year's growth after 14 seems clearly to be much less than a year's growth earlier on the scale. After about 14 or 15, the concept of height-age ceases to have any meaning. The same problem of a flattening growth curve is found, varying only in the age at which it occurs and in abruptness, for any trait that we can measure. The failure of the unit "one year's growth" to have uniform meaning is most apparent as one considers the extremes of age, but there is no guarantee that this unit has uniform meaning even in the intermediate range.

The problem introduced by the flattening growth curve is most apparent when we consider the individual who falls far above the average. What is the height-age of a girl who is 5 feet 10 (70 inches)? The average woman *never* gets that tall at any age. If we are to assign any age value, we must invent some hypothetical extension of our growth curve such as the lightly dotted line in Fig. 6.1. This line assumes that growth continues at about the same rate that was typical up to age 14. On this extrapolated curve, the height of 5 feet 10 is assigned a height-age of about 16 years, 6 months. But this is a completely artificial and arbitrary age equivalent. It does *not* correspond to the average height of 16½-year-olds. It does not correspond to average height at *any* age. It merely signifies "taller than average."

This same type of artificial age equivalent must be used for ability or achievement tests to express the performance of bright pupils in their teens. Mental growth curves also show a leveling off similar to that illustrated in Fig. 6.1. After the age of 14 or 15, increases become smaller and gradually disappear. The increase from age 15 to 18 may be no more than that from age 11 to 12, and after 18 there may be little or no further rise. Thus, a mental age of 18 or 20 does *not* mean performance corresponding to that of an average 18-year-old or 20-year-old. It is an arbitrary extension of the earlier growth curve. Such arbitrary and artificial age values are required if we are to be able to describe the performance of the upper half of our teen-age and adult population.

It is also true that growth curves are not entirely comparable for different functions. Rate of growth and time of reaching a maximum differ substantially. How shall we compare age scores on a vocabulary test and a maze-tracing test, for example, if the first continues to rise up to and into the twenties, while the second reaches a maximum in the early teens? For a 10-year-old to have reached the 12-year-old level may represent appreciably different degrees of superiority for different traits.

Two years' acceleration may also have quite different meaning, depending on the age level at which it occurs. A 5-year-old who is as tall as the 7-year norm is much more outstanding than the 10-year-old who reaches the 12-year norm. This fact has led to the development of the intelligence quotient and other types of quotients (which we shall consider presently) to allow for differences in age of the examinees. But the basic difficulty of inequality of the age unit at different points in the age scale still remains.

Of course, age norms are primarily appropriate for traits that depend on general normal growth. A trait showing no continuous improvement over an age range (such as acuity of vision) cannot possibly be expressed in terms of a scale of age units. One that depends primarily upon specific educational experiences, such as facility in arithmetical operations, seems to be more reasonably related to the educational framework of school grades than to the biological framework of years of growth.

Finally, though it does not directly concern the consumer of tests, it is worth noting that from the viewpoint of the test producer age norms present some serious practical problems. It is often difficult to get together a truly representative sample of individuals of a given age. Thus, if one wanted a cross-section of 12-year-olds one would have to look for some of them in the elementary school and some in the junior high school. They would have to be assembled from quite a range of school grades. Then as one moves toward the older ages the sample one needs to reach is widely scattered—some in school, some at college, some in the military establishment, and some in the world of work. To reach a representative sample of 18-year-olds, for example, is a very forbidding task. This is one more reason why the usual age norms for tests become suspect as one moves up into the teens.

In summary, age norms, which are based on the performance of the average person at each age level, provide a readily comprehended framework for interpreting the performance of a particular individual. However, the equality of the age units is open to serious question. As one goes up to adolescence and adulthood, age ceases to have any meaning as a unit in terms of which to express level of performance. Age norms are most appropriate for the elementary-school years and for abilities that grow as a part of the general development of the individual. Physical and physiological characteristics such as height, weight, and dentition, and psychological traits such as general intelligence appear to be ones for which this type of norm is most acceptable.

GRADE NORMS

Grade norms have many of the characteristics of age norms, differing only in that the reference groups are grade groups instead of age groups. That is, a test is given to representative groups in each of a series of school grades, and the average score is determined for each grade. Scores lying between the norm for two successive grades are assigned fractional credits by interpolation. The standard terminology assigns the value 5.0 to average performance at the beginning of the fifth grade, 5.5 to average performance at the middle of the grade, and so forth. A representative table of grade norms for the reading test of the *Metropolitan Achievement Test Battery* is shown in Table 6.3, p. 132. Thus, in this table a raw score of 9 corresponds to the performance of the average child at the beginning of the third grade, a raw score of 15 is average for beginning fourth grade, while 12 is average for the middle of grade three.

Grade norms have somewhat the same limitations as age norms. In particular, we have no guarantee that growth of one grade is the same amount of growth at all grade levels. The equality is even more suspect in the case of grade norms, because educational gains depend upon the content and emphasis in school instruction. The use of grade units to express growth only makes sense for those subject areas in which instruction is continuous through the school program. Since

Table 6.3. Grade Equivalents of Raw Scores for Reading Test of
Metropolitan Achievement Tests—Intermediate Battery, Form A

Raw Score	Grade Equiv.	Raw Score	Grade Equiv.
44	12.5	22	5.3
43	12.2	21	5.1
42	11.8	20	4.9
41	11.6	19	4.7
40	11.2	18	4.5
39	10.8	17	4.4
38	10.3	16	4.2
37	9.7	15	4.0
36	9.2	14	3.8
35	8.7	13	3.7
34	8.4	12	3.5
33	8.0	11	3.3
32	7.7	10	3.1
31	7.3	9	3.0
30	7.1	8	2.8
29	6.8	7	2.6
28	6.6	6	2.5
27	6.3	5	2.3
26	6.1	4	2.0
25	5.9	3	1.8
24	5.7	2	1.6
23	5.5	1	...

Reproduced by permission of Harcourt, Brace and World, Inc.

instruction in most of the basic skill subjects tapers off during high school, grade norms above the eighth or ninth have little direct meaning. In most cases, these are extrapolated values similar to those for the upper ages of age norms. Of course, grade norms for most high-school subjects would be essentially meaningless, since these are taught in only one or two grades.

The slowing down of gains at the upper grade levels makes it very difficult to express the performance of a very able child in terms of the grade framework. Many a superior child in the seventh or eighth grade can only be designated 11+ in terms of grade norms for standard school subjects. That is, his performance surpasses that of the average child in the highest grade for which norms are meaningful.

A further caution must be introduced with respect to the interpretation of grade norms. Consider a bright and educationally advanced child in the third grade. Suppose we find that on a standardized arithmetic test he gets a score for which the grade equivalent is 5.9. This does *not* mean that our child has a mastery of the arithmetic taught in the fifth grade. He got a *score* as high as that gotten by the average child at the end of the fifth grade, but this higher score was almost certainly obtained in part by superior mastery of third-grade work. The average child is sufficiently slow and inaccurate that a number of score points (and consequently a higher grade equivalent) can be earned merely by real mastery at his own grade level. This is worth remembering. The fact that our child has a grade equivalent of 5.9 need not mean that the child is ready to move ahead into sixth grade work. It is only the reflection of a score and does not tell in what way that score was attained.

Grade norms are relatively easy to determine, since they are based on the administrative groups already established in the school organization. In the directly academic areas of achievement, the concept of grade level is perhaps a more meaningful one than age level. It is in relation to his grade placement that a child's performance in these areas is likely to be used and interpreted. Outside of the school setting, grade norms have little meaning.

To summarize, grade norms, which relate the performance of an individual to that of the average child at each grade level, are useful primarily in providing a framework for interpreting the academic accomplishment of children in the elementary school. For this purpose they are relatively convenient and meaningful, even though we cannot place great confidence in the equality of grade units. They have little value for other types of groups or measures.

PERCENTILE NORMS

We have just seen that in the case of age and grade norms we give meaning to an individual's score by determining the age or grade group in which he would be just average. But it will often make more sense to compare him to his own age or grade group—to a group of which he may legitimately be considered a member. This is the type of comparison we make when we use percentile norms.

We saw in Chapter 5 how we could compute for any set of scores the median, quartiles, and any percentile. For each score value, we can compute the per cent of cases, p, falling below that score. Any person getting that score then surpasses p per cent of the group on which the percentile values were computed. We will say that he falls at the pth percentile, or has a percentile rank of p.

Table 6.4 shows percentile norms of ninth-grade boys for the eight subtests of the *Differential Aptitude Test Battery.* Look at the column headed "Verb. Reas." (Verbal Reasoning). The entries are scores. Thus, a score of 24 corresponds to the 75th percentile. An individual who gets this score surpasses 75 per cent of the group on which the norms were based. A score of 17 corresponds to the 50th percentile on this test. On the *Abstract Reasoning Test* (Abs. Reas.), a score of 26 corresponds to the 50th percentile. This score represents the same degree of excellence as the score of 17 on the *Verbal Reasoning Test.*

Note that not every percentile is given in Table 6.4. For most of the range, the percentiles are given by steps of 5, and sometimes several score points correspond to the particular percentile value. If more detailed tables were given, these scores would correspond to different percentiles. However, locating an individual to the nearest 5 percentiles is close enough for all practical purposes.

Table 6.4.　Percentile Norms for Differential Aptitude Tests

FORM A
GRADE 9

BOYS Percentile	Verb. Reas.	Num. Abil.	Abs. Reas.	Space Rela.	Mech. Reas.	Clerical S and A	LU-I: Spell.	LU-II: Sent.	N = 6900± Percentile
99	41+	35+	44+	87+	60+	73+	90+	59+	99
97	36–40	32–34	41–43	81–86	56–59	66–72	80–89	52–58	97
95	33–35	30–31	39–40	75–80	53–55	62–65	72–79	47–51	95
90	30–32	27–29	37–38	69–74	50–52	59–61	63–71	42–46	90
85	27–29	25–26	35–36	64–68	48–49	57–58	56–62	38–41	85
80	25–26	23–24	34	60–63	46–47	55–56	51–55	35–37	80
75	24	22	32–33	56–59	44–45	53–54	47–50	33–34	75
70	22–23	21	31	53–55	42–43	52	42–46	31–32	70
65	21	19–20	30	49–52	41	51	38–41	29–30	65
60	19–20	18	29	45–48	39–40	50	34–37	27–28	60
55	18	17	27–28	41–44	37–38	48–49	31–33	25–26	55
50	17	16	26	37–40	35–36	47	26–30	22–24	50
45	16	15	24–25	33–36	34	46	23–25	20–21	45
40	15	14	23	29–32	32–33	44–45	20–22	18–19	40
35	14	12–13	21–22	25–28	30–31	43	16–19	16–17	35
30	13	11	19–20	21–24	28–29	42	13–15	14–15	30
25	12	10	16–18	17–20	26–27	40–41	9–12	12–13	25
20	10–11	9	13–15	14–16	23–25	38–39	6–8	9–11	20
15	9	7–8	9–12	11–13	20–22	36–37	2–5	6–8	15
10	7–8	5–6	4–8	7–10	16–19	33–35	1	2–5	10
5	6	3–4	1–3	3–6	11–15	30–32	—	1	5
3	4–5	1–2	0	1–2	7–10	26–29	0	0	3
1	0–3	0	—	0	0–6	0–25	—	—	1
Mean	18.3	16.3	24.1	39.1	34.9	47.0	31.1	23.7	Mean
SD	8.7	8.2	11.3	23.4	12.6	10.5	24.1	14.6	SD

Percentile norms are very widely adaptable and applicable. They can be used wherever an appropriate normative group can be obtained to serve as a yardstick. They are appropriate for young or old, for educational or industrial situations. To surpass 90 per cent of the reference comparison group signifies a comparable degree of excellence whether the function being measured is how rapidly one can solve simultaneous equations or how far one can spit. Percentile norms are widely used. Were it not for the two points that we must now consider, they would provide a very nearly ideal framework for interpreting test scores.

The first problem that faces us in the case of percentile norms is that of the norming group. On what type of group should the norms be based? Clearly, we will need different norm groups for different ages and grades in our population. A 9-year-old must be evaluated in terms of 9-year-old norms; a sixth grader, in terms of sixth-grade norms; an applicant for a job as stock clerk, in terms of stock-clerk-applicant norms. The appropriate norm group is in every case the group to which the individual belongs and in terms of which his status is to be evaluated. It makes no sense to compare a medical-school applicant with norms based on unselected adults.

If we are to use percentile norms, then, we must have multiple sets of norms. We must have norms appropriate for each distinct type of group or situation with which our test is to be used. This is recognized by the better test publishers, who provide norms not only for different age or grade groups but also for special types of educational or occupational populations. However, there are limits to the number of distinct groups for which a test publisher can produce norms.

Published percentile norms will often need to be supplemented by the test user, who can build up norm groups particularly suited to his individual needs. Thus, a given school system will often find it valuable to develop local percentile norms for its own pupils. This will permit interpretation of individual scores in terms of the local group, a comparison that may be more significant for local problems than comparison with the national norms. Again, an employer who uses a test with a particular category of job applicants may well find it useful to prepare norms for this particular group of people. Evaluating a new applicant will be much facilitated by these strictly local norms.

The second problem in relation to percentile norms is more serious. Again, we are faced by the problem of equality of units. Can we think of 5 percentile points as representing the same amount throughout the percentile scale? Is the difference between the 50th and 55th percentile equivalent to the difference between the 90th and 95th? To answer this, we must notice the way in which test scores for a group of individuals usually pile up. We saw one histogram of scores in Chapter 5 (p. 102). This picture is fairly representative of the way the scores fall in many cases. There is a piling up of scores around the middle scores and a tailing off at either end. The ideal model of this type of score distribution, which is called the *normal curve,* was also considered in Chapter 5 (pp. 113–115) and is shown in Fig. 6.2. The exact normal curve is an idealized mathematical model, but many types of tests and measures distribute themselves in a manner that approximates a normal curve. You will notice the piling up of most of the cases in the middle, the tailing off at both ends, and the symmetrical pattern.

In Fig. 6.2, four score points have been marked. These are, in order, the 50th, 55th, 90th, and 95th percentiles. Note that near the median the 5 per cent of cases (the 5 per cent lying between the 50th and 55th percentile) fall in a tall narrow pile. Toward the tail of the distribution the 5 per cent of cases (the 5 per cent between the 90th and 95th percentile) make a relatively broad low bar. Five per cent of the cases spread out over a considerably wider range of scores in the second case than in the first. The same number of percentile points corresponds to about three times as many score points when we are around the 90th to 95th percentile as when we are near the median. The further out on the tail we go, the more extreme the situation becomes.

Thus, percentile units are typically and systematically unequal. The difference between being first or second in a group of 100 is many times as great as the difference between being 50th and 51st. Equal percentile differences do not represent equal differences in amount. Any interpretation of percentile ranks must take into account the fact

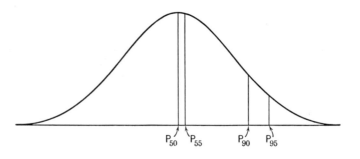

Fig. 6.2. Normal curve, showing selected percentile points.

that such a scale has been pulled out at both ends and squeezed in the middle. Mary, who falls at the 50th percentile in arithmetic and the 55th in reading, shows a trifling difference in these two abilities, whereas Alice, with percentiles of 90 and 95, shows a marked difference.

Percentile norms, to conclude, provide a basis for interpreting the score of an individual in terms of his standing in some particular group. If the percentile is to be meaningful, the group must be one with which it is reasonable and appropriate to compare him. We will usually need a number of tables of percentile norms based on different groups, if we are to use a test with different ages, grades, or occupations. As long as percentiles for appropriate groups are supplied, this type of norm is widely applicable. But interpretation of percentile values is made more difficult by the fact that we have a systematically "rubber" scale whose units are small in the middle range and large at the extremes.

STANDARD SCORES

Because the units of a score system based on percentiles are so clearly not equal, we are led to look for some other unit that does have the same meaning throughout its whole range of values. *Standard-score* scales have been developed to serve this purpose.

In Chapter 5, we became acquainted with the standard deviation as a measure of the spread or scatter of a group of scores. The standard deviation was a type of average of the deviations of scores away from the mean—the root-mean-squared deviation. Scores may be expressed in standard deviations away from the mean. Thus, if the mean of a set of scores is 65 and the standard deviation is 15, a score of 80 is 1 standard deviation above the mean. A score of 35 is 2 standard deviations below the mean. In standard deviation units, we could call them +1.0 and −2.0 respectively.

Suppose we have given two tests to a group. The means and standard deviations for the group are shown below, as are the scores made by Johnny and Mary.

	Test A	*Test B*
Mean	65	40
Standard deviation	15	10
Johnny's score	77	55
Mary's score	87	48

Let us see how we can use standard scores to compare performances on the two tests or of the two individuals.

On test A, Johnny is 12 points above the mean, or $12/15 = 0.8$ standard deviations above the mean. On test B he is 15 points, or $15/10 = 1.5$ standard deviations above the mean. Thus, Johnny does a good deal better on test B than on test A. For Mary, the corresponding calculations give

$$\text{Test A: } \frac{87 - 65}{15} = 1.5 \qquad \text{Test B: } \frac{48 - 40}{10} = 0.8$$

Thus, we may say that Mary did as well on test A as Johnny did on test B, and vice versa. Each pupil's level of excellence is expressed as so many standard deviation units above or below the mean of the comparison group. This is a standard unit of measure having essentially the same meaning from one test to another. For aid in interpreting the degree of excellence represented by a standard score, see Table 5.7 (p. 115).

The type of score in standard deviation units that we have just presented is satisfactory except for two matters of convenience: (1) it requires us to use plus and minus signs which may be miscopied or overlooked, and (2) it gets us involved with decimal points which may be misplaced. We can get rid of the need to use decimal points by multiplying every standard deviation score by some constant, such as 10. We can get rid of minus signs by adding to every score a convenient constant amount such as 50. Thus, for Johnny's scores on test A and test B, we have

	Test A	Test B
Mean of distribution of scores	65	40
Standard deviation of distribution	15	10
Johnny's raw score	77	55
Johnny's score in standard deviation units	+0.8	+1.5
Standard deviation score × 10	+8	+15
Plus a constant amount (50)	58	65

A table of standard scores for test A, based on this conversion, in which the mean is set equal to 50 and the standard deviation to 10, is shown in Table 6.5.

We could have used values other than 50 and 10 in setting up our conversion into convenient standard scores. The Army has used a standard-score scale with mean of 100 and standard deviation of 20 for reporting its test results. The College Entrance Examination Board has long used a scale with mean of 500 and standard deviation of 100. The Navy has used the 50 and 10 system.

Originally used in the Air Force, *stanine* scores have had some

Table 6.5. Standard-Score Equivalents for Test A

(Standard score mean = 50, SD = 10)

Raw Score	Standard Score	Raw Score	Standard Score	Raw Score	Standard Score
120	87	80	60	40	33
115	83	75	57	35	30
110	80	70	53	30	27
105	77	65	50	25	23
100	73	60	47	20	20
95	70	55	43	15	17
90	67	50	40	10	13
85	63	45	37	5	10

popularity in recent years. These are single-digit standard scores in which the mean is 5 and the standard deviation 2. The relationships among a number of the different standard score scales, and the relationship of each to percentiles and to the normal curve are shown in Fig. 6.3. The model of the normal curve is shown, and beneath it are a scale of percentiles and several of the common standard score scales. This figure illustrates the equivalence of scores in the different systems. Thus, a stanine score of 7 corresponds to an Army standard score of 120, a Navy standard score of 60, a College Board standard score of 600, a percentile rank of 84. The particular choice of score scale is arbitrary and a matter of convenience. It is too bad that all testing agencies have not been able to agree upon a common score unit. However, the important thing is that the same score scale and comparable norming groups be used for all tests in a given organization, so that results from different tests may be directly comparable.

Frequently standard-score scales are developed via the percentiles corresponding to the raw scores. The test maker assumes that the trait he is measuring is basically distributed in accordance with the normal curve. If he does not get a normal distribution of scores in his norming group, he assumes that this is because the raw-score units in which his test scores were expressed did not represent equal units throughout the range of scores. You will remember our discussion of this point in connection with our spelling test (pp. 125–126). He therefore takes steps to *make* his distribution of standard scores normal—he *normalizes* it. The actual calculations make use of percentiles and of tables of the normal curve. We shall not illustrate the details of procedure here.

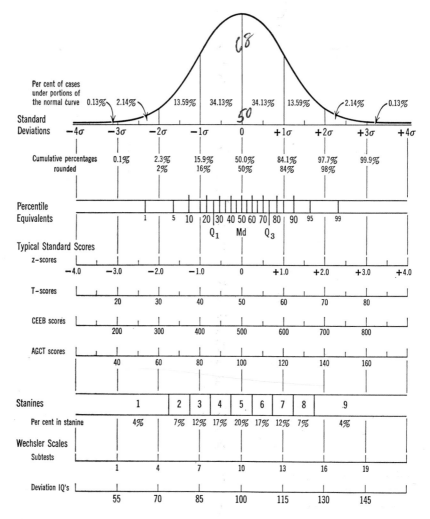

Fig. 6.3. Various types of standard-score scales in relation to percentiles and the normal curve. Reproduced by permission of the Psychological Corporation.

These standard scores have the distinctive feature that they are *guaranteed* to have a normal distribution, at least for a population comparable to that on which the original norms were obtained. The score scale has been stretched in some places and squeezed together in others so that finally a normal distribution results. This process of stretching and squeezing can take care of any inequality in the original units at different raw-score levels in the test. If the basic assumption of a normal distribution was justified, this transformation will produce a scale in which a point of score really represents the same amount at any point on the scale. These are *normalized standard scores*. The term *T-score* which the reader of testing literature quite often encounters refers to this type of normalized standard score based on a single age group.

In summary, standard scores, like percentiles, base the interpretation of the individual's score on his performance in relation to a particular reference group. They differ from percentiles in that they are expressed in presumably equal units. The basic unit is the standard deviation of the reference group, and the individual's score is expressed as the number of standard deviation units above or below the mean of the group. Different numerical standard-score scales have been used by different testing agencies.

INTERCHANGEABILITY OF DIFFERENT TYPES OF NORMS

Whichever type of norm is used, a table of norms will be prepared by the test publisher. This will show the different possible raw scores on the test, together with the corresponding score equivalents in the system of norms being used. Many publishers provide tables giving more than one type of score equivalent. An example is given in Table 6.6. Here we see the norms for the *Language Skills Test* of the revised *Metropolitan Achievement Test Battery*. Four types of norms are shown. The percentiles are based on a group tested early in the sixth grade. The standard-score scale assigns a mean of 50 and a standard deviation of 10 to a mid-sixth-grade group. Thus, a boy with a score of 21 can be characterized as

1. Having a grade equivalent of 8.6.
2. Falling at the 85th percentile in the sixth-grade group.
3. Receiving a standard score of 60.
4. Receiving a stanine of 7.

From Table 6.6 it is easy to see that the different systems of norms are different ways of expressing the same thing. We can translate from one to the other, moving back and forth. Thus, a child who falls at the 65th percentile in the sixth-grade group has a grade equivalent of 7.0. A grade equivalent of 7.0 corresponds to a standard score of 54. The different systems of interpretation support one another for different purposes.

Table 6.6. Norms for Language Study Skills Test of Metropolitan Achievement Tests—Intermediate Battery, Form A

Raw Score	Standard Score	Grade Equiv.	Grade 6 Percentile Rank (October testing)	Grade 6 Stanine (October testing)
28	80	12.5	. . .	
27	77	12.0	99+	
26	73	11.6	99	9
25	70	11.1	98	
24	67	10.6	95	
23	65	10.1	93	8
22	62	9.4	88	
21	60	8.6	85	7
20	58	8.0	80	
19	56	7.4	70	
18	54	7.0	65	6
17	52	6.6	60	
16	50	6.2	50	
15	49	5.9	45	5
14	47	5.6	40	
13	45	5.3	30	
12	43	5.0	25	4
11	42	4.8	20	
10	40	4.5	17	3
9	38	4.3	13	
8	36	4.0	10	
7	34	3.8	8	2
6	32	3.6	5	
5	30	3.3	2	
4	28	3.1	1	
3	24	2.9	1	1
2	20	2.6	1−	
1	16	2.4	. . .	

Reproduced by permission of Harcourt, Brace and World, Inc.

However, the different norm systems are not entirely consistent as we shift from one type of test to another. This is due to the fact that some functions mature more rapidly from one year to the next, relative to the spread of scores at a given age or grade level.

This can be seen most dramatically by comparing reading compre-

hension and arithmetic computation.   The phenomenon is illustrated
by the pairs of scores shown below that were taken from the Stanford

	Paragraph Meaning			Arithmetic Computation		
	John	Henry	Will	John	Henry	Will
Raw score	27	32	37	21	29	28
Grade equivalent	5.2	6.2	7.4	5.2	6.2	6.1
Grade 5.2 percentile	50	73	90	50	92	90

Achievement Test Battery.   It is assumed that the three boys were
tested at the end of 2 months in the fifth grade.   John received scores
on both tests that were just average.   His grade equivalent was 5.2
and he was at the 50th percentile for pupils tested after 2 months in
the fifth grade.   Henry shows superior performance, but how does he
compare in the two subjects?   From one point of view, he does equally
well in both; he is just one full year ahead of his grade placement.   But
in terms of percentiles he is much better in arithmetic than in reading,
i.e., 92nd percentile as compared with 73rd percentile.   Will, on the
other hand, falls at just the same percentile for both reading and arithmetic.   In his case, his grade equivalent for reading is 7.4 and for
arithmetic is 6.1.

The discrepancies that appear in the above example are due to differences in the variability of performance and rate of growth of reading
and arithmetic.   Reading shows a *wide* spread within a single grade
group, relative to the change from grade to grade.   Some fifth graders
read better than the average eighth or ninth grader, so a grade equivalent of 8 or 9 is not unheard of for fifth graders.   In fact a grade
equivalent of 8.0 corresponds to the 95th percentile for pupils at grade
5.2.   By contrast, a fifth grader almost never does as well in arithmetic
as an eighth or ninth grader—in part because he has not encountered
or been taught many of the topics that will be presented in the fifth,
sixth, seventh, and eighth grades.   Thus, fifth graders are more homogeneous with respect to arithmetic skills, or looked at another way,
arithmetic shows more rapid gains from fifth to eighth grade than does
reading.

This point must always be borne in mind, especially in comparing
grade equivalents for different subjects.   A bright child will often appear most advanced in reading and language, least so in arithmetic
and spelling—when the results are reported in grade equivalents. This
difference may result, in whole or in part, simply from the differences

in the growth functions for the subjects, and need not mean a genuinely uneven pattern of progress for the child.

QUOTIENTS

In the early days of mental testing, after age norms had been used for a few years, the need was felt to convert the age score into an index that would express rate of progress. The 8-year-old who had an age equivalent of $10\frac{1}{2}$ years was obviously better than average, but how much better? Some index was needed to take account of chronological age (actual time lived) as well as the age equivalent on the test (score level reached).

The expedient was hit upon of dividing test age by chronological age to yield a quotient. This procedure was applied most extensively with tests of intelligence where the age equivalent we were concerned with was a mental age and the corresponding quotient was an *intelligence quotient*. However, it was also used to some extent for achievement tests and for some other sorts of measures.

The formula for computing the intelligence quotient in this way is given below and is illustrated for the 8-year-old who reaches the $10\frac{1}{2}$-year level on the test.

$$IQ = \frac{100\,MA}{CA}$$

$$= \frac{100(10.5)}{8} = 131$$

A similar quotient could be computed for a reading test, general achievement battery, measure of strength, or any other testing instrument that yields age norms. The resulting value would be called a reading quotient (RQ), educational quotient (EQ), or the like.

How does an intelligence quotient come to have meaning? In the first place, it is obvious by the way in which the quotient was established that 100 should be average at every age group, since the average 10-year-old, for example, should fall exactly at the 10-year level on any test if the age equivalents were properly established. But how outstandingly good is 125? How poor is 80? Such questions as these can only be answered by becoming acquainted with the distribution of quotients that a particular test yields.

The intelligence quotient was originally developed in connection with the individual intelligence test of the type represented by the

Stanford-Binet (see Chapter 9). A typical distribution of intelligence quotients for the 1937 revision of that test, based upon the standardization group, is shown in Table 6.7. This table shows the per cent of

Table 6.7. Distribution of Revised Stanford-Binet IQ's

IQ Range	Per Cent of Cases	Cumulative Per Cent
140 and over	1.3	99.9
130–139	3.1	98.6
120–129	8.2	95.5
110–119	18.1	87.3
100–109	23.5	69.2
90– 99	23.0	45.7
80– 89	14.5	22.7
70– 79	5.6	8.2
60– 69	2.0	2.6
Below 60	0.6	0.6

From L. M. Terman and M. A. Merrill, *Stanford-Binet intelligence scale,* Boston, Houghton Mifflin Co., 1960.

cases falling within each 10-point IQ interval and the cumulative percentage through each interval. Thus, 1.3 per cent of cases got IQ's of 140 and over, 3.1 per cent from 130 to 139, and so forth. An IQ of 125 would surpass roughly 91 per cent of the group (fall at the 91st percentile), whereas one of 80 would surpass only about 8 per cent. The mean for this particular distribution of IQ's is 101.5, and the standard deviation is 16.3.

The circumstance that made intelligence quotients from such a test as the *Stanford-Binet* relatively interpretable was that the mean and standard deviation remained relatively uniform from age to age. For this reason, an IQ of 125 signifies about the same status, relative to his own age group, whether obtained for a 5-year-old or a 15-year-old. This situation would not necessarily be true and was not perfectly true even for this test, but in many instances quotients were found to maintain the same average and spread of values in different age groups sufficiently closely so that a common interpretation was appropriate at all age levels.

To all intents and purposes, such quotients represent a type of standard score. In the case of the 1937 revision of the *Stanford-Binet,* we have a standard score with a mean of approximately 100 and standard deviation of approximately 16 in a general sample of American children. This relationship of quotients to standard scores is explicitly recognized in most recent intelligence tests. For these, tables of IQ equivalents have been set up at each age level. These have been built so as to give a common mean and standard deviation for all age groups.

As a matter of fact, the most recent edition of the *Stanford-Binet,* brought out in 1960, also uses standard scores designed so that the mean is 100 and the standard deviation 16 at each age level, rather than the MA/CA ratio that was the basis for the IQ in earlier editions.

The quotients yielded by different tests are, unfortunately, not exactly equivalent. A variety of factors in the test and in the selection of norming groups have led to somewhat different means and standard deviations of intelligence quotients. Some evidence on the variability of quotients for five widely used tests for high-school groups is presented in Table 6.8. Experience with a test in a particular community

Table 6.8. Equivalent IQ's on Five Widely Used Group Intelligence Tests (From Engelhart [2])

Otis Quick-Scoring Beta, Form F_m	California Mental Maturity, Short Form, Intermediate Form S	Kuhlman-Anderson Battery Booklet G	Lorge-Thorndike Verbal, Level 4, Form A	Pintner General Ability, Intermediate Form A
140	145	140	142	151
130	134	130	132	139
120	123	121	121	126
110	113	111	111	113
100	102	101	100	100
90	92	92	90	87
80	81	82	79	74
70	70	73	69	61

setting will provide a further basis for interpreting quotients at different levels.

The notion of the intelligence quotient or IQ is deeply imbedded in the history of the testing movement, and, in fact, in twentieth-century American culture. The expression "IQ test" is a part of our common speech. We are probably stuck with the term. But in the future IQ's will in most cases really be standard scores. And this is how we should think of them and use them. We may hope that eventually the test publishers will agree upon a common standard score scale and will establish more clearly comparable normative groups, so that scores on different tests will be more directly comparable.

PROFILES

The various types of norms we have been considering provide a means of expressing scores on quite different tests in common units in such a way that they can be directly compared. There is no direct way of comparing a score of thirty words correctly spelled with one of twenty arithmetic problems solved. But if both scores are expressed in terms of the grade level to which they correspond or in terms of the per cent of some defined common group that gets scores below that point, then they may be compared. The set of different test scores for an individual, expressed in a common unit of measure, constitute his *score profile*. The separate scores may be presented for comparison in tabular form by listing the converted score values. Illustrations of record forms showing the manner of recording converted scores are given in Figs. 6.4 and 6.5. The comparison of different subareas of performance is made pictorially clearer by a graphic profile. Several ways of plotting profiles are shown in Figs. 6.6, 6.7, and 6.8.

Figure 6.6 shows the form for plotting the subscores of the *California Test of Mental Ability*. Each subtest is represented by a row. The scale of age equivalents appears across the top of the form. The broken vertical line portrays the performance of the particular individual. Peaks in performance are to the right and low points to the left.

Figure 6.7 shows a similar form for plotting part scores on the *Metropolitan Achievement Test*. This form differs in representing the different tests in successive columns and presenting the score scale in the vertical dimension. Grade equivalents are shown on the vertical scale.

Figure 6.8 shows a type of profile chart for the component tests of the *Differential Aptitude Test Battery*. This battery undertakes to appraise different aspects of ability important in a high-school guidance program. Note that in this case the different tests are represented by separate bars, rather than points connected by a line. The scale used in this case is a percentile scale, but in plotting percentile values appropriate adjustments have been made for the inequality of percentile units. That is, percentile points have been spaced in the same way as they are in a normal curve, being more widely spaced at the upper and lower extremes than in the middle range. This percentile scale corresponds to the percentile scale that is shown in Figure 6.3 (p. 140). By this process, the percentile values for an individual are plotted on

CLASS RECORD

In this Class Record achievement test results should be recorded in terms of grade or age equivalents. Mental Ages and IQ's should be determined from an intelligence test.

PUPIL'S NAMES	CHRONO-LOGICAL AGE	MENTAL AGE	IQ	1. Read.	2 Vocab.	Ave. Read.	3. Arith. Fund.	4. Arith. Prob.	Ave. Arith.	5. Lang. Usage	6. Spell.	AVE. ACHT.
1 Mary Anderson	11-8	12-3	105	6.5	6.7	6.6	5.6	6.0	5.8	6.5	6.3	6.3
2 Henry Baker	12-2	11-9	96	6.1	6.0	6.0	6.4	6.9	6.6	5.9	5.6	6.2
3 Carol Cohen	11-7	13-7	117	7.6	7.3	7.4	6.6	6.2	6.4	7.2	6.4	6.8
4 Harold Dominick	11-11	11-4	95	5.4	5.9	5.6	5.5	5.3	5.4	5.4	6.3	5.4
5 etc.												
6												
7												
8												
9												
10												
11												
12												
13												
14												
15												

Fig. 6.4. Class record form for *Metropolitan Achievement Test.* (Scores recorded as grade equivalents.)

California Test of Mental Maturity • Class Record Sheet

SERIES USED { Preprimary .... Primary .... Elementary .... Intermediate .... Advanced ....
Preprimary S.F. .... Primary S.F. .... Elementary S.F. .... Intermediate S.F. .... Advanced S.F. ....

School .... Date Given .... 19 ....

City .... Grade .... Teacher ....

PUPIL'S NAME	SEX	C. A.	M. A.			I. Q.			PERCENTILE RANK FOR AGE							
			TOTAL MENTAL	LANG-UAGE	NON LANG-UAGE	TOTAL MENTAL	LANG-UAGE	NON LANG-UAGE	MEMORY	SPATIAL RELATION-SHIP	LOGICAL REASON-ING	NUMERICAL REASONING	VERBAL CONCEPTS	TOTAL MENTAL	LANG-UAGE	NON LANG-UAGE
1																
2																
3																
4																
5																
6																
7																
8																
9																
10																
11																
12																
13																
14																

Fig. 6.5. Form for recording intelligence test results. (Reproduced by permission of California Test Bureau.)

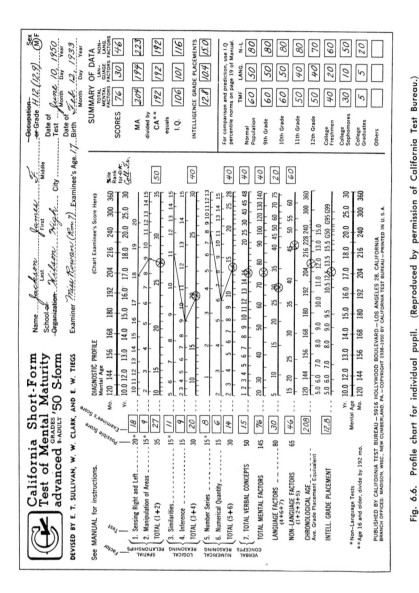

Fig. 6.6. Profile chart for individual pupil. (Reproduced by permission of California Test Bureau.)

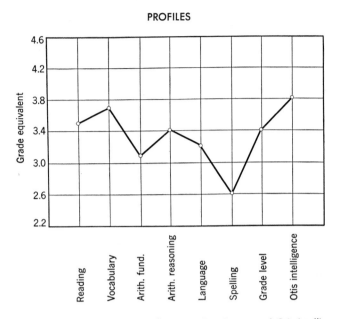

Fig. 6.7. Score profile for *Metropolitan Achievement Test Battery* and *Otis Intelligence Test.*

an equal-unit scale. A given linear distance can reasonably be thought of as representing the same amount of ability whether it lies high, low, or near the middle of the scale. By the same token, the same distance can be considered equivalent from one test to another.

Note that in Fig. 6.8 the bars have been plotted up and down from the 50th percentile. For this type of norm, the average of the group constitutes the anchor point of the scale, and individual scores can be referred to this base level. This type of figure brings out the individual's strengths and weaknesses very dramatically.

The profile chart makes a very effective way of representing the scores for an individual. In interpreting profiles, however, several cautions must be borne in mind. In the first place, procedures for plotting profiles assume that the norms for the several tests are comparable. Age, grade, or percentile scores must be based upon equivalent groups for all the tests. The best guarantee of equivalence is, of course, a common population used for all tests. This is the situation that commonly prevails for the different subtests of a test battery. Norms for all are established at the same time on the basis of testing a common group. The guarantee of comparability of the norms for the different component tests is one of the most attractive features of an integrated battery. If separately developed tests are plotted to-

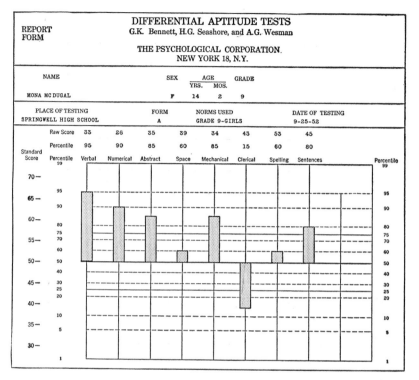

Fig. 6.8. Pupil profile chart for Differential Aptitude Tests. (Reproduced by permission of the Psychological Corporation.)

gether, we can usually only hope that the groups on which norms were established were comparable and that the profile is an unbiased picture of relative achievement in the different fields. Where it is necessary to use tests from several different sources, one solution is to develop our own local norms on a common population and to plot individual profiles in terms of the local norms.

A second problem is that of deciding how to interpret the ups and downs of a profile. Not all the differences that appear in a profile are meaningful, either in a statistical or a practical sense. We must decide which of the differences deserve some attention on our part and which should be ignored. This problem arises because no test score is completely exact. A full discussion of the problem of reliability and of the "error of measurement" in a test score will be provided in the following chapter. At this point, we shall merely note that test scores are not perfectly accurate, that performance on a reading test or an aptitude test will vary somewhat from form to form and from occasion to occasion. Thus, small differences from one score to another in a test profile should be largely ignored as having very probably arisen by chance. Only as the differences between scores become substantial in relation to the standard error (see p. 175) of the separate scores is there any justification for interpreting the differences as representing something real and significant.

Organizing the separate test scores of an individual into a graphic profile is, then, a very effective way of dramatizing the high and low points in a score pattern. Such a profile may be plotted whenever scores from several different tests are expressed in the same units. However, a profile must be interpreted with a good deal of caution, because even unreliable differences may look quite impressive.

USING NORMS

We have seen that norms provide a basis for interpreting the scores of an individual. Converting the score for any test taken singly into age or grade equivalent, percentile or standard score, permits an interpretation of the level at which the individual is functioning on that particular test. Bringing together the set of scores for an individual in a common unit of measure, and perhaps exhibiting these scores in a profile, brings out the relative level of performance of the individual in different areas.

The median performance for a class, a grade group in a school, or the children in a grade throughout a school system may be similarly reported. We then see the average level of performance within the group on some single function or the relative performance of the group in each of several areas. Norms provide a frame within which the picture may be viewed and bring all parts of the picture into the common frame. Now what does the picture mean, and what should we do about it?

Obviously we cannot, in a few pages, provide a ready-made interpretation for each set of scores that may be obtained in a practical testing situation. However, we can lay out a few general guiding lines and principles that may help to forestall some unwise interpretations of test results. The first points are phrased with an eye to the interpretation of group results. These are followed by some points relating primarily to interpretation of individual scores. However, the points overlap somewhat, and each has some reference to the other type of situation.

PRINCIPLES GUIDING INTERPRETATION OF GROUP PERFORMANCE

1. *In Evaluating Average Group Achievement, Consideration Must Be Given To Average Ability Level in the Group.* A sixth-grade class with an average mental age of 10 years could not be expected to do arithmetic as well as one with an average mental age of 12 years. Some adjustment must be made for the typical ability level. However, one must be somewhat conservative in making such adjustments, especially for classes superior on an intelligence test. The correspondence between intelligence and academic achievement is not perfect, and a group of bright youngsters will rarely be comparably outstanding in achievement. This will be true particularly in the more specialized and less academic subjects, such as spelling or handwriting. A group that deviates from average in ability can be expected to differ from the general norm in achievement also, and in the same direction, but it should not be expected to differ as much in achievement as it does in ability.

2. *A Further Factor That May Be Expected To Influence Achievement Is the Type of Cultural Background from Which the Children Come.* Home and community influences are strong. Foreign-language background, absence of pictures and books in the home, a negative family attitude toward schools and schooling may all be important. In a measure, these factors affect intelligence test score. But they affect achievement also, and perhaps more directly. Where a class is atypical in cultural background, either especially favored or especially deprived, allowance must be made for this in interpreting test results.

3. *Group Achievement Can Only Be Evaluated in the Light of Curricular Content, Emphases, and Objectives.* If a school system has delayed all formal instruction in arithmetic until the third grade in order to provide more time in the earlier grades for group projects, social experiences, and preparatory materials, it is unreasonable to expect the children in the third grades of that system to come up to national third-grade norms in arithmetic. If a school system has de-emphasized accurate spelling as an objective, has cut down or eliminated spelling drills, and has concentrated on other educational outcomes, it is inappropriate to evaluate that school by rigid application of national norms in a standardized spelling test. There is a good deal of evidence from test results themselves that schools in the more prosperous and privileged communities have de-emphasized the basic tool skills of arithmetic and spelling in the early grades. In these grades such communities often do no better in computation and spelling than much poorer communities with children of lower intelligence.

Of course, the communities giving less emphasis to arithmetic and spelling in order to achieve other less tangible educational outcomes may not actually be achieving them. Whether they are can only be answered as we develop measures to appraise such objectives as ability to follow directions, to work alone, to take care of property, to get along with other children, or to grow in social relationships, which are objectives given emphasis in the stated objectives of these communities. Instruments for appraising these objectives should receive the attention of the measurement specialist and the schools themselves. But one thing is clear. The school's objectives and curricular emphases must be taken into account in interpreting standardized test results.

4. *Use of Test Results Should Be Constructive, Not Punitive.* One continually encounters situations in which results on achievement tests are used as a basis for evaluating the professional worth of teachers. The test then becomes a sword held over the teacher's head, a recurring threat to his security. In such a situation, it should be no wonder if the test is resented, if the teacher teaches in order to "beat the test" or even gives illicit help at the time of testing. The teacher is now on the side of the pupils working against the test.

This type of situation is to be avoided at all costs. The threat arises in large measure out of administrative personnel and will disappear if administrators see the tests as primarily tools to help both pupil and teacher. This will be facilitated if tests are given in the fall, when they can be used to guide the work of the year to come, rather than in the spring, to judge the work of the past year.

PRINCIPLES GUIDING INTERPRETATION OF INDIVIDUAL PERFORMANCE

1. *Here Again, Achievement Must Be Evaluated in the Light of Evidences of Aptitude.* The 12-year-old who is reading at the 9-year level is not a *reading* problem if his mental age is also 9. He is then doing about what could be expected of him. Too many remedial classes are filled with children who are really performing at or even above the level that should be expected for them.

Again, the intellectually superior child cannot generally be expected to be *as* superior in achievement as he is on the measure of intelligence. In the first place, achievement depends upon exposure. Even the bright fourth grader cannot be expected to do sixth-grade arithmetic if he has never encountered or been taught the processes. In some subjects, at least, opportunity sets very real limits to the level that a person can reach. In the second place, abilities are to a degree specialized. The child who is picked out because he is bright is likely to be somewhat less outstanding in other specialized educational skills.

2. *For Individuals as Well as Groups, We Must Take Account of Family and Cultural Differentials.* The wide range of variation in language background, richness of home resources, and incentives to progress in school may be expected to have a great impact on educational skills and accomplishments, and allowance for IQ differences will only in part take account of these factors.

3. *The Individual Child's Performance, Too, Must Be Judged in Terms of the Curriculum To Which He Has Been Exposed.* The individual pupils cannot be expected to progress as rapidly in those areas in which teaching emphasis is less. Furthermore, in those skills that are closely dependent upon instruction, even the able pupils cannot be expected to move ahead at a tempo much faster than that at which the material is presented. Thus, the bright child may be expected to be more advanced in word knowledge and reading skills, which he can readily pick up on his own, than in the processes of arithmetic, which he is unlikely to master until he has been exposed to them in the school setting.

4. *In the Case of the Single Individual, We Must Be Acutely Aware of the Existence of Errors of Measurement.* A test score does not identify the exact level of ability for the child. It represents the most likely value within a fairly broad band of possible values. Differences between areas of achievement must be viewed as tentative as long as these bands overlap. Differences between standing on two testings— say, two reading tests a few months apart—should not excite us unduly unless they are quite substantial. We should be rather conservative in "explaining" differences that may represent nothing more than the fallibility of our measuring instrument.

5. *In the Very Nature of Things, by the Way Test Norms Are Developed We Must in General Expect Half of a Group to Fall Below the Norm.* The norm is the average, the typical. It is neither the ideal of satisfactory accomplishment nor the standard to which we can hold everybody. It is the typical performance of typical individuals at the present time. In any average there must be as many below as above. Educators must avoid the compulsion to bring everybody "up to the norm." We must be careful not to try to fit everybody into the Procrustean bed of the average.

SUMMARY STATEMENT

A raw score, taken by itself, has no meaning. It gets meaning only by comparison with some reference group or groups. The comparison may be with:

1. A series of age groups (age norms).

2. A series of grade groups (grade norms).

3. A single group, indicating what per cent of that group the score surpassed (percentile norms).

4. A single group, indicating standard deviations above or below the group mean (standard scores).

Each alternative has certain advantages and certain limitations, which we have considered.

To get an index of brightness from age norms, quotients such as the intelligence quotient and educational quotient were devised. These become meaningful and usable when they have approximately the same standard deviation for all age groups. In that case, they are essentially standard scores and should be thought of as such.

If the norms available for a number of different tests are of the same kind and are based on comparable groups, all the tests can be expressed in comparable terms. They can then be shown pictorially in the form of a profile. Profiles emphasize score differences within the individual. When profiles are used, care must be taken not to over-interpret minor ups and downs of the profile.

Norms represent a descriptive framework for interpreting the score of an individual, a class group, or some large aggregation. However, before a judgment can be made as to whether an individual or group is doing well or poorly, allowance must be made for ability level, cultural background, and curricular emphases. The norm is merely an average, not a strait jacket into which all can be forced to fit.

REFERENCES

1. Boynton, Bernice, The physical growth of girls, *Univ. Ia. Stud. Child Welf.*, **12**, No. 4, 1936.
2. Engelhart, Max D., *Equivalence of intelligence quotients of five group intelligence tests,* Bureau of Pupil Guidance, Chicago Public Schools (mimeographed report, 10 pp., no date).

SUGGESTED ADDITIONAL READING

Flanagan, J. C., Units, scores, and norms, Chapter 17 in E. F. Lindquist, Editor, *Educational measurement,* Washington, D. C., American Council on Education, 1951.

Harris, Chester W., Editor, *Encyclopedia of educational research,* 3rd ed., New York, Macmillan, 1960, pp. 922–926.

Mosier, Charles I., Batteries and profiles, Chapter 18 in E. F. Lindquist,

Editor, *Educational measurement,* Washington, D. C., American Council on Education, 1951.

Seashore, Harold G., Methods of expressing test scores. *Test Service Bulletin No. 48,* New York, Psychological Corp., 1955.

QUESTIONS FOR DISCUSSION

1. A pupil in the seventh grade received a raw score of 13 on the *Metropolitan Reading Test, Intermediate Level.* What additional information would be needed to interpret this score?

2. Why do standardized tests designed for use with high-school students almost never use age or grade norms?

3. What limitations would national norms have for use by a county school system in rural West Virginia? What might the local school system do about it?

4. What assumption or assumptions lie back of the development of age norms? Grade norms? Normalized standard scores?

5. In Fig. 6.8, p. 152, why are the standard scores evenly spaced whereas the percentile scores are unevenly spaced?

6. Using Tables 6.3 and 6.6, briefly characterize the following entering sixth-grade children:

	CA	MA	Reading Score	Study Skills
Pupil A	12.4	10.6	23	13
Pupil B	10.5	13.2	31	19
Pupil C	11.3	11.1	22	16

7. You are a guidance counselor and have given the *Differential Aptitude Battery* to a ninth grade. Using Table 6.4, prepare a summary report and interpretation for a boy with the following scores:

Verbal Reasoning	18	Mechanical Reasoning	54
Numerical Ability	23	Clerical Speed and Acc.	45
Abstract Reasoning	31	Spelling	14
Spatial Relations	72	Sentences	22

8. School A gives a battery of achievement tests each May in each grade from the third through the sixth. The median grade level in each subject in each teacher's class is reported to the superintendent. Should they be reported? If so, what else should be included in the report? In what ways might a superintendent use the results to advantage? What uses should he avoid?

9. Miss B prides herself that each year she has gotten at least 90 per cent of her fifth-grade group "up to the norm" in each subject. How desirable is this as an educational objective? What limitations or dangers do you see in it?

10. School C operates on a policy of assigning transfer students to a grade on the basis of their average grade standing on an achievement battery. Thus, a boy with a grade score of 6.4 on the battery as a whole would be assigned to the sixth grade, no matter what his age or his grade

in his previous school. What values do you see in this plan? What limitations?

11. The superintendent of schools in city D noted that school E fell consistently about a half grade below national norms on an achievement battery. He was distressed because this was the lowest of any school in his city. How justified is his dissatisfaction? What more do you need to know to answer this?

12. The board of education in city F noted that the second and third grades in their community fell substantially below national norms in arithmetic, though coming up to the norms in other subjects. They propose to study this further. What additional information do they need?

13. Look at the manual for some test, and study the information that is given about the norms.

a. How adequate is the norming population? Is adequate information given about this?

b. Figure out the chance score (i.e., the score to be expected from blind guessing) for each test, and note its grade equivalent. What limitations does this suggest on use of the test?

c. What limitations are there on the usefulness of the test at the upper end of its range?

d. How many raw score points correspond to one full grade?

14. Examine Fig. 6.6. What are the possible advantages of a profile such as this? What are its limitations and shortcomings? Is it desirable to plot it and use the results?

Chapter 7

▼

Qualities Desired in Any Measurement Procedure

Whenever a worker in psychology or education desires to measure some quality in a group or individual, he faces the problem of choosing the best instrument for his purpose. Ordinarily there will be several tests or testing procedures that have been developed for, or that seem to be at least possibilities for, his purpose. He must choose among these. He is also probably interested in determining not only which is the best procedure but how well it satisfies his needs by some absolute standard. On what grounds can he make his choice or his appraisal?

There are many specific considerations entering into the evaluation of a test, but we shall consider them here under three main headings. These are respectively validity, reliability, and practicality. Validity refers to the extent to which a test measures what we actually wish to measure. Reliability has to do with accuracy and precision of a measurement procedure. Indices of reliability give an indication of the extent to which a particular measurement is consistent and reproducible. Practicality is concerned with a wide range of factors of economy, convenience, and interpretability that determine whether a test is practical for widespread use. These three aspects of test evaluation will be considered in detail in the following sections.

VALIDITY

The first and foremost question to be asked with respect to any testing procedure is: How valid is it? When we ask this question, we are inquiring whether the test measures what we want it to measure, all of what we want it to measure, and nothing but what we want it to measure.

When we apply a steel tape measure to the top of our desk to determine its length, we have no doubt that the tape does in fact measure the length of the desk and does directly serve our purpose, which may be to determine whether the desk will fit between two windows in our room. Long experience with this type of measuring instrument has confirmed beyond a shadow of doubt its validity as a tool for measuring length.

Suppose now that we give to a group of children a test of reading achievement. This test requires the children to select certain answers to a series of questions about reading passages and to make little pencil marks on an answer sheet. We count the number of pencil marks made in the predetermined right places and give the child as a score the number of his right answers. We call this score his reading comprehension. But the score itself is not the comprehension. It is the *record* of a *sample* of behavior. Any judgment regarding comprehension is an inference from this number which is the number of allegedly correct answers. Its validity is not self-evident but is something we must establish on the basis of adequate evidence.

Consider again the typical personality inventory that endeavors to provide an appraisal of "emotional adjustment." In this type of inventory the respondent marks a series of statements as being characteristic of him or not characteristic of him. On the basis of various types of procedures, which we shall consider in some detail in Chapter 12, certain responses are keyed as indicative of emotional maladjustment. A score is obtained by seeing how many of these responses an individual selects. But making certain marks on a piece of paper is a number of steps removed from actually exhibiting emotional disturbance. We must find some way of establishing the extent to which the performance on the test actually corresponds to the quality of behavior in which we are directly interested. How can we determine the validity of such a measurement procedure?

TYPES OF EVIDENCE OF VALIDITY

A test may be thought of as corresponding to some aspect of human behavior in any one of three senses. For these three senses we shall use the terms (1) represent, (2) predict, and (3) signify. Let us explore each of these three, so that we may understand clearly what is involved in each case, and for what kinds of tests each of the three is relevant.

VALIDITY AS REPRESENTING

Consider a test that has been prepared to measure achievement in using the English language. How can we tell how well the test does in fact measure that achievement? First, we must reach some agreement as to the skills, knowledge and understanding that comprise correct and effective use of English, and that have been the objectives of language instruction. Then we must examine the test to see what skills, knowledge and understanding it calls for. Finally, we must match the analysis of test content against the analysis of course content and instructional objectives and see how well the former *represents* the latter. In proportion as the outcomes that we have accepted as goals for the course are represented in the test, the test is valid.

Since the analysis is essentially a rational and judgmental one, this is sometimes spoken of as *rational or logical validity*. Since the analysis is largely in terms of the content of the test, the term *content validity* is also sometimes used. However, we should not think of content too narrowly, because we may be interested in *process* as much as in simple content. Thus, in the field of English expression we might be concerned on the one hand with such "content" elements as the rules and principles for capitalization, use of commas, or spelling words with "ei" and "ie" combinations. But we might also be interested in such "process" skills as arranging ideas in a logical order, writing sentences that present a single unified thought, or picking the most appropriate word to convey the desired meaning. In a sense, *content* is what the pupil works with; *process* is what he does with it.

The problem of appraising content validity is closely parallel to the problem of preparing the blueprint for a test, as discussed in Chapter 3, and then building a test to match the blueprint. A teacher's own test has content validity to the extent that a wise and thoughtful analysis of course objectives has been made in the blueprint, and care, skill and ingenuity have been exercised in building test items to match the blueprint. A standardized test may be shown to have validity for a particular school or a particular curriculum insofar as the tasks that it presents to the examinee correspond to and represent the objectives accepted in that school or that curriculum.

It should be clear that validity evidenced as *representing*, i.e., rational or content validity, is important primarily for measures of achievement. When we wish to appraise a test of reading comprehension, of biology, or of American history, we can really do so only by asking: How well do the tasks of this test represent what we consider to be important outcomes in this area of instruction? How well do these tasks represent what the best and most expert judgment would consider to be important knowledge and skills? If the correspondence is good, we consider the test valid; if poor, the validity must be deemed to be low.

The responsible maker of a test for publication and widespread use goes to considerable pains to determine the widely accepted goals of instruction in the field in which his test is to be built. There are many types of sources to which he may, and often does resort. These include, among others: (1) the more widely used textbooks in the field, (2) recent courses of study for the large school units, i.e., states, counties, and city systems, (3) reports of special study groups, often appearing in yearbooks of one or another of the educational societies, (4) groups of teachers giving instruction in the course, (5) specialists in universities, cities, and state departments concerned with the training or supervision of teachers in the field.

Gathering information from these sources the test maker develops the blueprint for his test, and in terms of this blueprint he prepares his test items. Because of variations from community to community, no published test can be made to fit exactly the content or objectives of every local course of study. In this sense, a test developed on a national basis is always less valid for a specific community than an equally workmanlike test tailored specifically to the local situation. However, the well-made commercial test takes the common components that appear repeatedly in different textbooks and courses of study and builds a test around them. It *represents* the common core that is central in the different specific local patterns.

It should be clear from what has just been said that the relationship between teaching and testing is typically intimate. Test content is drawn from what has been taught, or what is proposed to be taught. The instructional program is the original source of test materials. Sometimes the thinking in a test may lead the thinking underlying a local course of study, as when a group of specialists have been brought together to design a test corresponding to some emerging trend in education. Sometimes the test may lag behind, as when the test is based on the relatively conventional objectives emphasized in established textbooks. But usually test content and classroom instruction are in close relationship to one another, and the test may be appraised by how faithfully it corresponds to the significant goals of instruction.

VALIDITY AS PREDICTING

Frequently we are interested in using a test to *predict* some specific future outcome. We use a scholastic aptitude test to predict how likely the high school student is to be successful in college X, where success is represented at least approximately by grade-point average. We use an employment test to pick machine operators who are likely to be successful employees, as represented by some such criterion as high production with little spoilage and low personnel turnover. For this purpose, we care very little what a test looks like.*   We are interested only in the degree to which it correlates with some chosen criterion measure of job success.   The higher the correlation, the better the test.

Our evaluation of a test as predicting is primarily an empirical and statistical evaluation, and this aspect of validity has sometimes been spoken of as *empirical* or statistical validity.   The basic procedure is to give the test to a group who are entering some job or training program, to follow them up later and get for each one some criterion measure of success on the job or in the training program, and then to compute the correlation between test score and criterion measure of success.   The higher the correlation, the more effective the test as a predictor.

This relationship can also be pictured in various ways.   For example, the bar chart in Fig. 7.1 shows the percentage of persons failing pilot training at each of nine score levels on a predictor-test battery. Examination of the chart shows a steady increase in the per cent failing training as we go from the high to the low scores.   The relationship pictured in this chart corresponds to a correlation coefficient of .49.

The Problem of the Criterion.   We said above that predictive validity can be estimated by determining the correlation between test scores and a suitable criterion measure of success on the job.   The joker here is the phrase "suitable criterion measure."   One of the most difficult problems that the personnel psychologist or educator faces is that of locating or creating a satisfactory measure of job success to serve as a criterion measure for test validation.   It may appear to the student that it should be a simple matter to decide upon some measure of rate of production or some type of rating by superiors.   It may also seem that this measure, once decided upon, should be obtainable in an easy and straightforward fashion.   Unfortunately, this is not so.   Finding or developing acceptable criterion measures usually involves the research worker in the field of tests and measurements in a number of troublesome problems.

Difficulties in obtaining satisfactory criterion measures arise from a variety of sources.   There are many types of jobs, such as those of physician, teacher, secretary, or stock clerk, that yield no objective

---

* This is not entirely true.   What a test "looks like" may be of importance in determining its acceptability and reasonableness to those who will be tested. Thus, a group of would-be pilots may be more ready to accept an arithmetic test dealing with wind drift and gasoline consumption than they would the same essential problems phrased in terms of costs of crops or of recipes for baking cakes.   This appearance of reasonableness is sometimes spoken of as "face validity."

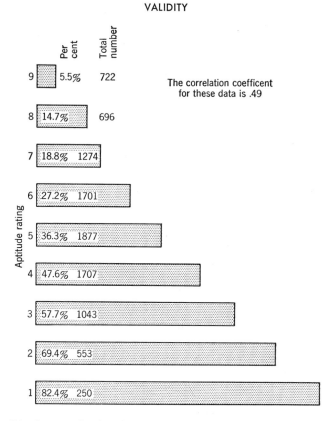

Fig. 7.1. Per cent of cadets eliminated from pilot training at each aptitude level.

record of performance or production. But even when such records are available, they are often influenced by a variety of factors outside the worker's control. Thus, the production record of a weaver may depend not only upon his own skill in threading or adjusting the loom but also on the condition of the equipment, the adequacy of the lighting where he must work, or the color of the thread he must weave. The sales of an insurance agent are not only a function of his own effectiveness as a salesman but also of the territory in which he must work and the supervision and assistance he receives. The problems of effective rating of personnel are discussed in detail in Chapter 13. It suffices to indicate here that ratings are often unstable and influenced by many factors other than the proficiency of the person being rated.

There are always many criterion measures that might be obtained and used for validating a selection test. In addition to quantitative performance records and subjective ratings, which have already been mentioned, we might use later tests of proficiency. This is the type of situation that is involved when a college entrance mathematics test is validated in terms of its ability to predict later performance on a comprehensive examination on college mathematics. Here the comprehensive examination serves as the criterion measure. Another common type of criterion is grades in some type of educational or training program. Thus, tests for the selection of engineers may be validated against course grades in engineering school.

All criterion measures are only partial in that they measure only a part of success on the job or only the preliminaries to actual job performance. This last is true of the engineering school grades mentioned above. They represent a relatively immediate but quite partial criterion of success as an engineer. The ultimate criterion is some appraisal of the man's lifetime success in his profession. In the very nature of things, such an ultimate criterion is inaccessible to us and we must be satisfied with substitutes for it. These substitutes are only partial and are never completely satisfactory. Our problem is always to choose the most satisfactory from among the measures that it appears feasible to obtain. We are faced, then, with the problem of deciding which of several criterion measures is most satisfactory. How shall we arrive at this decision?

Qualities Desired in a Criterion Measure. There are four qualities that we desire in a criterion measure. In order of their importance they are (1) relevance, (2) freedom from bias, (3) reliability, and (4) availability.

We judge a criterion to be relevant to the extent that score on the criterion measure is determined by the same factors that determine success on the job. In appraising the relevance of a criterion, we are thrown back once more upon rational considerations. There is no empirical evidence that will tell us whether a particular criterion measure is or is not relevant. For achievement tests we found it necessary to rely upon the best available professional judgment to determine whether the content of the test accurately represented our objectives. In the same way, with respect to a criterion measure it is also necessary to rely upon professional judgment to provide the appraisal of the degree to which any available partial criterion measure is relevant to the ultimate criterion of job success.

A second factor important in a criterion measure is that of freedom from bias. By this we mean that the measure should provide each person with the same opportunity to make a good score. Examples of biasing factors are such things as variation in wealth from one district to another in our previous example of the insurance salesman, variation in the quality of equipment and conditions of work of a factory worker, variation in generosity of the bosses rating private secretaries, or variation in the skill of teachers instructing pupils in different classes. We can see that it will be difficult to get meaning from the relationship of test results to a criterion score if that score depends upon factors in the conditions of work rather than factors in the individual worker.

The topic of reliability will be discussed in general terms later in this chapter. As it applies to the criterion scores, the problem is merely this: a measure of success on the job must be stable or reproducible if it is to be predicted by any type of test device. If the criterion performance is one that jumps around from day to day so that the person who shows high job performance one week may show low job performance the next, then there is no possibility of finding a test that will predict it. A measure that is fundamentally unstable itself cannot be predicted by anything else.

Finally, in the choice of criterion measure one always encounters practical problems of convenience and availability. How long is it going to take to get a criterion score for each individual? How much is it going to cost? Though a personnel research program can often afford to spend a substantial part of its effort in getting good criterion data, there is always a practical limit. Any choice of a criterion measure must take this practical limit into account.

THE INTERPRETATION OF VALIDITY COEFFICIENTS

Suppose that we have gathered test and criterion scores for a group of individuals and computed the correlation between them. Perhaps our predictor is a scholastic aptitude test, and the criterion is an average of college freshman grades. How shall we now decide whether the test is a good predictor?

Obviously, other things being equal, the higher the correlation, the better. In one sense, our only basis for evaluating any predictor is in relation to other possible prediction procedures. Does test A yield a higher or lower validity coefficient than other tests? Than other types of information, such as high-school grades or rating by school principals? We will look with favor on any measure whose validity for a particular criterion is higher than that of measures previously available to us.

Some representative validity coefficients are exhibited in Table 7.1. These give some picture of the size of correlation that has been obtained in previous work of different kinds. The investigator concerned with a particular course of study or a particular job criterion will, of course, need to become intimately acquainted with validities found for his particular criterion.

Table 7.1. Validity of Selected Tests as Predictors of Certain Educational
and Vocational Criteria

Predictor Test	Criterion Variable	Validity Coefficient
Pintner General Ability Test	*Metropolitan Achievement—*	
	Reading Comp. (Gr. 5)	.76
	Metropolitan Achievement—	
	Total Score (Gr. 5)	.84
ACE Psychological Exam—	College Grades—English	.48
L Score	College Grades—Math	.33
	College Grades—Art	.24
Seashore Tonal Memory Test	Performance test on stringed instrument	.28
Short Employment Test		
Word Knowledge Score	Production index—80 bookkeeping machine operators	.10
Word Knowledge Score	Job grade—106 stenographers	.53
Arithmetic Skill Score	Production index—80 bookkeeping machine operators	.26
Arithmetic Skill Score	Job grade—106 stenographers	.60
Differential Aptitude Tests		
Verbal Reasoning	English grades 3½ years later	.57
Space Relations	English grades 3½ years later	.01
Mechanical Reasoning	English grades 3½ years later	.17

The usefulness of a test as a predictor depends not only on how well it correlates with a criterion, but also on how much *new* information it gives. Thus, the *Differential Aptitude Tests' Verbal Reasoning Test* correlates on the average .48 with high-school English grades, and a test of sentence usage correlates .51 with the same grades. But the two tests have an intercorrelation of .62. They overlap and, in part at least, the information each test provides is the same as that provided by the other test. The net result is that pooling the two tests can give a validity coefficient of no more than .55. If the two tests were uncorrelated, each giving evidence completely independent of the other, the combination of the two tests would give a validity coefficient of .70.*

* Statistical procedures have been developed that enable us to determine the best weighing to give the two or more predictors and to calculate the correlation that will result from this combination. The procedures for computing the weights for the separate components (called regression weights) and the correlation (multiple correlation) resulting from them are beyond the scope of this discussion but will be found in standard statistics texts.

Clearly, the higher the correlation between a test or other predictor and a criterion, the more pleased we shall be. But in addition to this relative standard, we should like some absolute one. How high must the validity coefficient be for the test to be useful? What is a "satisfactory" validity? This is a little bit like asking, "How high is up?" However, we can try to give some sort of answer.

To an organization using a test as a basis for deciding whether to hire a particular job applicant or admit a particular student, the significant question is: How much more often will we make the right decision on whom to hire or admit if we use this test than if we operate on a purely chance basis or on the basis of some less valid measure? The answer to this question depends in considerable measure on the proportion of individuals who must be accepted. A selection procedure can do much more for us if we need to accept only the individual who appears to be the best one in every ten applicants than if we must accept nine out of ten. However, to provide a specific example, let us assume that we will accept half of the applicants. We may then ask what per cent of the ones we accept will fall in the upper half of the whole group in job success, i.e., in what per cent of our decisions do we make a "correct" choice? The per cent of correct choices that will result for correlations of different sizes is shown in Table 7.2.

Table 7.2. Per Cent of Correct Assignments When 50 Per Cent of Group Must Be Selected

Validity of Selection Procedure	Per Cent of Correct Choices
.00	50.0
.20	56.4
.40	63.1
.50	66.7
.60	70.5
.70	74.7
.80	79.5
.90	85.6

Table 7.2 indicates that when the correlation is zero, the per cent of correct decisions is 50. This is exactly the chance value. Fifty per cent of our cases are defined as successes, i.e., as falling in the upper half of the total group, and if we had picked our students or employees by just flipping a coin, we could have been right 50 per cent of the time. The improvement in our "batting average" as the correlation goes up is shown in the table. Thus, for a correlation

of .40 we will pick right 63.1 per cent of the time; with a correlation of .80 our percentage will be 79.5, and so forth.

The table shows not only our accuracy for any given correlation but our gain in accuracy if we raise the validity of our predictor. Thus, if we were able to replace a predictor with a validity of .40 by one with a validity of .60, we would increase our per cent of correct decisions from 63.1 to 70.5. All these percentages refer, of course, to the ground rules set in the previous paragraph. However, Table 7.2 gives a fairly representative basis for understanding the effects of a selection program from the point of view of the employing or certifying agency.

In many selection situations, the gain can be crudely translated into a dollars-and-cents saving. Thus, if it costs a company $500 to employ and train a new worker up to the point of useful productivity, a selection procedure that raised the per cent of successes from 56.4 to 63.1 would yield a saving in wasted training expenses alone of $3350 per 100 men tested. This takes no account of the possibility that the test-selected men might also be *better* workers after they had completed their training.

Another way of appraising the practical significance of a correlation coefficient, and one that is perhaps more meaningful from the point of view of the person being tested, is shown in Table 7.3. The rows in the little tables represent the fourths of a group of applicants, potential students or employees, with respect to a predictor test. The columns indicate the per cent of cases falling in each fourth on the criterion score. Look at the little table in Table 7.3 corresponding to a validity coefficient of .50. We see that of those who fall in the lowest fourth on our predictor 480 out of 1000 or 48.0 per cent fall in the lowest fourth on the criterion score, 27.9 per cent in the next lowest fourth, 16.8 per cent in the next to highest fourth, and 7.3 per cent in the highest fourth. The diagonal entries represent cases that fall in the same fourth on both predictor and criterion. The further we get from the diagonal, the greater the discrepancy between prediction and outcome.

This table emphasizes not so much the gain from using the predictor test as the variation in job success of those who are similar in predictor scores. From the point of view of schools or employers, the important thing is the improved percentage of accuracy illustrated in Table 7.2. Dealing in large numbers, they can count on gaining from any predictor that is more valid than the procedure currently in use. From the point of view of the single individual, the many marked discrepancies between predicted and actual success shown in Table 7.3 may

Table 7.3.   Accuracy of Prediction for Different Values of the
Correlation Coefficient

(1000 cases in each row or column)

Quarter on Predictor	$r = .00$ Quarter on Criterion				Quarter on Predictor	$r = .60$ Quarter on Criterion			
	4th	3rd	2nd	1st		4th	3rd	2nd	1st
1st	250	250	250	**250**	1st	45	141	277	**537**
2nd	250	250	**250**	250	2nd	141	264	**318**	277
3rd	250	**250**	250	250	3rd	277	**318**	264	141
4th	**250**	250	250	250	4th	**537**	277	141	45

Quarter on Predictor	$r = .40$ Quarter on Criterion				Quarter on Predictor	$r = .70$ Quarter on Criterion			
	4th	3rd	2nd	1st		4th	3rd	2nd	1st
1st	104	191	277	**428**	1st	22	107	270	**601**
2nd	191	255	**277**	277	2nd	107	270	**353**	270
3rd	277	**277**	255	191	3rd	270	**353**	270	107
4th	**428**	277	191	104	4th	**601**	270	107	22

Quarter on Predictor	$r = .50$ Quarter on Criterion				Quarter on Predictor	$r = .80$ Quarter on Criterion			
	4th	3rd	2nd	1st		4th	3rd	2nd	1st
1st	73	168	279	**480**	1st	6	66	253	**675**
2nd	168	268	**295**	279	2nd	66	271	**410**	253
3rd	279	**295**	268	168	3rd	253	**410**	271	66
4th	**480**	279	168	73	4th	**675**	253	66	6

seem at least as important.   If he has done poorly on the test, an applicant may be less impressed by the fact that the *probability* is that he will be below average on the job than by the fact that he *may* do very well.   He may always be the exception.

One further point can well be emphasized in conclusion.   Validity is always specific to a particular curriculum or a particular job.   When an author or publisher claims that his test is valid, it is always appropriate to ask: Valid for what?   A test in social studies that accurately

represents the content and objectives of one program of instruction
may be quite inappropriate for the program in a different community.
The test must always be evaluated against the objectives of a specific
program of instruction. Again, a test quite valid for picking department store sales clerks who will be pleasant to customers, informed
about their stock, and accurate in financial transactions may be entirely
useless in identifying effective insurance salesmen who will go out and
find or create new business. Validity must always be evaluated in
relation to the specific situation in which a measure is to be used.

VALIDITY AS SIGNIFYING

Sometimes we ask, with respect to a psychological test, neither
"How well does this test predict job success?" nor "How well does
this test represent our curriculum?", but "What does this test *mean
or signify?*" What does the score tell us about an individual? Does
it correspond to some meaningful trait or construct that will help us
in understanding him? For this question of whether the test tells us
something meaningful about people the term *construct* validity has
been used.

Let us examine one specific testing procedure and see how its validity as a measure of a useful psychological quality or construct was
studied. McClelland [5] developed a testing procedure to appraise the
individual's need or motivation to achieve—to succeed and do well.
The test used pictures like those in the *Thematic Apperception Test*
(see Ch. 15). The individual was called upon to make up a story
about each picture, telling what was happening and how it turned out.
A scoring system was developed for these stories, based on counting
the frequency with which themes of accomplishment, mastery, success,
and achievement appeared in the story material. Thus, each individual
received a score representing the strength of his motivation to achieve.
Now, how are we to determine whether this measure has validity in
the sense of truthfully describing a meaningful aspect of the individual's make-up? Let us see how McClelland and his co-workers proceeded.

In essence, the investigators proceeded to ask: "With what should
a measure of achievement motivation be related?" They made a
series of predictions. Some of the predictions were as follows:

1. Those high on achievement motivation should do well in college,
in relation to their scholastic aptitude.
2. Achievement motivation should be higher just after students
have been taking tests described to them as measuring their intelligence.

3. Those high on achievement motivation should complete more items on a motivated speeded test.

4. Achievement motivation should be higher for children of families emphasizing early independence.

Each of these predictions was based on a sort of "theory of human behavior." Thus, academic achievement is seen as a combination of ability and effort. Presumably those with higher motivation to achieve will exert more effort and will, ability being equal, achieve higher grades. A similar chain of reasoning lies back of each of the other predictions.

In general, McClelland found that most of his predictions were supported by the experimental results. The fact that the test scores were related to a number of other events in the way that was predicted from a rational analysis of the trait that the test was presumably measuring lent support to the validity of the test procedure as measuring a meaningful trait or construct, whose essential characteristics are well summarized by the label "achievement motivation."

A great many of our psychological tests, and, to a lesser extent, some educational tests, are intended to measure general traits or qualities of the individual. Verbal reasoning, spatial visualizing, sociability, introversion, mechanical interest are all designations of traits or constructs. Tests of these functions are valid insofar as they behave in the way that such a trait should reasonably be expected to behave. Some of the indicators of how a trait (and therefore a test of it) should behave are:

1. Its correlations with other tests, especially tests that are already accepted measures of the function in question. Thus, many group intelligence tests have been validated in part by their correlations with earlier tests, and especially with the individually administered *Stanford–Binet*.

2. Its correlations with outside facts about the individual, and its ability to differentiate between different groups. Thus, the fact that score on achievement need on the *Edwards Personal Preference Schedule* is higher for those with more education, those with higher incomes, those from urban rather than rural backgrounds, and those in their 30's rather than older groups seems consistent with the predictions that we would make, and supports the validity of the score.

3. Its response to changes in external conditions, especially to conditions that are experimentally induced for the specific purpose of testing the responsiveness of the instrument. Thus, flicker fusion has been proposed as an indicator of anxiety. One study [3] compared flicker

fusion in a group of subjects just before and sometime after a minor operation. In accordance with the prediction, it was found that the flicker fusion threshold was lower before the operation when the anxiety was presumed to be greater.

For any test that presumes to measure a trait or quality, we can formulate a network of theory, leading to definite predictions. These predictions can be tested. Insofar as they are borne out, the validity of the test as a measure of the trait or construct is supported. Insofar as the predictions fail to be verified, we are led to doubt the validity of our test, or our theorizing, or both.

RELIABILITY

The second question we raise with respect to a measurement procedure is: How reliable is it? We are now asking not what it measures but how accurately it measures whatever it does measure. What is the precision of our resulting score? How accurately will it be reproduced if we measure the individual again?

Suppose you were to weigh each child in a school class today and the school nurse were to weigh each child tomorrow on a good pair of beam scales. You would not agree perfectly. The two weights recorded for a child would differ somewhat in some cases. The differences would be due to a host of causes. One child might have had a heavy breakfast one morning and a light one the next. One child might be wearing heavier clothing one day than the other (if the weighing had been carried out with clothing on). When a reading on the scales was on the borderline, you might read it as 60½ pounds, whereas the nurse interpreted practically the same reading as 61. A whole collection of factors would operate to produce chance "errors" in the score—errors in the sense that they would not be repeated in another application of the measuring procedure.

In the situation just described—weighing children on a good pair of scales—the "errors" would be of relatively small size. The discrepancies in the two sets of weighings would probably be quite minor. Suppose, by way of contrast, you and the school nurse had each separately "hefted" each child and written down an estimate of his or her weight based on the hefting. Then the discrepancies between the two sets of values would have been much greater. Large elements of subjective judgment would now enter into each score, and the "error" of measurement would be correspondingly large. The second technique of measuring weight is very much less reliable.

There are two ways in which we can express the reliability or precision of a set of measurements. One indicates the amount of variation in a set of repeated measurements of a single specimen. If we were to weigh an individual not twice but 200 times, we would get a frequency distribution of scores to represent his weight. This frequency distribution has an average value, which we can think of as approximating the "true" weight. It also has a standard deviation, describing the scatter of these measurements. We shall call this the *standard error of measurement,* since it is the standard deviation of the "errors" of measurement. With psychological data, we can rarely actually make a whole set of measurements on each individual. Often we are fortunate if we can get two scores for each individual. But from such pairs of measurements it is possible to get an estimate of the scattering of scores that *would* be found if we *had* made repeated measurements.

Reliable measurement also implies that the individual stays in about the same place in his group. The child who is heaviest the first time should also be heaviest the next time, and each person in the group should stay in about the same position. We have already seen that the correlation coefficient provides us with a statistical index of the extent to which two things go together, high with high and low with low. If the two things we are correlating happen to be two applications of the same measure, the resulting correlation provides an indicator of reliability. We can designate it a *reliability coefficient.* The characteristics of the coefficient are those that we have already seen in Chapter 5 and in our discussion of validity. But the relationship now before us is that of two measurements with the same measuring instrument. The more nearly the scores are reproduced the second time, the higher the correlation and the more reliable the test.

A measure is reliable, then, to the extent that an individual remains nearly the same in repeated measurements—nearly the same as represented by a low standard error of measurement or by a high reliability coefficient. But what exact type of data do we need in order to get an appropriate estimate of this degree of stability or precision in measurement? We shall consider three distinct possibilities, noticing their similarities and differences and evaluating the advantages and disadvantages of each. The three are:

1. Repetition of the same test or measure.
2. Administration of a second "equivalent" form of the test.
3. Subdivision of the test into two or more equivalent fractions.

Let us examine each of these in turn.

If we wish to find how reliably we can evaluate an individual's weight, we can have him weighed twice. It may be a reasonable precaution to have the two measures taken independently by two persons. We don't want the experimenter's recollection of the first score to color the second score. It may be desirable to have the two weighings done on different days. That depends on what we are interested in. If we want to know how accurately we can carry out the process of weighing a person, the two measures should be carried out one right after the other. Then we know that the *person* has stayed the same and that the only source of variation or "error" is in the operation of weighing him. If we want to know how precisely a given weight characterizes a person from day to day—how closely we can predict his weight next week from what he weighs today, it would be appropriate to measure him on two separate occasions. Now we are interested in *variation within the individual* as well as *variation due to the operation of measurement.*

Sometimes we are interested in variation within the individual; sometimes we are not. We may ask: How accurately does our measurement characterize S at this moment of time? Or we may ask: How accurately does our measure of S today describe him as he will be tomorrow, or next week, or next month? Both are sensible questions. But they are not the same question. The data we must gather to answer one are different from the data we need to answer the other.

To study the reliability of such a physical characteristic of a person as weight, repetition of the measurement is a straightforward and satisfactory operation. It appears satisfactory and applicable also with some simple types of behavior, such as speed of reaction or muscular strength. But suppose now we are interested in the reliability of a test of reading comprehension. Let us assume that the test is made up of six reading passages with ten questions on each. We adminster the test once and then immediately administer it again. What happens? Certainly, the child is not going to have to reread all the material he has just read. He may do so in part, but to a considerable extent his answers the second time will involve merely remembering what answer he had chosen the time before and marking it again. If he had not been able to finish the first time, he will now be able to work ahead and spend most of his time on new material. These same effects will hold true to some degree even over a longer period of time. Clearly, this sort of test given a second time does not present the same task that it did the first time.

There is a second consideration entering into the repetition of such a test as a reading comprehension test. Suppose that one of the five passages in the test was about baseball and that a particular boy was an expert on baseball. The passage would then be especially easy for him, and he would in effect get a bonus of several points. The test would overestimate his general level of reading ability. But note that it would do it consistently on both testings because the material remains the same. The error for individual S is a *constant error* in the two testings. Since it affects both his scores in the same way, it makes the test look reliable rather than unreliable.

In such an area of ability as reading, we must recognize the possibility that an individual does not perform uniformly well throughout the whole area. His specific interests, experiences, and background give him strengths and weaknesses. A particular test is *one sample* from the whole area. How well individual S does on the test, relative to others, is likely to depend in some degree upon the particular sample of tasks chosen to represent the area of ability or personality we are trying to appraise. If the sample remains the same for both measurements, his behavior will stay more nearly the same than if the sample of tasks is varied.

Note that so far we have identified three main sources of variation in performance that will tend to reduce the precision of a particular score as a description of an individual:

1. Variation in response to the test at a particular moment in time.
2. Variation in the individual from time to time.
3. Variation arising out of the particular sample of tasks chosen to represent an area of behavior.

Retesting the individual with identically the same test can be arranged to reflect the first two types of "error," but this procedure cannot evaluate the effects of the third type. In addition, there may be the memory and practice effects to which we referred above.

PARALLEL TEST FORMS

Concern about this third source of variation, variation arising because of the necessity of choosing a particular sample of tasks to represent a whole area of behavior, leads us to another set of procedures for evaluating reliability. If the sampling of items may be a significant source of "error," and if, as is usually the case, we want to know with what accuracy we may generalize from the specific score to the area of behavior it is supposed to represent, we must develop some procedures that take account of this variation due to the sample of tasks. We may do this by correlating two equivalent forms of a test.

Equivalent forms of a test should be thought of as forms built according to the same specifications but composed of separate samples of behavior in the defined area.   Thus, two equivalent reading tests should contain reading passages and questions of the same difficulty.   The same sorts of questions should be asked, i.e., the same balance of specific fact and general idea questions.   The same types of passages should be represented, i.e., expository, argumentative, esthetic.   But the specific passages and questions should be different.

If we have two forms of a test, we may give each pupil first one form and then the other.   They may follow each other immediately if we are not interested in stability over time, or may be separated by an interval if we are.   The correlation between the two forms will provide an appropriate reliability coefficient.   If a time interval has been allowed between the testings, all three of our sources of variation will have had a chance to get in their effects—variation arising from the measurement itself, variation in the individual over time, and variation due to the sample of tasks.

To ask that a test yield consistent results under these conditions is the most rigorous standard we can set for it.   And if we want to use our test results to generalize about what Johnny will do on other tasks of this general sort next week and next month, then this is the appropriate standard by which to evaluate a test.   For most educational situations, this *is* the way we want to use test results, and so evidence based on equivalent test forms should usually be given the most weight in evaluating the reliability of a test.

The use of two parallel test forms provides a very sound basis for estimating the precision of a psychological or educational test.   This procedure does, however, raise some practical problems.   It demands that two parallel forms of a test be available and that time be allowed for administering two separate tests.   Sometimes no second form of a test exists, or no time can be found for a second testing.   To administer a second separate test is often likely to represent a somewhat burdensome demand upon available resources.   These practical considerations of convenience and expediency have made test makers receptive to procedures that extract an estimate of reliability from administration of only one form of a test.   However, such procedures are compromises at best.   The correlation between two parallel forms, usually administered with a lapse of several days or weeks in between, represents the preferred procedure for estimating reliability.

SUBDIVIDED TEST

The most widely used procedure for estimating reliability from a single testing divides a particular test up into two presumably equivalent halves. The half-tests may be assembled on the basis of careful examination of the content and difficulty of each item, making a systematic effort to balance out the content and difficulty level of the two halves. A simpler procedure, which is often relied upon to give equivalent halves, is to put alternate items into the two half-tests, that is, to put all the odd-numbered items in one half-test and all the even-numbered items in the other. This is usually a sensible procedure, since items of similar form, content, or difficulty are likely to be grouped together in a test. For a reasonably long test, say, of 60 items or more, splitting the test up in this way will tend to balance out factors of item form, content covered, and difficulty level. The two half-tests will have a good probability of constituting "equivalent" tests, as these are defined in the preceding section.

The procedures we are discussing now divide the test in half only for scoring, not for administration. That is, a single test is given at a single sitting and with a single time limit. However, two separate scores are derived—one by scoring the odd-numbered items and one by scoring the even-numbered items. The correlation between these two scores provides a measure of the accuracy with which the test is measuring the individual.

However, it must be noted that the computed correlation is between two half-length tests. This value is not directly applicable to the full-length test, which is the actual instrument prepared for use. In general, the larger the sample of a person's behavior we have, the more reliable the measure will be. The more behavior we record, the less our measure will depend upon chance elements in behavior of the individual or in the particular sampling of tasks. Single lucky answers or momentary lapses of attention will be more nearly evened out.

Where the two halves of the test, which gave the scores actually correlated, are equivalent, we can get an unbiased estimate of total-test reliability from the correlation between the two half-tests. This estimate is given by the formula

$$r_{11} = \frac{2r_{\frac{1}{2}\frac{1}{2}}}{1 + r_{\frac{1}{2}\frac{1}{2}}} \tag{1}$$

where r_{11} is the estimated reliability of the full-length test,

$r_{\frac{1}{2}\frac{1}{2}}$ is the actual correlation between two half-length tests.

Thus, if the correlation between the two halves of a test is .60, formula 1 would give

$$r_{11} = \frac{2(0.60)}{1 + 0.60} = \frac{1.20}{1.60} = .75$$

This formula, referred to generally as the Spearman-Brown Prophecy Formula from the names of its originators and function, makes it possible for us to compute an estimate of reliability from a single administration of a single test.

The appealing convenience of the split-half procedure has led to its wide use. Many test manuals will be found to report this type of reliability coefficient and no other. Unfortunately, this coefficient has several types of limitations, which we must now examine.

In the first place, when we have extracted two scores from a single testing, both scores necessarily represent the individual as he is at the same moment of time. Even events lasting only a few minutes will affect both scores about equally. In other words, variation of the individual from day to day cannot be reflected in this type of reliability coefficient. It can only give evidence as to the precision with which we can appraise him at a specific moment in time.

In the second place, a split-half reliability coefficient becomes meaningless when a test is highly speeded. Suppose we have a test of simple arithmetic, made up of problems like $3 + 5 = ?$, and that the test is being used with adults with a 2-minute time limit. We will get wide differences in score on such a test, but the differences will be primarily differences in speed. Errors will be a minor factor. The person who gets a score of 50 will very probably have attempted just 50 items, *and of these 25 will be odd and 25 will be even.* In other words, the two halves of the test will appear perfectly consistent, because opportunity to attempt items is automatically balanced out for the two half-tests.

Few tests depend as completely upon speed as does the one that we have chosen to illustrate our point. However, many involve some degree of speeding. This speed factor will tend to inflate estimates of reliability based on the split-half procedure. The amount of overestimation will depend upon the degree to which the test is speeded, being greater for those tests in which speed plays a greater role. However, speed enters in sufficiently generally so that split-half estimates of reliability should always be discounted. Test users should demand that commercial publishers provide reliability estimates based on parallel forms of the test.

RELIABILITY ESTIMATED FROM ITEM STATISTICS

The teacher or investigator who makes much use of tests and who reads extensively in test manuals will encounter one other type of procedure for estimating test reliability from a single test administration. This procedure, also named for its originators, yields what is referred to as a Kuder-Richardson reliability coefficient. The essential assumption in the procedure is that the items within one form of a test have as much in common with one another as do the items in that one form with the corresponding items in a parallel or equivalent form. This means that the items in a test are homogeneous in the sense that every item measures the same general factors of ability or personality as do the others. If this assumption is sound, the Kuder-Richardson procedure leads to a reliability estimate that has essentially the same interpretation as the odd-even coefficient we have just considered. The Kuder-Richardson estimate likewise (1) takes no account of variation in the individual from time to time, and (2) is inappropriate for speeded tests. Within these two limitations, it provides a conservative estimate of the split-half type of reliability.*

COMPARISON OF METHODS

A summary comparison of the different procedures for estimating reliability is given in Table 7.4. This shows four factors that may make a single test score an inaccurate picture of the individual's usual performance. The table shows which of the factors are represented in each of the procedures for estimating reliability we have discussed. It can be seen that the different procedures are not equivalent. Only administration of parallel test forms with a time interval between permits all sources of variation to have their effects. Each of the other

* A widely used form of the Kuder-Richardson procedure (their Formula 20) takes the form

$$r_{11} = \left(\frac{n}{n-1}\right)\left(\frac{s_t^2 - \Sigma pq}{s_t^2}\right)$$

where r_{11} is the estimate of reliability.
$\quad$ n is the number of items in the test.
$\quad$ s_t is the standard deviation of the test.
$\quad$ Σ means "take the sum of" and covers the n items.
$\quad$ p is the per cent passing a particular item.
$\quad$ q is the per cent failing the same item.

A formula involving simpler calculations (their Formula 21), which yields a reasonably close approximation to the above, is

$$r_{11} = \frac{n}{n-1}\left[1 - \frac{M_t\left(1 - \frac{M_t}{n}\right)}{s_t^2}\right]$$

where M_t is the mean score of the group and the other symbols have the same meaning as given above.

Table 7.4. Sources of Variation Represented in Different Procedures for Estimating Reliability

	Experimental Procedure for Estimating Reliability					
Sources of Variation	Immediate Retest, Same Test	Retest after Interval, Same Test	Parallel Test Form without Time Interval	Parallel Test Form with Time Interval	Odd-Even Halves of Single Test	Kuder-Richardson Analysis, Single Test
How much the score can be expected to fluctuate owing to: Variations arising within the measurement procedure itself	X	X	X	X	X	X
Changes in the individual from day to day		X		X		
Changes in the specific sample of tasks			X	X	X	X
Changes in the individual's speed of work	X	X	X	X		

methods masks some source of variation that may be significant in the actual use of tests. Retesting with the same identical test neglects variation arising out of the sample of items. Whenever all the testing is done at one point in time, variation of the individual from day to day is neglected. When the testing is done as a unit with a single time limit, variation in speed of responding is neglected. The facts brought out in this table should be borne in mind in evaluating reliability data found in a test manual or in the report of a research study.

INTERPRETATION OF RELIABILITY DATA

Analysis of data obtained from a general intelligence test for elementary-school children has yielded a reliability coefficient of .85. How shall we interpret this result? What does it mean concerning the precision of an individual's score? Should we be pleased or dissatisfied to get a coefficient of this size?

We have already tried to give some content and meaning to correlation coefficients in Fig. 5.7 and in Tables 5.8, 7.1, 7.2, and 7.3. These have shown typical values of the correlation coefficient, the scatter of scores for representative correlations, and the accuracy of prediction with correlations of different sizes. A further contribution to the interpretation of test reliability is found in the relationship between the reliability coefficient and the standard error of measurement.

It will be remembered that the standard error of measurement is an estimate of the standard deviation that would be obtained for a series of measurements of the same individual. (It is assumed that he is not changed by being measured.) The standard error of measurement can be calculated from the reliability coefficient by the formula

$$s_m = s_t\sqrt{1 - r_{11}} \qquad (2)$$

where s_m is the standard error of measurement.

    s_t is the standard deviation of test scores.

    r_{11} is the reliability coefficient.

Suppose that our test has a reliability of .85 and a standard deviation of 15 points. Then we have

$$s_m = 15\sqrt{1 - .85} = 15\sqrt{.15} = 5.7$$

In this instance, a set of measures of a particular person would have a standard deviation of 5.7 points. Remember that a fairly uniform proportion of observations fall within any given number of standard deviation units from the mean. Certain values for this relationship were given in Table 5.6. This table shows that for a normal curve 31.8 per cent of cases, or about 1 in 3, differ from the mean by as much as 1 standard deviation; 4.6 per cent by as much as 2 standard deviations. Applying this to our case, in which the standard deviation of our measurements is 5.7 points, we could say that there is about 1 chance in 3 that a score that we get for an individual differs from his "true" score by as much as 5.7 points (1 standard error of measurement). There is about 1 chance in 20 that it differs by as much as 11.4 points (2 standard errors of measurement).

The values shown above are fairly representative of what might be found for intelligence quotients from one of the commercially distributed group intelligence tests applied to children in the upper elementary grades. Note that even with this relatively high reliability coefficient, appreciable errors of measurement are possible in at least a minority of cases. Shifts of 5 or 10 points of IQ can be expected fairly frequently just because of errors of measurement. Anyone who is impressed by and tries to interpret an IQ difference of 5 points between two persons or two testings of the same person has been fooled into thinking the test has a precision that it simply does not possess. Further testing could perfectly well reverse the result. Any test score or comparison of test scores must be made with acute awareness of the standard error of measurement.

The manner in which the standard error of measurement is related to the reliability coefficient is shown in Table 7.5. We see that the magnitude of errors decreases as the reliability increases, but we also

Table 7.5. Standard Error of Measurement for Different Values of
Reliability Coefficient

Reliability Coefficient	Standard Error of Measurement	
	General Expression	When $S_t{}^* = 10$
.50	.71 $S_t{}^*$	7.1
.60	.63 S_t	6.3
.70	.55 S_t	5.5
.80	.45 S_t	4.5
.85	.38 S_t	3.8
.90	.32 S_t	3.2
.95	.22 S_t	2.2
.98	.14 S_t	1.4

* S_t signifies the standard deviation of the test.

see that errors of appreciable size will still be found even with reliability coefficients of .90 or .95. In interpreting the score of a particular individual, it is the standard error of measurement that must be kept in mind. If we think of a range extending from 2 standard errors of measurement above the obtained score to 2 below, we will have a band within which we can be reasonably sure (19 chances in 20) that the individual's true score lies. Thus, in the case of the intelligence test described in previous paragraphs, we can think of a test IQ of 90 as meaning rather surely an IQ lying between about 80 and 100. If we think in those terms, we shall be much more discreet in interpreting and using test results.

When interpreting the test score of an individual, it is desirable to think in terms of the standard error of measurement and to be somewhat humble and tentative in drawing conclusions from that test score. But for making comparisons between tests and for a number of types of test analysis, the reliability coefficient will be more useful. Where measures are expressed in different units, as height in inches and weight in pounds, the reliability coefficient provides the only possible basis for comparison. Since the competing tests in a given field, such as primary reading, are likely to use types of scores that are not really comparable, the reliability coefficient will usually represent the only satisfactory basis for test comparison. *Other things being equal,* we shall prefer the test with the higher reliability coefficient, that is, the test that provides a more consistent ranking of the individual within his group.

The other things that may not be equal are primarily considerations of validity and practicality. Validity, in so far as we can appraise it, is the crucial test of a measurement procedure. Reliability is important only as a necessary condition for a measure to have validity. The ceiling for the possible validity of a test is set by its reliability. A test must measure *something* before it can measure what we want it to measure. A measuring device with a reliability of .00 is reflecting nothing but chance factors. It does not correlate with itself and cannot correlate with anything else. The theoretical ceiling for the validity coefficient of a test (i.e., its correlation with some criterion measure representing success in learning or on the job) is the square root of its reliability coefficient. Thus, a test with reliability coefficient of .36 could not give a validity coefficient above .60, and one with a reliability coefficient of .64 could not possibly yield a validity coefficient above .80. Only to the extent that a test measures something accurately can it measure it validly.

The converse of the relationship we have just presented does not follow. A test may measure with the greatest precision and still have no validity for our purposes. Thus, we can measure head size with a good deal of accuracy, but the measure is still useless as an indicator of intelligence. Validity is something over and beyond mere accuracy of measurement.

Considerations of cost, convenience, etc. may also sometimes lead to a decision to use a less reliable test. We may accept a less reliable 40-minute test in preference to a more reliable 3-hour one because the 3 hours of testing time is too much of a burden in view of the purpose the test is designed to serve.

Within the limitations discussed in the preceding paragraphs, we shall prefer the more reliable test. There are several factors that must be taken into account, however, before we can fairly compare the reliability coefficients of two or more different tests. These will be discussed in the paragraphs that follow.

1. *Range of the Group.* The reliability coefficient indicates how consistently a test places each individual relative to the others in the group. When there is little shifting from test to retest or form A to form B, the reliability coefficient is high and vice versa. But the extent to which individuals will switch places depends on how closely similar they are. It does not take very accurate testing to differentiate the reading ability of second graders from that of seventh graders. But to place each second grader accurately within his own class is much more demanding.

If children from several different grades are pooled together, we may expect a much higher reliability coefficient. For example, the manual for the *Otis Quick-Scoring Mental Ability Test—Beta* reports alternate-forms reliabilities for single grade groups ranging from .65 to .87. The average value is .78. But pooling the complete range of grades (4–9), the reliability coefficient is reported as .96. These data are all for the same test. They reflect the same precision. Yet the coefficient for the combined groups is strikingly higher. Similar data are reported for the *Durrell-Sullivan Reading Achievement Test.* The data in this case involve a range of four grades—from grade three through grade six. Reliability coefficients are split-half reliabilities based on a single testing. In the case of the *Word Meaning Test,* the average coefficient for a single grade is .93, whereas the correlation for all four grades together is .97. For the test of *Paragraph Meaning* the corresponding values are .87 and .94.

In evaluating a reported reliability coefficient, the range of ability in the group tested must be taken into account. If the reliability coefficient is based upon a combination of age or grade groups, it must usually be sharply discounted, as can be seen above. But even in less extreme cases, account must be taken of the variability of talent within the group. Reliabilities for age groups will tend to be somewhat higher than for grade groups, because an age group will usually contain a greater spread of talent than a single grade. A sample made up of children from a wide range of socio-economic levels will tend to yield higher reliabilities than a very homogeneous one. In comparing different tests, one must take account of the type of sample on which the reliability data were based, in so far as this can be determined from the reported facts, and judge more severely the test whose reliability is based on the more heterogeneous group.

2. *Level of Ability in the Group.* Precision of measurement by a test may be related to the ability level of the persons being measured. However, no simple rule can be formulated for stating the nature of this relationship. It depends upon the way in which the particular test was built. For those people for whom the test is very hard, so that they are doing a large amount of guessing, accuracy is likely to be low. At the other extreme, if a test is very easy for a group, so that all of them can do most of the items very easily, it may be expected to be ineffective in discriminating among the members of the group. When everyone can do the easy items, it is as if we had shortened the test to just the few harder items that some can do and some cannot.

It is possible, also, that a test may vary in accuracy at different intermediate difficulty levels. The meticulous test constructor will report the standard error of measurement for his test at different score levels. When separate values of the standard error of measurement are reported in the manual, they provide a basis for evaluating the precision of the test for different types of groups. They permit a more appropriate estimate of the accuracy of a particular individual's score. Each individual's score can be interpreted in relation to the standard error of measurement for scores of that level. For example, from data provided by Terman and Merrill [8] the standard error of measurement for the 1937 edition of the *Stanford-Binet* for different IQ levels is found to be as follows:

IQ Level	Standard Error of IQ
130 and over	5.2
110–129	4.9
90–109	4.5
70– 89	3.8
Below 70	2.2

For this test, the variation that may be expected from one testing to another is very much higher for children with average and above average IQ's than for the retarded child. In the case of the *Wechsler Intelligence Scale for Children,* the standard error of measurement depends upon the age of the group tested. The manual reports values as follows:

7½-year-olds	4.2 points of IQ
10½ " "	3.4 " " "
13½ " "	3.7 " " "

The test is most accurate for an age group in the middle of the age range for which it was intended.

3. *Length of Test.* As we saw on p. 179 in discussing the split-half reliability coefficient, test reliability depends on the length of the test. If we can assume that the quality of the test items and the nature of the examinees remain the same, then the relationship of reliability to length can be expressed by a simple formula. The formula is

$$r_{nn} = \frac{n r_{.1}}{1 + (n-1)r_{11}} \tag{3}$$

where r_{nn} is the reliability of a test n times as long as the original test.

r_{11} is the reliability of the original test.

n is, as indicated, the factor by which the length of the test is increased.

This is a more general form of formula 1 found on p. 179.

Suppose we have a spelling test made up of 20 items which has a reliability of .50. We want to know how reliable the test will be if it is lengthened to contain 100 items comparable to the original 20. The answer is

$$r_{nn} = \frac{5(.50)}{1 + 4(.50)} = \frac{2.50}{3.00} = .83$$

As the length of the test is increased, the chance errors of measurement more or less cancel out; score comes to depend more and more completely upon the characteristics of the person being measured; and a more accurate appraisal of him is obtained.

Of course, how much we can lengthen a test is limited by a number of practical considerations. It is limited by the amount of time available for testing. It is limited by factors of fatigue and boredom on the part of examinees. It is sometimes limited by the stock of good test items that it is possible to construct. But within these limits, reliability can be increased as needed by lengthening the test.

One special type of lengthening is represented by increasing the number of raters who rate an individual or a product he has produced. If several raters of equal competence or equal familiarity with the ratee are available, a pooling of their ratings will produce increased reliability in the composite rating, and this increase will be described by the same formula we have just been considering.

4. *Operations Used for Estimating.* How high a value will be obtained for the reliability coefficient depends also upon which of the several possible sets of experimental operations is used to estimate the reliability. We saw in Table 7.4 that the different procedures treat different sources of variation in different ways, and that it is only the use of parallel forms of a test with a period intervening that includes all four sources of variation in "error." That is, this procedure of estimating reliability represents a more exacting definition of the test's ability to reproduce the same score. The individual must then show consistency both from one sample of tasks to another and from one day to another. We have gathered together a few examples that show reliability coefficients for the same test when these were computed by two different procedures. These are shown in Table 7.6.

The two procedures compared in Table 7.6 are correlation of alternate forms and correlation of half-tests made up from a single form. It will be noted that the alternate-forms correlation is lower in every case. This is consistent with our earlier discussion, in which we pointed out that the alternate-forms procedure constitutes a more demanding test of an instrument's precision. The difference between

Table 7.6. Comparison of Reliability Coefficients Obtained from Equivalent Forms and from Fractions of a Single Test

Test	Alternate Forms	Single Test
Otis Quick-Scoring Intelligence Test—Beta	.84	.90
Pintner-Durost Intelligence Test		
Scale 1, Picture Content	.78	.92
Scale 2, Reading Content	.92	.97
Essential High School Content Battery		
Mathematics	.88	.92
Science	.75	.85
Social Studies	.85	.89
English	.86	.90

the two procedures varies from test to test, being as small as .04 in one instance and as large as .14 in another. But in every instance, it is necessary to discount the odd-even correlation.

HOW HIGH MUST THE RELIABILITY OF A MEASUREMENT BE?

Obviously, other things being equal, the more reliable our measuring procedure is, the better satisfied we are with it. A question that is often raised is: What is the *minimum* reliability that is acceptable? Actually, there is no general answer to this question. If we *must* make some decision or take some course of action with respect to an individual, we will do so in terms of the best information we have, however unreliable it may be, provided only that the reliability is better than zero. (Of course, here as always the crucial consideration is the validity of the measure.) The appraisal of any new procedure must always be in terms of other procedures with which it is in competition. Thus, a high-school mathematics test with a reliability coefficient of .80 would look relatively unattractive if tests with reliabilities of .85 to .90 were already available. On the other hand, a procedure for judging "leadership" that had a reliability of no more than .60 might look very attractive if the alternative were a set of uncontrolled ratings having a reliability of .45 to .50.

Although we cannot set an absolute minimum for the reliability of a measurement procedure, we can indicate the level of reliability that is required to enable us to achieve specified levels of accuracy in describing an individual or a group. Suppose that we have given a test to two individuals, and that individual A fell at the 75th percentile of the group while individual B fell at the 50th percentile. What is the probability that A would still surpass B if they were tested again?

Table 7.7. Per Cent of Times Direction of Difference Will Be Reversed in Subsequent Testing for Scores Falling at 75th and 50th Percentile

Per Cent of Reversals with Repeated Test

Reliability Coefficient	Scores of Single Individuals	Means of Groups of 25	Means of Groups of 100
.00	50.0	50.0	50.0
.40	40.3	10.9	0.7
.50	36.8	4.6	0.04
.60	32.5	1.2	
.70	27.1	0.1	
.80	19.7		
.90	8.7		
.95	2.2		
.98	0.05		

In Table 7.7 the probability is shown for different values of the reliability coefficient. Thus, where the correlation is .00, there is exactly a fifty-fifty chance that the order of our two individuals will be reversed. When the correlation is .50, the probability of a reversal is 1 in 3. For a correlation of .90, there is still 1 chance in 12 that we will get a reversal on repetition of the testing. To have 4 chances in 5 that our difference will stay in the same direction, we require a reliability of about .80.

Table 7.7 also shows the situation when we are comparing two groups of 25. That is, in class A the average fell at the 75th percentile of some larger reference group, whereas in class B the average fell at the 50th percentile. We ask what the probability is that we would get a reversal if the testing were repeated. Here we still have a fifty-fifty chance when the correlation is .00. However, the security of our conclusion increases much more rapidly as the reliability of our test is increased. When the reliability is .50, the probability of reversal is already down to 1 in 20; with a correlation of .70 it is only 1 in 1000. Thus, a test with relatively low reliability will permit us to make useful studies of and draw accurate conclusions about groups, but relatively high reliability is required if we are to have precise information about individuals.

RELIABILITY OF DIFFERENCE SCORES

Sometimes we are less interested in single scores than we are in the relationship between scores taken in pairs. Thus, we may be con-

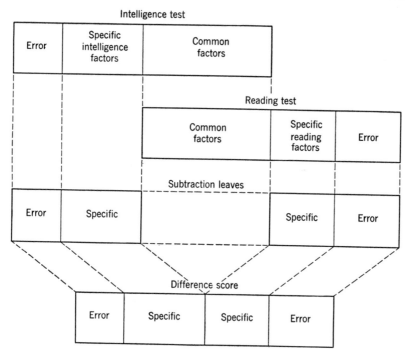

Fig. 7.2.   Nature of a difference score.

cerned with the differences between scholastic aptitude and reading achievement in a group of pupils, or we may wish to study gains in reading from an initial test given in October to a later test given the following May.   In these illustrations, the significant fact for each individual is the difference between two scores.   We must inquire how reliable our estimates of these differences are, knowing the characteristics of the two component tests.

It is, unfortunately, true that the appraisal of the difference between two tests usually has substantially lower reliability than the reliability of the two tests taken separately.   This is due to two factors: (1) the errors of measurement in both separate tests affect the difference score, and (2) whatever is common to both measures is canceled out in the difference score.   We can illustrate the situation by a diagram.   Look at Fig. 7.2.

Each bar in Fig. 7.2 represents performance * on a test, broken up into a number of parts to represent the factors producing this per-

* More precisely, variance in performance.

formance. The first bar represents an intelligence test, and the second a reading test. Notice that we have divided reading performance into three parts. One part, labeled "common factors," is a complex of general intellectual abilities that operate both in the reading and the scholastic aptitude test. A second part, labeled "specific reading factors," is abilities that appear only in the reading test. The third part, labeled "error," is chance error of measurement. Three similar parts are indicated for the intelligence test. Now look at the third bar, which represents the difference score. In this bar, the common factor has disappeared. It canceled out in our process of subtraction. Only the specific factors and the errors of measurement remain. These are the factors that determine the difference score. And the errors of measurement bulk relatively much larger in this third bar. In the limit, where two tests measured exactly the same common factors, only the errors of measurement would remain in the difference scores, and the differences would have exactly zero reliability.

The reliability of the difference between two scores can be expressed in a fairly simple formula, which reads

$$r_{Diff.} = \frac{\dfrac{r_{11} + r_{22}}{2} - r_{12}}{1 - r_{12}}$$

where r_{11} is the reliability of one measure.

r_{22} is the reliability of the other measure.

r_{12} is the correlation between the two measures.

Thus, if the reliability of test A is .80, the reliability of test B is .90, and the correlation of A and B is .60, for the reliability of the difference score we have

$$r_{Diff.} = \frac{\dfrac{.80 + .90}{2} - .60}{1 - .60}$$

$$= \frac{.25}{.40} = .62.$$

In Table 7.8 the value of $r_{Diff.}$ is shown for various combinations of values of $\frac{r_{11} + r_{22}}{2}$ and r_{12}. Thus, if the average of the reliabilities of our two tests $\left(\frac{r_{11} + r_{22}}{2}\right)$ is .80, the reliability of the difference score is .80 when the two tests have zero intercorrelation, is .60 when

Table 7.8. Reliability of a Difference Score

Average of Reliability of Two Tests

Correlation between Two Tests (r_{12})	$\left(\dfrac{r_{11} + r_{22}}{2}\right)$					
	.50	.60	.70	.80	.90	.95
.00	.50	.60	.70	.80	.90	.95
.40	.17	.33	.50	.67	.83	.92
.50	.00	.20	.40	.60	.80	.90
.60		.00	.25	.50	.75	.88
.70			.00	.33	.67	.83
.80				.00	.50	.75
.90					.00	.50
.95						.00

the intercorrelation is .50, and is .00 when the intercorrelation is .80. It is clear that, as soon as the correlation between the two tests begins to approach the average of their separate reliability coefficients, the reliability of the difference score drops very rapidly.

The low reliability that tends to characterize difference scores is something to which the psychologist and educator must always be sensitive. It becomes a problem whenever he wishes to use test patterns for diagnosis. Thus the judgment that Herbert's reading lags behind his scholastic aptitude is a judgment that must be made a good deal more tentatively than a judgment about either his IQ or his reading grade taken separately. The conclusion that Mary has improved in reading more than Jane must usually be a more tentative judgment than that Mary is now a better reader than Jane. Any difference needs to be interpreted in the light of the standard error of measurement of that difference.*

Many differences will be found to be quite small relative to their standard error, and are consequently quite undependable. The interpretation of profiles and of gain scores are places where this caution especially applies.

EFFECTS OF UNRELIABILITY ON CORRELATION BETWEEN VARIABLES

There is one further effect of unreliability which merits brief attention here because it affects our interpretation of the correlations be-

* The standard error of measurement of a difference is roughly equal to $\sqrt{S^2_{m_1} + S^2_{m_2}}$, where S_{m_1} is the standard error of measurement of one test and S_{m_2} is the standard error of measurement of the other.

tween different measures. Let us think of a measure of reading comprehension and one of arithmetic reasoning. In each of these tests,
the individual differences in score are due in part to "true" ability and
in part to chance "errors of measurement." But if the errors of measurement are really chance matters, the reading test errors and the
arithmetic test errors must be uncorrelated. There is no relationship
between one toss of a coin and a later toss of a coin. So we have
these uncorrelated errors in the total score. This means that they
must water down any correlation that exists between the true scores.
That is, the actual scores are a combination of true score and error,
so the correlation between actual scores is a compromise between the
correlation of the underlying true scores and the .00 correlation that
characterizes the errors.

We would like to extract an estimate of the correlation between the
underlying true scores from our obtained data in order to understand
better how much the functions involved have in common. Fortunately,
we can do this quite simply. Such an estimate is provided by the
formula

$$r_{1_\infty 2_\infty} = \frac{r_{12}}{\sqrt{r_{11}r_{22}}} \tag{4}$$

where $r_{1_\infty 2_\infty}$ is the correlation of the underlying "true" scores.

r_{12} is the correlation of the obtained scores.

r_{11} and r_{22} are the reliabilities of the two measures in question.

Thus, if the correlation between our reading test and arithmetic test
is .56, and the reliability coefficients of the tests are respectively .71
and .90, we have

$$r_{1_\infty 2_\infty} = \frac{.56}{\sqrt{(.71)(.90)}} = .70$$

Our estimate is that the correlation between error-free measures of
arithmetic and reading would be .70. In thinking of these two
functions, it would be appropriate to think of the correlation as .70
rather than .56, though the *tests* correlate only .56.

FACTORS MAKING FOR PRACTICALITY IN ROUTINE USE

Though validity and reliability may be all-important in measures
that are to be used for special research purposes, when a test is to be
used in classrooms throughout a school or school system a number of
down-to-earth practical considerations must also be taken into account.

It is easy for the administrator to pay too much attention to small financial savings or to economies of time that make it possible to fit a test into the standard class period with no shifting of schedules, but, nevertheless, these factors of economy and convenience are real considerations. Furthermore, there are other factors relating to the readiness with which the tests may be given, scored, and interpreted that bear more importantly on the use that will be made of the tests and the soundness of the conclusions that will be drawn from them.

ECONOMY

The practical significance of dollar savings does not need to be emphasized. Dollars are of very real significance for any educational or industrial enterprise. Economy in the case of tests depends in part on cost per copy. It depends in part on the possibility of using the test booklets over again. From the junior high school on, and possibly even in the upper elementary grades, it is feasible to administer a test using a separate answer sheet. Such a separate answer sheet permits reuse of the test booklets. If a test will be used in successive years or if testing can be scheduled so that different classes or schools will be tested on successive days, an important economy can be effected by using the same test booklet over again several times.

A second aspect of economy is saving of time in test administration. However, this is often false economy. We saw in the previous section that the reliability of a test depends on the length of the test. As far as testing time is concerned, we get about what we give. Some tests may be a little more efficiently designed, so that they give a little more reliable measure per minute of testing time, but, by and large, any reduction in testing time will be accomplished at the price of loss in the precision or the breadth of our appraisal.

A third, and quite significant, aspect of economy is ease of scoring. The clerical work of scoring a battery of tests can become either burdensome if it is done by the already busy teacher or expensive if it is carried out by clerical help hired for the purpose. A well-designed test should be planned so as to simplify and speed up the scoring operation. In tests for young children in the first two or three grades of school, there is not a great deal that can be done to streamline scoring procedures. Any attempt to separate the answers from the problems, so that the answers will be more convenient to score, is likely to confuse the young child and affect his score. By the upper elementary grades, however, it is practical to provide answer spaces at the side of the page, preferably the right, so that all answers appear in a column and can be scored by placing an answer key beside them.

The separate answer sheet referred to in an earlier paragraph, and also discussed and illustrated in Chapter 4, represents a further major economy in time. It completely eliminates time-consuming turning of pages by the scorer. When score is the number correct, the test can be scored by placing over the answer sheet a simple stencil with holes punched in the spaces corresponding to the right answers. There are also special types of answer sheets prepared to further simplify the scoring operation. Three main types should be noted.

1. *Carbon-Backed Answer Sheets.* (*Clapp-Young, Scoreze,* etc.) In these, two sheets are fastened together. On the inside certain parts of one or both sheets are covered with carbon. When the examinee marks in the answer spaces, the marks are transferred to the inside of the page by the carbon paper. The inside has the key printed upon it, in the form of boxes or circles placed opposite the correct answers. Scoring consists merely of counting the number of marks that appear in the boxes.

2. *Pin-Prick Answer Sheets.* These operate in essentially the same way, except that a pin is pushed through the answer sheet in the specified place. This technique is especially effective in the case of a multiscore test. It has been used with the *Kuder Preference Record,* where the pin is pushed through several sheets of paper, each one of which is printed with the scoring key for a different interest area. Counting the number of holes appearing within the printed circles on the different sheets gives the score for the different areas of interest without the necessity of using key or stencil.

3. *The IBM Answer Sheet and Test-Scoring Machine.* For a number of years the International Business Machines Corporation has made available a test-scoring machine that operates electrically through the conductivity of pencil marks on a special answer sheet. The sheet has 750 answer positions, which may be grouped in different ways but which most commonly represent 150 five-choice test items. The answer sheets must be rather carefully marked with a soft pencil, preferably a special one developed for the purpose, if they are to score accurately. Various other mechanical difficulties have been encountered, for example, current leakage due to a damp climate. However, when these conditions are watched for, the machine can considerably accelerate large-scale test-scoring jobs. The basic IBM machine can be bought for $3000.00, or rented for $50.00 per month.* This means that the equipment must be used quite a good deal of the time if it is

---

* 1960 prices.

to pay for itself.   It is especially useful in organizations having a large and fairly steady flow of test scoring.

For large-scale testing programs, there are a number of agencies that maintain scoring services.   These are commented on further in the discussion of school testing programs in Chapter 16.

FEATURES FACILITATING TEST ADMINISTRATION

In evaluating the practical usability of a test, one factor to be taken into account is the ease of administration.   A test that can be handled adequately by the regular classroom teacher with no more than a session or so of special briefing is much more readily fitted into a testing program than a test requiring specially trained administrators.   Several factors contribute to the ease of giving and taking a test.

1. A test is easy to give if it has clear, full instructions.   The instructions for the administrator should be written out substantially word for word, so that all the examiner must do is read them and follow them.   Instructions for the examinee should also be complete and should provide appropriate practice exercises.   The amount of practice that should be provided depends upon how novel the test task is likely to be for those being tested.   Where it is a familiar type of task or a simple and straightforward instruction, no more than a single example will be needed.   However, for an unusual item format or test task more practice will be desirable.

2. A test is easy to give if the number of units to be separately timed is few, and close timing is not critical.   Timing a number of brief subtests to a fraction of a minute is a bothersome undertaking, and the timing is likely to be inaccurate unless a stop watch is available for each tester.   Some tests have as many as eight or ten parts, each taking only 2 or 3 minutes.   A test made up of three or four parts, with time limits of 5, 10, or more minutes for each, will be easier to use.

3. The layout of the test items on the page has a good deal to do with the ease of taking the test.   Items in which response options are all run together on the same line, items with small or illegible pictures or diagrams, items that are crowded together, and items that run over from one page to the next all make difficulty for the examinee.   Print and pictures should be large and clear.   Response options should be well separated from one another.   All parts of an item and all items referring to a single figure, problem, or reading passage should appear on the same page or double-page spread.   Shortcomings on any of

these points represent black marks against a test as far as ease of taking it is concerned.

It seems axiomatic, though the point is sometimes overlooked, that a test is given to be used. If the score is to be used, it must be interpreted and given meaning. The author and publisher of the test have the responsibility of providing the user with information that permits him to make a sound appraisal of the test in relation to his needs and to give appropriate meaning to the score of an individual. This they do primarily through the *test manual* and other collateral materials that are prepared to accompany the test. What may the test user reasonably expect to find in the manual for a test, together with its supporting materials? We have outlined below the aids we believe the test user should expect.

1. *A Statement of the Functions the Test Was Designed to Measure and of the General Procedures by Which It Was Developed.* This is the author's statement of what he considers the test to be valid for and the evidence that proper steps have been taken to achieve that validity. Particularly for achievement tests, in which we are concerned primarily with content and process validity, the author should tell us the procedures by which he arrived at his choice of content or his analysis of the functions being measured. If he is unwilling to expose his thinking to our critical scrutiny, we may perhaps be skeptical of the thoroughness or profundity of that thinking.

Procedures involve not only the rational procedures by which range of content or types of objective were selected, but also the empirical procedures by which items were tried out and screened for final inclusion in the test.

2. *Detailed Instructions for Administering the Test.* We have discussed in an earlier section the need for this aid to uniform and easy administration by the teachers or others who will have to use the test.

3. *Scoring Keys and Specific Instructions for Scoring the Test.* The problems of scoring have also been discussed, under the heading of economy. The manual and supporting materials should provide detailed instructions as to how the score is to be computed, how errors are to be treated, and how part scores are to be combined into a total score. Scoring keys and stencils should be planned to facilitate as much as possible the onerous task of scoring.

4. *Norms for Appropriate Reference Groups,* together with infor-

mation as to how they were obtained and instructions for their use. Chapter 6 was devoted to a full consideration of types of test norms and their use. It will, therefore, be sufficient at this time to point out the responsibility of the test producer to develop suitable norms for the groups with which his test is to be used. General norms are a necessity, and norms suitable for special types of communities, special occupational groups, and other more limited subgroups will add to the usefulness of a test in many cases.

5. *Evidence as to the Reliability of the Test.* This evidence should indicate not only the bald reliability statistics but also the operations used to obtain the reliability estimates and the descriptive and statistical characteristics of each group on which reliability data are based. If a test is available in more than one form, it is highly desirable that the producers report the correlation between the two forms, in addition to any data that were derived from a single testing. If the test yields part scores, and particularly if it is proposed that any use be made of these part scores, reliability data should be reported for the separate part scores. It is good procedure for the author to report standard errors of measurement as well as reliability coefficients. An author who indicates what the standard error of measurement is at each of a number of score levels is particularly to be commended, since this information shows over what range of scores the test maintains its accuracy.

6. *Evidence on the Intercorrelations of Subscores.* If the test provides several subscores, the manual should provide evidence on the intercorrelations of these. This is important in guiding the interpretation of the subscores and, particularly, in judging how much confidence to place in *differences* between the subscores. If the scores are correlated to a substantial degree, measuring much the same things, the differences between them will be largely meaningless and uninterpretable.

7. *Evidence on the Relationships of the Test to Other Factors.* In so far as the test is to be used as a predictive device, correlations with criterion measures constitute the essential evidence on how well it does in fact predict. Full information should be provided on the nature of the criterion variables, the group for which data are available, and the conditions under which the data were obtained. Only then can the reader fairly judge the validity of the test as a predictor.

It will often be desirable to report correlations with other measures of the same function as collateral evidence bearing on the validity of the test.   Thus, correlations with individual intelligence test score are relevant in the case of a group intelligence measure.

Finally, indications of the relationship of test score to age, sex, type of community, socio-economic level, and similar facts about the individual or the group are often helpful.   They provide a basis for judging how sensitive the measure is to the background of the group and to circumstances of their life and education.

8. *Guides for Using the Test and for Interpreting Results Obtained with It.*   The developers of a test presumably know how it is reasonable for the test to be used and the results from it to be evaluated. They are specialists in that test.   For the test to be most useful for others, especially the teacher with limited specialized training, suggestions should be given of ways in which the test results may be used for diagnosing individual and group weaknesses, forming class groupings, organizing remedial instruction, counseling with the individual, or whatever other activities may appropriately be based on that particular type of instrument.

SCHEDULES FOR EVALUATING A TEST

The potential user, who is trying to select the best test for a particular purpose, might welcome a standard form or procedure for evaluating the various tests that are candidates for his patronage.   A standard and somewhat objective procedure for rating tests would be very attractive if an appropriate one could be devised.   There have been several attempts to apply the technique of quantification to tests themselves, and score cards have been developed to be used in appraising tests.[4, 6, 7]   These allocate so many points to aspects of validity, so many to factors associated with reliability, so many to ease of use and interpretation, and so forth.

One can question how useful this standard scheme of adding up points is in this situation.   Certainly, if a test has low validity, no amount of elegance and polish in other respects can make it a satisfactory instrument.   And the importance of different qualities for a measure varies, depending upon the purpose for which the instrument is to be used.   For that reason, we are not proposing any numerical scheme for arriving at a score on each test being considered.   However, a systematic outline should help in assuring that the significant factors are all taken into account and that the analysis is organized in such a way that comparison of different tests will be facilitated.   The schedule given below provides such an outline.   If answers are sought to all the questions raised in the outline, the potential user should have a good basis for comparing the suitability for his needs of different available measurement devices.

An extensive and analytically critical set of criteria for an acceptable psychological test has been developed by the Committee on Test Standards of the American Psychological Association, and published by the Association. This article gives a full statement of the standards that a commercially distributed test may be expected to meet. Similar standards for educational tests have been prepared by the American Educational Research Association and the National Council on Measurements Used in Education.[1]

SCHEDULE FOR EVALUATING A TEST

GENERAL REFERENCE INFORMATION

1. Name of test.
2. Author's name (and position, if available)
3. Publisher.
4. Date of publication.
5. Cost.
6. Time for administration.

VALIDITY

A. *Evidence from the Plan for the Test.* What were the procedures for determining the scope of the test? For determining the particular content to be covered? For determining the functions and processes to be represented? How adequate do these appear to be? How closely do the test objectives correspond to objectives that *you* are interested in for *your* school?

What provisions were made for editorial review of the test materials? How adequate do these appear?

B. *Evidence from the Test Blank Itself.* Do the test items appear appropriate for the objectives that *you* are trying to evaluate? Do the test items appear to be well constructed? Are they free from ambiguity? Do they have attractive wrong-answer choices?

C. *Evidence from Statistical Studies of the Test in Use.* With what concurrent measures has the test been correlated? For what sort of groups? How substantial are the correlations?

With what later criterion measures has the test been correlated? For what sorts of groups?

How does the evidence on statistical validity compare with that for other tests?

How accurate a prediction does it give of significant outside criteria? How do these results compare with those of other tests that try to measure the same trait?

D. *Evidence from Outside Authority.* What have reviewers and critics said about the validity of the test?

RELIABILITY

A. *How Adequately Are Data Reported?* Do the authors indicate size and nature of groups for which data are reported? Do they indicate type of reliability coefficient computed? Do they give mean and standard deviation for the groups? Do they report reliabilities for single age and grade groups?

B. *What Are the Facts on Reliability?* What actual data on reliability are reported? (Indicate, as far as given, the age or grade, size of group, mean and standard deviation, procedures by which reliability was computed, and resulting values obtained.) How do the data compare with other competing tests?

PRACTICAL CONSIDERATIONS IN ADMINISTRATION AND USE OF TEST

A. *Factors in Administration*

    1. Adequacy of manual.

    2. Complexity of procedures.

        a. Complexity of process required of students.

        b. Adequacy of instructions and practice exercises.

        c. Complexity of process required of examiner. Timing, giving instructions, and interpreting responses of subjects examined.

    3. Time requirements.

    4. Legibility, attractiveness, and convenience of format.

B. *Factors in Scoring*

    1. Time required (i.e., form of answer, type of key, etc.).

    2. Special skills required (subjective scoring and qualitative interpretation).

C. *Factors in Interpretation*

    1. Type of norms. Appropriateness to uses, completeness, representativeness of sample. How readily may raw scores be converted into derived scores?

    2. Aids to interpretation provided by manual.

D. *Factors in Continued Use*

    1. Are there comparable forms? How many? How well is comparability established?

    2. Cost. Does this permit routine continued use? Can blanks be used a number of times?

SUMMARY STATEMENT

We have discussed the requirements of a good test under the headings of validity, reliability, and practicality. A test is valid in so far as it measures the qualities we wish to measure. It is reliable in so far as it measures with precision.   It is practical in so far as it is economical of time and money and simple to give and interpret.

The crucial requirement for a test is validity.   In some tests, especially achievement tests, we may have to judge how well the test *represents* the content and processes we wish to measure.   For other tests, especially aptitude tests, we may evaluate how well the test *predicts* some measure that serves as a later criterion of success.   In still others, where we are interested in the test as *describing* some trait or aspect of the individual, appraisal of validity is more complex.   A "theory" of the trait or construct must be developed, and the test is evaluated by how well it fits into the pattern of relationships that would be predicted from this theory.

There are several different procedures available for obtaining estimates of the *reliability* or precision of a measure.   The most rigorous procedure is to administer two *equivalent forms* of the test on two separate occasions.   The correlation between the two forms provides a reliability coefficient that tells how closely individuals maintain their position in the group from one testing to the other.   Less exacting procedures include (1) repetition of the same test and (2) extracting two scores from a single test, usually by scoring odd and even items separately.   Reliability estimates based on these last procedures are less satisfactory and should usually be discounted somewhat.

The value obtained for the reliability coefficient will depend on the range and level of ability in the group tested and the length of the test, as well as upon the particular procedure used for estimation.   It is particularly necessary to discount a coefficient based on the pooling of several grades.

To describe the accuracy of an individual's score, the *standard error of measurement* is often preferable to the reliability coefficient.   It tells the variation to be expected if we were able to make repeated measurements of a particular individual.   This variation must always be borne in mind when interpreting the score an individual receives

Practicality is a function of economy, ease of administration, and readiness of interpretation.   Economy is affected by initial cost, by the possibility of reusing materials, and by time required for scoring and analyzing the results.   Ease of administration results from full directions, simple procedures for the examinee, and an objective record of performance.   Readiness of interpretation is facilitated by good norms and by a full guide of suggestions for interpretation.

The potential test user should examine the tests from among which he must choose in the light of the above criteria and pick the one that best fits his needs.

REFERENCES

1. American Educational Research Association and National Council on Measurements Used in Education, Committee on Test Standards, *Technical recommendations for achievement tests,* Washington, D. C., National Education Association, 1955.
2. American Psychological Association, Committee on Test Standards, Technical recommendations for psychological tests and diagnostic techniques, *Psychol. Bull.,* **51,** No. 2, Pt. 2, 1954.
3. Buhler, R. A., Flicker fusion threshold and anxiety level, unpublished doctor's dissertation, Columbia University, 1953.
4. Cole, R. D., and F. von Borgersrode, A scale for rating standardized tests, *Sch. of Educ. Rec. of Univ. of North Dakota,* **14,** 1928 (Oct.), 11–15.
5. McClelland, David, John W. Atkinson, Russell A. Clark, and Edgar L. Lowell, *The Achievement Motive,* New York, Appleton-Century-Crofts, 1953.
6. Otis, A. S., *Scale for rating tests,* Yonkers, N. Y., World Book, 1926.
7. Rinsland, H. D., Form for briefing and evaluating standardized tests, *J. educ. Res.,* 1949, **42,** 371–375.
8. Terman, L. M., and Maud A. Merrill, *Measuring intelligence,* Cambridge, Mass., Houghton Mifflin, 1937.

SUGGESTED ADDITIONAL READING

American Educational Research Association and National Committee on Measurements Used in Education, *Technical recommendations for achievement tests,* Washington, D. C., National Education Association, 1955.

American Psychological Association, Committee on Test Standards, Technical recommendations for psychological tests and diagnostic techniques, *Psychol. Bull.,* **51,** No. 2, 1954, Pt. 2.

Bennett, George K., Harold G. Seashore, and Alexander G. Wesman, *Differential Aptitude Tests manual,* New York, Psychological Corp., 1959, Chapters 4 and 5.

Cronbach, Lee J., *Essentials of psychological testing,* 2nd ed., New York, Harper, 1960, Chapters 5 and 6.

Cureton, Edward E., Validity, Chapter 16 in E. F. Lindquist, Editor, *Educational measurement,* Washington, D. C., American Council on Education, 1951.

Doppelt, Jerome E., How accurate is a test score? *Test Service Bulletin No. 50,* New York, Psychological Corp., 1956.

Harris, Chester W., Editor, *Encyclopedia of educational research,* 3rd ed., New York, Macmillan, 1960, pp. 1038–1047, 1551–1554.

Thorndike, Robert L., Reliability, Chapter 15 in E. F. Lindquist, Editor, *Educational measurement,* Washington, D. C., American Council on Education, 1951.

Wesman, Alexander G., Expectancy tables—a way of interpreting test validity, *Test Service Bulletin No. 38,* Psychological Corp., 1949, 1–5.

QUESTIONS FOR DISCUSSION

1. If the College Entrance Examination Board were developing a general survey test in science for high-school seniors, what might they do to establish the validity of the test?

2. What type of validity is indicated by each of the following statements which might be found in a test manual?

a. Scores on Personality Test X correlated +.43 with teachers' ratings of adjustment.

b. The objectives to be appraised by Reading Test Y were rated for importance by 150 classroom teachers.

c. Scores on Clerical Aptitude Test Z correlated +.57 with supervisors' ratings after 6 months on the job.

d. Intelligence Test W gives scores that correlate +.69 with *Stanford-Binet* IQ.

e. Achievement Battery V is based on an analysis of 50 widely used texts and 100 courses of study from all parts of the U. S.

3. Comment on the statement "The classroom teacher is the only one who can judge the validity of a standardized achievement test for his class."

4. Look at the manuals of two or three tests of different types. What evidence on validity is presented? How adequate is it for each test?

5. Using Table 7.3 on p. 171, determine what per cent of those selected would be above average on the job if a selection procedure with a validity of .40 were used and only the top quarter were accepted for the job. What per cent would be above average if the top three-quarters were selected? What would the two per cents be if the validity were .50? What does a comparison of the four percentages bring out?

6. Air Force personnel psychologists are doing research on the selection of jet-engine mechanics. What might they use as criterion measures of success as a mechanic? What are the advantages and limitations of each possible measure?

7. What advantages and disadvantages do school grades have as criterion measures?

8. A test manual contains the following statement: "The validity of test X is shown by the fact that it correlates .80 with the *Stanford-Binet.*" What additional information is needed to evaluate this assertion?

9. Look at the evidence presented on reliability in the manuals of two or three tests. How adequate is it? What are its shortcomings?

10. The manual for test T presents reliability data based on (a) retesting with the same test form a week later, (b) correlating odd with even items, and (c) correlating form A with form B, the two forms being given a week apart. Which procedure may be expected to yield the *lowest* coefficient? Why? Which to yield the most *useful* estimate of reliability? Why?

11. A student has been given the *Stanford-Binet Intelligence Test* four different times during his school career, and his cumulative record card shows the following IQ's: 98, 107, 101, and 95. What significance should be attached to the fluctuations in IQ?

12. A school plans to give form A of a reading test in October and form B in May, in order to study individual differences in improvement during the year. The reliability of each form of the test is known to be about .85 for a grade group. The correlation between the two forms turned out to be .80. How much confidence can be placed in the "gain" scores?

13. You are considering three reading tests for use in your school. As far as you can judge, the three are equally valid. The reliability of each is reported to be .90. What else would you need to know to make a choice among the tests?

14. Examine several tests of intelligence or of achievement that would be suitable for a class you are teaching or might teach. Write an evaluation of one of these tests, following the guide on pp. 201–202.

Chapter 8

▼

Where to Find Information about Specific Tests

THE NATURE OF THE PROBLEM

The production of educational and psychological tests has been going on for only half a century, but during that time literally thousands of different tests have been produced. In a comprehensive bibliography which covered up to about 1945, Hildreth [9, 10] included entries for 5294 different tests. The number could probably now be increased by at least another thousand. Of course, many of the earlier published tests are obsolete now, or only of historical interest, but the number of currently available tests is still very great.

Not only is the total number of tests great. So also is the variety. Tests vary widely in testing procedures, in content, and in group for which designed. There are paper-and-pencil tests, individual performance tests, rating scales, self-rating procedures, observational procedures, and projective techniques. There are measures of attitude, of interest, of temperament, of personal adjustment, of intellect, of special aptitudes, and of all aspects of school achievement. There are tests designed for infants, for preschool children, for school children and adolescents, and for adults.

No one book can hope to introduce a student to even a representative sampling of tests of all types, covering all sorts of content for all age levels. The following chapters will introduce some of the most important and most widely known tests, discussing them as examples of many others. But this book cannot give a complete treatment of any particular age group or subject area, and there are so many special situations in which a reader may be interested or for which he may need a test that the tests discussed here may include not even one that fits his particular need.

Since it is impossible to list and evaluate all or even most of the tests that might be of concern to an audience with varied interests, we shall approach the problem at a different level. We shall try to guide the reader to sources in which he can find the available tests listed, and in some cases evaluated, and we will try to guide the reader in evaluating the tests he locates. The present chapter discusses re-source materials for finding tests and for finding out about them. Chapter 7 has given an orientation in the factors to be considered in evaluating the suitability of a particular test for a particular purpose.

The knowledge of where to go to find out about tests of a particular type and how to evaluate one when found is probably more important than predigested information about a particular test. Tests change and the purposes of the test user change. It is impossible to anticipate what type test will be required for some future need. The important thing is to know how to go about finding the tests available for that need when it arises and how to evaluate their relative merits.

There are several different types of questions about a test or an area of measurement for which one may seek answers. Some of the types of questions are:

1. What tests have been developed that might serve my present need or purpose?

2. What are the *new* tests in my field of interest?

3. What is test A, of which I have heard, like? For what groups and purposes was it designed? Who made it? How long does it take and how much does it cost? What skills are needed to give and use it?

4. What do specialists in the field of measurement have to say about test A? How do they evaluate it, in comparison with competing tech-niques?

5. What basic factual material do we have on test A? What are its statistical attributes? What are its relationships to other measures?

6. What research has been done studying or using test A?

Let us see what materials are available to us as we try to answer questions such as these. These resources include (1) text and ref-erence books in special areas of testing, (2) the *Mental Measurements Yearbooks,* (3) test reviews in professional journals, (4) publishers' test catalogues, (5) each test itself together with its accompanying manual, (6) articles in professional journals reviewing a broad field of testing, (7) comprehensive bibliographies of tests and the testing lit-erature, and (8) educational and psychological abstract and index series. These will be considered in turn, the most useful items will be identified, and the information to be obtained from each type of source will be indicated.

TEXT AND REFERENCE BOOKS IN SPECIAL AREAS

There are a number of text and reference books covering more specialized areas of testing. When the scope is limited to include only elementary-school tests, tests for diagnosis of individual maladjustment, or tests for vocational placement, it becomes possible to cover the field in more detail. A book dealing with tests of a particular type provides a good general introduction to the materials of the field. Such a book usually acquaints the reader with a representative selection of established tests in the area—those which the author considers worthy of mention. In addition, some evaluation of each test is usually given, indicating the purposes for which it may well be used, and what the writer considers to be its strengths, weaknesses, and distinctive characteristics. The book will usually also contain some discussion of the problems of testing in the field it covers, apart from discussion of specific tests.

It is not possible to consider all the books that might prove useful to some reader. However, a number of them have been listed below with brief annotations. The titles have been chosen in terms of their recency and the quality of their treatment. In addition, an attempt has been made to get books that represent a wide range of specialized interests. The annotations are designed to bring out the distinctive quality of each book.

Allen, Robert M., *Personality assessment procedures,* New York, Harper, 1958. Surveys methods and techniques for evaluating personality, and is a source book of tests and instruments used to assess personality. For each test, the purpose, reliability, validity, and standardization procedures are given.

Arny, Clara Brown, *Evaluation in home economics,* New York, Appleton-Century-Crofts, 1953. Although the examples given in the first half are related to home economics, the excellent discussion of purposes and methods of evaluating student progress are applicable to any class. Commercially published standardized tests, check lists, and rating scales are described and uses indicated in an appendix.

Bauman, Mary K., *A manual of norms for tests used in counseling blind persons,* AFB Publications, Research Series, No. 6, New York, American Foundation for the Blind, 1958. Information is given on tests that have been adapted or developed for use with the adult blind. Also includes bibliography of source material on tests, testing, and test interpretation for adult blind.

Blair, Glenn M., *Diagnostic and remedial teaching: a guide to practice in elementary and secondary schools,* rev. ed., New York, Macmillan, 1956. Gives selected lists of tests which Blair judges to be of value for diag-

nosis of difficulties in the basic skills.   Comments on each test are given
indicating strengths and weaknesses and suggested ways of using.

Bond, Guy L., and Eva Bond Wagner, *Teaching the child to read,* 3rd ed.,
New York, Macmillan, 1960.   Appendix contains information on reading readiness tests, diagnostic and survey tests of reading, group and
individual intelligence tests.

Clarke, H. Harrison, *Application of measurement to health and physical
education,* 3rd ed., Englewood Cliffs, N. J., Prentice-Hall, 1959.   Describes a variety of performance tests for physical fitness and skills, paper-
and-pencil tests for knowledge of sports techniques and health education, and rating scale techniques.   Emphasizes use of tests and need for
planning an efficient program for evaluating students in physical education.

Froehlich, Clifford P., and Kenneth B. Hoyt, *Guidance testing,* 3rd ed.,
Chicago, Science Research Associates, 1959.   Chapters in book are devoted to scholastic ability, multifactor aptitude batteries, single aptitude
tests, achievement tests, interest inventories, and personal and social adjustment inventories.   At the end of each chapter is a list of tests judged
by Froehlich and Hoyt to be the most useful and best in the area.

Hardaway, Mathilde, and Thomas Maier, *Tests and measurements in business education,* 2nd ed., Cincinnati, South-Western Publishing Co., 1952.
Provides lists of achievement and prognostic tests available in business
education.

Super, Donald E., and John O. Crites, *Appraising vocational fitness,* New
York, Harper, in press.   Reports on selected tests in a wide variety of
fields that may be used in educational or vocational guidance.

One limitation of books, such as those just annotated, becomes apparent from an examination of the publication dates.   At the time
that these were selected (1960), each was judged to be the most recent
good book in its field and yet some were already eight years old.   When
one adds to this the time that has elapsed in the preparation and
printing of the book, it is easy to see that a book reviewing a field cannot be relied upon for current materials.   The typical textbook gives
information about well-established and accepted tests, but recently
published devices or techniques that are still in the experimental stages
are not likely to be represented.   There is a lag of several years between production of a device and the reporting of it in books reviewing an area of testing.

Another feature of most books surveying a field, which may be in
some cases an advantage and in others a disadvantage, is that they are
selective.   They must be.   The author cannot discuss everything, so he
must pick the items he wishes to present.   He selects for discussion the
tests which he considers valuable.   In so far as his judgment is sound,
he does a real service to the novice in the field, who is thus led directly
to the more important and valuable material.   However, this means
that the reader cannot expect to use a textbook as a source to lead him

to all the tests in an area and permit him to compare them. For a full listing of the tests of any particular type he will have to look elsewhere.

THE MENTAL MEASUREMENTS YEARBOOKS

Probably the most useful single reference source for the person needing to make choices and plan programs in the field of testing is the series of *Mental Measurements Yearbooks* prepared by Buros.[3, 4, 5, 6, 7] Five *Yearbooks* have now been pubished, and they were preceded by two more modest volumes of the same type. The *Yearbooks* undertake to provide a listing and one or more frank and critical reviews of each new standardized test that is published.

A large panel of reviewers has cooperated in the preparation of these volumes, each reviewer evaluating two or three tests in an area in which he is presumed to be competent. The tests of more general interest are appraised by two and sometimes even more reviewers. The reviews are fairly full, pointing out strengths and weaknesses of a test, comparing it with others in the field, and indicating the purposes for which the reviewer considers it useful.

In addition to reviews of tests, the *Yearbooks* also include the factual items about each test that a potential user is likely to need—such items as author, publisher, publication date, cost, time to administer, grades for which suitable, and number of forms available. Finally, for each test the *Yearbooks* give a bibliography of books and articles that have appeared dealing with that particular test. These bibliographies are quite extensive, amounting in the case of one test to 2297 titles.

The *Yearbooks* have two other features that add to their value to the test user. One is a section on books and monographs related to measurement problems. This section undertakes to list all the significant books on measurement for the period covered and in addition gives excerpts from the reviews of these books that have appeared in psychological and educational journals. The bibliography and reviews provide a guide to, and evaluation of, publications in the field.

Also valuable is a very complete index and directory section. This includes (1) a directory and index of the publishers of the tests and of the books on measurement reviewed in the volume, (2) a directory and index of the periodicals that have included reviews of tests or books on testing, (3) an index of titles of books and tests, (4) an index of names occurring in any connection, and (5) a classified index of tests organized by content or type. These indices make it possible to locate any test or type of test, to locate the complete original of any excerpted test review, and to get in touch with the publisher of any test.

When a question arises about a test or a type of test, the *Mental Measurements Yearbooks* are the volumes for which one reaches almost automatically. They are a "must" for any individual or any office that must answer frequent questions about tests or testing.

The *Yearbooks* are not too convenient to use if one wishes to cover early as well as current tests in a particular area. At the present writing, there are five of them, published in 1938, 1941, 1949, 1953, and 1959. To cover the tests in any field, the reader must search all five volumes and may in fact need to go back to antecedent publications.[1,2]

A new test is ordinarily reviewed in the first *Yearbook* that came out after it was published, and reviews may sometimes also appear in subsequent volumes. Space limitations did not permit review in the 1938 *Yearbook* of all the older tests that were thought to merit review, and reviews of some of these first appeared in later volumes. Even the set of volumes taken together does not undertake to be *exhaustive* in its coverage of tests of a given type. However, if he brings together the material in the complete series, the reader will probably find an appraisal of any test that he is likely to consider using, published up to the time that planning for the last *Yearbook* was completed. The first two *Yearbooks* cover tests up to about 1939; the third covers the period from 1940 through 1947; the fourth deals with material from 1948 through 1951; and the fifth brings us up to 1958.

JOURNAL TEST REVIEWS

We still face the problem of getting information on the *latest* tests and testing developments. One way of keeping up with important new tests is through reviews in professional journals. Tests of interest to the psychologist and the counselor have been reviewed for a number of years in the *Journal of Consulting Psychology* and the *Journal of Counseling Psychology*. In late 1959, a test review section, called "Testing the Test," was initiated in the *Personnel and Guidance Journal*. These sources should keep the test user up to date on the most significant new psychological tests within a year or so of their appearance.

TEST PUBLISHERS

The most up-to-date information on what tests are available is probably to be obtained from the test publishers themselves, either through correspondence or through their catalogues. There are many publishers, too many to list here, so that gathering information from all of them would be quite an undertaking. However, the number who publish *extensively* in the testing field is a good deal more limited. A number of the most important publishers are listed in Appendix IV together with their addresses and some indication of the types of material and the services they supply.

The limitations of a test publisher as an entirely unbiased source of information on the *values and limitations* of his own publications are, of course, obvious. Reversing Marc Antony, we may say he comes to praise his tests, not to bury them. However, as a source of information about, rather than evaluation of his tests, he can be very helpful. In Chapter 7 we have considered how the potential user may go about appraising a new test for himself in the light of the information he can get from the test producer and from other sources.

TEST AND MANUAL

The individual who is seriously considering using a particular test will certainly need to examine the test itself and the manual the publisher has prepared to go with it. Each publisher's catalogue will indicate the price for which a specimen set of each test may be obtained. The specimen set contains a copy of the test itself, the instructions for administering and scoring, and part or all of the supplementary materials available to the user to help in interpreting the test.

The amount of supplementary materials included in a specimen set varies from one publisher to another. The potential user can legitimately expect the publisher to include materials in a specimen set that will provide all the information he needs in order to arrive at a decision as to the suitability of the test for his purposes. He should be skeptical of any test for which the information supplied him is incomplete. The individual who wishes to examine a number of different tests without buying specimen sets of each may be able to find a test file in the library or the guidance department of his local university.

To obtain specimen sets of tests, the applicant must ordinarily present some sort of credentials. A letter on the official letterhead of his school or institution will often suffice. A note from the university where he is studying may serve the function. The limitations that publishers place upon the distribution of their materials depend upon the nature of the materials. They will often refuse to distribute tests that require special skills to administer and interpret unless the applicant can give evidence that he has the training and skills that qualify him to use the materials.

A detailed examination of the test itself will provide the potential user with a basis for judging how well the content of the test and the form of test exercises correspond to the objectives and functions he wishes to measure. The accompanying material, which we have collectively called the test manual, is a very important part of any test. It varies enormously in quality and comprehensiveness from one test to another. In some of the better current tests, this collateral material becomes almost a book. It provides a great variety of important information to help in using and interpreting a test. We have indicated in Chapter 7 (pp. 202–203) the types of information a test user has a right to expect to find in the test manual. A manual that provides all this information becomes a very important source for information about the test.

Manuals differ greatly not only in comprehensiveness but also in impartiality and integrity. Probably no test manual is entirely free of a promotional element. However, sometimes the manual becomes to a very large extent a promotional device focused on increasing the sales of the test. The potential user must always be aware of this aspect of the manual and must endeavor to discount appropriately claims made for the test. There often appears to be an inverse relationship between the grandeur of the claims that are made and the evidence on which they are based. The reader will do well to keep his attention focused on the evidence presented in the manual, to view claims in the light of this evidence, and to be extremely suspicious of the test whose manual makes sweeping claims but presents very little data.

JOURNAL REVIEW ARTICLES

It is sometimes useful to refer to summary articles covering recent developments in tests and testing. The most regular of these in recent years has been the triennial summary in the *Review of Educational Research*. This journal undertakes to summarize research in a number of different sectors of education. Its publication schedule is arranged so that a given area is treated every 3 years. Material on tests and measurements was reviewed in the February, 1959, issue, which was devoted to educational and psychological testing. Similar reviews appeared in 1956, 1953, and every third year back to 1932. Because of the volume of material to be covered, these reviews are very condensed, but they do introduce the reader to new tests and testing research and provide him with a bibliography of original references to which he can go for a fuller report on any topic in which he is interested.

Since 1950, the *Annual Review of Psychology* has provided a yearly review and bibliography on selected psychological topics. Chapter headings such as "Individual Differences" and "Theory and Techniques of Assessment" suggest sources for material of possible interest to the psychological tester.

Gray has for many years prepared an annotated bibliography on reading, which has appeared in recent years in the *Journal of Educational Research*. This deals with reading tests—as well as with other reading problems.

COMPREHENSIVE BIBLIOGRAPHIES ON TESTS AND TESTING

There have been, from time to time, comprehensive bibliographies on tests and testing. However, the most complete of these, by Hildreth [9, 10] is badly out of date, covering material only up to 1945, and is of interest primarily to a person having a historical interest in tests of a given type. Its coverage up to the time of its publication was quite complete. The bibliography merely lists and gives a reference source for each test, and provides no further information about it.

One fairly extensive bibliography dealing with the technical aspects of testing (i.e., such issues as the appraisal of reliability, item analysis techniques, etc.) has been prepared by Goheen and Kavruck.[8] This source provides over 2500 references covering the period from 1929 to 1949.

These extensive bibliographies will be useful primarily to the person who wants to dig fairly deeply into tests of some particular type, or into some technical testing problem.

ABSTRACTS AND INDICES

Two final sources that must be brought to the attention of the serious student are the *Psychological Abstracts* and the *Education Index*. These are basic bibliographic sources in the fields of psychology and education respectively. Each undertakes to provide a complete listing of current publications in its respective field. The field for the *Psychological Abstracts* is rather more narrowly defined, being restricted to scientific and technical publications in psychology. Each publication is represented not merely by title but also by an abstract indicating the nature of the report and the major findings. An annual subject index and author index aid in locating desired material. The *Psychological Abstracts* provides a monthly listing of new tests. This appears in the "General" section at the beginning of each issue under the heading New Tests. The *Abstracts* also covers the literature of research using tests and of findings with respect to them.

The *Education Index* covers a considerably wider range of material, since it deals with the whole broad area of education and includes popular and professional materials as well as those of a more technical and scientific nature. It gives references only, providing no information about the nature and content of the item. Material is topically organized, and the user who looks under such topics as ability tests, educational measurement, mental tests, or personality tests will find most of the material relating to measurement in education.

The joint use of the *Psychological Abstracts* and the *Education Index,* supplemented by the other sources discussed previously, should enable the student who wishes to dig to the roots of a measurement problem to locate the bulk of the work that has been done on that problem.

SUMMARY STATEMENT

At the beginning of this chapter a number of questions were suggested to which a test user might wish answers. The important sources of information about tests and testing have now been discussed. By way of summary, we may try to relate the sources to the questions. An attempt has been made to do this in Fig. 8.1. At the top of this chart are listed various questions one might raise about a test, type of test, or testing problem. On the side are listed the most important types of source material referred to in this chapter. In each cell is a symbol to represent the extent to which the source should help in answering the question. The symbol ** is used to designate one of the sources that would probably be *most* helpful and to which one would turn first. Sources marked * are ones that would also be expected to contribute to the needed answer. Sources marked ? are ones that might perhaps provide some useful information. Where there is *no* entry at all, the source is not likely to be helpful in that connection. A critical study of this table, with analysis of the reasons for the various entries, should leave the reader well prepared to go out and get for himself the information he needs in order to select a test or as background for a specific testing problem.

Sources	To Find Out, in Any Field					
	What tests there are	What *new* tests there are	What test X is like	What specialists think of test X	What facts we have about test X	What research has been done on or with testing problem Y
Texts in special areas of measurement	*		*	?	*	*
Mental Measurements Yearbooks	**	?	*	**	*	**
Reviews in current professional journals		**	*	*		
Publishers' catalogues	*	**	*			
Test blank and manual			**		**	*
Review articles in *Review of Educ. Research*, etc.		*		?	?	*
Hildreth's bibliography of tests	*					
Goheen and Kavruck's bibliography						*
Psychological Abstracts		*			*	**
Education Index		*				*

Key: **—Most helpful.   *—Somewhat helpful.   ?—Possibly helpful.

Fig. 8.1. Appraisal of sources of information about tests and testing.

REFERENCES

1. Buros, O. K., Educational, psychological, and personality tests of 1933, 1934, and 1935, *Rutgers Univ. Bull.*, Vol. 13, No. 1, Studies in Education, No. 9, New Brunswick, N. J., School of Educ., Rutgers University, 1936.
2. Buros, O. K., Educational, psychological, and personality tests of 1936, *Rutgers Univ. Bull.*, Vol. 14, No. 2A, Studies in Education, No. 11, New Brunswick, N. J., School of Educ., Rutgers University, 1937.
3. Buros, O. K., *The 1938 mental measurements yearbook*, New Brunswick, N. J., Rutgers University Press, 1938.
4. Buros, O. K., *The 1940 mental measurements yearbook*, Highland Park, N. J., The Mental Measurements Yearbook, 1941.
5. Buros, O. K., *The third mental measurements yearbook*, New Brunswick, N. J., Rutgers University Press, 1949.
6. Buros, O. K., *The fourth mental measurements yearbook*, Highland Park, N. J., Gryphon Press, 1953.

7. Buros, O. K., *The fifth mental measurements yearbook,* Highland Park, N. J., Gryphon Press, 1959.
8. Goheen, Howard W., and Samuel Kavruck, *Test construction, mental test theory, and statistics,* Washington, D. C., U. S. Government Printing Office, 1950.
9. Hildreth, Gertrude H., *A bibliography of mental tests and rating scales,* New York, Psychological Corp., 1939.
10. Hildreth, Gertrude H., *A bibliography of mental tests and rating scales. 1945 supplement,* New York, Psychological Corp., 1946.

QUESTIONS FOR DISCUSSION

1. Using the sources indicated in the text, prepare as complete a list as you can of currently available standardized tests for a specific grade and purpose (i.e., tests in first-year Spanish, reading readiness tests, tests in American history for the twelfth grade, etc.).

2. Using the *Mental Measurements Yearbooks,* find out what reviewers think of a particular test that you are interested in.

3. Using the *Fifth Mental Measurements Yearbook,* find out what reviewers have to say about one of the following titles that interests you:

Doll, E. A., *The Measurement of Social Competence.*
Eysenck, H. J., *The Scientific Study of Personality.*
Remmers, H. H., *Introduction to Opinion and Attitude Measurement.*
Sarason, S. B., *The Clinical Interaction: With Special Reference to Rorschach.*
Strong, E. K., Jr., *Vocational Interests 18 Years After College.*

4. To what sources would you go to try to answer each of the following questions? To which would you go first? What would you expect to get from each?

    a. What test should I use to study the progress of two class groups in beginning French?

    b. What kinds of norms are available for the *Stanford Achievement Tests?*

    c. Is the *Rorschach Test* of any value as a predictor of academic success in college?

    d. Has a new revision of the *Wechsler Adult Intelligence Scale* been published yet?

    e. What intelligence tests have been developed for use with the blind?

    f. What are the significant differences between the *Metropolitan Achievement Tests* and the *California Achievement Tests?*

    g. How much does the *Otis Quick-Scoring Intelligence Test—Beta,* cost?

    h. What do testing people think of the *Brainard Occupational Preference Inventory?*

5. Look at two or three publishers' catalogues. Compare the announcements of tests of the same type. How adequate is the information that is provided? How objective is the presentation of the tests' values and limitations?

Chapter 9

▼

Standardized Tests of Intelligence or Scholastic Aptitude

ACHIEVEMENT AND APTITUDE

Ability tests are designed to appraise what an individual *can* do under favorable conditions when he is trying to do his best. All any ability test measures is performance at the time of testing. From this performance we may hope to make one or more of a variety of different inferences. We may want to infer how effective a program of school instruction has been in teaching new knowledges or skills, i.e., how much progress the pupils have made in some kind of achievement. We may want to infer how well each individual will do in learning some new task, i.e., a prognosis of future achievement. We may want to make inferences about the organization or structure of human abilities, i.e., what goes with what. We may hope to unravel the causal factors in individual abilities or disabilities, i.e., why the individual fails or succeeds with a particular task. All these are different sorts of *inferences*. The basic *evidence* in every case is performance on a set of test tasks.

Performances are tied with varying degrees of closeness to specific, organized instruction. At one end of the scale are those knowledges and skills that are the direct outcome of organized teaching, usually in schools but sometimes on the job. To decipher the meaning of: *Arma virumque cano* or of

$$6 \cdot r \big(\ ) \ c \ \frown \ \text{———} \ \frown \frown \ r \, \delta \ \delta \, 6.$$

are accomplishments that will be developed almost exclusively in a high-school course in Latin, on the one hand, or Gregg shorthand, on the other. Even the ablest individual with a wealth of general life experiences is unlikely to acquire abilities such as these unless they have been specifically taught. We frequently want to measure the extent to which abilities such as these, dependent directly upon formal instruction, have been acquired. Tests thus tied to instruction and concerned with evaluation of past progress are spoken of as *achievement* tests or *proficiency* tests. We shall consider them in some detail in Chapter 11.

At the other end of the scale are abilities that are developed through the general experiences of life, quite apart from any formal instruction. Consider the two pictures in Fig. 9.1*A* and *B*. Suppose we were to ask a child, concerning each of them: What is wrong with this picture? What is silly about it? As we went up the age range, we would find more and more children who could give us a satisfactory answer. But probably no child would have been specifically taught in school that shadows extend away from the sun or that in a wind flags and smoke will be blowing in the same direction. The background to apprehend the absurdity in these situations and the ability to isolate the critical elements in the pictures come with maturity from the general experiences of growing up in our society.

It should be emphasized that any performance depends in some degree upon experience. A child from a culture that had provided no experience with books and pictures would be less likely to suc-

A   B

Fig. 9.1A and B. Picture-absurdity-test items.

ceed with the tasks of Fig. 9.1 because he had never learned to interpret a picture as corresponding to real things in a real world. A child who had had no experience with chimneys or with flags would be severely handicapped on picture B since he would not be able to interpret the picture or know how these things should behave. These two absurdities items assume (1) a general familiarity with pictures and the representation of things by pictures and (2) experience with trees, shadows, houses, flags, smoke, and wind. Any child in a *normal* American environment will have had these experiences in abundance. For him, therefore, the test provides a measure of perception, analysis, and understanding of his environment. Differences between individuals in performance on these tasks may then reasonably be expected to reflect fairly basic differences in certain aspects of intellectual ability.

The examples we have given have illustrated two points quite far apart on the scale ranging from "directly taught" to "acquired entirely from general life experiences." Many abilities fall at intermediate points along this scale. The meanings of words, for example, are taught in school in connection with almost every segment of the school program. But a very large part of our stock of word meanings is picked up in the reading and listening done out of school as an incidental by-product of just living in our society. Again, reading is usually first learned in school, but a large part of the growth in fluency of reading and depth of understanding of printed matter comes from out-of-school reading and from the general acquiring of experience and maturity as a part of growing up. There is no clear boundary line marking off the ability that is a school achievement from the one that is not.

Psychologists and educators are interested in measuring the underlying *aptitudes* of human beings. The interest is sometimes in using these aptitude measures to predict later achievements. It is sometimes in studying the aptitudes for their own sake. But the concept of aptitude is a tricky one. Aptitude implies some natural or innate capacity for a particular type of performance—scholastic aptitude, mechanical aptitude, or artistic aptitude. But all we can observe is performance on a set of tasks. As stated above, this performance inevitably depends in some measure upon the experiences that the individual has had. If we want to get at basic individual differences in *capacity* to do a certain type of task, our only hope is to seek for test items based on experiences so common and general in our culture that almost every person will have had the requisite experiences. We must build upon the common core of experience available to all. This is what aptitude tests aspire to do. They try to base their items upon experiences, mostly out of school but overlapping to some extent those provided in school, that are uniformly provided for individuals growing up in our society. They use these present abilities, based inevitably on a variety of past learnings, as indicators of what the individual can learn to do in the future.

The difference between *aptitude* measures and *achievement* measures is, then, one of degree and emphasis. Any test of ability is to some extent an aptitude test and to some extent an achievement test. The difference between the two designations is perhaps as much in the type of inference that we want to make as in the specific content or the "innateness" of the measure. A test can be thought of as an achievement test when we wish to draw conclusions about past progress and as an aptitude test when we wish to estimate future potentialities. The remainder of the present chapter will be devoted to tests of general intellectual ability, or scholastic aptitude. Chapter 10 will be concerned with other types of special abilities, and Chapter 11 will be devoted to standardized tests of educational achievement.

TASKS USED TO MEASURE ABSTRACT INTELLIGENCE

Much of the research and development of aptitude measures has been devoted to devising and studying tests of "general intelligence," familiarly known as "IQ tests." General intelligence, in this context, has typically meant abstract intelligence—the ability to see relations in, make generalizations from, and relate and organize ideas represented in symbolic form. What general intelligence has meant to those who have tried to test it can be seen from the types of tasks they have used. Examples of a number of the common types of tasks are given below. The keyed answers for multiple-choice items are underlined.

VOCABULARY

A word meaning nearly the same as *robust* is

A. cheerful.　　B. strong.　　C. fat.　　D. small.　　E. wealthy.

VERBAL ANALOGIES

Branch is to tree as brook is to

A. water.　　B. root.　　C. bank.　　D. river.　　E. babble.

SENTENCE COMPLETION

The sun rises in the ——— and sets in the west.

   A. summer.   B. morning.   C. east.   D. end.   E. sky.

ARITHMETIC REASONING

A boy bought candy bars at 90 cents for a box of 24 and sold them at 5 cents each. How much did he make on each bar?

   A. 30 cents.   B. 3¾ cents.   C. 1¼ cents.   D. ⅘ cents.

                E. None of these.

NUMBER SERIES

What number should come next to continue the series 1 2 4 7 11?

   A. 14.   B. 15.   C. 16.   D. 18.   E. 22.

FIGURE ANALOGIES

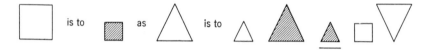

Fig. 9.1C.

CLASSIFICATION

Look at the three words on the left. Which word on the right belongs with these three?

Doctor. Lawyer. Engineer.   Farmer. Architect. Mechanic.
                                      Salesman. Laborer.

"MULTIMENTAL"

Which one of the figures does not belong with the other four?

Fig. 9.1D.

PICTURE ARRANGEMENT

The pictures below tell a story. Which picture comes first in the story?

Fig. 9.1E.

COMPREHENSION (COMMON SENSE)

What is the thing to do if you bump into someone and hurt him?

SIMILARITIES

In what way are wool and cotton alike?

INFORMATION

What month in the year has the fewest days?

DIGIT SPAN

"I will say some numbers. Listen carefully, and when I am through repeat exactly what I said. Listen—

3   8   7   1   5

Now repeat what I said."

DIGIT SYMBOL SUBSTITUTION

This is a code test. Each figure stands for a particular number. You are to put the right numbers in the boxes as fast as you can.

Fig. 9.1F.

OBJECT ASSEMBLY

These pieces, if put together correctly, will make a boy. Go ahead and put them together.

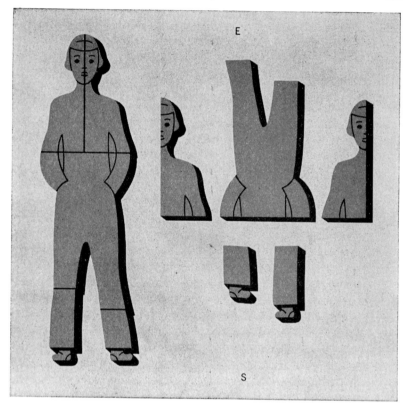

Fig. 9.1G. Object Assembly Test item from *Wechsler Intelligence Scale for Children.* (Reproduced by permission of the Psychological Corporation.)

GROUP INTELLIGENCE TESTS

Most of the intelligence testing carried on in this country is done with group tests. These are paper-and-pencil tests much like the objective type of school examination. They usually consist of 75 to 100 multiple-choice items of the types illustrated in the previous section. Ordinarily, the examinee must read the problem to himself, must work along and do the tasks one after another, and must do as many as he can within a fixed time limit. However, some group tests call for oral instructions from the examiner, and some are paced by the rate at which the examiner presents the test tasks.

Some group intelligence tests (e.g., *California, Kuhlmann-Anderson, Lorge-Thorndike, Pintner*) are made up of several separately timed subtests, in each of which all the items follow the same pattern; i.e., all are vocabulary items or all are number series items. Others (e.g., *Henmon-Nelson, Otis*) have the different types of items mixed in together, a vocabulary item being followed by a number-series item, that by a figure-analogies item, etc. The cycle of different types of items is repeated, the items gradually becoming more difficult. This type of test is called a "spiral omnibus" test because of the cyclical pattern.

The typical group test is designed to cover a range of three or four school grades, i.e., 4 to 6, 7 to 9, 10 to 13. Tests for elementary-school children usually call for responses marked in the test booklet itself, but many of the tests for older groups use separate answer sheets that can be machine scored.

There are a number of different series of group tests on the market that are quite satisfactory to use. The number is too great to permit discussion of each one here. Several are listed, together with annotations describing and providing some evaluation of each, in Appendix III.

In the remainder of this chapter we will first describe the two individual tests, i.e., tests given to one examinee at a time in a face-to-face setting, that are currently most widely used in the United States. These are the *Stanford-Binet Intelligence Scale* and the *Wechsler Adult Intelligence Scale*. Next, we will discuss some of the special types of intelligence measures—tests avoiding reading and language, tests for the very young, tests designed to be free from cultural biases. Then we will compare group and individual tests, considering the advantages of each. Finally, the remainder of the chapter will be concerned with evaluation, interpretation, and use of intelligence test results.

THE REVISED *STANFORD-BINET* TESTS OF INTELLIGENCE

The individual test that over the years has had the widest use with school-age children is the *Stanford-Binet,* brought out by Lewis M. Terman in 1916. A revised version of the test was published in 1937 by Terman and Merrill, and this has been somewhat further revised in 1960.[25] The current revision, which uses the best items from the two forms of the test brought out in 1937, is known as *Form L-M.* It provides a set of tests for each of twenty levels of ability, starting with tests suitable for the average 2-year-old and going up to four levels suitable for differentiating the abilities of average and superior adults. To illustrate the content of the test, we have picked four levels at different points on the scale and listed the tests of each level with brief descriptions.

TWO-AND-A-HALF-YEAR LEVEL

1. *Identifying Objects by Use.* (Card with 6 small objects attached.)
   "Show me the one that we drink out of." etc.
   Three out of 6 for credit at this level.
2. *Identifying Parts of Body.* (Large paper doll.)
   "Show me the dolly's hair." etc.
   Six out of 6 parts for credit at this level.*
3. *Naming Objects.* (Five small objects.)
   "What is this?" (Chair, automobile, etc.)
   Five out of 5 for credit.
4. *Picture Vocabulary.* (Eighteen small cards with pictures of common objects.)
   "What's this? What do you call it?"
   Eight out of 18 for credit at this level.*
5. *Repeating Two Digits.*
   "Listen; say 2." "Now, say 4, 7." etc.
   One out of 3 for credit.
6. *Obeying Simple Commands.* (Four common objects on table.)
   "Give me the dog," "Put the button in the box."
   Two out of 3 correct for credit.

SIX-YEAR LEVEL

1. *Vocabulary.* (Graded list of 45 words.)
   "When I say a word, you tell me what it means. What is an orange?" etc.
   Six words correct to receive credit at this level. Words like tap, gown.*
2. *Differences.*
   "What is the difference between a bird and a dog?" "Wood and glass?"
   Two out of 3 correct for credit.
3. *Mutilated Pictures.* (Five cards of objects with part missing.)
   "What is gone in this picture?" or "What part is gone?"
   Four out of 5 for credit.
4. *Number Concepts.* (Twelve 1-inch cubes.)
   "Give me 3 blocks. Put them here."
   Four out of 5 different numbers correct.
5. *Opposite Analogies.*
   "A table is made of wood; a window of _____."
   Three out of 4 correct for credit.
6. *Maze Tracing.* (Mazes, with start and finish points marked.)
   "The little boy wants to go to school the shortest way without getting off the sidewalk. Show me the shortest way."
   Two right out of 3 for credit.

* Scored also at one or more other levels.

TWELVE-YEAR LEVEL

1. *Vocabulary.* (Same as 6-year level.)
   Fifteen words correct for credit at this level. Words like juggler and brunette.
2. *Verbal Absurdities.* (Five statements.)
   "Bill Jones' feet are so big that he has to pull his trousers on over his head. What is foolish about that?"
   Four out of 5 right for credit at this level.
3. *Picture Absurdities.*
   Picture showing person's shadow going wrong way. "What is foolish about that picture?"
4. *Repeating 5 Digits Reversed.*
   "I am going to say some numbers, and I want you to say them backwards."
   One out of 3 correct for credit.
5. *Abstract Words.*
   "What do we mean by pity?"
   Three out of 4 for credit at this level.
6. *Sentence Completion.* (Four sentences with missing words.)
   "Write the missing word in each blank. Put just one word in each."
   Three out of 4 required for credit at this level.

SUPERIOR ADULT—LEVEL II

1. *Vocabulary.* (Same as 6-year level.)
   Twenty-six words for credit at this level. Words like mosaic, flaunt.
2. *Finding Reasons.* (Two parts.)
   "Give three reasons why a man who commits a serious crime should be punished."
   Both parts right for credit.
3. *Proverbs* (Pearls before swine, etc.)
   "Here is a proverb and you are supposed to tell what it means."
   One out of 2 correct for credit.
4. *Ingenuity.*
   A 5-pint can and a 3-pint can to get exactly 2 pints of water.
   Three out of 3 problems correct for credit.
5. *Essential Differences.*
   "What is the principal difference between work and play?"
   Three out of 3 correct for credit.
6. *Repeating Thought of Passage.*
   Short paragraph on the value of life.
   Four out of 7 essential ideas must be reproduced for credit.

The above examples illustrate the variety of material included in the test. Note that the specific tests vary from one level to another. Many of the tests at the lower age levels are quite concrete, dealing with little objects and pictures. At the upper levels, the tests tend to be more abstract and quite heavily verbal. The various tests include tasks calling for display of past learnings, perception of relations, judgment, interpretation, sustained attention, immediate memory, and other cognitive processes.

The tasks were selected so as to be of appropriate difficulty for the average child of the age level to which they were assigned. In testing a child, the examiner begins at a level where the child is likely to succeed, but only with some effort. If the child fails these and appears discouraged, the examiner will drop back to an easier level. Otherwise, he will move ahead level by level until he reaches a level at which the child fails all tests. When the upper limit has been established, the examiner will be sure to go back and establish the level at which the child can do all the tasks. Often, a few quite easy tests will be given at the end to build up the child's morale.

The child is credited with the basal age at which he passes all tasks plus a credit for tasks passed at more advanced levels. Each task passed at a given level credits the child with the same number of months of mental age. Thus, where there are 6 tests at each year age level, passing a single test gives a credit of 2 months of mental age. For example, child A

Passed all tasks at 6-year level	= 6 yrs. basal age
Passed 3 of 6 tasks at 7-year level	= 6 mos. credit
Passed 1 of 6 tasks at 8-year level	= 2 mos. credit
Failed all tasks at 9-year level	= 0 credit
Resulting in a mental age of	6 yrs., 8 mos.

Level of achievement is expressed as a mental age, arrived at as indicated above. The mental age describes the level at which the child is performing. But this takes no account of the child's life age. Performance in relation to a group of children of his own age is expressed as an IQ. The IQ's for this latest revision of the Stanford-Binet are deviation IQ's, i.e., they are essentially standard scores for which the mean is 100 and the standard deviation 16 at each age level. In so far as the normative groups are adequate and comparable from one age to another, an IQ has the same meaning at one age as at any other. Tables for converting MA's to IQ's are provided from age 2-0 (2 years, no months) up to age 16-0. For individuals over 16 years of age the table is entered with a chronological age of 16-0. The way IQ's spread out is shown in Table 6.7 (p. 145). Thus, a child with an IQ of 130 would surpass about 95 per cent (95.5 per cent by Table 6.7) of children of his age; one with an IQ of 90 would surpass about 23 per cent (22.7 per cent by Table 6.7).

THE WECHSLER INTELLIGENCE SCALES

The second major individual intelligence test is the *Wechsler Adult Intelligence Scale (WAIS)*.[28]   This test was originally developed for adults, and the materials and tasks were chosen with an eye to their appropriateness for adults.   The pattern of organization of the test differs from that of the *Binet*.   Whereas the *Binet,* developed for children, is organized in successive age levels, the *WAIS* is organized by subtests representing types of tasks.   The subtests are the following:

Verbal Subscale	*Performance Subscale*
1. General Information.	7. Digit-Symbol Substitution.
2. General Comprehension.	8. Picture Completion.
3. Arithmetical Reasoning.	9. Block Design.
4. Similarities.	10. Picture Arrangement.
5. Digit Span.	11. Object Assembly.
6. Vocabulary.	

Tasks like those in a number of the subtests will be found among the examples on pp. 222–225.

Each subtest of the *WAIS* yields a separate score, which is then converted into a standard score for that subtest.   The subtest standard scores are combined in three different groupings to yield total scores, and from these total scores three different types of IQ's may be read from norm tables.   The three IQ's are (1) a verbal IQ from subtests 1 through 6, (2) a performance IQ from subtests 7 through 11, and (3) a total IQ from all the subtests put together.   The separate verbal and performance IQ's may have diagnostic significance in the case of certain individuals with verbal, academic, or cultural handicaps.   The IQ on the *WAIS* is also a standard score, set to make the mean of the normative sample 100 and the standard deviation 15.

As we have indicated, the original *Wechsler Intelligence Scale* was designed for adults.   It was suitable for use with adolescents and with adults of all ages.   Subsequently, however, the material has been extended downward to make a test for children.[29]   The same general pattern of subtests has been used, though with minor variations.   In particular, the nature of the tasks in several of the subtests changes as one goes down to the easiest items.   The *Wechsler Intelligence Scale for Children (WISC)* is designed to be usable from age 5 to 15.

The features that distinguish the *WAIS* from the 1937 edition of the *Stanford-Binet* are:

1. Original test items specifically designed for adults.
2. Organization by subtests rather than by age levels.
3. Provision for separate verbal and non-verbal IQ's.

All these features seem like sound adaptations in a test for adults. Most psychometricians would probably agree now in preferring the *WAIS* as a measure for adolescents and adults, though its relation to academic success is perhaps not as clearly established as is the *Binet's*. (As a matter of fact, at these ages a printed group test would usually seem more appropriate for academic prediction.)

The *WISC* cannot be used with children below 5 and is probably not very satisfactory below the age of about 7. For young children the *Binet* would be generally preferred. In the age range from 7 to 15, a decision between the two tests is not an easy one. The *Binet* is reported to be somewhat more difficult and time-consuming to give. The usual *Binet* procedure of carrying the examinee through to the point where he encounters a long series of failures is judged to be a seriously upsetting matter for some emotionally tense children. The separate verbal and performance IQ's of the *WISC* should be quite useful in some cases in understanding children whose verbal development is either very accelerated or retarded. It has diagnostic value for some children with special educational disabilities. However, the *Binet* is probably a somewhat more reliable measure. (No directly comparable data are available.) The test items entering into the *Binet* have had the benefit of trial in earlier forms, with opportunity to revise and select on the basis of that experience. The ultimate basis for choice will be the validity of the inferences that can be made from each in the situations in which they are actually used. Prediction of academic success can apparently be made about equally well from either test. It seems likely that the two tests are about equally useful for children with mental ages of 7 or above.

NON-LANGUAGE AND PERFORMANCE TESTS

Most of the widely used intelligence tests depend to some degree upon language and include tasks presented in verbal terms. This is natural, since the bulk of our learning and thinking makes use of language. For the usual person and in relation to the usual type of academic learnings, aptitude for learning can be tested more efficiently by tasks that involve language than by those that do not. However, for some groups or situations this is not so. The most obvious example is that of groups who do not speak the language or speak it only slightly. When an individual has limited command of English, results from a verbal test in English are in large measure meaningless. Children who have had little opportunity to attend school may suffer a special handicap on a test that relies upon materials close to school learnings. For groups of this sort, tests have been developed that do not require language. In some of these, only the test tasks are non-language in character; in others the instructions can be given by panto-mime and no language need be used at any point during the testing.

A group test that requires no language in solving the test problems, though the instructions are presented in words, is the *Lorge-Thorndike Intelligence Test, Non-Verbal Series.* Types of tasks that are included are figure analogies, figure classification, and number series. (See examples on p. 223.) A group test that dispenses with language in both instructions and test is the *Pintner Non-Language Test,* in which all instructions may be given by pantomime. The test includes the following types of tasks, which are illustrated in Fig. 9.2.

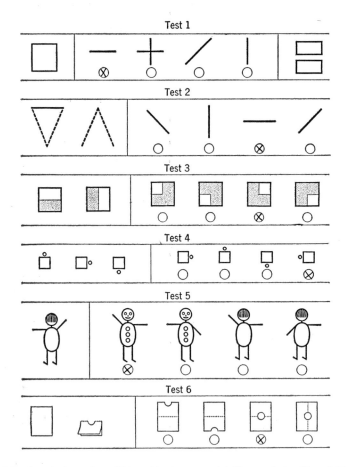

Fig. 9.2. Sample items from *Pintner Non-Language Intelligence Test.* (Copyright 1941, World Book Co., Yonkers, N. Y. Reproduced by permission.)

1. *Figure dividing,* indicating which line or lines will divide a figure up to give a specified set of parts.

2. *Reverse drawings,* indicating the line or lines needed to complete a mirrored drawing.

3. *Pattern synthesis,* indicating the figure that will result from super-imposing two figures.

4. *Movement sequence,* selecting the figure that follows the movement sequence established by three figures in the stem of the item.

5. *Manikin,* selecting the manikin that is the same as the one in the stem, except rotated in some way.

6. *Paper folding,* selecting the diagram that shows how a paper folded and cut in a specified way will look when unfolded.

When used with ordinary school groups, a test such as the *Pintner Non-Language* provides an appraisal of intelligence somewhat distinct from that provided by a verbal measure. Thus, this test correlates only about .65 with the *Pintner General Ability Test, Language Series,* a test made up of verbal and arithmetical material. With usual groups, the non-language test may be expected to be somewhat less effective as a predictor of school achievement. The value of the non-language test is for atypical individuals or groups, i.e., the deaf, the foreign born, or the academically retarded.

Individual tests are also available that do not require the use of language. We have already described the *Wechsler Adult Intelligence Scale* and referred to the performance IQ provided by this test. The performance IQ is based upon five subtests that do not require the subject to use language once he has been instructed as to the nature of his task. A performance test that is widely used with children, as a supplement to the *Binet* when a verbal handicap is suspected, or for groups with which the *Binet* would not be appropriate is the *Arthur Point Scale.*[2] We shall describe it in some detail, since it is a good representative of individual performance tests.

The *Arthur Point Scale* consists of two forms, which contain some-what different tests. Form I has nine subtests, as follows:

1. *Knox Cubes:* The examiner taps four cubes in a specified sequence, and the subject must reproduce the sequence.

2. *Seguin Form Board:* Ten geometric figures are to be placed into the corresponding holes in the board as rapidly as possible.

3. *Two-Figure Form Board:* Cut-up pieces are to be fitted into a square and cross cut out of the board.

4. *Casuist Form Board:* Similar to the above, only four figures.

5. *Manikin or Feature Profile* (depending on level): Cut-up figure of man or cut-up face is to be assembled.

6. *Mare and Foal:* Picture has cut-outs that are to be fitted into place.

7. *Healy Picture Completion I:* Picture has square cut-outs, and subject must select the appropriate block to make the most meaningful picture.

8. *Porteus Mazes:* Simple pencil mazes are to be traced without retracing or crossing a line.

9. *Kohs Block Design:* Designs are to be reproduced using colored cubical blocks, like those in sets for children.

Form II of the test also uses the *Knox Cube, Seguin Form Board, Healy Picture Completion,* and *Porteus Mazes,* presenting a different form or a different set of tasks from *Form I.* In place of the other tests, however, it substitutes the *Arthur Stencil Design Test.* In this test, the subject is supplied with a set of colored cards and a set of cut-outs of different designs and colors. The subject is shown a design that can be produced by superimposing certain ones of the cards provided to him. He must select the right cut-outs and background and put them together in the right order to produce the master design.

A point score is allowed the subject for his performance on each subtest of the *Arthur Scale.* The score depends in some subtests upon the speed with which the task was completed, in others upon the correctness of the solution or the number of graded tasks solved. The point credits for the subtests are summed to give a total point score, and this is converted to a mental age equivalent. An IQ is computed by dividing mental age by chronological age. The IQ's appear to have about the same distribution as for the *Revised Binet.*

There have been a number of other attempts to evaluate intellectual ability through performance tasks, ideally ones that would be usable in different countries and different cultures. One of the most widely known is the *Goodenough Draw-a-Man Test,*[13] in which the child is told simply, "Draw a man—the best man you can draw." The performance is scored on completeness and maturity of representation, not on esthetic qualities.

The individual performance test must generally receive the same evaluation as group non-language tests. For an English-speaking person with normal environmental opportunities and without specialized language or reading handicap, it represents a less efficient way of appraising mental development than the more widely used verbal test. However, as a way of checking on whether there *is* a specialized language handicap it represents a valuable supplemental tool. It makes it possible to check upon individuals who appear retarded on the verbal type of test to see whether the retardation is general or whether it is a localized deficiency in the language area. A performance test such as the *Arthur Point Scale,* which can be given with pantomime instructions, is also useful in testing deaf children, non-English-speaking children, and other types of special groups.

INFANT AND PRESCHOOL TESTS

The first intelligence tests were made for school-age children. However, it was not long before the theoretical interests of child psychologists and the practical needs of child-care and placement agencies stimulated the attempt to develop procedures for appraising intelligence in preschool children and even in infants. Any appraisal procedures with young children obviously had to be individually administered. Also, they had to be based upon behavior that was spontaneously exhibited by or could be elicited from children of the age being studied. Infant tests, therefore, had to take on a very different character from later appraisals. Arnold Gesell [11] pioneered in designing tests based on observation of the child's postural, perceptual, manipulative, and social responses. Does he sit up? Stand up? Walk? Will he turn to look at a light? Notice a face? Can he pick up a block? A spoon? A little pellet? By what type of a grasping motion? How does he react to strange adults? To another infant?

Observations of large numbers of infants showed a typical developmental sequence in the different aspects of the child's development. Performance B followed A, and was followed by C. Norms have been established representing the average age at which a particular behavior manifests itself. The child may be assigned a developmental age, based upon the behavior he shows. Retests after a short interval show the child to be fairly consistent in his level of performance. If he is advanced at one testing, he will tend to be advanced at the other. The developmental schedules provide a moderately reliable picture of the individual *at that point in time.*

What significance does acceleration or retardation in development during the first year or so of life have for predicting later intelligence? The answer is well presented in Table 9.1, which shows the correlation of infant tests given at the ages of 1 to 12 months with intelligence tests at various later ages. The tests during the first 15 months were those of the *California First-Year Mental Scale,* those from 18 months to 5 years were the *California Pre-school Scale,* and those from 6 years on were the *Stanford-Binet.*

The picture seems quite clear. The infant tests give a fairly good prediction of developmental status a few months later, but their value as predictors drops rapidly as the interval increases. The infant tests provide essentially *no* prediction of intellectual status at school age. Whatever factors produce differences in rate of development during the first year or so of life are entirely distinct from those that deter-

Table 9.1.   Correlation of Intelligence Tests During First Year of Life with
Later Measures *

(Correlations based on pooling of successive tests)

Age at Later Test	Age at Initial Test			
	1, 2, 3 mos.	4, 5, 6 mos.	7, 8, 9 mos.	10, 11, 12 mos.
4, 5, 6 mos.	.57			
7, 8, 9 mos.	.42	.72		
10, 11, 12 mos.	.28	.52	.81	
13, 14, 15 mos.	.10	.50	.67	.81
18, 21, 24 mos.	−.04	.23	.39	.60
27, 30, 36 mos.	−.09	.10	.22	.45
42, 48, 54 mos.	−.21	−.16	.02	.27
5, 6, 7 yrs.	−.13	−.07	.02	.20
8, 9, 10 yrs.	−.03	−.06	.07	.19
11, 12, 13 yrs.	.02	−.08	.16	.30
14, 15, 16 yrs.	−.01	−.04	.01	.23
17, 18 yrs.	.05	−.01	.20	.41

* Tests used were: 1–15 months, *California First-Year Mental Scale;* 18
months–5 years, *California Pre-school Scale;* 6 years and older, *Stanford-Binet.*   From Bayley.[3]

mine intellectual level at school age.   It seems, then, that little practical significance can be attached to results from infant developmental
schedules.   They describe an aspect of the child which is temporary
only, not lasting.

There have been a number of different tests prepared primarily for
use with preschool children, i.e., the age range from about 18 months
to 5 years.   As a matter of fact, as we have seen, the *Stanford-Binet
Intelligence Scale* has tests going down to the 2-year level and may be
considered a preschool test.   It would compare very favorably with
the other tests available for this age level, though it is somewhat more
verbal than many of the others.   A good many of the preschool tests
have tended to get away from the verbal material that appears so
heavily in group tests for older children and also in the *Stanford-Binet.*

One test for preschool children that has received wide use is the
Merrill-Palmer Scale.[24]   This is most suitable for children from 2 to
4, though it can be used with children slightly older and slightly
younger.   The test is made up of 38 little subtests, of which only 4
call for verbal response by the child.   A number of the tasks call for

gross motor coordination (standing on one foot) or finer eye-hand coordination (building block tower, cutting with scissors). Form and object perception and motor control combine in a number of form-boards in which cut-outs must be fitted into the appropriate hole. The tasks make use of a variety of materials interesting to the child, blocks, pictures, scissors, balls, etc., so that cooperation can usually be obtained, a real problem with children at these ages.

The *Merrill-Palmer Scale* has fairly satisfactory reliability, especially above about 30 months. Correlations with retests 6 months later have been reported [9] as follows for different age groups:

24 months	.63
30 months	.76
36 months	.78
42 months	.80

The correlation with school-age *Binet* is about .40 for a *Merrill-Palmer* test at age 2; about .45 to .50 for one at age 4.

The *Minnesota Preschool Scale* [15] is another example of a test designed for preschool groups. The 26 tests in this scale tend to be more like those of the *Binet*. Six tests taken at random from one form of the *Scale* are described briefly. They are

Test 2: Pointing Out Objects in Pictures. Card with man, chair, apple, house, and flower on it. Child is asked to point to each in turn.

Test 5: Imitative Drawing. Experimenter makes vertical stroke; then a cross. Child is asked to imitate each in turn.

Test 8: Imitation. A set of 4 cubes, on which experimenter taps in specified sequence. Child instructed to imitate the sequence of taps.

Test 14: Colors. Cards colored red, blue, pink, white, and brown. Child is asked to name the color.

Test 20: Paper Folding. Examiner folds paper with three consecutive folds. Child is asked to copy exactly.

Test 24: Giving Word Opposites. Child is asked to give words meaning opposite of cold, bad, thick, dry, dark, and sick.

Test materials are quite simple. Copying, imitating, and responding to simple verbal relations enter into a number of the tests.

This test appears to be somewhat more reliable than the *Merrill-Palmer*. Correlation between two forms of the test given within a few days of each other was found to be .89. Below 3 years, this test did not correlate very well with later *Binets,* but the *Minnesota* given between 3 and 4 gave a correlation with *Binets* at school age of about .60. However, IQ's on the *Minnesota Preschool Scale* have quite a different spread from those for the *Binet* so a preschool IQ on this test is not readily equated to later *Binet* performance. (See reference 14.)

CULTURE-FREE AND CULTURE-FAIR TESTS

Many workers in the field of aptitude testing have been distressed by the fact that test performance depends upon the experiences the person has had. Every test maker has recognized this to a degree and has tried to base test items upon experiences that would be common to the group for whom the test was planned. But some have perhaps taken too narrow a view of the group for whom the experiences should be common. Certainly the test that incorporates pictures of the usual American house, automobile, or football is not suitable for an Australian Bushman who has seen none of these objects. The typical American test assumes the common core of an American culture. Some critics have gone further and asserted that the typical test is based upon an urban middle-class American culture. Both in its highly verbal content and its emphasis upon speed, competition, and doing one's best, it is said to be centered in the middle-class culture and values.

Several attempts have been made to develop tests that are "culture free," or if not that at least "culture fair." These are closely related to the non-verbal and performance tests described in the previous section, because a culture-free test is almost necessarily non-verbal. It must not only be non-verbal but must also be free of the content of any particular culture.

One attempt to develop such a test is the *Cattell Culture Free Intelligence Test*. The *Cattell Test* is based on the premise that general intelligence is a matter of seeing relationships in the things with which we have to deal, that the ability to see relationships can be tested with simple diagrammatic or pictorial material, and that for a test to be usable in different cultures the pictures should be of forms or objects which are fairly universal, i.e., not peculiar to any cultural group. Items illustrating the different types of tasks are shown in Fig. 9.3. The evidence that the test is in fact useful for widely different cultures is largely lacking, but the tasks constitute one further interesting non-verbal group test that may prove usable, particularly in research studies.

One test that was developed in Great Britain and has been used in many countries is the *Progressive Matrices Test*.[20] The type of item is similar to the last two samples in Figure 9.3. Two types of progression or relationship are established, one in the horizontal and one in the vertical direction. The examinee is required to pick the choice that correctly fills the missing entry in the lower right-hand corner of the matrix.

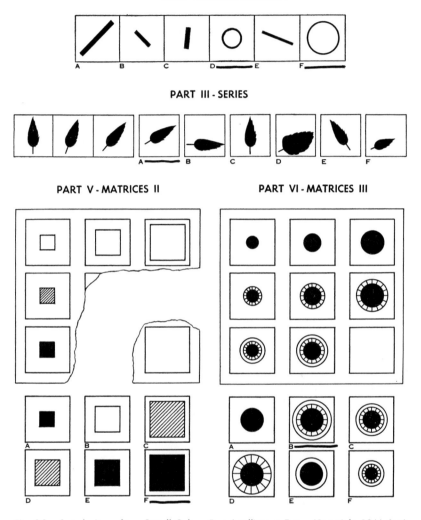

Fig. 9.3. Sample items from *Cattell Culture-Free Intelligence Test*. (Copyright 1944, Institute for Personality and Ability Testing, 1602 Coronado Drive, Champaign, Ill. Reproduced by permission.)

An attempt to develop a test that imposes no penalty on different classes in American society is found in the *Davis-Eells Games*. (Presumably the child is supposed to be naive and not realize that this is a test.) This test series involves no written language but does require quite long oral directions. Types of items include:

1. *Best ways,* in which three pictures are shown in the test booklet, and the examinee is orally instructed to mark the one that is the best way to carry a pile of packages, get over a fence, etc.

2. *Analogies,* in which the analogies are presented in pictures and are of the type, "Glove is to hand as sock is to: arm, leg, foot."

3. *Probabilities,* in which a picture is shown and the examinee must select the one of three orally presented choices that indicates what probably led up to or is represented in the picture.

4. *"Money,"* a task based on complex directions for following certain rules for combining coins to make specified sums.

This test was designed to avoid the cultural biases, particularly socio-economic biases within the American culture, thought to characterize previously existing tests. However, studies of the test in recent years have failed to confirm that it does so. IQ's from the *Davis-Eells Games* are found to have about as high a correlation with indices of socio-economic status as those for any other test. We must conclude that either there basically *is* a relationship between mental ability and socio-economic status, or that the *Davis-Eells Games* has failed to eliminate the bias which its authors believed to characterize other tests. Since this type of test is laborious to give and relatively unreliable, it has little to recommend it on other grounds. We must conclude that it does not appear very useful as a measurement tool at the present time.

GROUP VERSUS INDIVIDUAL TESTS AS MEASURES OF INTELLIGENCE

We have seen that intelligence tests fall into two main patterns, group tests and individual tests. The types of tasks presented to the examinee are a good deal alike in both patterns. However, the two procedures have certain significant differences. These may be summarized as follows:

Group Tests	*Individual Tests*
Problems presented in printed booklet. Read by examinee. Personal contact with examiner a minimum.	Problems presented orally by examiner in face-to-face situation.
Tasks presented and test timed as a unit, or separate time limits for each subtest.	Problems presented one at a time, usually without indication of time limits.
Individual usually responds by selecting one of a limited set of response options printed in the test booklet.	Individual usually responds freely, giving whatever response seems appropriate to him.

These differences in procedure have several important implications for the conduct of testing and for the results that may be obtained from such testing. In the first place, when test tasks are presented orally to the subject and he does not have to read them for himself, his performance is much less dependent upon his reading skills. The child who has lagged behind in acquiring these skills is not penalized for this specific failure. The effect of reading disability upon intelligence test performance is shown clearly in a study [8] comparing individual *Stanford-Binet* scores and group-test scores of retarded, normal, and accelerated readers in the sixth grade. For those children whose reading was a year or more accelerated (in relation to *Stanford-Binet* mental age), group-test IQ averaged 15 points higher than the individual *Stanford-Binet* IQ. Where reading was within + or − 1 year of *Stanford-Binet* mental age, the group test IQ was 2 points higher. Where reading was retarded a year or more, group test IQ fell 8 points below the *Stanford-Binet* IQ. Thus, in this study the accelerated reader received a 15 point bonus, the retarded reader an 8 point penalty in IQ on the printed group test as compared with the individual test orally administered.

The results reported above are probably somewhat extreme, because the particular group test was very verbal in nature and because the study was carried out with elementary-school children, for whom the actual operation of reading still represents something of a task. One may anticipate that less difference would be found for high-school or college students. Furthermore, some current group tests are either partly or wholly non-language in their content and would be relatively independent of reading skills. However, this study points out very clearly the caution with which a group test IQ must be interpreted for a person who departs markedly from the average in his reading skills. A low group test IQ for a poor reader cannot be taken at face value. It should always be checked with a test that does not involve reading.

The presentation of problems one at a time by an examiner is also a factor of some significance in determining what the test is likely to yield. Especially with younger children, maintaining continuity of attention and effort on a group test may be a problem, and variations in this respect are certainly a significant factor in test score. When each problem is separately presented by the examiner, this serves to re-establish the child's orientation to the task and to maintain his effort. What is equally important, the examiner is in a position to observe lapses of interest and effort and to take some account of them in interpreting the results.

The individual intelligence test is essentially a well-standardized interview situation. The tasks to be presented to the examinee are specifically formulated, and detailed standards are provided for evaluating his responses. However, at the same time, the face-to-face relationship of an interview prevails. This offers the alert examiner a wealth of opportunities for observing the examinee and noting poor motivation, distractability, signs of anxiety and upset, and other cues that will help in interpreting the actual test performance. At the same time, the demands upon the examiner are considerably heavier. If valid testing is to result, the tasks must be presented in a standard way, interest and cooperative effort must be maintained, and a uniform standard must be applied in evaluating responses.

The free-response item in the individual test fits into the interview setting of the individual test and reinforces both its strengths and its limitations. Potentially, the free response of the examinee can tell us more about him than the mere record of which option he has chosen from a set of five. There is more of the quality of his own behavior available to us. We can see just how he goes about defining a word, whether by class and differentia (i.e., an orange is a round, orange-colored, citrus fruit) or by use (an orange is to eat). We can note the speed and sureness of his attack on a problem task. But we must also depend on the examiner to interpret and evaluate the responses, and at this point subjectivity is likely to creep into the examining. Careful attention must be paid to the standard samples provided in the test manual, and experience under supervision is indicated before an examiner can expect to give and score an individual intelligence test in a way that will yield results comparable to those of other examiners.

In general, the limitations of group tests are most acute and the advantages of individual tests most pronounced with young children. Printed group tests cannot be used successfully with children below school age. They cannot read and have difficulty in manipulating a pencil, following instructions, or maintaining sustained attention for the period that is required for taking a test. These same factors continue to present fairly serious problems for testing in the primary grades. However, the factor of cost makes individual testing impractical for most large-scale users of tests, so that with older individuals the overwhelming majority of the intelligence tests used are paper-and-pencil group tests.

RELIABILITY AND STABILITY OF MEASURES OF INTELLIGENCE

We have already presented some evidence on the reliability of measures of intelligence in our discussion of infant and preschool tests. The reliability of those early measures is found to be quite modest.

For tests at school age, reliabilities are more promising. Considering the group tests first, we find that when correlations between two forms of the same test are reported for an age group or a grade group they usually fall between .80 and .90. A few are higher. Unfortunately, the authors of some tests report only odd-even reliabilities, and it is difficult to estimate how much these are inflated. (See discussion on pp. 180–181.) Comparisons of different tests are made difficult by variations in the procedure used for estimating reliability and in the type of group for which results are reported.

The correlations reported by the authors [25] between Form L and Form M of the *Stanford-Binet Intelligence Scale* ranged from .85 to .95 for different age groups. For ages from 2 to 6, the median value was .88, whereas for ages above 6 the median was .93.

Since Form L-M was prepared by selecting the better items from both Form L and Form M, one may anticipate that the reliability of the new form is at least as high as these values. The reliability reported in the manual for the *Wechsler Adult Intelligence Scale* is .96 for the verbal IQ, .93 for the performance IQ, and .97 for the full scale IQ. These are split-half reliabilities, and consequently should be discounted somewhat in relation to the reliability of the *Binet*. Split-half reliabilities for the *Wechsler Intelligence Scale for Children* are reported to be .92 at age $7\frac{1}{2}$, .95 at age $10\frac{1}{2}$, and .94 at age $13\frac{1}{2}$.

Though the variations in procedure for estimating reliability and in type of group tested make it difficult to arrive at an unequivocal answer, it does seem that the individual intelligence tests yield a somewhat more reliable measure than do the commonly used group tests. This is probably in part a reflection of the somewhat longer actual testing time, in part a result of more uniform motivation and effort when working under the eye of the examiner.

The reliabilities of intelligence tests are reasonably satisfactory, and they are among the most dependable psychological measuring instruments. However, the chance errors in an IQ are still enough to require that we be quite tentative in our interpretation. Thus, Table 9.2 shows the spread of IQ's that could have been expected on Form M of the *Binet* if that form had been given to a group of pupils all of whom had received exactly the same IQ on Form L. Note that the IQ's spread over a range of more than 25 points, and that less than a third of the cases fall in the center 5-point interval. And it must be remembered that these figures are for the *Stanford-Binet,* one of our most reliable tests. Thus, an IQ of 100 must not be thought of as meaning "exactly 100," but rather "probably between 95 and 105, *very* probably between 90 and 110, almost certainly between 85 and 115."

Table 9.2.   Distribution of Stanford-Binet Form M IQ's for Cases with Identical Form L IQ's

IQ	f
113+	3
108–112	9
103–107	23
98–102	30
93–97	23
88–92	9
87 and below	3

STABILITY OVER A PERIOD OF YEARS

In addition to knowing the precision with which an intelligence test appraises an individual's abilities at a particular time, we would like to know how consistently the individual maintains his position in his group from one year to the next or over a considerable span of years. How confidently can we predict what scholastic aptitude an individual

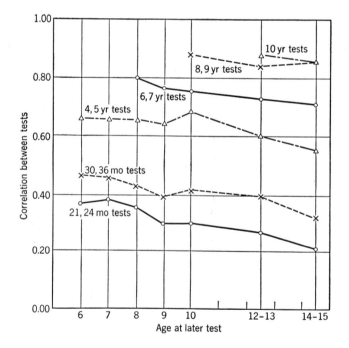

Fig. 9.4.   Effect of age at initial testing and test-retest interval on prediction of later *Stanford-Binet* IQ from earlier test. (Adapted from Honzik, McFarlane, and Allen.[16])

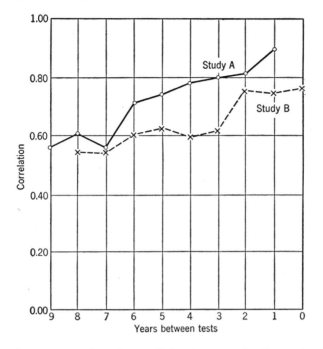

Fig. 9.5. Effect of test-retest interval on prediction of group test intelligence at end of high school from earlier group tests. (Study A adapted from J. E. Anderson.[1]   Study B adapted from R. L. Thorndike.[26])

will show when he is of college age from his performance on a test at age 2?   Age 6?   Age 10?   Evidence on this point is presented in Figs. 9.4 and 9.5.

Figure 9.4 shows the findings from one extensive study using individual tests.   The final test is the *Stanford-Binet* in every case.   The initial test is the *California Pre-school Scale* up through 5 years and the *Stanford-Binet* after that age.   Note that for the early tests the prediction is rather poor and drops as the interval is increased.   A test at age 2 correlates only .37 with one at age 6 and .21 with one at age 14 or 15.   As we go up the age range, however, the correlations are higher and the drop is less.   A test given at age 8 or 9 correlates .88 with one at age 10 and still correlates .86 with one at age 14 or 15. For normal children in a typical environment, a *Stanford-Binet* at age 8 or 9 appears to provide almost as accurate a forecast of ability near the end of high school as would the same test given several years later.

Two sets of data on stability of group-test performance over time are presented in Fig. 9.5.   The two follow the same general pattern, though they differ a good deal in detail.   As we go back further in time, the correlation coefficients tend to drop more or less steadily. The earlier tests at around grade 3 or 4 correlate perhaps .50 to .60 with the final test, but for a test in grade 9 or 10 the correlation is .70 to .80. In these studies of group tests, the tests that were used differed at the different ages. For this reason, it is not clear how much the lower correlation over the longer intervals is due to growth changes in the subjects over a span of years and how much it is due to changes in the material included in the tests. From the practical point of view, Fig. 9.5 suggests that a group intelligence test needs to be supplemented by new testing every 3 or 4 years if pupil records are to provide an accurate indication of current ability level.

THE PRACTICAL IMPORTANCE OF INDIVIDUAL DIFFERENCES IN MEASURES OF INTELLIGENCE

To what extent are the individual differences that are brought out by tests of intelligence of importance in the practical affairs of life? Do they enable us to predict to a useful degree how an individual will perform in school, on a job, or in other life adjustments?

INTELLIGENCE AND SCHOOL SUCCESS

First, let us consider academic success. From the many hundreds of investigations of intelligence test scores in relation to academic success, a number of conclusions can safely be drawn. These may be summarized as follows:

1. *The Correlation of Intelligence Test Score with School Marks Is Substantial.* Viewing all the hundreds of correlation coefficients that have been reported, a figure of .50 to .60 might be taken as fairly representative. Though this constitutes a very definite relationship, it is only necessary to turn back to Fig. 5.7 and the discussion of correlation on p. 119 to realize that there are still many marked discrepancies between intelligence test score and what a particular youngster does in school.

2. *Higher Correlations Have Been Found in Elementary Schools Than in High Schools and in High Schools Than in Colleges.* Past studies have indicated a drop in correlation from perhaps .70 in elementary school to .60 in high school and .50 in college. The drop in correlation is probably to be explained by the decreased range of intellectual ability in the college groups. A relatively small percentage from the lower half of a school population go on to college, and specific colleges draw from an even more restricted ability range. Though

more and more young people are going to college, the clientele of specific colleges continues to be fairly homogeneous in ability.

3. *Previous School Achievement Has Given Correlations with Later School Success as High as or Higher Than Intelligence Test Score.* In predicting college marks, for example, high-school record has usually shown correlations at least as high as those resulting from a scholastic aptitude test at entrance.

4. *Intelligence Test and Achievement Combined Give Still Better Prediction.* By pooling information on previous school achievement and intelligence test score, the correlation with later school achievement can be raised above that yielded by either factor alone. The two types of information supplement one another.

5. *Intelligence Tests Correlate Higher with Standardized Measures of Achievement Than with School Marks.* Correlations between an intelligence test and total score on an achievement battery in the .70's or even .80's are not unusual. Thus, for one large eleventh-grade group the correlation between the *California Test of Mental Maturity* and total achievement on the *Progressive Achievement Test* was found to be .71,[4] whereas for a group from grades 4, 5, and 6 it was .84. Another report [7] gives correlations of .84 and .78 for grades 5 and 7 for the correlation between the *Pintner General Ability Test* and the *Metropolitan Achievement Test.*

6. *The Degree to Which Intelligence Tests Are Related to Academic Success Depends Upon the Subject Matter.* As one would expect, the more academic subjects, which depend more completely upon the same kinds of verbal and numerical symbols as those that bulk so large in intelligence tests, show the higher correlations. Thus, one summary of studies in secondary and higher education [21] reports an average correlation of .46 with natural science grades and .38 with English grades and foreign language grades but only .28 with shop work and .22 with grades in domestic science.

The fact that intelligence tests correlate with academic achievement and school progress is unquestioned. From the very way in which the tests were assembled it could hardly be otherwise. How these facts should be capitalized upon in educational planning and individual guidance is a more troublesome matter. We will return to it later in the chapter.

INTELLIGENCE IN RELATION TO OCCUPATIONAL LEVEL

We turn our attention now to out-of-school accomplishments and consider how intelligence test scores relate to achievement in the world of work. There are two types of questions that we may raise: (1)

How do workers in different kinds of jobs compare in measured intelligence? (2) Within a given kind of job, to what extent is intelligence related to job success?

In relation to the first question, we have a good deal of evidence stemming from the testing of recruits carried out during World Wars I and II. Data for a selection of representative jobs are shown in Table 9.3. This table shows the 10th, 25th, 50th, 75th, and 90th per-

Table 9.3. AGCT Standard Scores of Occupational Groups in World War II

Occupational Groups	Percentile				
	10	25	50	75	90
Accountant	114	121	129	136	143
Teacher	110	117	124	132	140
Lawyer	112	118	124	132	141
Bookkeeper, general	108	114	122	129	138
Chief clerk	107	114	122	131	141
Draftsman	99	109	120	127	137
Postal clerk	100	109	119	126	136
Clerk, general	97	108	117	125	133
Radio repairman	97	108	117	125	136
Salesman	94	107	115	125	133
Store manager	91	104	115	124	133
Tool maker	92	101	112	123	129
Stock clerk	85	99	110	120	127
Machinist	86	99	110	120	127
Policeman	86	96	109	118	128
Electrician	83	96	109	118	124
Meat cutter	80	94	108	117	126
Sheet metal worker	82	95	107	117	126
Machine operator	77	89	103	114	123
Automobile mechanic	75	89	102	114	122
Carpenter, general	73	86	101	113	123
Baker	69	83	99	113	123
Truck driver, heavy	71	83	98	111	120
Cook	67	79	96	111	120
Laborer	65	76	93	108	119
Barber	66	79	93	109	120
Miner	67	75	87	103	119
Farm worker	61	70	86	103	115
Lumberjack	60	70	85	100	116

Adapted from N. Stewart.[23]

centiles on *Army General Classification Test* standard score (based on standardization with an average value of 100 and a standard deviation of 20). A marked gradient is noticed from such occupations as accountant, teacher, and lawyer to such occupations as barber, miner, and lumberjack. The gradient follows fairly closely the educational requirements or average educational background for each occupation. In general, one may say that occupations select out individuals jointly on the basis of educational level and of intelligence. Whether intelligence enters as a significant factor excepting as it determines educational level is more difficult to determine. In any event, the net result is appreciable difference between different occupational groups in performance on intelligence tests.

While noticing the differences between groups, one must not forget the substantial range of score within each group. Individuals differing widely in abstract intelligence function together in the same occupation. Thus, the upper 10 per cent of meat cutters did as well on the *AGCT* as the average lawyer. The bottom 10 per cent of lawyers showed no more intellectual ability than the upper 10 per cent of miners. In spite of group differences in average score, there are still wide *individual* differences *within* groups.

INTELLIGENCE AND JOB SUCCESS

What can we say about the relationship of intelligence test score to success within particular jobs? A summary of the findings reported in a number of different studies is presented in Table 9.4. With the

Table 9.4. Relationship of Intelligence Test Score to Measures of Job Success

Type of Job	Median Correlation with Job Success	Per Cent Significantly Positive Correlations *	Number of Coefficients
Clerical workers	.35	70	84
Supervisors	.40	78	9
Salesmen	.33	100	4
Sales clerks	−.09	6	18
Protective services	.25	33	6
Skilled workers	.55	100	6
Semiskilled workers	.20	47	45
Unskilled workers	.08	31	13

Adapted from E. E. Ghiselli and C. W. Brown.[12]
* Significant at 5 per cent level.

exception of sales clerks, the median correlation is positive in each case. But for unskilled and semiskilled workers the correlations are quite small. They are higher for clerical workers, supervisors, and skilled workers, though only in the case of the skilled workers are they as high as the typical correlations with school success. In part this may be due to limitations in the *criterion* of job success. Whether success is measured by supervisors' ratings, as is usually the case, or by some index of production on the job, the indicator is likely to be unreliable and biased by a number of considerations that have nothing to do with the real efficiency of the worker. In so far as this is true, no test given to the individual can be expected to predict the criterion.

All in all, we may conclude that (1) intelligence is related to occupational group membership and (2) though the relationship of intelligence test score to job success is usually positive, it is likely to be quite low. Prediction of out-of-school achievement appears a good deal less accurate than prediction of school achievement.

INTERPRETATION OF GROUP DIFFERENCES IN MEASURED INTELLIGENCE

As soon as the first intelligence tests were developed, investigators started administering them to different kinds of groups and studying group differences in performance on the tests. They compared the sexes, different age groups, groups of different racial or national origin, urban and rural groups, groups from different parts of the country, groups from different socio-economic levels, and so forth. The findings from these studies were fairly consistent in showing appreciable group differences. Lower score on intelligence tests was associated with lower socio-economic status, living in a rural area, living in the Southern or Southwestern United States, being an Indian or Negro, being in an immigrant family from the south of Europe, or being over 40 years old. However, the interpretation of these findings has been a source of a good deal of confusion and conflict.

The first naive tendency was to interpret group differences in intelligence test performance as an indication of innate hereditary differences between the groups in question. For example, the lower test performance of the children of laboring class parents was interpreted as indicating basic genetic differences between that group and the white-collar group. Now, such basic genetic differences have not been *disproved,* but many lines of evidence have made psychologists much more cautious in interpreting group differences in intelligence test performance. Many studies have pointed out the role of life experience in influencing test scores and have made us realize how dangerous it is to make any comparison of groups whose experiences differ radically. We shall consider some of the relevant evidence.

The testing in the United States in World War I and in World War II has made possible a comparison of the level of performance of the military recruit population in 1918 with that in 1940 to 1945. Using a somewhat revised edition of the 1918 *Army Alpha Test* with a sample of World War II recruits, it was possible to estimate the *Army General Classification Test* equivalents of different scores on *Army Alpha* and thus to compare the performance of the two recruit populations. It was found [27] that the average World War II recruit surpassed 83 per cent of the World War I group.

A similar comparative study, on a smaller scale, was made of children in certain mountain counties of eastern Tennessee.[30] When 1940 performance was compared with that in 1930, it was found that the average IQ for children in these counties had risen from 82.4 to 92.2, a gain of 9.8 points. This gain paralleled a very considerable increase in accessibility and cultural opportunities in the counties in question.

Comparisons of national groups in their own countries have failed to substantiate differences found between immigrant groups in the U. S.[10] Studies of Negro children in New York City have shown a tendency for the IQ's to be higher for those children who had spent a longer time in New York.[18] Studies of foster children have found a level of intelligence for these youngsters above what would have been predicted from the intelligence or social level of their biological parents.[22]

All these findings point to the fact that intelligence test score depends upon experience. Where groups differ widely in experience, differences in test score may be expected to result. Thus, in the United States between 1918 and 1940 the median schooling of 18-year-olds increased from about 8½ years to about 10½ years. In addition, radio sets appeared in over 80 per cent of the homes of the country. Good roads pushed out into the rural areas, so that it was relatively easy to get to town. These are only some of the social and cultural changes. These changes had their impact upon test performance. A more educated population, exposed to more experiences and perhaps especially to more extensive and varied use of language, did better on the tests.

The present discussion does not negate the significance of intelligence test differences in *individuals*. These differences are large even for individuals who have had closely similar environmental opportunities. Environment and experience are not the whole story or perhaps even a major part of the story. However, the discussion should make us slow to accept group differences uncritically on their face value. It should also make us realize that in interpreting the performance of an individual, some allowance must be made for the environmental opportunity he has had. An IQ of 90 has a rather different meaning for a Negro child who spent his early years in a share-cropper's cabin in the rural South from what it has for the son of the local banker.

USING INTELLIGENCE TEST RESULTS IN SCHOOLS

There are, in general, three types of settings in which standardized tests are used in schools, and intelligence tests should be considered in relation to each of these. Standardized tests may enter into administrative policy as a basis for administrative decisions on such matters as class grouping, promotion, eligibility for certain classes and curricula, and the like. Standardized tests may be used by the classroom teacher as aids to understanding the individual pupils with whom he must deal and in making adaptations and adjustments to their individual needs. Tests may be used by the guidance staff of the school in planning the most effective use of special resources for diagnostic and remedial teaching, in helping the pupil and his family arrive at sound and realistic educational and vocational plans, and in helping understand personal adjustment crises when they arise. We may consider intelligence tests in each of these contexts.

INTELLIGENCE TESTS AND THE SCHOOL ADMINISTRATION

Intelligence tests are likely to enter into the actions of the school administration either (1) through a policy of using test results as one basis for forming the group for a classroom or (2) through regulations specifying score levels that permit or require some special action, e.g., assignment to a slow-learning class, eligibility to take algebra, eligibility for a special school, etc. What is an appropriate attitude toward administrative actions of these sorts?

Grouping by Intellectual Ability. The policy of forming class groups at least in part on the basis of the intellectual level of the pupils remains a common one. In 1947 to 1948 more than half of city school systems reporting [19] used ability grouping in some form in one or more schools. However, the procedure remains a controversial one. In part this is due to the varied and somewhat contradictory results obtained in studies of the effects of ability grouping.[5] In part it is due to the variety of specific practices subsumed under the same label of "ability grouping" or "homogeneous grouping." In part it is based upon the different initial biases of those discussing the problem.

It is probably impossible to make any single general evaluation of ability grouping that would apply to all instances of the practice. It can be pointed out that grouping together pupils of like mental ages is only a *first step* to permit adapting class program and procedures to the abilities of the pupils in the class. What is most important is the adaptations that are actually made in materials and procedures after the grouping has been carried out—and also what attitudes exist or can be developed in the community toward the grouping and the adjustments that accompany it. It should also be noted that groups formed on the basis of intelligence-test scores will still be quite heterogeneous with respect to academic skills. The correlations of intelligence and achievement, and of different aspects of achievement are low enough so that forming groups on any one measure will still leave quite a range of performance on any of the others. In a departmentalized program, as in high school, effective grouping in separate subject areas can be based on a combination of an intelligence test and a measure of achievement in the subject area. Though a general evaluation of achievement can be combined with intelligence test score for elementary school pupils, it is not possible to get a group homogeneous for all subject areas.

Many of both the gains and hazards of ability grouping have been claimed to lie in relatively intangible areas of interest, attitude, and adjustment. Evaluations in these areas have generally been quite inadequate. Thus, it is still largely a matter of opinion whether the bright child develops better work habits and leadership traits or feelings of snobbishness and superiority from being in a special class group.

Ability grouping for the bulk of pupils is one issue, and special classes for the relatively extreme deviate is a somewhat different one.

How about the highest and lowest 2 or 3 or 5 per cent in intelligence? Here we must recognize that special administrative provisions are possible only in a community of some size. Unless there are perhaps 500 children per grade in the school system, there will not be enough extreme deviates to fill a class group. The problem of the extreme deviate becomes most acute in the case of the low deviate, because of the obvious problems that the slow learners have in adapting to the activities and tempo of a regular classroom. Special class groups have not been a universal panacea, but they do permit adaptation of the type of class activities and the rate of progress to the interests and abilities of the slower learners.

The very bright child is usually a less conspicuous problem in the regular class. He gets the regular work done. His boredom is less apparent. Furthermore, the alert teacher can often provide supplementary activities which will keep him profitably occupied. However, there is evidence [17] that children of high ability who are placed in special groups can master the regular school curriculum more rapidly than they would in regular classes, or engage in a wide range of enrichment activities without falling behind children in regular schools. Furthermore, there is no real evidence that membership in special class groups results in undesirable personality attributes in these children. In view of the importance of individuals of high ability for our society and in view of the long period of training that most of them must undergo to take a role in the professional groups of our society, special provisions to accelerate or enrich their early training would seem to be a sound social provision where such provisions are administratively feasible.

Intelligence Test Score as an Administrative Prerequisite. Intelligence test results enter into administrative actions when a certain level of intelligence is specified as a prerequisite for some action in relation to a pupil. Generally speaking, the relationship of intelligence test score to educational progress or success is low enough and the variety of factors involved is great enough so that rigid administrative standards on intelligence seem rather questionable. Intelligence is often a factor that should receive consideration, together with other factors, in arriving at a decision with respect to any individual. But room for flexibility of action is needed, in the light of all relevant factors. An administration should formulate general policy with respect to the use of intelligence tests for admitting pupils to special groups, but the policy should be one which permits actions on individual cases to be taken in the light of a variety of relevant factors.

INTELLIGENCE TESTS AND THE CLASSROOM TEACHER

The classroom teacher will want to use intelligence test results as an aid to understanding each pupil in the class and to providing the school experiences that will be most helpful to that pupil. The child's level as measured by an intelligence test provides probably the best single clue available to the teacher as to the child's potentialities for learning the abstract symbolic aspects of the school curriculum. The test results provide a guide as to what can reasonably be expected of each pupil: whether the pupil should be expected to move along as rapidly as the rest of the class, whether the pupil's achievement is falling enough behind expectation to suggest the need for special diagnostic or remedial procedures, or whether the pupil's abilities are enough ahead of those of the bulk of the class so that the teacher should try to provide special activities and opportunities for enriching the regular program.

There are certain cautions that need to be observed when the classroom teacher makes use of intelligence test scores for his pupils. An enumeration of the pitfalls may help the reader to avoid them.

1. The general intelligence test, especially the group test, is a measure of ability to work with symbols, abstract ideas, and their relationships. This is one quite limited type of ability. The test does not encompass ability to work with things or people, or perhaps the ability to solve many types of concrete and practical problems. The child who is low on an intelligence test will probably have trouble with the academic aspects of the conventional school curriculum. However, he may have a good level of skill or ability in the many non-abstract aspects of living—mechanical, social, artistic, musical. The teacher should seek these strengths, capitalize upon them, and build upon them. *Above all, the teacher must recognize that intelligence test score is not a measure of personal worth and must avoid rejecting the child whose aptitude for academic pursuits is low.*

2. The verbal group intelligence test that is ordinarily used for school-wide testing is sufficiently dependent upon reading and arithmetical skills that a low test score must be interpreted cautiously for a poor reader or low achiever in arithmetical skills. If possible, individuals of this sort should be tested also with an individual test or a non-verbal group test to determine whether the low performance is due to limited ability, or whether it is a reflection of limited reading and number skills.

3. Intelligence test results for a child whose social and cultural background differs radically from that of the rest of the group should be interpreted with caution. The possibility of some degree of environmental deprivation should be borne in mind.

4. If it is known or suspected that a child was emotionally disturbed at the time of testing, results should be considered quite tentative. Motivation and effort are needed for sound test results.

5. The standard error of measurement should always be very real to the test interpreter. An IQ of 90 should always signify to the teacher "IQ somewhere between 80 and 100."

INTELLIGENCE TESTS AND THE GUIDANCE STAFF

Intelligence tests have their most obvious function in the educational program as sources of information important to persons responsible for counseling and helping the child with problems of personal and social adjustment, making provisions for special educational activities for him, helping him to decide on appropriate educational objectives, and working with him to formulate vocational plans. In plans and decisions of all these types, it is important to have a clear picture of the pupil's intellectual abilities as one aspect of the total picture of the pupil as an individual.

In educational guidance information about scholastic aptitude is especially important. This information should receive very serious consideration in deciding what is an appropriate educational objective for the pupil; i.e., whether to plan for college and if so the kind of college to plan for, or what type of high school curriculum to select. In vocational counseling, more specialized ability measures, of the kinds we shall consider in the next chapter, are desirable as a supplement to the general intelligence test, but these specialized tests are not so important for educational planning. For understanding a child who is having problems in school, whether with his school work or his personal adjustments, an estimate of his intellectual level is essential. As we have indicated elsewhere, individual tests and non-language tests are highly desirable supplements to the usual group test when any reading or language handicap is suspected.

The specific situations and circumstances under which intelligence tests may be used in guidance are so many and varied that they cannot each be discussed here. Some further consideration is given to tests in the guidance program in Chapter 18.

SUMMARY STATEMENT

Tests of ability include tests of achievement and of aptitude. Though aptitude tests usually depend less directly upon specific teaching than do achievement tests, it must be recognized that any test performance is in some degree a function of the individual's background of experience. Aptitude tests are distinguished at least in part by their function—to predict future accomplishments.

Among the most thoroughly explored and widely used aptitude tests are tests of intelligence. As these have been developed, they tend to emphasize abstract intelligence, the ability to deal with ideas and symbols, and may even be thought of as scholastic aptitude tests.

The two main patterns of tests have been group tests and individual tests. Group tests, resembling the short-answer achievement test in format, are much more economical to use and are satisfactory for many purposes when the examinees are normal groups of school age or older.

However, the individual tests have a number of advantages and are useful particularly with (1) young children, (2) emotionally disturbed cases, and (3) cases with special educational disabilities.

Special tests have been developed for infant and preschool groups, for groups with educational and language handicaps, and for groups from varied cultures and social classes. These may be of practical value in special cases, though they serve more often as research tools.

Intelligence test results for school-age children are about as reliable as any of our psychological measurement tools. The widely used individual tests such as the *Stanford-Binet Intelligence Scale* and the *Wechsler Intelligence Scales* are probably somewhat more reliable than the typical group test, though the differences are not large. In spite of the high reliability, appreciable differences may be expected between one testing and another.

When intelligence test scores are studied in relation to achievement in the world, the most clear-cut relationships are with academic achievement. However, it is also true that there are substantial differences in test performance between persons in different types of jobs. Furthermore, success in at least some types of jobs has been found to be related to the abstract intelligence measured by our tests.

Group differences in intelligence (i.e., sex, race, age differences) must be interpreted quite tentatively, in view of the differences in background for these different groups. However, *individual* differences in intelligence are important facts, which we need to use wisely in helping individuals in their adjustment to the world of the school and of work.

REFERENCES

1. Anderson, J. E., The limitations of infant and preschool tests in the measurement of intelligence, *J. Psychol.,* 8, 1939, 351–379.
2. Arthur, Grace, *A point scale of performance tests,* 2nd ed., New York, Commonwealth Fund, 1943.
3. Bayley, Nancy, Consistency and variability in the growth of intelligence from birth to eighteen years, *J. genet. Psychol.,* 75, 1949, 165–196.
4. Clark, W. W., *Questions and answers regarding the California Test of Mental Maturity,* Los Angeles, California Test Bureau, 1948.
5. Cornell, Ethel L., Effects of ability grouping determinable from published studies, in The grouping of pupils, *Nat. Soc. Study Educ., 35th Yrbk.,* Pt. I, 1936, 289–304.
6. Derner, G. F., M. Aborn, and A. H. Canter, The reliability of the Wechsler-Bellevue subtests and scales, *J. consult. Psychol.,* 14, 1950, 172–179.

7. Durost, W. N., and G. A. Prescott, An improved method of comparing a capacity measure and an achievement measure at the elementary school level, *Educ. Psychol. Meas.*, **12**, 1952, 741–751.
8. Durrell, D. D., The influence of reading ability on intelligence measures, *J. educ. Psychol.*, **24**, 1933, 412–416.
9. Ebert, E., and Katherine Simmons, The Brush Foundation study of child growth and development, I, Psychometric tests, *Monogr. Soc. Res. Child Develpm.*, **8**, No. 2, 1943,
10. Franzblau, R. N., Race differences in mental and physical traits, *Arch. Psychol.*, 1935, No. 177.
11. Gesell, A., et al., *The first five years of life: A guide to the study of the pre-school child*, New York, Harper, 1940.
12. Ghiselli, E. E., and C. W. Brown, The effectiveness of intelligence tests in the selection of workers, *J. appl. Psychol.*, **32**, 1943, 575–580.
13. Goodenough, Florence L., *Measurement of intelligence by drawings*, Yonkers, N. Y., World Book, 1926.
14. Goodenough, Florence L., and Katherine M. Maurer, The mental growth of children from two to fourteen years; a study of the predictive value of the Minnesota Preschool Scales, *Univ. Minn. Inst. Child Welf. Monogr.*, No. 19, 1942.
15. Goodenough, Florence L., Katherine M. Maurer, and M. J. Van Wagenen, *Minnesota Preschool Scales: Manual of instructions*, Minneapolis, Minn., Educational Test Bureau, 1940.
16. Honzik, Marjorie P., Jean W. McFarlane, and Lucille Allen, The stability of mental test performance between two and eighteen years, *J. exp. Educ.*, **17**, 1948, 309–324.
17. Justman, J., A comparison of the functioning of intellectually gifted children enrolled in special progress classes in the junior high school, unpublished doctor's dissertation, Columbia University, 1953.
18. Klineberg, O., *Negro intelligence and selective migration*, New York, Columbia University Press, 1935.
19. National Education Association, Research Division, Trends in city school organization, 1938 to 1948, *Res. Bull.*, **27**, 1949, 4–39.
20. Raven, J. C., *Progressive matrices*, London, H. K. Lewis, 1956 (U. S. Distributor, Psychological Corp.).
21. St. John, C. W., Educational achievement in relation to intelligence as shown by teachers' marks, promotions and scores in standard tests in certain elementary grades, *Harvard Univ. Stud. Educ.*, **15**, 1930.
22. Skodak, Marie, Children in foster homes: A study of mental development, *Univ. Ia. Stud. Child Welf.*, **16**, No. 1, 1939.
23. Stewart, Naomi, A.G.C.T. scores of army personnel grouped by occupations, *Occupations*, **26**, 1947, 5–41.
24. Stutsman, Rachel, *Mental measurement of pre-school children, with a guide for the administration of the Merrill-Palmer Scale of Mental Tests*, Yonkers, N. Y., World Book, 1931.
25. Terman, Lewis M., and Maud A. Merrill, *Stanford-Binet Intelligence Scale, Manual for the Third Revision, Form L-M*, Boston, Houghton Mifflin, 1960.

26. Thorndike, R. L., The prediction of intelligence at college entrance from earlier tests, *J. educ. Psychol.*, **38**, 1947, 129–148.
27. Tuddenham, R. D., Soldier intelligence in World Wars I and II, *Amer. Psychologist*, **3**, 1948, 54–56.
28. Wechsler, David, *Wechsler Adult Intelligence Scale*, New York, Psychological Corp., 1955.
29. Wechsler, David, *Wechsler Intelligence Scale for Children: Manual*, New York, Psychological Corp., 1949.
30. Wheeler, L. R., A comparative study of the intelligence of east Tennessee mountain children, *J. educ. Psychol.*, **33**, 1942, 321–334.

SUGGESTED ADDITIONAL READING

Bayley, Nancy, On the growth of intelligence, *Amer. psychologist*, **10**, 1955, 805–818.

Bradway, Katherine P., C. W. Thompson, and R. B. Cravens, Preschool IQ's after 25 years, *J. educ. psychol.*, **49**, 1958, 278–281.

Cronbach, Lee J., *Essentials of psychological testing*, 2nd ed., New York, Harper, 1960, Chapters 7 and 8.

Dreger, Ralph Mason, and K. S. Miller, Comparative psychological studies of Negroes and Whites in the United States, *Psychol. Bull.*, **57**, 5, 1960, 361–402.

Eells, Kenneth Walter, et al., *Intelligence and cultural differences*, Chicago, University of Chicago Press, 1951.

Froehlich, Clifford P., and K. B. Hoyt, *Guidance testing*, 3rd ed., Chicago, Science Research Associates, 1959, Chapter 5.

Harris, Chester W., Editor, *Encyclopedia of educational research*, 3rd ed., New York, Macmillan, 1960, pp. 59–62, 715–717, 817–822.

Miner, John B., *Intelligence in the United States*, New York, Springer, 1957.

QUESTIONS FOR DISCUSSION

1. It has been proposed that all intelligence tests should really be called scholastic aptitude tests. What are the merits and the limitations of this proposal?

2. Why is it better to depend upon a good intelligence test for an estimate of a pupil's intelligence than upon ratings by teachers?

3. In each of the following situations would you elect to use a group intelligence test or an individual intelligence test? Why?

a. You are studying a boy with a serious speech impediment.

b. You are selecting students for a school of nursing.

c. You are preparing to counsel a high-school senior on his educational and vocational plans.

d. You are making a study of the Mexican children in a school system in Arizona.

e. You are working with a group of delinquents in a state institution.

4. In which of the following situations would you routinely first give the *Arthur Point Scale* rather than the *Stanford-Binet?* Why did you decide as you did?

    a. For testing Puerto Rican children entering school in New York City.
    b. For selecting children for a special class of gifted children.
    c. For evaluating intelligence in a school for the deaf.
    d. For studying children who have reading problems.

5. What are the implications for child placement agencies of the data on infant tests presented on p. 236?

6. Why do two different intelligence tests given to the same pupil quite frequently give two different IQ's?

7. Are the usual group intelligence tests more useful for guidance for professional occupations or for skilled occupations? Why?

8. A news article reported that a young woman who had been committed to a mental hospital with an IQ of 62 had been able to raise her IQ to 118 during the 3 years she had spent there. What is misleading about this news statement? What factors could account for the difference between the two IQ's?

9. In what respects are intelligence tests better than high-school grades as predictors of college success? In what respects are they less good?

10. Why do intelligence tests show higher correlations with standardized achievement tests than they do with school grades?

11. Comment on the statement: "College admissions officers should discount scholastic aptitude test scores of applicants who come from low socio-economic groups."

12. You are a fourth-grade teacher. You have given a group intelligence test to your class and gotten IQ's from it. What additional information would you want to have on the pupils. What sorts of specific action and plans might grow out of the test results?

13. An eighth grader has received the following IQ's on the *Lorge-Thorndike Intelligence Test, Verbal:* Grade 4—98, Grade 6—112, Grade 8—102. What would be the best figure to represent his "true" scholastic aptitude?

14. A school in a prosperous community gave *Stanford-Binet* intelligence tests to all entering kindergartners and all first graders who had not been tested in kindergarten within the first week or two of school. How desirable and useful a procedure is this? Why?

Chapter 10

▼

The Measurement of Special Aptitudes

The tests that we reviewed in Chapter 9 were tests of general mental ability. In most cases they resulted in a single score that represented an over-all appraisal of the individual's ability to deal with abstract ideas and relationships. However, we found that some of them did produce two or more scores of a more specialized nature that were designed to provide more specific and analytical information about the individual, i.e., the verbal and performance IQ's of the *Wechsler* scales. The concern for specific information on more restricted segments of the ability domain has led to the development of test batteries and single tests to measure specialized aptitudes. It is these tests that we shall consider in the present chapter. We will direct our attention first to batteries and tests designed for vocational guidance and vocational selection. Then we will consider specialized tests for prognosis and prediction in special school subjects and in special types of schools. Finally, we will take a brief look at tests in the specialized fields of art and music.

VOCATIONAL APTITUDE BATTERIES AND TESTS

One of the early practical concerns of psychologists was in guiding young people into the types of work in which they would be happy and successful and in selecting for an employer those men who would be efficient and satisfied in the jobs that he was trying to fill. As psychologists began to study jobs, it seemed apparent that different ones required different special abilities as well as different levels of general mental ability. The automotive mechanic required a good deal of mechanical knowledge, but little verbal fluency, while the lawyer needed verbal comprehension but not mechanical skill. The bookkeeper needed good ability with numbers, while the watchmaker needed fine coordination in his finger movements. The ability requirements of jobs appeared to differ along a number of specialized dimensions.

At the same time, research demonstrated that human abilities are to some degree specialized. This has been shown in studies of the correlations between different tests. Consider the correlations shown in Table 10.1 between six tests of a battery used for classification of

Table 10.1. Intercorrelations of Selected Air Force Aptitude Tests

	1	2	3	4	5	6
1. Reading Comprehension	. . .	.50	.05	.23	.13	.11
2. Navigator Information	.50	. . .	.16	.25	.17	.15
3. Numerical Operations	.05	.16	. . .	.44	.27	.11
4. Dial and Table Reading	.23	.25	.44	. . .	.39	.23
5. Speed of Identification	.13	.17	.27	.39	. . .	.43
6. Spatial Orientation	.11	.15	.11	.23	.43	. . .

men in the U. S. Air Force.[5] Note that the correlations between the first two tests are relatively high. These are both tests that are quite verbal in nature and they appear to define a factor of ability to deal with verbal relationships. Tests 3 and 4 are both numerical tests and are substantially correlated. Tests 5 and 6, which correlate substantially with each other, both involve speed of visual perception. Note that the correlations of tests 1 and 2 with 3 through 6 are quite low. The verbal tests are measuring abilities quite different from those measured by the other four. The numerical and perceptual tests are not as clearly distinct from one another, but the correlations of tests 3 and 4 with 5 and 6 are less than the intercorrelation of 3 and 4 or the intercorrelation of 5 and 6. Thus, it appears that our six tests measure three somewhat distinct abilities: a verbal ability measured by 1 and 2, a numerical ability measured by 3 and 4, and a perceptual ability measured by 5 and 6. These abilities are not *entirely* independent but are tied together, perhaps by a common element of general mental ability running through all of them. However, the three are sufficiently different to justify separate measurement of them.

There has been a large volume of research on the organization and structure of human abilities during the last 50 years. Much of it has employed a technique known as *factor analysis* to try to tease out the underlying mental factors. Factor analysis starts with a table of correlations such as we have shown in Table 10.1 (usually, however, a much larger table) and tries to identify the pattern of underlying factors that could have produced the observed relationships. The techniques are computationally laborious and statistically involved, and we shall not go into them in any detail here.*   We shall report merely that the research has indicated that one can distinguish quite a number of special ability factors, such as verbal comprehension, word fluency, numerical fluency, perceptual speed, mechanical knowledge, spatial visualizing, and inductive and deductive reasoning.   It is also true that most of these abilities are to some degree related to each other.   The tests of general intelligence discussed in the last chapter reflect a pooling of several of these separate factors, together with accentuation of their common core.

Through theoretical research on the nature of abilities on the one hand and the applied research on the validity of specific tests for specific jobs on the other, psychologists have been guided in the design of aptitude test batteries for use in educational and vocational guidance and in personnel selection and classification.   Since about 1940, these batteries have come to occupy quite central positions in the testing scene, so we will need to study them in some detail.   First, we will examine two of the most widely used batteries, one oriented primarily toward school use and the other toward industrial use.   Then we will review some of the evidence on validity and consider the advantages and limitations of a battery of this sort.

The Differential Aptitude Test Battery.   This battery was produced by the Psychological Corporation in 1947 as a guidance battery for use at the secondary-school level.   Some attention was paid to getting measures of separate and relatively uncorrelated abilities, but the main attempt was to get measures that would be meaningful to high school counselors.   As a result, the intercorrelations of the tests, with the exception of a test of clerical speed and accuracy, are about .50.   However, the reliabilities of the separate tests average about .90 and are enough higher than the test intercorrelations to assure us that each test measures abilities somewhat distinct from those measured by the others.   The eight subtests are briefly described and illustrated below.

1. *Verbal Reasoning.*   Items are of the double-analogies type, i.e., ? is to A as B is to ?.   Two sets of answer choices are provided and one must be picked from each set to complete the analogy.

Example

3.   . . . . .is to wide as thin is to. . . . .

1. store	2. narrow	3. nothing	4. street
A. fat	B. weight	C. man	D. present

* For an introductory exposition of factor analysis see Guilford, J. P. *Psychometric Methods.* New York, McGraw-Hill Book Co., 1954.

2. *Numerical Ability.* Consists of numerical problems emphasizing comprehension rather than simple computational facility.

Example

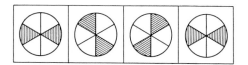

$$\frac{1}{4} \div \frac{1}{8} =$$

A $\frac{1}{32}$
B $\frac{1}{8}$
C $\frac{1}{2}$
D 2
E none of these

3. *Abstract Reasoning.* A series of problem figures establishes a relationship or sequence, and the examinee must pick the choice that continues the series.

Example

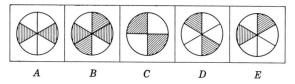

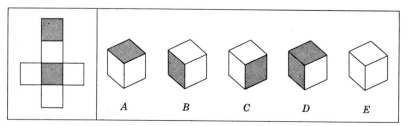

    A   B   C   D   E

4. *Space Relations.* A diagram of a flat figure is shown. The examinee must visualize and indicate which solid figure or figures could be produced by folding the flat figure.

Example

    A   B   C   D   E

5. *Mechanical Reasoning.* A diagram of a mechanical device or situation is shown, and the examinee must indicate which choice is true of the situation.

Example

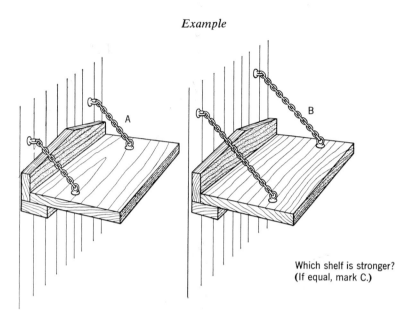

Which shelf is stronger?
(If equal, mark C.)

6. *Clerical Speed and Accuracy.* Each item is made up of a number of combinations of symbols, one of which is underlined. The examinee must mark the same combination on his answer sheet.

Example

Test Items

V.	AB	AC	AD	AE	AF
W.	aA	aB	BA	Ba	Bb
X.	A7	7A	B7	7B	AB
Y.	Aa	Ba	bA	BA	bB
Z.	3A	3B	33	B3	BB

Sample of Answer Sheet

	AC	AE	AF	AB	AD
V	:::::	:::::	:::::	:::::	:::::
	BA	Ba	Bb	·aA	aB
W	:::::	:::::	▬	:::::	:::::
	7B	B7	AB	7A	A7
X	▬	:::::	:::::	:::::	:::::
	Aa	bA	bB	Ba	BA
Y	:::::	▬	:::::	:::::	:::::
	BB	3B	B3	3A	33
Z	:::::	:::::	:::::	:::::	▬

7. *Language Usage: Spelling.* A list of words is given, some of which are misspelled. The examinee must indicate for each word whether it is correctly or incorrectly spelled.

Example

                                                Right   Wrong

definate

8. *Language Usage: Sentences.*   A sentence is given, containing one or more errors in usage or punctuation.   The sentence is divided into subsections, and the examinee must indicate all the sections that contain an error.

Example

Ain't we / going to the / office / next week / at all.
A   B   C   D   E

Sample of Answer Sheet

A	B	C	D	E
▌	‖	‖	‖	▌

The tests of the *DAT* are essentially power tests, with the exception of the Clerical Speed and Accuracy Test, and time limits are in most cases 30 minutes.   Total testing time for the battery is about 5 to $5\frac{1}{2}$ hours, and requires at least two separate testing sessions.   Percentile norms are available for each grade from the eighth through the twelfth. Norms are provided for each of the subtests, and also for the combination of V and A, which may be used as a general appraisal of scholastic aptitude.   An illustration of the profile form on which results may be plotted is shown on p. 152.

The General Aptitude Test Battery (GATB).   The *General Aptitude Test Battery* was produced by the Bureau of Employment Security, U. S. Department of Labor, in the early 1940's.   It was based upon previous work in which experimental test batteries had been prepared for each of a number of different jobs.   Analysis of the more than 50 different tests that had been prepared for specific jobs indicated that there was a great deal of overlapping among certain ones of them, and that only about 10 different ability factors were measured by the complete set of tests.   The *GATB* was developed to provide measures of these different factors.   In its most recent form it includes 12 tests and gives scores for 9 different factors.   One is a factor of general mental ability (G), resulting from scores on three tests (*Vocabulary, Arithmetic Reasoning,* and *Three-Dimensional Space*) that are also scored for more specialized factors.   The other factors, and the tests that contribute to each are described below.

Verbal Aptitude. Score is based on one test, Number 4, *Vocabulary.* This test requires the subject to identify the pair of words in a set of four that are *either* synonyms or antonyms.

Examples

a. cautious   b. friendly   c. hostile   d. remote
a. hasten   b. deprive   c. expedite   d. disprove

Numerical Ability. The appraisal of this aptitude is based upon two tests. The first of these, Number 2, *Computation,* involves speed and accuracy in simple computations with whole numbers.

Examples

$$\text{Subtract } (-) \quad \begin{array}{r} 256 \\ 83 \\ \hline \end{array} \qquad \text{Multiply } (\times) \quad \begin{array}{r} 37 \\ 8 \\ \hline \end{array}$$

The second test entering into the *Numerical Ability* score, Number 6, *Arithmetic Reasoning,* involves verbally stated quantitative problems.

Example

John works for $1.20 an hour. How much is his pay for a 35-hour week?

Spatial Aptitude. One test, Number 3, *Three-Dimensional Space,* enters into appraisal of this aptitude. The examinee must indicate which of four 3-dimensional figures can be produced by folding a flat sheet of specified shape, with creases at indicated points.

Example

Example of Spatial Aptitude

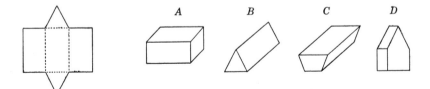

Form Perception. This aptitude involves rapid and accurate perception of visual forms and patterns. It is appraised in the *GATB* by two tests, Number 5, *Tool Matching,* and Number 7, *Form Matching,* which differ in the type of visual stimulus provided. Each requires the examinee to find from among a set of answer choices the one that is identical with the stimulus form.

Examples

Tool Matching:

Form Matching:

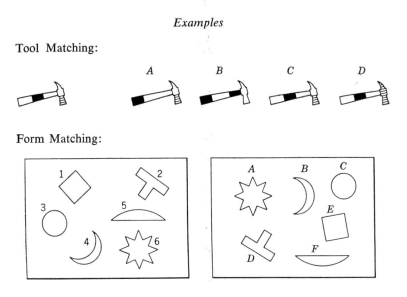

Clerical Perception. This aptitude also involves rapid and accurate perception, but in this case the stimulus material is linguistic instead of purely spatial. The test, Number 1, *Name Comparison,* presents pairs of names and requires the examinee to indicate whether the two members of the pair are identical, or whether they differ in some detail.

Examples

John Goldstein & Co.—John Goldston & Co.
Pewee Mfg. Co.—Pewee Mfg. Co.

Motor Coordination. This factor has to do with speed of simple but fairly precise motor response. It is evaluated by one test, Number 8, *Mark Making.* The task of the examinee is to make three pencil marks within each of a series of boxes on the answer sheet to yield a simple design. The result appears approximately as follows:

etc.

Score is the number of boxes correctly filled in a 60-second test period.

Manual Dexterity. This factor involves speed and accuracy of fairly gross hand movements. It is evaluated by two pegboard tests, Number 9, *Place,* and Number 10, *Turn.* In the first of these, the examinee uses both hands to move a series of pegs from one set of holes in a pegboard to another. In the second test, the examinee uses his preferred hand to pick a peg up from the board, rotate it through 180°, and reinsert the other end of the peg in the hole. Three trials are given for each of these tests, and score is the total number of pegs moved or turned.

Finger Dexterity. This factor represents a finer type of dexterity than that covered by the previous factor, calling for more precise finger manipulations. Two tests, Number 11, *Assemble,* and Number 12, *Disassemble,* use the same piece of equipment. This is a board with 50 holes in each of two sections. Each hole in one section is occupied by a small rivet. A stack of washers is piled on a spindle. During *Assemble,* the examinee picks up a rivet with one hand, a washer with the other, puts the washer on the rivet, and places the assembly in the corresponding hole in the unoccupied part of the board. He assembles as many rivets and washers as he can in 90 seconds. During *Disassemble,* he removes the assembly, returns the washer to its stack, and returns the rivet to its original place. Score is the number of items assembled or disassembled as the case may be. The apparatus tests are all arranged so that at the completion of testing the equipment has been returned to its original condition, and is ready for the testing of another person.

A comparison of the *GATB* and the *DAT* brings out that the *DAT* has tests of mechanical comprehension and language which the *GATB* lacks, while the *GATB* includes form perception and several types of motor tests that are missing in the *DAT.* Thus the *GATB* is more work oriented and less school oriented in its total coverage. Inclusion of the several types of motor tests results in somewhat lower correlations, on the average, for the *GATB,* though the "intellectual" tests correlate about as highly as those of the *DAT.* The correlations among the different aptitude scores of the *GATB* are shown in Table 10.2 for a group of 100 high school seniors. Excluding the correlations with G, which involves the same tests appearing in V, N, and S, the correlations range from $-.03$ to $.66$. The three motor factors show fairly marked correlations, but they are practically unrelated to the remaining tests. The perceptual and intellectual tests also show quite a bit of relationship to one another, and this is most marked between the two types of perceptual tests.

Table 10.2. Intercorrelations of GATB Aptitude Scores for
100 High-School Seniors *

	G	V	N	S	P	Q	K	F	M
G–Intelligence									
V–Verbal	73								
N–Numerical	74	42							
S–Spatial	70	40	34						
P–Form Percept.	43	34	42	48					
Q–Clerical Percept.	35	29	42	26	66				
K–Motor Coord.	−04	13	06	−03	29	29			
F–Finger Dext.	−05	−03	−03	01	27	20	37		
M–Manual Dext.	−06	06	01	−03	23	16	49	46	

* Decimal points have been omitted.

There are quite substantial correlations between the corresponding factors of the *DAT* and the *GATB*. Representative values from one study [8] are as follows:

Verbal	.70
Numerical	.56
Space	.69
Clerical	.56

However, the correlations are low enough so that it is clear that the tests cannot be considered identical. One important difference is the fact that the *DAT* tests are in most cases purely power tests, while the *GATB* tests are quite highly speeded.

Other Aptitude Batteries. A number of other aptitude batteries have been produced, mostly since 1950. There is generally less information available on these than on the *DAT* or the *GATB,* so their usefulness is less fully established. The batteries are briefly described in Appendix III.*

There are also a good many single aptitude tests. Many of these are much like the tests that have been described as components of the *DAT* or *GATB*. The batteries have, of course, usually adapted ideas from the most effective single tests and incorporated measures that have been successful in previous use. Thus, the *Bennett Mechanical Comprehension Test* was the predecessor and model for the *DAT Mechanical Reasoning Test*. The *Minnesota Vocational Test for*

* Fuller reports on each of seven different batteries, together with an evaluation by one outside expert, appeared in the *Personnel and Guidance Journal* from September 1956 through September 1957, and have been brought out as a separate monograph entitled *The Use of Multifactor Tests in Guidance.*

Clerical Workers provided the model for the *Clerical Perception* factor in the *GATB*. The various early mechanical aptitude and clerical tests have been reviewed by Bennett and Cruickshank,[2,3] and of course more recent tests will be found reviewed in the *Mental Measurements Yearbooks*.

VALIDITY OF APTITUDE BATTERIES

Now we must inquire into the usefulness of aptitude batteries such as the *DAT* and the *GATB*. We must inquire to what extent such a battery can provide us information that permits us to make better, more varied, and more differentiated predictions than those that are possible from a test of general mental ability or scholastic aptitude. The types of predictions with which we are most likely to be concerned are predictions of success in specific school subjects or major fields, predictions of success in specific jobs for which the individual is an applicant, and predictions of success in general fields of the world of work.

Differential Prediction of Academic Success. We have seen that scholastic aptitude tests have fairly good over-all validity for predicting academic success. One thing that we might hope is that an aptitude battery would tell us in *which* subject areas a student is *most* likely to be successful. Will Walter do better in English or in mathematics, in science or in French, in mechanical drawing or in history? A battery can do this to the extent that different tests in the battery are valid for different subjects. To what extent is this the case?

The manual for the *DAT* provides extensive data on the correlations of each of the subtests with achievement in a number of school subjects. Some of these results are summarized in Table 10.3. This

Table 10.3. Median Correlation of Differential Aptitude Test Scores with School Grades in Different Subjects

Test	English	Mathematics	Science	Social Studies, History	Languages	Typing	Shorthand
Verbal Reasoning (VR)	.50(2) *	.39(2)	.54(1)	.50(1)	.30(4)	.19(6)	.44(3)
Numerical Ability (NA)	.48(3)	.50(1)	.51(2)	.48(2)	.42(1)	.32(1)	.27(4)
Abstract Reasoning (AR)	.36(5)	.35(4)	.44(4)	.35(5)	.25(5)	.27(3)	.24(5)
Space Relations (SR)	.27(6)	.32(5)	.36(6.5)	.26(6.5)	.15(8)	.16(7)	.16(6)
Mechanical Reasoning (MR)	.24(7.5)	.22(7)	.38(5)	.24(8)	.17(7)	.14(8)	.14(7.5)
Clerical Speed & Accuracy (CSA)	.24(7.5)	.19(8)	.26(8)	.26(6.5)	.23(6)	.26(4.5)	.14(7.5)
Spelling (Spell.)	.44(4)	.29(6)	.36(6.5)	.36(4)	.31(3)	.26(4.5)	.55(1)
Sentences (Sent.)	.52(1)	.36(3)	.48(3)	.46(3)	.40(2)	.30(2)	.49(2)

* Number in parentheses shows rank of that test for that subject.

table shows the median value of the correlations, and also ranks the eight subtests with respect to their correlations with each subject.

The first thing that we notice is that certain subtests are among the highest for almost all the subjects. Thus, *Verbal Reasoning* ranks near the top for all subjects except typing and *Numerical Ability* for all except shorthand. The *Sentences* test is one of the three most valid for all subject areas. This means that in large part the abilities that underlie academic performance are general abilities, and that a single general scholastic aptitude test will be effective in predicting success. The authors of the *DAT* have recognized this by printing the combined *Verbal Reasoning* and *Numerical Ability* tests as a single booklet and preparing separate norms for them. The combination of these two provides an effective measure of general scholastic aptitude.

At the same time, Table 10.3 does show *some* indication of differential validity. The *Mechanical Reasoning Test* is more valid for science than for the other subjects. The *Spelling Test* comes into its own in predicting success in shorthand. The *Numerical Ability Test* is more valid for mathematics than it is for English. A specific test does have a modest amount of differential validity, and does provide some suggestion that a pupil is likely to be more successful in one field than in another. However, it must be admitted that for much of educational guidance a general measure of scholastic aptitude will prove quite serviceable, and a battery of specialized aptitude tests will make only a limited additional contribution.

Prediction of Specific Job Success. We may next ask how successful a battery of aptitude tests will be in predicting the success of workers in a specific job in a specific company. Will the tests have validities high enough to make them useful to employers? Will different tests predict success in different jobs? The manual for the *GATB* provides quite an array of validities for job criteria. The data fall short of being ideal because the validation is often concurrent, based upon men already employed; because the samples are small; because the sample is typically limited to workers in a single plant or company; and because there is rarely any independent cross-validation.* However, they provide about as good a pool of data as we have in which a common battery was validated against criteria of success in a number of different jobs. We have abstracted from the original report those instances in which validities are available against job (as distinct from school or training) criteria for samples of as many as seventy

---

* Especially in exploratory studies in which a battery of tests is being tried out, it is important to verify validities discovered in an initial study by checking the same tests with a new independent sample.

cases and display them in Table 10.4. Only those correlations are shown in the table that are of a size that would be unlikely to have occurred by chance.*

Table 10.4. Validity of GATB Scores for Specific Occupations

	Number of Cases	General Intelligence	Verbal	Numerical	Spatial	Form Perception	Clerical Perception	Motor Coordination	Finger Dexterity	Manual Dexterity
Boarding Mach. Op.	103	−.21						.21	.23	.38
Bomb Fuse Parts Assembler	90		.34	.25		.33	.23	.26	.37	.31
Chemist's Assistant	118	.30			.43			−.24		
Compositor, Hand and Machine	107	.39	.37	.40	.20		.34	.25		.22
Laborer, Poultry	72	.24		.42			.25		.50	.56
Machinist	71	.29			.37	.27	.30			
Mounter	281						.12	.22	.28	.38
Pottery Decorator	70				.25			.28		
Pressman, Cylinder	102	.49	.43	.52	.29	.39	.41	.27		.31
Sewing Mach. Op.	133	.27	.29	.36			.30	.26		.22
Survey Worker	130	.50	.41	.44	.29					
Tabulating Machine Operator	203	.34	.22	.36	.20		.15			
Telephone Operator	88	.45	.38	.40	.27	.25	.35	.44	.23	
Underwriter	81			.24			.25			

From Table 10.4 we see that for every job two or more of the scores show significant validity. For some jobs all the validities are quite low, as for Pottery Decorator and Underwriter. For others, more encouraging values are obtained, as for Survey Worker. It is also clear that the factors that are valid for different jobs differ. Thus, manual dexterity appears to be important for a number of assembly and production line jobs, spatial ability counts relatively heavily for the machinist and chemist's assistant, clerical perception is relevant to the printing trades and to the underwriter, general intelligence discriminates the good from the poor survey worker, etc. In so far as these results are representative of the whole range of jobs, and within the limitations stated in the previous paragraph, they support the position that different specific abilities are valid for different jobs, and that a battery can be useful to an employer in picking men for a specific job or in assigning new workers to a type of assignment in which they will be effective and productive. Differences in success in certain jobs in single companies are predicted to a useful degree by an appropriate selection of aptitude tests.

A large number of separate studies of aptitude tests in relation to job

* Correlations are exhibited that are statistically significant at the .05 level.

success have been summarized by Ghiselli.[7]   Where a number of different sources provided correlations between scores on some type of test and success in a general category of job, he combined all the available data to produce a kind of pooled composite validity index. Selections from his report are shown in Table 10.5.   Each entry is

Table 10.5.   Selected Data on Average Validity of Different Sorts of Tests for Different Categories of Job (Adapted from Ghiselli)

Type of Job

Type of Test	Super-visory	Cleri-cal	Sales	Pro-tective	Vehicle Operator	Trades and Crafts	Indus-trial
Intelligence	28	31	02	27	14	20	20
Arithmetic	20	26	(06) *	(15)	(04)	23	13
Spatial Relations	21	10	. . .	(11)	. . .	19	14
Name Comparison	. . .	30	(−15)	(24)	. . .	(20)	16
Mechanical Principles	24	. . .	. . .	(27)	21	40	(50)
Finger Dexterity	. . .	24	. . .	(19)	. . .	20	18
Arm Dexterity	. . .	(18)	. . .	. . .	. . .	15	21

* Correlations based on less than 500 cases are placed in parentheses.

an average, often of a number of correlations.   The correlations have been enclosed in parentheses when they are based on less than five hundred persons.   For some combinations of test and occupation no data could be found, so these entries have been left blank.

The pooled correlations reported by Ghiselli rarely go above .40, and then only for the smaller groups.   Correlations in the twenties are fairly typical.   For a given category of job, the variation in validity from one type of test to another is rather modest.   Thus, these results present a rather less optimistic picture of the value of tests of special aptitudes than that portrayed in the *GATB* results in Table 10.4.

The less promising picture may stem in part from the blurring resulting from combining quite a span both of jobs and of tests within a single coefficient.   It may be, however, that the larger numbers of cases represented in Ghiselli's composite correlations are less likely to yield large correlations than the rather small U. S. Employment Service samples. The true picture of validity of tests as predictors of success at a given job in a given company, and of the distinctiveness of different abilities as predictors for different types of jobs probably lies somewhere between the pictures presented in these two tables.

Forecasting Success in the World of Work. For the school or college guidance counselor, special aptitude tests are useful in so far as they permit him to forecast some years in advance the general field of work for which a student will be able to complete training and in which he will be successful. The counselor cannot know what *specific* company the student will work for, or what exact job position he will fill. He deals in relatively long range forecasts over relatively broad categories. What evidence can be offered on the long-range forecasting effectiveness of aptitude test results?

Probably the most extensive study bearing on this problem is one in which approximately 10,000 men, who had originally been given an extensive battery of aptitude tests in the Air Force during World War II, were followed up some 13 years after the time of testing.[11] Test results were related to entry into and persistence in an occupation and to reported income and other indicators of success in that occupation. Even in a group of 10,000 men, samples in many occupations were small. However, it was possible to assemble samples large enough to merit analysis for about 125 occupational groupings.

The results on prediction of occupational *success* contrast rather sharply with those reported in the previous section. There was *no* convincing evidence of *any* relationship of test scores to success within an occupation for those men who had entered a specific occupation. Correlations were generally small, about as often negative as positive, and the total set of correlations could quite possibly have arisen as a result of chance deviations from a true correlation of zero. It appeared that when the men might enter an occupation such as law anywhere in the country, in many different kinds of settings both public and private, the test battery was quite unable to predict who would achieve the largest income, report the most satisfaction, or perceive himself as most successful in his field. It is important for the counselor to realize that such predictions are probably not possible for him.

For another type of occupational prediction the results were much more positive. Differences *between* occupations in average test score profile were real and quite marked for a number of occupations. Table 10.6 reproduces the results for selected occupations. Results for closely related tests have been combined into a factor score, and the table shows data for five distinct factors. Scores are standard scores in which the mean for the complete population of aviation cadet applicants is set equal to zero and the standard deviation for this group is set equal to 100.   Thus, a score of $+50$ represents a score half a standard deviation above the cadet applicant mean.   The profiles of several of the occupations are shown graphically in Figure 10.1.

From Table 10.6 and Figure 10.1 we can see that there are substantial differences between one occupation and another.   Most of these make good sense.   The accountants as a group are highest on numerical ability, while the architects are highest on visual perception. Engineers are highest on the general intellectual measures that bulk so large in success in engineering school, while machinists are highest in mechanical and psychomotor skills.   Some profiles have quite marked peaks and hollows, as, for example, the ones for accountant and machinist.   Others are quite flat, exemplified by the sales engineer and

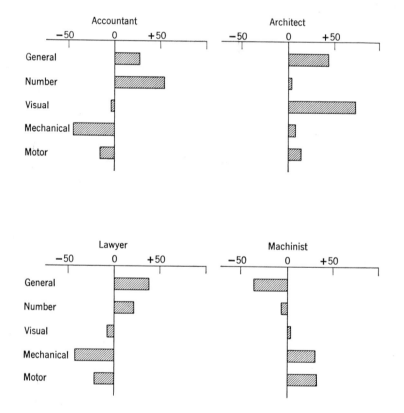

Fig. 10.1. Ability profiles for four occupations.

Table 10.6. Ability Profiles of Occupational Groups *

Group	General Intellectual	Numerical Fluency	Visual Perception	Mechanical	Psychomotor
Accountants and auditors	28	54	− 4	−46	−16
Architects	44	4	74	8	14
Artists and designers	− 7	−12	51	− 4	8
Bricklayers	−24	− 5	−38	10	−32
Carpenters	−44	−17	− 4	24	− 1
College professors	75	38	38	−33	1
Contractors	− 7	−10	−10	34	5
Dentists	28	20	15	−19	1
Draftsmen	1	−14	31	14	15
Drivers, bus and truck	−53	−11	−23	−14	−20
Engineers, chemical	106	42	30	19	20
Engineers, civil	75	31	56	36	14
Engineers, sales	57	33	35	39	40
Farmers, general	− 6	− 7	−29	38	−36
Lawyers	39	22	− 7	−42	−21
Machinists	−35	− 6	4	31	32
Mach. ops., fabricating	−45	−25	−25	−39	9
Managers, credit	− 5	22	25	−27	0
Managers, office	4	33	9	−29	11
Mechanics, vehicular	−72	−65	− 7	19	− 6
Physicians	59	20	18	2	0
Plumbers	−42	−21	−31	− 7	− 5

* Expressed as standard scores: mean = 0; standard deviation = 100.

plumber profiles. These last two differ more in level than in any clear-cut patterning. Thus, we find some occupations with quite distinctive ability patterns, some with rather nondescript ones, some at a generally high level and some at a generally low level. Jobs vary noticeably both in the level of demand that they make and in their degree and type of specialization.

The differences shown in Table 10.6 and Figure 10.1 probably represent a minimum estimate of differences between occupations. This is because the Air Force group had already been screened by a test of general ability, so that the less intellectually able men who would ordinarily have been heavily represented in the semi-skilled and unskilled occupations had been screened out. On the other hand, it must always be remembered that although substantial differences can be shown *between* group means there is still a wide range of scores *within* each group. Some artists will be found with numerical ability higher than the typical accountant, some accountants with higher mechanical ability than the typical engineer. Differences between occupations are real, but so is variability within occupations.

PROGNOSTIC TESTS

One group of aptitude tests is made up of tests designed to predict readiness to learn or probable degree of success in some specific subject or segment of education. These are called prognostic tests. A group of tests in this category that have been widely heralded and have received considerable use are the "reading readiness" tests. These tests are designed to be used with children, usually shortly after their entry into the first grade, to give the school as accurate an indication as possible of the child's ability to progress in reading. They provide information the teacher can use in assembling working groups within the class, in deciding upon the amount and type of prereading activities to provide, and in judging how soon to start a formal reading program. In some communities where kindergarten attendance is quite general, tests at the end of kindergarten are looked to as one basis for organizing first-grade groups for the following year. The sorts of tasks that appear in these tests may be seen from Table 10.7.

The reader who compares the tasks in Table 10.7 with the sample intelligence test items shown on pp. 222–225 will be aware of a substantial degree of similarity. In both, knowledge of word meanings appears. Both deal with recognition of sameness and differences, with analysis and classification. However, the reading readiness tests tend to emphasize more exclusively the materials of reading, letters and words. They include the components or early stages of the reading task. The basic question now becomes: Does the special slant which is given in the reading readiness test result in increased validity? Is the special test an improvement over a measure of general or academic aptitude? This is the question that must be raised for any type of prognostic test or special aptitude test.

Table 10.7. Types of Tasks Included in Representative Reading Readiness Tests

Type of Test Task	Gates	Lee-Clark	Metropolitan	Stevens	Murphy-Durrell
Oral vocabulary or directions, using pictures	x	x	x		
Rhyming or matching sounds	x				x
Visual matching of figures, letters, or words	x	x	x	x	x
Visual perceiving of figures, letters, or words ("Which one is different?")		x		x	
Learning words in a standard lesson				x	x
Ability to read letters and words	x				

Whether a reading readiness test provides a better guide to later reading success than does a general intelligence test remains somewhat unclear. One fairly extensive investigation [6] indicates that tests requiring pupils to perceive and match words, to complete a story, and to select rhyming words gave better prediction of reading achievement one, two, or three terms later than did *Stanford-Binet* mental age. The validities reported for the *Gates Reading Readiness Test,* developed on the basis of this research, have been about .70, whereas *Stanford-Binet* MA showed a correlation of only .40 in the original study. This would indicate that the test tasks closely resembling the tasks faced by the beginning reader *do* have higher predictive effectiveness.

Another set of data [10] indicates, by contrast, that the *Pintner-Cunningham Intelligence Test* had a higher correlation with sixth-grade reading achievement than did the *Lee-Clark Reading Readiness Test.* However, these two sets of results need not be considered contradictory. The reading readiness test undertakes to predict ability to profit from reading instruction in the near future and is not used to forecast ultimate level of reading achievement. It may well be that it is more effective as an indicator of progress in reading within the next few months, even though an intelligence test is a better indicator of ultimate level of reading achievement.

Prognostic tests have been developed for various other subjects and levels, and the last few years have witnessed some renewal of interest in these tests.   Carroll and Sapon [4] have brought out a battery of foreign language prognosis tests and the *Symonds Foreign Language Prognosis Test* has been restandardized.   The older Orleans prognostic tests for algebra, geometry and foreign languages continue to be available.   The authors of all these tests offer evidence to show that the specialized tests provide a better prediction of achievement in the special subject area than is possible from a general measure of scholastic aptitude.   However, one may still question whether, within the areas of academic achievement, special prognostic tests can improve the predictions based upon a combination of measures of general intelligence and previous academic achievement in related areas enough to justify their use.   The demonstration that they can has not been sufficiently impressive to result in widespread adoption of the tests.

Special prognostic tests seem likely to be more useful as predictors of success in rather special types of academic tasks that have had no counterparts at earlier levels of school experience.   Thus, the *Turse Shorthand Aptitude Test,* for which a correlation of .67 with later achievement in shorthand has been reported, may be useful as a supplement to other information about the pupil in evaluating probable success in shorthand training.   The *ERC Stenographic Aptitude Test* and the *Bennett Stenographic Aptitude Tests* have given comparable results.   These tests include such tasks as spelling, transcribing symbols, dictation under speed pressure, and word discrimination.

PROFESSIONAL-SCHOOL APTITUDE BATTERIES

One other group of aptitude tests, so-called, are the tests that have been developed to select individuals for particular types of professional training.   Many types of professional schools, sometimes individually but more often operating through their professional organizations, have instituted testing programs for the selection of their students.   Testing programs are in operation for selecting students for engineering, law, medicine, dentistry, veterinary medicine, nursing, and accounting, to mention a few.

The tests used in these professional-school batteries tend to be tests of reading, quantitative reasoning, and apprehending abstract relationships, with the balance and emphasis shifted somewhat to conform to the academic emphasis of the particular training program.   They are largely minor variations upon the same theme—a relatively high-level measure of scholastic aptitude and achievement.   The different professional aptitude tests would correlate very substantially with one another or with a measure of general intelligence, and, indeed, it should be expected that they would because the abilities required to succeed in training for the different professions have much in common. The similarities outweigh the differences. The common core is adapted to the professional field, as by giving more emphasis to quantitative materials for engineering and more to verbal materials for law. It is supplemented in some cases by rather highly specialized tests, for example, a test of chalk-carving for dentistry. These variations are superimposed upon the basic theme of scholastic aptitude and achievement.

MEASUREMENT OF MUSICAL APTITUDE

When we come to such fields as music and art, the need for special measures of aptitude becomes quite apparent. Grades in these subjects are usually among those least well predicted by general measures of scholastic aptitude. Furthermore, the specialized nature of outstanding talent in these fields has long been recognized. Our problem is to determine what the components of this talent are and devise ways of appraising them.

In musical ability one large component is executive or motor, the ability to master the patterns of action required for playing an instrument. Aptitude measures have largely avoided this domain, perhaps because of its specificity to a particular instrument. Most measurement has been directed toward the perceptive and interpretive aspects of music.

Hearing music involves in the first place various types of sensory discrimination—discrimination of pitch, of loudness, of temporal relations. It involves in the second place perceiving the more complex musical relations in the material, interval relationships, the pattern of a melody, the composition of a chord, the relationship of a harmony to a melody. Third, it involves esthetic judgments about the suitability and pleasingness of a melody or harmony, a rhythmic pattern, or a pattern of dynamics.

The most thoroughly investigated musical aptitude test battery, the *Seashore Measures of Musical Talents,* is directed primarily toward measuring simple sensory discriminations, though with some attention to perceiving slightly more musical material. The tests have analyzed music down so far that very little music remains. Thus, there are the following subtests:

1. *Discrimination of Pitch:* judging which of two tones is higher.
2. *Discrimination of Loudness:* judging which of two sounds is louder.

3. *Discrimination of Time Interval:* judging which of two intervals is longer.

4. *Judgment of rhythm:* judging whether two rhythms are the same or different.

5. *Judgment of Timbre:* judging which of two tone qualities is more pleasing.

6. *Tonal Memory:* judging whether two melodies are the same or different.

The items are on phonograph records, with a series of items of each type. Within each type, the judgments become progressively more difficult.

The analytic approach to musical aptitude is evident in the above list of subtests. Critics have contended that the analysis has removed the tests a great way from any genuinely musical material and that fine discriminations of pitch, time, and intensity are really not called for in the activities of the musician. Validity studies of the Seashore tests have been somewhat conflicting, yielding appreciable correlations with measures of musical success in some instances and very low correlations in others. The value of the analytic test is still a matter of doubt and controversy.

Contrasting rather markedly with the Seashore type of test are the *Wing Standardised Tests of Musical Intelligence.* These tests, developed in England, were designed to stay as close as possible to the actual materials of music. The following subtests are included:

1. *Chord Analysis:* detecting the number of notes in a single chord.

2. *Pitch Change:* detecting the direction of change of one note in a repeated chord.

3. *Memory:* detecting which note is changed when a short melodic phrase is repeated.

4. *Rhythmic Accent:* judging which of two performances of the same piece has the better rhythmic pattern.

5. *Harmony:* judging which of two harmonies is more appropriate for a melody.

6. *Intensity:* judging which of two playings of the same piece has the more appropriate pattern of dynamics.

7. *Phrasing:* judging which of two renditions has the more appropriate phrasing.

This test is made up in part of tests that call for perceiving musical relationships and in part of tests that call for esthetic choices in intact musical material. Information on the validity of the test is still limited, but what there is seems very promising. Thus, the author reports [12] correlations of .64, .78, and .82 with teachers' rankings in three small samples. If these are maintained in future studies, a test like the *Wing* test would appear to have a very real place in guidance of young people who have musical aspirations or whose families hold such aspirations for them.

TESTS OF ARTISTIC APTITUDE

Several types of tests are available relating to aptitude for art. In the first place, there have been tests of esthetic judgment. That field is now fairly well dominated by the *Meier Art Judgment Test.* Each item consists of a pair of pictures of art objects. One is an acknowledged masterpiece. The other is that same masterpiece systematically distorted in some specified way. The examinee must choose the better picture in each pair, the test blank indicating the respect in which the two specimens differ.

A test of the judgmental aspect of art ability is the *Graves Design Judgment Test.* This differs from the *Meier Test* in that all the items consist of abstract and non-representational material. The members of a pair differ in some single aspect of design, i.e., balance, symmetry, variety. Judgment of design is presumably divorced from any particular object or content.

In an attempt to get at the productive, as distinct from the purely judgmental, aspect of art, several tests (*Horn, Knauber, Lewerenz*) require the subject to produce drawings, based on certain limiting "givens." Thus, in the *Horn Art Aptitude Inventory,* a pattern of lines and dots is provided, and from this material the examinee must produce a sketch. The type of item is indicated in Fig. 10.2. The products must be evaluated by subjective rating, according to standards given by the authors, but they present some evidence that this can be done rather reliably even by non-artists.

The *Lewerenz Tests in Fundamental Abilities of Visual Art* use dot patterns to elicit drawings, whereas the *Knauber Art Ability Tests* use various assigned drawing tasks. Both these last two tests also present problems in shading, perspective, and composition.

Art tests have been rather generally successful in differentiating art students or art teachers from other groups. However, it has been argued that they accomplish this because they are in large measure achievement tests rather than aptitude measures. There has been relatively little study of these tests as aptitude measures with untrained individuals. Studies of art students have indicated that test perform-

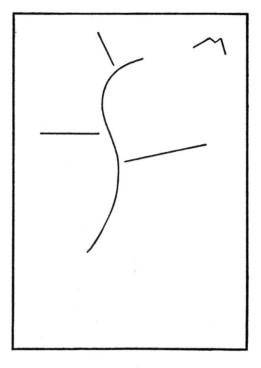

Fig. 10.2. Example of type of item used in *Horn Art Aptitude Inventory*.

ance is reasonably predictive of later art-school success. Thus, Horn and Smith [9] found a correlation of .66 between score on the Horn test at the beginning of the year and average faculty rating of success in a special high-school art class at the end of the year. Barrett [1] correlated four art tests with grades in a ninth-grade art course and with ratings of pupils' art products, with the following results:

	Course Grade	Ratings of Product
McAdory Art Test	.10	.13
Meier Art Judgment Test	.37	.35
Knauber Art Ability Test	.33	.71
Lewerenz Fundamental Art Abilities Test	.40	.76

Thus the last two tests, requiring production of drawings by the examinee, had about the same correlation with grades as did the *Meier Art Judgment Test* but much higher correlations with appraisals of student products.

We can see from the above that the test tasks that require art students to do the sorts of tasks they will be taught to do in art class predict their later achievement. How far down to untrained pupils this can be pushed remains to be determined.

Since the keying of art tests of all types depends upon a pooling of judgments, obtaining a high score requires conformity to the accepted esthetic standards. There is real question as to the applicability of these tests (or the tests of musical aptitude) in a distinctly different culture. There is also the possibility, though it is a fairly unlikely one, that a highly talented but unconventional person will be penalized on the tests.

SUMMARY STATEMENT

Though general intelligence tests bear some relationship to success in many fields, efficient vocational guidance or personnel classification calls for tests more specifically directed at the abilities called for by each kind of job. Analytical studies of human abilities support the genuineness and importance of these special abilities. Numerous tests of special abilities have appeared, and more recently tests of this sort have been organized into comprehensive aptitude batteries for use in vocational guidance or personnel classification.

Special tests to evaluate readiness to undertake particular educational tasks have also been developed. The most widely used of these are reading readiness tests. Other types of prognostic tests have been less widely used, perhaps because their function is reasonably well served by measures of scholastic aptitude and academic achievement. Professional school aptitude batteries appear to be variations upon the basic theme of scholastic aptitude tests.

The fields of music and art have produced a number of ability tests. However, highly analytic tests have not been very clearly successful. More complex tests involve an unknown admixture of previous training. These show reasonably good validity and may provide an improved and at least relatively objective way of appraising status and, hence, promise in the field.

REFERENCES

1. Barrett, H. O., An examination of certain standardized art tests to determine their relation to classroom achievement and to intelligence, *J. educ. Res.,* **42,** 1949, 398–400.
2. Bennett, G. K., and Ruth M. Cruickshank, *A summary of clerical tests,* New York, Psychological Corp., 1948.

3. Bennett, G. K., and Ruth M. Cruickshank, *A summary of manual and mechanical ability tests,* New York, Psychological Corp., 1942.

4. Carroll, John B., and Stanley M. Sapon, *Modern language aptitude test,* New York, Psychological Corp., 1958.

5. DuBois, Philip, Editor, *The Classification Program,* Army Air Forces Aviation Psychology Program Report No. 2. Washington, D. C., U. S. Government Printing Office, 1947.

6. Gates, A. I., G. L. Bond, and D. H. Russell, *Methods of determining reading readiness,* New York, Teachers College, Columbia University, Bureau of Publications, 1939.

7. Ghiselli, Edwin E., *The measurement of occupational aptitude,* University of California Publications in Psychology, 1955, 8(2), pp. 101–216.

8. *Guide to the use of the general aptitude test battery, section III,* Bureau of Employment Security, U. S. Department of Labor, Washington, D. C., 1955.

9. Horn, C. A., and L. F. Smith, The Horn Art Aptitude Inventory, *J. appl. Psychol.,* **29,** 1945, 350–355.

10. Lee, M. J., and W. W. Clark, *Lee-Clark Reading Readiness Test: Manual,* Los Angeles, Calif., California Test Bureau, 1951.

11. Thorndike, Robert L., and Elizabeth P. Hagen, *10,000 careers,* New York, John Wiley, 1959.

12. Wing, H., Tests of musical ability and appreciation: An investigation into the measurement, distribution, and development of musical capacity, *Brit. J. Psychol. Monogr. Suppl.,* **8,** No. 27, 1948.

SUGGESTED ADDITIONAL READING

Froehlich, Clifford P., and K. B. Hoyt, *Guidance testing,* 3rd ed., Chicago, Science Research Associates, 1959, Chapter 6.

Harris, Chester W., Editor, *Encyclopedia of educational research,* 3rd ed., New York, Macmillan, 1960, pp. 59–62, 1084–1085.

Super, Donald E., *Appraising vocational fitness by means of psychological tests,* New York, Harper, 1949, Chapters 4, 6, 8–11, and 15.

Super, Donald E., *The use of multifactor tests in guidance,* Washington, D. C., American Personnel and Guidance Association, 1958.

QUESTIONS FOR DISCUSSION

1. A number of aptitude test batteries have been developed for use at the secondary-school level, but almost none for the elementary school. Why is this? Is it a reasonable state of affairs?

2. What are the advantages in using a battery such as the *Differential Aptitude Tests* instead of tests selected from a number of different sources? What are the limitations?

3. Step by step, what would need to be done to set up a program for selecting students for a dental school?

4. How could a high-school counselor use the data of Table 10.3? What are the limitations on the usefulness of this material?

5. How might the counselor use the data of Table 10.2? What are its limitations?

6. How sound is the statement: "The best measure of aptitude in any field is a measure of achievement in that field to date."? What are its limitations?

7. What are the differences between a reading readiness test and an intelligence test? What are the advantages of using the readiness test rather than an intelligence test for first-grade pupils?

8. To what extent are tests like the *Horn Art Test* and the *Wing Music Test* measures of aptitude? To what extent are they measures of achievement?

9. What factors tend to make tests of artistic and musical aptitude somewhat less useful than other types of aptitude tests?

10. In what ways could a follow-up study of graduates of a high school help in improving the school guidance program?

11. Why have aptitude test batteries shown up better in discriminating *between* jobs than in predicting success *within* a single job category?

Chapter 11

▼

Achievement Tests

STANDARDIZED VERSUS TEACHER-MADE TESTS

We turn now to tests of school achievement. We shall be concerned particularly with commercially available standardized tests, though we shall need to consider other types of appraisal devices in order to see how the standardized test fits into the total picture. As we indicated in the previous chapter, the distinction between an aptitude test and an achievement test is a somewhat blurred one. However, we shall be interested now in measures of knowledges and skills that are closely tied to organized school instruction, and in measures that are being used primarily to appraise present status in those school-taught knowledges and skills.

Standardized tests do not represent anything new and strange in the measurement of academic achievement. They are blood brothers of the short-answer teacher-made tests that were discussed in Chapter 4. They are made up of the same types of items and cover many of the same areas of knowledge. In what ways, then, do they differ from teacher-made tests? What are the advantages and limitations of each? For what purposes should each be used?

DISTINCTIVE FEATURES OF STANDARDIZED TESTS

There are four main ways in which commercially distributed standardized tests differ from the tests that the individual teacher would prepare for his own class.

1. The standardized test is based on the general content and objectives common to many schools the country over, whereas the teacher's own test can be adapted to content and objectives specific to his own class.

2. The standardized test deals with large segments of knowledge or skill, whereas a teacher-made test can be prepared in relation to any specific limited topic.

3. The standardized test is developed with the help of professional

writers, reviewers, and editors of test items, whereas the teacher-made test must usually rely upon the skill of one or two teachers.

4. The standardized test provides norms for various groups that are broadly representative of performance throughout the country, whereas the teacher-made test has usually been given only to the pupils in a single class or school.

The distinctive features of the standardized test represent important advantages for some purposes and disadvantages for others. Basing the test upon a careful analysis of the common objectives expressed in textbooks, courses of study, and reports of committees of professional societies should guarantee that the thinking of many specialists has entered into the test plan. However, a published test is fixed for a period of years in terms of *broad, common* objectives. It is not a flexible tool. It cannot be adapted to special current needs, to local emphases, or to particular limited units of study.

The value of standardized tests lies particularly in situations in which comparisons must be made—comparisons of a school with other schools, comparison of achievement in different areas by a pupil or by a school group, or comparison of achievement with the potentiality for achievement indicated by an aptitude test. The norms provided with standardized tests make such comparisons readily possible. For a school, achievement may be compared with national norms. The standing of a single pupil, or of several pupils coming from different schools, may be determined by reference to the norms for the test. The age or grade equivalents, percentiles or standard scores of a pupil on tests in different subjects may be compared to establish his relative level of achievement, or these converted scores may be compared with a similar score from an aptitude test to see whether achievement is consistent with what we would expect from the pupils' aptitude.

FUNCTIONS OF STANDARDIZED AND TEACHER-MADE TESTS

In the light of these differences, we propose that chief reliance should be placed on teacher-made tests when we want to test in order to

1. See how well students have mastered a limited unit of instruction.
2. Determine the extent to which distinctive local objectives have been achieved.
3. Provide a basis for assigning course marks.

Standardized tests should be used when we wish to test in order to

1. Compare achievement with potentiality for an individual or a group.

2. Compare achievement of different skills or in different subject areas.

3. Evaluate the status of pupils from different schools or classes on a common basis, as when a pupil transfers to a new school.

4. Make comparisons between different classes and schools.

5. Study pupil growth over a period of time to see whether progress is more or less rapid than might be expected.

For some purposes, such as pupil diagnosis, we may wish to use not only standardized and teacher-made tests but a variety of informal testing and observational procedures as well.

We see, therefore, that standardized and teacher-made tests both have important functions to perform in the educational economy. To a large extent they are different functions. The two types of evaluation supplement one another. They are not competitors.

Standardized tests of achievement have been developed for practically every subject in the school curriculum. It would be impossible to give even a brief treatment of all subject areas in the pages that can be allotted to achievement tests in this book. We have decided, therefore, to concentrate on tests in a single area, in the belief that a fairly full treatment of this area will serve to introduce almost all the major problems and issues that would be encountered in dealing with tests in any area. We have chosen to discuss reading tests for two reasons. In the first place, these tests are more widely used than those in any other subject area. In the second place, a great variety of both survey and diagnostic procedures have been developed in this area, so that we shall get an introduction to a wide spectrum of testing techniques. Readers especially interested in tests in other areas can get names and evaluations of available tests in their field from Buros' *Mental Measurements Yearbooks* (see Chapter 8).

ANALYZING THE OBJECTIVES OF AN AREA: THE FIRST STEP

Before we can proceed intelligently with either the preparation of a test in an area or the choice of one from among those already existing, we must analyze and define clearly the objectives of our instruction in the field in question.

Is test A a good test? Good for what? What are we trying to produce in children? What do we want or need to evaluate? Only when we have in our minds a clear answer to these further questions can we answer the question: Is this a good test? An analysis of objectives helps us to identify the strengths and weaknesses of any single test or any complete evaluation program.

When we look at our statement of objectives, we will see some for which an existing test seems appropriate, some for which testing procedures might be devised if sufficient ingenuity were available, and some that seem obviously inaccessible by test procedures. Consider the following statement of objectives in the field of reading.*

Essential Knowledge, Attitudes, Skills, and Procedures in Reading

I. Basic attitudes, skills, and procedures involved in securing meaning in both reading and listening.
  A. To respond to the motive, problem, or purpose.
  B. To direct attention to the meaning of what is read.
  C. To develop fluent, accurate perception of word forms.
    1. Accurate discrimination of word forms.
    2. Accurate perception of both form and meaning.
    3. Association of right meanings with word forms.
    4. Accurate perception of words in context.
    5. Fluent perception of words.
  D. To secure an adequate understanding of what is read.
    1. A clear grasp of meaning, involving:
      a. Selection of meanings of words appropriate to the context.
      b. Fusion of the meanings of words into a chain of related ideas.
      c. Recognition of the importance and relationship of the ideas acquired.
    2. Coping successfully with such factors as:
      a. Unusual word order.
      b. Complexity of sentence structure.
      c. Abstract ideas.
    3. Interpreting meaning in the light of its broader context. This ability implies an understanding of:
      a. The total setting of the ideas expressed.
      b. The author's mood, tone, and intention.
    4. Supplementing the specific meanings apprehended.
      a. Reading between the lines.
      b. Seeing implications.
  E. To react critically to what is read.
    1. Recognizing the value, usefulness, timeliness, and significance of what is read.
    2. Judging the validity or truthfulness of the ideas presented in the passage.
    3. Judging the accuracy or completeness of the author's conclusions.

* Adapted from Greene, Harry A., and William S. Gray, "The measurement of understanding in the language arts," *The Forty-Fifth Yearbook of the National Society for the Study of Education*, Part I, 1946.

      4. Recognizing whether or not the reasoning of the author is sound.

      5. Identifying and resolving propaganda.

   F. To integrate the ideas acquired with previous experience so that the following evidences of understanding may be noted immediately, or later:

      1. New insights are acquired.

      2. Previous understandings are reaffirmed or modified.

      3. Challenging problems are solved.

      4. Rational attitudes are acquired.

      5. Behavior is modified.

      6. Interests are broadened.

      7. Richer and more stable personalities are developed.

II. Supplementary attitudes, skills, and procedures essential in many silent-reading activities.

   A. To locate needed information.

      1. Using an index.

      2. Using a table of contents.

      3. Using the dictionary.

      4. Using card files.

      5. Using reference books.

   B. To gather and evaluate information in the light of a given purpose.

      1. Recognizing the purpose to be achieved.

      2. Applying appropriate fact-finding techniques.

      3. Sorting essential from non-essential information.

      4. Judging the validity and significance of relevant information.

      5. Organizing the information in terms of the purpose or problem.

      6. Drawing tentative conclusions.

      7. Deciding when the purpose has been achieved.

   C. To adjust reading attitudes and procedures to different purposes.

      1. Modifying interpretative processes in light of the purposes to be achieved. As, for example,

        a. Reading to answer factual questions.

        b. Reading an organized body of material to report.

        c. Reading to determine the accuracy of the facts or events described.

      2. Adjusting rate of reading to the purpose.

As we scan this list of objectives, we see some that can obviously be measured quite readily and directly. Objective I C has to do with perceiving and comprehending words. Discrimination of word forms (I C 1) is appraised in tests for the primary grades by various types of word-picture or word-word matching tests. Accurate perception of form and meaning (I C 2) and association of form and meaning (I C 3) are central to the conventional vocabulary tests. One element entering into paragraph comprehension measures is accurate perception of words in context (I C 4). Fluent perception of words (I C 5) contributes to rapid reading and is appraised indirectly in a test of reading speed.

By the same token, most of the components under I D (to secure an adequate understanding of what is read) can be appraised by a well-designed test of comprehension of connected material. Thus, questions can be asked not only about the meaning of words in their context (I D 1a), but also about the sequence and relationship of parts of the passage (I D 1c) and about the author's mood or purpose (I D 3b). A teacher can test not only for facts explicitly stated, but also for implied conclusions (I D 4). A student can be called on not merely to comprehend the author's statement, but to judge the accuracy of his facts (I E 2), to appraise the soundness of a chain of reasoning (I E 4), or to identify the presence of propagandistic techniques (I E 5).

Though the better reading tests cover a wide range of skills of perceiving symbols, of getting meaning from them, and of evaluating and interpreting this meaning, no test can cover all of the objectives of reading. Thus, a reading test can hardly determine the pupil's responsiveness to reading (I A), or the extent to which he does in fact integrate reading into his total life experience (I F). Though certain components of study skills can be incorporated into a test (II A), a test will be less useful in appraising how the student actually uses these skills to solve an intellectual problem (II B).

Even more difficult might be the appraisal of the extent to which the individual *will* read and the type of reading he will select, as distinct from the extent to which he *can* read.

In this discussion we have been trying to make four main points. These points refer not only to reading but to any segment of the school program. The points are these:

1. The teaching of reading, or of any segment of the school program, is a complex undertaking looking to a variety of different outcomes.

2. A specific existing test will provide an appraisal of only certain ones of the desired outcomes.

3. Some of the desired outcomes are not likely to be reached by any test procedures.

4. The evaluation of any test of achievement requires a formulation of *your* objectives and an analysis of the test to see to what extent its content conforms to those outcomes that you are seeking to achieve.

SURVEY READING TESTS

One of the most widely used types of standardized test is the survey reading test. Because of the importance of reading skills in all aspects of the school program, many schools make a special effort to appraise these skills as a basis for planning group activities and individual remedial action. As was suggested on pp. 291–292, reading is a complex and far-reaching enterprise. The commercial survey tests undertake to appraise only certain aspects of this range of skills. In Appendix III a number of the better-known and more widely distributed reading tests are listed, showing the grade levels for which forms are available, the types of subtests that are included in each, and certain other items of practical interest about each.

The subtests most frequently included in survey reading tests are word knowledge and paragraph reading. The test of paragraph reading usually involves paragraphs of some length with questions based upon each, though the pattern of a missing word or words to be supplied is sometimes used (*Stanford*) and the technique of requiring the reader to identify the word which *spoils* the meaning has also been tried (*Science Research Associates*). The paragraph with questions seems to correspond most naturally to the normal reading task.

The paragraph-with-questions pattern still leaves room for a wide range of variation in the processes that are actually tapped by the test. Only a critical examination of the single test items will enable the potential user to tell how many items call merely for knowing a word meaning, how many call for selecting the particular meaning which fits the context, how many for the answer to a specific factual question that is answered in the passage, how many for an inference based upon information given in the passage, how many for getting the main idea or theme of the passage, how many for sensing the author's mood or purpose, and how many for recognizing literary devices used in the passage. Reading with understanding is all these things and more. The different components are represented in different tests in very different proportions. The potential user of a reading test must examine the actual test items to get a real understanding of what abilities the test is measuring. And this is true not only for reading tests. In any area of achievement, it is only as the potential user examines critically the individual items on the test that he can judge whether this is a valid test for *his* purposes.

Fortunately, these different skills are all positively correlated, so that a survey based on some one combination of the skills will tend to rank pupils in fairly much the same way as a survey based on a rather different balance of them. The child who does well on a test made up of directly factual items will in most cases tend to do well on one involving items of inference and synthesis. But the correlation is far from perfect. The potential user must examine each test in which he is interested, bearing in mind the specific types of comprehension skills that he deems important, in order to judge whether that particular test is the one best suited for his purposes. In the same way, a test in any subject matter must be scrutinized to see whether the test items represent the balance of information, understanding, and application that corresponds well with the objectives of teaching in the using school.

MEASURING SPEED OF READING

An additional factor that enters in to complicate the appraisal of reading achievement is the factor of speed. Speed of performance is a complicating factor in measuring achievement in any area, but perhaps especially so in the case of reading. To what extent do we want speed per se to enter into our score? Do we wish to penalize the person who is a slow worker but can accomplish a good deal if we give him time? Or do we want to get a pure measure of *power,* uncontaminated by speed of work?

Different tests resolve this problem in somewhat different ways, but generally speaking good testing practice accepts as its goal the separate measurement of *speed* of performance and *level* of performance. In measuring level, the objective is to provide enough time on any test so that each individual has had an opportunity to progress as far as his ability permits. This means either that he has had time to try all the items on the test or, if the items are graded in difficulty, that he has had time to work along to the point where he can no longer succeed with any of the test tasks.

In practical testing, this goal can only be approximated. Tests must be given with a definite time limit if they are to be fitted into a school program. Furthermore, it does not make for good testing conditions to have time limits so long that half the group is sitting around fidgeting. Time limits for a test designed to be a power test are usually figured so that *most* of the pupils have time to try *most* of the items.

But in the case of reading, we are also interested in speed for its own sake. Slow, laborious reading is inefficient and time-consuming. With some materials, it is desirable to be able to skim rapidly in order to cover a large amount of material in a short time. For this reason, a number of tests have undertaken to include separate measures of speed of reading.

The measurement of speed presents its own special problems. We start a group of pupils reading an extended passage. At the end of 2 minutes we stop them and tell them to mark the word they were reading when the signal was given. But how do we know that they actually read the intervening material? Some may have read it word for word, others only skimmed, and others just read parts. What does "reading the passage" really mean?

Various devices have been tried in the attempt to make the task more uniform for different examinees. In some tests, such as the *Iowa Silent Reading Tests* and the *Traxler High School Reading Test,* the reader is instructed to read in such a way that he will be able to answer questions. The *Gates Reading Survey for Grades 3 to 10* uses very brief paragraphs, each ending with a multiple-choice question, and score is the number of questions answered within the time limit. The *Michigan Speed of Reading Test* includes in each two-sentence unit one word that spoils the meaning of the unit. The reader must cross out these words. Any of these devices is only partly satisfactory. Any device that doctors up the actual text tends to distort the normal process of reading. Yet we cannot rely upon instructions alone to bring about comparable care and thoroughness by different readers. The reading speed test is at best very dependent upon the instructions given to the examinees and provides only an approximate indication of the relative speeds at which different people *can* read when degree of care and comprehension are uniform for each person.

SUMMARY STATEMENT

The survey test is, then, a sampling of the tasks that comprise a particular skill or knowledge. Only certain aspects of the total skill are represented, and the balance is a little different in each test. Most survey achievement tests have reasonably satisfactory reliability. The main problem is to pick the one that, in its content, provides the best balance of skills for your particular objectives.

DIAGNOSTIC TESTING

A survey achievement test undertakes to provide a general, over-all appraisal of status in some area of knowledge or skill. A diagnostic test undertakes to provide a detailed picture of strengths and weaknesses in an area. Furthermore, it is anticipated that this detailed analysis will suggest *causes* for deficiencies and provide a guide for remedial procedures. A survey reading test tells us that Johnny, who is starting the fourth grade, performs on our test of reading paragraphs at a level typical of the usual child beginning the second grade. A series of diagnostic tests indicates that Johnny has a fair sight vocabulary of common words but no skills for working out unfamiliar words, that he is unable to blend sounds to form words, that he does not recognize the sounds that correspond to letter combinations, and that he makes frequent reversal errors. These findings, together with others, provide the basis for planning remedial teaching of word analysis and phonic skills that are specifically directed toward Johnny's deficiencies. Development of diagnostic tests involves two steps (1) analysis of the complex performance—be it reading, multiplying fractions, or using a microscope—into its component subskills and (2) developing tests for the component skills, free as far as possible from any other source of difficulty.

It has become fashionable in recent years to call many tests "diagnostic tests." In a sense, any test that yields more than a single overall score is diagnostic. Even if there are only two part scores, say, one for word knowledge and one for paragraph comprehension, the test makes it possible for us to say that Johnny showed better ability in word knowledge than he did in reading connected prose. This is certainly *one* diagnostic clue. Diagnosis is, after all, a matter of degree. We may probe and analyze with varying degrees of thoroughness and detail. We must ask concerning any test purporting to be diagnostic: How complete and how adequate are the diagnostic cues that this test provides? It is easy to overstate the value of the diagnostic information provided by a particular test.

Diagnostic testing faces a very troublesome dilemma. How is the test to provide sufficient diagnostic detail and yet appraise each separate ability with sufficient reliability? The essence of good diagnosis is that one should get many distinct and relevant facts about the individual. One wishes an appraisal of each of the component abilities into which the complex performance has been analyzed. At the same time, it is important that the separate appraisals have adequate reliability.

Reliable appraisal is particularly important in diagnostic testing for two reasons. In the first place, in diagnostic work we are in almost every instance interested in the *individual*. It is his personal strengths and weaknesses with which we are concerned. Group averages or group comparisons are of no particular interest to us in this context. We cannot fall back upon averages to balance out the chance errors in measuring a particular pupil. We need an accurate appraisal of the specific individual. This is made more acute by the fact that we are dealing with *differences* between the individual's performance in related tasks. We are interested in making such a statement as: "This pupil's ability to pick out the main idea in what he has read is poorer than his ability to answer questions on specific factual details." But the two abilities are quite closely related. How reliably can we measure the differences between the two?

At this point, the student could well refer to the discussion of profiles on pp. 147–152. A set of diagnostic scores is a specific instance of a profile. All the issues about the reliability of a difference score that were raised in that discussion apply very acutely to the case of diagnostic tests. Since we are dealing with different aspects of a single field, correlations between tests are likely to be fairly substantial and the loss of reliability to be considerable when we have to think about differences. One would think, this being so, that authors of diagnostic tests would have been particularly concerned about the reliability of their instruments. But, alas, this has not generally been the case. The temperament that becomes excited about problems of diagnosis appears to be different from the temperament that grows concerned about issues of reliability of measurement. It must be confessed that in many cases the reliability of diagnostic tests is quite modest and that in many others it is unreported.

All this means that diagnostic test results must be interpreted with caution. The tests provide some rough and quite tentative hypotheses as to the individual's strengths and weaknesses. But these must be clearly recognized as tentative hypotheses and nothing more. The test profile suggests possible causes for the present difficulty and a jumping-off place for remedial work. If the remedial activities are successful, well and good. If not, the remedial teacher must stand ready to review his hypotheses and to explore other leads. Diagnostic test results are suggestions, not commands.

We find several types of diagnostic instruments in reading, and these serve also to illustrate the varieties of diagnosis in other areas. In the first place, we find tests with somewhat specialized subtests yielding scores for some aspect of the total function. This type is well illustrated by the *Iowa Silent Reading Tests* (*Advanced Level*). These have the following subtests, each supposed to represent a somewhat different aspect of reading skill.

Test 1. *Rate and Comprehension* of connected prose.
Test 2. *Directed Reading* of connected prose to locate answers to factual questions.
Test 3. *Poetry Comprehension,* including mood, metaphor, etc.

Test 4. *Word Meaning* in different content areas.

Test 5. *Sentence Meaning* of brief sentences out of context.

Test 6. *Paragraph Comprehension:* selecting central idea and comprehending essential details.

Test 7. *Location of Information:* using an index, selecting key words.

How many of these are in fact both sufficiently reliable and sufficiently different to be usefully diagnostic is a real question. For example, the reliabilities of *Test 5, Sentence Meaning,* and *Test 6, Paragraph Comprehension,* are reported (probably somewhat optimistically, since the coefficients are based on odd versus even halves and the tests have quite short time limits) as .751 and .759. The correlation between the two tests is reported as .48. From these values, we may estimate the reliability of the difference score to be .53. Inferences from a datum having this level of reliability should be made very cautiously.

The use of subtest scores such as those on the *Iowa* is probably most justifiable for a class or larger group. With a group average, chance errors tend to cancel out, and the low reliability of the scores becomes less important. If the group as a whole shows some marked weakness, as in the use of indices and library aids, for example, this may point out areas in which instruction has been neglected and suggest directions for instruction for the group as a whole.

A second approach to the diagnostic study of reading is through standard oral reading passages. One test of this type that has been used for many years is *Gray's Oral Reading Passages.* The test consists of a standard set of passages, ranging from easy and simple to quite difficult. The child who is being studied reads the passages aloud. The examiner uses a standard code to record on a copy of the passages all the errors and hesitations made by the pupil. Mispronounced words are underlined. Mispronounced vowels are shown by appropriate diacritical marks. Omissions are encircled. Substitutions and insertions are written in. Repetitions are indicated by a wavy line. A sample record with a number of errors indicated upon it is shown in Fig. 11.1.

The sun pierced into my large windows. It was the opening of October, and the sky was of a dazzling blue. I looked out of my window and down the street. The white houses of the long, straight street were almost painful to the eyes. The clear atmosphere allowed full play to the sun's brightness.

Fig. 11.1. Example of reading passage taken from *Gray's Oral Reading Passages.* (Reproduced by permission of the Public School Publishing Co.)

The record of the child's oral responses is valuable for the insight that it gives us into the actual *process* of reading. The usual objective written test shows us only the *product* of a child's efforts, the marks he makes on a test booklet or answer sheet. If he does poorly or makes mistakes, we are often at a loss to know why. In the oral test we can see the errors as they happen—each hesitation, each omission, each reversal. In this way we can identify more specifically the components that are giving the child trouble. They are not lost in the one final result, that the child is slow in reading the passage or does poorly on comprehension questions based on it.

The oral test as a basis for diagnosis can be illustrated in arithmetic also by the *Buswell-John Diagnostic Test for Fundamental Processes in Arithmetic*. This test consists of a series of graded examples. The examples are to be worked out by the child "thinking out loud," telling what he is doing and why he is doing it at each step. The examiner has a record sheet, with a code for types of erroneous processes. One page of the record sheet is illustrated in Fig. 11.2. The examiner uses this form to record errors made by the pupil as he speaks out his solution of the problem. A study of the types of errors that the pupil is making may suggest specific points at which the pupil needs help. This opportunity to gain insight into the way in which the pupil is attacking the task and to understand the nature of his errors is an advantage of oral testing procedures in whatever field they may be used.

In a third type of diagnostic test the test maker tries to analyze the complex task, such as reading, into its simpler components and test these components one at a time. Thus, the *Gates Reading Diagnosis Tests* include tests of recognition of words, recognition of separate syllables, ability to blend the sounds of letter combinations, and recognition of the single letters. The complex skill is pushed back to smaller and smaller segments of the total task. The thought is that when a person fails on the complex task we test to see whether he is able to show the component skills of which the larger task is built.

This type of approach may be illustrated in another field by the *Compass Diagnostic Arithmetic Tests*. In these the authors undertake to break up each complex skill in arithmetic into its components —to test the simplest components first, and then to add on additional elements until the full task has been tested. Thus, the diagnostic test concerned with division of whole numbers has subsections testing the child upon the following contributing skills and understandings: (1) the vocabulary of division, (2) fundamentals of short division, (3) short division with carrying, (4) the addition, subtraction, and multiplication used in later subtests, (5) estimating the first quotient fig-

Published by the
Public School Publishing Co.
Bloomington, Illinois

Teacher's Diagnosis

for Pupil

DIAGNOSTIC CHART
FOR
INDIVIDUAL DIFFICULTIES
FUNDAMENTAL PROCESSES IN ARITHMETIC
Prepared by G. T. Buswell and Lenore John

Name_____ School_____ Grade_____ Age_____ IQ_____

Date of Diagnosis: _____ Add._____; Subt._____; Mult._____; Div._____

Teacher's preliminary diagnosis_____

ADDITION: (Place a check before each habit observed in the pupil's work)

_____ a1 Errors in combinations
_____ a2 Counting
_____ a3 Added carried number last
_____ a4 Forgot to add carried number
_____ a5 Repeated work after partly done
_____ a6 Added carried number irregularly
_____ a7 Wrote number to be carried
_____ a8 Irregular procedure in column
_____ a9 Carried wrong number
_____a10 Grouped two or more numbers
_____a11 Splits numbers into parts
_____a12 Used wrong fundamental operation
_____a13 Lost place in column
_____a14 Depended on visualization

_____a15 Disregarded column position
_____a16 Omitted one or more digits
_____a17 Errors in reading numbers
_____a18 Dropped back one or more tens
_____a19 Derived unknown combination from familiar one
_____a20 Disregarded one column
_____a21 Error in writing answer
_____a22 Skipped one or more decades
_____a23 Carrying when there was nothing to carry
_____a24 Used scratch paper
_____a25 Added in pairs, giving last sum as answer
_____a26 Added same digit in two columns
_____a27 Wrote carried number in answer
_____a28 Added same number twice

Habits not listed above_____

(Write observation notes on pupil's work in space opposite examples)

(1) 5 6 2 3		(5) 6+2= 3+4=	
(2) 2 8 9 4		(6) 52 40 13 39	
(3) 12 13 2 5		(7) 78 46 71 92	
(4) 19 17 2 9		(8) 3 8 5 7 8 9 2 7	

Fig. 11.2. Example of record sheet used in the *Buswell-John Diagnostic Test for Fundamental Processes in Arithmetic.* (Reproduced by permission of the Public School Publishing Co.)

ure, (6) fundamentals of long division and checking, and (7) finding errors in long division. A study of scores on these subsections may provide insight as to where the trouble *really* lies.

Related to this type of test is the test that is loaded with opportunities to make a particular type of error. Thus, one test used by Gates in reading diagnosis is one in which the examinee reads a set of words that lend themselves to reversal errors, i.e., was—saw, on—no. Such a test gives a concentrated exposure and permits a judgment of the susceptibility of the examinee to that particular type of error. Informal tests of this sort in such fields as language usage, spelling, etc., are, of course, familiar to any teacher who tries to check upon the effectiveness of his teaching of particular usages, rules, generalizations, and understandings.

Finally, diagnostic testing in any given field must go beyond the immediate field of skill or knowledge and seek information on all the background factors that contribute to success or difficulty in the particular area. Thus, to understand the child with reading difficulty we need information on his vision, his hearing, his general intellectual level, even his interests and his emotional adjustment. So a thorough diagnostic study will include tests of visual acuity, muscular balance and fusion, testing with an audiometer to be sure the child can hear adequately, a non-reading intelligence test, and interview or questionnaire information about factors in the child's background and present life that may prove relevant. Diagnostic testing spreads out beyond subject boundaries and a full diagnostic study becomes essentially a directed case history of an individual, directed in that it is focused on the academic problem but comprehensive in that it covers all potentially significant features of both the skill area and the individual's personal life.

We have described a variety of diagnostic procedures in reading and in arithmetic. It is in these fields that the most work on diagnostic procedures has been done. There are, in fact, few published diagnostic tests outside these fields, though there is certainly informal teacher diagnosis. Even in the fields of reading and arithmetic, relatively little information about the specific diagnostic tests is provided by the authors. Evidence on reliability is meager, and norms are rather crude and fragmentary. Most diagnostic tests are not very elegant psychometric devices. They have not been sufficiently widely used to support the large investment in development and analysis that characterizes the more popular survey tests. Interpretation of test scores must, therefore, be made with particular care and a good deal of tentativeness.

ACHIEVEMENT MEASURED THROUGH PUPIL PRODUCTS

One type of achievement measure that cannot be well illustrated within the field of reading is the product scale. We can illustrate this type of appraisal in the field of handwriting. Here, the plan is to evaluate some performance of an individual, in this case his handwriting, by comparing it with a set of standard samples. The standard samples are chosen by using the pooled judgments of a number of judges. The judges are usually asked to consider specimens in pairs and decide which is better. The basic idea in this type of scaling is that the larger the per cent of judges who agree in noticing a difference, the larger the difference. Thus, if 90 per cent of judges consider specimen A to be better than specimen B and only 80 per cent consider B to be better than C, the difference between A and B is greater than the difference between B and C. If 50 per cent consider C better than D and 50 per cent consider D better than C, then C and D must be considered of equal merit. Equally perceptible differences are considered to be the same size. Thus, a difference that is agreed upon by 75 per cent of our group of judges would be considered to be the same size wherever it occurred on our scale. Basing our scale units on this ease-of-perception standard, we can set up a scale of specimens from very poor to very good and assign a numerical value to each.

When we use a product scale, the procedure is to compare the specimen of a pupil's performance with the set of standard samples. His product is moved up and down the set of standard samples until the judge decides which one it most nearly resembles. It is then assigned the scale value of the one that it matches most closely. If greater accuracy is desired, each specimen may be compared to the set of standard samples by two or more judges independently and their judgments averaged to give the final value.

Product scales have been used for such performances as handwriting, sewing, drawing, and manual arts. They are potentially applicable to any area of skill in which a permanent tangible product is the end result.

ACHIEVEMENT TEST BATTERIES

The tests that are probably most widely used in programs of achievement testing are survey achievement test batteries. These batteries represent "package" achievement testing programs ready-made for the schools' use. The typical battery is made up of from four to eight or ten separate tests covering the core knowledge and skill segments of the curriculum. We shall examine the content of several batteries in more detail presently. The attempt of the authors and publishers is to produce an integrated instrument that will cover the general achievement testing needs of the typical community.

The chief virtues of the single battery of tests, as compared with a program made up of separate tests chosen from a variety of different sources, are those of unity and of convenience. A test battery is unified in two important respects. In the first place, it is based upon a unified and integrated plan. The parts have been selected and the content of each planned with an eye to the whole. Within the limits of the professional skill and understanding of the team of authors, the product is a unified whole in which the parts fit together to cover the range of objectives that they deem important and feasible to appraise with a standardized test.

A battery is unified in one other important respect. It has a unified set of norms. The norms for all the subtests are based upon the same population and expressed in the same form. This makes direct comparison between the different subtests possible with a minimum of question. We do not have to ask whether our reading test was tried out on the same type of group as our arithmetic test, or how the standard scores of our spelling test compare with the percentile equivalents of our language usage measure. When tests are assembled from different sources, these problems can be matters of real concern. Particularly in the past, when norming populations for tests were assembled in a somewhat haphazard manner, the comparability of a grade score of 4.0, for example, from one test to another was subject to serious question. The large, broadly representative groups used in norming recent achievement batteries assure both breadth of representation for the norms as a whole and equivalence of meaning from one test to another.

Of course, the "package" testing program based on a standard battery has certain limitations. The chief one is rigidity. Some sections of a battery may fit a particular local curriculum better than others. Some subtests of one battery may fit modern curricular objectives, whereas another battery may seem better in another area. The user of the battery gets the good with the bad, "the bitter with the sweet." Short of omitting certain sections completely, he must use what the battery offers him, even though in certain respects it may not fit his needs, as he sees them, as well as some other specific test covering that area. How serious this is the consumer must judge for himself when he compares the subtests of the battery that he is using or proposes to use test by test with other tests that are available for measurement in those same areas. The general verdict of users, particularly in the elementary school, has been that the convenient and unified program represented in a survey battery has more advantages than drawbacks, and in practice such instruments are very widely used.

COMPARISON OF ELEMENTARY SCHOOL BATTERIES

We propose to try to give a picture of the common features of some of the widely used achievement batteries. Since content changes somewhat at different levels, and space does not permit a comparison at all levels, we have chosen the tests designed for use at about the fifth and sixth grades. The upper elementary school is probably the level at which achievement test batteries are most widely used. We have elected to compare the following batteries, with publishers and approximate publication dates as indicated:

California Achievement Tests, California Test Service, 1957
Iowa Tests of Basic Skills, Houghton Mifflin Co., 1956
Metropolitan Achievement Test, World Book Co., 1960
Sequential Tests of Education Progress (STEP), Educational Testing
   Service, 1957
SRA Achievement Test, Science Research Associates, 1956
Stanford Achievement Test, World Book Co., 1956

The tests will be compared area by area, to bring out the elements that are common and the features that are distinctive.

MEASUREMENT OF WORD KNOWLEDGE

Each of the tests except the *STEP* provides for the appraisal of word knowledge. However, the tests vary in the degree to which this ability is kept separate for scrutiny as a significant fact about the individual. On the one hand, the *SRA* tests appraise vocabulary only in paragraph context, and include the items only as part of a total appraisal of reading ability. By contrast, the *Iowa* and *Metropolitan* tests yield a separate vocabulary score, and provide *no* procedure for putting it together with paragraph reading in a single reading score. The others (*California, Stanford*) provide a separate word knowledge score, but also provide for combining this with paragraph reading in a total reading score.

MEASUREMENT OF READING

Every one of the tests provides for the measurement of reading ability as represented by the reading of connected passages. The tests vary quite widely, however, in the length of the passages, and the type and range of test items based on each. At one extreme, appraisal in the *Stanford Achievement Test* is based on passages only 50 to 100 words long with two or three items on each passage. (These follow the somewhat unusual format of omitting words or phrases from the passage and requiring the subject to pick the word or phrase that best fills in the gap—an activity rather different from the normal process of reading.) At the other extreme, the reading test of the *SRA Achievement Series* is based upon a small number of long passages (500 or 600 words) with as many as twenty test items referring to a single passage. The other tests use passages of intermediate length with six to ten comprehension items testing various aspects of the comprehension of each passage.

As noted above, a number of the tests combine word knowledge with paragraph comprehension into a single global reading score. One may question whether it is desirable to have knowledge of words *per se* bulk so large in an appraisal of reading. Of course, word knowledge is quickly and easily measured, but real reading comprehension would seem to be better exemplified by ability to get meaning and draw inferences from connected material.

MEASUREMENT OF ARITHMETICAL SKILLS AND UNDERSTANDINGS

All achievement batteries make some appraisal of ability in arithmetic. The older batteries tended to break the total area of arithmetic up into computational skills and problem solving, and to provide two subtests corresponding to these two areas. Provision was usually made for combining the subtests into a single global appraisal of arithmetical ability. Among many of the newer tests, however, there is an additional concern with arithmetical concepts and understandings. In the *Iowa* tests, the computational subtest has been entirely replaced by a test dealing with arithmetical concepts. In others (*Metropolitan, SRA*) a section dealing with concepts is included in either the skills or the problem-solving subtest. Addition of the material on concepts reflects the increased emphasis within the arithmetic curriculum on developing meaning and understanding, as distinct from simply facility in carrying out mechanical operations.

In arithmetic it is often difficult to free appraisal of problem-solving ability from the influence of reading skills. This is illustrated by the mathematics test of the *STEP*. In a commendable attempt to incorporate the arithmetical tasks in real and meaningful problems, the authors have introduced a reading level such that the resulting score has a higher correlation with a verbal than a quantitative score on the parallel aptitude series (*SCAT*).

LANGUAGE SKILLS

Another common denominator in all the batteries is appraisal of various skills in using language. The batteries vary in detail, but typically they cover capitalization, punctuation, elements of usage such as case, number and tense, and spelling. As in other subtests, there is a tendency here too to present all tasks in multiple choice form. Thus, most of the spelling tests call in some manner for the recognition of error. The examinee must decide which word in a set, if any, is misspelled (*Iowa*); or he must decide whether or not a given word is misspelled, and if it is he must correct it (*Metropolitan*). Recognition of the correct form is also typical of the usage items, and it is assumed that the ability to recognize error is a good indicator of ability of the student to avoid error in his own writing.

The psychometrician is fairly happy with this assumption, on the basis of the correlation of recognition test scores with ratings of quality of actual writing, and is impressed by the greater reliability, efficiency and objectivity of the recognition test. The English teacher, however, would still prefer to appraise writing ability through an actual sample of writing—an essay of some sort. The only one of the achievement batteries that provides for this is the *STEP*. The essay test is supported in part because it may measure, though unreliably, something that is not reached by the objective tests. It is justified further as having a healthy effect on the curriculum, the argument being that we must evaluate writing if we are to expect the schools to continue to teach it.

One further aspect of language skill that appears in the *STEP* is a test of listening comprehension. Learning through listening has always bulked fairly large in school, and the expansion of radio, television and sound movies as instructional media in recent years has increased the importance of the aural channel. Skills of listening are probably less directly related to school instruction than other communication skills, but appraisal of ability to comprehend and retain what has been heard is certainly of some educational importance.

MEASUREMENT OF STUDY SKILLS

Knowledge about and skills in obtaining information have found a place in most of the recent achievement tests. The emphasis in many schools upon individual and group projects, and upon gathering information from all parts of a book—not just the words in it—has supported the need for tests dealing with such skills.   In one way or another, most current batteries appraise such skills as: reading graphs and charts; reading tables; reading maps; picking appropriate reference sources; finding information in a reference source; using a dictionary. These skills are occasionally incorporated in tests of content areas such as social studies, science and mathematics (*STEP*) or included only as a brief subtest in some other major test (*California*), but usually some combination of them now appears as a distinct test in the battery, yielding one or more distinct scores.   Thus the *Iowa* provides three subtests which between them cover all of the six skills referred to above.   This is one major respect in which the widely distributed batteries of the present differ from those of the 30's—a place in which achievement tests have adapted to, and perhaps even helped to foster certain types of curriculum emphases.

MEASUREMENT IN CONTENT AREAS

The six batteries that we use as illustrations split evenly on the matter of including tests of information in content areas.   Three (*STEP, Metropolitan, Stanford*) include tests in social studies and science; the other three do not.   However, the three that do provide these content subtests also provide a "partial" battery, a more limited set of tests from which the content subtests have been omitted, in recognition of the fact that some schools are not interested in them.

Tests in content areas have tended to play a less prominent part in standardized testing in recent years, reflecting a feeling that in the common core of the curriculum items of information are a good deal less universal than skills.   Thus, at one time a "Literature" section appeared in some tests, but it now has disappeared because of the feeling that the stories and books read will vary too much from school to school to provide any dependable common core in terms of which the schools may be compared.   The common core is undoubtedly larger for science and social studies, but one may still question whether it is large enough to permit meaningful comparisons between different school systems.   This has been handled in the *STEP* by making the science and social studies tests into reading and study skills tests in the science and social studies areas.   That is, the role of information and specific knowledge in the area is held to a minimum, and the tests become primarily tests of ability to comprehend and work with ideas in the specific subject matter field.

BATTERIES FOR HIGH-SCHOOL ACHIEVEMENT

The batteries that have been discussed so far are for the elementary school and junior high school. It is at these levels that survey batteries have been most widely used. The more departmentalized and specialized program of the high school and college appears to call more for specific tests in particular subject areas. The Cooperative Test Division of the Educational Testing Service markets a range of such specific achievement tests all tied to a common score scale.

There are, however, several comprehensive batteries at the secondary and higher levels. Summary information on four of these is presented in Appendix III. The four batteries suitable for secondary-school use have in common tests of content knowledge in natural sciences, social studies, and mathematics. Three of them also provide an evaluation of achievement in English, tending to emphasize correctness and effectiveness of expression. The *Sequential Tests of Educational Progress (STEP)*, which include a battery for grades four through six, as well as batteries for seven through nine, ten through twelve, and the first 2 years of college, emphasize communication skills, with objective tests of reading, writing, and listening, as well as a subjectively graded essay. The *Iowa Tests of Educational Development* go beyond the fields of content knowledge and undertake to appraise abilities to locate, read, and understand materials in the different subject areas, thus attempting to test ability to get and use knowledge as well as the amount of knowledge already obtained. Tests of this sort were found especially useful in evaluating the educational level of individuals much of whose education had occurred outside the usual school setting, specifically soldiers in World War II who had acquired various amounts and types of training while in military service. Evidence is reported by the test authors that score on this battery predicts college achievement at least as well as grades during 4 years of high school.

USING THE RESULTS OF A SURVEY BATTERY

Since the survey achievement battery is one of the two or three most widely used types of standardized test, it is fitting that we consider ways in which the results from this testing may be used and appraise the soundness of each. Various things are done with the results from achievement testing, some useful, some relatively futile, and some perhaps positively harmful. Let us examine some of the possibilities. One possibility, of course, is that the tests are just given, scored, incorporated in some type of summarizing report, and filed away. This is one of the forms of futility referred to above. We shall dismiss this possibility and assume that at least *something* will be done with the test results. Let us examine various uses that might be made of them.

USE TO EVALUATE THE CURRICULUM OF SCHOOL OR SCHOOL SYSTEM

As part of a total appraisal of the effectiveness of its program, a school system may well wish to include measures of progress in basic skills. An achievement battery provides a convenient tool for doing this. The results will show how well the particular school or school system has progressed on the several components of the battery in relation to the norming groups. However, in interpreting this progress, three cautions must be borne in mind.

1. The evaluation is only partial, not complete. The battery can give information only on the range of skills that it covers, and these skills represent only a fraction of the objectives of the modern school. Because they are so conveniently measurable, they may become overvalued. This is an insidious danger. The school system must seek to supplement standardized achievement tests with broader and more informal appraisals of other objectives if it is to obtain a well-rounded evaluation of its program.

2. Local emphases may differ from those that characterized the national sample. The particular school system may have placed heavier emphasis upon reading or may have delayed the introduction of formal instruction in arithmetic. In so far as local emphasis and effort are atypical, local accomplishment may be expected to be atypical. Evaluation of achievement in the single school or system must take account of distinctive local emphases.

3. Evaluation of pupil performance in a school must take account of the characteristics of the pupil population. Schools, communities, even regions differ in the economic and cultural level of the population served. Associated with these differences are differences in average level of ability as measured by our intelligence tests. The expectancy for achievement must be tempered to take these factors into account. This may be approximated by developing regional norms or norms for schools of a particular type.

USE TO PLAN THE PROGRAM FOR A CLASS GROUP AND THE PUPILS IN IT

Every fall each teacher in most schools faces a new group of pupils. Within the limits set by the course of study (which may in some instances be quite rigid limits) he must plan a program of activities for the group as a whole and must adapt that program as best he can to each of the children in the group. He must decide where to pick up the various skill subjects, how much time to devote to review of materials presumably taught in the previous year, and how fast to move ahead. He must plan appropriate enrichment experiences and materials for independent work and free time. He will probably want to form informal groupings within the class for work together at a common level.

To do these things he needs to get to know the pupils in the group as quickly, thoroughly, and accurately as possible. Administration of a standard achievement battery is an efficient way of laying the foundations for that picture of the class which will permit him to adapt his plans to the individuals with whom he has to deal. The scores will provide a guide as to whether the group as a whole is superior, average, or retarded in each of the basic skills he is trying to develop. They may indicate group areas of relative strength and weakness. They will pick out the children who could profit from more challenging tasks than those presented to the class as a whole, those who need less demanding materials, and those who should be considered for special help either within the classroom or through a remedial teacher if one is available.

It should be understood that this function of informing the teacher about his pupils is not to depend on tests alone. Every contact with the children helps the teacher to get a "feel" for the class group and the pupils in it. A richness of understanding of individual pupils can only come from working with them as persons. But the set of standard test scores provides an objective reference framework within which to see the rest of the picture of the class and the pupils. This function can, of course, be served by tests given the preceding spring and forwarded to the teacher when he meets the class in the fall. Technically, test results from spring testing would be quite serviceable, since pupils' skills are not likely to shift around greatly during the few summer months. But it is likely that tests given early in the fall will seem more current and alive than results from the preceding spring and will be more likely to be used by the teacher in determining his plans for the class.

USE TO IDENTIFY INDIVIDUALS FOR MORE DETAILED STUDY

One function of an achievement battery is to help screen out a fraction of the group of children for more intensive study. Though every child should be studied as an individual, there are in every school system some children more in need of special help than others. In those cases in which the symptom is failure to progress in school skills, the problem may be first identified by poor performance on a standardized test.

Gross irregularities in performance on different subtests, performance far below his age or grade level, or performance well below his aptitude as indicated by an intelligence test are cues suggesting further study. But they are only cues. They are only symptoms suggesting that something may be wrong. The significance of the symptom must be investigated further. In the first place, the educational achievement must be related to a measure of aptitude to see that the child is falling behind what should be expected of *him*. Where it is reading achievement that is at issue, his achievement should be related to performance on an aptitude test not involving reading. Then if the deficiency appears to be a specific retardation in some school skill, further diagnostic procedures need to be applied to determine the exact nature and causes of the deficiency.

UNDERSTANDING THE INDIVIDUAL PUPIL

Though special study and remedial activities may be possible for only part of the children in a class, the school and teacher have the responsibility of knowing every child as well as possible so as to provide the best possible guidance for him in his present school activities and in plans for the future. Level of educational achievement is one facet of the picture that is needed in understanding and guiding each pupil. Appraisal of present adjustment, planning for future education, and counseling about a life career can all be helped by information about educational progress.

MAKING UP CLASS GROUPS AND PLACING INDIVIDUAL PUPILS

In a large school where there are enough pupils to fill several classes in a grade or several sections in a subject, some procedure must be adopted for assigning pupils to particular groups. Fashions with respect to grouping together children of similar ability have changed several times over the past 50 years. At present, this procedure seems to be a relatively respectable one in educational circles. When the basic decision has been made to try to achieve homogeneous groups within each classroom, a standardized achievement test or battery provides one useful tool for achieving this end.

Of course the term "homogeneous group" is rather misleading, because the most we can do is to make a group somewhat less heterogeneous. Whether we use over-all level on an achievement battery, reading level, score on a scholastic aptitude test, or some combination of these, the children in any group will still vary markedly. They will vary in part because it will always be necessary to include children with a range of scores in any group. They will vary in even larger part because different abilities are not perfectly correlated. The child who is most outstanding in reading may be fairly mediocre in arithmetic or spelling, and vice versa. Grouping will not do away with the need to treat pupils as individuals, or to group them *within* the class for some special purposes, but it may reduce the range of individual differences enough so that the whole group can work together better and participate effectively in common academic enterprises. At the high-school level, where separate grouping is possible by subject areas, a specific measure of achievement in the subject area is likely to provide a more useful basis for grouping than a measure of over-all achievement.

The problem of placement in a class also arises for transfers into a school system. Here it may be a question not only of the section into which to place the pupil, but even of the grade level at which he can perform adequately. Results from standardized achievement tests can help in this decision. They make it possible to compare his achievement with that of the groups into which he may be placed in a way that is not possible from school marks above.

EVALUATING THE TEACHER

It is reported that in some school systems a standardized achievement battery is used, either openly or covertly, to evaluate the success of the teacher. He is judged by the performance his class shows on standardized tests given at the end of the school year. He is expected, with varying degrees of unrealism, to bring his class "up to the norm" on these tests.

This procedure seems questionable at best, and quite possibly vicious. It fails to take account of a number of important considerations. In the first place, the achievement of a class group is a function of their whole previous educational history, not merely of the year just past. It is unreasonable to hold the teacher who has taught a group for a single year solely responsible for their present status. In the second place, achievement depends upon aptitude and upon out-of-school cultural experiences as well as upon schooling. Unless the evaluator is prepared to make an appropriate adjustment for the intellectual and socio-economic level of a particular class—and class groups can differ widely in these respects—no reasonable base-line can be provided for evaluating what the teacher has accomplished. In the third place, the skills measured by an achievement battery represent only a fraction of the objectives of a modern school. Comparison of teachers with respect to this partial criterion neglects much of their work and may provide a very unfair evaluation of relative worth of two teachers whose strengths lie in different directions. Fourth, placing a premium upon easily testable skills when evaluating the teacher is almost inevitably going to lead the teacher to overvalue those skills in his teaching. As he is judged, so will he judge. Skills will tend to become the one central theme of his teaching, at the expense of all the other outcomes the school is trying to achieve. He will, with varying degrees of directness, teach for the tests. Finally, one may mention the demoralizing effect upon teachers of a mechanical, external evaluation that is subject to all the technical limitations discussed above.

SUMMARY STATEMENT

The typical standardized achievement test is superficially much like an objective test made by the classroom teacher. However, it is based on large segments of knowledge or skill common to the programs of many schools, and it provides norms. These features mean that it is appropriately used in making broad comparisons—between schools or classes, between areas of achievement, or between achievement and aptitude.

Just as an analysis of the objectives to be measured was indicated as the first step in thoughtful construction of a classroom test, so an analysis of objectives is a prerequisite for evaluating a published test. The test can only be evaluated in terms of the objectives that the teacher or school is trying to achieve.

Most widely used standardized tests are survey tests, giving a general appraisal of level of accomplishment in a broad area. If the teacher is to work constructively with the pupil, such survey results need to be supplemented by more specific and diagnostic information. Some published diagnostic tests exist, and these can be supplemented by informal teacher appraisals. However, the reliability of difference scores and consequently of differential diagnoses is often low. Diagnostic clues should be considered quite tentative.

Certain skills, such as those of handwriting, shop work, or domestic arts, can be appraised effectively by comparing a pupil product with a scaled set of standard samples.

Standardized achievement test batteries are very popular for school use. In these the advantage of unity in plan and standardization must be weighed against the inflexibility of a single total battery. The published batteries are similar in general design, though they differ in (1) content subjects included, (2) emphasis on work-study skills, (3) balance of emphasis among different areas, and (4) specific pattern of items in each field.

When used with discretion and proper reservations, a standardized achievement battery can serve a useful purpose as *one* type of evidence (1) to evaluate a school's educational program and its several components, (2) to help the teacher plan the work of his class and the grouping of pupils within it, and (3) to provide an understanding of the individual pupil. Standardized test results should rarely, if ever, be used as a basis for evaluating the effectiveness of individual teachers.

SUGGESTED ADDITIONAL READING

Harris, Chester W., Editor, *Encyclopedia of educational research*, 3rd ed., New York, Macmillan, 1960, pp. 72–73, 464–466, 804, 881–883.

Katz, Martin R., *Selecting an achievement test: principles and procedures*, Princeton, Educational Testing Service, 1958.

Lindquist, E. F., and A. N. Hieronymus, *Manual for administrators, supervisors, and counselors, Iowa Tests of Basic Skills*, Boston, Houghton Mifflin, 1956.

Sequential tests of educational progress, teacher's guide, Cooperative Test Division, Educational Testing Service, Princeton, N. J., 1958.

Traxler, Arthur E., *The use of test results in diagnosis and instruction in the tool subjects*, rev. ed., Educational Records Bulletin No. 18, New York, Educational Records Bureau, 1949.

Traxler, Arthur E., et al., *Introduction to testing and the use of test results in public schools*, New York, Harper, 1953, pp. 89–95.

QUESTIONS FOR DISCUSSION

1. For which of the following purposes would a standardized test be useful? For which should a teacher expect to make his own test? Why?

a. To determine which pupils have mastered the addition and subtraction of fractions.

b. To determine which pupils in a class are below standard in arithmetic computation.

c. To determine the subjects in which each pupil in a class is strongest and weakest.

d. To determine for a class which punctuation and capitalization skills need further teaching.

e. To form subgroups in a class for the teaching of reading.

2. Examine some standardized reading test. In view of the tasks it presents, which of the objectives outlined on pp. 291–292 does it measure adequately? Which does it measure to some extent? Which does it fail to measure at all?

3. Examine a standardized achievement test for a subject that you are

teaching or plan to teach. Which of the objectives that are important in the subject are measured adequately by the test? Which ones are not?

4. Make a critical comparison of two achievement test batteries for the same grade. How do they differ? What are the advantages of each from your point of view?

5. What are the advantages and disadvantages of a dictation as opposed to a multiple-choice type of spelling test?

6. Suppose you are teaching mathematics in the first year of junior high school. List the steps you would take to diagnose the achievement level of the pupils and plan for remedial instruction.

7. The manual of test W states that it can be used for diagnostic purposes. What should you look for to determine whether it has any real value as a diagnostic aid?

8. Why should we be specially concerned about the reliability of the scores resulting from a set of diagnostic tests? What implications does this have for using and interpreting such tests?

9. Suppose that you are a college chemistry teacher and are interested in the laboratory skills of glass blowing that your students have developed. How might you develop a product scale for evaluating their skill?

10. Before you can make a sound evaluation of the grade equivalents made on a battery of achievement tests by a class or pupil, what information do you need beside the converted scores themselves?

11. The town of M gives the *Stanford Achievement Tests* to pupils in grades four and six and records on the cumulative record card only the grade equivalent for the whole test. What are the disadvantages of this type of record?

12. You have given a standardized achievement battery in October to your fourth-grade class. What might you, as teacher, do on the basis of the results?

13. In city K, the *Metropolitan Achievement Test* is given to all schools in April. The average grade level for each class group and for each subject is reported to the superintendent of schools' office, and these results are mimeographed and distributed to all schools. What are the gains from this procedure, and what are the dangers in it? What changes would you suggest?

14. In a fourth-grade group you have data from a group intelligence test and from an achievement test battery. On what basis would you select individuals to receive special remedial work, either in your class or with a special teacher? What are the hazards of this procedure?

15. What should be the role of standardized test results in evaluating the performance of the classroom teacher?

Chapter 12

▼

Questionnaires and Inventories for Self-Appraisal

The last three chapters have been devoted to measures of ability: what the individual *can* do under test conditions and motivation to do his best. We shall move on now to measurement of other aspects of personality—to the appraisal of what he *will* do under the natural circumstances of life. Both in our discussions of personality and in our efforts to develop instruments of appraisal, we must recognize that the person is a unified whole. Any aspects or traits that we may separate out are separated out for our convenience. They do not exist as separate entities. They are only aspects of or ways of looking at the unitary person. However, it is inevitable that we do pick the person to pieces to study and understand him. We cannot look at everything at once.

In Chapter 2 we identified five segments of personality; to wit:

Temperament refers to the individual's characteristic mood, activity level, excitability, and focus of concern. It includes such dimensions as cheerful-gloomy, energetic-lethargic, excited-calm, introverted-extroverted, and dominant-submissive.

Character relates to those traits to which definite social value is attached. They are the "Boy Scout" traits of honesty, kindliness, cooperation, industry, and such.

Adjustment is a term that we shall use to indicate how well the individual has been able to make peace with himself and the world about him. In so far as the individual can comfortably accept himself and his world, in so far as his ways of life do not get him into trouble in his social group, he will be considered well adjusted.

Interests refer to tendencies to seek out and participate in certain activities.

Attitudes relate to tendencies to accept or reject particular groups of individuals, sets of ideas, or social institutions.

317

METHODS OF STUDYING PERSONALITY

Most of the evaluation techniques we shall consider in this and the following chapters have to do with one or more of the aspects of personality identified above. To what sources may we go for evidence on these aspects when we wish to study an individual? First, we can see what the individual has to say about himself. Second, we can find out what others say about him. Third, we can see what he actually does, how he behaves in the real world of things or people. Fourth, we can observe how he reacts to the world of fantasy and make-believe.

WHAT THE INDIVIDUAL SAYS ABOUT HIMSELF

One obvious source for information about a person is that person himself. No one else has as intimate and continuous a view of Johnny as Johnny has of himself. He is aware of hopes and aspirations, worries and concerns that may be well hidden from the outsider. To get at the individual's view of himself we may interview him, probing those areas that seem sensitive or significant. Another approach is to incorporate the questions that might be asked in a face-to-face interview into a uniform questionnaire or personality inventory. The choices the individual makes in responding to the set of questions are scored in various ways to provide a picture of him as he describes himself. These procedures will be elaborated in this chapter, and their strengths and weaknesses pointed out.

APPRAISAL THROUGH THE OPINION OF OTHERS

For some purposes, we may be interested in how a person is perceived by his fellow beings. Is he seen as a friendly fellow worker? A fair teacher? An industrious pupil? A convincing salesman? A generally desirable employee? The opinion of others may be the significant fact in certain settings. It is also a very convenient way of getting a summary appraisal of a fellow man. For these reasons, rating procedures have been widely used. We shall consider their values and limitations in the next chapter.

MEASURES OF BEHAVIOR

It can be argued that for practical purposes an individual's personality is what he does, rather than what he says or what is said about him. The problem is to develop procedures for appraising genuine behavior, not distorted for the purpose of making a good impression. Some attempts have been made to do this with objective tests, and we shall consider these briefly in Chapter 14. Of more importance and current interest are procedures for observing the individual and for recording or evaluating his responses as they are seen by an observer.

THE WORLD OF IMAGINATION AND FANTASY

What an individual will tell about himself in response to questions is limited by his willingness to reveal himself, his understanding of himself, and his understanding of the language in which the questions are presented. For this reason, indirect methods have been sought to avoid these limitations and permit him to "open up" more fully. One indirect avenue is that of fantasy, imagination, and make-believe. We may study what the person sees in ink blots, what stories he tells about an ambiguous picture, what play scenes he acts out with dolls, what he does with paints and modeling clay. These materials and others have been used to elicit imaginative productions that psychologists have studied as a source of understanding of children and adults. The individual is allowed to express himself through play materials or to project his own interpretations into ambiguous stimuli, and thus to reveal himself to us. These are expressive and projective techniques for personality appraisal. We shall undertake to describe and evaluate them in Chapter 15.

INTERVIEW

If we wish to find out about a person, one obvious way to do so is to ask him questions and evaluate his answers. If the questions are asked orally in a face-to-face situation, we are carrying out an interview. The interview has been a perennial favorite as a way of studying people. It is widely used by colleges and professional schools, by employers, and by clinicians working with disturbed individuals. Why is the interview looked upon with such widespread favor?

The popularity of the interview is *not* based primarily upon its demonstrated validity as a device for appraising people. In fact, evidence for the validity of the impressions or conclusions derived from interviews is spotty and rather contradictory. Interview procedures are basically subjective, variable and heavily dependent upon the skill of the interviewer. It has repeatedly been demonstrated that different interviewers interviewing the same person come up with quite varied impressions of him. The variability arises in part from variation in the questions asked and the lines of inquiry intensively pursued. It arises in part from differences in interpretation and evaluation of the responses the individual makes. The typical interview is not a precise or efficient psychometric technique.

The appeal of the interview lies rather in its great flexibility and adaptability. The interviewer can structure the interview in whatever way seems to him most suitable, in the light of the purposes of the interviewing and of the responses elicited to prior questions. He can skim over certain areas; probe intensively in others. He can give full play to his "clinical insight" and "intuition."

There is no doubt that the flexibility possible in the interview situation has certain elements of strength. It permits the wise interviewer to take full advantage of everything he has learned about the interviewee as he directs the further course of the interaction. But this same flexibility contains elements of weakness. It tends to destroy comparability from one interviewer to another and from one interviewee to the next. It makes it possible for an interviewer to ride a personal hobby and ignore many obvious areas of inquiry. Just as it permits full scope to the wisdom of the wise, so also it gives abundant rope to the foolishness of the foolish or the biases of the biased.

One approach that undertakes to reduce the subjectivity and variability of interview procedures, while still maintaining the flexibility and vividness of direct personal contact, is the *structured interview*.[4] Structured interview procedures give the interviewer a fairly detailed guide of topics to be covered and areas of inquiry to be included. These may include, for an employment interview, family patterns and interrelationships, school interests and activities, sports participation, previous work history, reasons for leaving previous jobs, and other similar areas. Within any one of these rather broad areas there may be several more specific questions to which the interviewer is to find an answer. The interviewer retains freedom and flexibility with respect to the order in which he attacks the different topics and the depth to which he pursues each. At the same time, he has a guide to make sure that a standard set of areas of inquiry is covered in each interview. The structured interview is a compromise between the free interview on the one hand and the printed biographical data blank or personality inventory on the other.

The questions during an interview session elicit responses that are descriptive of the individual. However, these responses require some degree of interpretation if they are to provide a useful picture of him. The interpretation may sometimes flow quite directly from the manifest content of the responses. This would be the case when the interviewer interprets a report of membership in many school organizations, the holding of many school offices, out-of-school experience in selling, and membership in the debating team as evidence of assertiveness and social leadership. Sometimes the interpretation may be quite indirect, and dependent upon the latent or concealed, rather than the manifest or obvious content of the response. This is true of many of the psychoanalytic interpretations of the communications from patient to analyst. In these variable and unstandardized interpretations lie potential strengths and frequent weaknesses of the interview as an appraisal technique.

The clinical interview is an unstandardized inquiry, highly dependent upon the particular interviewer both for the way it is carried out and for the way it is interpreted. Furthermore, individual interviews place very heavy demands upon the time of interviewing personnel, demands which may be prohibitive in a number of situations. To economize on interviewer time, then, and to provide an inquiry that is uniform in presentation and procedure for evaluation, the printed questionnaire has been developed. The self-report questionnaire or inventory is essentially this: a standard set of questions about some aspect or aspects of the individual's life history, feelings, preferences, or actions, presented in a standard way and scored with a standard scoring key.

THE BIOGRAPHICAL DATA BLANK

An obvious and important use of the questionnaire is as a means of eliciting factual information about the individual's past history. Place and date of birth, amount and type of education and degree of success with it, nature and duration of previous jobs, hobbies, special skills, and a host of other biographical facts can be determined most economically through a blank filled out by the individual himself. It is the economy and efficiency of this approach that makes it particularly appealing. Though his reports may be inaccurate in some respects, the individual himself is probably the richest single repository for the factual information we would like to have about him.

The problems in using questionnaires to elicit facts are primarily problems of communication. When questions are preformulated and appear in printed form and answers are written down, misunderstanding may occur either in the respondent's interpretation of the question or in the using agency's interpretation of his response. If there is no personal interaction, these misunderstandings cannot be cleared up with an oral question or a further probing into the area of uncertainty. It is important, therefore, that a fact-finding questionnaire be very carefully worded and that it be tried out in preliminary form with small groups to make sure that the ambiguities have been cleared out of it.

An interview to supplement the questionnaire is often desirable in order to permit clarification of any of the responses to questionnaire items that are puzzling to the user or to get fuller information on some points. As a matter of fact, one appropriate use of self-report inventories of all types is to provide a jumping-off place for an interview, the questionnaire providing leads that may be followed up in the interview.

Sometimes the factual information on an application blank or other fact-finding questionnaire has been used to determine whether the individual meets certain stated requirements to be eligible for a job, educational program, or the like. Sometimes it has been used as part of the raw material from which the personnel officer, director of admissions, or scholarship committee makes a clinical judgment of the individual's desirability as an employee or student. In a few instances, however, biographical data blanks have been analyzed item by item to determine to what extent particular responses to each item actually predict some criterion of job success. Items found to discriminate more successful from less successful individuals are given a score credit, and the separate items are summed to give a score for the blank as a whole. Thus, the World War II programs for selecting pilot trainees for both the Army and the Navy used a scored biographical data blank that was treated just as if it were a test. The life-insurance companies have for a number of years used an *Aptitude Index* in selecting insurance salesmen, one section of which consists of factual items about the individual applicant. Thus, the individual is asked about the amount of insurance he himself carries, his net worth, etc. A scoring system assigns scores for each response in terms of the success experienced by those in the validation group who had given that response

In the examples given above, objective scoring of a biographical data blank provided one of the most valid predictors of job success. These results suggest that there may be a number of other selection situations in which a standard scoring procedure could be used with advantage The development of scoring weights is a major undertaking, but once a scoring system has been developed the scoring of individual blanks proceeds rapidly It has even been possible in military use of biographical inventories to prepare them in multiple-choice form and score them like any standard test

INTEREST INVENTORIES

One aspect of the individual's make-up that we would like to study, both to understand him as a person and to help in such immediately practical problems as educational and vocational guidance, is the domain of interests and aversions, preferences for activities and surroundings. Of course, in the matter of vocational interests, the simplest procedure would seem to be to ask the individual how much he would like to be an engineer, for example. However, this doesn't work out very well in practice. In the first place, people differ in the readiness with which they exhibit enthusiasm. "Like very much" for person A may signify no more enthusiasm than "like" for person B. In the second place, people differ substantially in the nature and completeness of their understanding of what a particular job means in terms of activities and conditions of work. "Engineer" to one person may signify primarily out-of-doors work; to another it may carry a flavor of the laboratory or drafting board; to still another it may signify vaguely a high-prestige, science-oriented job. These varied and incomplete meanings cause a response to the single question, "How much would you like to be an engineer?" to be a rather unsatisfactory indicator of the degree to which the individual has interests really suitable for the profession of engineering. It is for these reasons that psychometricians have undertaken to broaden the base of information and to ask a whole array of questions about the individual's likes and dislikes, rather than simply to ask directly about preference for particular jobs.

THE STRONG VOCATIONAL INTEREST BLANK

One of the best known instruments for appraising interests is the *Strong Vocational Interest Blank for Men*. This inventory is made up of 400 items, broken up into the following types: liking for occupations, liking for amusements, liking for activities, reaction to peculiarities of people, choice or preference between activities, and evaluation of personal abilities and characteristics. To most of the 400 items in the *Strong Blank* the individual responds by marking one of the three given options L, I, and D (Like, Indifferent, Dislike). A response is called for to each item. Over 40 different scoring keys have been developed for the men's blank. Most of these are for specific occupations, largely at the professional level, such as architect, chemist, lawyer, or YMCA secretary, though there are also keys for interest maturity, masculinity of interests, and occupational level.

The scoring key for each occupation was developed by comparison of a group of men who were successfully engaged in that occupation with a reference group of men-in-general. Thus, the per cent of men in occupation A choosing the L, I, and D options to item 1 is compared with the per cent of men-in-general choosing these same options. If enough more men in occupation A choose a particular option, that option receives a plus score for occupation A. If the per cent is smaller for occupation A, the option receives a minus score. If the per cent for occupation A is very much larger or smaller than for men-in-general, the score may be as much as $+4$ or -4. Smaller scores are assigned to smaller differences. Thus, responses are weighted to take account of the sharpness with which the item discriminates.

Table 12.1 shows the scoring key for the first ten items in the blank for four different occupational keys. Note the range of weights for the different items. Note that some or all of the options for a given item may receive a zero weight.

Table 12.1. Scoring Weights for Sample Items and Keys of *Strong Vocational Interest Blank for Men*

Scoring Key

Item	Engineer			Social Science Teacher			Farmer			Production Manager		
	L	I	D	L	I	D	L	I	D	L	I	D
Actor (not movie)	−1	0	1	1	0	−1	0	0	1	0	0	0
Advertiser	−2	0	2	0	1	−1	−2	1	1	−1	0	1
Architect	2	−1	−1	−1	0	1	0	0	0	0	0	0
Army officer	1	0	−1	1	0	−1	0	0	0	0	0	0
Artist	0	0	0	−1	0	0	−1	0	1	−1	0	0
Astronomer	1	0	−1	−1	0	0	−1	0	1	0	0	0
Athletic director	−1	1	0	2	−1	−2	0	0	0	0	0	−1
Auctioneer	−1	−1	2	0	1	−1	0	1	−1	0	0	1
Author of novel	−1	1	0	1	0	−1	−1	0	1	−1	0	0
Author of technical book	3	−1	−2	0	1	0	−1	0	1	1	0	−1

An individual's score is obtained by summing up the plus and minus credits corresponding to the responses he has chosen. Since the weights are different for each occupation, a separate scoring key is required, and a separate score is obtained for the examinee for each scale. Thus, a series of scores is obtained showing how closely the responses given by our examinee correspond to those typically given by each specific occupational group. Raw scores are translated into a standard score scale in which 50 represents the mean for men in the specific occupation. A scale of letter grades is also provided, in which A represents close resemblance to the particular occupational group, B+, B, and B− lesser degrees of resemblance, and C+ or C interest patterns quite different from those of the particular occupational group.

Table 12.2 shows the standard scores and letter ratings on the occupational scales of the blank for one college freshman. This young man shows interest patterns resembling closely (A) those of chemists,

Table 12.2. Scores on *Strong Vocational Interest Blank* for a College Freshman

Occupation	Standard Score	Letter Rating
I. Artist	26	C+
Psychologist	22	C
Architect	29	C+
Physician	42	B+
Dentist	41	B+
II. Mathematician	26	C+
Engineer	44	B+
Chemist	52	A
III. Production manager	39	B
IV. Farmer	59	A
Carpenter	44	B+
Math and science teacher	48	A
V. YMCA physical director	34	B−
Personnel manager	21	C
YMCA secretary	Low *	C−
Social-science teacher	17	C
City school superintendent	Low *	C−
Minister	Low *	C−
VI. Musician	25	C+
VII. CPA	16	C
VIII. Accountant	25	C+
Office worker	25	C+
Purchasing agent	28	C+
Banker	22	C
IX. Sales manager	19	C
Real estate salesman	17	C
Life-insurance salesman	Low *	C−
X. Advertising man	19	C
Lawyer	20	C
Author-journalist	24	C

* "Low" designates a standard score of 15 or lower.

farmers, and mathematics and science teachers. His interests are also quite like (B+) those of physicians, dentists, engineers, and carpenters. His interests are very *unlike* (C−) those of YMCA secretaries, city school superintendents, ministers, and life-insurance salesmen.

Strong has developed a companion *Vocational Interest Blank for Women* that follows closely the pattern of the blank for men. However, the blank has been rather less thoroughly developed than the men's blank, and seems to have been rather less successful. This may be due to the fact that specifically vocational interests are less central in the lives of many women, being contaminated by general "homemaker" interests, so that interest profiles in women tend to be less clear-cut and meaningful.

Originally, scoring the *Strong Vocational Interest Blank* was a very time-consuming task because of the large number of different scores that are called for. Hand-scoring a blank was a matter of several hours' work. But twentieth century electronics has hit the test-scoring field, and a special device developed by E. J. Hankes has made it possible to score the blanks at very high speed. This scoring machine is available only at Engineers Northwest, Minneapolis, Minnesota. The special answer sheets must be sent to this organization, where they will be scored at a cost that is a fraction of what the cost would be by hand methods.*

There are two points about the construction of the *Strong Blank* to which we wish to call especial attention at this time. In the first place, the person taking the test responds by choosing one of a set of response categories for each item (L, I, D). A particularly effusive individual *could* choose all L's, and a particularly jaundiced one *could* choose all D's. There is a certain amount of freedom to impose one's own standards upon the task. Secondly, the keys are externally determined. That is, they are defined by the responses of a particular job group and not by any internal logic. We wish now to contrast with the *Strong Blank* the *Kuder Preference Record,* which is different with respect to both of these features.

THE KUDER PREFERENCE RECORD (VOCATIONAL)

The *Kuder Preference Record (Vocational)* is made up of triads, or sets of three options. Typical sets might read:

> Go for a long hike in the woods.
> Go to a symphony concert.
> Go to an exhibit of new inventions.

* A price of 70¢ per answer sheet was quoted in 1960 for scoring blanks in quantity lots.

Fix a broken clock.
Keep a set of accounts.
Paint a picture.

In each set the individual is required to mark the one he would like to do *most* and the one he would like to do *least*.

Scoring keys were established on the basis of the *internal* relationships of the items. Thus, a study of the responses to the items showed that a number of items dealing with mechanical activities tended to hang together. If a person chose one he was likely to choose others, and if he rejected one he was likely to reject the others. Moreover, items in this group showed relatively little relationship to the remaining items. The items grouped together in a distinct cluster. From the nature of the items it was evident that this cluster related to mechanical interest. Those items having a substantial correlation with this cluster were included in a scoring key that gave a score for mechanical interest.

In the same way, other clusters were identified and built up in which the items went together but were largely independent of items not in the cluster. Scoring keys were developed for these. The *Preference Record* now yields scores for the following interest clusters: outdoor, mechanical, computational, scientific, persuasive, artistic, literary, musical, social service, and clerical. Raw scores are converted into percentiles, separate norms being supplied for male and female high-school students and for male and female adults.

In Table 12.3, the *Kuder* scores are given for the same college freshman whose *Strong* scores were shown in Table 12.2. On the *Kuder*,

Table 12.3. *Kuder Preference Record* Scores of a College Freshman *

Interest Area	Raw Score	Percentile Equivalent
Outdoor	71	95
Mechanical	58	87
Computational	17	16
Scientific	60	93
Persuasive	25	07
Artistic	30	68
Literary	23	78
Musical	12	45
Social Service	36	46
Clerical	19	01

* Scores for same individual shown in Table 12.2.

this young man stands highest on outdoor, scientific, and mechanical interest. He is very low on clerical and persuasive interests. These findings can be studied in relation to his interest in specific occupations, as shown in Table 12.2. The two sets of results are obviously consistent and support one another.

COMPARISON OF STRONG AND KUDER INVENTORIES

Note that in the *Kuder Preference Record,* the examinee is *forced* to pick a most liked and a least liked activity in each set. No matter how much or how little he likes all three, one must be preferred and one rejected. This forced-choice pattern appears in a number of inventories and should be contrasted with the category-response pattern found in the *Strong.* The forced-choice pattern forces a common frame of reference upon everyone. Differences in general optimism are controlled. Everyone must express the same number of preferences and rejections. Thus, superficial differences in standards of judgment, or what has been called "response set," are eliminated. But so also are genuine differences in interest level. Whether the forced-choice pattern produces a net gain in this respect is still a matter of debate.

Note again that in the *Preference Record* the several scores relate to coherent interest clusters rather than to something outside the individual or the test. The scores carry their own relatively direct meaning in terms of the common theme running through the cluster of items. The meaning does not have to be inferred by thinking what lawyers or salesmen are like. If our purpose is to build up a meaningful description of an individual, the internally consistent scales appear more satisfactory than those that are externally oriented. To say that a person is high on mechanical, scientific, and out-of-doors interests and low on clerical and persuasive is more directly interpretable than to say he is high on interests characteristic of farmers, chemists, and mathematics-science teachers and low on those characterizing ministers and YMCA secretaries. Internally coherent clusters definable in terms of their common theme "make sense" better than job-oriented appraisals.

When it comes to rating the individual for a specific job, however, the balance of advantages is radically changed. If our concern is to help the individual decide whether he would be content in the job of engineer, it is much more directly relevant to know how well his interests correspond to those of successful engineers than to know how high his mechanical and scientific interests are. In the first case, the scoring key itself defines what the interests of engineers are; in the second case we must either infer this or determine it from a separate study.

Either the internally consistent or job-oriented approach to inventorying interests is possible; which will work better depends on our particular purpose. If our purpose is to appraise appropriateness of interests for a limited number of specific jobs, this may be done effectively with a specific job key for each job. If, however, our concern is to get a meaningful description of a person and perhaps to be prepared to use that description to make inferences as to his suitability in any one of a very large number of jobs, then the homogeneous cluster scores seem preferable.

RELIABILITY, VALIDITY, AND PERMANENCE OF INVENTORIED INTERESTS

The *Strong Vocational Interest Blank* is one of the most thoroughly investigated psychometric tools we have, and, though the history of the *Kuder Preference Record* is shorter, it too has been intensively studied. Both instruments yield scores that are reasonably reliable for individuals in their teens or over. Thus, for 285 Stanford University seniors Strong [16] reports odd-even reliabilities for the separate occupational scales ranging from .73 to .94, with an average value of .88. A number of reliability studies with the *Kuder,* based on analysis of a single testing, give values averaging about .90. The reliability of the scores extracted from these interest inventories compares favorably with that of scores on ability tests.

For the *Strong* [9,12,13,14,16] there is evidence that interests show a good deal of stability over time, at least in adolescents and adults. Data on the average correlation at different ages and over different periods may be summarized as follows:

	Upper Elementary School	High School	College Freshmen	College Seniors
1 or 2 years	.55	.65	.80	. . .
3 to 5 years	.30	. . .	.75	.75
6 to 10 years	. . .	.50	.55	.70

The stability is low in the elementary school, but for persons of college age stability compares favorably with that for intelligence tests.

In appraising the validity of an interest inventory as a *description* of how the individual feels about activities and events in the world about him, the main issue is the truthfulness of his responses. There isn't really any higher court of appeal for determining a person's likes and preferences than the individual's own statement.

A number of studies have indicated that inventories such as the *Strong* [6,8] *can* be faked. If a group of examinees is told to try to respond the way that life-insurance salesmen would, they are generally rather successful in making themselves appear like life-insurance salesmen. However, this is no indication that the blank *will* be faked, even when used as an employment device.

When the inventory is used for counseling and to help the respondent, as is most often the case, there is probably little reason to anticipate intentional faking. The individual may be expected to report his likes and dislikes as he knows them. His self-knowledge is perhaps imperfect, so his reports may be inaccurate in some respects. Thus, he may say that he would like to attend symphony concerts because he feels that that is the thing to say, but his actions may belie his statement; he may in fact avoid concerts whenever they come his way. This lack of self-insight is a real problem. But it is probably mitigated somewhat, in the inventory approach to interests, where isolated points of poor insight will have only minor effects upon a final score.

The validity of interest inventories as predictors of later behavior is another matter. Scoring keys for the *Strong* were established by comparing men who were already in the occupation with men-in-general. *Kuder* occupational interest profiles have also been prepared by determining the average level in each of the interest areas for individuals already working in the occupation. But the common interest patterns of individuals in a field of work may have grown out of their work. The men may have come to exhibit certain common patterns from the very nature of their work experience. The crucial evidence on predictive validity would come from testing a group *before* they entered the world of work and determining whether those who later entered and continued in a particular occupation had distinctive interest patterns *before* they entered the occupation. This is an expensive operation, expensive in the time that must elapse before men can become settled in their occupation and expensive in the dissipation of cases among literally hundreds of occupations.

Strong [15] has been able to follow some groups who were tested as college undergraduates and does have some evidence on the extent to which students with interests characteristic of a particular occupation tended to enter that occupation and to persist in it. For the typical individual, the occupation in which he was actually working 10 years later ranked second or third for him among all the scales of the *Strong*. Considering group averages, those who remained in an occupation received higher interest scores for that occupation than for any other occupation and higher than those who switched to some other occupation.

McCully [10] followed up a group of men who had been given the *Kuder* as a part of Veterans Administration counseling at the end of

World War II. They were located several years later, and their occupation determined. Table 12.4 shows the average standard scores on each of the ten *Kuder* interest areas for those occupational groups that were large enough to justify study. The results show clear-cut

Table 12.4. Mean *Kuder* Standard Scores of Different Occupational Groups *

	Mechanical	Computational	Scientific	Persuasive	Artistic	Literary	Musical	Social Service	Clerical
Accounting and related	−78	152	−32	37	−82	19	2	−14	118
Engineering and related	56	45	82	−16	7	1	−21	−46	−41
Managerial work	−28	44	−18	56	−27	19	−15	−2	42
Clerical— computing and recording	−27	67	−9	9	−50	4	3	−14	68
General clerical work	−19	−3	−31	−9	−14	22	3	17	30
Sales—higher	−65	−14	−40	111	−54	38	17	18	30
Sales—lower	−19	−12	−25	79	−32	10	6	15	16
General farming	22	−25	−16	−37	−4	−49	−42	12	−10
Mechanical repairing	81	−21	3	−40	28	−28	−30	−40	−29
Electrical repairing	66	−3	27	−35	5	−41	−13	−19	−29
Bench crafts (fine)	63	−5	12	−24	38	−23	−20	−33	−2

* Based on a mean of 0 and a standard deviation of 100 for the reference group of 2797 employed veterans.

and fairly substantial differences in pattern of interest for different occupations. Thus, evidence with respect to both the *Strong* and the *Kuder* indicates that they have a certain amount of validity as predictors of occupational choice.

INTEREST AND ABILITY

It is important not to confuse measures of interest and ability. The fact that a boy scores high on the scientific interest scale of the *Kuder* or on the physicist scale of the *Strong* is no guarantee that he possesses the intellectual and other aptitudes required to master the concepts of physics and become a physicist. Interest measures tell us nothing directly about abilities, though, as we shall see in a moment, there are certain relationships between abilities and interests. Interest measures and ability measures deal with two quite distinct aspects of fitness for a field of study or work. Each provides information that supplements the other.   Interest is not a substitute for ability, and, conversely, ability to learn the skills of a job is no guarantee of success or satisfaction in the job.

There have been many studies of the relationship between interest and ability.*   Most of these have related to aspects of academic work. In general, the relationship between achievement in a field such as science and the corresponding interest (i.e., scientific interest on the *Kuder*) is positive but low.   Correlation of achievement with interest in the corresponding area will run about .30 to .50.   Thus, there is some slight tendency for those with high ability for a field of knowledge to show high interest in it.   But the relationship is much too low for either type of measure to serve in place of the other.   Both types of information are needed for any sound evaluation of an individual's suitability for a particular program of study or plan for work.

Standardized interest inventories have been developed primarily for their contribution to vocational counseling and job placement.   With this purpose in mind, they are directed at groups of high-school age or older.   The *Kuder,* with its relatively general interest areas, has been used satisfactorily at about the ninth grade and above.   The *Strong,* focusing on specific occupations and with a particular emphasis upon occupations at the professional level, is suitable primarily for senior high school pupils with definite plans to go to college and for college groups.   As in almost all inventories, these instruments involve a good deal of reading.   Their use with individuals who fall below eighth or ninth grade reading level would probably present serious problems.

Several other interest inventories are listed and briefly described in Appendix III.

TEMPERAMENT AND ADJUSTMENT INVENTORIES

Self-report inventories have been extensively developed in the areas of temperament and personal adjustment.   In these areas we again encounter instruments developed to yield scores for internally consistent clusters of behaviors, as did the *Kuder Preference Record,* and instruments built with keys based on reference to some external criterion, as was the *Strong Vocational Interest Blank.*

The basic material of all temperament and adjustment questionnaires is much the same.   They draw from an extensive catalogue of statements about actions and feelings.   To these the individual re-

* See Frandsen [5] for a review of some of this material.

sponds by indicating whether each is or is not characteristic of him. In many cases, a "?" or "uncertain" category is provided for the person who does not wish to endorse an unequivocal "Yes" or "No" answer. In the case of adjustment questionnaires, questions are culled from case studies, writings on various types of adjustment problems, suggestions of psychiatrists, and similar sources. For the normal dimensions of temperament, a review of psychological and literary treatments of personality differences and a systematic scrutiny of previous questionnaires, together with the personal insights of the investigator, provide the raw material for assembling items.

There are a large number of temperament and adjustment inventories. We will describe three in some detail, illustrating distinctively different patterns. These are the *Guilford-Zimmerman Temperament Survey,* the *Minnesota Multiphasic Personality Inventory (MMPI),* and the *Edwards Personal Preference Schedule (EPPS).* Then we will undertake a more general evaluation of the validity of inventories in this area and of the conditions under which we may expect them to be of value.

THE GUILFORD-ZIMMERMAN TEMPERAMENT SURVEY

The *Guilford-Zimmerman Temperament Survey* is the most recent development in a series of instruments on which Guilford has worked, each of which has attempted to identify and measure a number of internally coherent dimensions of personality that are clearly distinct from one another. Guilford has started with a pool of items and studied the intercorrelations among them, using the methods of factor analysis to which we referred on p. 262. He has identified distinct personality factors or foci, and tried to build up clusters of items to measure each. The objective is to get separate scales that are internally coherent and that are relatively independent of other scales. Thus, if a factor of "sociability" is identified, one attempts to get a cluster of items focussing on "sociability" that correlate substantially with each other, so that the person who subscribed to one item is likely also to subscribe to others. This cluster should be quite independent of other clusters relating to "dominance," "impulsiveness," and so forth, so that the correlations between the different clusters are quite low. This is the same basic approach as the one we saw in the *Kuder Preference Record.*

The *Guilford-Zimmerman* inventory provides scores appraising the clusters named and characterized below. Each cluster is characterized both by descriptive phrases and by two illustrative items.

General Activity. A high score indicates rapid pace of activities; energy, vitality; keeping in motion; production, efficiency, liking for speed; hurrying; quickness of action; enthusiasm, liveliness.

Sample Items

You start to work on a new project with a great deal of enthusiasm. (+)
You are the kind of person who is "on the go" all of the time.   (+)

Restraint. A high score indicates serious-mindedness; deliberateness; persistent effort; self-control; *not* being happy-go-lucky or carefree; *not* seeking excitement.

Sample Items

You like to play practical jokes upon others.   (−)
You sometimes find yourself "crossing bridges before you come to them."   (+)

Ascendance. A high score indicates habits of leadership; a tendency to take the initiative in speaking with others; liking for speaking in public; liking for persuading others; liking for being conspicuous; tendency to bluff; tendency to be self-defensive.

Sample Items

You can think of a good excuse when you need one.   (+)
You avoid arguing over a price with a clerk or salesman.   (−)

Sociability. A high score indicates one who has many friends and acquaintances; who seeks social contacts; who likes social activities; who likes the limelight; who enters into conversations; who is *not* shy.

Sample Items

You would dislike very much to work alone in some isolated place. (+)
Shyness keeps you from being as popular as you should be.   (−)

Emotional Stability. A person with a high score shows evenness of moods, interests, etc.; optimism, cheerfulness; composure; feelings of being in good health; *freedom from* feelings of guilt, worry, or loneliness; *freedom from* day dreaming; *freedom from* perseveration of ideas and moods.

Sample Items

You sometimes feel "just miserable" for no good reason at all.   (−)
You seldom give your past mistakes a second thought.   (+)

Objectivity. The high scorer is defined as *free from* the following: egoism, self-centeredness; suspiciousness, fancying hostility; ideas of reference; a tendency to get into trouble; a tendency to be thin-skinned.

Sample Items

You nearly always receive all the credit that is coming to you for things you do. (+)
There are times when it seems everyone is against you. (−)

Friendliness. High scores signify respect for others; acceptance of domination; toleration of hostile action; *freedom from* hostility, resentment, or desire to dominate.

Sample Items

When you resent the actions of anyone, you promptly tell him so. (−)
You would like to tell certain people a thing or two. (−)

Thoughtfulness. The high-scoring person is characterized as reflective, meditative; observing of his own behavior and that of others; interested in thinking; philosophically inclined; mentally poised.

Sample Items

You are frequently "lost in thought." (+)
You find it very interesting to watch people to see what they will do. (+)

Personal Relations. High scores signify tolerance of people; faith in social institutions; *freedom from* self-pity or suspicion of others.

Sample Items

There are far too many useless laws that hamper an individual's personal freedom. (−)
Nearly all people try to do the right thing when given a chance. (+)

Masculinity. The high-scoring person is interested in masculine activities; not easily disgusted; hardboiled; inhibited in emotional expression; resistant to fear; unconcerned about vermin; little interested in clothes, style, or romance.

Sample Items

You can look at snakes without shuddering. (+)
The sight of ragged or soiled fingernails is repulsive to you. (−)

Since each of these clusters can be thought of as a dimension having two ends, just as we have north and south, east and west, there is an opposite end of each dimension that can be characterized as just the reverse of the description given above. Items marked (−) characterize this opposite end. Of course, most people do not score at either extreme on these dimensions. Here, as elsewhere, a continuous range of variation with most people occupying an intermediate position is the characteristic pattern. Most people are neither outstandingly active nor conspicuously lethargic, neither clearly ascendant nor clearly submissive. People can rarely be well described by clear-cut personality *types*. They are described as showing different *traits* in varying *degrees*.

Choosing the names for the clusters presented above was a bit of a problem, because the clusters do not correspond exactly to the language labels we bring with us. Each cluster is defined by the items that went into it and that were grouped together because they actually went together in the responses of people taking the inventory. The titles are approximate. Each cluster can be understood more exactly only by a close study of the items of which it is composed.

Table 12.5 * shows the reliabilities of the separate scores, and the intercorrelations of the scores. The reliabilities cluster about .80 and are adequate, though not strikingly high. The attempt, in developing this inventory, was to identify a number of relatively independent aspects of personality. This means that the correlations of the different scores should be low. They tend to be. However, certain of the scores show rather substantial correlations. Attention may be directed to Ascendance and Sociability, Emotional Stability and Objectivity, Friendliness and Personal Relations, and Restraint and Thoughtfulness. These pairs of scores are far from independent, and the information provided by the scores is overlapping. In a sense, the inventory is only partially efficient because of the duplication in the different scores. It is as if we were in part saying the same thing over

---

* People who read about tests and testing will frequently have occasion to study tables of correlations like Table 12.5. In the table the column at the left lists the different variables and numbers them in order. The numbers (but not the names) are repeated across the top of the table. Look at the row labeled "1 General activity." The numbers that appear in this row are the correlations of "general activity" with each of the other variables. The first figure, −.16, is the correlation between "general activity" and variable 2, "restraint." This means that there is a slight tendency for high scores on the general activity scale to go with low scores on the restraint scale. The next figure, .34, is the correlation of "general activity" with "ascendance," and the other entries are to be read in the same way. The correlation between any two variables will be found in the row and column whose numbers correspond to those variables. In this table, the reliability coefficients for the variables are shown in a column at the extreme right.

Table 12.5.   Intercorrelations and Reliabilities of the Ten Scales of the
Guilford-Zimmerman Temperament Survey

	Scale	Intercorrelations									Relia-bility *
		2	3	4	5	6	7	8	9	10	
1	General activity	−.16	.34	.35	.34	.14	−.17	.24	−.03	.30	.79
2	Restraint		−.08	−.21	.08	.05	.25	.42	.14	−.01	.80
3	Ascendance			.61	.35	.41	−.25	−.19	−.04	.29	.82
4	Sociability				.23	.36	−.06	.04	.18	.21	.87
5	Emotional stability					.69	.37	−.13	.34	.37	.84
6	Objectivity						.34	−.04	.43	.32	.75
7	Friendliness							−.03	.50	.26	.75
8	Thoughtfulness								.22	−.12	.80
9	Personal relations									.35	.80
10	Masculinity										.85

* Kuder-Richardson formula, based on 912 college students.

again.   In most cases, however, each score provides information about a new and distinctive aspect of the individual.

The *Guilford-Zimmerman Inventory* has several characteristics that it may be well to summarize at this time.

1. It is based upon the responses of normal everyday people, not of the overtly maladjusted or the institutionalized.

2. Its scales are set up by internal analysis, by study of the "going together" of groups of items.

3. Responses are taken at face value.   Their significance is assumed to be given by their obvious content.

4. The respondent may endorse as many or as few of the items as he wishes; his choices are not forced or constrained.

By contrast, let us consider the *Minnesota Multiphasic Personality Inventory,* which differs radically with respect to the three first features.

THE MINNESOTA MULTIPHASIC PERSONALITY INVENTORY

The *Minnesota Multiphasic Personality Inventory* was developed to identify a number of distinct categories of abnormal behavior.   A pool of items was gathered which referred to different types of psychopathology: hysteria, depression, hypochondriasis, paranoid tendencies. The pool of items was tried out on a group of "normals" * and upon

* The problem of selecting a group of normal and well-adjusted persons is often a harder one than selecting people with a particular type of pathology.   A particular type of disease can be identified with a good deal of definiteness, but absence of disease is a fuzzier notion, harder to define and to identify.   The "normals" in this case were mostly people who had come to visit relatives at the Univ. of Minnesota Hospital.

a number of different groups with specific patterns of symptoms of maladjustment. The procedure was essentially the same as that for the *Strong*. Items were scored when they distinguished a given pathological group from the group of "normal" control cases.

The different scales of the *MMPI* are described below and illustrated with sample items. It must be remembered that the scales were established by using groups of patients showing behavior that was judged to be definitely abnormal. We cannot automatically apply the same labels to the variation in these traits that appears among normal individuals. The interpretation of scores found for normal persons must be made with great caution.

Hypochondriasis Scale (Hs). This scale assesses the amount of abnormal or excessive concern with bodily functions. A high score indicates undue worry about health, often accompanied by reports of obscure pains and disorders that are difficult to identify.

Sample Items

I do not tire quickly.   (−)
The top of my head sometimes feels tender.   (+)

Depression Scale (D). This scale appraises a tendency to be chronically depressed, to feel useless and unable to face the future.

Sample Items

I am easily awakened by noise.   (+)
Everything is turning out just like the prophets of the Bible said it would.   (+)

Hysteria Scale (Hy). This scale gets at the tendency to solve personal problems by developing physical symptoms, such symptoms as paralyses, cramps, gastric or intestinal complaints, or cardiac symptoms. The symptoms tend to appear under emotional stress and to be used as an escape mechanism.

Sample Items

I am likely not to speak to people until they speak to me.   (+)
I get mad easily and then get over it soon.   (+)

Psychopathic Deviate Scale (Pd). This scale was based upon a group who showed absence of deep emotional response, inability to profit from experience, and disregard for social pressures and the regard of others. They were individuals who, from their disregard of social pressures, had tended to get into trouble of various sorts.

Sample Items

My family does not like the work I have chosen.   (+)
What others think of me does not bother me.   (+)

Paranoia Scale (Pa). The qualities evaluated by this scale are suspiciousness, oversensitivity, and feelings of being picked on or persecuted.

Sample Items

I am sure I am being talked about.   (+)
Someone has control over my mind.   (+)

Psychasthenic Scale (Pt). This scale was based on patients who were troubled with excessive fears or with compulsive tendencies to dwell on certain ideas or perform certain acts.   High score indicates resemblance to this group.

Sample Items

I easily become impatient with people.   (+)
I wish I could be as happy as others seem to be.   (+)

Schizophrenic Scale (Sc). This scale is based upon a group of patients characterized by bizarre and unusual thought or behavior, and a subjective life tending to be divorced from the world of reality.   High scores indicate responses similar to this group.

Sample Items

I have never been in love with anyone.   (+)
I loved my mother.   (−)

Hypomania Scale (Ma). This scale evaluates a tendency to be overactive both bodily and mentally, with a tendency to skip around rapidly from one thing to another.

Sample Items

I don't blame anyone for trying to grab everything he can get in this world.   (+)
When I get bored I like to stir up some excitement.   (+)

Masculinity-Femininity Scale (Mf). This scale measures interests characteristic of the one or the other sex.

Sample Items

I like movie love scenes.   (F)
I used to keep a diary.   (F)

The *MMPI* has a number of additional features, and these focus attention on certain problems that arise in using adjustment questionnaires.   The first of these features is a *lie scale (L)*.   This is based upon fifteen items, imbedded in the questionnaire, that relate to socially approved and virtuous activities that are generally approved of but not frequently carried out.   General population norms indicate what may reasonably be expected on a set of items of this sort. If a person marks an excessive number of these socially approved behaviors, it is considered to be an indication that he tends, consciously or unconsciously, to distort his report so that he appears in a favorable light. That is, he tends to "fake good."

Another score, the *K* scale, was built up by keying items that distinguished known abnormals who had presented normal score profiles from a control group of normals. A high score on this scale is thought to indicate a tendency to be very defensive in self-evaluation, whereas a low score brings out the tendency to be extremely self-critical, i.e., to "fake bad."

The *?* score is based upon the number of *?* or undecided responses. A very high number is thought to indicate a tendency to evade the task imposed by the inventory: to withdraw from it and fail to face up to it.

One further control scale is the *F* scale, made up of an assortment of unrelated items, each of which is marked as true only rarely in the general population. A high score on this scale is thought to be symptomatic of careless and superficial marking of the inventory: of marking items at random or misunderstanding the statements.

Thus, the authors of the *MMPI* have introduced a whole series of control scales, designed to isolate individuals whose responses are untrustworthy for one of several different reasons. They recognize, first, that good adjustment (and also bad adjustment) can be faked with at least partial success and that before an attempt is made to interpret scores on an inventory some guarantee is needed that there was not intentional faking. They recognize also that quite unintentionally individuals differ in the severity of the standards by which they judge themselves and that some control is needed on this difference in severity of standards. They recognize unwillingness to cooperate and inability to comprehend the task or to read the written items, which may show up as superficial and meaningless patterns of responses. All of these issues represent real problems to users of an inventory, and the control scores represent one well-conceived attempt to identify untrustworthy answer sheets.

In contrast with the *Guilford-Zimmerman,* we note that the *MMPI:*

1. Is based upon the distinctive responses of selected groups of persons—in this case, groups each presenting a particular psychopathology.

2. Has scales that are defined by these abnormal groups.

3. Is not concerned with the apparent meaning of an item, but only with whether it functions—whether it serves to differentiate between the abnormal and the control group.

It thus follows the general pattern of the *Strong Vocational Interest Blank*. In common with the *Guilford-Zimmerman,*

4. It permits any number of items to be endorsed, leaving the respondent free of constraint in this regard.

Let us look now at an inventory that makes use of the forced-choice pattern of response.

THE EDWARDS PERSONAL PREFERENCE SCHEDULE

The *Edwards Personal Preference Schedule* tries to assess the strength of various needs or motives in the life economy of the individual. Fifteen needs were selected from among those listed by Murray,[11] and items were developed to exemplify each. These are presented to the individual in pairs, each need being paired twice with each of the 14 others (to make a total of 210 items). Sample pairs are:

A I like to help my friends when they are in trouble.
B I like to do my very best in whatever I undertake.

A I like to conform to custom and to avoid doing things that people I respect might consider unconventional.
B I like to talk about my achievements.

The examinee must respond to each pair by indicating which statement is more true or more characteristic of him. Knowing how many times (out of 28) the examinee chose the option referring to achievement, for example, the examiner can refer to the norms and express *need-achievement* as a percentile of the norm group. Edwards made a systematic attempt to equate the statements in a given pair for *social desirability,* so that individuals would respond as they really felt, and not in terms of what is the approved or accepted thing to say. This was one way of trying to free scores of the element of defensiveness or "faking good" that has been a problem in many of the inventories that have been developed over the years.

The distinctive features of the *EPPS* are, then,

1. The "forced choice" pattern, which means that each respondent must make the same number of choices and the same number of rejections. Thus, no profile can be high on all scales, and each profile must have about the same number of highs and of lows. Everyone is brought to the same general base line. This is true also of the triads of the *Kuder*.

2. Equating "social desirability," so that any pressure or incentive to distort responses or "fake good" is held to a minimum.

PROBLEM CHECK LISTS

The instruments we have just been describing yield one or several scores, representing traits or aspects of the individual. There are also several recently published "problem check lists," which are essentially catalogues of problems that are fairly often mentioned by children or young people. Examples are the *Mooney Problem Check List, SRA Junior Inventory* and *Youth Inventory,* and *Billett-Starr Youth Problems Inventory.* Responding to the comprehensive list of problems provides a kind of uniform problem-finding interview. The items that a child marks as matters of concern to him can serve as the starting point for more intensive inquiry in a face-to-face interview, while the problems that are marked as troublesome by several in a class group can serve as the focal point for group guidance sessions.

EVALUATION OF TEMPERAMENT AND ADJUSTMENT INVENTORIES

How well can we hope to describe temperamental characteristics and personal adjustment through the individual's responses to a series of questions? Perhaps we can clarify the issue by asking what a person must do to fill out an inventory adequately. Completing one of these inventories usually requires that the respondent be (a) able to read and understand the item, (b) able to stand back and view his own behavior and decide whether the statement is or is not true of him, and (c) willing to give frank and honest answers. Each of these points raises certain issues about the validity of self-report instruments.

One problem in inventories of all types is that of reading load. This problem is partly one of sheer amount of reading. Especially in those inventories that try to appraise several different traits, it is usually necessary to have several hundred items to provide enough scope and reliability. The slow reader may have trouble getting through so much verbiage, or may start responding without really reading through the item. The problem is partly one of level of reading, i.e., of the complexity of structure and abstractness of ideas involved. If the vocabulary or concepts are beyond the respondent's comprehension, he may again give up the attempt really to understand and may respond in a superficial or random fashion. (The F scale of the *MMPI* was designed to protect against this hazard.) Thus, inventories are of questionable value for those of low literacy, be they adults or children.

A second problem is that of self-insight. Inventories require the individual to conceptualize and classify his own behavior—to decide whether certain descriptions or classifications of behavior are true of him. This implies a certain ability to stand back from himself and view himself objectively that may be difficult to achieve. In fact, the person whose adjustment is most unsatisfactory may be the one who is least able to achieve this objectivity and to face his own deficiencies. Studies have shown repeatedly that those who are rated low by their associates on some desirable trait tend to grossly over-rate themselves. Thus, the ill-tempered girl is likely not to recognize her own irascibility; the overbearing boy may be unaware of his boorishness.

When inventories are built according to the pattern of the *Strong VIB* or the *MMPI,* such a lack of self-insight may not be of crucial importance. For these inventories, the keying of an item is based not on its obvious content but on the empirical fact that it did distinguish between criterion groups. If Henry has marked that he would like to be an architect, he has behaved in the way engineers typically behave. The question of whether engineers on the one hand or Henry on the other *really* want to be architects is not central to our interpretation. The point is that they have both reacted to the question in the same way, so we give Henry a credit on the engineer key of the Strong. On the other hand, where items and scores are interpreted on the basis of their manifest content and taken at face value, as is true of the *Guilford-Zimmerman* inventory or the *Kuder Preference Record,* non-insightful responses will lead to an untrue picture of the person who makes them.

A third problem is the willingness of the respondent to reveal the way he perceives or feels about himself. For personality inventories, frank and honest response by the examinee is essential for a valid picture. In most cases, the general significance of the items is reasonably apparent to the reader. Most subjects can follow successfully instructions to fake in a particular way. Even when the subject cannot fake successfully, if he tries to do so he will certainly give a distorted picture of himself. Inventory scores will only be useful when most respondents are answering in the way that they consider to represent themselves. The importance of providing protection against distortion is sufficiently great so that control scores to detect it have been introduced into the *MMPI* and certain other inventories.

This means that personality or adjustment inventories cannot be used, or can be used only with caution, when the examinee feels threatened by the test or feels that it may be used against him. Inventories have not generally proved useful in an employment situation, perhaps for this reason. If an inventory is given to elementary school pupils (and perhaps in high school and college) in the typical school setting, in which a test is something to do your best on and the teacher is often someone to get the best of, one is inclined to doubt whether many of the pupils will be willing to reveal personal shortcomings that they may be aware of. Generally speaking, in any practical situation we should consider an adjustment inventory to be no more than a preliminary screening device that will locate a group of individuals who *may* be having problems of adjustment or *may* be in conflict with their environment. Final evaluation should always await a more personal and intensive study of the individual. Furthermore, a good score on an adjustment inventory is not a guarantee of good adjustment; it may characterize a person who is protective, defensive, or unable to face and to acknowledge very real problems.

Personality inventories are a product of the middle-class American culture. The extent to which items have equivalent meaning for other national cultures, or even for the lower socio-economic level in America, has not been fully explored. Some additional caution is necessary in interpreting results for members of other cultural groups.

Evidences of Validity. Those inventories that have been developed as measures of adjustment usually show a moderate level of *concurrent* validity. That is, they differentiate between groups established on other grounds as differing in adjustment. Thus, the *MMPI* was set up to distinguish between diagnosed pathological groups and normals and continues to do so in new groups. Other inventories have been tested by their ability to differentiate less extreme groups and have stood up fairly well under the test.

When it comes to *predictive* validity, the results are less encouraging. In civilian studies,[1, 2, 7, 17] inventory scores have generally failed to predict anything much about the future success of the individual either in school, on the job, or in his personal living. Military experience [3] with these instruments has been somewhat more promising. There have been a number of studies showing substantial relationship between scores based on inventories and the subsequent judgment resulting from a psychiatric interview. Relationships to subsequent discharge from the service have also been sufficiently good to indicate that an inventory could serve a useful function as a device to screen for careful interview those who appeared to be potential misfits.

The Practical Use of Temperament and Adjustment Inventories. We must now ask what use should be made of temperament and adjustment inventories in and out of school. In the light of the factors that can distort scores and the limited validity these instruments have shown as predictors, we must conclude that they should be used very sparingly. Our feeling is that an adjustment inventory should be used only as an adjunct to more intensive psychological services. If facilities are available to permit intensive study of some of the group by psychologically trained personnel, an inventory may serve as a means of identifying persons likely to profit from working with a counselor. However, there is little that a classroom teacher can do to dig behind and test the meaning of an inventory score. Accepted uncritically, the score may prove very misleading. We believe that little useful purpose is served by giving an adjustment inventory and making the results available to the teacher, especially the teacher of an elementary-school child.

The multi-dimensional temperament inventories are still too new for us to have much evidence on the social or practical validities of the different scales. Their use for vocational guidance or personnel selection can hardly be recommended at the present time. It *may* be that persons having certain patterns of temperamental characteristics should be guided towards or away from certain types of jobs. This seems plausible to many people. However, our information about the personality patterns in specific occupations is too limited, and the range of variation within occupations is probably too wide to make much practical use of such personality appraisals at the present time.

ATTITUDE QUESTIONNAIRES

One further type of self-report inventory deserves brief mention. This is the attitude questionnaire, designed to appraise an individual's favorableness toward some group, proposed action, social institution, or social concept. Opinion polling has become commonplace in the last 25 years. However, this involves attitude *measurement* in only the most rudimentary sense. One or more questions are asked, and a count is made of the frequency of responses in two or three broad categories. Polls of this sort may be used in the schools to get an appraisal of public opinion of the school's patrons, or to study the status or change of pupils' expressed beliefs after instruction. The schools express a good deal of concern about development of attitudes and ideals as educational objectives, so there is need for good devices to appraise the extent to which such outcomes are being achieved. Industrial morale surveys are another point at which practical use may be made of attitude measurement. But the greatest use of attitude appraisal devices up to the present time has probably been for research studies of factors related to attitude differences, types of experiences that produce changes in attitude, or the influence of attitudes upon our perception of our world.

The typical attitude questionnaire is made up of a series of statements which the individual may either endorse or reject. There are two main patterns:

1. *Scaled Statements.* In this form, statements are scaled in terms of their degree of favorableness on the basis of extensive preliminary work. Thus, if we are preparing this type of attitude scale toward the United Nations, we start with a large pool of items. They may include the following:

> The UN is a strong influence for peace.
> The UN is a waste of time and effort.
> The UN does about as much harm as good.
> The UN is the most important force for good in the world today.

A corps of judges is assembled and each judge is asked to sort these statements into a set of piles, each pile representing a different degree of favorableness toward the UN. The judge is *not* indicating his agreement or disagreement with the statement; he is giving his interpretation of its meaning and significance. Each statement receives a scale value based on the average of these judgments and an ambiguity index based upon the spread of the ratings. (The more the judgments spread out, the more ambiguous the statement is.) From the pool of items tried out, about twenty are chosen that spread out over the range of scale values and are relatively unambiguous. These constitute the attitude scale.

When this type of attitude scale is administered, the respondent marks all the statements with which he agrees. His score is the average of the scale values of the statements he endorses.

2. *Summed Score.* In the other common format, the basic statements are much the same, except that neutral statements are avoided. Each statement is unequivocally either favorable or unfavorable. The respondent reacts to each statement on a five-point scale, ranging from strong agreement to strong disagreement. Thus, a section of a questionnaire in this format might read:

| The UN is a strong influence for peace. | Strongly agree | Agree | Uncertain | Disagree | Strongly disagree |
| The UN will only make trouble. | Strongly agree | Agree | Uncertain | Disagree | Strongly disagree |

The questionnaire can be scored quite simply by giving five points for strong endorsement of a favorable statement, four points for agreement, three points for uncertainty, and so forth. The scoring is reversed for the unfavorable statements. An individual's raw score is the sum of his scores for the separate items. The raw score can, of course, be converted into a percentile or standard score if this seems desirable.

Both forms of attitude scale usually have satisfactory reliabilities, typically in the .80's. The two types of scales yield scores that intercorrelate very highly, and for most practical purposes there does not seem to be a great deal of choice between them. The greater simplicity of preparation of a summed-score type of inventory will commend it to most persons who wish to use an attitude scale as an aspect of some type of educational evaluation or research project. In either case, the scale will yield only a single general favorableness–unfavorableness score for an attitude area. Any qualitative variations within the broad area are blurred. Recent investigations on attitude scale development have been concerned with identifying more restricted and more homogeneous subscales within a larger attitude domain. A series of homogeneous subscales within a larger attitude area (toward the UN, for example) should permit mapping out in a more analytic and diagnostic way the profile of an individual's or a group's attitudes.

The big qualification about attitude scales is that they operate purely on a verbal level. The individual doesn't *do* anything to back up his stated attitude. The scales deal with verbalized attitudes rather than actions. Of course, an attitude scale is obviously fakeable. If we recognize that they represent the verbalized attitude that the individual is willing to express to us and work within that limitation, attitude scales appear to be a useful research tool or tool for experimental evaluation of educational objectives lying outside the domain of knowledges and skills.

SUMMARY AND EVALUATION

In this chapter we have considered self-report inventories as instruments for studying personality. An inventory of this sort is essentially a standard set of interview questions presented in written form.

The individual's report about himself has one outstanding advantage. It provides an "inside" view, based on all the individual's experience with and knowledge about himself. However, self-reports are limited by the individual's limited

1. Ability to read the questions with understanding.
2. Self-insight and self-understanding.
3. Willingness to reveal himself frankly.

One type of questionnaire that has proven valuable in selection and placement is the biographical data blank, in which the individual provides factual information about his past history. A scoring key developed for the particular job has been found to have useful validity in several different instances.

Interest inventories provide satisfactorily reliable descriptions of interest patterns. These patterns persist with a good deal of stability, at least after late adolescence, and appear to be significant factors for vocational planning.

The validity of adjustment and temperament inventories is more open to question. Inventories of all types can be distorted to some extent if the individual is motivated to distort his responses. Thus, the integrity of the responses depends upon the motivation of the person examined. This depends, in turn, upon the setting in which and purposes for which the inventory is used. In school, industrial, or military use of adjustment inventories, one suspects that the motivations may often favor distorted responses. In any event, inventories of this type have not generally shown high validity. They should be used only with a good deal of circumspection.

Attitude questionnaires have been developed to score the intensity of favorable or unfavorable reaction to some group, institution, or issue. Though these represent only verbal expressions of attitude, they are useful research tools.

REFERENCES

1. Ellis, A., Recent research with personality inventories, *J. consult. Psychol.*, **17**, 1953, 45–49.
2. Ellis, A., The validity of personality questionnaires, *Psychol. Bull.*, **43**, 1946, 385–440.
3. Ellis, A., and H. S. Conrad, The validity of personality inventories in military practice, *Psychol. Bull.*, **45**, 1948, 385–426.
4. Fear, Richard, *The evaluation interview: prediction of job performance in business and industry*, New York, McGraw-Hill, 1958.
5. Frandsen, A., Interests and general educational development, *J. appl. Psychol.*, **31**, 1947, 57–65.
6. Garry, R., Individual differences in ability to fake vocational interests, *J. appl. Psychol.*, **37**, 1953, 33–37.
7. Ghiselli, E. E., and R. P. Barthol, The validity of personality inventories in the selection of employees, *J. appl. Psychol.*, **37**, 1953, 18–20.
8. Longstaff, H. P., Fakability of the Strong Interest Blank and the Kuder Preference Record, *J. appl. Psychol.*, **32**, 1948, 360–369.
9. Mallinson, G. G., and W. M. Crumrine, An investigation of the stability of interests of high school students, *J. educ. Res.*, **45**, 1952, 369–383.

10. McCully, C. Harold, *The validity of the Kuder Preference Record.* Ed. D. Dissertation, George Washington University, Washington, D. C., 1954.
11. Murray, H. A., et al., *Explorations in personality,* New York, Oxford University Press, 1938.
12. Rosenberg, N., Stability and maturation of Kuder interest patterns during high school, *Educ. psychol. Meas.,* **13,** 1953, 449–458.
13. Strong, E. K., Interest scores while in college of occupations engaged in 20 years later, *Educ. psychol. Meas.,* **11,** 1951, 335–348.
14. Strong, E. K., Nineteen-year followup of engineer interests, *J. appl. Psychol.* **36,** 1952, 65–74.
15. Strong, E. K., Permanence of interest scores over 22 years, *J. appl. Psychol.,* **35,** 1951, 89–91.
16. Strong, E. K., *Vocational interests of men and women,* Stanford, Calif., Stanford University Press, 1943.
17. Super, D. E., The Bernreuter Personality Inventory: a review of research, *Psychol. Bull.,* **39,** 1942, 94–125.

SUGGESTED ADDITIONAL READING

Allen, Robert M., *Personality assessment procedures,* New York, Harper, 1958, Chapters 2–7.
Bass, Bernard M. and Irwin A. Berg, Editors, *Objective approaches to personality assessment,* New York, Van Nostrand, Chapters 1, 3, 5 and 6.
Cronbach, Lee J., *Essentials of psychological testing,* 2nd ed., New York, Harper, 1960, Chapters 14–16.
Darley, John G., and Theda Hagenah, *Vocational interest measurement,* Minneapolis, The University of Minnesota Press, 1955, Chapters 2, 4, 6.
Harris, Chester W., Editor, *Encyclopedia of educational research,* 3rd ed., New York, Macmillan, 1960, pp. 102–112, 728–732.
Guilford, J. P., *Personality,* New York, McGraw-Hill, 1959, Chapters 8–9.
Kuder, Frederic G., *Kuder preference record occupational, Form D, research handbook,* 2nd ed., Chicago, Science Research Associates, 1957.
Layton, Wilbur L., Editor, *The strong vocational interest blank: research and uses,* Minneapolis, University of Minnesota Press, 1960.

QUESTIONS FOR DISCUSSION

1. How satisfactory is the method that was used in validating the *Strong Vocational Interest Blank?* What limitations do the procedures have? In what ways should they be checked?

2. What are the relative advantages of the *Strong Vocational Interest Blank* and the *Kuder Preference Record?* Under what circumstances would you choose to use one and under what circumstances the other?

3. What is the relationship between measures of interest and measures of ability? What does this suggest as to the ways in which the two types of tests should be used?

4. Most civilian studies have failed to find interest or adjustment inventories very useful in personnel selection. What are the reasons for this?

5. Why are most published interest inventories intended for use with secondary-school pupils, college students, and adults rather than elementary-school students?

6. What uses could a classroom teacher make of results on the *Kuder Interest Inventory* other than in giving vocational and educational guidance?

7. In what ways could a biographical data blank help a teacher in understanding the pupils in a class? What types of information would be useful to include on such a blank?

8. What conditions must be met if a self-report inventory is to be filled out accurately and give meaningful results?

9. How much trust can we place in adjustment inventories given in school to elementary-school children? What factors limit their value?

10. What important differences do you notice between the *Guilford-Zimmerman Temperament Survey* and the *Minnesota Multiphasic Personality Inventory?* For what purposes would each be more suitable?

11. What purposes are served by the control scales (*L, K, F, ?*) on the *Minnesota Multiphasic Personality Inventory?* What would be the comparable issues in personality rating scales? How might one adapt the ideas of control scales to ratings?

12. What factors limit the usefulness of paper-and-pencil atttitude scales? What other methods might a teacher use to evaluate attitudes?

13. Prepare the rough draft for a brief attitude scale to measure teachers' attitudes towards objective tests.

14. With what kinds of groups can adjustment inventories be used most satisfactorily?

Chapter 13

▼

The Individual as Others See Him

In the last chapter we considered the information about personality that could be gotten from inventories in which the individual describes himself. A second main way in which an individual's personality shows itself is through the impression he makes upon others. The second person serves as a reagent reacting to the first personality. How well does A like B? Does A consider B a pleasing person to have around? An effective worker? A good job risk? Does A consider B to be conscientious? Trustworthy? Emotionally stable? Questions of this sort are continually being asked of every teacher, supervisor, former employer, minister, or even friend. We must now inquire how fruitful it is to raise such questions and what precautions must be observed if the questions are to receive useful answers.

We shall first give brief consideration to the unstructured letter of recommendation. Then we shall examine rating scales and rating procedures. Finally, we shall consider some special forms of rating: nominating techniques and forced-choice rating procedures.

LETTERS OF RECOMMENDATION

The most fluid form for getting an impression of one person through the eyes of a second person is to invite the second person to talk or write to you about him. Such a communication could be obtained in any setting. However, the setting in which it most commonly does occur is when person A is a candidate for something: admission to a school, a scholarship or fellowship, a job, membership in a club, or a security clearance. He then furnishes the institution, placement agency, or employer the names of people who know him well or know him in a particular capacity, and that agency obtains statements about A from B and C, who know him.

How useful and how informative is the material that is included in free, unstructured communications describing another person? Actu-

351

ally, in spite of the vast numbers of recommendations written every year, very little of a solid and factual nature is known about their adequacy or the effectiveness with which they discharge their function. Opinion covers the full gamut from a belief that a free and unconstrained letter about an applicant is the best possible way to get an evaluation of him to the conviction that letters of recommendation are completely worthless, from a conviction that the letter of recommendation is the core of any selection program to a feeling that the best thing to do with recommendations is to burn them. But factual studies of the reliability and validity of the information that is gotten from a letter of recommendation or of the extent to which recommendations influence the action taken with respect to an applicant are fragmentary in the extreme.

The letter of recommendation is such an unstructured document that it is very hard to study by sound research techniques. However, several investigators have attempted to make analyses of the content of the letters and to scale them with respect to the enthusiasm of the endorsement they provided. A moderate degree of agreement has been found [4] between different letters written about the same person. Within a group of applicants for jobs in secondary-school teaching from one teacher-training institution the between-letters reliability would be represented by a correlation of about .40. There was some evidence in this same study that the letters of those who *got* the jobs were a little higher on the enthusiasm scale than letters of applicants who were *not* employed. However, another study failed to find any difference between the terms used to describe job getters and other applicants.

The extent to which a letter of recommendation provides a *valid* appraisal of an individual and the extent to which it is accurately diagnostic of outstanding points, strengths or weaknesses, is almost completely unknown. However, we cannot be very sanguine. Most of the limitations that we shall presently discuss in connection with more structured rating scales apply with at least equal force to uncontrolled letters. In addition, each respondent is free to go off in whatever direction his fancy dictates, so that there is no core of content common to the different letters about a single person or to the letters dealing with different persons. One letter may deal with A's social charm; a second, with B's integrity; and a third, with C's originality. On what common base are we to compare the three? Add to this the facts that (1) the applicant usually is more or less free to select the persons who will write about him and may be expected to pick those who will support him and that (2) recommenders differ profoundly in their propensity for using superlatives, and the prospect is not a very rosy one.

Further research studies of the validity of free descriptions of one person by his fellows are urgently needed. In the meantime, recommendations will continue to be written—and perhaps to be used. We must turn our attention to more structured evaluation procedures.

RATING SCALES

Undoubtedly it was in part the extreme subjectivity of the unstructured statement, the lack of a common core of content or standard of reference from person to person, and the extraordinary difficulty of quantifying the materials that gave impetus to the development of rating scales. Rating procedures attempt to overcome just these deficiencies. They attempt to get appraisals on a common set of attributes for all raters and ratees and to have these expressed on a common quantitative scale.

We all have had experience with ratings, either in making them or in having them made about us or, more probably, in both capacities. Rating scales appear in a large proportion of school report cards, more clearly in the non-academic part. Thus, we often find a section phrased somewhat as follows:

	1st Period	2nd Period	3rd Period	4th Period
Effort	_____	_____	_____	_____
Conduct	_____	_____	_____	_____
Citizenship	_____	_____	_____	_____
Cooperation	_____	_____	_____	_____
Adjustment	_____	_____	_____	_____

H = superior   S = satisfactory   U = unsatisfactory

Many civil service agencies and industrial firms send rating forms out to persons listed as references by job applicants, asking for evaluations of the individual's "initiative," "originality," "enthusiasm," or "ability to get along with people." These same companies or agencies often require supervisors to give merit ratings of their employees, rating them as "superior," "excellent," "very good," "good," "satisfactory" or "unsatisfactory" on a variety of traits or in over-all usefulness. Colleges, medical schools, fellowship programs, and still other agencies call for ratings as a part of their selection procedure. Beyond these practical operating uses, ratings have been involved in a great many research projects. All in all, vast numbers of ratings are called for and given, often reluctantly, in our country week by week and month by month. Rating other people is a large-scale operation.

The most common pattern of rating procedure presents the rater with a set of trait names, perhaps somewhat further defined, and a range of numbers, adjectives, or descriptions that are to represent levels or degrees of possession of the traits. He is called upon to rate one or more persons on the trait or traits by assigning him or them the number, letter, adjective, or description that is judged to fit best. Two illustrations are given of rating scales, drawn from a program being developed for evaluation of management personnel.* The first is one of a series of trait ratings. This part of the evaluation instrument calls for ratings of the following traits: job know-how, judgment, leadership, ability to plan and organize, communication ability, initiative, dependability, and human relations. For the trait of leadership, the rater is instructed as shown below. The actual rating scale follows these instructions.

LEADERSHIP

Consider his ability to inspire confidence. How much respect does he command as an individual, not merely because of his position? Do people look to him for decisions? Is he afraid to "stick his neck out" for what he believes? Does he have teamwork?

| Completely lacking. Definitely a follower with equals. Does not try to convince others that his way is best. ☐ | Tries to lead with some success, but has never achieved a strong position. Is passive in directing his subordinates. ☐ | Good leader. People wait to hear what he has to say. Respected by colleagues. People call for his opinion. ☐ | Exceptional leader. Able to take over and pull things into shape. People seem to enjoy going along on his side. Is respected by subordinates and colleagues. ☐ |

An over-all summary rating is also called for, and this takes the form shown below.

Please place a mark on the scale to best show the over-all rating of this man in his present position.

Not meeting the requirements	Fair, but needs to improve	Satisfactory	Doing good work	Excellent job

---

* These have been made available through the courtesy of the Personnel Department of Mack Trucks, Inc.

These are only illustrations of a wide range of rating instruments. We shall turn presently to some of the major variations in rating patterns. Right now, however, let us consider some of the problems that arise when we try to get a group of judges to make these appraisals.

PROBLEMS IN OBTAINING SOUND RATINGS

The problems in obtaining valid appraisals of an individual through ratings are of two main sorts. There are first the factors that limit the rater's *willingness* to rate honestly and conscientiously, in accordance with the instructions given to him. There are secondly the factors that limit his *ability* to rate consistently and correctly, even with the best of intentions. We shall need to consider each of these in turn.

FACTORS AFFECTING THE RATER'S WILLINGNESS TO RATE CONSCIENTIOUSLY

When ratings are collected, it is commonly assumed that each rater is trying his best to follow the instructions that have been given him, and that any shortcomings in his ratings are due entirely to human fallibility and ineptitude. However, this is not necessarily true. There are at least two sets of circumstances that may impair the integrity of a set of ratings: (1) The rater may be unwilling to take the trouble that is called for by the appraisal procedure; and (2) the rater may identify with the person rated to such an extent that he is unwilling to make a rating that will hurt him. Each of these merits some elaboration.

Unwillingness to Take the Necessary Pains. At best, ratings are a bother. Careful and thoughtful ratings are even more of a bother. In some rating procedures the attempt is made to get away from subjective impressions and superficial reaction by introducing elaborate procedures and precautions into the rating enterprise. Thus, in one attempt to improve efficiency rating procedures for Air Force officers,[13] an elaborate form was introduced that was to serve as a combined observational record and rating form. Fifty-four specific critical behaviors were described relating to officer efficiency. Scales were prepared describing degrees of excellence in each type of behavior. The accompanying instructions called upon raters to observe their ratees for a period before the official ratings were to be given and to tally on the rating form instances that had been observed of desirable and undesirable acts within each of the behavior categories described on the scale. After a year or two of use this form was discarded, in part at least because of its complexity and because raters were not willing to devote the time and thought that would have been required to maintain the preliminary observational records on which the ratings were to be based.

In a lesser degree, one suspects that perfunctoriness in carrying out the operation of rating is a factor contributing to lowered effectiveness in many rating programs. Particularly if the number of pupils or employees to be rated is large, the task of preparing periodic ratings can become a decidedly onerous one. Unless raters are really "sold" on the importance of the ratings, the judgments are likely to be hurried and superficial ones, given more with an eye on finishing the task than with a concern for making accurate and analytical judgments.

Identification with the Persons Being Rated. Ratings are often called for by some rather remote and impersonal agency. The Civil Service Commission, the Military Personnel Division of a remote Headquarters, the personnel director of a large company, or the central administrative staff of a school system are all pretty far away from the first line supervisor, the squadron commander, or the classroom teacher. The rater is often closer to the persons being rated, the workers in his office, the junior officers in his outfit, the pupils in his class, than to the agency that requires the ratings to be made. One of the first principles of supervision or leadership is that the good leader looks out for the needs and welfare of his followers or subordinates. Morale in an organization depends upon the conviction that the leader of the organization will take care of the members of the group. When ratings come along, "taking care of" becomes a matter of seeing to it that one's own men fare as well as—or a little better than—those in competing groups.

All this boils down to the fact that in some situations the rater is more interested in providing a "break" for the people whom he is rating and in seeing that they get at least as good treatment as other groups than he is in providing accurate information for the using agency. This situation is aggravated in many governmental and official agencies by a policy of having the ratings public and requiring that the rater discuss with the person being rated any unfavorable material in the ratings. A further aggravation is produced by setting up administrative rulings in which a minimum rating is specified as required for promotion or pay increase. No wonder, then, that ratings tend to climb or to pile up at a single scale point. Thus, in certain governmental agencies during World War II the typical rating, accounting for a very large proportion of the ratings given, was "excellent." "Very good" became an expression of marked dissatisfaction, while a rating of "satisfactory" was reserved for someone you would get rid of at the first opportunity.

It is important to realize that a rater cannot always be depended upon to work wholeheartedly at giving valid ratings for the benefit of the using agency, that making ratings is usually a nuisance to him, and that he is often more committed to his own subordinates than to an outside agency. A rating program must be continuously "sold" and policed if it is to remain effective. And there are limits to the extent to which even an active campaign can overcome a rater's natural inertia and interest in his own little group.

FACTORS AFFECTING THE RATER'S ABILITY TO RATE ACCURATELY

Even when a group of raters are presumably well motivated and doing their best to provide valid judgments, there are still a number of factors that operate to limit the validity of those judgments. These center around the lack of opportunity to observe, the covertness of the attribute, ambiguity of the quality to be observed, lack of a uniform standard of reference, and specific rater biases and idiosyncrasies.

Opportunity to Observe the Person Rated. One factor that must always be borne in mind as a consideration limiting the accuracy of rating procedures is limited opportunity on the part of the rater to observe the person being rated. Thus, the high-school teacher teaching four or five different class groups of 30 pupils each and seeing many pupils only in a class setting may be called upon to make judgments as to the "initiative" or "flexibility" of these pupils. The college instructor who has taught a class of 100 pupils will receive rating forms from an employment agency or from the college administration asking for similar judgments. The truth of the matter is that effective contact with the person to be rated has probably been too limited to provide any adequate basis for the judgment that is being requested. True, the ratee has been physically in the presence of the rater for a good many hours, possibly several hundred, but these have been very busy hours, concerned primarily with other things than observing and forming judgments about pupil A. Pupil A has had to compete with pupils B, C, D, and on to Z and also with the primary concern with teaching rather than judging.

In a civil service or industrial setting much the same thing is true. The primary concern is with getting the job done, and although in theory the supervisor has had a good deal of time to observe each worker, in practice he has been busy with other things. We may be able to "sell" supervisors on the idea of devoting more of their energy to observing and evaluating the persons working for them, but there are very real limits to the amount of effort that can be withdrawn from a supervisor's other functions to be applied to this one.

We face not only the issue of general opportunity to observe, but also that of specific opportunity to observe a particular aspect of the individual's personality. Any person sees another only in certain limited contexts, in which only certain aspects of his behavior are displayed. The teacher sees a child primarily in the classroom, the foreman sees a workman primarily on the production line, and so forth.

We might question whether a teacher in a thoroughly conventional classroom has seen a child under circumstances which might be expected to bring out much "initiative" or "originality." The college instructor who has taught largely through lectures is hardly well situated to rate a student's "presence" or "ability to work with individuals." The supervisor of a clerk doing routine work is poorly situated to appraise "judgment." Whenever ratings are proposed, either for research purposes or as a basis for administrative actions, we should ask with respect to each trait being rated: Has the rater had a chance to observe these people in enough of the sorts of situations in which they could be expected to show variations in this trait so that his ratings can be expected to be meaningful? If the answer is "No," we would be well advised to abandon the ratings.

In this connection, it is worth while to point out that persons in different roles may see quite different aspects of the person to be rated. Her pupils see a teacher from quite a different vantage point than does the principal. Classmates in Officer Candidate School have a different view of the other potential officers than does the drill instructor. In getting ratings of some aspect of an individual, it is always appropriate to ask who has the best chance to see the relevant behavior displayed. It would normally be to this source that we should go for our ratings.

Covertness of Trait Being Rated. If a trait is to be appraised by an outsider, someone other than the person being rated, it must show on the outside. It must be something that has its impact on the outside world. Such characteristics as appearing at ease at social gatherings, having a pleasant speaking voice, and participating actively in group projects are characteristics that are essentially social. They appear in interaction with other persons and are directly observable. They are *overt* aspects of the person being appraised. By contrast, attributes such as "feeling of insecurity," "self-sufficiency," "tension," or "loneliness" are inner personal qualities. They are private aspects of personality and can only be crudely inferred from what the person does. They are *covert* aspects of the individual.

An attribute that is largely covert can be judged by the outsider only with great difficulty. Little of inner conflict or tension shows on the surface, and where it does show it is often in masquerade. Thus, a child's deep insecurity may express itself as aggression against other pupils in one child, or as withdrawal into an inner world in another. The insecurity is not a simple dimension of overt behavior. It is an underlying dynamic factor that may break out in different ways in different persons or even in the same person at different times. Only a thorough knowledge of the individual, combined with a good deal of psychological insight, makes it possible to infer from the overt behavior the nature of his underlying covert dynamics.

One can see, then, that rating procedures will be relatively unsatisfactory for the inner, covert aspects of the individual. Qualities that depend upon very thorough understanding of a person plus wise inferences from his behavior will be rated with low reliability and little validity. Ratings have most chance of being accurate for those qualities that show outwardly as a person interacts with other people, the overt aspects. Experience has shown that these can be rated more reliably, and one feels confident that they are rated more validly. The validity lies in part in the fact that these social aspects of behavior have their meaning and definition primarily in the effects of one person or another.

Ambiguity of Meaning of Dimension to Be Rated. Many rating forms call for ratings of quite broad and abstract traits. Thus, in our illustration on p. 353 we included, among others, "citizenship" and "adjustment." These are neither more nor less vague and general than the attributes included in other rating schedules. But what do we mean by "citizenship" in an elementary-school pupil? By what actions is "good citizenship" shown? Does it mean not marking up the walls? Or not spitting on the floor? Or not pulling little girls' hair? Or bringing newspaper clippings to class? Or joining the Junior Red Cross? Or staying after school to help the teacher clean up the room? What *does* it mean? Probably no two raters would have just exactly the same things in mind when they rated a group of pupils on "citizenship."

Or consider "initiative," "personality," "supervisory ability," "mental flexibility," "executive influence," or "adaptability." These are all examples from rating scales in actual use. Though there is certainly some core of uniformity in the meaning that each of these terms will have for different raters, there is with equal certainty a good deal of variability in meaning from one rater to another. In proportion as a term becomes abstract, its meaning becomes variable from person to person, and such qualities as those listed above are conspicuously abstract.

The rating that a given child will receive for "citizenship" will, then, depend upon what "citizenship" means to the rater. If it means to rater A conforming to school regulations, he will rate certain children high. If to rater B it means taking an active role in school projects, the high ratings may go to quite different children. A first problem in getting consistent ratings is to achieve consistency from rater to rater in the meanings of the qualities being rated.

Uniform Standard of Reference. A great many rating schedules call for judgments of the persons being rated in some set of categories such as

Outstanding, above average, average, below average, unsatisfactory.
Superior, good, fair, poor.
Best, good, average, fair, poor.
Outstanding, superior, better than satisfactory, satisfactory, unsatis-
   factory.
Superior, excellent, very good, good, satisfactory, unsatisfactory.

But how good is "good"? Is a person who is "good" in "judgment" in the top tenth of the group with whom he is being compared? The top quarter? The top half? Or is he just *not* one of the bottom tenth? And what *is* the group with whom he is supposed to be compared? Is it all men of his age? All employees of the company? All men in his particular job? All men in his job with his length of experience? If the last, how is the rater supposed to know the level of judgment that is typical for men in a particular job with a particular level of experience?

The problem that all these questions are pointing up is that of forming a standard against which to appraise a given ratee. Variations in interpretation of terms and labels, variations in definition of the reference population, and variations in experience with the members of that background population all contribute to variability from rater to rater in their standards of rating. The phenomenon is a familiar one in academic grading practices. Practically every school that has studied the problem has found enormous variations among faculty members in the per cent of A's, B's, and C's that they give. The same situation holds for any set of categories, numbers, letters, or adjectives, that may be used. Standards of interpretation are highly subjective and vary widely from one rater to another. One man's "outstanding" is another man's "satisfactory."

Raters differ not only in the level of ratings that they assign, but also in how much they spread out their ratings. Some raters are conservative, and rarely rate anyone very high or very low; others tend to go to extremes. This difference in variability of ratings serves also to reduce the comparability of ratings from one rater to another.

Specific Rater Idiosyncrasies. Not only do raters differ in general "toughness" or "softness." They also differ in a host of specific idiosyncrasies. The experiences of life have built up in each of us an assortment of likes and dislikes and an assortment of individualized interpretations of the characteristics of people. You may distrust anyone who does not look at you while he is talking to you. Your neighbor may consider any man a sissy who has a voice pitched higher than usual. Your boss may consider that a firm handshake is the guarantee of a strong character. Your golf partner may be convinced that blonds are flighty. These are rather definite reactions that may be explicit and clearly verbalized by the person in question. But there are myriad other more vague and less tangible biases that we carry with us and that influence our ratings. These biases help to form our impression of a person and color all aspects of our reaction to him. They enter into our ratings too. In some cases, our rating of one or two traits may be affected. But often the bias is one of general liking for or aversion to the person, and this generalized reaction colors all our specific ratings. Thus, the ratings reflect not only the general subjective rating standard of the rater, but also his specific biases with respect to the person being rated.

THE OUTCOME OF FACTORS LIMITING RATING EFFECTIVENESS

What is the net result of these factors affecting the raters' willingness to rate conscientiously and ability to rate accurately? The effects show up in certain pervasive distortions of the ratings, in relatively low reliabilities, and in doubt as to the basic validity of rating procedures.

The Generosity Error. We have pointed out that the rater is often as much committed to the people he is rating as he is to the agency for which ratings are being prepared. Over and above this, there seems to be a widespread unwillingness on the part of raters to damn a fellow man with a low rating. The net result is that ratings tend quite generally to pile up at the high end of any scale. The unspoken philosophy of the rater seems to be "one man is as good as the next, if not a little better," so that "average" becomes in practice not the mid-point of a set of ratings but near the lower end of the group. One finds quite generally the paradox of a great majority of the group being rated above average.

If the generosity error operated uniformly for all raters, it would not be particularly disturbing. We would merely have to remember that ratings cannot be interpreted in terms of their verbal labels and that "average" means "low" and "very good" means "average." Makers of rating scales have countered this humane tendency with some success by having several steps on their scale on the plus side of average, so that there is room for differentiation without having to get disagreeable and call a person "average."

It is differences between raters in the degree of their "generosity error" that are more troublesome. To correct for such differences is a good deal more of a problem. We shall consider presently some special techniques that have been developed for that purpose.

The Halo Error. Limitations in our experience with the person being rated, lack of opportunity to observe the specific qualities that are called for in the rating instrument, and the influence of personal biases that affect our general liking for the person all conspire to produce another type of error in our ratings. This is a tendency to rate in terms of over-all general impression without differentiating specific aspects, of allowing our total reaction to the person to color our judgment of each specific trait. This is called "halo."

We can illustrate halo by a set of data on embryo airplane commanders in World War II. Students were rated by their instructors for such qualities as "eagerness," "foresight," "leadership," "instrument flying," "formation flying," "lead crew potentiality," and "over-all value." The correlation between *two* raters for the *same* attribute was, on the average, about .60. This serves as a measure of the reliability of the ratings. We may speak of it as the between-raters reliability. The average correlation between *different* attributes for the *same* rater was about .75. That is, the correlation between ratings of different qualities was higher than the reliability of the separate ratings. This consistency can only be accounted for by a general halo that made instructor A's appraisal of student B much the same no matter what attribute was being rated.

Of course, some relationship among desirable traits is to be expected. We find correlation among different abilities when these are tested by objective tests and do not speak of the halo effect that produces a correlation between verbal and mechanical ability. Just how much of the relationship between the different qualities on which we get ratings is genuine and how much of it is spurious halo is very hard to determine. That some of the relationship is due to inability to free oneself from general biases seems clear, however, from examples such as the one we have just given.

Reliability of Ratings. Studies have shown repeatedly that the between-raters reliability of conventional rating procedures is low. Symonds,[17] writing in 1931, summarized a number of studies and concluded that the correlation between the ratings given by two independent raters for the conventional type of rating scale is about .55. There seems to be no good reason to change this conclusion after the lapse of years. When the two ratings are uncontaminated; i.e., the raters have not talked over the persons to be rated, and where the usual type of numerical or graphic rating is used, the resulting appraisal shows only this very limited consistency from rater to rater.

If it is possible to pool the ratings of a number of independent raters who know the persons being rated about equally well, reliability of the appraisal can be substantially increased. Studies have shown [15] that pooling ratings functions in the same way as lengthening a test, and that the Spearman-Brown formula (p. 179) can legitimately be applied in estimating the reliability of pooled independent ratings. Thus, if the reliability of one rater is represented by a correlation of .55, we have the following estimates for the reliability of pooled ratings:

2 raters	.71
3 raters	.79
5 raters	.86
10 raters	.92

Unfortunately, in many important practical situations it is impossible to get additional equally qualified raters. An elementary-school pupil has only one regular classroom teacher; a worker has only one immediate supervisor. Adding on other raters who have limited acquaintance with the ratee may weaken rather than strengthen the ratings.

Reliability data on some of the newer types of rating devices to be discussed presently appear somewhat more promising. These data will be presented as the methods are discussed. One of the gains from basing ratings on specific tangible behaviors will be, it is hoped, that the objectivity, and hence the reliability, of the judgments will be increased.

Validity of Ratings. All the limiting and distorting factors that we have been considering make us doubtful about the validity of ratings. Rater biases and rater unreliability operate to lower validity. However, it is usually very difficult to make any statistical test of the validity of ratings. The very fact that we have fallen back on ratings usually means that no better measure of the quality in question is available to us. There is usually nothing else against which we can test the ratings.

In one context, the validity of ratings is axiomatic. If we are interested in appraising how a person is reacted to by other people, i.e., whether a child is well liked by his classmates or a foreman by his work crew, ratings *are* the reactions of these other persons and are directly relevant to the point at issue.

When ratings are being studied as predictors, statistical data can be obtained as to the accuracy with which they do in fact predict. This is something that must be determined in each setting and for each type of criterion that is being predicted. That ratings are in some cases the most valid available predictors is shown in studies of the ratings of aptitude for military service that are given at the U. S. Military Academy.[12] These ratings by tactical officers and by fellow cadets correlated more highly with later ratings of performance as an officer than did any other aspect of the man's record at West Point. Correlations with ratings of effectiveness in combat in the war in Korea were about .50. This criterion is again a rating, but it is probably as close to the real "pay off" as we are likely to get in this situation. In other situations, of course, ratings may turn out to have no validity at all. Each type of situation must be studied for its own sake.

IMPROVING THE EFFECTIVENESS OF RATINGS

So far we have painted a rather gloomy picture of rating techniques as devices for appraising personality. It is certainly true that the hazards and pitfalls in rating procedures are many. But for all their limitations, there are and will continue to be a host of situations in which we will have to rely on the judgments of other people as a means of appraising our fellow men. The sincerity and integrity of a potential medical student, the social acceptability of a would-be salesman, the conscientiousness of a private secretary can probably only be evaluated through the judgment that someone makes of these qualities in the individuals in question. What can be done, then, to mitigate the defects of rating procedures? We shall consider first the design of the rating instrument and then the planning and conduct of the ratings.

REFINEMENTS IN THE RATING INSTRUMENT

The usual rating instrument has two main components: (1) a set of stimulus variables (the qualities to be rated) and (2) a pattern of response options (the ratings that can be given). In the simplest and most conventional rating forms, the stimulus variables consist of trait names and the response options consist of numerical or adjectival categories. Such a form was illustrated on p. 353. This type of format appears to encourage most of the shortcomings that we have been discussing in the preceding section. Consequently, many variations and refinements of format have been tried out in an attempt to overcome or at least minimize these shortcomings. The variations have manipulated the stimulus variables, the response options, or both. Some of the main variations are described below.

REFINEMENTS IN PRESENTING THE STIMULUS VARIABLES

Bare trait names represent unsatisfactory stimuli for a rater for two reasons. In the first place, as we pointed out on p. 359, the words mean different things to different people. The child who shows "initiative" to teacher A may show "insubordination" to teacher B, whereas teacher B's "good citizen" may seem to teacher A a "docile conformist." In the second place, the terms are quite abstract and far removed in many cases from the realm of observable behavior. Consider "adjustment," for example. We do not observe a child's adjustment. We observe a host of reactions to situations and people. Some of these reactions are perhaps symptomatic of poor adjustment. But the judgment about the child's adjustment is several steps removed from what we have a chance to observe.

Workers with ratings have striven to get greater uniformity of meaning in the traits to be rated, and they have attempted to base the ratings more closely upon observable behavior. These attempts have modified the stimulus aspect of rating instruments in three ways.

1. *Trait Names Have Been Defined.* A phrase, sentence, or several sentences have been appended to each trait name to give it greater uniformity of meaning. Thus, we might have:

> *Citizenship.* Participation in school projects. Willingness to do his share. Responsibility for work and property.

This represents a somewhat more objective and behavioral statement and should produce at least *some* more uniformity in meaning among a group of raters. However, we may doubt that a brief verbal definition will completely overcome the individual differences in meaning that different raters bring to the task.

2. *Trait Names Have Been Replaced by Several More Concrete and Limited Descriptive Phrases.* Thus, the abstract and blanket term "citizenship" might be broken down into the several components suggested above, i.e.:

> Participation in school projects.
> Willingness to do his share.
> Responsibility for completing work.
> Carefulness with school property.

A judgment would now be called for with respect to each of the more limited and more concrete aspects of pupil behavior.

3. *Each Trait Name Has Been Replaced by a Substantial Number of Descriptions of Specific Behaviors.* This carries the move toward concreteness and specificity one step farther. Following out our analysis of "citizenship," we might replace it with a set of behaviors somewhat as follows:

  a. Works well with other children in groups and committees.
  b. Brings materials to school.
  c. Does his work without complaining.
  d. Gets assigned work in on time.
  e. Keeps desk and work area neat.
  f. Uses materials without wasting.
  g. Works steadily, even when not watched.
  h. When one task is done, finds other work to do.
  i. Takes care of school property.

This list is still more tangible and specific. There should be relatively little opportunity, in each case, for ambiguity as to what it is that is being observed and reported on.

The replacement of one general term with many specific behaviors gives promise of achieving more uniformity of meaning from one rater to another. It may also bring the ratings in closer touch with actual observations that have been made of the behavior of the individual who is being appraised. Where the trait to be rated is one that the rater has really had no opportunity to observe, the attempt to replace the trait name with specific observable behaviors will often make this fact painfully apparent and will force the designer of the instrument to rethink the problem of relating his instrument to the observations that the rater has really had an opportunity to make.

The gains that a list of specific behaviors achieves in uniformity of meaning and concreteness of behavior judged are not without cost. The cost lies in the greatly increased length and complexity of the rating instrument. There are limits to the number of different judgments that can be asked of a rater. Furthermore, the lengthy, analytical report of behavior may be confusing to the person who tries to use and interpret it. The lengthy list of specific behaviors will probably prove most effective when (1) judgments are in very simple terms, such as simply present-absent and (2) there are provisions for organizing and summarizing the specific judgments into one or more *scores* for broad areas.

REFINEMENTS IN FORM OF RESPONSE CATEGORIES

Expressing judgments about a ratee by selecting some one of a set of numbers, letters, or adjectives is still common on school report cards or in civil service and industrial merit rating systems. However, these procedures have little other than simplicity to commend them. As we saw on p. 360, the categories are arbitrary and undefined. No two raters interpret them in exactly the same way. A rating of "superior" may be given to 5 per cent of employees by one supervisor and to 25 per cent by another. One man's A is another man's B. Subjective standards reign supreme.

Various attempts have been made to manipulate the response options to try to achieve a more meaningful scale or greater uniformity from rater to rater.

1. *Percentage of Group.* To try to produce greater uniformity from rater to rater and to produce greater discrimination among the ratings given by a particular rater, judgments are sometimes called for in terms of percentage of a particular defined group. Thus, the professor rating an applicant for a fellowship is instructed to rate each candidate according to the following scale:

> Falls in the top 2 per cent of students at his level of training.
> In top 10 per cent, but not in top 2 per cent.
> In top 25 per cent, but not in top 10 per cent.
> In top half, but not in top 25 per cent.
> In lower half of students at his level of training.

Presumably, the specified percentages of a defined group provide a uniform standard of quality for different raters. However, the stratagem is usually only partially successful. Individual differences in generosity are not that easily suppressed.

2. *Graphic Scale.* A second variation is more a matter of form than clarity of definition. Rating scales are often prepared so that judgments may be recorded as a check at some appropriate point on a line, instead of by choosing a number, letter, or adjective. For example:

| *Responsibility for* | Very | | | Average | | | Very |
| *Completing Work* | high | | | | | | low |

The pattern often makes a fairly attractive page layout, is compact and economical of space, and seems somewhat less forbidding than a form which is all print. However, this particular variation does not seem to have much advantage other than attractiveness and convenience.

3. *Behavioral Statement.* We have seen that the stimuli may be in the form of relatively precise behavioral statements. Statements

of this sort may also be used to present the choice alternatives. Thus, we may have an item of this type:

Participation in School Projects

Volunteers to bring in materials. Suggests ideas. Often works overtime.	Works or brings materials as requested. Participates, but takes no initiative.		Does as little as possible. Resists attempts to get him to help.	

In this case, three statements describing behavior are combined with a graphic scale, and are used to define three points on the scale. The descriptions may be expected to lend more concreteness and uniformity of meaning to the scale steps. However, these editorial provisions do not completely overcome rater idiosyncrasies, which continue to plague us.

  4. *Man-to-Man Scales.* An early attempt to get more uniformity of meaning into the response scale, developed in World War I, used men instead of numbers, adjectives, or descriptions to represent the scale points. The rater is asked to think of someone he has known well who was very high on the quality being rated. That person's name is then entered on the rating form to define the "very high" point on the scale. In the same way, the names of other persons known well by the rater are entered in spaces to define "high," "average," "low," and "very low." The five names then define levels for the trait. When a person is to be rated, the rater is instructed to compare him with the five persons defining the levels on the trait. The rater is to judge which man he most closely resembles on the trait in question. He is assigned the value corresponding to the step on the scale which that man occupies.

  It was thought that the man-to-man feature would lend concreteness to the comparisons and overcome the tendency of some raters to be consistently generous. In cases in which all raters have a wide range of acquaintance, so that their scale persons may be expected to be fairly comparable, the procedure may make for more uniformity from rater to rater. But such scope of acquaintance and thoroughness of familiarity with suitable scale persons is likely to be somewhat unusual in the practical situations in which ratings must be made. Implicit comparison with other persons is involved in any rating enterprise, but explicit use of particular persons to define the steps on a rating scale has not been widely adopted.

  5. *Present—Absent.* When a large number of specific behavioral statements are used as the stimuli, the response that is called for is

often a mere checking of those that apply to the individual in question. The person is then characterized by the statements that are checked as representing him. The rating scale becomes a behavior check list. The set of items on p. 366 might constitute part of such a check list.

If this type of appraisal procedure is to yield a score, the statements must be scaled or assigned score values in some way. The simplest way is merely to score them $+1$, -1, or 0, depending upon whether they are favorable, unfavorable, or neutral with respect to a particular attribute (i.e., perseverance, integrity, reliability, etc.) or a particular criterion (i.e., success in academic work, success on a job, responsiveness to therapy, etc.). An individual's score can then be the sum of the scores for the items checked for him.

If the additional elegance seems justified, more refined scaling procedures can be applied to the statements. Scale values can be based on their judged significance or the degree to which they had actually discriminated between successful and unsuccessful individuals. The score an individual receives is then based on an averaging of the scale values of the items that were checked as describing him. The reliability of such a check list of scaled items has been found to be quite satisfactory in some instances, Richardson and Kuder [16] reporting a correlation of .83 between two independent raters of groups of salesmen.

Only limited use has been made of check lists as devices to yield scores on each individual, but they seem to present a promising pattern. They come the closest of any of the rating procedures to self-report inventories on the one hand and to ability tests on the other. A behavior check list is in a sense a personality inventory that has been filled out by someone other than the person being described. The items can be selected and scored in much the same way. The resemblance to an ability test can be seen in one well-known behavior check list, the *Vineland Social Maturity Scale.*[3] This check list is made up of items relating to self-help, self-direction, communication, socialization, and the like. Selected items from different levels of the scale are shown in Table 13.1.

Norms for the scale were established for each item, representing the age at which the behavior appears on the average. The check list is filled out by a rater who knows the child being appraised. Items the person does or can do are checked. A basal age is established for which all items are positive, and the person being rated is automatically given credit for all earlier items. Points are given for additional items passed. The table of norms gives developmental age equivalents for

Table 13.1. Items Selected from the Vineland Social Maturity Scale

Item No.	Age Level (in years)	Item
1	0–1	"Crows," laughs
6	0–1	Reaches for nearby objects
11	0–1	Drinks from cup assisted
15	0–1	Stands alone
19	1–2	Marks with pencil or crayon
28	1–2	Eats with spoon
34	1–2	Talks in short sentences
37	2–3	Removes coat or dress
40	2–3	Dries own hands
44	2–3	Relates experiences
51	4–5	Cares for self at toilet
53	4–5	Goes about neighborhood unattended
68	7–8	Disavows literal Santa Claus
70	7–8	Combs or brushes hair
78	10–11	Writes occasional short letters
80	10–11	Does small remunerative work

the point scores, and a developmental quotient may be computed that indicates the individual's rate of progress toward self-sufficiency and independence.

The check-list pattern has been used as a simple descriptive instrument, as in school reports to the home. The procedure is attractive in this setting because it can give information on specific aspects of pupil development. However, forms tend to become complicated and to confuse many parents, so this type of reporting has not been widely adopted.

6. *Frequency of Occurrence, or Typicality.* Instead of reacting in an all-or-none fashion to an item, as in the check list, response can be qualified as being "always," "usually," "sometimes," "seldom," or "never" characteristic of the ratee. Or the ratee may be characterized as "very much like," "a good deal like," "somewhat like," "slightly like," or "not at all like" the behavior described in the statement. (The terms of frequency or resemblance may vary; the ones given are only suggestive.) An individual's score would now take account both

of the significance of the statement and the point on the scale that was checked. That is, an important attribute would receive heavier credit than a minor one, and a check at the "always" step more credit than a check at "usually."

Indefinite designations of frequency or degree of the sort that are being discussed here will be differently interpreted by different raters, so the old problem of differences in rater standards is still with us. Moreover, when the number of specific behaviors being checked is substantial, a simple present-absent checking correlates quite highly with the more elaborate form.

7. *Ranking.* In those cases in which each rater knows a substantial number of ratees, he may be asked to place them in rank order with respect to each attribute being studied. Thus, a teacher may be asked to indicate the child who is most outstanding for contributing to the class projects and activities "over and beyond the call of duty," the one who is second, and so on. Usually, the ranker will be instructed to start at both ends and work in toward the middle, since the extreme cases are usually easier to discriminate than the large group of average ones in the middle. In order to ease the task of the ranker, tie ranks may be permitted. If no tie ranks are permitted, the ranker may feel that the task is an unreasonable one, especially in a group of some size.

Ranking is an arduous task for the ranker, but it does achieve two important objectives. It forces the person doing the evaluation to make discriminations among those being evaluated. The ranker cannot place all or most of the persons being judged in a single category, as may happen with other reporting systems. Secondly, it washes out individual differences among raters in generosity or leniency. No matter how kindly the ranker may feel, he must put somebody last, and no matter how hardboiled he is, someone must come first. Individual differences in standards of judgment are eliminated from the final score.

If scores based on rankings by different judges are to be combined, there is one assumption that is introduced in rankings that may be about as troublesome as the individual differences in judging standards that have been eliminated. If we are to treat rankings by different judges as comparable scores, we must assume that the quality of the group ranked by each was the same. That is, we assume that being second in a group of twenty represents the same level on the trait being appraised, whichever group of twenty it happened to be. Usually we do not have any direct way of comparing the different subgroups, so about all we can do is assume that they are comparable. If the groups are fairly sizable and chosen more or less at random from the same sort of population, this may be a reasonable assumption. But with small groups or groups selected in different ways, the assumption of comparability may introduce substantial amounts of error into any scores based on ranks.

Ranks as such do not represent a very useful score scale. The meaning depends upon the size of the group: being third in a group of three is very different from being third in a group of thirty. Furthermore, steps of rank do not represent equal units of a trait. As we saw in our discussion of percentile norms (Chapter 6), in the usual bell-shaped distribution, one or two ranks at the extremes of a group represent much more of a difference than the same number of ranks near the middle of the group. For that reason, it is common practice to convert ranks into normalized standard scores in order to get a type of score that has uniform meaning without regard to the size of the group and uniform units throughout the score range. Special tables have been prepared to facilitate this conversion, and tables for groups of all sizes up to twenty-five may be found on pp. 90–92 of Symonds (ref. 17).

THE "FORCED-CHOICE" PATTERN

All the variations considered so far operated on the same basic pattern. The rater considered one attribute at a time and assigned the ratee to one of a set of categories or placed him relative to others on that particular attribute. We shall now consider a major departure from that pattern. The essence of the procedure we consider now is that the rater considers a *set* of attributes at one time and decides which one (or ones) most accurately represents the person being rated. Thus, an instrument developed for evaluating Air Force technical-school instructors [5] included sets of items such as the following:

> a. Patient with slow learners.
> b. Lectures with confidence.
> c. Keeps interest and attention of class.
> d. Acquaints classes with objective for each lesson.

The rater's assignment was to pick out the two items from the set that were *most descriptive* of the person being rated.

Note that all the statements in the above set are nice things to say about an instructor. As a matter of fact, they were carefully matched, on the basis of information from a preliminary investigation, to be just about equally nice to say about an instructor. But they differ a good deal, again based on preliminary investigations, in the extent to which they actually distinguish between persons who have been identified on other evidence as being good and poor instructors. The most discriminating statement is (a) and the least discriminating is (b). Thus, we could assign a score value of 2 to statement (a), 1 to (c) and (d), and 0 to (b). A person's score for the set would be the sum of the credits for the two items marked as most descriptive of him. His score for the whole instrument would be the sum of his scores for 25 or 30 such blocks of four statements. Such a score was found to have good split-half reliability (.85 to .90), so that this instrument provided a reliable score for the individual's desirability as an instructor in the eyes of a single rater. This does not, of course, tell anything about the agreement that would be found between different raters.

By casting the evaluation instrument into a forced-choice format, the maker hopes to accomplish three things:

1. He hopes to eliminate variation in rater standards of generosity or kindliness. Since the items in a set are all equally favorable things to say about a person, the kindly soul should have no particular tendency to choose one rather than another, and the true nature of the ratee should be the controlling factor.

2. He hopes to minimize the possibility of a rater intentionally biasing the score. In the ordinary rating scale, the rater is in pretty complete control of the situation. He can rate a man up or down as he pleases. In the forced-choice type of instrument, it is hoped that the rater will be unable to identify which are the significant choices and that therefore he will be unable to throw the score one way or the other at will. However, though there are some indications that a forced-choice instrument is less fakeable than an ordinary rating scale, it is still far from tamper-proof in the hands of a determined rater.

3. He hopes to produce a better spread of scores and a more nearly normal distribution of ratings. By making all options equally attractive, one minimizes the effect of the generosity error, it is hoped, and gets a more symmetrical spread of scores. Again, there is indication that this result is achieved at least in part.

Forced-choice rating instruments are a relatively new development, dating from World War II, though the forced selection of one of a set of alternates had been used before that time in self-report inventories. The close similarity in the pattern of these forced-choice ratings to self-report instruments such as the *Kuder Preference Record* and the *Edwards Personal Preference Schedule* should be apparent. Because of the relative novelty of the forced-choice pattern, evaluation of its usefulness in merit rating procedures and in personality appraisal is still incomplete. This format does appear to get away from some of the most troublesome limitations of conventional rating procedures.

However, it has some limitations of its own.[1] It has a tendency to create rater resistance, because of the difficulty of the judgments that the rater is called upon to make. Where the options are negative, i.e., "Is this worker more stupid or more lazy?," the instrument has a good deal of the "Have you stopped beating your wife yet?" flavor. And even the judgment as to whether employee A is more intelligent or more industrious is not easy to make. There often seems to be no basis for comparing two quite different traits.[2] The score that results from this type of instrument does not have any clear trait label or psychological interpretation, even if it is a relatively good predictor of some particular criterion. It gives us little help in building a descriptive picture and an understanding of the individual.

Developmental and exploratory work with forced-choice rating instruments continues. For example, a recent version produced in the Standard Oil Company of New Jersey as a Management Performance Report combines forced-choice with numerical rating. A set of four items would appear as follows:

	Fits poorly								Fits well
Follows work schedule closely	0	1	2	3	4	5	6	7	8	9
Has good work habits	0	1	2	3	4	5	6	7	8	9
Is a credit to his department	0	1	2	3	4	5	6	7	8	9
Makes decisions promptly	0	1	2	3	4	5	6	7	8	9

The numerical scale runs from a low of *0* to a high of *9*. The rater may use any part of the scale, with the one restriction that he may not use the same scale point for two statements. Thus, he can rate a man relatively low on all or relatively high on all. This takes some of the onus out of the forced ranking so far as the rater is concerned. In using the results, we may treat them either as conventional ratings, paying attention to the level checked, or as pure forced-choice rankings, ignoring the numerical values completely.

REFINEMENTS IN THE RATING PROCEDURES

The best-designed instrument cannot give good results if used under unsatisfactory rating conditions. Raters cannot give information they do not have and cannot be made to give information they are unwilling to give. We must, therefore, try to pick raters who have had close contacts with the ratees and ask them for judgments on attributes they have had an opportunity to observe. We should give them some guidance and training in the type of judgments we expect them to make, and if possible they should have opportunity to observe the ratees *after* they have been educated in the use of the ratings. When there are several people who know the ratees equally well, ratings should be gathered from all of them and pooled. Every effort should be made to motivate the raters to do an honest and conscientious job. Let us consider these points further.

Selection of Raters. For most purposes, the ideal rater is the person who has had a great deal of opportunity to observe the person being rated in situations in which he would be likely to show the qualities on which ratings are desired. (Occasionally it may be desirable to get a rating of the impression which a person makes on brief contact or in a limited experimental situation.) It is also desirable that the rater take an impartial attitude toward the ratee. The desirability of these two qualities, thorough acquaintance and impartiality, is generally recognized in the abstract. However, the goals may be only partially realized in practice.

Administrative considerations usually dictate that the rating and evaluation function be assigned to the teacher in the school setting and to the supervisor in a work setting. The relationship here is in each case one of direct supervision. There is generally a continuing and fairly close personal relationship. But the relationship is a one-directional and partial one. The teacher or supervisor sees only one side of the pupil or worker, the side that is turned toward the "boss."

Those qualities that a boss has a good chance to see, primarily qualities of work performance, can probably be rated adequately by the teacher or supervisor. Thus, in one study [7] of airplane mechanics it was found that the ratings by a pair of supervisors on "job know-how" were as reliable as the pooled ratings by eight coworkers in a plane maintenance crew and that the supervisors' pooled rating correlated .53 with a written proficiency test, whereas the pooled rating for the coworkers correlated only .43. However, those qualities that show themselves primarily in relationships with peers or subordinates will probably be evaluated more soundly by those same peers and subordinates. The validity of the U. S. Military Academy peer ratings described on p. 364 is a case in point.

The lack of agreement between supervisor and pupil ratings of teachers is suggested in some of the following correlations from different studies:

Pupil's rating of excellence versus principal's rating [2]	.39
Pupil's rating of excellence versus composite of 5 judges [8]	.28
Mean pupil rating of effectiveness versus administrator's rating [1]	.08
Student versus administrator rating on general teacher effectiveness [14] School I	.40
School II	.50

A certain amount of overlap does exist, but the ratings appear also to have a good deal of uniqueness. The bird's eye and worm's eye views are not the same.

Who Should Choose the Raters? The selection of persons to rate applicants for jobs or fellowships requires consideration from another point of view. In this setting, the applicant is usually asked to supply a certain number of references or to submit evaluation forms filled out by a certain number of individuals. The choice of the individuals is usually left up to him, and we may anticipate that he will select persons he believes will rate him favorably. It might be more satisfactory if the applicant were asked to supply the names and addresses of persons who stood in particular relationships to him and who should be able to supply relevant information, rather than leaving the applicant free to pick his own endorsers. Thus, a job applicant might be asked to give the names of his immediate supervisors in his most recent jobs; a fellowship applicant, to list the name of his major advisor and of any instructors with whom he had taken two or more courses. Thus, we are shifting the responsibility of determining who shall provide the ratings from the applicant to the using agency. Such a shift should reduce the amount of special pleading for the applicant.

Selection of Qualities to Be Rated. Two principles appear to apply in determining the types of information to be sought by rating procedures. In the first place, it seems undesirable to use rating procedures to get information that can be provided satisfactorily by some more objective and reliable indicator. Score on a well-constructed intelligence test is a better indicator of intellectual ability than a supervisor's rating of intellect. When accurate production records exist, they are to be preferred to a supervisor's rating for productivity. Ratings are something to which we resort when we do not have any better indicator available.

Secondly, we should limit ratings to relatively overt qualities, ones that can be expressed in terms of actual observable behavior. We cannot expect the rater to look inside the ratee and tell us what goes on within. Furthermore, we must bear in mind the extent and nature of the contact between rater and person rated. For example, a set of ratings to be used after a single interview should be limited to the qualities that can be observed in an interview. The interviewee's neatness, composure, manner of speech, and fluency in answering questions are qualities that are observable in a single interview. His industry, integrity, initiative, and ingenuity are not, though these qualities might be appraised with some accuracy by the person who has worked with him for a time. Ratings should be of observable behavior—observable in the setting in which the man has been observed.

Educational Program for Raters.   Good ratings do not just happen, even with the proper raters and the proper instrument for recording the ratings.   Raters must be "sold" on the importance of making good ratings and taught how to use the rating instrument.   Pointing out the importance of "selling" a rating program is easier than telling how to do it.   As we have indicated earlier, inertia on the one hand and identification with the ratee on the other are powerful competing motives.   We cannot provide a course in direct selling at this point, but a job of selling needs to be done in almost any program for gathering ratings.   Furthermore, the selling must continue if thoughtfulness and integrity of the appraisals are to be maintained.

It is desirable that raters have practice with the specific rating instrument.   A training session, in which the instrument is used under supervision, is often desirable.   The meanings of the attributes can be discussed, sample rating sheets can be prepared, and the resulting ratings reviewed.   The prevailing generosity error can be noted, and raters cautioned to avoid it.   Further practice can be given, in an attempt to generate a more symmetrical distribution of ratings.   Training sessions will not eliminate all the shortcomings of ratings, but they should reduce somewhat the more common distortions considered earlier.

Observations Made as a Basis for Ratings.   One objection to ratings is that they are usually made after the fact and are based on general unanalyzed impressions about the person rated.   An attempt to get away from this dependence on general memory is sometimes made by introducing the rating program well in advance of the time at which the final ratings are to be called for.   It is hoped that the raters will then be on the alert for and take specific note of behavior relating to the qualities that are to be rated.   As noted on p. 354, the attempt has even been made to provide for systematic recording of such observations over a period of time.   However, recording of this type calls for a high level of commitment to, and cooperation in, the rating program.   Where that level of involvement is achieved, advance notice and systematic recording may be expected to improve the rating process.   Situations of this sort are probably rare, however.

Pooling of Ratings by Several Raters.   One of the limitations of ratings is low reliability.   In those situations in which there are a number of persons who have all had approximately equal chance to observe the ratee, it may be possible to get independent ratings from each potential rater and to pool these into a composite rating.   Studies have shown [15] that the effect on reliability of pooling independent ratings is essentially the same as the effect of lengthening a test.   The formula given in Chapter 7 (p. 187) applies.   Thus, theoretically we could achieve any needed level of reliability in our appraisal merely by increasing the number of raters.

The catch is found in the phrase "equal chance to observe the ratee." Unfortunately, the number of persons well placed to observe a person in some particular setting, school, job, camp, etc., is usually limited. Often only one person has been in close contact with the ratee in a particular relationship. He has had only one homeroom teacher, only one foreman, only one tent counselor. Others have had some contact with him, but it may be so much less that their judgments add little to the judgment of the rater most intimately involved.

Note that we specified the pooling of *independent* ratings. If the ratings are independently made, the "error" components will be independent and will tend to cancel out. If, however, the judgments are combined through some sort of conference procedure, we cannot tell just what may happen. Errors may cancel out, wisdom may win, or the prejudices of the most dogmatic may prevail. Pooling independent judgments is the only sure way of balancing out individual errors and has been found in several studies [10, 11] to be more satisfactory than the conference type of procedure.

NOMINATING TECHNIQUES

If a teacher is to understand pupils, he must have some awareness of the values and standards that the group sets for its members—the peer culture—and of the role that each child plays in the group of his contemporaries—the peer group. The standards and values of his peers provide the sanctions and the rewards that are very influential in determining how a person will act and how content he will be in the group setting. The peer group can be quite a cohesive unit. In such a group any action by a teacher with respect to an individual child is often viewed not only as an action for or against him but also as an action for or against the group to which he belongs and which identifies with him. Thus, in order both to understand the individual and to understand how acts with respect to individuals affect the group climate, it is important to appraise the role of the individual in the group.

It is far from easy for the teacher or other outsider to get an accurate appraisal of group structure and of the place of the individual in it. The child's role is likely to be seen only from an adult point of view and that adult viewpoint to be projected upon the group of his contemporaries. Thus, when a child is helpful, friendly, and generally acceptable to the teacher, the teacher is likely to attribute to that child a level of influence with other children that he does not have. It is often difficult for the teacher to attribute to an active and troublesome child his true level of influence with his peers. Teachers are often only dimly aware of the pattern of social interplay in their classroom, the reputation of each pupil among his peers, the factors determining prestige in the peer group, the patterns of attraction and repulsion, or the individual social aspirations.

In the understanding of these relationships, peer ratings are often helpful. A rating procedure that is very simple and quite effective for obtaining appraisals by peers is the *nominating technique*. We will consider this technique first as applied to social choices and rejections and then as applied more generally to trait ratings.

To improve their understanding of the social structure in a classroom, the patterns of friendship and leadership, teachers may use the simple expedient of asking pupils to name their choices of best friends or of work partners. For example, a teacher might say to a class: "For our unit on Mexico, we are going to need some committees of children who will work together on some part of the project. I would like to know which children you would like to have on a committee with you. Put your name on the top of the piece of paper I gave you. Then under it put the names of the children you would especially like to have on your committee."

We now have a series of nominations or choices for work partners. It is possible to show these choices pictorially by a diagram such as that shown in Fig. 13.1. This is called a *sociogram* and the procedure of constructing a sociogram is called *sociometry*.

Procedures to help in the construction of sociograms can be found in Moreno [9] and in a booklet by the staff of the Horace Mann Lincoln Institute. [6]

From the sociogram shown in Fig. 13.1, we see that A and B are the most sought after members of the group: these are the "stars." Pupils J and O did not choose anyone and were not chosen by any other pupils: they are isolates. Pupils H and I chose each other but were not chosen by any other pupils. Except for the mutual friendship between them, they too are isolates. Pupils P, Q, M, and N are fringers: they do not really belong to any of the groups but do make choices within the group.

Figure 13.1 shows the pattern of choices and attractions within the group. It would also be possible to have children indicate those class members whom they would definitely *not* want in their group. Calling for rejections presents some slight risks to individual and class morale but does permit a more complete picture of group structure.

The sociogram in Fig. 13.1 indicates that this is not a closely-knit

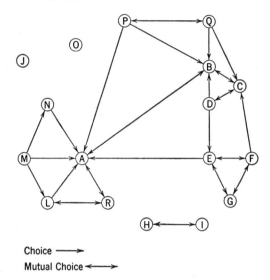

Choice ——→
Mutual Choice ←——→

Fig. 13.1. Sociogram of fourth-grade class.

group. The rather large number of isolates and fringers and the link-
ages across from one "clique" to the other suggest an unstable pattern
which is in the process of changing and reforming. Thus, the sociogram might represent a class at the beginning of the school year, in
which a residue of last year's friendships is mixed with new currents
and in which pupils from other class groups and other schools are not
yet integrated into the group. It is in such a setting as this that the
teacher can be most effective in bringing isolates into the group or
promoting new friendships.

After the teacher has determined which children are without friends
or are relatively isolated in the group, he should try to find out why
this is the case. Sometimes the explanation may be very simple. The
child may be new to the group and have not yet had time to find his
place in it. The normal opportunities to get acquainted, furthered by
the teacher's efforts to bring out the new child's assets, may be all that
is required. The child may be older or younger than the rest of the
group, having friends in other classes or outside of school. The child
may not live near any of the other children in the class. At other
times, the reasons may be more subtle, and it may take a good deal
of discreet sleuthing for the teacher to find out why Willie or Alice
are not chosen by their classmates.

When the reasons are understood, the teacher can often help to remove them.   Sometimes the simple process of coaching the child so that he develops competence in athletics may turn the trick.   The teacher can arrange seats so that a child is placed near one for whom he expressed preference.   Sometimes helping a child to develop every-day social graces or to improve his personal appearance is all that is needed to make him acceptable.   If an isolate or fringer has special mechanical or artistic skills, giving him an opportunity to use these in class group activities may be effective.

In general, the teacher can help a child become integrated with and accepted by his peer group by (1) providing opportunity for develop-ing friendly relations, (2) improving social skills, and (3) building up a sense of accomplishment or competence.

Sociometric choices describe the present flow of interaction among children rather than indicating any strong and permanent emotional structuring.   However, the structuring of a class group affects the general emotional climate of the classroom.   In a class where there are many isolates or children who are "fringers," i.e., not completely accepted by a clique, the morale of the group tends to be low and group planning and coordinated group action is made more difficult. It is also true that the teacher in dealing with one child is quite fre-quently dealing with the clique to which the child belongs.

Sociograms frequently point up mistakes that a teacher makes in characterizing a child.   Thus, when the teacher has judged a child and his position in his peer group by adult standards, sociometric devices point out these mistakes and give the teacher a framework for understanding behavior that taken by itself may seem unexplainable.

Sociograms have been used in various non-school situations.   In industry they have been used to form work groups and have been found to stimulate production.   They have been used in institutions, especially those for juvenile offenders, to select house groups.

The sociogram by itself tells the teacher only what children are selected or rejected, not the reasons for selection and rejection.   It is most useful when used in conjunction with good anecdotal records. For successful use, especially when rejections are asked for, there needs to be a friendly feeling between the teacher and the class.   Fur-thermore, the teacher should actually use the nominations as far as possible in the way in which he has told the class he would use them.

The teacher should also remember that group structure is not static, especially in younger age groups.   One sociogram made at the begin-ning of a school year will rarely provide an adequate picture of group structure through the year.   Furthermore, neither choices nor rejec-tions can be taken entirely at face value.   When, as is sometimes the procedure, the number of choices is limited to "three best friends," failure to choose a particular pupil need not mean lack of friendly feeling for him.   Choices may reflect the prestige of the person chosen and a desire to be associated with that prestige, rather than a link of friendship.   The culture pattern in certain age groups dictates that rejections follow sex lines.   Class and caste distinctions also introduce cultural factors influencing choice and rejection.   A sociogram is at best a rough and tentative picture of the social currents and climate of the group.

A final word of caution should be sounded about attempting to use sociometric data to reconstruct a group or modify a child's role in it. We have offered some suggestions as to ways in which a teacher may try to help the relatively isolated child.   However, any such manipulations call for a good deal of subtlety.   Heavy-handed attempts by the teacher to manipulate the pupils in the group may only aggravate the ills he is trying to cure.

Other patterns for obtaining peer evaluations have been developed, and they have been used for other purposes beside the preparing of sociograms and the studying of social currents within the group.   A slightly more complex form is the *Ohio Social Acceptance Scale,* in which each pupil reacts to each other pupil in the group, checking him under one of the following six categories: (1) My very, very best friends, (2) My other friends, (3) Not friends, but okay, (4) Don't know them, (5) Don't care for them, (6) Dislike them. From the pooled pupil responses, a score may be obtained for each child indicating the extent of his acceptance within the group.   This or some other similar format provides a simple procedure for obtaining ratings by a group of peers, and their simplicity makes them usable even with elementary school children.

Nominations may be used at any age level, and may be made with respect to any type of characteristic.   For example, they have frequently been used in the armed services in Officer Candidate School, where each member of a unit may be asked to nominate a specified number of individuals in his unit who have shown the greatest evidence of "leadership" during the training course.   He may also be asked to nominate those who have shown the *least* indication of leadership.

Taking all the nominations for the group as a whole, it is possible to arrive at a score for each individual, giving a plus for each favorable nomination and a minus for each unfavorable nomination.

A variation of the nominating procedure that has been used with school children has usually been referred to as the "Guess Who" technique or as "Casting Characters." In this procedure, the children are instructed somewhat as follows:

> Suppose we were going to put on a class play. The characters in the play are described below. For each character, you are to put down the names of one or more children in the class who would be good for that part because he or she is just like that anyway.
>
> "This person is always cheerful and happy—never grouchy or cross.
> "This person is always butting in and telling other people how to do things. He cannot mind his own business.
> "This person is very quiet and doesn't get into games or do things with other children."

The number of characters can be extended as desired. Each "character" is a description in fairly concrete terms of a quality of behavior in which the investigator is interested. Descriptions of opposite ends of a scale can be included—i.e., friendly versus unfriendly, dominating versus submissive, etc.—and can be treated as positive and negative nominations on a single scale. Each child receives a score for each "character," based on the number of nominations he receives.

The attractive feature of the nominating pattern is its simplicity, which makes it rather painless to administer and usable with young groups or groups with little sophistication or experience in rating. It is feasible because the large number of raters make it possible to use a simple count of nominations instead of a rating of the usual type.

SUMMARY AND EVALUATION

In spite of all their limitations, evaluations of persons through ratings will undoubtedly continue to be widely used for administrative evaluations in schools, civil service, and industry, as well as in educational and psychological research. We must recognize this fact and learn to live with it. Granting that we shall continue to use ratings of different aspects of personality, we should do so with full awareness of the limitations of our instruments, and we should do so in such a way that these limitations are minimized.

The limitations of rating procedures arise out of:

1. A humane unwillingness to make unfavorable judgments of our fellows, which is particularly pronounced when we identify to some extent with the person being rated (generosity error).

2. Wide individual differences among raters in "humaneness" or, in any event, in leniency or severity of rating (differences in rater standards).

3. A tendency to respond to other persons as a whole in terms of our general liking or aversion and difficulty in differentiating out specific aspects of the individual personality (halo error).

4. Limited contact between the rater and person being rated—limited both in amount and in type of situation in which seen.

5. Ambiguity in meaning of the attributes to be appraised.

6. The covert and unobservable nature of many of the inner aspects of personality dynamics.

7. Instability and unreliability of human judgment.

In view of these limitations it is suggested that ratings will provide a most accurate portrayal of the person being rated when:

1. Appraisal is limited to those qualities that appear overtly in interpersonal relations.

2. The qualities to be appraised are analyzed into concrete and relatively specific aspects of behavior, and judgments are made of these behaviors.

3. A rating form is developed that forces the rater to discriminate and/or that has controls for rater differences in judging standards.

4. Raters are used who have had the most opportunity to observe the individual in situations in which he would display the qualities to be rated.

5. Raters are "sold" on the value of the ratings and trained in the use of the rating instrument.

6. Independent ratings of several raters are pooled when there are several persons qualified to carry out ratings.

Evaluation procedures in which the significance of his ratings is somewhat concealed from the rater present an interesting possibility for civil service and industrial use. This is true particularly when controls on rater bias are introduced through "forced-choice" techniques or a correction score.

Peer-nominating techniques have interesting possibilities for use in schools and other group settings. They permit sociometric analyses of the interpersonal relations of pupils in a classroom or the workers in a shop. "Guess Who" nominations permit a simple type of rating in the early grades.

REFERENCES

1. Brookover, W. B., Person-person interaction between teachers and pupils and teaching effectiveness, *J. educ. Res.*, **34**, 1940, 272–287.
2. Cook, W., and C. H. Leeds, Measuring the teaching personality, *Educ. psychol. Meas.*, **7**, 1947, 399–410.

3. Doll, E. A., *Measurement of social competence,* Minneapolis, Minn., Educational Test Bureau, Educational Publishers, 1953.
4. Harrington, W., Recommendation quality and placement success, *Psychol. Monogr.,* No. 252, 1943.
5. Highland, R. W., and J. R. Berkshire, *A methodological study of forced choice performance rating,* San Antonio, Texas, Human Resources Research Center, Lackland Air Force Base, May 1951 (Research Bulletin 51–9).
6. Horace Mann Lincoln Institute of School Experimentation, *How to construct a sociogram,* New York, Teachers College, Columbia University, Bureau of Publications, 1950.
7. Judy, C. J., *A comparison of peer and supervisory rankings as criteria of aircraft maintenance proficiency,* Doctor of Education Project Report, Teachers College, Columbia University, 1952.
8. Lins, L. J., The prediction of teaching efficiency, *J. exp. Educ.,* **15,** 1946, 2–60.
9. Moreno, J. L., *Who shall survive?,* Washington, D. C., Nervous and Mental Disease Publishing Co., 1934.
10. Personnel Research Section, AGO, *Analysis of an Officer Efficiency Report (WD AGO Form 67–1) using multiple raters,* Washington, D. C., Adjutant General's Office, 1952 (PRS Report 817.)
11. Personnel Research Section, AGO, *A study of officer rating methodology, validity and reliability of ratings by single raters and multiple raters,* Washington, D. C., Adjutant General's Office, 1952 (PRS Report 904).
12. Personnel Research Section, AGO, *Survey of the Aptitude for Service Rating system at the U. S. Military Academy, West Point, New York,* Washington, D. C., Adjutant General's Office, 1953.
13. Preston, H. O., *The development of a procedure for evaluating officers in the United States Air Force,* Pittsburgh, Pa., American Institute for Research, 1948.
14. Reed, H. J., An investigation of the relationship between teaching effectiveness and the teacher's attitude of acceptance, *J. exp. Educ.,* **21,** 1953, 277–325.
15. Remmers, H. H., N. W. Shock, and E. L. Kelly, An empirical study of the validity of the Spearman Brown formula as applied to the Purdue Rating Scale, *J. educ. Psychol.,* **18,** 1927, 187–195.
16. Richardson, M. W., and G. F. Kuder, Making a rating scale that measures, *Person. J.,* **12,** 1933, 36–40.
17. Symonds, P. M., *Diagnosing personality and conduct,* New York, Century, 1931.

SUGGESTED ADDITIONAL READING

Cronbach, Lee J., *Essentials of psychological testing,* 2nd ed., New York, Harper, 1960, pp. 506–528.
Gronlund, Norman E., *Sociometry in the classroom,* New York, Harper, 1959.

Guilford, J. P., *Psychometric methods,* 2nd ed., New York, McGraw-Hill, 1954, Chapter 11.

Harris, Chester W., Editor, *Encyclopedia of educational research,* 3rd ed., New York, Macmillan, 1960, pp. 809–812, 929–931, 1320–1322.

QUESTIONS FOR DISCUSSION

1. If you were writing to someone who had been given as a reference by an applicant for a job in your company or for admission to your school, what should you do in order to obtain the most useful evaluation of the applicant?

2. Make as complete a list as you can of the different ratings used in the school that you are attending or the school in which you teach. What type of a rating scale or form is used in each case?

3. In the light of such evidence or opinion as you can obtain, how effective are the ratings that you identified in the previous question? How adequate a spread of ratings is obtained? How consistently is the scale used by different users? What is your impression of the reliability of the ratings? Of their freedom from halo and other errors?

4. What factors influence a rater's willingness to rate conscientiously? How serious is this issue? What can be done about it?

5. Why would three *independent* ratings from separate raters ordinarily be preferable to a rating prepared by the three persons working together as a committee?

6. In the personnel office of a large company, employment interviewers are called upon to rate job applicants at the end of the interview. Which of the following characteristics would you expect to be rated reasonably reliably? Why?

    a. Initiative.
    b. Appearance.
    c. Work background.
    d. Dependability.
    e. Emotional balance.

7. In a small survey of the report cards used in a number of communities the following four traits were most frequently mentioned as found on the report cards: (a) courteous, (b) cooperative, (c) health habits, (d) works with others. How might these be broken down or revised so that the classroom teacher could evaluate them better?

8. Which of the following would influence your judgment of a person in an interview? In what way?

    a. A very firm grip in shaking hands.
    b. Wearing a "loud" necktie.
    c. Generally pausing for a moment before replying to a question.
    d. Playing with keys on a key ring.
    e. Having a spot on his vest.
    f. Looking at the floor all during the interview.

9. Compare the reactions of several class members or of several acquaintances on the items of question 8. How general are the reactions? What basis in fact is there for them?

10. What advantages do ratings by peers have over ratings by superiors? What disadvantages?

11. What are the advantages of ranking over rating on a rating scale? What are the disadvantages?

12. Suppose that a forced-choice rating scale had been developed for use in rating the teachers in a city school system in order to get an evaluation of their effectiveness. What advantages would this rating procedure have over other types of ratings? What problems would be likely to arise in using it?

13. Make up a "Guess Who" form that might be useful to a teacher in finding out about the pupils in his class. If a class group is available to you, try the form out and analyze the results. What precautions should be taken in using the results?

14. Using a class group taught by some class member or made available by the instructor, get each child's choices for other children to work on a committee with him. Plot the results in a sociogram. What do the results tell you about the class and the pupils in it? What limitations would this sociogram have for judging the status of an individual child among his classmates?

15. Suppose you have been placed in charge of a merit rating plan which is being introduced in some company. What steps would you take to try to get as good ratings as possble?

Chapter 14

▼

Behavioral Measures of Personality

We have tended to define personality as the typical quality of an individual's behavior. It would be natural, then, to go directly to the behavior of the individual to get an appraisal of his personality. Two possibilities are available to us. We may set up especially designed "test" situations, in which the individual's behavior may be scored or rated. Or we may plan to observe his behavior as it occurs spontaneously in his natural environment. Each of these has received attention from psychologists and educators, and we shall consider each in turn.

BEHAVIOR TESTS

In personality testing we are concerned with the typical behavior of the individual—what he *will* do under the ordinary conditions of life, rather than what he *can* do if he is trying to do his best. Under these circumstances, it is obvious that any test must usually be indirect and disguised, so that the examinee does not know what is being appraised. This appears especially clearly in the field of character testing.

Traits of character relate to behaviors in which society sets up definitions of what is "good" and what is "bad." We can hardly expect a child to report his dishonesties, for example, or to show them in a test situation in which he knows his honesty is being observed and appraised. Furthermore, he has probably managed to conceal most of his transgressions from teacher, camp counselor, or other adult who might be asked to rate him. We are almost forced back upon a concealed test to elicit such socially disapproved behavior. We shall describe in some detail the honesty tests devised by May and Hartshorne for the Character Education Inquiry,[5] in part for their intrinsic interest and in part because they illustrate the virtues and many of the limitations of this type of measurement procedure.

388

May and Hartshorne developed a comprehensive series of tests of honesty. These included situations in which the individual had a chance to cheat, situations in which he had an opportunity to lie, and situations in which it was possible for him to steal. Some of the situations are described below.

Situation A: Cheating on a test by copying. A test is given dealing with some topic related to school work, word knowledge, for example. The papers are collected. The next day the papers are passed out, and each pupil is allowed to score his own paper when the answers are read aloud. As a matter of fact, however, the papers have been accurately scored before they are returned without any marks being made on the paper. The amount that the pupil copies in and scores his own paper above the correct score is used as an indication of cheating.

Situation B: Cheating on a test by adding on. A speeded arithmetic test is given, and at the end of 2 or 3 minutes pupils are told to stop work. However, for several minutes papers are left on their desks while the teacher or test administrator is busy doing something else. Later a second test is given after which the papers are immediately collected. When performance on the first testing surpasses performance on the second test by a specified amount, this is taken as evidence that the examinee added onto his work after the time limit was up and before the papers were collected.

Situation C: Cheating in a game—peeking. The game is illustrated in Fig. 14.1. The stunt is to shut one's eyes and put a dot in each

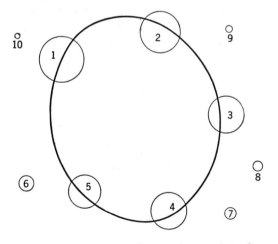

Fig. 14.1. Aiming test. (After Hartshorne and May.[5])

circle in turn. Norms are prepared, based upon children tested with their view blocked so that they cannot peek. A child who performs unduly well, as determined by the "peek-proof" norms, is assumed to have peeked and helped himself.

Situation D: Cheating in an athletic contest. As a part of a "field day," each child is given a hand dynamometer to squeeze as a test of strength of hand. Three "practice" squeezes are given, and the adult observer notes and later records the best performance on these. Then the pupil is told to make additional squeezes "for the record." While he makes the squeezes, the adult is obviously busy with another child and not watching him. The child records his own performance on a record blank. Since fatigue tends to set in on successive squeezes, it is unlikely that he will show improvement. If the performance he reports surpasses his practice squeezes by a specified amount, it is assumed that he has been unduly optimistic in recording his performance.

Situation E: Lying—self-glorification. In this test the child is asked a series of questions. Each question has to do with standards of behavior that are universally applauded but seldom achieved. Thus, one question reads "Do you always obey your parents cheerfully and promptly?" and another, "Do you always smile when things go wrong?" It is hard to know how many of a set of statements like this a child might truthfully endorse, but an attempt was made to determine this by having groups of graduate students think back to their childhood and respond as would have been true of them then. The child who marks an excessive number of items is deemed to be not angelic but untruthful.

Situation F: Stealing. A game is devised which uses a number of coins. These are in a box, and one box is passed out to each child. After the game is over, each child is told to put the coins back in the box and fasten it up. The boxes are collected. They have been unobtrusively coded, so it is possible to tell which child had which box. A check of the coins in the boxes makes it possible to determine which children have helped themselves to one or more of the coins.

As can be seen from the brief descriptions, the tests are quite involved and require rather extensive stage-managing. The details of the testing situation seem fairly critical, i.e., how sure the child feels that he is free from observation, the manner in which the children are occupied when they are stopped in their work, and so forth. And it is crucial that the "security" of the test be maintained, for if the true purpose of the test were suspected, examinees could immediately conform to the approved social standard.

How reliable and how valid are these situational tests of honesty? Reliability estimates are shown in Table 14.1. We can see that the reliabilities of single tests are rather modest, averaging about .50. In comparison with the aptitude and achievement tests we have been considering in the preceding chapters, these reliabilities are disappointing. The score of a pupil on any single test of the set used by May and Hartshorne would provide only the roughest indication of the typical behavior of that child. A single test would need to be extended by adding on several additional tests of the same sort if a satisfactorily stable and dependable measure were to be obtained. The tests would appear to be useful primarily for the comparison of different groups of pupils.

Table 14.1. Reliabilities of Tests Used for Measuring Deception

(From May and Hartshorne [5])

Type of Test	Reliability Coefficient
1. Copying from a key or answer sheet	.70
2. Adding onto one's score on a speeded test	.44
3. Peeping when one's eyes should be shut	.46
4. Faking a solution to a puzzle	.50
5. Faking a score in a physical ability test	.46
6. Lying to win approval	.84
7. Getting illicit help at home	.24

When it comes to validity, we are put to it to find any outside standard against which to evaluate the tests. Teachers' ratings of pupils may be taken as one limited and imperfect criterion, and the classroom cheating tests showed a modest correlation with this criterion (average about .35). But before we look for outside criterion measures, we should perhaps ask how the different kinds of honesty tests correlate with each other.

Considering four different types of cheating tests carried out in the classroom situation, the authors found that on the average a test of one type correlated with a test of one of the other types only to the extent of .26. When some type of classroom cheating test was correlated with cheating in an athletic contest, the average correlation was found to be only .16, and with the stealing test the average correlation was .17. The lying test, also given in the classroom, averaged .23 with the other classroom tests and .06 with the two out-of-classroom tests.

Even though the reliabilities of the single tests are low, the correlations between the different sorts of tests are a good deal lower. When the correlations involve different settings (i.e., classroom versus gymnasium) or different types of behavior (i.e., cheating versus stealing), the correlations drop still further. Many of them are not far from zero. The common factor running through all these tests is of quite limited significance, and to a very considerable extent the different tests are measuring different specific factors.

These results can be thought of as telling us something about the "trait" of honesty (and probably about the nature of other personality and character traits), and something about performance testing of personality. So far as the general trait is concerned, it is of limited significance in determining and predicting behavior in a specific situation. Behavior is determined to a very considerable extent by the specifics of the situation, and by specific factors (habits or response patterns) in the individual that have developed in response to that situation. Our characterization of a person in general terms will be only partially effective in predicting what he will do in a given specific setting.

So far as personality testing is concerned, we find that each performance test behaves much like an *item* on an ability test or a personality inventory. Thus, in a sense, the test that permits a pupil to revise his answer sheet as he scores it really asks a specific question, in behavioral terms, to wit: Would you change the answers if you scored your own paper? Each honesty test asks a somewhat different question, and collectively they might be thought of as a twenty-item questionnaire on honesty. The reliabilities of the separate tests, and their intercorrelations are not so different from those that we find for the single items of a personality questionnaire. If we think of the single tests as items, we will appreciate better the relatively modest reliabilities and the quite considerable specificity that they show.

The low correlations among specific honesty tests make it necessary to include a number of separate tests if we hope to get an adequate representation of different honesties. Because of this fact, together with the complexities of testing procedure, the use of behavior tests of character has been limited largely to research projects. They have not been adapted to any extent for routine use in schools or for any type of personnel selection.

SELECTED RESULTS FROM MAY-HARTSHORNE STUDIES

As research tools, behavior tests have provided a wealth of interesting data, notably in the original studies of May and Hartshorne. Some of the more interesting findings from these studies are summarized below. Readers are referred to the original studies for details.

1. Honesty was essentially unrelated to age or sex over the range of grades studied. There was no tendency for children to learn to be more honest as they got older.

2. The more intelligent children received higher honesty scores. Of course, school pressures were probably less severe for brighter children. How much the difference in behavior reflects a difference in motivational pressures cannot be determined.

3. Honesty was associated with socio-economic status, children from higher socio-economic levels evidencing less dishonesty than those from lower levels.

4. Siblings resembled one another in honesty, and this resemblance was more than could be accounted for by familial resemblances in intelligence or by the common socio-economic background.

5. Children in a school following progressive educational practices cheated less than comparable children in a conventional school program.

6. The children within a school as a whole or a class group within a school tended to resemble one another in level of honesty displayed. There appeared to be a factor of school or class morale.

7. There was no indication that children who participated in organized programs of religious education or who were members of groups expressing character education aims were more honest than non-participants or non-members.

OTHER TYPES OF PERFORMANCE TESTS

A number of psychologists have recently been exploring indirect performance measures as indicators of personality variables. Eysenck[4] has developed a battery of performance measures to predict neuroticism. Some of the measures that have tended to discriminate between normal and neurotic groups are (1) the amount of body sway in response to a direct suggestion of falling, (2) the number of unusual responses on a multiple-choice free association test, (3) the speed of dark adaptation, (4) the number of food aversions, and (5) the length of time breath could be held. From a battery of eight or ten such specific tests Eysenck was able to get quite high reliability and fairly sharp discrimination between a normal and a neurotic group. Cattell[3] has attempted to develop batteries of performance measures to appraise the same personality factors that he had identified in personality rating and inventory procedures. These approaches are appealing, in that they presumably cannot be distorted by the subject to give a desired impression. However, the procedures are complex and time-consuming, and the value of the tests is still largely undetermined. Indirect, objective testing to appraise personality remains primarily an area for further research.

SITUATIONAL TESTS AND ASSESSMENT PROGRAMS

During and since World War II a number of assessment programs have been set up for making a comprehensive appraisal of candidates for a particular type of training or assignment. Perhaps the most publicized of these was the program set up to screen personnel for the Office of Strategic Services during World War II. The program has been fully described,[1] and some features of it will be worth considering here. Assessment programs have generally made use of a wide variety of techniques for evaluating the individual. They have included ability tests of several sorts, detailed interviews, and various types of fantasy and projective materials. However, one central element has been the situational test, in which the individual is placed in a more or less standardized task situation where his behavior can be observed, his responses recorded, or various aspects of his reactions rated by observers.

SITUATIONAL TESTS IN THE OSS ASSESSMENT PROGRAM

For assessment by the OSS staff, each candidate was brought to an assessment center for a 3-day period of testing and evaluation. During this period he was continuously under observation and was subjected to a wide range of tests and stresses. In addition to ability tests of a number of kinds—tests of intelligence, mechanical ability, ability to observe and remember details—he was exposed to a number of "situational" tests. These consisted of staged situations, with fairly complete instructions and ground rules, presenting problems that the candidate was to solve, either individually or as a member of a group. The variety of situational tests used in the program was wide. Selected examples are described briefly in the following paragraphs.*

The Brook. Individuals worked in teams composed of five or six men. The group was brought to a stream about 8 feet wide. On the

* For fuller descriptions and verbatim instructions, the reader is referred to *The Assessment of Men.*[1]

banks were a log, a rock, various boards, ropes, a pulley, and other items. They were instructed somewhat as follows:

> In this problem you have to use your imagination. Before you you see a raging torrent so deep and so fast that it is quite impossible to rest anything upon the bottom of the stream. The banks are sheer, so it will be impossible for you to work except from the top of them.
>
> You are on a mission in the field, and having come to this brook you are faced with the task of transporting this delicate range-finder, skillfully camouflaged as a log, to the far bank, and of bringing that box of percussion caps, camouflaged as a rock, to this side. In carrying out this assignment, you may make use of any materials you find around here. When the job is done, all of you, as well as any material you have used, are to be back on this side.
>
> The limits within which you are to work are marked by the two white stakes on each bank (the stakes were approximately 15 feet apart), and you are not permitted to jump across the stream.

The behavior of each man in the group was observed, as the group went about solving the task, and each man was rated on such factors as energy and initiative, effective intelligence, social relations, leadership, and physical ability.

Construction. A single candidate was presented with the task of building a structure, using materials resembling oversized Tinker Toy. His task was described to him, and then he was told that the test was primarily one of leadership, since the work was to be done by two helpers whom he was to supervise. The "helpers" were called in, and the construction project began. However, the "helpers," who were carefully coached assistants, turned out to be sensitive, stupid, and obstructive, and their behavior ranged from "gold-bricking" to systematically heckling their supervisor. Again, the responses of the examinee to these frustrations were observed, and he was rated for emotional stability and leadership.

Improvisations. This test was one of role-playing. Working in pairs, examinees were assigned roles in a dramatic situation and were told to enact the scene as they would handle it in real life. Thus, one situation was set as follows:

> A moved to a small city about 3 months ago and opened a business there. He has been doing quite well and one month ago sent in an application for membership in a club in the town. He has heard nothing in response to this application and goes to the home of B, a prominent member of the club, with whom he is pleasantly acquainted. (A is then sent out of the room and B is told that A has received several blackballs. A is then called back into the room.)

As before, aspects of each individual's personality, as they exhibited themselves in the role-playing situations, were rated by observers.

Stress Interview. Candidates were instructed to assume that the following situation had occurred.

> A night watchman at 9:00 P.M. found you going through some papers in a file marked "SECRET" in a Government office in Washington. You are NOT an employee of the agency occupying the building in which the office is located. You had no identification papers whatsoever with you. The night watchman has brought you here for questioning.

The examinee was given 12 minutes to prepare a cover story to account for his presence in the compromising situation. Then he was subjected to an intensive and grueling interrogation, in which his statements were questioned, inconsistencies brought out, and every attempt made to trip him up and to make him feel foolish. He was rated on the quality of his story and his ability to maintain it and upon his evidence of emotional stability.

Further examples of situational tests might be cited, but these serve to show the essential characteristics of this type of approach to personality appraisal. The attempt is made to develop situations that approach realistic lifelike situations but still permit a reasonable amount of control from person to person. The OSS staff considered desirable characteristics of situations to be that they (1) have a number of alternative solutions, (2) do not require highly specialized abilities, (3) reveal kinds of behavior that cannot be registered by mechanical means, (4) force the candidate to reveal dominant dispositions of his personality, (5) involve interaction with other persons, and (6) require the coordination of numerous components of personality.

LEADERLESS GROUP DISCUSSION

One procedure that provides a somewhat simplified version of the situational test, and consequently one that is more widely adaptable for practical use, is the "leaderless group discussion." This approach has been used when a number of individuals are to be appraised for some type of administrative or executive position, such as a school principalship. The candidates are assembled in small groups, a group of about six apparently working best. The group is assigned a topic to discuss or a problem to solve relevant to their background and the position for which they are candidates. They are allowed a substantial block of time—perhaps an hour—to carry on their discussion. During that time they are observed by a team of observers and a record is kept of the nature and extent of each man's contributions to the work of the group, or summary ratings are made of each group member on those traits and behaviors that can be exhibited in the group situation. A good deal of research has been done [2] on this type of group situation as a personality appraisal device, and the results suggest that the behaviors shown in the limited test situation do have some validity as indicators of life behavior. However, the values and limitations of this type of situational test have still not been completely explored.

EVALUATION OF SITUATIONAL TESTS

Situational tests like the leaderless group discussion and those used in the OSS differ from the *May-Hartshorne* character tests in that, though they still deal with behavior in a somewhat disguised situation, they do not yield an actual record or product. Thus, in the *May-Hartshorne* stealing test, it was necessary only to count the coins left in the box to determine the examinee's score. The tests were highly objective as far as the scoring was concerned. Situational tests are not objective. Though an attempt is made to present a relatively standard task situation, the evaluation of each examinee's behavior is through the observations and ratings of the staff of examiners.

The gain from this approach, which offsets the loss in objectivity, is a great increase in the range of behaviors that can be studied. Much that the individual does, especially in his relations with others, leaves no record once the behavior is past. An action showing aggression or resistance to domination, an integrating suggestion that promotes group harmony, assumption of the initiative, or lapsing into passive followership are actions that occur and are gone. We must observe them on the wing if we are to get them at all. This is what the situational test hopes to achieve—to provide the situations that will elicit behavior of this sort and to provide for its immediate observation and rating.

Situational tests appear to be adaptable to eliciting a variety of types of social and emotional behavior that have resisted measurement by any more objective form of test. However, they present a number of problems. A program involving a number of situational tests is costly. The tests are likely to be costly in the facilities and arrangements they require. They are almost certain to be costly in the time of professional personnel to supervise their administration and to evaluate the behavior exhibited in the test situation. The staging of the situations may call for a certain amount of dramatic skill on the part of the examiners, and there is a real problem in maintaining the uniformity of the situations from individual to individual and from group to group. Another problem is that of preventing leakage of information about the test tasks, so that the task is a novel one to each group as it is tested and is approached by each group with the same background. In view of the practical difficulties involved, it is not surprising that the use of situational tests has been limited to rather elaborate assessment programs, arranged for evaluation of special types of personnel—undercover agents, clinical psychology trainees, or executives and administrators.

The actual value of situational tests and, in fact, of the whole elaborate assessment program remains somewhat of a question. Psychologists who have participated in the programs have been, in many cases, enthusiastic about the procedures. Whether the information that is elicited has real value in predicting important facts about the individual is another matter. In the OSS program, it was possible to obtain only a limited amount of evidence on the extent to which men who had gone through the assessment program turned out well in their job assignments. Ratings from overseas colleagues and evaluations by commanding officers were obtained in a fraction of the cases. Predictions of success did correlate significantly with success on the job. The evaluation that showed the highest correlation was rating for *effective intelligence*. The final rating for effective intelligence based on the complete 3-day program had a somewhat higher correlation with rated success on the job than did scores based on a brief objective test of verbal ability, but the difference was not great.

In another extensive program of situational testing, designed for the selection of clinical psychology trainees [8] there was no evidence that the addition of situational tests improved prediction beyond what was possible from the individual's credential file, selected objective tests and a personal autobiography. In summary then, the situational type of test is an interesting additional tool for personality assessment. It seems to provide a direct opportunity to see the individual functioning in lifelike situations and thus to appraise a variety of aspects of leadership, cooperation, and social functioning. However, evidence for the value of the results as improving our prediction of the individual's success on the job is largely lacking. Because its practical value has not been demonstrated and because the techniques are costly in preparations required and in the time of testing personnel, situational testing must be considered a subject for research at the present time, rather than a proven tool for personnel evaluation.

SYSTEMATIC OBSERVATION

The situational test has introduced us to observation as a technique for studying the typical behavior of the individual. Observation in that instance was of what he did in specified test situations. We turn now to observation in the naturally occurring situations of everyday life. The situations of everyday life are probably less uniform from person to person than the test situations that we stage. Also, they are not loaded to bring forth the behaviors in which we are specially interested. However, the very naturalness of real life events and the fact that we do not have to stage special events just for testing purposes make observation of natural situations appealing to us.

Of course, we observe the people with whom we associate every day of our lives, noticing what they do and reacting to the ways in which they behave. Our impressions of people are continuously being formed and modified by our observations of them. But these observations are casual, unsystematic, and undirected. If we are asked to document with specific instances our judgment that John is a leader in his group or that Henry is undependable, we are usually put to it to provide more than one or two concrete observations of actual behavior to document our general impression. Observations must be organized, directed, and systematic if they are to yield dependable information about an individual.

We should perhaps pause to draw a distinction between the observational procedures that we discuss now and the rating procedures that we considered in Chapter 13. The basic distinction is this: when we are collecting observations, we want the observer to function as nearly as possible as an objective and mechanical recording instrument, whereas when we gather ratings we want the rater to synthesize and integrate the evidence that he has. The one function is purely that of providing an accurate record of the number of social contacts, suggestions, aggressive acts, or whatever the category of behavior may be in which we are interested. The *observer* serves merely as a somewhat more flexible and versatile camera or recording machine. In *rating,* by contrast, the human instrument must judge, weigh, and interpret.

Systematic observational procedures have been most fully developed in connection with studies of young children. They seem particularly appropriate in this setting. On the one hand, the young child has not developed the covers and camouflages to conceal himself from public view as completely as has his older brother or sister, so there is more to be found out by watching him. On the other hand, he is less able to tell us about himself in words. So it has been in the study of infants and nursery-school children that observational procedures have had their fullest development.

STEPS TO IMPROVE OBSERVATIONAL PROCEDURES

Many of the early studies of young children were accounts of the development of a particular child or of two or three children based on observations by a psychologist parent. These provided a general descriptive background for understanding the young child, but they were qualitative and lacking in precision. Careful research with the child or investigations to determine the effect of particular preschool environments or experiences require that we know not merely that he shows negativism and resistance, for example, but also how much or how often. The needs of measurement, as distinct from those of qualitative description, require observational procedures that will permit a statement of quantity, of amount. The procedures should be as objective and reliable as possible, with a minimum of dependence upon the whims and idiosyncrasies of the individual observer. To accomplish this, several precautions are typically undertaken. These are discussed below.

1. *Selecting the Aspect of Behavior to Be Observed.* One problem of the general observer of human behavior is that he does not know what he is looking for. So much is happening in any situation involving one or more active human beings that some part of it must inevitably be missed. We cannot notice everything that happens, and we cannot record everything that we notice. In any program of systematic observation, we must first select certain aspects or categories of behavior to be observed. Thus, in a study of nursery-school pupils, we may be interested in aggressive behavior and may limit ourselves to instances of aggressiveness. In a research project to evaluate a school program, we may be interested in observing evidences of cooperation or of independently initiated activity and may restrict our observation to these.

2. *Defining the Behaviors That Fall within a Category.* If we turn two observers loose without further ado to observe the occurrence of "aggressive acts" or "nervous behavior" in preschool children, we will find that there are many disagreements between them in the observations they make. Our categories must be further specified. They must become more behavioral if we are to get good agreement be-

tween observers. What is an "aggressive act," a "nervous habit"? Do we wish to include name-calling in the first instance? Fidgeting in one's seat in the second? Just as we must analyze "ability to get and interpret data" into specific testable skills of using an index or making inferences from a bar chart, so must we translate "aggressive acts" into hitting, kicking, biting, pushing, grabbing, name-calling, and the like. An advance agreement on what is to be included, based upon prior studies of the domain in question, is a necessary condition of objective and reliable observation.

3. *Training Observers.* Even with a carefully defined set of behaviors to be observed, disagreements arise between observers. Some of these are unavoidable due to fluctuations of attention or variation of scoring on close judgments. Others can, however, be eliminated by training. Practice sessions in which two or more observers make records of the same sample of behavior, compare notes, discuss discrepancies, and reconcile differences provide one means of increasing uniformity. Practice sessions watched and later criticized by an already trained observer represent another. Such procedures make for uniformity of interpretation and standard application of the observation categories.

4. *Quantifying Observations.* If observations of some aspect of the child's behavior, his aggressive acts or his social contacts, for example, are to provide a measurement of the child, some form of quantification is required. The quantification usually takes the form of counting. The count may be of the number of times that a child shows a particular form of behavior during a period of observation. However, in this case one often has difficulty in deciding when one act ends and the next one begins. Johnny slaps Henry and then kicks him. Is this one aggressive act or two? If the actions flow over from one to the other, the decision may not be an easy one.

An expedient that has appeared to work well in a number of cases has been to break the period of observation up into quite short segments. These may be no more than a minute or even half a minute in length. Then the observation that is made is merely the occurrence or non-occurrence of the particular category of behavior during each small segment of time. Thus, we might observe each child for ten 5-minute periods, each on a different day. The 5-minute periods might each be subdivided into ten ½-minute periods. For each of the ½-minute periods we would observe whether the particular child did or did not exhibit any of a set of defined aggressive behaviors. Each child would then receive a score, with a possible range from 0 to 100, indicating the extent of his overt aggressiveness. Such scores, based on an adequate number of short samples of observed behavior, have been found to show quite satisfactory reliability. Thus, Olson found [9] the reliability for twenty 5-minute observations of children's nervous habits to be .87 in one case and .82 in another.

5. *Developing Procedures to Facilitate Recording.* An essential for accurate observational data is some procedure for immediate recording of what was observed. The errors and selectivity of memory enter in to bias the reporting of even outstanding and unusual events. In the case of the rather ordinary and highly repetitive events that are observed in watching a child in preschool, for example, an adequate account of what was observed is only possible if the observations are recorded immediately. There is so much to see and one event is so much like others that to rely upon memory to provide an accurate after-the-fact account of a child's behavior is fatal. This is certainly the case in any attempt at complete and systematic recording, though we shall find a place for selective observation and anecdotal recording of significant incidents of behavior some time after they have taken place.

Any program of systematic observation must, therefore, provide some technique for immediate and efficient recording of the events that are observed. There are many possibilities for facilitating recording of behavior observations. One that has been widely used has been to develop a systematic code for the categories of behavior that are of interest. Thus, preliminary observations will have served to define the range of aggressive acts that can be expected from 3- and 4-year-olds. Part of the code might be set up as follows: h = "hits," p = "pushes," g = "grabs materials away from," n = "calls a nasty name," and so forth. A record blank can be prepared, divided up to represent the time segments of the observations, and code entries can be made quickly while the child is observed almost without interruption.

If the observer is skilled in standard shorthand, of course, fuller notes of the observation can be taken. These can be transcribed and coded or scored later. In some cases, where a research project has liberal financial backing, more complete photographic or sound-tape recordings of the observations may make possible a permanent record of the behaviors in a relatively complete form. These records can then be analyzed at a later date. Such resources are likely to be the exception, however, and in many cases it will be necessary to plan a simple and efficient code to provide an immediate and permanent record of what was observed. The important objectives here are to do away with dependence on memory, to get a record that will preserve as much as possible of the significant detail in the original behavior, and to develop a recording procedure that will interfere as little as possible with the process of observing the child.

ILLUSTRATIVE STUDIES USING DIRECT OBSERVATION

The ways in which direct observation has been used in studying aspects of the child's behavior and the impact of educational experiences upon him can best be indicated by selected illustrations. We have chosen three examples of quite different types of observational procedures and quite different problems to illustrate the applications of direct observation.

NURSERY-SCHOOL CHILDREN'S SOCIAL BEHAVIOR

First let us describe a study of the social behavior of nursery-school children and the impact of nursery-school experience on that social behavior. This study [6] deals with a group of eighteen children in one nursery school. Nine of the children were "veterans" who had attended nursery school before; the other nine were "novices" who were at school for the first time. The procedure was one of direct observation, in which a running diary account was kept of a child's activities on the playground. One child was observed at a time. In the fall, the observation period was 15 minutes and there were ten such periods. However, the record was kept by separate half-minutes and could be analyzed by half-minute units. An additional series of eight 5-minute observations was carried out with each child in the spring.

The behavior that was particularly observed was "social contacts." A social contact was taken to mean "any occasion which, to all appearances, involves an actual interchange between two or more children; this includes all cooperative organized play, sharing of materials or activity, physical contacts, or conversation." The records were scored to determine the per cent of half-minute periods during which a social contact occurred. Observations were made independently by two observers, so it was possible to determine observer consistency as well as the consistency of the child from day to day.

We shall report briefly some of the quantitative data that are of interest in characterizing the observational method as used here. The reader who is interested in details of the substantive results and particularly in qualitative materials and interpretations is referred to the original study.

The two observers agreed in their report of an item of behavior in approximately 95 per cent of the instances. That is, there were about 5 per cent of the items that were reported by one observer but not by the other. The reliability of the score for a child based upon ten 15-minute periods of observation was estimated (by split-half procedures) to be about .80. In the fall, the "novices" showed social contacts in only 26 per cent of the periods, on the average, whereas the "veterans" showed contacts in 47 per cent. By spring the average for both groups was 58 per cent. Though previous nursery-school experience gave the "veteran" group a large early advantage, this was apparently completely overcome by the "novices" by the end of the school year. However, the correlation of fall score with spring score was .60 for the "veterans" and .82 for the "novices." Individual rank in the group showed marked stability over this period of time.

AN EVALUATION OF A SCHOOL "ACTIVITY PROGRAM"

Our next illustration of the use of direct observation deals with an attempt to evaluate certain changes in curriculum and procedure in the New York City elementary schools.[7] In 1935 the Board of Education of New York City introduced into a number of schools an experimental "activity program" in which units of pupil activity were to supplement, and in a measure replace, the traditional textbook learnings. As a part of the total experiment, a project was undertaken to evaluate on a broad base the effects of this program, as compared with the standard program that had been in effect and was continued in many "control" schools. In addition to paper-and-pencil tests of abilities and skills, both conventional standardized tests and some of a more experimental character, classroom observations were carried out. The hope was that the observations would get at some of the differences between the schools that were not well represented in paper-and-pencil tests.

The categories of behavior that were observed were:

1. *Cooperative Activities:* helping pupils or teacher; offering objects to teacher, pupil or visitor; responding quickly to requests for materials, quiet, etc.
2. *Critical Activities:* praising or challenging work of others; defending own point of view; asking pertinent questions of teacher or other pupils.
3. *Experimental Activities:* trying out new things, putting things together in new combinations; creating or constructing an original poem, story, diagram, instrument, etc.
4. *Leadership Activities:* organizing, directing, or controlling persons.
5. *Recitational Activities:* responding to question on assigned text; volunteering answer on assigned text or subject matter.

6. *Self-Initiated Activities:* bringing voluntary contributions to class activities; submitting data gathered outside school; presenting a report on a self-directed investigaton; suggesting methods, materials, etc. for developing a project.

7. *Negative Work-Spirit Activities:* wasting time; requiring undue help; not working when teacher is absent; leaving paper on floor; etc.

Behavior was observed during a series of half-hour periods by an observer seated unobtrusively in one corner of the room.   The observer undertook to observe the whole class at the same time, coding behaviors as they occurred.   Under these circumstances, some items of behavior were certainly missed.   However, analysis of a number of periods of joint observation by two independent observers showed that there was substantial agreement in the items that were recorded. The percentages of agreement were reportd as follows:

	Per Cent
Recitational activities	90
Cooperative activities	82
Self-initiated activities	87.5
Critical activities	82.5
Leadership activities	100
Experimental activities	96
Negative work-spirit activities	61

A further analysis of reliability was made by correlating frequency of a particular item of activity for successive samples of observation (first 5 versus second 5 of 10 periods).   Correlations were computed for class averages of 51 classes and for individual scores of 1833 pupils.   The estimates of the reliability of a score based on a complete series of ten 30-minute periods of observation were as shown.

	Class Total	Individual Pupil
Cooperative activities	.88	.56
Critical activities	.82	.54
Experimental activities	.44	.39
Leadership activities	.90	.32
Recitational activities	.68	.46
Self-initiated activities	.60	.47
Work-spirit activities	.94	.54

Thus, although in most cases this procedure gave scores having fairly satisfactory reliability for studying the group as a whole, the procedure was quite undependable when it came to providing a score for a specific individual.   Fortunately, in the context in which the results were used it was groups rather than individuals that were the matter of primary concern.

The reader may be interested in a brief summary of the results from the observational procedures as far as differences between the two educational programs were concerned. The "activity" classes showed consistently and dependably more critical, experimental, leadership, and self-initiated activities. The "control" classes showed consistently and dependably more recitational behavior. Differences in cooperative and negative work-spirit activities were small and inconsistent from one semester to the next. Readers interested in other aspects of similarity or difference between the two groups are referred to the original report of the investigation.

BEHAVIORAL EFFECTS OF A UNIT ON COMMUNICABLE DISEASES

The third and final illustration shows how direct observation may be used to aid in evaluating the outcomes from a specific unit of instruction.[10] The unit was a 6 weeks' one on communicable diseases and was taught in a high-school course in biology. The purposes of the unit were not merely to provide the pupils with certain items of factual information and certain generalizations and understandings, but also to change their overt behavior in ways approved by health officers. Certain frequently occurring behaviors were selected for observation. Undesirable behaviors included putting fingers in the mouth, putting other objects in the mouth, biting fingernails, putting fingers in the nostrils, rubbing an eye with a finger. A desirable behavior that was observed was using one's handkerchief when one sneezed or coughed.

Observations were carried out on all the pupils in a class group at one time. Each period of observation was 20 minutes in length, and there were ten periods in a series. One series of observations was carried out prior to teaching the unit; one, immediately after teaching the unit; and one, after a lapse of 12 weeks. Concurrent observations were made on control groups who were taught a unit dealing with quite different content. Observations were carried out both in the biology class, in which pupils had received the actual instruction, and in English class, to check on the generality of any changes produced. As in the previous studies, some observations were carried out with a check observer to test the reliability of the procedure, and very high consistency was indicated.

Results are summarized in Table 14.2. The fact that teaching had an impact on pupils' behavior is brought out dramatically by this table. In the experimental group a number of disapproved behaviors all but disappeared and the esteemed actions came strongly into the picture.

Table 14.2. Behavioral Changes in High-School Pupils Taught a Unit on Communicable Diseases Compared with Those for a Control Group [10]

| | Frequency | | | | | |
| | Experimental Group | | | Control Group | | |
Behavior	Pre-test	End of Unit	After 12 wks	Pre-test	End of Unit	After 12 wks
In Biology class:						
Put fingers in mouth	692	163	172	717	739	813
Put objects in mouth	237	16	16	217	272	229
Bit fingernails	44	4	6	61	90	73
Put finger in nostril	60	8	2	27	51	48
Rubbed eye with finger	99	25	30	67	96	129
Used handkerchief to cough	0%	82%	79%	0%	0%	3%
Used handkerchief to sneeze	15%	84%	86%	7%	12%	8%
In English class:						
Put fingers in mouth	907	283	327	941	888	860
Put objects in mouth	290	111	107	241	304	317
Bit fingernails	63	7	6	43	61	57
Put finger in nostril	41	7	5	58	63	55
Rubbed eye with finger	155	60	48	196	181	184
Used handkerchief to cough	0%	78%	76%	0%	1%	0%
Used handkerchief to sneeze	0%	48%	59%	0%	9%	0%

The changes carried over in large measure at least to another classroom setting, and persisted with little change 3 months after the unit was over. No comparable effects appeared in the control group. Evidence of this sort is an important supplement to tests of the conventional types, if we wish to get a well-rounded picture of the effects of our teaching.

The three illustrations we have just sketched in have shown methods of direct observation used in rather different ways and applied to quite different problems. These examples are representative of many specific studies from among which the selection was made. They suggest the range of usefulness of this way of studying the individual person or groups of persons.

EVALUATION OF SYSTEMATIC OBSERVATION AS AN APPROACH TO PERSONALITY MEASUREMENT

We have described the nature of systematic observation, outlined some of the precautions necessary if the procedure is to be satisfactorily reliable and objective, and illustrated the application of the method to three quite different sorts of research studies. Now let us undertake an appraisal of the method, indicating some of its strengths and some of its limitations as a way of studying personality.

ADVANTAGES OF DIRECT OBSERVATION

Procedures based on direct observation of the behavior of others have a number of features that make them attractive as personality evaluation devices. Some of the more significant points are considered below.

A Record of Actual Behavior. When we observe an individual, we get a record of what he actually *does.* We are not dealing with his rationalizations and protestations. If our observational procedures have been well planned and our observers carefully trained, our score is in large measure free from the biases and idiosyncrasies of the particular observer. Our record of the individual is not a reflection of what he thinks he is, or of what someone else thinks he is. His actions speak to us directly. If, as will be true in many cases, our concern is in what the person does or the way in which his behavior has been changed, then observation of his behavior is the most direct, and in many ways the most satisfying, way of getting the relevant information.

Applicable in a Natural Situation. One great advantage of observational techniques is that they can be applied to the naturally occurring situations of life. Observation is not restricted to a test situation, though we saw when we were describing situational tests that observation is often an important adjunct to a test situation. Observation can be carried out in the nursery school, in the classroom, in the cafeteria, on the playground, at camp, in the squadron day room, or anywhere individuals work or play in a public setting. There are, as we shall point out presently, practical difficulties and limitations that arise in stage-managing the observations. But in spite of these, direct observation is a widely applicable approach to studying individual personalities operating in a normal non-test setting.

Usable with Young Children and Others for Whom Verbal Communication Is Difficult. Observation is possible with small children, no matter how young. As a matter of fact, the younger the child, the easier it is to observe him.   The infant is completely unselfconscious, and we can sit and watch what he does with no special procedures or precautions.   With older children, it becomes necessary either to screen the observer from the subjects being observed or adapt them to him.   The observer may be separated by a one-way vision screen so that he can see the child or children but they cannot see him.   However, the requirement to provide such a physical setting seriously restricts the situations in which observation may be done.   More often, and more simply, the observer may be present long enough and function sufficiently unobtrusively so that the subjects come to pay no attention to him, accepting him as a natural part of the surroundings.

The value of direct observation is greatest where its application is most feasible—with young children.   Young children are quite limited in their ability to communicate through language.   They do not have much experience or facility in analyzing or reporting their feelings or the reasons for their actions.   They are often shy and resistant with strangers.   For these groups especially, direct observation provides an important avenue of approach.

LIMITATIONS OF DIRECT OBSERVATION

The factors we have just described contribute to the attractiveness of direct observation as a technique for studying individuals.   However, it is by no means the answer to all our measurement problems. A number of factors seriously limit the usefulness of observational techniques.   These range from very practical and down-to-earth considerations, which we shall consider first, to more fundamental theoretical issues.

Cost of Making the Observations.   Observation is costly primarily in the demands that it makes on the time of trained observers.   In the illustrations we gave, each child or class was observed for a minimum of 3 hours and for a maximum that extended well beyond this amount. When observations are to be made of a substantial number of individuals or class groups, the hours rapidly mount up.   Systematic direct observation and recording of behavior is for this reason alone limited in its use to research projects, in which the necessary time commitments can be made.   In routine school operations it is not practical to find the manpower required to make direct observations routinely of each pupil.

The cost of direct observation lies not merely in the observer time required in making the recordings.   Any form of special setting or any form of mechanical recording represents an additional cost.   Furthermore, when the original record is a running diary account of activities, a motion picture of activities, or a sound track of a discussion or conversation, analysis of the records is also likely to be time-consuming.

Fitting the Observer Into the Setting.   There is always a question of whether having an observer in any setting, watching and making notes of what goes on, will actually change what happens.   In many of the situations one wishes to observe, it is not practical to have the observer invisible.   One hopes, often with justification, that after an initial period of getting used to the observer all persons being observed will take him completely for granted and ignore him.   However, this is easier in some situations than others.   When the group is small, when it is necessary for the observer to follow its activities very closely, or when the group meets for too short a time to get used to being observed, the members may not be too successful in coming to think of the observer as a piece of the furniture.

Eliminating Subjectivity and Bias.   When observational procedures are used, it is found necessary to use all possible precautions to keep the observer's interpretations and biases out of the observation.   Our objective is to have the observer function purely as a recording instrument that is sensitive to, and makes a record of, certain categories of behavior.   Most of the precautions we described on pp. 400–402 are directed toward that end.   But at best we are only partially successful.   The observer is always human.   We may minimize his influence, but we cannot eliminate it.   Especially when the phenomena we are studying are complex or involve an element of interpretation, we must beware of the role of the observer in the final result.

Determining a Meaningful and Productive Set of Behavior Categories to Observe.   Any observation is selective.   Only certain limited aspects of the individual's behavior can be observed and recorded.   Furthermore, if observations are to be treated quantitatively they must be classified, grouped, and counted.   Any system of classification is a more or less arbitrary framework that we impose upon the infinitely varied events of life.   It is not always easy to set up a framework that serves our purposes well.   Thus, the reader may very well feel that the categories of behavior described on p. 405 do not indicate important outcomes of a progressive school program or that the types of activities included under a given heading are inappropriate to that heading.   Or we may have classified aggressive acts in terms of the overt behavior, hitting, pushing, or grabbing, whereas for our purposes it might have been better to classify by the precipitating event (if we could observe it): aggression in response to conflict over property, or as a reaction to verbal disparagement, or after thwarting of some activity in progress.   In any event, scores based upon observations of behavior can be no more significant and meaningful than the categories we have devised for analyzing that behavior.

Determining the Significance of an Isolated Item of Behavior.   Because of the need to achieve reliability and objectivity, the tendency has been to focus observation upon rather small and discrete acts, or at least to break the analysis of observational material up into small and discrete acts.   There is a real danger that when this is done the meaning of the behavior, the true significance of the action, will be lost.   Thus, we observe that 3-year-old A hugs 3-year-old B.   Is this an act of affection?   Or is it, as seems frequently the case at this age, an act of aggression?   If the observation stands alone, we have no way of telling.   Or suppose that A hits B.   This is fairly clearly an aggressive act, but what does it signify in the life economy of A?   Is it a healthful and adjustive reaction to earlier domination by B, a bursting of bonds that have shackled A?   Or is it a displaced aggression built up by domination at home by a parent or older sibling?   Or does it signify any one of a number of other things?

The External Character of Observation.   What the illustration we have just given brings out is that observation is external.   The "outsideness" is exaggerated when little bits of behavior are analyzed out of context.   But the "outsideness" is a fundamental feature of any observational approach to studying behavior.   We always face the problem of determining the meaning of the behavior and must recognize that what we have before us is only what the person does, not what it signifies.

INFORMAL OBSERVATION—THE ANECDOTAL RECORD

The systematic and continuous observations of pupil behavior that we have considered in the previous section are essentially research tools.   They are too time-consuming to be practical and usually too specialized to be useful to classroom teachers trying to build up a better understanding of their pupils.   However, every teacher is observing his pupils from day to day, and there is no reason why those observations should not be informally recorded as a guide to his own increased understanding or to that of others who will later deal with the pupils.   Such reports of informal teacher observations of pupils have been called *anecdotal records.*

But why should the observations be *recorded?*   Who should be observed?   What should be recorded?   How should the records be kept?

What steps should be taken to organize and summarize them? What problems are commonly encountered in making and using anecdotal records? These are some of the points we shall need to consider.

WHY MAKE A RECORD?

Of course teachers learn from observing pupils, but why record the separate observations? Why not trust to the teacher's memory to summarize in his own mind the observations he makes from day to day and allow him to report his evaluation of a pupil in a term-end descriptive statement or set of ratings?

The answer lies partly in the fallibility of human memory and the inadequacy of human beings as assemblers and combiners of facts about another person. We make many observations of other people, but we make *so* many that they all melt together in our memory, and only a rare few of the most striking experiences continue to retain their individuality. Even these become warped and distorted with the lapse of time. And the way the sharper memories are distorted, together with the flavor of the stew that is made of our blurred recollections of ordinary day-to-day experiences, depends as much on the rememberer as on the event. Our general reaction to a child, flavored by all our ingrained prejudices and warped by what we have heard about him or by our initial experiences with him, provides the framework into which our observations are fitted. All of the sources of difficulty with personality ratings that we discussed in the previous chapter bear witness to the fallibility of general impression and unguided memory. A record of an event is one dependable datum that will remain unchanged from the time we made it until the time we want to refer to it. A set of such records provides stable evidence on which later appraisals can be based.

A further reason for not relying upon summary impressions of a child, as reported by the teacher at intervals, is that such reports have generally not proved too informative or useful. They are likely to be couched in general terms, often moralistic in tone, evaluating rather than describing, and telling more about the teacher's reactions to the child than about the child.

> Wilhelmina does not work nearly as hard as she should. She seems to be a bright child, and does well when she really tries. She can be very annoying at times.

What do we now really know about Wilhelmina? What chance do we have of understanding her or of working with her more effectively?

We have a fairly good picture of a teacher's dissatisfaction, but know very little of a factual nature about the child.

Making a record of an observation of child behavior, a prompt record while the behavior is still fresh in the mind, can be a corrective for the limitations and distortions of memory. Such a record can come, with practice, to provide a relatively direct and objective report of actions, with the reactions of the observer kept down to a minimum.

> During art class Wilhelmina was very slow in starting work. She stopped her own work several times during the period to wander around the room and look at what other pupils were doing and tell them what was wrong with their pictures. Mary and Jane each told her to mind her own business and leave them alone.

This notation provides an item of factual information that can help us to know and understand Wilhelmina. It is a specific excerpt of behavior. Put together with a number of others, it may yield a factual and meaningful picture of the child.

WHO SHOULD BE OBSERVED?

Anecdotal records may serve two rather different sorts of purpose. A first purpose may be to give teachers practice in studying children, with a view to deepening their understandings and increasing their sympathetic insights. If the records are serving as part of an in-service educational program in child study, it may be well to concentrate observations on two, or at most three or four, pupils. This will permit a completeness of observation and a fullness of reporting that would not otherwise be possible. The children will ordinarily be selected for observation in terms of the teacher's special interest in them. However, it would probably be unfortunate to focus exclusively or even primarily upon "problem" cases. There is much to be learned and much light to be cast on the child with special problems by studying the "normal" child, with his or her normal problems, quirks, and idiosyncrasies.

In schools in which anecdotal records have become a part of the basic cumulative record system, anecdotes should be reported for each child in the class group. In this case, it will naturally be necessary to be content with a much more limited sample of observations for any single child.

WHAT SHOULD BE RECORDED?

This question divides into two. Which incidents should be made a matter of record? What should be included in the record of each?

Items Worthy of Recording.   Anecdotal records provide an informal and largely qualitative picture of certain aspects of an individual's behavior.   There is no point in using them for aspects of his behavior that can be appraised by more objective and accurate methods.   Intellectual ability, academic achievement, and creative skills are better shown by standardized tests on the one hand or by pupil products on the other.   It is primarily aspects of social functioning or adjustment to personal problems that one hopes to illuminate by records of incidents of school behavior.   The interactions of a child with the other children in the room, evidences of acceptance or rejection, aggression or withdrawal, events that throw light on the child's role in the group and his reaction to it are fit material for our pen.   Indications of personal tensions and adaptations to them, habitual mood and temper, or special crises and adjustments are worth recording.   We may ask in each case: What can this incident tell a reader who does not know the child—a guidance worker, a subsequent teacher—that he could not find out in some simpler, more objective way?

Material to Be Included in an Anecdote.   An anecdotal record should be an accurate factual report of an event in a child's life, reported with enough of the setting and enough detail so that it is a meaningful item of behavior.   Such a report is far from easy to prepare.   Experience with teachers who are starting to try to write anecdotes about their pupils indicates that there are three common deviations from the prescription we have given.

1. *The anecdote evaluates, instead of reporting.*   It tells the teacher's reaction to the child.   "John was a very difficult child today" is a report of how the teacher felt about John, not what he did.

2. *The anecdote interprets, instead of reporting.*   It gives the teacher's conclusions as to the reasons for behavior, instead of or as well as a report of what actually occurred.   For example, we may see an item that reads: "Oscar simply cannot keep still in class now.   He is growing so fast that he is restless all the time."   The second sentence is pure interpretation, based upon extremely meager evidence, as far as we can tell.   It tells us nothing about what happened.   Explanations and interpretations are all very well in their place, if they are kept tentative and thought of only as hypotheses for further testing.   But they should be clearly distinguished from description.   The primary function of an anecdotal record is to describe a child's behavior.

3. *The anecdote describes in general terms, rather than being specific.*   A report of this type would be the following: "Mary is not well accepted by the other children in the class.   She usually stands on the

sidelines at recess and does not take part in the games." This summarizing statement may be of some value in providing a picture of the child. However, it lacks the objectivity and concreteness that characterize the description of a single specific event. It incorporates more of selection and evaluation than we would like in our basic raw material.

A good anecdotal record has the following features:

1. It provides an accurate description of a specific event.
2. It describes the setting sufficiently to give the event meaning.
3. If it includes interpretation or evaluation by the recorder, this interpretation is separated from the description and its different status is clearly identified.
4. The event it describes is one that relates to the child's personal development or social interactions.
5. The event it describes is either representative of the typical behavior of the child or significant because it is strikingly different from his usual form of behavior. If it is unusual behavior for the child, that fact is noted.

The following three anecdotes are presented as conforming fairly well to the above specifications. Note that no attempt is made to phrase the anecdotes in full sentences. The emphasis is on ease of recording rather than on grammatical elegance. The reader may find it worthwhile to check them off point by point and see how he would like each changed to make it a more useful and meaningful piece of data about a child.

Class: 5A   *Pupil:* Henry K.   *Date:* 3/15/58

Class working as a group, Richard serving as chairman, discussing plans for class exhibit for local "Visit Your School Week." Henry's hand up and trying to talk almost continuously. Interrupted other children four or five times. Interruptions largely caustic or facetious comment. When Richard told him he was "out of order" because someone else was talking, he said, "Aw, nuts to you," and paid no more attention to the discussion.

(Typical of Henry's behavior a number of times lately. Aggressively seeking attention, then withdraws if rebuffed.)

Class: 8B   *Pupil:* Peter Y.   *Date:* 4/25/57

Peter drowsed off in social studies discussion period after lunch today. Far-away look; then eyes closed. Came to with a start when spoken to. Seemed attentive for few minutes, then dropped off again. Sleepy throughout the period.

(Same sort of thing several times in past two weeks. Is something preventing him from getting enough sleep? What is it?)

Class: 6B   *Pupil:* Betsy R.   *Date:* 10/6/57

Coming into class after morning recess Betsy slapped Sue, reason unknown. While getting seated, had a row with Jane about ownership of a pencil. Later in morning, pinched Ellen. Two or three other squabbles before lunch. Standing by herself after lunch, not playing with other girls.

(Very unusual for Betsy. Usually even tempered, well liked, and the center of the group.)

HOW SHOULD ANECDOTAL RECORDS BE KEPT?

The exact mechanical format of anecdotal records is of secondary importance compared with the considerations of content. However, the usefulness of records will depend upon the ease with which the records for a particular pupil may be assembled, studied, and summarized. It is also important that the sheer mechanical burdens of keeping the records be kept to a minimum. One of the main practical problems in the use of anecdotal records has been the clerical problems they impose.

The appropriate form for keeping records will depend upon the primary purpose for which they are being kept. If the records are serving to guide the teacher's study of two or three particular pupils, they may well be kept in the form of two or three separate logs or diaries. Successive entries should then be dated and entered in sequence in a notebook, on sheets of typewriter paper, or on file cards. When records are being made from time to time on all the pupils in a school, as a part of the regular cumulative record system of the school, a uniform method of recording that facilitates filing the records of each child in his individual file folder will be needed. The record form should be evaluated in terms of the total record system. If an individual file folder is used, an 8½ x 11 sheet of paper will often prove suitable. The record form should provide space for identifying information (class, pupil, data, person making the record), the anecdote itself, and possibly for an evaluating comment.

WHAT SHOULD BE DONE TO ORGANIZE OR SUMMARIZE RECORDS?

Each original anecdotal record is an item of information about an individual. A series of records provides a whole set of such items. But for data to be useful they must be organized, summarized, and interpreted. The data in such an intelligence test as the *Binet* consist of a series of responses to specific items that are summarized in a mental age or IQ. Although the significant elements in a set of anecdotal records cannot be summarized as simply, some attempt at bringing the items together into an organized picture of the individual will usually be desirable.

At intervals, perhaps once a semester or possibly oftener if a child is being studied intensively, the anecdotes on an individual should be reviewed carefully. Recurring patterns should be noted. Any progressive changes should be brought out. A thumb-nail sketch of the individual, as shown by the anecdotes, should be prepared. The attempt should be made to relate the anecdotal material to other facts that are known about the child: his health, intellectual ability, academic achievement, home surroundings, and family pattern. A tentative interpretation of the patterns may be attempted, if it is recognized that any interpretation is to be thought of as a set of very tentative hypotheses. In the summary, as in the records themselves, the descriptive summary and the interpretation of it should be kept clearly differentiated.

WHAT PROBLEMS ARISE IN MAKING AND INTERPRETING ANECDOTAL RECORDS?

We have already indicated a number of the problems in making and using anecdotal records in the previous sections. These and some other issues will be considered in this section.

Problems Arising out of the Selection of Items. The number of anecdotes that could be written about any individual is almost limitless. The written record must consist of a relatively small fraction of these, chosen by the observer as being significant or as typical of the child. The quality of the accumulated data depends upon the shrewdness and impartiality of this selection. Both the significance and the truthfulness of the picture will depend upon the ability of the observer to select items to record that are illuminating and truly representative. Bias by the observer can easily creep into both the selection and the recording of the items. For a child whom the teacher dislikes, it is easy to pick out and record only situations in which he appears in a bad light. If the teacher is unduly preoccupied with academic achievement or an orderly classroom, incidents relating to non-achievement or disorder may take a dominant role in the record. It is hard to know how much bias is introduced in a set of anecdotes by selectivity of this sort, but the problem is certainly a very real one.

Problems Relating to the Phrasing of the Anecdote. Difficulties here center around the tendencies, which we have already considered, to include evaluation, interpretation, and generalities and to leave out the specific factual description. Problems of literary style are also occasionally a matter of concern. In this regard, the thing to remember is that anecdotes are valued not as literary gems but for the information they convey. Brevity and clarity, not literary elegance, are the objectives even to the point of writing in phrases rather than sentences.

Problems Relating to the Clerical Burden. One of the most serious practical problems in any school program of anecdotal records is the sheer clerical burden of preparing, filing, and summarizing the records. With this problem in mind, any school system should move into anecdotal recording cautiously. Recording should be tried first for a few pupils in each class and gradually expanded if it seems to be yielding useful information. Recording procedures should be kept as simple as possible. Literary style and elegance of format should be minimized.

Problems Relating to Use. Like any other evaluation procedure, anecdotal records are useful only if they are used. One must take care that the records do not become an end in themselves. The records must be accessible. They must be summarized periodically, so that the user can refer to a concise summary. School personnel should be encouraged and trained to use them.

One specific problem is a feeling on the part of some teachers that they do not wish to be biased by what a previous teacher has said about a child. When what the previous teacher has said is primarily an expression of his reactions to the child, with a strong admixture of personal prejudice, this unwillingness is understandable. When the anecdotes and the summary become factual and descriptive, there is no longer any reason to object to having the information. It is as important for the teacher to start the year with information about the status of a child's personal and social development as it is to be informed about his reading and number skills.

SUMMARY EVALUATION OF ANECDOTAL RECORDS

An anecdotal record provides a medium for recording the observation of a significant item of pupil behavior. When teachers have developed skill in selecting incidents and in describing them objectively, when the mechanics of record-keeping and summarizing are kept within reasonable bounds, and when the records are available for use by those whose concern it is to understand the individual pupil, such records can be a significant aid to working with children.

SUMMARY STATEMENT

One approach to personality appraisal is the direct measurement or the observation of some aspect of behavior. We may attempt to elicit typical behavior by actual test situations, such as those represented by the honesty tests of May and Hartshorne. These have the advantage that they can be scored as directly and objectively as an ability test. However, the tests are complex to develop and stage, have rather modest reliability, yield results which seem to be rather specific to the particular test situation, and are not readily adaptable to many of the aspects of personality in which we are interested.

The situational test represents a compromise between a standard test and an observational procedure. A lifelike test situation is developed, into which the examinee is placed. Typically, it is a social situation involving some type of interaction with other individuals and structured to emphasize the facets of the personality in which the investigator is particularly interested. Group discussion or group problem-solving represents one promising type of situation. For evaluation of the examinee's behavior, however, reliance is placed on observation and ratings. This permits a good deal more freedom in planning the test situations, and many sorts of interpersonal behavior may be observed. In large measure, however, the predictive value of the observations that can be made in such settings remains to be demonstrated.

Behavior in naturally occurring situations has been studied by techniques of direct observation. Steps that have been taken to refine the everyday observations we make of people include (1) limitation of observations to a single aspect of behavior, (2) careful definition of the behaviors falling within this category, (3) training of observers, (4) quantification of observations, as by a procedure of taking many short samples, and (5) development of procedures for coding and recording the observations.

Direct observation has the advantages of (1) representing actual behavior, (2) being applicable to natural life situations, and (3) being usable with young children and others with whom verbal communication is difficult. However, observational procedures present a number of problems, including (1) cost, (2) difficulty of fitting the observer into the situation, (3) difficulty of eliminating observer bias, (4) difficulty of setting up meaningful and productive categories to observe, (5) difficulty in determining the meaning of isolated bits of behavior, and (6) the fact that an observer inevitably has an outside view of the person whom he observes.

Systematically scheduled observation is rarely practical for teachers, job supervisors, or other persons for whom personality appraisal is secondary to other aspects of their job. Such a person may use informal anecdotal records to accumulate factual information about a pupil or employee. Informal observations should be factual reports of significant items of behavior; they should avoid evaluation, interpretation, and vague generalities. Records of observations should be kept as simply as possible and reviewed and interpreted periodically to give an organized picture of the person who has been observed.

REFERENCES

1. Assessment Staff, U. S. Office of Strategic Services, *Assessment of men*, New York, Rinehart, 1948.
2. Bass, Bernard M., The leaderless group discussion, *Psychol. Bull.*, **51**, 1954, 465–492.
3. Cattell, Raymond B., The principal replicated factors discovered in objective personality tests, *J. abnorm. soc. Psychol.*, **50**, 1955, 291–314.
4. Eysenck, H. J., *The scientific study of personality*, New York, Macmillan, 1952.
5. Hartshorne, H., and M. A. May, *Studies in deceit*, New York, Macmillan, 1928.
6. Jersild, A. T., and Mary D. Fite, The influence of nursery school attendance on children's social adjustments, *Child Develpm. Monogr.*, No. 25, 1939.
7. Jersild, A. T., R. L. Thorndike, B. Goldman, and J. J. Loftus, An evaluation of aspects of the activity program in the New York City public elementary schools, *J. exp. Educ.*, **8**, 1939, 166–207.
8. Kelly, E. L., and D. W. Fiske, *The prediction of performance in clinical psychology*, Ann Arbor, University of Michigan Press, 1951.
9. Olson, W. C., The measurement of nervous habits in normal children, *Univ. of Minn. Inst. of Child Welfare Monogr.*, 1929, No. 3.
10. Urban, J., Behavior changes resulting from a study of communicable diseases, *Teachers College Contrib. Educ.*, 1943, No. 896.

SUGGESTED ADDITIONAL READING

Allen, Robert M., *Personality assessment procedures*, New York, Harper, 1958, Chapters 16, 17, and 18.

Almy, Millie, *Ways of studying children*, New York, Bureau of Publications, Teachers College, Columbia University, 1959, Chapter 2.

Cronbach, Lee J., *Essentials of psychological testing*, 2nd ed., New York, Harper, 1960, Chapters 17 and 18.

Harris, Chester W., Editor, *Encyclopedia of educational research*, 3rd ed., New York, Macmillan, 1960, pp. 927–932, 954–955.

Prescott, Daniel A., *The child in the educative process*, New York, McGraw-Hill, 1957, Chapter 6.

Stern, George G., Morris I. Stein, and Benjamin S. Bloom, *Methods in personality assessment*, Glencoe, Illinois, The Free Press, 1956, Chapters 1, 2, and 3.

Thomas, R. Murray, *Judging student progress,* 2nd ed., New York, Longmans, Green, 1960, Chapter 8.

Willey, Roy DeVerl, *Guidance in elementary education,* rev. ed., New York, Harper, 1960, Chapter 3.

QUESTIONS FOR DISCUSSION

1. In their studies of honesty, Hartshorne and May report quite low correlations between different behavior tests of honesty. If this is true for other qualities as well, what does it mean for our understanding of people?

2. What implications do the findings of May and Hartshorne have for the classroom teacher when it comes to writing descriptions or evaluations of students for permanent school records?

3. Try to plan a number of behavior tests for some trait other than honesty.

4. Plan a situational test for use in a school or industrial situation. What would you hope to get from this test that you could not get in other ways? What would be the difficulties of using such a test as you have proposed?

5. How could the class discussion that takes place in most classes serve as the basis for systematic observation? Make a plan for recording these observations.

6. In a research study, you propose to use systematic observations of school children as a method of studying their social adjustment. What problems would you encounter? What precautions would you need to take in interpreting the results?

7. What advantages do systematic observations or short sample observations have over the observations of everyday life? What limitations do these more specialized procedures have?

8. If you are working in a classroom, make anecdotal records on some one child over a 1-week period. Observe as well as you can the guides for making anecdotal records given on pp. 413–415. What difficulties did you encounter in making the records?

9. Criticize the following anecdotal records:

a. "Mary continues to be a nuisance in class. She is noisy and not only fails to do her own work but keeps other children from doing theirs. I don't know what I am going to do about it."

b. "John had a good deal of trouble with his arithmetic today. He didn't seem to be able to get the idea of reducing fractions to a common denominator. Out of several problems he was able to identify the lowest common denominator only once."

Chapter 15

▼

Projective Tests

In the last three chapters, we have considered the possibilities of studying a person through (1) what he tells us about himself, (2) the impression he makes on others, and (3) his observable actions. There is one further avenue of approach that we must now examine. We may be able to learn about the individual by exploring his world of fantasy and make-believe. We shall do this by providing him with relatively indefinite and unstructured stimuli and observing how he structures them for us. The various techniques for doing this may be collectively identified as *expressive and projective techniques*.

Psychologists have long recognized that the perceiving of even quite definite stimuli—an accident, a scene staged before a class, the content of a picture—is dependent upon the individual perceiver. He sees what he is set to see. The report reflects his readinesses and predispositions. The vaguer the stimulus, the more opportunity there is for the individual to project himself into the report. Projective tests take advantage of this situation. They operate with quite unstructured materials: a vague and ambiguous picture, an ink blot, a word or two of a sentence, some modeling clay, or paper and finger paints. Furthermore, the instructions place very little restriction or constraint upon the respondent. Under these conditions, there is the greatest diversity of product produced. The basic assumption of projective methods is that under these circumstances the production depends in large measure upon basic personality factors in the person being tested and that an appropriate analysis of the productions can reveal that personality structure. The basic procedure common to projective techniques is, then,

1. to present the subject with a series of fluid, weakly structured stimuli

2. under instructions that emphasize freedom of response, and

3. to analyze his productions for insight into his basic personality dynamics.

For at least some of the projective media, materials and procedures have been standardized and are widely used. In addition, there are numerous exploratory and unstandardized projective media. We shall describe in some detail the two that are probably most extensively used, mention briefly several others, and then try to apply to projective tests the same criteria of evaluation that we have used with other measurement procedures.

THE RORSCHACH TEST

The *Rorschach Test* [16] has been so widely publicized now that it is probably familiar in a general way to most readers of this book. The basic material is ten ink blots, nonsense patterns produced by putting blobs of ink on a piece of paper and folding the paper over so the two halves blot. But these are not just ordinary ink blots. They were selected by Hermann Rorschach, the original investigator, after trying out thousands of different blots with patients in mental institutions, because they appeared particularly effective in eliciting a richness of diagnostic material.

Sample ink blots, like those in the *Rorschach Test,* are shown in Fig. 15.1. These blots are entirely black and white, as are five of the blots in the *Rorschach* series. Two *Rorschach* blots contain bright red blotches in addition to the black and white, while three are made up only of colored patches of various hues. The symmetrical blots are mounted in the center of white cards and may be turned and viewed from any angle. The cards are presented to the subject one at a time in a specified order. The order of presentation is considered important because the subject's reaction to the sudden appearance of color is thought to be a significant element in his reaction to the test materials.

The test is introduced to the subject in a rather ambiguous way— "People see all sorts of different things in these cards. I'd like you to tell me what you see." When the subject is seated, the examiner hands him card I with instructions: "Tell me what you see? What might this be?" The subject is allowed as much time as he wants for a given card and is permitted to give as many responses to it as he wishes. He is also allowed to turn the card around and look at it from any angle to find things in it. However, he is not instructed to look for many items and is not told that he may rotate the card. Instructions are kept to the barest minimum, this presumably making the performance depend more completely on the person being examined.

During the initial presentation, the examiner keeps a record of the time between presentation of each card and the initial response to it.

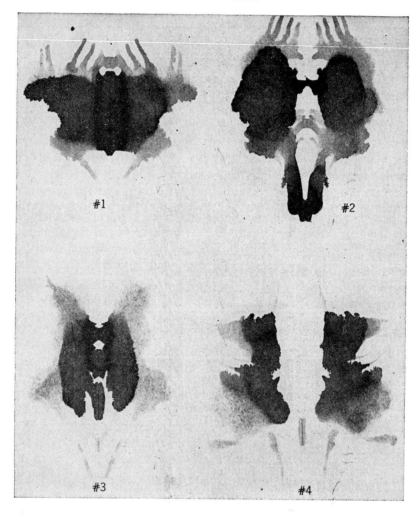

Fig. 15.1.   Rorschach-type ink blots.

He records each response as it is given and the position of the card when the response is seen. Notes are also made of any significant behavior by the subject during testing, i.e., evidences of upset, rejection of a card, etc.

After the initial presentation of the cards, the examiner goes over them with the subject again, questioning him about his responses. The questioning helps the examiner to find out where each item was seen in the blot and what aspect of the blot (form, color, etc.) primarily determined what the subject saw. It gives an opportunity for further clarification of anything that may have been obscure in the subject's initial response. Notes are made as needed and become part of the raw test record.

SCORING A RORSCHACH RECORD

The raw *Rorschach* record contains a mass of diverse material, and procedures of analysis must be applied to bring some order out of the chaos of details. Several different scoring schemes for the *Rorschach* have been developed.[1, 9, 10] The scoring procedure described here is the one developed by Klopfer. Only the major features of the scoring procedure are discussed in this section.

Rorschach and his followers have identified a number of different categories of response which are thought to have diagnostic significance. In addition to the simple count of number of responses, three main aspects of each response are considered important. These are location, determinant, and content.

In general, location is scored by determining the area of the blot to which the response corresponded. The subject can use the whole blot (W) for his response, as when he calls blot 1 of Fig. 15.1 a "crab's shell." He may base his response on a large subdivision of the blot (D), as when he reports each half of blot 2 to be "an Indian's head." He may base his response on some small usual detail (d), as when the upper center part of blot 2 is seen as two witches talking.

The determinant refers to the characteristic of the blot that caused the subject to see it as he did. The principal determinants are the shape or form of the blot (F), color (C), movement (M) and shading (k). As a rule, the greatest number of responses in a record are elicited by the shape of the blot. A further coding may be assigned to form responses depending upon whether the form of the blot appears to fit the response well (F+) or quite poorly (F−). It is quite common to have a response based jointly on two determinants. Thus, a response may depend upon both the shape and color of the blot, or the shape and shading of the blot. Thus, a subject may see blot 3 as a reflection of a bear in the water. The response would be coded for both determinants, the dominant one being listed first (i.e., if this response was made primarily because of the shape of the blot, it would be coded FK, F for form and K for the depth or vista response).

The content categories refer to what it is that is seen in the blot. Among the categories used are human beings, animals, parts of human beings, parts of animals, nature, and inanimate objects. Recurrent content themes are particularly noted, as are content elements that appear to tell a story.

In addition to the three aspects of analysis noted above, each response is also classified as a frequently occurring or popular response (P) or as a rarely given or original response (O). There are a number of additional categories which are noted in the analysis of the record, i.e., use of white space, rare edge details, etc. It is not possible or desirable to try to indicate the complete scoring procedure here.

After the single responses have been coded, a summary tabulation is prepared for the record. The frequency of each category is determined, and a number of ratios between different categories are calculated. It is this quantitative summary, plus the qualitative notes on the subject's reactions, on which interpretation is primarily based. The single response has significance only as it becomes part of this total.

INTERPRETING THE RORSCHACH RECORD

Rorschach specialists would agree that the heart of the *Rorschach* method is the final integrative synthesis of the material that results from scoring the test. This is also the most difficult part of the undertaking, calling as it does for the evaluation and synthesis of many separate cues. Writers about the *Rorschach* insist that adequate interpretations can be made only by persons who have both a broad psychological background and extensive experience with the instrument itself. Just how much training is required would probably be a matter of debate, but clearly the interpretation of a record is not something to be undertaken by the teacher, the usual guidance worker, or many psychologists without the required special training. Any abbreviated presentation of the manner of interpretation must necessarily represent an oversimplification and do the method some injustice.

The *Rorschach* record is considered by its exponents to provide information about the whole functioning personality. We may ask and expect help on questions like the following: How does this person usually attack a problem? Does he characteristically first look at the problem as a whole and then break it down into component parts or does he build up the total solution from its main parts? Does he deal with the main features of a problem or does he bog down in details and never reach the main problem? Does he approach problems in a rigid, set manner, or is his approach flexible? What is his intellectual level and how effectively does he use his intelligence? Is he overly ambitious? How does he handle his emotions?

Factors that are considered to be associated with the intellectual level of the subject are clearness of perception of form, ability to organize the blot into forms using the whole of the blot, number of original responses, total number of responses, and variety of content.

The location of the response in the blot and the approach in responding to each blot are said to represent the individual's way of solving problems. Using the whole blot is associated with intellectual ambition, and a person who is striving beyond his ability is expected to produce poor whole responses (i.e., to force a high level of organization even where it is not appropriate). Breaking the blot into small, unusual details is considered to be characteristic of compulsive people who insist that the response must exactly match the form of the blot. The common-sense approach is illustrated by the frequent use of D, or usual details. Exponents of the *Rorschach* consider it to be particularly effective in revealing how well the individual uses his intelligence. However, estimates of intelligence based on the *Rorschach* have shown only rather modest correlations with scores on the conventional intelligence test.

The subject's use of color, texture, and shading are thought to give evidence about his emotional life. Pure color or color naming responses are considered to indicate a lack of emotional control. When color is combined with form but the form predominates, it is taken to indicate that the individual has a lively emotional life but that he has control of his emotions. Texture and shading responses are usually interpreted as indications of anxiety, feelings of inadequacy, or depression. Vista or three-dimensional responses receive much the same interpretation.

The movement (M) responses are associated with the inner life of the individual. Rorschach expressed the belief that movement responses represent a strongly felt wish experience. Many interpreters feel that M is a correlate of the color (C) response and shows internalized emotion whereas the C response represents the externalized emotional reaction.

The content of the *Rorschach* responses provides cues for understanding other types of responses. In the different content of the responses, the subject reveals his different personal experiences. It is from the content or symbolism of the content that the analogy is made between a *Rorschach* record and a dream.

THE THEMATIC APPERCEPTION TEST

The *Thematic Apperception Test,* usually referred to as the *TAT,* was originally described by Murray and Morgan [13] in 1935. The basic material of the *TAT* is a set of pictures, 30 in all, each rather vague and indefinite, showing one or two human figures in different poses and actions. Some of the pictures are specifically for boys, some specifically for girls, some for males over 14, some for females over 14, and some for all groups. For a particular age and sex, there are 20 of the pictures that are supposed to be used, though in many cases the examiner limits himself to a smaller number of pictures that he considers particularly appropriate for his subject. A sample picture from Murray's *Thematic Apperception Test* is shown in Fig. 15.2. This particular picture is one used in the series for women.

The subject's basic task is to tell a story based on the picture. Before any of the pictures are shown to the subject, the examiner instructs him somewhat as follows: "I am going to show you some pictures. I want you to tell me a story about what is going on in each picture. What led up to it, and what will the outcome be?" The exact instructions may vary from time to time, but they always include the directions to produce a setting for the action in the picture and to indicate the outcome. The story told by the subject is recorded verbatim, either by the examiner or with a recording machine. There

Fig. 15.2. Sample picture from *Murray Thematic Apperception Test.*

are no time limits and no limits on the length of the story. The example given below is a sample of the responses given to the picture in Fig. 15.2.

> This young girl wants to go out on her own and lead a good life, but this old woman wants to control her and make her do things as the old woman wants them done. Some of the things the old woman has told the girl were bad, but the girl had to do them anyway. She hates the old hag and gets tired of the control that the old woman has over her and kills the old hag. No one ever found out that the girl killed the woman so she is free to do what she wants.

Points that should probably be noted in the above story are submission to another, an unwillingness to assume responsibility for personal behavior, hostility, and a socially unacceptable method of solving the problem situation. It must be remembered that a single story is not especially significant in understanding the person. However, if these elements recurred in a number of stories, then the pattern would be considered to have much greater significance.

SCORING AND INTERPRETATION OF THE TAT

A number of different scoring schemes have been worked out for the *TAT*.[17] Most of these are elaborate and time-consuming. One thing that all the scoring schemes have in common is that the *content* of the stories plays a central role in interpreting the record. This contrasts with the *Rorschach,* where the center of attention is not *what* the subject sees but *how* he sees it. Beyond this, there is little uniformity in procedure for analysis, the method of interpretation and aspects analyzed depending upon the original purpose of giving the test.

Originally Murray analyzed the stories according to needs and presses, the needs of the hero and the environmental forces (presses) to which he is exposed. Each story was analyzed; from the total set of stories each need and press received a weighted score; and the needs and presses were then arranged in rank order. At the same time, the relationships between the needs were investigated. Although this type of analysis appeared to yield a wealth of data, it is not generally followed today. Mastery of the need concept is difficult to achieve, and the analysis is quite laborious, requiring about 5 hours to interpret a set of twenty stories, on the average.

Most currently used scoring systems take account of the following:

1. The style of the story, including such factors as length of story, language used, originality, variation of content, and organizational qualities.

2. Recurring themes in the story: such themes as retribution, struggle and failure, parental domination, etc.

3. Relation of the outcome of the story to the rest of the plot.

4. Primary and secondary identification, the choice of hero for the story and person second in importance.

5. The handling of authority figures and sex relationships.

Whatever method of interpretation is used, it is recognized that the single response has significance only as an element in the total pattern. It is the recurring themes and features that are important for interpretation.

OTHER PROJECTIVE TECHNIQUES

During the last 25 years, a host of other projective procedures have been proposed and have been developed to a greater or lesser degree. A number of these bear a close resemblance to the *TAT*. The *Four-Picture Test* of Van Lennep requires the subject to use four vague water-color pictures involving persons in different grouping and relationships in composing a story. This is alleged to bring out the subject's attitude toward life. The *Schneidman Make a Picture Story Test (MAPS)* requires the subject to make his own picture and corresponding story from a set of 67 cardboard figures presented one at a time by the examiner. The more active participation by the subject is reported to result in longer and richer stories than those from the *TAT,* but the unstandardized nature of the task makes it difficult to arrive at any norms or any standard way of scoring the product. Symonds has prepared the *Picture Story Test,* a set of pictures involving adolescent characters, designed for use with adolescents. Special sets of pictures have also been prepared for use with children and for use with Negroes, using figures with which the respondents are expected to identify themselves more readily.

A number of adaptations of the *Rorschach* test have been developed. It has been adapted for group presentation with a projector, with the necessarily curtailed freedom for manipulation of materials by the subject and detailed inquiry by the examiner. Multiple-choice versions have been prepared, in which the examinee must select one or more choices from a list provided on the test blank. Most recently, Holtzman [7] has developed a version in which the number of blots is greatly increased, but only one response is called for to each blot. The hope is that by this procedure the reliability will be increased and factors of sheer fluency of response can be held constant.

Graphic and plastic art materials have also been used to provide the raw material for projective analyses. Children's painting and finger painting and various types of clay modeling have provided unstructured media into which the child could project himself. Doll play also has provided an opportunity for dramatic expression for young children. The child is provided a set of dolls representing the various members of a family constellation and is given the materials with which to construct a stage setting. He is encouraged to act out any type of story or scene that appeals to him. Acting out problem situations in the make-believe setting is used not only as a source of information about the child's problem, but also as a form of therapy through which the child is provided with an opportunity to express, and presumably eventually relieve, his anxieties and tensions.

Verbal materials have also been used to some extent as media to elicit the individual's projections. The classical form of verbal projective test is the word association test, in which stimulus words are read one after another and the subject responds to each with the first word he thinks of. Cues to problem areas are obtained from words to which the subject responds very slowly, words on which he blocks and makes no response, and words to which he responds with unusual associations. The word association procedure is not widely used at the present time because it does not appear to provide very rich insights into the person being studied.

Sentence completion is another form of verbal test that has received some attention since 1940. The subject is given a series of incomplete sentences. The beginning of each sentence is provided, and the subject is to go through the list quickly, writing an ending for each sentence. The sentences may be in first person or third person, very unstructured or quite complete. Illustrations of the sort of materials used are the following:

I wish ————————————————————————.
John felt ———————————————————————.
When I am alone I ——————————————————.
When Mary's mother left she —————————————.

The sentence completion test is usually analyzed for the content of the responses in much the same way as the *TAT* and gives indications of feelings, attitudes, and reactions to things and people rather than indicating underlying personality structure and dynamics. The ease with which it can be administered to a group makes it attractive, but the verbal production required limits its use to fairly literate individuals. The nature of the response that he is making is fairly apparent to the subject, and it is relatively easy for him not to reveal himself on the test if he does not choose to.

THE ESSENTIAL NATURE AND PRESUMED ADVANTAGES OF PROJECTIVE TESTS

We have seen something of the diversity of projective methods and of the wide range of materials and media they use. Now we must ask what the common core running through them is and determine what advantages they may claim over other methods of studying the individual. Four points will be noted.

In the first place, the tasks presented to the individual are usually both somewhat novel and quite unstructured. The subject cannot depend upon established, conventional, and stereotyped patterns of response. Rather, he is thrown back upon himself and must delve within himself for the response. He must create it anew in the test situation.

In the second place, the nature of the appraisals being made is usually well disguised. The subject is ordinarily not aware of the true purpose of the test, and even if he does have a general idea of the nature of the appraisal he does not know what aspects of his response are significant or what significance they have. The test is usually given under a neutral guise as one of imagination or artistic ability. The individual is not called upon to verbalize his anxieties or emotions or to reveal himself directly and consciously to the tester. What revelation occurs is largely indirect and outside the subject's awareness. Thus, inhibitions and conscious controls may be by-passed, and intentional distortion of the picture presented is difficult for any but the most sophisticated subject.

Third, most of the tests make little or no demand on literacy or academic skills. They are non-reading, largely independent of any particular language, and in some cases do not involve speech at all. This extends greatly their scope of usefulness. They may be used with children, even quite young children below school age. They may be used with illiterates or non-English speaking persons. They may be used in different cultures. Thus, their scope is much wider than that of self-report or rating procedures.

Fourth, they provide a view of the total functioning individual. They do not slice off one piece or trait for analysis. They preserve, it is alleged, the unity and integration of the total personality. To the clinically oriented user this appears a great virtue. In practical work, one must deal with the whole person, not just his limited intelligence, or his lack of emotional control, or his strong identification with his father. There is an appeal to a test that aspires to appraise the individual as a total functioning unity. Whether this is, in fact, the best way to understand him is another matter. We may be seduced by the shibboleth of "the whole child" into vagueness and fuzziness that results in a poorer picture of the whole than if we had looked more analytically and carefully at one aspect at a time. In buying a house, there are considerations of basic construction, type of roof, size of rooms, quality and adequacy of heating plant, plumbing and electrical equipment, accessibility and quality of schools and shopping areas, character of the neighborhood, esthetic appeal of the structure, cost, and many others. A more rational choice of house could probably be made by identifying these components and considering them one at a time than by reacting to the proposition as a totality. In the same way, it is possible that the total individual may be appraised more accurately and a truer description of him prepared if we concentrate our information-gathering upon one aspect at a time. It is, in any event, a fundamental issue and one on which no agreement is currently available as to how analytical an approach should be to provide the best basis for viewing the whole.

EVALUATION OF PROJECTIVE METHODS

We must now attempt to evaluate projective methods in terms of the criteria which we set forth in Chapter 7, attempting to see how they meet our requirements of validity, reliability, and practicality. Most of our data and illustrations will refer to the *Rorschach,* since this test has been studied longer and much more intensively than the others. The general problems we encounter in attempting to evaluate this test apply pretty generally to all. However, information on many of the varied techniques is fragmentary in the extreme.

VALIDITY OF PROJECTIVE TECHNIQUES

In the general discussion of validity in Chapter 7, we distinguished three broad aspects of validity. These we designated validity as *representing,* validity as *signifying,* and validity as *predicting.* Let us examine the validity of projective techniques, and specifically of the *Rorschach* under these three general headings.

Validity as Representing. We said that a test such as a high school biology test has high validity when the knowledges and skills called for by the test match accurately the knowledges and skills that we have set up as the objectives of our instruction. The test then accurately represents what we are trying to teach. It has high content validity, because the obvious, manifest content of the test corresponds well with our most thoughtful analysis of what the pupil is expected to have learned.

This type of validity—validity exemplified by the direct matching up of test content with life behavior—has no application in the case of projective techniques. The essence of projective testing is that it deals with the inner, concealed aspects of personality dynamics, and that these are revealed only indirectly by the interpretation of subtle signs in the fantasy behavior of the individual. Thus, we must exclude content validity, or validity as representing, as an approach to the evaluation of projective techniques. Their validity must be appraised in other ways.

Validity as Signifying. Projective techniques are alleged to provide a basis for describing inner personality dynamics. The prominence of various determinants in a *Rorschach* record, for example, is thought to have significance for understanding manner of attacking problems, level of anxiety and ways of dealing with it, control of tensions, creativity, or some of a host of other aspects of the dynamic interplay in the personality. The projective techniques are esteemed for what the responses are presumed to *signify,* so the primary focus of inquiry into the validity of the techniques will be upon their validity as signifying.

We have used the word "technique" rather than "test" in the last few paragraphs to set the stage for a distinction we wish to make between the projective procedures and those that we might speak of as psychometric tests. An instrument such as the *Guilford-Zimmerman Temperament Survey* yields a set of scores. Each score is based on a separate set of items, and can be thought of as a measure of an hypothetical distinct trait. Validation consists of trying to obtain other evaluations of the trait, as by ratings, and correlating the test scores with them, or of trying to predict the reasonable life correlates of such a trait and seeing whether these correlates do in fact appear. The validation of each score is a separate enterprise, and there is little or no interaction between the scores.

By contrast, a projective technique such as the *Rorschach* yields a mass of response material that is initially quite unstructured. The twenty or thirty responses to the blots may be classified in a variety of ways—by location, by use of color, by content—and one may study not only the single responses and single aspects, but also various relations among them. There is almost no limit to the number of different scores and indices, of varying degrees of subtlety and complexity, that can be obtained from this sample of behavior. And by the same token, there is no limit to the number and variety of hypotheses that can be generated concerning the *significance* of these indices. These hypotheses may relate not merely to single indices, such as the per cent of W, or whole card, responses, but to ratios, patterns, and interrelationships of indices of any degree of complexity.

Validation of the *Rorschach* is, then, not an all-or-none proposition, but a piecemeal undertaking of validating each of the interpretive hypotheses. If one is to have confidence in the significance of a *Rorschach* record, each of the hypotheses as to what signifies what must be individually validated. This is an imposing undertaking, and one that is fraught with many difficulties.

A first major difficulty is to translate the hypotheses, originally expressed in terms of inner personality dynamics into behavior. Thus, it has been hypothesized that M (human movement) responses are related to a "creative personality." What does a "creative personality" mean in terms of observable behavior? One interpretation is that those whose behavior has resulted in socially approved artistic production, i.e., professional artists, could be thought to have demonstrated creativity by their behavior, and Roe [15] studied such a group to see if they generally showed a large number of M responses. Her results were generally negative. But what does this mean? Is the test faulty? Is the hypothesis linking M with "creativity" in error? Or is artistic production an inadequate indicator of a "creative personality"? The *Rorschach* enthusiast prefers the last alternative, and asserts that creativity in the *personality* cannot be judged by creative *production*.

This is not altogether satisfying to the hard-headed critic, who senses a certain reluctance to abandon, or in some cases even to modify, hypotheses even in the light of negative evidence. On the other hand, our general understanding of personality dynamics is not far enough advanced to permit us to predict with certainty the behavioral outcomes that *should* result from certain personality structures, so that faulty translations from inner life to observable behavior are quite possible. Furthermore, difficulties in observing and appraising behavior, together with the impact of situational factors outside the individual, may attenuate and obscure even logically sound predictions. So the tendency of *Rorschach* hypotheses to survive in spite of a good deal of negative evidence is not surprising.

In the balance of research results, it is always a problem to judge whether negative outcomes should be written off as faulty predictions from the underlying hypotheses or as results of inadequate experimental design; whether they should encourage one to make modifications and adaptations of theory to accommodate the new findings, or whether they should cause one to abandon the whole structure (and perhaps the methodology that supports it) and begin again.

Among psychologists, one will find almost all shades of opinion represented with respect to the *Rorschach,* and similarly, to other projective tests. There are those who dismiss most of the negative findings in attempts to validate *Rorschach* hypotheses as due to experiments that were inadequate or inappropriately conceived to really test the hypotheses that they were designed to test. There are those who would respond to the negative results by doctoring up the hypotheses, so that a new one sprouts out hydra-like as soon as one is chopped off. There are those who would view the balance of confirmation and non-confirmation as indicating that projective materials are a rich source of behavior samples, but that the structure of interpretation of these behavior samples still includes much that is questionable, unverified, and perhaps unverifiable, and that they hardly merit the central role they have come to hold for many clinical psychologists. There are those who would feel that the personality theory associated with projective tests is so esoteric, so out of touch with the picture of personality drawn from other sources, and so inadequately supported by the voluminous research literature on these procedures that psychologists would be well advised to concentrate their efforts elsewhere.*

It is the feeling of the authors that research on the verification of *Rorschach* hypotheses has yielded enough that is positive to justify continued research on this (and other) projective types of instruments. At least some of the hypotheses suggested by clinical use of the test have been supported in systematic studies designed to test them out. At the same time, there have been enough instances in which studies to test *Rorschach* hypotheses have yielded negative results so that the critic looks with some concern on the widespread use and glib interpretation of this instrument in clinical practice. We would counsel a good deal of caution and scepticism in accepting as truth the personality pictures drawn from a *Rorschach* record.

There is one thing on which all can agree—enthusiast and critic alike, and that is that interpretation of *Rorschach* and other projective records is no enterprise for a novice. The structure of hypotheses

---

* For several extended reviews, reflecting quite varied evaluations of the *Rorschach,* see the *Fifth Mental Measurements Yearbook,* pp. 273–289.

based upon the indices is sufficiently subtle and complex that none but the well-trained can hope to arrive at valid personality descriptions from these instruments. If they are used at all, the use should be limited to the well-trained specialist. The teacher and counselor will do well to concentrate on behavior in life situations and limit interpretations to the fairly direct and manifest significance of the behavior. Attempts to interpret behavior samples in depth can lead the novice far astray.

Validity as Predicting. A third type of validation of test devices is found in their ability to predict socially significant outcomes. Thus, a scholastic aptitude test is valued in proportion as it gives a good prediction of academic success. We may ask how effective projective tests have proven in predicting significant outcomes for individuals.

One type of outcome that we might reasonably expect to find predicted by an appraisal of personality structure and personality dynamics is the psychiatric classification in which a person falls. Though there may not be a one-to-one correspondence between personality structure and form of psychiatric disability, there should be enough of a correspondence so that a good measure of the one would give a good prediction of the other. What have been the findings in this regard?

In different studies, in which experienced *Rorschach* analysts attempted to make "blind diagnoses" merely from the records, the degree of success has varied from quite high to little if any better than chance. Thus, Benjamin and Ebaugh [2] reported agreement in 85 per cent of 46 cases in which blind diagnoses based on the *Rorschach* alone were checked against independent diagnoses by a psychiatrist.

In one well-planned study Chambers and Hamlin [3] sent to each of twenty well qualified judges a set of 5 *Rorschach* protocols. Different specific protocols were sent to the different judges, but each judge's set of five included the same five diagnostic categories: involutional depression, anxiety neurosis, paranoid schizophrenia, syphilitic brain damage, and simple feeblemindedness. Each judge knew the categories represented in his set of records and had the fairly straightforward task of matching *Rorschach* record and diagnosis. Results were better than chance, but far from perfect. The imbecile was correctly matched by eighteen of the twenty judges— but one wonders whether they might not have done as well from the results of a 5-minute vocabulary test. The other four diagnoses were correctly matched in 51 per cent of the instances, a good deal better than chance, but very far from perfect.

On the other hand, a study [6] in which two experienced *Rorschach* analysts tried to separate the records of 60 neurotic boys from those of a control group matching the neurotic cases for age and intelligence yielded percentages of success of 63 and 48. Flipping a coin could have been expected to give 50 per cent accuracy in this two-way classification.

As in so much of the research with projective procedures, sometimes they seem to work and sometimes not. It is hard to say why. Many factors vary from one study to another—skill of analysts, heterogeneity of groups compared, sharpness and clarity of the criterion, among others. But the total impression is that though the test provides some cues to diagnostic groupings, these cues are far from clear and dependable.

Another social outcome that clinicians have been interested in predicting is improvement under various types of therapy, and projective techniques have been studied with this end in view. Results have been generally discouraging. One or another sign may appear promising in one study, but when checked in a new sample these rarely hold up.

College success was an outcome that was predicted quite effectively by Munroe [12] in one study. A correlation of $-.49$ was found between number of signs of maladjustment devised from an inspection technique of scoring the *Rorschach* and freshman grades at Sarah Lawrence College. However, Cronbach [4] was unable to achieve any useful prediction with University of Chicago freshmen, and it may be noted that Munroe has not reported confirmation of her results with new groups.

A quite different social outcome, elimination from flying training because of emotional disturbance, was studied by Holtzman and Sells.[8] A number of clinical psychologists were each asked to examine a series of case records for aviation cadets, each of which included among other things a *Rorschach* protocol. Some were men who had successfully completed training, and some were men who had been eliminated for fear of flying or some other personal reason (i.e., not for lack of skill). The clinicians were asked to study the records on each man and classify him into the success or failure group. It was found that, although the clinicians showed some agreement in the way in which they portrayed a given man, they could do essentially no better than chance in picking those who would crack up in the training program. Though the procedures appeared to have some reliability, so far as personality description was concerned, this description had no validity as a predictor of flying success. These results are consistent with those from other attempts to use the *Rorschach* as a predictor during World War II.

In general, the conclusion on predictive validity at this time must apparently be that the *Rorschach,* and probably other projective tests, have some validity as predictors of psychiatric diagnoses, though just how much seems quite uncertain.   For other practical criteria we must be more pessimistic.   There appears to be no *verified* evidence that they have validity for any other practical outcome in the world of events.

RELIABILITY

Arriving at a satisfactory basis for appraising the reliability of projective methods has also proved to be a tricky business.   Separate equivalent or near-equivalent forms of the tests have rarely been prepared.   The devotees of the tests protest that it is not possible to divide the test into equivalent halves.   Memory of a previous testing is likely to distort retesting over a short time.   And the test enthusiast is likely to protest that the total personality is changing from day to day, so that test results cannot be expected to remain stable over a period of time.   One senses a certain flight from reality in all of this, a well-formed mechanism of defense.   The tough-minded psychometrician would like to know what magic there is about one set of ink blots or one set of pictures that makes them irreplaceable.   Why should it be essentially more difficult to produce a parallel set of blots than a parallel set of intelligence test items?   He would also contend that aspects of personality so fleeting that they cannot legitimately be appraised by a retest after some lapse of time are probably also so superficial that they are of no importance.

But real problems in evaluating the reliability of projective methods do remain.   These center around the question of what it is whose reliability is being appraised.   Is it the reliability of some relatively objective component score, or is it the reliability of some inference from the test materials, or is it the reliability of the total descriptive picture?   Probably each of these is worth studying.   The last, the reliability of the descriptive picture, does not fit into the usual statistics of reliability, and one must fall back on matching or similar techniques.   Let us inquire into reliability at each of the several levels.

Reliability of Single Score Components.   Evidence on the reliability of single score components is available chiefly for the *Rorschach.*   A number of split-half and retest reliability studies are available.   Values reported differ from study to study and for the different types of subscores. However, correlations are quite uniformly positive and, in many instances, quite substantial. One would conclude that the major score components show a within-test consistency that is comparable with that of other personality measures.

Perhaps the most satisfying evidence of reliability is correlation of two comparable or near-comparable forms. A separate set of blots, the *Behn-Rorschach,* was designed to parallel the original *Rorschach Test.* Correlations between the two were determined by Eichler. [5] For total number of responses the correlation was about .70. Separate scoring categories showed correlations of from .45 to .70. The values were not greatly different when a retest was given with the original *Rorschach.* The relationships were all significantly positive but lower than we have come to expect with other test materials, particularly tests that are to be used for detailed individual diagnosis. Comparable figures were obtained by Meadows [11] for the main score components. However, Meadows found many of the rarer and subtler scores to give reliability coefficients ranging from .40 down to zero.

Reliability of Predictive Inferences. It is *possible* that the single components of a projective test record may be of rather modest reliability, and yet that consistent inferences may be drawn from the total record. If we work with a single sample of the subject's behavior and two or more interpreters, we are studying only the reliability of the interpretation. If we provide the independent interpreters records from different testings, then we are testing the reliability of the test-interpreter combination. Few studies of the reliability of inferences from projective tests have been made. One related study by Palmer [14] had trained interpreters make judgments about the persons whose *Rorschach* records they studied on a check list of different attributes. Palmer found very low correlations between judges for judgments of this sort based on the same set of records.

Reliability of Personality Descriptions. How accurately does the total picture given by a projective test maintain itself from one testing to another, or from one interpretation to another? Such evidence as we have presented on the extent to which *Rorschach* records can be matched with case materials or with diagnostic categories is indirect evidence of reliability. There must be some stability in the basic *Rorschach* record if it can be dependably matched with anything else. What *level* of precision the descriptive picture achieves, however, is almost impossible to determine from this sort of evidence. Little direct evidence on the problem is available.

PRACTICALITY

Projective tests are viewed by their proponents as clinical techniques that can be expected to give valid results only in the hands of persons having both special training in the technique and a high level of general sophistication in dynamic psychology. Furthermore, the tests are generally time-consuming both to give and to score. It seems clear, therefore, that whatever use may be justified by the validity that they demonstrate will be limited to mental hygiene clinics, mental institutions, private clinical practice, and similar settings in which adequate resources are available. They are not, and probably never will be, techniques to be widely applied in schools. The teacher and the school administrator are interested in these approaches only as consumers. They may have occasion to hear some test or the interpretation of a test discussed in connection with a particular child. Their need is to know something of what the clinician hopes to be able to do with the test and to have some sense of the level of confidence to be placed in the results. It is hard to decide, at the present state of our knowledge, what the answer is on this last point. Certainly, a substantial admixture of scepticism seems to be indicated. But clearly, these procedures are for specialists in special situations, and the story of the help that they can provide even then is far from complete.

SUMMARY STATEMENT

During the last 25 years, the invention, exploration, and development of projective tests of personality has been for many psychologists the most exciting adventure in personality evaluation. The tests have many ardent supporters and many severe critics. A sound appraisal of their contribution to our understanding of the individual is difficult to arrive at at the present time. Both claims and results are conflicting.

A great many of the procedures have received very little by way of rigorous and critical testing and are supported only by the faith and enthusiasm of their backers. In those few cases, most notably that of the *Rorschach,* where a good deal of critical work has been done, results are varied and there is much inconsistency in the research picture. Modest reliability is usually found, but consistent evidence of validity is harder to come by.

In any event, these techniques are the tools of the trained specialist. They are not likely ever to become part of a general testing program. The specialist must appraise them with a critical thoroughness that is not possible within the limits of this single chapter.

REFERENCES

1. Beck, S. J., *Rorschach's test: Vol. I, Basic processes,* New York, Grune and Stratton, 1944.
2. Benjamin, J. D., and F. G. Ebaugh, The diagnostic validity of the Rorschach test, *Amer. J. Psychiat.,* **94,** 1938, 1163–1178.
3. Chambers, Guinevere S., and Roy W. Hamlin, The validity of judgments based on "blind" Rorschach records, *J. consult. Psychol.,* **21,** 1957, 105–109.
4. Cronbach, L. J., Studies of the Group Rorschach in relation to success in the college of the University of Chicago, *J. educ. Psychol.,* **41,** 1950, 65–82.
5. Eichler, R. M., A comparison of the Rorschach and Behn-Rorschach inkblot tests, *J. consult. Psychol.,* **15,** 1951, 185–189.
6. Eysenck, H. J., *The scientific study of personality,* New York, Macmillan, 1952, pp. 162–163.
7. Holtzman, Wayne H., Objective scoring of projective techniques, in Bass, Bernard M. and Irwin A. Berg, *Objective approaches to personality assessment,* Princeton, N. J., Van Nostrand, 1959, pp. 136–140.
8. Holtzman, Wayne H., and S. B. Sells, Prediction of flying success by clinical analysis of test protocols, *J. abnorm. soc. Psychol.,* **49,** 1954, 485–490.
9. Klopfer, B., and D. M. Kelley, *The Rorschach technique,* Yonkers, N. Y., World Book, 1942.
10. Klopfer, B., *Developments in the Rorschach technique,* Yonkers, N. Y., World Book, 1954.
11. Meadows, A. W., An investigation of the Rorschach and Behn tests; cited in Eysenck, H. J., *The scientific study of personality,* New York, Macmillan, 1952.
12. Munroe, Ruth L., Prediction of the adjustment and academic performance of college students by a modification of the Rorschach method, *Appl. Psychol. Monogr.,* 1945, No. 7.
13. Murray, H. A., et al., *Explorations in personality,* New York, Oxford University Press, 1938.
14. Palmer, J. O., A dual approach to Rorschach validation: a methodological study, *Psychol. Monogr.,* No. 325, 1951.
15. Roe, Anne, The personality of artists, *Educ. psychol. Measmt,* **6,** 1946, 401–408.
16. Rorschach, H., *Psychodiagnostics* (translation by P. Lemkau and B. Kronenburg), New York, Grune and Stratton, 1942.
17. Tompkins, S. S., *The Thematic Apperception Test,* New York, Grune and Stratton, 1947.

SUGGESTED ADDITIONAL READING

Allen, Robert M., *Personality assessment procedures,* New York, Harper, 1958, Chapters 8–14.

Anderson, H. H., and Gladys L. Anderson, *An introduction to projective techniques,* Englewood Cliffs, N. J., Prentice-Hall, 1951.

Guilford, J. P., *Personality,* New York, McGraw-Hill, 1959, Chapter 12.

Henry, William E., *The analysis of fantasy,* New York, Wiley, 1956, Chapters 1–6.

QUESTIONS FOR DISCUSSION

1. What is projection? Give several examples from your own experience or your observations.

2. What basis is there for expecting a projective test to work? Why should we be able to tell anything about a person from the types of responses that he gives to projective test materials?

3. Why has there been such a divergence of opinion between clinical psychologists and specialists in measurement as to the value of projective tests?

4. In what ways are the situational tests described in Chapter 14 similar to projective techniques? In what ways do they differ?

5. Write down all the different things you can see in the four ink blots in Fig. 15.1. If possible, get three or four other people to do the same thing. Try to make a rough scoring in terms of the determinants given on pp. 425–426. Do you find common responses? Whole responses and detail responses? Movement responses? How do the different records compare?

6. Is it possible or desirable for you to make a psychological interpretation of the material obtained under question 5? What factors limit the interpretability of this sort of material?

7. Collect several stories in response to the picture in Fig. 15.2. What aspects of these look as if they might tell you something about the person? What cautions would need to be observed in interpreting this kind of material?

8. Pictures such as those used in the *TAT* have frequently been used to measure attitudes. What are the advantages and disadvantages of this method?

9. In what ways is the play of children a projective technique?

10. What should be the role of the teacher in regard to projective tests? In regard to the informal projective material in pupils' compositions, art work, and other activities through which they express themselves?

Chapter 16

Planning a School Testing Program

We want to give some standardized tests in our school. What would you recommend?

I am on a committee to revise the testing program for our schools. These are the tests we plan to use, and the grades in which we plan to use them. Will you criticize this plan?

Probably every teacher of tests and measurements faces requests like these each semester. What standardized tests should be used? When should they be used? What constitutes a sound testing program?

THE CART AND THE HORSE

The trouble is that there is really no answer to such a question. Or, rather, the only answer is another series of questions. What do you want test results for? How are you hoping to use them? What decisions or actions are you proposing to base on them? What needs for information have led you to decide upon a testing program? For a program can only be planned in terms of the purposes it is to serve. Tests given with no particular purpose *may* find a use, *may* create their own market, but it hardly seems likely. A functioning testing program should grow out of the needs felt and functions to be served in the particular school or school system and should be directed toward meeting those needs and serving those functions.

The first step, then, in planning a testing program for a school or school system should be to find out what types of information about pupils are felt to be needed by the school staff and how test results are to be used. Before asking, "What tests should we give?" one asks, "What information do we need that we do not now have? When do we need it? How will we use it?" There are many situations in which giving tests can be a rather futile enterprise. What profit is there in a reading readiness test if all members of a class study reading together from the same primer at the same rate and time? Will it pay to give reading tests if there are no provisions for differentiated individual work or remedial instruction?

The starting place is the school and its curriculum, the staff and their needs. Of course, it cannot be expected that each single teacher will have seen in advance how test data are to be used in forwarding his activities with his class. Learning to use test information represents one aspect of in-service growth. But a testing program unrelated to local needs, local resources, and local levels of sophistication is unlikely to function effectively. Planning that does not center around the ways the staff are to be brought into using the test information is likely to be sterile. For tests are given to be used, not to be filed. More important than planning *what* tests are to be *given* is planning *how* the tests are to be *used*.

This is why planning a testing program in the abstract or in a vacuum is so unsatisfactory. The first question one always needs to raise is: For what purposes will the tests be used in your schools? Defining functions and purposes is the horse. Let us put him out in front, and the cart carrying a program of tests will follow after.

FUNCTIONS OF A TESTING PROGRAM

As we use the phrase *testing program* in this chapter, we are referring to an organized school-wide or system-wide program for the administration of standardized tests. We are not thinking of the wide variety of teacher-made tests that are prepared for use within a single school nor of the specialized testing procedures that may be carried on to study single pupils. Teacher-made tests have been discussed at some length in Chapters 3 and 4 and will receive some further consideration in Chapter 17, in which we consider marking and reporting.

Of course, many of the needs for the information that tests can supply and many of the functions to be served by a testing program are common from one school system to another. We present, in Table 16.1, a brief catalogue of functions often served by tests. This catalogue may serve as a check list to guide a review of local needs and uses. However, the applicability of these functions must always be checked in the local setting. We must ask, "Can we, or do we wish to, use tests for this purpose in our schools?"

A brief discussion of the nature and appropriateness of each function follows.

Table 16.1. Possible Functions of a Testing Program

Classroom Functions	Guidance Functions	Administrative Functions
Grouping pupils for instruction within a class.	Preparing evidence to guide discussions with parents about their children.	Forming of and assigning to classroom groups.
Guiding the planning of activities for specific individual pupils.	Building realistic self-pictures on the part of pupils.	Placing new students. Helping determine eligibility for special groups.
Identifying pupils who need special diagnostic study and remedial instruction.	Helping the pupil with immediate choices. Helping the pupil to set educational and vocational goals.	Helping determine which pupils are to be promoted. Evaluating curricula, curricular emphases, and curricular experiments.
Determining reasonable achievement levels for each pupil and evaluating discrepancies between potentiality and achievement.	Improving counselor, teacher, and parent understanding of problem cases.	Evaluating teachers. Evaluating the school as a unit.
Assigning course grades.		Improving public relations. Providing information for outside agencies.

CLASSROOM FUNCTIONS OF A TESTING PROGRAM

A number of the functions of a testing program center around the work of the classroom teacher. These have to do with grouping for instruction, individualization of instruction, selection for special diagnostic and remedial services, and the assignment of marks.

Grouping Pupils for Instruction within a Class. One of the effective techniques teachers have developed for dealing with individual differences in pupils is to form within the class small groupings of pupils who have about the same level of skill. Pupils in these groupings may work on the same materials and at the same speed. Standardized tests are often called upon to aid in forming these within-class groups. They provide information quickly and objectively at the beginning of the school year and make it possible to short-circuit the slower and more subjective process of getting acquainted with each pupil's abilities and skills. Readiness tests serve this function in the first grade, and achievement tests at later levels.

Guiding the Planning of Activities for Specific Individual Pupils. Many teachers report that they use test results to help in individualizing instruction. This is carrying the small-group procedure still further. Programs of work in the skill subjects are adjusted to the present level of the individual pupil. The gifted child is encouraged to move ahead at his own speed, and enrichment activities are provided for him. The child of limited achievement is permitted to move more slowly toward more limited objectives. Both measures of scholastic aptitude and of educational achievement play a role in this type of planning.

Identifying Pupils Who Need Special Diagnostic Study and Remedial Instruction. When a school system has resources for special diagnostic study of individual pupils and special teachers to provide remedial instruction, the testing program will usually provide important data to help in identifying the pupils most likely to profit from that instruction. If the classroom teacher must pick pupils for such special services, he is likely to pick the pupils whom he considers most below par in achievement. It is very difficult for him to distinguish between general low ability and specialized deficiency in a particular limited skill. A testing program that appraises both achievement and aptitude is an aid in picking out those pupils who have a remediable defect.

Evaluating Discrepancies Between Potentiality and Achievement. Picking pupils for special remedial training is a special case of the more general problem of identifying discrepancies between potential and actual achievement. Such discrepancies may serve to focus the efforts of the teacher upon particular pupils in his class, may help to orient and guide the teacher's discussions in a conference with parents, or may influence the statements or ratings in the periodic report to the home. This last situation is encountered in those school systems in which the report card attempts to evaluate the individual pupil's achievement in relation to his potentiality. Any attempt to evaluate achievement in relation to potentiality requires good measures of both potentiality and achievement. One function of a testing program may be to help supply these.

Assigning Course Grades. A number of teachers, especially in the secondary school, report using standardized test results as one consideration in assigning course grades. This may be appropriate in certain specific courses for which standardized tests exist whose content parallels closely the objectives of instruction in the course. However, the school-wide or city-wide program of standardized testing ordinarily seems less well fitted to serve this purpose. Standardized test content is typically general content, not directly related to the teaching in any single school or grade. It covers broadly a whole range of knowledges and skills. For that reason, the standardized test is not particularly well adapted to measuring the particular things a pupil has learned in a particular class or period of instruction.

GUIDANCE FUNCTIONS OF A TESTING PROGRAM

Much school testing is carried out primarily to service the school's program of guidance and counseling. The tests are useful in discussing a pupil's school progress with parents. The results serve to help the pupil build up a more accurate and realistic self-picture, to make immediate choices between alternatives offered by the school, and to formulate appropriate long-range goals and plans. They help school personnel to understand and plan for problem cases, providing material for staff discussion and for case conferences.

Reporting Progress to Parents. The school has the responsibility of keeping parents informed of the progress of their children. This information needs to be conveyed whether the pupil is doing well or ill. In many schools, and we hope the number is increasing, there are regular opportunities for all parents to meet with their child's teacher and discuss his progress. Whether the setting be one of sweetness and light or whether the conference grows out of some distressing problem, it helps if the teacher can document his report with concrete, objective evidence on performance. This removes the teacher's appraisal from the realm of individual, subjective (and in the eyes of the parent perhaps very biased) opinion and sets it on a foundation of fact. We shall consider in some detail later in the chapter the manner in which the results can best be expressed.

Building Realistic Self-Pictures. A general function of the guidance program is to improve each individual's understanding of his own assets and liabilities—his strengths and weaknesses. A testing program can provide the school objective evidence on these strengths and weaknesses to be interpreted to the individual pupil.

Helping the Pupil with Immediate Choices. The pupil at the secondary-school level usually has a certain number of choices to make. He must decide whether to take certain courses or determine in which of alternative curricula he wishes to enroll. The evidence provided by a testing program can enter into the thinking about these choices by pupil and counselor.

Helping the Pupil to Set Educational and Vocational Goals. In addition to providing information for immediate choices, a testing program can contribute to the individual's long-range planning for further education or for work.   The self-picture that is built up in part by the counselor's interpretation of test results will influence these plans and the actions to implement them.   "Shall I go on to college, and if so what type?"   "Shall I seek a mechanical or a clerical type of job?"   These are the kinds of questions to which ability and interest tests may help provide answers.

Improving Understanding of Problem Cases.   In each school, some pupils present more or less acute problems of educational or social adjustment.   They are the unruly, the withdrawn, the unhappy, the educationally retarded, and the other children who are not fitting into the educational and social pattern of the school.   A testing program provides some basis for counselors and teachers to understand these cases.   In particular, a systematic testing program combined with an adequate record system can provide some of the historical background for understanding the present problem.   Every present problem has its roots in the past.   Records of regular testing permit us to follow back at least some of these roots and to throw some light on the present problem.

Another aspect of the testing resources of a school system should consist of facilities for more intensive study of children who present special problems.   Here, availability of a wide variety of testing techniques to fit the needs of the specific case is the desideratum.   This special testing is distinct from and should supplement the uniform program applied to all children.

ADMINISTRATIVE FUNCTIONS OF A TESTING PROGRAM

So far we have seen ways in which a program of standardized testing may help the teacher in dealing with the children of his class or may contribute to the guidance activities in a school.   There are also a number of administrative functions for which a testing program has at times been used.   These include forming class groups, assigning transfer students, determining eligibility for special groups, determining who is to be promoted, evaluating the curriculum, evaluating teachers, evaluating a school as a unit, improving public relations, and providing service to agencies outside the school.

Forming and Assigning to Classroom Groups.   When a school is large enough to have several groups at the same grade level or several sections of a particular course, a decision must be reached on some grounds as to who goes into which group.   We have discussed elsewhere the issue of homogeneous grouping (see pp. 252–253).   Grouping is probably likely to be more effective in single special courses, i.e., mathematics, English, science, etc., at the secondary or higher level than for a total school program. Grouping on the basis of initial level of achievement in the subject permits real differentiation in content covered and rate of progress. In any event, if an administrative decision has been made to form class groups on the basis of aptitude or of initial level of achievement, the testing program can be organized so as to serve those ends.

Placing Students Transferred from Other Schools. When a pupil transfers from one school to another, a decision must be reached as to the grade level and group into which he is to go. Of course, he may be assigned purely on the basis of age or of his grade in the previous school. However, if a school system ever takes into account the student's level of achievement in determining grade placement, these transfers would appear to be particularly appropriate cases in which to do so. The break in continuity represented by a change in school and in schoolmates should reduce any upset associated with repeating or skipping a grade. Plans for prompt testing of transferred students should be included in a program that proposes either to consider achievement level in determining grade placement or to adapt instruction in the class group to the particular needs of the new child.

Helping to Determine Eligibility for Special Groups. The school may have certain special groups or special courses for which prerequisites have been set. On the one hand, there may be classes for slow-learning children, and admission to these classes may be contingent upon having an IQ below a specified level. On the other hand, admission to certain subjects such as algebra may be restricted to those falling above a certain minimum in IQ, arithmetic achievement, or score on a specific prognostic test. Rigid and mechanical adherence to exact score standards seems justifiable more in terms of administrative convenience than educational policy. However, *some* basis is required for determining eligibility for any special program. The information yielded by a testing program can provide part of the basis for determining this eligibility.

Helping to Determine Which Pupils Are to Be Promoted. We cannot at this point enter into a discussion of the pros and cons of having a pupil whose educational achievement is far below that of his class group repeat a grade. Certainly since 1925 there has been a great reduction in the amount of repeating and a tendency to give weight to factors other than just educational achievement when the decision to repeat is made. However, if the issue of non-promotion is being considered for a child, objective appraisal of achievement and aptitude on standardized tests can serve to supplement and document the teacher's judgment of school progress.

Evaluating Curricula, Curricular Emphases, and Curricular Experiments. So far we have been considering administrative evaluations of the individual pupil and actions with respect to him. Using standardized tests for these purposes has been under some attack, and the value of such procedures is at least open to question. Evaluation of the local curriculum or of curricular experiments or innovations is a happier administrative function for a testing program. Application of test results to the evaluation of a local curriculum or of a curricular experiment or innovation must be made judiciously. Standardized tests appraise at best only part of the range of desired curricular outcomes. They need to be supplemented by other more informal techniques of appraisal. Test results should be interpreted in terms of the total picture of tangible and intangible objectives. However, in any experimentally minded program it will be important to determine how adequately the basic common skills are being maintained.

Evaluating Teachers. Some administrators have used the results of a standardized testing program as one basis for evaluating the competence of individual teachers. The reasons for considering this an undesirable procedure have already been discussed rather fully in Chapter 11 (p. 313).

Evaluating the School as a Unit. A testing program can serve the school administrator as a type of educational quality control. Summary tabulations for the separate schools and classes in a system, reviewed in the light of the aptitude and the background characteristics of each group, can serve to point out strengths and weaknesses of particular schools and classes. The information can guide supervisors to places or persons needing special help or needing to make some shift in emphasis. If this quality control function of tests is applied in a punitive way, it may have the same disruptive effect that is likely to accompany the use of tests to judge teachers. But if the orientation of the central administration is toward helping rather than judging, the testing program can serve a valuable function in directing that help where it is needed.

Improving Public Relations. The schools of a community are always fair game for critics. It is always "open season" for the schools. One of the recurring themes, especially when a school deviates from traditional patterns, is that pupils are no longer learning the basic three R's, which is what the parents see as the objective of going to school. A program of standardized testing provides the basis for answering such criticisms. Since the skills with which the critics are most likely to be concerned correspond rather closely to those measured by standardized tests, standardized test results provide very relevant information for answering or forestalling many critics. If the schools are in fact maintaining the expected level in basic skills, this fact can be demonstrated and the administration can move on into an exposition of the further outcomes it is trying to achieve.

The public relations function of testing becomes particularly important when a school is introducing some departure from the tried and true way of doing things. When curricular innovations are introduced, the administration must be prepared to meet cries that the fundamental skills are no longer being mastered by pupils under the new system. If it is a fact that they are not being mastered, the administration certainly needs to know it; if it is not, the administration needs to be able to refute the charge.

The role of the classroom teacher as a front-line worker in the battle of public relations should not be forgotten. Relevant evidence from studies of achievement in the schools of the community or of evaluations of curricular changes should be put in the hands of the teachers, so that they may be able to respond to criticisms and present to the community a true and authentic picture of achievement in the schools.

Providing Information for Outside Agencies. The school is frequently called upon to supply information to other agencies—to social agencies, to potential employers, to other schools and colleges. A testing program, coupled with an adequate system of cumulative records, permits supplying needed information in standard terms as it is requested. Objective information on aptitude and achievement can be made available as needed.

PARTICIPATION IN PLANNING A PROGRAM

We have seen the great variety of functions for which the results of a testing program may be used. We have seen how test scores may be useful to the classroom teacher in working with individual pupils and groups of pupils, how test results enter into the guidance program, and how test results serve functions relating to supervision and administration. This outline indicates functions that tests *may* serve. Whether they will serve these functions effectively depends upon whether the testing program is planned with these objectives in view and whether it is understood and supported by the potential users. For these reasons, we believe that within a school system there should be widespread participation in the original planning and periodic review of a testing program.

Since the main categories of potential users are (1) administrative and supervisory personnel, (2) guidance personnel, and (3) classroom teachers, we believe that representatives of these three groups should participate in the planning.   The needs of each group should be considered in planning the tests to be used, the time of their administration, and the manner in which the test results are handled.   Participation should not cease when a specific testing program has been introduced but should continue in the form of periodic review of the adequacy of the tests and the ways of handling them and in in-service development of better ways of using the test results.   One may anticipate that when teachers participate in planning and reviewing the testing program there will be the greatest likelihood that the test scores will function in important ways in classroom activities and the least chance that test papers will be filed away or scores entered on record cards and forgotten.

QUALITIES DESIRED IN A TESTING PROGRAM

What are the general characteristics of a good school testing program?   We shall consider three briefly: relationship to use, integration, and continuity.

RELATION TO USE

We have outlined in the previous section a number of functions for which standardized tests are used in some school systems.   The first step in planning a testing program for your schools is to review these and possibly other functions and determine for which of them tests are needed and will be used in your schools.   The testing should then be planned in relation to these uses.   Tests should be selected and the times at which they are given should be chosen so that the needed information will be available and as up to date as possible at whatever time it is needed.

Thus, suppose teachers in the first grade wish to use test results to help them form in their classes subgroups that will move into reading at different rates.   Our need is then for a reading readiness test. If almost all pupils go to kindergarten, the test might be scheduled for the end of the kindergarten year, say, in May.   But more likely we will want to give the test in the first grade early in the fall, say, about the beginning of October, as soon as the pupils have settled down in their new class.

Or again, suppose that a differentiated high-school program is available for the 3 years of senior high school, and that counselors and pupils work out plans for the high-school program during the spring of the ninth grade in the light of available information on pupil aptitudes and achievement. In this setting, a program of aptitude and achievement testing during the first semester of the ninth grade will provide relevant and current information. Here, as everywhere, the important thing is to provide *what* will be used *when* it will be used.

INTEGRATION

The testing program should be seen as a whole. Information that is needed in the sixth grade is not unrelated to the information that was obtained in the fifth grade or to information that will be useful in the seventh grade. Each item of information gathered should be obtained at such a time and in such a way that it will make the maximum contribution to the total. Several aspects of integration merit consideration.

In an integrated program, it will usually be desirable to use the same series of tests over the grade range for which the series is appropriate. Thus, if the *Metropolitan Achievement Tests* are being used to measure progress in basic skills, it will probably be desirable to use them in any grade from first up to sixth, and possibly to eighth or ninth, in which an achievement battery is being used. The advantages are that norms are based upon the same sampling of communities from grade to grade, and the tests conform to a common outline of content and format. Thus, scores from one grade to the next are more nearly comparable, so that a truer picture may be obtained of pupil growth.

Integration implies particularly integration between the several divisions of the school program. Tests in junior high school should be planned in relation to those already given in the elementary school, and those in senior high should take account of junior high testing. An intelligence test given in the sixth grade need not be followed by a similar test at the beginning of the seventh grade. If aptitude tests are given in the ninth grade, there is limited gain from a similar battery in the tenth.

Integration between divisions of the school implies continuity of school records. The records accumulated about a pupil in the elementary school should follow him, in whole or in part, when he goes on to the secondary school. It may be that the complete record, especially if it is a very full one, should not stay in the active record file. However, key information should carry over into the record system of the higher school, and the full record should be available for reference if need be.

Integration means, finally, timing testing so that in so far as possible multiple purposes can be served.   An attempt to serve two masters is always a compromise.   However, it sometimes represents a sound use of limited resources.   Thus, an intelligence test fairly early in the sixth grade can serve adequately for sectioning and guidance in the seventh grade and still be available as a resource for studying problem cases and issues of promotability in grade six.   A scholastic aptitude test in grade ten or eleven gives as good a prediction of college success as one taken in May of the senior year and is also available for counseling purposes during two or three years of high school.

CONTINUITY

The potential values of a testing program increase as it is continued over a period of years.   Advantages of continuity in the program are two-fold.   On the one hand, data accumulate in the records of the individual pupil.   There are available to contribute to an understanding of the youngster not merely the results of tests given during the present year but also the data from earlier testings one or more years ago in lower grades.   Present status can be seen in perspective in relation to earlier records.   Thus, we can see whether Jerry's academic problems in the sixth grade have developed recently or whether they represent merely the continuation of an early trend; we can determine whether the difficulty Mary is having with long division is new or whether it has its roots in early difficulties with arithmetic fundamentals.

Continuity also is of importance in permitting a school system to get to know the particular tests it is using.   We have emphasized at various points that a good deal of caution must be exercised in applying national norms to a local setting.   Continued local use of a test or test series permits the development of local standards of expectancy.   This may take the form of an informal and implicit tempering of national norms in interpreting local performance.   It may take the form of an actual set of local norms.   Thus, a suburban community with a very high percentage of pupils going on to college may find that percentiles based on its own school population provide a more appropriate framework for judging the academic status of one of its pupils than do national age or grade norms.

Getting to know tests implies getting to know what they measure, as well as establishing local standards of expectancy.   If teachers work with the tests and test results, they will come to know what the test covers, what cues for diagnosing group strengths and weaknesses can be drawn from it, and what its limitations are.   Both types of familiarity are desirable when teachers are using test results to help them with their work. For this reason, a school system will ordinarily wish to continue to use the same tests over a period of years, changing them only when they become out of date òr when a study of other available tests indicates that there are ones available that represent a definite improvement over those that have been used in past years.

MECHANICS OF A SCHOOL TESTING PROGRAM

A program of standardized testing that is carried out throughout a grade, a school, or a school system is a fairly complex undertaking. If the testing is to proceed smoothly, and if standard testing conditions are to be maintained, a certain amount of advance planning is needed, and consideration must be given to a number of points. Some of these may seem fairly obvious, but it is perhaps well to view them briefly— as reminders, if nothing more.

CENTRALIZED DIRECTION

Though many people can well have been involved in the original planning of a testing program and many will participate in carrying it out, responsibility for administration of the program should be centralized, so that there is one person in the system (and perhaps one person at each school) who will see that all the administrative details are taken care of on schedule. These administrative details may include (1) ordering the necessary tests, answer sheets, special pencils and other auxiliary materials, (2) arranging for the packaging and distribution of materials to separate schools and classes, (3) preparing and distributing any supplementary local instructions, (4) arranging schedules of time and place for testing, (5) providing training for testers and proctors, (6) training and supervising scorers, (7) seeing that the test results are appropriately recorded in pupil record cards, (8) supervising any analyses and tabulations of test results, and (9) taking responsibility for the storage and security of the tests when they are not being used. Clearly, a person with some training and experience in testing is needed for this job.

We will comment at this point on a few issues that arise with respect to some of the above-mentioned responsibilities.

SCHEDULING OF TESTS

After the original decision has been reached as to what tests are to be given, in which grades they are to be given, and at what time of year they are to be given, an exact testing schedule must be worked out.

Since the scheduling problem can become fairly complex—especially if separate answer sheets are used, and if the same test booklets are to be used over in several classes or schools—schedules should be planned in detail well ahead of time.

The most fundamental concerns in scheduling are that tests be given under standard conditions and that these conditions permit each examinee to perform at his best level. Thus, any unit of time scheduled for testing should be long enough to permit administration of a complete test, including a realistic allowance for distributing and collecting papers and for giving instructions. The novice is likely not to realize how much time is required beyond the basic testing time. Testing schedules should not be made too tight.

When more than a single test is to be given, however, as in the case of standardized aptitude or achievement test batteries, it is undesirable to give too many of the tests in one day or at a single sitting. For younger children especially, a break should be provided between parts of the test, and the program of testing should be divided into several segments and spread over several days. A number of the manuals for test batteries suggest ways in which the total testing time can be divided advantageously for children at different age levels. The purpose of the spread-out schedule is, of course, to minimize loss of interest and effort especially on the part of young children and of children who find the tests somewhat difficult and frustrating.

Secondary to the above considerations are those of economy and administrative convenience. Economy is achieved by re-using the same test booklets several times. When tests with separate answer sheets are to be used in several classes, a fairly complex testing schedule may be necessary in order to permit this re-use. (This schedule should provide some time for screening out booklets that have been marked up by examinees.) Greater flexibility of scheduling will be possible if the tests are purchased as separates, rather than bound together in a single booklet, because one class can use one part of the battery while some other class is using another part.

In departmentalized schools with class periods of a fixed length, it is administratively convenient if a unit of testing fits into a single class period. Many test publishers have taken account of this in designing their tests. However, this type of convenience should not be permitted to distort or interrupt the administration of any test. Enough time should be provided to permit the completion of a test at a single sitting. If the program of testing is worth doing, it is worth the upsetting of administrative routines.

It is usually helpful if the complete schedule for testing is reproduced well in advance of the testing dates and distributed to all those who will be concerned.

PREPARATION OF STUDENTS FOR TESTING

Advance preparation of students for testing has as its objectives (1) establishing optimum motivation and cooperation during testing and (2) assuring that students are familiar with the procedures for the test, so that they will not be handicapped by novel and unfamiliar procedures.

Optimum motivation is that which results in serious and sustained effort without undue anxiety and tension. Because of wide pupil differences, it is not possible to achieve this ideal with every examinee. However, some advance explanation of and discussion about the tests may help to achieve it. The attitude should be conveyed that the tests are genuinely important, but not a desperate "life-or-death" matter. Constructive uses of the test results for individual guidance and educational adaptation can well be stressed. The older the students, the more complete the advance briefing that can profitably be given to them.

Since tests are designed to measure aptitudes and achievements rather than the tricks and skills of test-taking, it is desirable that all examinees have an opportunity to get acquainted with the general character of the test items and the mechanics of testing in advance. Some of the large-scale testing agencies, such as the Educational Testing Service and the Educational Records Bureau, prepare for distribution to examinees leaflets that describe the tests and give sample items. A school system might find it profitable to prepare similar practice materials for its own testing program.

When separate answer sheets are to be used by students for the first time, it may help to give advance practice with the mechanics of the answer sheet. The teacher might provide a similar answer sheet to be used with one of his own tests, or with sample items prepared to resemble those of the test itself.*

ENVIRONMENT FOR TESTING

The desirable environment for testing is one in which examinees are (1) physically comfortable and emotionally relaxed, (2) free from interruptions and distractions, (3) conveniently able to manipulate their test materials, and (4) sufficiently separated to minimize tendencies to copy from one another.

* Special practice materials are available from some publishers of standardized tests.

The conditions of lighting and ventilation for testing should be at least as good as those maintained for teaching in a normal classroom. Especially for young children, the familiar surroundings of their own classrooms are to be preferred to those of cafeterias or auditoriums, where crowding and lack of good conditions for writing and for handling test materials may also be problems.

Casual interruptions in the classroom can be minimized by a "Test in progress—Do not disturb" sign on the door. Arrangements should be made with the school administration to suspend fire drills, public address announcements and, in so far as possible, bells and other unrelated signals during a period when testing is being carried out in one or more classes. Other steps to minimize delays and distractions include (1) seeing either that each examinee has an extra pencil, or that spare pencils are readily available, (2) making sure that children (especially young ones) have had a chance to visit the toilet before testing starts, and (3) providing clear instructions as to what to do for those examinees who finish their work completely before the time limit is up.

To be able to manipulate test materials conveniently, the examinee should have a desk or table on which to write, and enough room so that he can spread both the test and the answer sheet out before him. Working in chairs, perhaps with a lap-board, in an auditorium or gymnasium is far from ideal, especially if tests are speeded so that delays in paper-handling can lower the score of the examinee.

The problem of proctoring an examination (and sometimes of maintaining order) is made a good deal easier if desks or seats are well separated.

SELECTION AND PREPARATION OF TEST ADMINISTRATORS

The administration of most group tests is simple enough so that any teacher should be able to handle it satisfactorily after a little special preparation and practice. However, some schools may find it more convenient administratively to have this function discharged by special personnel from the guidance staff or from the school psychologist's office. No matter who administers the tests, all prospective administrators should have some in-service training with the specific tests that are to be used. The training has the objectives of (1) making the examiners thoroughly familiar with the tests and test manual and (2) standardizing procedures with respect to certain recurring problems and questions that frequently arise.

One worthwhile familiarization experience for examiners is "giving the test" to each other, that is, by reading the directions aloud exactly as they are given in the manual, and raising questions with one another. Taking the tests, at least in part, is another way of anticipating problems that are likely to arise in giving them. A few of the issues that are likely to arise in assuring standard and optimum testing conditions are the following:

Verbatim Directions. The examiner should follow the manual exactly and should read directions verbatim, rather than relying upon his memory.

Answering Questions. The principle to guide the examiner in answering student questions is that the student should have a clear understanding of what he is supposed to do. He should not be confused by the mechanics of testing or at a loss as to what the nature of the test is. Therefore, before testing starts, the examiner should use his best efforts to make the procedures and the task clear. He can repeat or paraphrase instructions, go over the practice examples, and, possibly, even supplement them. He should encourage questions at this point, and make every effort to clear up any misunderstandings.

Once a specific test starts, questions should be discouraged. Obviously, no help may be given on specific items, and no cues should be provided as to whether a pupil's answer is right or wrong. Questions on general procedure can be dealt with by repeating or paraphrasing the directions, but when a child expresses perplexity on a specific item he must be stalled off with "I'm sorry. I can't answer that. Do the best you can. If you get stuck go on to the next item."

Timing. If the test has sections with very short time limits, i.e., one or two minutes, each examiner should be provided with a stop watch. For other tests, a watch with a second hand will suffice. When using an ordinary watch, a written record should be made of the exact time that a subtest was started and of the time that it is to stop, so that timing will not be thrown off by memory lapses. A simple home-made form will facilitate such recording.

Proctoring. The examiner should circulate around the room, especially when a new subtest is being started, to check on the work of the examinees. He should check to make sure that each student is working on the correct pages, and that he is marking his responses in the proper place if a separate answer sheet is being used. Individual children may need to be encouraged to keep working or to go back and check their work.

CENTRALIZED ADMINISTRATION

In the last few years, an increasing number of schools have been using the intercommunication system of the school to administer tests from a central point to all pupils being tested. The justification for this procedure is that it presumably guarantees uniformity in directions and timing, and reduces the amount of training that needs to be provided for classroom teachers. However, these gains are obtained at the cost of a serious loss in flexibility and personal contact. No opportunity is provided to give extra instruction to slow groups on the procedures for handling the test materials. There is no possibility of adapting to such a minor crisis as a passing fire engine that may have made part of the directions inaudible. We feel that efficiency and pseudostandardization are often gained at too high a cost.

SCORING

In many parts of the country, test-scoring service can be bought from university testing bureaus, test publishers, or other private agencies. These organizations are usually better equipped to do accurate scoring than the typical school system. The cash outlay that this involves may not be practical for some school systems, or there may be other reasons for wishing to do the scoring within the system. If it is done internally, adequate controls should be set up to guarantee that it is done accurately. The original scoring should be at least spot-checked by rescoring a sample of papers. Errors are particularly likely to creep into such operations as: subtracting a correction for errors, adding part scores to make a total score, and going from raw to converted scores. It is especially important to check these steps. Surveys have repeatedly indicated the inaccuracy of teachers in scoring tests, and have pointed out the need for careful checking of the clerical and arithmetical operations.

RECORDING RESULTS OF TESTS

Since test results are meant to be used, not only immediately but in the more remote future, and since the meaningfulness of any one test increases in proportion as it can be compared with the results of other tests given at the same time or at earlier dates, a pupil's score should be recorded on a permanent record card. A convenient layout for a record card is one in which like tests are kept together, i.e., all achievement test records in one part of the card and all intelligence and aptitude test results in another. Space should also be provided for recording special scores, such as those resulting from an individual intelligence test or from diagnostic tests.

The record of testing should give all essential information, so that it will be most meaningful when referred to at some later date. The following information is desirable:

1. Grade in which test was given.
2. Date (month and year) of the testing.

3. Complete identification of the test, including name, form, and designation of the specific subtests.

4. Norm group used for converting raw scores, where this is relevant.

5. All meaningful and reliable part scores, in addition to the total score. Part scores are needed because of their diagnostic and guidance value, much of which is lost in the total score.

CHECKING ON DISCREPANT RESULTS

A certain number of errors are made in scoring, converting, or transcribing results of tests, and a certain number of instances of error or inadequacy are due to the testing conditions. One way of identifying these is to scrutinize test results, as they are recorded, for implausible or inconsistent results. A test may be inconsistent with others given at the same time, as when a pupil who has consistently scored a year or more above his grade level on all parts of an achievement battery gets an IQ of 85 on a group intelligence test. A test may be inconsistent with results from earlier tests of the same type, as when a child who had gotten an IQ of 130 on an intelligence test given in the fourth grade receives an IQ of 90 on a sixth-grade test of the same sort.

A list should be made up of all cases showing seriously discrepant results, and these results should be carefully checked. The papers should be rescored to make sure that the scoring is accurate. Computations or reading of norm tables involved in obtaining converted scores should be verified. Transcription of the scores should be checked. If no error is found in any of these steps, and if the discrepancy is very marked, it may be desirable to refer the examinee for retesting with another form of the suspect test, before a permanent record is made of the results.

SUGGESTED PRIORITIES IN A TESTING PROGRAM

At the beginning of the chapter we indicated an unwillingness to prescribe a particular pattern for a testing program. This unwillingness stemmed in part from the different functions which the program may serve in different schools. It stemmed also from the wide variation in financial and professional resources available in different school systems. However, there is a general core of uniformity, in spite of diversity, and the same types of tests are available to all schools. That being so, we shall offer some suggestions on the tests we consider likely to prove most generally useful in a program at the different levels.

A PROGRAM FOR THE ELEMENTARY SCHOOL

In the elementary school, our concern centers in helping the individual to master the tools of learning and communicating while he is learning to live and work in a group of his peers. At the same time, the individual is building up a background of experience, knowledge, and understanding at his own level. It is in this setting that tests must function. Though it is difficult to arrange choices in an ordered sequence, since tests relate to each other and function in teams, we have attempted to do so roughly.

In all subsequent discussion it is assumed that children have been adequately examined for vision and hearing and general health status. We have thought of these measures as part of the physical examination rather than as part of the school testing program. They are, of course, of fundamental importance in guaranteeing a profitable educational experience for each child. There is nothing more tragic than the so-called "stupid" child in the back row, who got nothing out of school because he could not hear what the teacher was saying or see what was written on the blackboard.

Reading Tests. We are disposed to give first place in our program of elementary-school testing to tests of reading ability. Reading has always been the key avenue for acquiring all types of organized knowledge. Though in the present-day world its supremacy is challenged somewhat by movie, radio, and television, learning from books will continue to be at the heart of education, especially at the higher levels. For this reason, aiding the school in making early identification of poor progress in reading and in keeping track of reading progress through the school years seems to be among the most useful services a testing program can perform.

If very meager resources permitted only a single reading test, we suspect that we would give it at the end of the second or beginning of the third grade, so that it might be available to identify individuals for special help for a year or so before they reached the greater variety of content and the more extensive demands upon independent reading during the later elementary grades. However, we would like to be able to give a reading test every year or two from the beginning of the second grade throughout the elementary school.

Group Intelligence Test. To aid in interpreting reading test results and other aspects of academic achievement, to help in setting expectations for pupils, and to aid in understanding problem cases, we would like to have results from intelligence testing. When we are thinking in terms of a minimum program and are considering the practical realities of time and cost, we must settle for a group test. If it is to be used in conjunction with our early third-grade reading test, it must be a non-reading test of intelligence. But group tests given as early as the beginning of the third grade do not have too satisfactory reliability or stability over time. If we can afford only a single group intelligence test, we would probably do well to delay it until the fourth or fifth grade, when the results will be more dependable. If a test is to be given in the second or third grade, we would want to be able to include at least one more group intelligence test during the upper elementary grades, fourth, fifth or sixth, the choice of grade depending upon plans for testing in junior high school. We would not object to additional tests, given fairly adequate resources. These would serve primarily to increase the reliability of our appraisal. We would be glad to have both verbal and non-verbal measures of intellectual ability.

Basic Skills Battery. Competing with the intelligence test for second place in our program would be a battery covering the basic skill subjects. This would, of course, include reading and could replace the separate reading test. If the battery could be given only once, we would probably choose to give it in grade three or four, where the results could be used by the school for planning individual programs of instruction for pupils or for fitting pupils into special programs of remedial instruction. However, we would like to be able to test children with such a battery every year, starting in the third grade or possibly the second. We have a certain bias in favor of carrying out this testing in the fall, so that the fresh results may be available for use by the teacher who has worked with the testing.

Reading Readiness Test. On the assumption that the teachers in our school have an individualized program of instruction in reading for the first grade, we would place a reading readiness test next upon our list. We might possibly move it higher. We would view this test as a partial guide to the first-grade teacher in organizing subgroups for reading instruction and as a basis for helping her to evaluate the progress of individual pupils.

The four types of tests we have listed so far are the ones commonly found in school testing programs. Other types of tests will be found much less frequently. Some are not used because of cost; some, because what they have to offer seems less important.

Individual Intelligence Tests. Individual intelligence tests have certain advantages over group tests, particularly in the early grades. If a community has adequate resources and trained personnel, it would be well worth while to have an individual test administered to each child toward the end of kindergarten or in the first grade. An individual test later in the elementary school could be used to replace one of the group tests.

Achievement Tests in Content Subjects. Some of the achievement tests for the upper elementary grades include sections dealing with content areas of science, literature, and social studies. Measures in these areas may have some value for administrative appraisals of the school program, though they are probably too general in content to help the classroom teacher greatly in her work with individual pupils. Other special achievement tests may appeal to certain schools, but we do not recommend them as general features of an elementary-school program.

Other Types of Measures. Other types of tests may be called for in the case of individual children. These include the diagnostic tests used in the special study of children with disability in a particular subject. They include also the techniques of clinical testing, projective and otherwise, used by the clinical psychologist in studying a problem case. However, these represent supplements to the testing program, rather than a basic part of it.

We have not recommended paper-and-pencil personality questionnaires because of serious doubts as to (1) the validity of the information they provide in the typical school situation and (2) the soundness of interpretations that school personnel can make from the results. This does not mean that personality development of the elementary-school child is of no concern to the school. Rather, it means that understanding the child as a person must depend upon the direct and more informal observations of each pupil by the teacher and other school personnel.

A PROGRAM FOR THE SECONDARY SCHOOL

In the secondary school, the pupil has reached a point where usually a number of educational choices and decisions must be faced. He may have to make choices of particular subjects or between different curricula. At the same time, he must start thinking about future plans: how long to stay in school, whether to go on to college, what to plan for in the world of work. The curriculum has, to a considerable extent, moved beyond the basic skills and deals with various types of special content. However, reading, writing, and, to a somewhat lesser extent, arithmetic are still called for in the service of these later content learnings. These shifts in emphasis appear to call for a corresponding shift in the pattern of the school testing program. The order of priority we propose is outlined below.

Scholastic Aptitude Test. A major decision for each individual is how far up the educational ladder he shall seek to go. A related decision, where several distinct high-school curricula are available, is whether he shall continue with a college preparatory program or enter a commercial, industrial, or general program. A scholastic aptitude test is of value, as a supplement to school grades, in arriving at these decisions. It is, of course, also of value in interpreting the pupil's school progress and setting the standard of expectancy for him.

By high-school age, the abilities measured by a scholastic aptitude test have become pretty well stabilized. There is little systematic shift from one year to the next. Thus, a tenth-grade test will serve to estimate scholastic aptitude at the end of the twelfth grade as well as one given later. For this reason, if only a single test is to be given, it may be given early, so that it can be used throughout the school program. If more than one testing can be provided for, the tests may be spread fairly evenly through the high-school years.

Reading Test. In secondary and higher education, the role of reading becomes, if possible, even more critical. There is relatively little to be gained by giving a reading test unless the school has some provisions for taking action on the basis of the results and providing guidance in remedial activities. Where such resources are available, however, suitable reading tests to identify candidates for the reading program can play an important role. Since the constructive use of this testing implies remedial action, it is desirable that the testing be early in the program of the particular school—in the seventh grade for the junior high school, the tenth grade for the senior high.

Tests of Special Aptitudes. With an eye to vocational counseling, especially for those who will not go on to college, a high-school testing program can well include measures of aptitudes important for job success. These may be separate tests of mechanical, clerical, and spatial aptitudes. They may be incorporated into a single battery such as the *Differential Aptitude Test Battery*. If such a complete battery is used, it can take the place of the scholastic aptitude test, since certain of the subtests can be combined to give a suitable estimate of scholastic aptitude.

Tests of specialized aptitudes are usually not well adapted to use below the eighth or ninth grade. The particular time at which they are used will depend upon the total program of guidance in the school. Testing should be carried out so that results will be available and as up to date as possible in the grade in which counseling is focused and in which major decisions must be made. This may well be the ninth grade in a junior-senior high-school system. Additional data from further testing in the eleventh grade would make possible more reliable estimates of aptitude, to be used in counseling before the pupil leaves school.

Interests. Interests join with aptitudes in providing the background for vocational planning. For this reason, an interest inventory seems an appropriate supplement to aptitude measures, and evidence on interest could appropriately be gathered at the same time that the evidence on aptitudes is assembled. At the secondary level, an instrument that evaluates in terms of general interest areas, such as the *Kuder Preference Record,* seems preferable to one that provides ratings for specific jobs.

Achievement Tests in Content Areas. We have placed standardized achievement tests in the content areas somewhat lower down on the list for testing in the secondary school, because we believe that they have somewhat less to contribute to the guidance of pupils than the types of tests we have already considered. However, evaluation of achievement by standardized tests in the general areas of secondary education, science, social studies, and the arts and letters, does have value in appraising potential for higher education. A set of such tests would have value in the ninth grade if choices are to be made with respect to the particular program in the senior high school. A survey achievement battery might be included again in the eleventh or twelfth grade, in connection with the final decision as to collegiate education.

Prognostic Tests. There are several subjects for which special prognostic tests appear to have some merit. These include algebra, foreign languages, and shorthand. A school may perhaps wish to give such tests the year before the particular program of instruction starts and use them as one factor in screening students.

Personality and Adjustment Inventories. We have serious reservations about the practical value of paper-and-pencil techniques for assessing personality at this level also. However, they are probably more usable in the secondary school than in the elementary grades. Their use might prove of some value if counseling personnel with good background are available and the inventories are used merely as rough screening devices to pick up pupils for more thorough study.

A TESTING PROGRAM FOR THE COLLEGE

Standardized testing for or by colleges tends to serve three main functions: (1) admissions, (2) academic placement, and (3) educational, vocational and personal guidance of the individual student.

The content and administrative organization of testing programs reflect these three purposes.

Admissions Testing. In contrast with the public schools, which in the United States have been for "all the people," the colleges have always been designed for those with special academic capabilities. Soon after standardized tests had been developed, they were put to work as tools to select students with those capabilities. As both the per cent and number of young people aspiring to go to college have increased, standardized testing programs have come to play a larger and larger role in this massive screening process. With the bumper crop of "war babies" hitting the colleges in the 60's, and with limited spaces to accommodate them, screening of applicants becomes an even more hectic undertaking.

Much of the admissions testing is done for the colleges by one of several independent testing agencies. The oldest and best known of these is the College Entrance Examination Board. The Board began in 1900 to administer entrance tests for a limited number of "Ivy League" colleges. Early tests were essay in character, but an objective *Scholastic Aptitude Test* was introduced in 1926, and subsequently the achievement tests were gradually converted to objective format. The volume of College Board testing increased slowly at first, but then more and more rapidly as the number of schools requiring the tests increased and the per cent of young people aspiring to go to college mounted. Between 1956 and 1960, the number of examinees taking CEEB *Aptitude* and *Achievement* tests doubled, reaching almost half a million in the latter year.

The College Entrance Examination Board administers its tests at testing centers all over the world. Papers are centrally scored, and the results reported to the colleges the individual has designated, to his school and to the individual himself. Generally, these tests are taken by the student during his senior year in high school. However, there were always some who took the tests as juniors and in 1959–60 the College Board formalized a *Preliminary Scholastic Aptitude Test* to be administered to college-bound juniors in secondary schools and used for guidance purposes and for early admission to college. Further information about the tests in the series can be obtained from the publications of the College Board.[1,2]

A second and newer program for college admissions, designed for smaller and less selective colleges than those for which the College Board program was tailored, is the American College Testing Program. The battery for this program consists of four tests of general skills in English, mathematics, social studies, and science, respectively. Tests are administered at centers spread over the United States. Further information about the program can be obtained from the American College Testing Program, Iowa City, Iowa. The *College Qualification Tests* were prepared by the Psychological Corporation for those colleges wishing to handle their own admissions testing.

Certain of the states also run programs for admission to state-operated colleges in that state. These vary considerably from state to state. Information about them can usually be obtained either from the major state university or the state Department of Education.

Finally, there are various programs for admission to graduate schools or professional schools. The most widely used admission tests for graduate schools are the *Graduate Record Examination* administered by the Educational Testing Service and the *Miller Analogies Test* administered by the Psychological Corporation. Special tests are used by professional schools in such fields as law, medicine, dentistry, and accountancy. Information about the relevant tests can usually be obtained from the national association of the profession, from the admissions office of a professional school, or from one of the agencies mentioned above.

Testing for Placement in College. The problem of placing students in the proper courses or sections of courses after their admission to college arises in three general situations: (1) placement in freshman courses, (2) advanced placement for those students who have taken college-level courses in secondary school, and (3) placement of students transferring from another college at the sophomore or higher level.

Help with certain of these problems is available from the nation-wide testing agencies. Thus, the College Board offers an achievement examination program to assist in the selection of candidates for advanced placement as well as a testing program for transfer students. The *National Sophomore Testing Program* administered by the Educational Testing Service may also be useful in the placing of transfer students.

Some colleges undertake to section certain freshman introductory courses, particularly English, foreign languages and mathematics, on the basis of the ability of the entering students. Such sectioning permits differentiation of content and methods of instruction for the extreme groups. If all entering students have taken the relevant College Board *Achievement Tests* or the tests of the American College Testing Program, these may be used for this purpose. If not, colleges often find it desirable to give standardized tests in the subject areas to their entering students, and to use them in accomplishing grouping into sections.

Testing for Guidance. The major function of standardized testing in colleges is for guidance of individual students. This guidance may be educational, vocational or personal. Problems of educational guidance are especially likely to arise for students who have deficiencies in aptitude for college work, in the skills that are the tools of learning, and in techniques, habits, and attitudes of study. These problems are sufficiently widespread so that a testing program to identify weaknesses may be appropriate for all entering freshmen. This testing ties in closely with placement testing, since one of the adaptations to reading or writing deficiency, for example, may be placement in a special remedial section.

Vocational and personal guidance tend to present individual rather than common problems. Furthermore, especially with college-age students, these services are likely to be offered as needed or requested by specific individuals. This suggests a relatively heavy emphasis upon individualized testing services, available as needed, rather than upon uniform college-wide testing programs. However, some types of tests are likely to be of more general concern than others. In the light of common guidance needs, we suggest certain priorities in the material that might with advantage be gathered for all students.

Scholastic Aptitude. Since a substantial number of college students have difficulty in maintaining satisfactory scholastic standing, evidence on scholastic aptitude is often needed as a basis for counseling with respect to academic difficulties. Separate appraisal of verbal and quantitative abilities may be of value in permitting a more diagnostic appraisal. The test should be given at the time of admission so that the results may be available for use throughout the college course.

A battery of special aptitude tests could be used in place of the scholastic aptitude test. However, there appears to be somewhat less need for special aptitude tests in a college population than at the secondary level. The decision to go on to college has already somewhat narrowed down the range of occupations for which the group is preparing, and tests of mechanical, spatial, and clerical abilities are of rather less significance for college students than for a high-school group.

Reading. A measure of reading ability contributes some further basis for understanding problems of academic failure. It has a special function if the college provides a reading clinic in which remedial instruction may be obtained. A reading test given at the time of college entrance and interpreted in conjunction with the scholastic aptitude test provides one basis for locating students who might advantageously receive such special help.

Interests. With final vocational choices drawing close, early in college appears to be a time at which a vocational interest test can advantageously be given to all students. Thus, if a test of interest in specific vocations, such as the *Strong Vocational Interest Blank,* is given during the sophomore year, the results can be available for consideration at the time that choices of major field are made. Since interest patterns at that age remain quite stable, the scores will be suitable for special counseling throughout the remainder of the college course.

Adjustment Inventory. The typical adjustment inventory is better suited to college students than it is to less mature and less educated groups. Where extensive counseling services exist, such an inventory might be used to screen out individuals for further study. However, we have serious reservations as to the value of such a procedure. Ordinarily at the college level counseling is initiated at the request of the client. We question how effective or useful college-wide screening and bringing in students for conferences is likely to be. Use of the scores by departmental advisers and others without special training is hardly to be recommended.

SUMMARY OF SUGGESTED PROGRAMS

Let us emphasize again that any testing program needs to be formulated by personnel in the local situation aware of local conditions, local purposes, and local resources. The proposals that have been outlined in this section are at most rough general guides. The highlights of this discussion have been organized in tabular form in Table 16.2. The most highly recommended tests are marked with a double asterisk. Tests considered useful supplements in an extensive testing program or of value for certain special purposes receive a single asterisk. Procedures deemed of doubtful value are indicated by a question mark. Where no mark is made, it indicates that the type of test is considered inappropriate, impractical, or of little value at that level for a class-wide or school-wide testing program.

LARGE-SCALE TESTING PROGRAMS

A matter of some concern to educators in recent years has been the proliferation of large-scale external testing programs, imposed upon the schools and serving some purpose other than those of the school itself. We have already discussed the college admission testing

Table 16.2. Suggested Tests for School Testing Program

Type of Test	Educational Level		
	Elementary	Secondary	College
General intelligence or scholastic aptitude	**	**	**
Reading	**	**	**
Basic academic skills	**		
Reading readiness	**		
Individual intelligence	*	?	?
Achievement in content subjects	*	*	*
Personality inventory		?	?
Interest inventory		**	**
Special aptitude tests or battery		**	*
Prognostic tests for special subject		*	

programs, which are carried out in behalf of the colleges. In addition, there are national scholarship testing programs, large-scale research testing programs, and "quality control" testing programs administered by states or by large city units. Each of these is designed to serve a valid educational purpose, but one may ask whether these purposes do not at times conflict with other purposes of the schools where the tests are administered.

Concern about the impact of these testing programs upon students, especially during the last year or two of their secondary-school program, arises on two counts. On the one hand, it is sometimes felt that the pupil spends too much time taking tests, or that the time spent on tests interferes with his regular school work. We cannot feel that this is an important objection. Many of the outside tests are scheduled for Saturdays. Pupils are likely to take, at most, two or three during a year. Though scheduling the tests may be a nuisance for school administrators—and testing agencies must give some consideration to this—the burden on the time of the student can hardly be considered serious.

The second concern is that the external tests may pervert the educational program of the school, because the tests come to control the curriculum and the teachers focus on preparing for the tests. This problem is most likely to arise when the external tests are concerned with specific segments of the school curriculum, as is the case with the *New York State Regents Examinations*. Since the performance of student, teacher, and school are all judged to some extent by performance on the tests, they assume a disproportionate importance.

Anyone acquainted with secondary schools in New York State knows of classes that spend weeks, even months, in review of past *Regents Examinations*. One can certainly question whether this is the most rewarding investment of time for student and teacher.

Even when the test is less closely tied to the curriculum, the test may affect it through what the test does and does not emphasize. Thus, it had been argued that the relatively small role for actual writing in recent English tests of the College Board had reinforced a tendency to reduce the number and variety of compositions called for in high school English courses, and had thus strengthened an undesirable trend. Certainly, it is important that external testing programs present desirable models, emphasizing the important goals of education and not distorting the pattern of the school program. When the testing programs deal with achievements of a nature sufficiently broad and basic so that they go beyond specific courses and course objectives, the danger of an unfavorable impact seems reduced.

TESTING PROGRAMS FOR SCHOLARSHIP AWARDS

Testing programs used in connection with scholarship awards represent one special development of some interest. The need for these programs arises from the fact that substantial scholarship funds come from sources outside of any particular university—from foundations, industry, and federal and state governments—so that some general appraisal of applicants is needed not related to the programs or policies of any single institution. The most ambitious testing program of this type is the one administered by the National Merit Scholarship Corporation. In 1958, this Corporation distributed over $5,000,000 in awards to high school graduates. In the same year, almost 500,000 high-school juniors and seniors took the qualifying tests. Identification of "semi-finalists" has been based on a test that as of 1960 resembled closely the *Iowa Tests of Educational Development*. Since it has been the policy of the Corporation that awards be pro-rated by states, in proportion to the number of high-school seniors, the standard to qualify as a semi-finalist has varied fairly widely from one state to another. (It has also been the policy that the cash value of the award vary depending upon the financial status of the family.)

Final award of scholarships has been based upon performance on College Entrance Examination Board tests, and upon such other factors as the evaluating panels chose to consider.

Other less extensive scholarship testing services have been developed and offered to the public by the College Board, the Educational Testing Service and the Psychological Corporation.

A number of cities, and some states have centrally administered programs of aptitude and/or achievement tests. We have already discussed some of the disadvantages of uniform, narrowly course-centered achievement tests for a large educational unit. With respect to aptitude or more general achievement tests, the situation is somewhat more favorable. The great advantage of a centralized and uniform testing program is the comparability of records from one school to another. Thus, if the records of a pupil who transfers to a new school follow him, his new principal and teacher find that they have the same records for him that they have for the rest of their pupils, and so they can readily place him in his new setting.

If a rigid uniform testing program is applied somewhat mechanically throughout a large educational unit, there is danger that the tests may not fit very well in some specific schools. They may not fit the needs and backgrounds of the teachers; they may not fit the characteristics of the school population. Furthermore, teachers may feel less identification with such a remotely controlled testing program. Some states and cities, by contrast, provide only advisory service for local educational units. In these places the department of education may formulate a number of different possible testing programs and offer them as guides to the local community, or they may maintain files or lists of tests suitable for different purposes and help local communities select tests to meet their own needs. They may also offer consultant and advisory help to the local unit. Since many communities cannot provide testing experts on their own staff, these advisory and consultative functions may be more important for a really functional testing program than a centrally directed program handed down from above.

"PACKAGED" TESTING PROGRAMS

Another kind of large-scale testing program that has grown in recent years is the packaged testing program offered by many test publishers to schools at all levels. Many schools feel inadequate when it comes to selecting tests and planning testing programs, so personnel in these schools have turned to the test publishers for help.

The kinds of programs made available from different test publishers vary considerably both in the variety of tests and in the services offered. For elementary schools, the package usually consists of a general scholastic aptitude test and achievement tests in the basic skills. For secondary schools, the package usually consists of a general scholastic aptitude test or a multi-factor aptitude battery and achievement tests in reading, mathematics, language, science and social studies.

If the school buys the "package," the cost of so much per pupil tested usually includes rental or purchase of test materials, scoring the tests, and making up score distribution and report forms by grades or classes.

A school that is thinking about buying a packaged program should examine each test in the package carefully to determine whether the test meets its needs adequately and whether each test has desirable characteristics.   If the tests in the package are of good quality, and if they will give the school the information it needs, then buying the package may be both economical and efficient.   However, it should not be assumed that the purchase of a packaged program will result in a good testing program for a specific school.   This can only be determined by comparing the components of the package with the needs and objectives of the purchasing school.

PRESENTING THE RESULTS OF TESTING TO THE PUBLIC

When we speak of presenting test results to the public we may be thinking of reporting on the performance of the school system as a whole or of a major segment of it.   On the other hand, we may be thinking of presenting the test results for a particular individual to a specific interested public, the parents or, possibly, the pupil himself. Each type of public use of test results has its place, and each presents its problems.   We shall give a little attention to each in turn.

REPORTING THE RESULTS OF A PROGRAM OF TESTING

Test results are often used as one basis for an over-all appraisal of a school and its curriculum.   The appraisal may be a within-school one, and the report may be planned to stimulate self-evaluation and self-criticism.   Or the report may be to lay groups, the board of education, groups of parents, or the general public that supports the schools.

Whatever the audience, the purpose of the report should be to summarize, organize, and interpret the test results so that a meaningful picture of the school's accomplishments will emerge.   Scores will need to be tallied for each class and school, separately for each significant subtest, and for the test as a whole.   The scores of interest will ordinarily be converted scores, i.e., age or grade scores or percentiles for a particular grade group.   Measures of average score (mean or median) will need to be obtained for each group of interest. These will then be organized for the audience in tabular or graphic form.

In presenting test results to an audience, we may be interested in various types of comparisons. Comparisons that may be of significance include:

1. Comparison of local group performance with national norms or more specialized norms if they are available.

2. Comparison of local group performance with level of ability in the group.

3. Comparison of achievement in different subject areas.

4. Comparison of different schools in a system or possibly different class groups in a school.

5. Comparison of groups taught in different ways—using different methods or materials.

6. Comparison of groups at different grade levels.

7. Comparison of the same group at different times to show pupil growth.

If an effective presentation is to be achieved, graphic representations will be needed as a supplement to the relatively formal and forbidding tabular presentation of evidence. Presentation of group data falls most naturally into the pattern of the bar chart or of the profile (see Chapter 6, pp. 151–152).

Suppose that we had tested all the pupils in grades two through six of an elementary school in April, and that the results were as shown in Table 16.3 below.

Table 16.3. Median Performance of Each Grade of School W on Intelligence Test and Achievement Battery

(Tested in eighth month of school year)

Test	Grade Medians				
	2	3	4	5	6
Intelligence test	3.3	4.4	5.4	6.3	7.6
Word knowledge test	3.7	4.6	5.9	6.6	7.8
Paragraph reading test	3.6	4.8	5.6	6.5	8.1
Arithmetic fundamentals test	2.2	3.6	5.1	6.2	7.5
Arithmetic reasoning test	2.5	3.7	5.0	6.4	7.7
Language usage test	3.2	4.3	5.4	6.2	7.8
Spelling test	2.5	3.6	4.9	5.9	6.8

This table shows a school in which the pupils are generally of above-average intelligence. (For example, when the tests were given in grade 2.8, the median intelligence grade level was 3.3.) Reading achievement is generally superior, above both national norms for the grade level and the intelligence level of the group. Arithmetic is below national norms in the early grades but is above in the later grades, approximately equaling the intelligence level. The reader can note other details of the table.

Figures 16.1 and 16.2 show two types of graphic representation of these data. The first figure shows a profile of separate test medians for the second-grade group. The upper profile in the figure shows

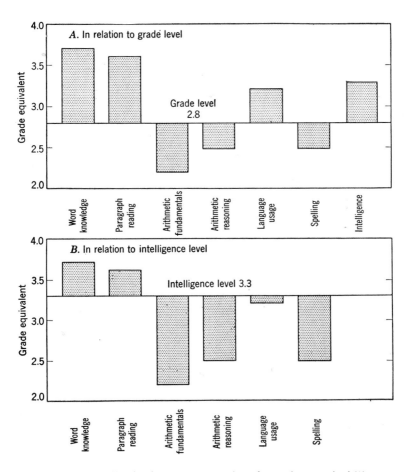

Fig. 16.1. Profile of Achievement Test medians for grade two, school W.

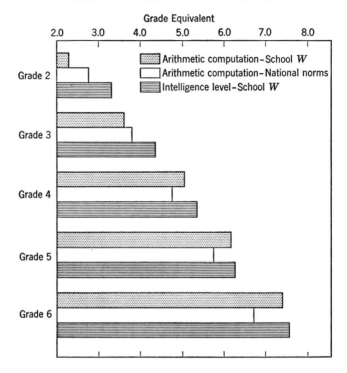

Fig. 16.2. Median arithmetic computation scores by grade for school W compared with national norms and grade intelligence level.

performance in relation to national norms for the grade level. The lower profile shows performance in relation to the ability level for the group. Similar profiles would, of course, be prepared for other grades.

Figure 16.2 is a bar chart comparing achievement in arithmetic fundamentals in the different grades. In order to include a reference standard for each grade, the national norm for the grade and the grade level of the group on intelligence are both indicated. This type of bar chart could, of course, be used for comparing different schools, groups taught in different ways, or other different types of groups.

An effective popular presentation should usually contain much graphic and pictorial material but few tables, hiding these in appendices or other odd corners where they will not distract the audience.

It is perhaps worth re-emphasizing here that the test results brought out in any set of charts constitute only raw facts, not meaningful interpretations or conclusions. These interpretations must be supplied by the educator, who is acquainted with the circumstances surrounding the test scores. Thus, in our illustration the *interpretation* of the arithmetic achievement in the second and third grades would be vastly different for a school that had given little formal instruction in those grades than for one that had emphasized arithmetic. It is easy to give a false impression of the significance of test results if meaningful background facts are not taken into account.

REPORTING TEST RESULTS FOR THE INDIVIDUAL

The teacher, guidance worker, or principal is faced at frequent intervals with the problem of reporting test results to pupils or to parents. He must decide how much to report and in what way to report it. In particular, the question is often raised whether exact score equivalents should be reported. Should the parent be told his child's IQ or reading grade level? Should the high-school pupil see his percentile rank on a scholastic aptitude test?

We can perhaps best answer this question by asking another one. What information does the parent or pupil need in order to have a true picture of the situation or to reach a sound decision? In practically every instance we will have to conclude that an exact score is not needed, and would be of no practical value. The need is for a sound *interpretation* of the pupil's or client's standing. Except in rare instances, this interpretation is better provided by school personnel than by parent or pupil. The need is for an interpretation of the score in terms of its educational or vocational significance.

In addition to not needing specific information there is the very real possibility that the lay person will misinterpret and misuse it. A precision may be attributed to test scores that they do not have. Differences may be noted and given significance that they do not in reality possess. The importance and scope of the test score may be overvalued. Invidious comparisons may be encouraged.

Generally, then, results of testing a particular individual should be reported to the lay public, and especially to the parent or pupil, by statements of general level or range of ability: "about average," "somewhat below most of those in his group," "not as well as we would expect in terms of what we know about his abilities." Emphasis should be on an interpretive reporting of results—on what the scores signify in terms of school progress or vocational plans. Exact scores should be played down. Presented in this way, the potential misuses of test results are held to a minimum, while their values in providing understanding of the pupil are maintained.

There are three qualities that we would like to see in any interpretation of a score to a pupil or parent.

1. The interpretation should be set in the frame of reference of the particular pupil. Thus, standardized achievement test results should be interpreted in terms of what is known about the pupil's aptitude and about his educational and vocational goals. A reading score at the 50th percentile of a ninth-grade group means quite different things for the boy who aspires to go to medical school and for the boy who plans to become a mechanic.

2. The interpretation should be directed toward positive and constructive action. It should emphasize the assets in an aptitude profile, or it should be oriented toward remedial action when achievement falls below what aptitude would lead one to expect. It should point toward possible educational or vocational outlets, even if the chosen one may be impossible of achievement.

3. It should be factual and dispassionate, rather than appearing to pass judgment on the individual. Test results and other evidence should be reported truthfully and accurately, but with a friendly and accepting attitude. The flavor should be one of working with the pupil to realize common goals rather than one of passing judgment on him.

Consideration should be given to making more general provision for feeding back to pupils information about their performance on tests that they have taken. All too often, pupils take a battery of tests and that is the last that they hear of them. Testing will be more meaningful and significant to pupils if they can see something of the outcomes and uses of the testing. Of course, any report must be adapted to the maturity of the group. However, several ways of reporting back to the group merit consideration.

1. The classroom or homeroom teacher might give a simple summary report and interpretation of the performance of the group as a whole. Strengths and weaknesses could be indicated. Comparisons could be made with general norms for the grade level. Some indication could be given of the way the results could help the work of the group and planning for particular individuals in the group.

2. An invitation could be extended for pupils to talk over the tests with the teacher. In individual conference, pupils could be given a general picture of the significance of their test results and how they relate to plans for the pupil.

3. In cases where the test results have important implications, i.e., large discrepancy between aptitude and achievement, large discrepancy between test performance and what the teacher believes the child to

hold as a self-picture, the teacher could take the initiative and make a point of discussing test results individually with the pupil and perhaps also with his parents.

SUMMARY STATEMENT

Our central theme in this chapter has been that tests are given to be used, and that uses are determined by local needs. A testing program must, therefore, be developed for local needs in terms of local resources and with active participation by the local personnel, who will be the users and interpreters of the test results.

In Table 16.1 we listed a wide variety of functions that tests are often called upon to serve. The discussion of these functions may guide a local group in defining their purposes in testing. In terms of common needs, we proposed tentative priorities for different types of tests. These were summarized in Table 16.2.

An effective testing program means not only sound choice of the tests to be given, but good planning for their administration and for recording the results. Some of the provisions important for standardized but favorable testing conditions, conditions that will permit each examinee to show what he is truly capable of, were reviewed.

Finally, adequate procedures are needed by which the results of testing programs can reach interested publics. Group results need to be organized effectively in graphs and charts centering about the significant comparisons, and the whole organized into a report that can be presented to school board, PTA, and other interested lay groups. Presentation of results for individual pupils to pupils and parents should be facilitated. However, in this presentation results should be in general terms, and emphasis should be on an interpretive synthesis rather than on specific details.

REFERENCES

1. Dyer, Henry S., and Richard G. King, *College Board scores: their use and interpretation,* Princeton, N. J., College Entrance Examination Board, 1955.
2. Fishman, Joshua A., *1957 Supplement to College Board scores No. 2,* New York, College Entrance Examination Board, 1957.

SUGGESTED ADDITIONAL READING

American Council on Education, *College testing,* Washington, D. C., American Council on Education, 1959.

Dyer, Henry S., and Richard G. King, *College Board Scores No. 2,* Princeton, N. J., College Entrance Examination Board, 1955.

Froehlich, Clifford P., and Kenneth B. Hoyt, *Guidance testing,* 3rd ed., Science Research Associates, Chicago, 1959, Chapter 4.

Hill, George E., and John D. Scott, *School testing program inventory,* Athens, Ohio, Center for Educational Service, Ohio University, 1960.

Kent Area Guidance Council, *A proposed 12-year testing program,* Columbus, Ohio, Ohio Scholarship Tests, State Department of Education, 1959.

Science Research Associates, *National merit scholarship qualifying test; interpretive manual for counselors and school administrators,* Chicago, Science Research Associates, 1959.

Science Research Associates, *National merit scholarship qualifying test, technical report,* Chicago, Science Research Associates, 1960.

Traxler, Arthur E., *Techniques of guidance,* rev. ed., New York, Harper, 1957, Chapters 9, 10, and 11.

Traxler, Arthur E., et al., *Introduction to testing and the use of test results in public schools,* New York, Harper, 1953, Chapters 2, 3, 5, 8, and 9.

QUESTIONS FOR DISCUSSION

1. Suppose you are starting to teach a new group of students. Make a list of the types of information you would like to have about the new class. For which could standardized tests contribute the information either wholly or in part?

2. Assume that you are on a testing committee to plan a testing program for your school system. What would you want to know as a basis for planning the program? What part should the teachers in the system have in the planning?

3. How are planning a testing program and planning curriculum revision for a school similar?

4. How sound and how generally true is the statement "standardized tests are less satisfactory in the content than in the skill areas"? What is the basis for your answer?

5. In a school system where you are in charge of testing, funds make it possible to give only one group intelligence test in the elementary school. When would you give it? What are the reasons for your choice? When would you give one test in the junior-senior high school?

6. What are the relative merits of giving a battery of achievement tests in the fall (October or November), as compared with giving them in the spring (April or May)?

7. In an elementary-school class that you are teaching, an intelligence test and an achievement battery have been given in October. In what different ways might you as teacher use the test results with your class?

8. Under what circumstances would it be appropriate to have a school mark depend in whole or in part upon standardized test results?

9. What are the potential advantages and dangers of a uniform statewide program

   (a) of standardized aptitude and achievement tests?

   (b) of subject-matter end-of-course examinations?

10. To what extent should standardized test results be reported to parents? To elementary-school pupils? To secondary-school pupils? To college students? If they are reported, in how much detail and how precisely should they be reported?

11. What should be the role of aptitude and achievement tests in forming classroom groups for instructional purposes? In forming special groups of high or low deviates?

12. School A is experimenting with a new type of core program in the secondary schools. Those who have set up the program wish to evaluate its effectiveness. What place should standardized achievement tests such as the *Essential High School Content Battery, Iowa Tests of General Educational Development,* or *Sequential Tests of Educational Progress* (*STEP*) have in such an evaluation? What cautions should be observed in basing the evaluation on these?

13. School B makes a policy of using the *Metropolitan Achievement Test* one year, the *California Tests* the next, and the *Iowa Tests of Basic Skills* the next. What advantages do you see in this policy? What disadvantages?

14. How would you describe the shift in emphasis in a standardized testing program as one goes from the fourth grade to the twelfth grade?

15. Do colleges place too much emphasis upon standardized tests in their admissions policies? What is good or bad about this?

16. A school system gave the *Stanford Achievement Tests* to all pupils in the sixth grade in May. The *Otis Quick-Scoring Mental Ability Test* had been given at about the same time. Grade equivalents for the 10th, 25th, 50th, 75th and 90th percentiles for each test are shown below. Prepare a report to interpret these results to the Board of Education or a group of interested parents.

Test	P_{10}	P_{25}	P_{50}	P_{75}	P_{90}
Stanford-Paragraph Meaning	5.5	6.3	7.4	9.2	10.1
Word Meaning	5.7	6.7	7.8	8.8	10.2
Spelling	5.0	6.0	7.2	8.4	9.4
Language Usage	4.0	5.9	7.2	8.2	9.1
Arithmetic Reasoning	5.6	6.8	7.3	8.4	9.8
Arithmetic Computation	6.0	6.8	7.8	8.7	10.2
Otis—IQ	86	100	107	116	124

Chapter 17

▼

Marking and Reporting

One educational phenomenon closely related to problems of measurement is that of grades and report cards. In this chapter we shall start out by examining the basic nature of school marks. Then we shall consider the functions that marks and reporting systems are supposed to serve and try to evaluate how well these functions are in fact served by various marking and reporting practices. Finally, we shall consider several technical problems relating to the assignment of marks.

What we shall have to say in this chapter will not stem to any large extent from experimental research. The problems involved are largely problems calling for thoughtful analysis of needs to be met and the resources available for meeting them.

WHAT A MARK IS

A mark or grade in school, college, or university is, in the last analysis, a judgment of one person by another. The judgment may sometimes be formulated rather intuitively and subjectively, as when the teacher reads and evaluates various literary productions known as essay tests, reacts in an unanalyzed way to classroom activities and participation, and puts in a little credit for "effort" to leaven the mixture. In other cases, the final appraisal may be arrived at quite mechanically and objectively, as when the teacher sums certain objective test scores with specified weights, arranges the totals in rank order, and gives the top 10 per cent A. But judgment was involved in the second case as truly as in the first. In the second case judgments that were made early in the game were: (1) that objective tests provided the appropriate basis for arriving at a rank order, (2) that certain items represented suitable evidences of achievement, (3) that the appropriate responses to these items were thus and so, and (4) that for this group it would be appropriate to assign the label A to 10 per cent of the group.

We see, then, that the manner in which the final appraisals are reached differs. Judgment may enter primarily into the planning of objective test procedures and may be made for the class as a whole, or it may enter into the appraisal of performance by specific pupils. The types of evidence judged will vary from class to class, consisting in some instances largely of test papers, in others of tangible pupil products, and in still others of pupil activity and participation in the work of the group. The qualities appraised and the weight assigned to each may vary markedly from one instructor or class to another. But the basic fact of passing judgment is common. Any mark is a judgment of a student by a teacher.

Furthermore, a mark is ordinarily a *relative* judgment. The relativity of a score was brought out in detail at the beginning of Chapter 7, when we were discussing norms. It was pointed out then and illustrated with a pair of spelling tests that a test score of 75 per cent could represent a high score or a low score, depending upon the nature of the test and the relation of the test to the person or group being tested. This is equally true of marks. What does a mark of E signify? In one system it may denote "excellent," whereas in another it denotes "failure but subject to re-examination." Here the difference lies in the structure and meanings of the two symbol systems. However, in other cases even though the symbol system is *nominally* the same the *real* meaning of a symbol may vary widely. Thus, B+ has quite a different real significance for the course of instructor X who habitually gives A's to half his class than for the course of instructor Y who habitually gives A's to only 10 per cent of his class. And the variation from school to school is often even more striking. A performance that would be evaluated as meriting a C− at Harvard might very well be judged as constituting A work at Eastern Arkansas State College. Evaluation is relative to the general student population of the institution and to the standards held by the particular instructor.

The variation from teacher to teacher and place to place bears witness to the fact that no fundamental anchor or reference point exists for grades. The standard of reference may be the group itself when grades are explicitly assigned in terms of proportion of the total group, e.g., 20 per cent A's, 30 per cent B's, 40 per cent C's, and 10 per cent D's. The standard may be some shadowy inner picture the instructor carries with him of the performance by his previous classes and of the accomplishment that may reasonably be expected from individuals at this level of advancement. But in either case, the standard is a relative one. There is no "sea level," no fixed standard to which we can refer each individual's performance.

The school can never escape making these relative judgments about pupils. Such judgments will always be necessary for guiding the pupil in his school work, for understanding his personal trials and tribulations, for helping him to plan his educational and occupational future, and for cooperating with later schools and employers in selecting the individuals who may most suitably be instructed or employed. No, the schools cannot escape their responsibility for making these judgments. On this we can agree. But we will find agreement on little else.

The issues revolve around the following questions, taken singly or in combination:

1. When should judgments be made?
2. In what form should judgments be recorded?
3. What factors should be covered?
4. On what sorts of evidence should the judgments be based?
5. Who should be responsible for making the judgments?
6. To whom should they be reported? Who is the appropriate consumer of the information?

We shall start by seeing who has need for the information that judgment of pupils by teachers is supposed to provide and shall try to consider the other questions in the context of the functions to be served.

THE FUNCTIONS OF MARKING AND REPORTING SYSTEMS

The functions of marking and reporting systems change quite a bit as one goes from the primary grades on up to college. Some of what we have to say will apply most directly to earlier educational levels and some to later. With varying emphasis at different educational levels we can identify five categories of persons who will normally be users of the information represented by the judgments that a school makes about a pupil. These are (1) the pupil being evaluated, (2) the pupil's parents, (3) some school that the pupil will attend later, (4) a potential employer or similar outside community agency, and (5) the school itself. If we now try to determine what information each of these potential users needs, we should be better able to decide what sorts of judgments should be made and how they should be reported.

Why does the pupil need to be informed about the school's appraisal of him? What information does he need? Information conveyed to the pupil would appear to serve four functions: (1) motivation of school work, (2) guidance of learning, (3) guidance of future educational and vocational planning, and (4) guidance of personal development. For each of these needs, what information should the school give him, at what times, and in what forms?

Motivation. The motivations underlying work in school are manifold and complex. They include satisfactions in participating with the group, in exploring and investigating new fields, in succeeding, in receiving social approval, in conforming and doing what is expected, and many others. The negative incentives are also quite real—of frustration, failure, boredom, or rejection.

Testing, evaluation, marking, and systems of reporting enter into pupil motivation in at least four related ways.

1. Through experiences of success and failure in the day-by-day recitations, tests, and exercises of the school.

2. Through the awareness that others are appraising his work and forming their opinions of him at least in part on the basis of that work.

3. Through the awareness that his performance in whatever ways it is appraised by the school is becoming a matter of permanent record and part of his official past history.

4. Through the anticipated and actual impact of school reports upon his world, the world of family and classmates.

Daily experiences of success and failure with the tasks he meets in school represent the most direct and intrinsic motivating effect of measurement procedures. The teacher sets the tasks by which the pupil tries out his abilities and reflects back to the pupil his evaluation of the pupil's performance. This teacher appraisal, made known to the pupil through corrections on papers and through oral comments, provides a continuing set of cues on success or progress that motivate daily activities.

The importance of success and achievement as motives to sustain interest and effort is indicated in both laboratory and clinical research. The goal of the school should be, therefore, so to set the daily tasks and the standard of expected performance for each pupil as to provide a reasonable proportion of experiences of success. The teacher has the responsibility of knowing the potentialities and past performances of each child well enough so that he can adopt and help the child to adopt standards of performance that are reasonable for him. If the most effective motivation is to be maintained, the school must set flexible standards adapted to individual pupils.

Maintaining the favorable opinion of others represents another aspect of school motivation. The pupil values the good opinion of adults who are important to him—his parents and, usually, his teachers. At higher educational levels, he is aware that the impression of him held by his instructors may be important when they are later called upon as references to support his application for higher education or a job. The motivation to be thought well of by teachers operates no matter what formal reporting or marking procedure is used. However, a system of periodic grades and reports makes teacher reactions more explicit and visible to the pupil, and may make this aspect of motivation more tangible and effective.

Associated with an awareness that his reputation with his teachers is important is an awareness that his academic record may be important: the record that follows him in transcripts through further education and out into the world of work. Motivation to leave a good record is another aspect of the picture, an aspect whose importance probably increases the higher up the educational ladder we go.

Periodic grades and report cards represent administrative devices to write into the record the evaluations that teachers are making of pupils and to transmit them to pupil and parents. What further value do these reports have in motivating student learning, over and above the awarenesses to which we have referred in the preceding paragraphs?

One cannot be too sure. It is undoubtedly true that the prospect of the report card stimulates *some* additional effort on school work by *some* pupils, especially in the higher grades. How widespread, how profound, and how effective this additional effort is is another matter, however, and is a point on which we have little, if any, direct information. Evidence on the point is largely indirect, stemming from the experience of those schools that have done away with the traditional forms of marks and marking. There is no indication that these schools find the motivating of pupils a more serious problem than do the more conventional and marks-oriented schools.

Informal contacts between school and parent, between teacher or counselor and pupil can serve to transmit the type of appraisal that is commonly recorded in a mark. At the same time, an adequate program of testing and cumulative records guarantees that the pupil's performance is a matter of record. When such contacts and records are adequate, periodic marks may well be superfluous as motivating devices.

In addition to harboring some doubts as to the *effectiveness* of marks as motivating devices, many educators would raise serious questions as to the *desirability* of the motivation they provide. The motivation of the marks given in the traditional school has been criticized as being (1) individual and competitive, emphasizing individual achievement and superiority at the expense of cooperation and joint achievement, (2) extraneous and not related to any genuine purposes or needs for learning things for their own sake, and (3) a barrier to organizing the work of the school around genuine interests and pupil needs.

We would conclude that frequent opportunities to test himself against the tasks of the school program and prompt evaluation of his performance are important and functional aspects of the motivation of the pupil in school, but that as far as motivation is concerned a periodic report card grade is a questionable addition to this regular and immediate appraisal.

Guidance of Learning. Information about his successes and his errors is important also for guiding the pupil's learning activities. Here, again, it is prompt information that is important—prompt and, preferably, specific. Research has shown repeatedly the value of specific identification of pupil errors or deficiencies and of practice directed toward replacing those errors with a correct performance. In handwriting, practice on those letter combinations that produce illegibility in *his* handwriting; in English, practice to eliminate the punctuation or capitalization errors found in *his* writing; in spelling, practice on the words *he* has misspelled represent efficient learning procedures. Techniques for diagnosing individual weaknesses promptly so that they may be identified and corrected represent key tools in guiding the learning process. This is one part of the rationale in the recent emphasis on "teaching machines"—devices that permit an individual to identify his errors and correct them as soon as they are made. *Testing* serves this function in proportion as the tests provide diagnostic cues and those cues are fed back to the pupil to direct his learning activities.

As far as the guidance of learning is concerned, the summary appraisals represented by periodic marks would appear to have no function. They are removed in time from the actual learning activities, global, and quite lacking in diagnostic value. *Marks* cannot help to direct day-by-day learning activities in the school.

Guidance of Future Educational and Vocational Plans. To make intelligent, realistic plans about his educational and vocational future, the student needs, among other things, a realistic understanding of his level of educational achievement. He needs this information most crucially at times of decision and action. However, decisions and plans crystallize gradually, so that all times are suitable for reflecting to the individual a realistic picture of himself in relation to his educational and vocational expectations.

Periodic marks, regularly and systematically reported, do represent *one* way of reporting to the individual judgments about him that are significant for his educational and vocational planning. The relationship of judgments at an earlier level (e.g., high-school marks) to judgments at a later stage (e.g., college marks) has been demonstrated repeatedly. As the individual considers whether he should plan to go to college, seek professional training, or aspire to a professional job, evaluations of his current academic success represent important guideposts. The question is how that academic achievement can best be appraised and how the appraisal can best be communicated to the student.

With respect to manner of appraisal, one possibility is to rely upon the judgment of individual teachers, based on whatever types of evidence they may see fit to use in arriving at their judgment. Another possibility is to make the single inclusive judgment that a particular standardized test or group of tests gives a sound appraisal of prospects for success. Tests have the great advantage that the score scale has a uniform meaning independent of the particular teacher or the particular school. Teachers' judgments based on a class setting have, perhaps, more in common with future teacher judgments also based on class activities. However, there are data showing that as far as statistical prediction is concerned, a thorough achievement battery at the high-school level, such as the *Iowa Tests of General Educational Development,* gives as good a prediction of college success as the full four-year record of high-school grades. Thus, at least through the high school, a prediction equivalent to that provided by grades could be obtained from standardized test results.

Reporting academic achievement to the pupil only through a periodic report card is a rather unsatisfactory way of communicating to him the significance of this evidence for his own plans. What does a B average at Centerville High signify with respect to probable success at State University or prospects of becoming an engineer? Some translation or interpretation is needed, and the student cannot be expected to make it for himself. The important thing as far as the student is concerned is the *meaning of his record* rather than the raw grades themselves. For a standardized test score, it is even more true that we need to provide the pupil with an interpretation rather than with the raw facts.   Here many counselors would make it their policy to report to the student *only* the interpretation, feeling that the bare test scores would be without meaning to the student.   But for the guidance of the pupil, this meaning must also be put into the teacher's evaluation of class performance.   Grades are at best only raw materials that enter into the formulation of educational and vocational plans.   These raw materials need to be processed by someone with greater breadth of experience than the typical pupil if they are to contribute to valid decisions.

One main responsibility of the high-school counselor is to build up a fund of experience that will permit him to make sound interpretations of evidence available at the high-school level in the form either of marks or of standardized test results.   He should do at least an informal follow-up of the graduates from his school to see what degree of success his B students do have at the State University or what sorts of jobs the C students appear to find and hold successfully.

Guidance of Personal Development.   We learn how to live with other people by the way other people react to our actions.   What is acceptable and desirable behavior is defined by our group.   The school also has a responsibility of reflecting to the individual pupil its appraisal of his ways of acting, so that he may develop in socially desirable directions.   This reflecting is implicit in every contact that school personnel have with the student.   Every expression of interest, approval, enthusiasm, or the reverse is a subtle guidepost indicating the way the school community defines desirable behavior patterns and appraises pupils.   These appraisals can be formalized by anecdotal records or by periodic use of rating scales or check lists to provide a permanent record of the appraisal of the individual pupil.   It seems doubtful, however, whether such periodic appraisals are likely to be really understood by the pupil or to have much impact on him.   The direct person-to-person contact in the school, largely in day-to-day interaction but also in special conference as that seems needed, is probably the way in which the school exerts whatever effect it can upon personal growth and development.

Relation of Self-Evaluation to School Evaluation.   Some educators have contended that evaluation of the student should be primarily self-evaluation.   It is contended that the pupil should set his own goals and should evaluate his own progress toward them.   There is a good deal to be said for this point of view as far as some of the functions of evaluation are concerned.   The pupil's own goals certainly represent more intrinsic motivators than arbitrary and external goals.   Guidance of his learning activities can perhaps be satisfactorily achieved by reference to the objectives he himself has set up.

However, there are many pitfalls to self-evaluation, and many situations in which it seems quite out of place. In the first place, the pupil often lacks the background to define the objectives he should seek, or the experience to set for himself realistic standards of progress toward them. How can the typical ninth grader know what values are to be gained from beginning algebra or how fast he should be able to proceed toward them? The good teacher will try to make the objectives explicit, but the pupil can be expected to see them only "through a glass darkly" until he has had the course and can see in retrospect what it was all about. Furthermore, the pupil is an interested party in many evaluations. We could hardly expect the medical school applicant to be an unbiased judge of his own suitability for admission, or the job applicant to give his projected employer a completely dispassionate evaluation of his strengths and weaknesses. Self-appraisal is not a substitute for school appraisal.

In summary, we have seen rather little use for marks or a report card as far as informing the student of the school's appraisal of him is concerned. Motivation and direction of learning can best be served by the tasks and tests of school itself. Guidance of personal development is best provided in direct personal contact. Marks may have a function in guiding educational and vocational planning, but this function can also be served, and perhaps more effectively, by the uniformly based information from standardized tests. Either type of information needs to be interpreted to the pupil in relation to particular educational or vocational objectives.

REPORTING SCHOOL APPRAISALS TO PARENTS

Marks and report cards have had as one of their main functions that of maintaining communication between the school and the home. Effective communication between these two chief agencies concerned with the growth and development of the child is vital for his best development. The school needs an adequate picture of each child's home: the physical circumstances under which he lives, the family constellation, the attitudes of parents toward him, and parental goals and aspirations for him. At the same time, if parents are to cooperate with the school and to work intelligently for the child's good, they need to know what the school is trying to accomplish, what problems it is encountering in the case of their child, and what plans and programs are reasonable for that child.

Two-way communication of the type just described is an ideal that is only likely to be achieved in an alert and enterprising school and with cooperative parents. It does, however, define the goal. What place do marks and a report card have in moving toward such a goal?

Fundamentally, the objectives of communication between school and home and home and school are that both agencies shall understand the pupil better. Reports from the school to parents have as their objective letting parents know how the pupil appears to school personnel in the school setting, so that the parents may be better able to

1. Accept, support, and strengthen the child as he meets the problems of growing up.

2. Understand and cooperate in the school's program for the child.

3. Adopt realistic and constructive educational and vocational goals for him.

In appraising any reporting system, we must ask how well it achieves these objectives.

The Traditional Report Card. The traditional school grading system and report card measure up rather poorly by these standards. A parent is not encouraged to understand, support, and feel closer to a child by a string of 75's and 80's or A's, B's, and C's. They are coldly and impersonally evaluative. They provide no interpretation of strengths and weaknesses, no relating of performance to potentiality, no encouragement to "accentuate the positive." For many children, the effect of the report of grades is to alienate parents from their child, rather than to enlist them in his support. Failure by parent standards, which are often quite unrealistic, is frequent. The popular humorist has long recognized the role of the report card as a destroyer of family morale, and though we cannot accept caricature as a picture of life, we must recognize the core of truth in this disruptive picture of the report card.

A report of numerical or letter grades may have some value in helping the parents to adopt realistic goals for each child. If marks are low, this may suggest that a limited objective be set, and vice versa. But as in the case of the pupil's own definition of his objectives, here also grades need interpretation. The typical parent has little notion of what significance a particular set of grades at a particular school level has for success at higher academic levels. Furthermore, the appraisal of achievement as seen by the teacher needs to be combined with other evidence from measures of scholastic aptitude and from standardized achievement tests if the most adequate appraisal is to be made of future academic prospects.

It must be admitted that the translation of marks and standardized test scores into a prognosis of later achievement is not easy to make, even by trained personnel with all the evidence available. But the untrained parent given only a school report card is in a much poorer position still to make a sound judgment. If the school is to help the parent plan realistically for the child, it must provide *interpretations* of his academic and vocational potential based on *all* the available evidence. These interpretations cannot well be conveyed by a report card.

We see, then, that the traditional report card serves rather unsatisfactorily the needs of the school to communicate with parents. It is a one-way message lacking the interpretation and the orientation toward constructive attitudes and constructive action that are needed in such a communication. But to be dissatisfied with marks and report cards does not guarantee an easy solution to the problem of communication with the home. Schools have tried many experiments in their search for an ideal medium of communication without finding any that is satisfactory from all points of view. We may consider briefly some of the variations that have been tried.

Modification of the Number and Meaning of Marks. The traditional report card, as we are using that term here, reports grades in subject areas (i.e., reading, arithmetic, history, etc.) either in percentage values or in the A, B, C, D, E letter system. Whichever system is used, some value is defined as a passing mark that constitutes the minimum acceptable from the school's point of view.

The simplest modification of this system, and one that has been tried in many schools, especially at the elementary-school level, is to make some change in the number and definition of the categories in which apraisals are reported. The change is typically a reduction to four, three, or even two categories. The simplest two-category system is usually just S = satisfactory and U = unsatisfactory. An extra category for superior achievement is often added, and sometimes a category indicating improvement. Many specific variations have been tried, but the common theme in all of them is a broader, rougher grading, and less detailed appraisal of specific level of accomplishment.

This type of modification may have value in a negative sort of way, in that it reduces the emphasis upon marks as indicators of status and relative achievement. Pressures on pupils tend to be reduced. But little of a constructive nature has been accomplished in improving communication from the school to the home. Parents are given less, rather than more, information about the child's activities in school and his accomplishments and progress.

Supplementing Grades with Ratings on Other Factors. Many report cards, even quite traditional ones, call for ratings of pupils on non-academic factors. Examination of report cards from a number of communities showed the number of qualities to be appraised to be as many as 16 or 18 in some cases, but the usual number was 4 to 6. The factors appearing in different reports were many and varied. Some of the traits appearing in one or more report forms are shown below:

Accepts changes	Considerate
Accepts group decision	Cooperative
Accepts responsibility	Courteous
Appearance	Dependable
Attentive	Effort
Care of materials	Finishes on time
Careful	Gets along well with others
Cleanliness	Health habits
Completes work	Independent work
Conduct	Initiative
	etc.

What are we to say about ratings such as these? Little can be added to our discussion of rating procedures in Chapter 13. The difficulties of ambiguity of meaning, subjectivity of standards, lack of opportunity to observe, and unreliability of judgment that typically harass ratings are at work just as much here. The variations in interpretation afflict not only the teachers who give the ratings but also the parents to whom they are transmitted. Furthermore, the teacher who is expected to remember her observations of and record ratings on thirty or more youngsters as part of her task of making out a set of report cards can hardly be blamed if she becomes rather perfunctory by the time she gets to Arthur Young or Susie Zabriskie. In summary, then, ratings on aspects of personality represent a very subjective and often perfunctory appraisal in terms of a set of ambiguous and ill-defined traits.

Check-List Forms. Some schools have tried to get more information into their report to parents by breaking down broad skill or content areas and vague personality traits into a large number of more limited and specific components. Thus, one report breaks up the broad area of language arts into the following ten facets:

1. Shows growing interest in reading materials.
2. Understands what he reads.
3. Reads well aloud.
4. Takes part in discussions intelligently.

5. Has methods of attacking new words.
6. Expresses himself in writing.
7. Writes legibly.
8. Learns the spelling of new and review words.
9. Uses correct spelling in written work.
10. Is learning to read independently.

In this particular report form, the teacher had the following four alternatives to check:

> Capable of doing better.
> Finds work difficult.
> Shows satisfactory progress.
> Shows high-quality work.

The development of a form such as this is ordinarily based on analysis by the school of its objectives at each level and the attempt to state them in concrete and specific terms. The form is designed to give the parents information both on what the school is trying to accomplish and what success it is encountering in the case of a particular child.

Report forms of this general type are potentially a good deal more informative than those of the traditional variety. However, they encounter several sorts of difficulties. A major one is complexity. As goals are broken down into more and more specific outcomes, the number of such outcomes increases rapidly. A report may well call for 40 or 50 separate judgments of each child. This tends to become burdensome for the teacher who must make them. It is both burdensome in clerical detail and exacting in the thoroughness of knowledge of the pupil that it calls for. It is also frequently confusing for the parent who receives the report. Particularly in the case of the less well-educated parent, the complexities of format and the volume of detail are likely to be overpowering.

When a report form is based on a detailed analysis of objectives and covers many specific points, the categories for evaluating each point are usually quite broad and simple. In the illustration we gave there were four categories of response, but the number is often less. However, phrasing these alternatives so that they present clear and significant evaluations of a child is a problem. This is true especially when the attempt is made to take account of individual aptitude and to appraise the pupil in terms of his potential achievement. How, for example, do we use the category "capable of doing better" in the set of four categories in our illustration? Do we use it for the slow-learner who is not keeping up with the group? For the above-average youngster who is only doing average work? Or for the very able child who is doing better than most of the group but not as well as we believe he could? Any mechanical evaluation system that tries to take account of both accomplishment and potentiality runs into some such difficulties.

All in all, an analytic check-list type of report form appears a commendable move toward providing the parent detailed information about the child. If it can be interpreted to parents so that they will not feel confused and frustrated and if the burden for the teacher can be distributed, it can represent a partial solution. In the development of such a form, it is important to keep in mind not only the types of appraisals it would be nice to have about each pupil but also the types of observations that a teacher can be expected to make. There is little point in burdening the form with evaluations for which the teacher will have no adequate evidence.

Teacher-Parent Conference. From many points of view, the ideal way of maintaining communication between the school and the home is to have periodic conferences between parent and teacher, home-room teacher, counselor, or other school representative. Such conferences may, of course, supplement other more formal communications. On the other hand, the school may elect to rely entirely upon this channel. The advantages are several:

1. *Communication is flexible.* It can be adapted to the needs of the particular case. The teacher may emphasize whatever particular point she wishes to get over for this particular pupil.

2. *Interpretation is possible.* The report can indicate not merely isolated facts but interrelationships and evaluations of these facts. Long-range plans can be considered in the light of evidence available to date.

3. *The communication is a two-way affair.* The school cannot only inform parents but learn from them. It is possible to bring together the two views of the child and see how each illuminates the other. Home facts can throw light on school facts, and vice versa.

4. *Misunderstandings can be cleared up.* If the parent appears not to understand the school's message, it can be clarified by further discussion.

The difficulties in relying on conferences as the chief or only method of communicating with the home are chiefly practical ones. They are factors of time and skill of teachers and cooperation by parents.

1. *Time.* If a program of parent-teacher conferences is to function really effectively, the teacher must have time for several unhurried conferences with parents of each child during the course of the year.

Some planning for the conference is desirable so that the teacher may have in mind the points to be discussed. Furthermore, notes on the conference would be a useful item to have in the permanent record folder for the child. A record of points discussed, information obtained from the parent, or impressions of the parent and home should be available for reference. This means that an allowance of 2 or 3 hours of teacher time per pupil per year is not excessive for this function. Some special provision to release teacher time may need to be made if time is to be available for this purpose.

2. *Skill.* Carrying out effective conferences with parents calls for special skills on the part of the teacher. A parent conference is essentially a counseling situation. It involves skills in establishing rapport, empathy—a sensitivity to the other individual's feelings and point of view—and ability to adapt a communication to the particular audience. These skills can be improved somewhat with practice and training, but large individual differences in skill will remain. The effectiveness of a conference system depends on the personal security, sensitivity, and understanding of the teachers who will hold the conferences with parents.

3. *Parent cooperation.* Some parents are eager to come to school and meet with their child's teacher or guidance counselor. Others are very hard to reach. The reasons are varied: both parents working, inconvenience in leaving the family, lack of interest, or hostility toward the school, but the net result is that there will be parents who do not come. This problem has been reported to become more serious as time goes by. Cooperation for a first interview is relatively good. But as the novelty wears off and the parent gets no dramatic information from the interview, interest tends to wane. Fewer parents come back for second and third conferences. Since those who fail to come are often the ones with whom the school particularly needs to communicate, it seems unlikely that interviews can serve as the only, or perhaps even as the basic, medium of communication for most schools. If a school has a very active and devoted parent group, this procedure may work successfully, but in other schools conferences would appear to serve best as an important supplement to some other communication medium.

Informal Teacher-to-Parent Letters. An informal letter has sometimes been used to replace or supplement the conference with the parent. The letter is probably less time-consuming, and the parents of each child can be reached more surely.

Some of the same flexibility that seemed so desirable in the interview is still present in the letter. But many of the advantages of a face-to-face conference are lost. There is no opportunity for interchange of ideas or clarification of misunderstandings. Negative or critical notes seem more absolute and threatening when they are committed to paper. Furthermore, writing good letters to parents is an art at which some teachers have limited skill. Phrasing a letter that will convey the desired tone and message and elicit understanding and cooperation is not easy. The task can also become quite burdensome.

The burden of letter writing can be eased somewhat if it is spread out in time. And for any reporting system we may well ask why all the reports need to go out on the same date. There seems to be no good reason other than tradition and administrative convenience. Spreading reporting over a period of several weeks will serve to break some of the traditional report card attitudes and will also ease the burden on the teacher.

Both conferences and letters seem more feasible in the elementary school, where the classroom teacher works with a single group of 25 or 30 pupils through the major part of the day, than in the departmentalized program of high school or college. At these levels, a single teacher may deal with 150 or 200 different pupils. The numbers to be evaluated and the limited contact with each pupil limit sharply the amount of information that a teacher can be expected to provide. A simple appraisal of subject-matter achievement as shown through recitations, exercises and tests may be all that the teacher can be expected to provide.

Summarizing, as we review the possibilities for communicating with parents the most desirable way of doing this appears to be by face-to-face conference. Because of practical difficulties in scheduling such conferences and getting parents to attend, some supplementary form of communication will usually be needed. Provided teachers can be given help in developing skills to prepare them and time to do the work, the best type of supplement is probably a personal letter from teacher to parent. If this is not practical, some type of check list will permit a certain amount of fullness and flexibility of report. The most sterile form of report, as far as helping the parent to help the child, is probably the traditional form of report card. However, in secondary or higher education if no one person knows the student well enough to organize a more integrated and understanding report of his progress, we may have to be content with traditional report forms. No revising of forms will substitute for intimate acquaintance with the pupil.

Colleges maintain records (in part, at least) for the benefit of graduate and professional schools; high schools for the benefit of colleges; and, presumably, elementary schools for the benefit of high schools and kindergartens for the benefit of elementary schools. It is entirely reasonable that an institution at a higher level expects the schools from which it recruits its students to provide it with appraisals of candidates for admission. It is reasonable that the higher schools expect the lower ones to provide as valid indicators of probable success in the later school as they can.

Since the criterion of success at the higher level is based in considerable measure upon ability to master the more abstract and demanding studies at that level, a good deal of emphasis can legitimately be placed on aptitude for studying abstract subject matter. The questions we face center largely around the most useful information and the best way in which to convey it.

Information likely to be useful is information about scholastic aptitude and scholastic achievement. For information about aptitude, there is little competition with standardized tests of scholastic aptitude. Subjective teacher judgments, based on a limited sample of cases, are an inferior substitute for objective performance expressed in a uniform way by reference to a common table of norms.

In the area of achievement, a case can be made both for informal teacher appraisals and for standardized tests. Teacher appraisals are more flexible and adaptable to a wide range of activities: to skills of oral participation, laboratory and workshop activities, and skills of composition and expression, to mention only a few. However, here also the objectivity and uniformity of standardized tests in the basic skill and content areas are strong arguments for their use at least to supplement the teacher's own appraisals. Standardized tests of reading skills, arithmetical and mathematical skills, and knowledge of science and social studies have been found to predict success [2] in later education with accuracy that compares favorably with teachers' grades.

It is hard to know how much detail with respect to academic achievement a higher educational institution can usefully use. Most studies of grades as predictors deal with an over-all measure of academic success as a predictor. Some types of specialized schools probably tend to weight certain areas more heavily than others because those areas are more closely related to their curricula, e.g., mathematics and science by engineering schools, history and English by law schools.   For these special purposes, a report of success in particular subjects appears to have some meaning.   But in most in·· stances, what is needed is a summary appraisal of total performance, i.e., percentile rank in class or some similar statistic.

It is possible for colleges to get along very happily with no report of formal grades from secondary schools and with no prescription of specific content for the secondary-school program.   This was demonstrated in the special Eight-Year Study carried out under the auspices of the Progressive Education Association.[1]   In this study thirty secondary schools were exempted for the period of the experiment from all formal course and credit requirements, and a group of colleges agreed to accept graduates from these schools on the basis of the principal's recommendation alone.   Follow-up studies in college indicated that the graduates did as well, on the average, as students of comparable ability from other schools.   The school's recommendation represented an adequate basis for admission.

The schools in the Eight-Year Study were well-staffed and well-supported schools.   They carried out extensive programs of standardized testing.   In addition, a number of special appraisal devices were developed for and used in the study.   Cumulative records were unusually complete.   Evaluation within this freer setting needed to be more, rather than less, thorough than usual.   But given this careful and continuing evaluation by a competent staff, the judgment of the school staff, rendered by the principal constituted a satisfactory basis for indicating to the colleges which pupils could be expected to succeed with college work.

In conclusion, then, in order to select students for admission, higher-level schools need the information that schools at the lower levels can supply about the pupil.   However, class grades are only one form for such information.   Standardized test scores have certain advantages over grades, and a comprehensive appraisal by the lower school is another possible substitute.   Grades have value chiefly in those cases in which adequate objective appraisals are not available and serve as a reasonably satisfactory substitute for such appraisals.   Their accrediting function increases in importance as we go up the educational ladder.

SCHOOL APPRAISALS FOR THE BENEFIT OF EMPLOYERS

As a service both to the student and to society, the schools must stand ready to provide information about students to potential employers.   The information that an employer believes he needs will vary from case to case.   Often the employing or placing agency will have its own recommendation form. The school administration or a particular staff member will fill this out as accurately and completely as available information permits. School records that permit an adequate and objective reply to such inquiries are to be desired. However, detailed information on specific phases of academic achievement is not likely to be required in many cases. A summary appraisal of level of performance will usually suffice.

The employer will often want information about non-academic aspects of the student. This is where the school is hardest pressed to provide useful answers. Perhaps the most important resource is good factual information about out-of-class activities: club memberships, offices held, and other evidences of participation or responsibility. If anecdotal records have been maintained, some judicious use of these may supplement the record of activities. Beyond this, for non-academic appraisals one is largely thrown back on ratings by teachers and staff members who may still remember the student. These possess the usual limitations that plague rating procedures, with the additional factor of forgetting thrown in. Retrospective ratings of a student who sat in the back row 5 years ago are not likely to be models of precision.

SCHOOL APPRAISALS FOR THE SCHOOL'S OWN USE

To a considerable extent, a school's appraisals of its pupils are to help the school itself to do a better job of teaching and guiding the pupils. To understand Johnny, who is now in the sixth grade, it is useful to know what Johnny was like in the fifth grade, the fourth grade, and on back to the school's first contact with him. Whether Johnny as a sixth grader is presenting serious problems or is getting along very well, the present situation can be better understood if its roots in the past are known.

Here again, a variety of appraisals are possible. For broad skill and content areas, use can be made of standardized tests. For classroom work as seen by the teacher, a written comment and evaluation may become part of the cumulative record. Or a letter or number grade may be recorded. The class grade is a clerically convenient way of summarizing the judgment of the pupil's work. What it gains in compactness, convenience, and ease of manipulation it loses in vitality and descriptive detail. However, practical administrative routines may require this convenient, compact single-letter or single-number summary appraisal.

As a matter of realistic fact, in secondary or higher education, the instructor may not know the student well enough to give more than the most general appraisal. Classes may be large, contact with students slight, and evidences of student accomplishment limited to performance on tests, exercises, and papers. When the instructor knows the pupil only through limited samples of academic work, it is unrealistic to expect anything more than a summary global rating of achievement. In this case, a report in one of a few broad categories is probably as much as we can realistically hope to get. The use of letter grades is then a frank acknowledgment of our limited bases for appraisal of the student.

If the school's records are to be most helpful to the school in dealing with the pupil, they will be (1) continuous and cumulative, (2) descriptive and diagnostic, (3) comprehensive, and (4) organized. In such a program, grades for subject-matter achievement will have at most a small place.

TECHNICAL ASPECTS OF GRADING AND MARKING PROCEDURES

In the previous section we have expressed a number of reservations about the suitability of traditional grading and reporting practices for the purposes for which they are used. However, in many schools and for some time to come practical administrative considerations may dictate that grades be given and reported. If this is to be done, it should be done in as competent and workmanlike a manner as possible. The present section will be devoted, therefore, to improving the workmanship in assigning grades if the basic decision to give them has been made. We shall give some consideration to (1) the factors to be included in arriving at a mark, (2) the types of evidence to be considered, (3) the weighting of components of evidence, and (4) the final distribution of grades.

FACTORS TO BE INCLUDED IN A COURSE GRADE

When a course grade consists of a single number or letter, what factors should be taken into account in arriving at the final evaluation? In particular, should the grade reported be specifically restricted to the level the student has reached in the outcomes that the instructor hopes to achieve in the course? Or should consideration also be given to the student's potentialities, to attitude and effort, to amount of improvement, to writing and speaking skills?

The answer to this question can only be given in the light of a decision as to the functions which the grade is to serve. It is our conviction that a grade functions most adequately

1. To help guide the student and his parents with respect to future educational plans.

2. To help a school decide upon a pupil's readiness to enter certain selective programs or courses, e.g., a college preparatory program or a special mathematics or science course.

3. To help higher educational levels to appraise an applicant's acceptability for the program they present.

4. To help a potential employer to decide upon the suitability of the student for certain jobs that depend upon academic skills.

These purposes would appear to be served best by a grade that is as pure and uncontaminated a measure of competence in the field as can be obtained.

A grade that is a pure measure of competence has a unity of meaning that makes it interpretable and usable. The grade in algebra expresses competence in algebra. The algebra teacher may know other equally important things about the pupil: that he is highly intelligent, that he is disinclined to work on class assignments, that his written work is barely legible, and that he speaks and writes ungrammatically. It may be desirable that these impressions also be a matter of record. But they should not be concealed within the algebra grade. A grade that is based in unknown proportions upon competence, effort, attitude, and collateral skills is an uninterpretable and unusable hodgepodge. A grade is not a tool of discipline to be used as a reward or punishment, but a record of achievement. If a single grade is to be reported, it should represent a single thing, the best available estimate of competence in the field of instruction.

What is meant by competence in the field is something each teacher or group of teachers must determine. We saw in Chapter 3 that the first step in preparing a test in any field is that of defining the objectives of instruction and translating those objectives into behaviors that can be tested. In the same way, the first step in deciding what should be represented in a course grade is to define the several objectives of the course and decide upon the relative emphasis to be given to each. What weight is to be given to acquisition of information? To understanding of concepts and generalizations? To ability to apply information in solving problems? To ability to organize and express ideas? To laboratory or manipulative skills? Though in any course the grade should constitute an appraisal of competence, the specific elements going to make up competence must be identified for each course.

TYPES OF EVIDENCE AND THE WEIGHTING OF EACH

Once the instructor has defined his objectives and decided upon the weighting he wishes to give to each in his over-all evaluation of competence, he must determine what evidence he wishes to gather to represent each objective and how the different types of evidence are to be weighted in his composite appraisal. He must allocate weights as between a comprehensive terminal examination; exercises, quizzes, and partial examinations throughout the course; papers and reports prepared out of class by the student; participation in classroom discussion and other classroom activities; and performance observed or tested in laboratory or workshop activities.

Terminal Examination. Those who would give major weight to a final examination at the conclusion of a course argue that the significant appraisal of the individual's competence in a segment of instruction is what he can do at the end of that instruction or, even better, after some lapse of time. When and how the individual achieved his competence is deemed of no importance. Learnings are considered of no value unless they persist at least to the end of the course. Terminal ability is deemed the important ability.

The University of Chicago has carried this viewpoint through to its logical conclusion and certifies achievement in the major areas covered in the first two years of college entirely by comprehensive terminal examinations. Comprehensive certifying examinations also play a central role in evaluation of students in many programs of graduate training. State-wide testing programs, such as the *New York State Regents Examinations,* are based on this same point of view that final level of ability is the crucial appraisal.

As far as evaluation of the pupil is concerned, it seems hard to object to the point of view that final *competence* is the important competence. However, we will find less disposition to accept a terminal comprehensive *examination* as the only, or perhaps even the primary, basis for determining a final grade. Objections are on several grounds.

1. It is impossible to appraise certain types of competence within the limits of a scheduled examination. Ability to find and organize materials in relation to a problem, ability to demonstrate certain skills —whether of using a microscope or of baking a cake—and ability to participate effectively in a group discussion or group project are examples of outcomes not adapted to appraisal in a scheduled examination.

2. The sample of behavior that can be obtained in an examination

of a practical length is limited, and the reliability of the appraisal will be correspondingly restricted. Including evidence available from other sources may permit a more reliable appraisal. This will be true if the additional evidence is of as high quality as that provided by the examination. However, both quantity and quality of evidence must be borne in mind if reliability of appraisal is to be a maximum.

3. A sample so limited in time may do injustice to certain individuals. Certain examinees may be ill, tired, under pressure from outside circumstances, or below par for other reasons at the time of the examination. Their performance at a particular day and hour may fail to represent their usual level of performance. These cases are likely to be infrequent, but a concern lest we do injustice to even an occasional pupil makes us hesitate to place exclusive emphasis upon appraisal at a single point in time.

4. Performance under examination pressure may fail to represent the individual's competence under more relaxed and normal life conditions. An examination is inevitably a somewhat stressful situation. The stress is heightened in the case of a single major examination, the outcome of which has important effects upon the individual's future. People differ in the extent to which they are disturbed by such stress. Though a case can be made for basing an appraisal in part on ability to perform under pressure, it is hard to justify basing it *completely* on performance under stress conditions.

5. The crucial terminal examination may have an unwholesome effect upon teaching and learning activities during the year. At best, the correspondence between what it is possible to test in an examination and the objectives of instruction is imperfect. As we indicated above, some objectives do not lend themselves to testing. When the examination is one set by an outside agency, the correspondence may be even poorer. The competences that seem important as judged by the tasks set by the examining agency may not correspond at all closely to the objectives that seem real and significant to the teaching group. This is particularly likely to be true when the representatives of a higher, more selective, and more academically oriented level control the terminal examinations for a lower level of the educational structure.

Such control of examinations from above is more common in foreign countries than it is in the United States. In India, for example, the universities, which enroll an extremely small fraction of the population, have controlled the examinations that represent the final hurdle for graduation from the secondary school and have made them in their own academic image. The nature of these terminal examinations has determined the character of year-end examinations through the secondary school, and these in turn have set the pattern for year-end testing in the elementary grades. Thus, the pattern of evaluation and to a considerable extent the program of instruction for the large group of elementary-school pupils, most of whom will never come near a university, has been controlled by an examining system structured in the last analysis to pick individuals who will pursue academic work at the university level. Entirely apart from the technical quality of the examining, which is reported to have been none too good, the direction of its orientation almost guarantees that it will cramp and pervert the education provided in the elementary and secondary schools upon which its influence is felt.

Any program of terminal examinations will have an influence upon the instruction that the examinations are set up to evaluate. This influence may be positive and constructive if the examinations are based upon a more enlightened and forward-looking analysis of educational objectives than is characteristic of the single schools to which the appraisal is applied. However, it is more common for the schools to view the terminal examination imposed by an outside agency as a restrictive and limiting influence that prevents them from working toward the most significant educational objectives.

Quizzes and Examinations During the Course. Quizzes and examinations during the course can give additional evidence on the achieving of the same sort of objectives that can be appraised on a final examination. The en-route examinations have the advantage that they can be used for instructional as well as evaluation purposes. One's errors on an in-course examination can serve as a diagnostic guide for restudy of course materials. Furthermore, many short tests are certainly less traumatic than a single terminal one. However, tests on a particular unit shortly after it has been taught measure immediate mastery. They cannot appraise lasting retention and are not well adapted to evaluating mastery of large concepts or integration of parts into the total framework of the field. These limitations would suggest that in-course examinations of the paper-and-pencil variety should carry less weight in arriving at a final grade than the terminal examination appraising mastery at the end of the course and should be thought of in considerable measure as instructional tools.

Papers and Reports. The report, essay, or literary product prepared by the student "on his own" out of class provides material for appraising a number of objectives that can be evaluated only poorly, if at all, in a scheduled examination. The individual may be called on to gather and organize evidence. He has an opportunity to dig relatively deeply into a topic. He has time to express his thoughts in the most polished form of which he is capable. The area of inquiry or topic for creative effort may be freely adapted to individual interest.

At certain levels and in certain fields, appraisal of these skills of finding facts, selecting evidence, organizing a thorough and logical presentation, and expressing ideas in clear and literate fashion may be deemed very important. Then the evaluation of appropriate types of independent reports should receive a substantial weight in a final grade.

A sense of the importance of such appraisals should not blind us to the difficulty of making them reliably. The difficulties are those that plague the grading of essay examinations but are compounded by the fact that the topic or task is now usually different for each individual. Reliability in appraising individual compositions, papers, and reports is typically rather low. There is the further problem of knowing how completely work done out of class represents the competence of the individual student, as distinct from family, friends, or academic predecessors.

Participation in Group Activities. One type of student behavior that a teacher should report on in any complete and analytical description of a student is the nature and extent of his participation in the activities of the class. How well does he work with others in small group projects and enterprises? How active a role does he take in class projects or discussions? Is he a leader or a follower? Active or passive? How astute are his comments? How deep is his apparent understanding of what has been discussed? A descriptive report of a student could well pay attention to such matters.

Whether such evidence should have any appreciable role in a course grade seems more debatable. Nature and extent of class participation is perhaps more a matter of temperament and attitude than of competence. And those skills that are represented are perhaps better evaluated for their own sake than incorporated in an over-all mark. To evaluate an individual's knowledge and understanding by listening to what he has to say in a discussion is not easy. Unless skills of working in a group represent one of the specific objectives of instruction, it seems doubtful that evaluation of oral contributions in class or group should enter into a class grade. They will probably only have the effect of watering down our measure of competence.

Laboratory and Workshop Activities. In many areas of school work, competence is represented at least in part by what the individual can *do* with concrete objects or materials of one sort or another. Can the student saw a board straight? Make a buttonhole? Cook an edible cake? Machine a part to specified tolerances? Set up a microscope and prepare materials for observation with it?   Such skills as these must usually be tested in the laboratory or workshop setting.   In certain fields, this type of evaluation may appropriately receive substantial weight in a total grade.

Evaluation of performance skills by unaided subjective judgment is likely to be quite unreliable.   There are two approaches that can sometimes be used to improve the accuracy of appraisal of such skills.

1. A standard task may be set up, a scale of examples of different levels of goodness be prepared, and individual performance be judged by comparison with the set of standard samples.   This type of product scale was discussed briefly in Chapter 11.

2. A detailed check list or score card may be prepared to cover the performance or product.   The check list can then be used to evaluate an individual's performance as it occurs.   Thus, we can check step by step as he sets up work on a lathe to see that each operation is done correctly and in proper sequence.   A scoring schedule can apply penalties for errors and omissions.   Or a score card can be applied to the product.   Thus, in evaluating a cake baked by a student, point allocations and scoring standards could be set up for texture, flavor, consistency of frosting, and appearance.   Analytical scoring schemes and uniform reference standards will help to improve reliability of judgments that are at best rather subjective.

THE MECHANICS OF WEIGHTING PARTS IN A TOTAL

Let us assume that we have decided upon the weight we wish to allocate to each of several evidences of pupil competence.   For example, suppose we decide that we wish to assign one fourth of the total weight to laboratory work, one fourth to a series of short quizzes, and one half to the sum of points earned on a midterm and final examination.   Our problem is to combine these three scores in such a way that this weighting is in fact achieved.

Achieving the desired weighting becomes a problem because the separate components may differ widely in variability.   Suppose, in the illustration we have given, the three components had the following statistical characteristics.

	Range of Scores	Standard Deviation
Laboratory work	63 to 86	4.2
Quizzes	32 to 147	21.0
Exams	48 to 105	10.5

Suppose we now combine these three scores with weights of 1, 1, and 2.   What will happen?

Let us concentrate for the moment on the laboratory work and quizzes. Suppose that the man who is best in one is worst in the other, and vice versa. If we combine them with equal weight, we find that the sum for the man who is at the top in quizzes and at the bottom in laboratory work is $63 + 147 = 210$, whereas the sum for the man at the top in laboratory work and the bottom in quizzes is $86 + 32 = 118$. There is a gross difference. This is due to the much greater variability of quiz scores, a variability that is in this instance 5 times as great as that for lab work. The more variable quiz grades have swamped out the less variable lab grades and affect the final composite 5 times as much.

The point we are making is that the *effective* weight of a component in the total depends not only on its *nominal* weight but also upon its *variability*. If the variability is great, the weight applied to a raw score must be reduced if the component is to have the desired effective weight in the composite. In the example we have given, in order for the effective weights to stand in the ratio 1–1–2, the weights applied to raw scores would have to stand in the ratio 1–⅕–⅘. Thus, if we multiplied the quiz grades by ⅕, the two cases we considered above would have totals of $63 + \frac{1}{5}(147) = 92.2$ and $86 + \frac{1}{5}(32) = 92.4$ and would turn out approximately equal.

In determining the relative weights to be applied to the raw scores on any component of a score composite, the desired effective weights must be divided by a measure (or some rough estimate) of the variability of each of the components. For this purpose, even the range of scores can be used as an approximate estimate. However, the semi-interquartile range or standard deviation is a better estimate. In our illustration, the desired effective weights were 1, 1, and 2, and the standard deviations were 4.2, 21.0, and 10.5. Dividing, we get $1/4.2 = 0.24$; $1/21.0 = 0.048$; $2/10.5 = 0.192$. Thus, the appropriate *raw score* weights stand in the ratio 1–⅕–⅘ or 5–1–4. This is in sharp contrast with the *effective* weights of 1–1–2. The contrast shows that one can go badly astray if one takes scores at their face value and weights them without any regard to their variability.

THE ASSIGNMENT OF GRADES

Suppose we have now scored all the tests, exercises, papers, products, observations, and other behaviors that seem significant to us as evidences of competence in a field. We have put the separate scores together into a single composite score, weighting the separate types of evidence in the way that seems most appropriate to us. We have one score for each individual, constituting our best judgment of that individual's competence. The scores rank the individuals in the group from most to least competent, according to our definition of competence. Now, how shall we arrive at a grade for each student? How many shall get A, how many B, and so on?

Underlying Considerations.   Before we can attack this question, there are two fundamental facts of life that we must face.

1. The composite score representing our pooled appraisal of competence is a *relative* appraisal only, not an absolute one. It permits a comparison of one individual with another and a judgment of more or less. It does *not* permit a judgment of absolute amount or of level of excellence by an absolute standard. The score shows relative performance only in the group for which common evidence is available. By intuitive judgment or by collateral evidence, we may have some impression of how this group compares with other groups. Inevitably, such judgment entered into the tasks we set for the group or the standards by which we appraised performance. But this reference to other groups or broader standards is fuzzy and undependable at best.

2. The meaning we give to numbers, letters, words, or other symbols as standards of excellence is a matter of *completely arbitrary convention.*   It is utterly futile to argue whether 10 per cent or 25 per cent of a student group *should* receive A's, as if there were some eternal verity that determined this. Each teaching group must *define* what the symbols they use are to mean. Furthermore, in view of the relativity of our appraisals, in the last analysis the only definition that can be defended is a definition expressed as *a range of percentiles in a defined group.*   Thus, A might be defined as "the top 10 per cent of a representative group of freshmen at W college," or as "the top 25 per cent of the group of M.A. candidates." There are no right or wrong definitions; there are only more and less socially useful and expedient definitions.

In measurement textbooks in the past, there has been a good deal of talk about the normal curve and "grading by the curve." Much of this has been nonsense. What we have is a rank order of pupils and a rank order of evaluation categories. Where in the first rank order we set the dividing lines of the second rank order is a completely arbitrary decision and should be based on considerations of practical utility. Suppose that E signifies "Unsatisfactory. Does not receive credit. May take re-examination, with possibility of raising to D." The decision as to what per cent of a representative group in a particular institution should be given E is not a statistical decision. It is a practical administrative decision. To make the decision realistically one would have to answer the question: Considering the type of students whom we receive, the social functions which our institution serves, and the implications for the individual that attach to the grade E as we use it, to what per cent of students does it seem appropriate that this grade be given? The answer rests primarily upon the social and educational philosophy of the institution or of a segment of it.

To assign grades rationally and consistently, we must

1. Explicitly recognize the arbitrary social judgment that is implied in defining grading categories and make that judgment for our school and college on the basis of full understanding and rational analysis of the implications of our decision.

2. Establish general adherence to the definition among the individual faculty members of the institution.

3. Devise techniques to assist the instructor in adapting and applying the definition to each specific class.

Making the Meaning of Grades Explicit. Currently in most institutions the definition of grading categories is either in terms of verbally described levels of performance (e.g., A, superior; B, good; C, satisfactory; etc.) or in terms of a completely inappropriate assumption of absolutism in which 100 per cent is perfect, 75 is three-fourths of perfect and is just acceptable, and so forth. The interpretation of grades in terms of relative performance is ill defined and highly individual from instructor to instructor. But the relative meaning is basically there. It sneaks in as raised marks on tests, as make-up tests when the original one was too hard, as standards of grading written work, and in other guises. This relative standard should be brought out into the light, closely and critically examined, and made clear and explicit for all. That is, some agreement should be reached as to what a grading symbol does mean in terms of standing in relation to a standard reference group. A consensus must be sought within the institution that an A, for example, or a grade of 90 or above signifies being in the top 10 per cent of typical general introductory courses and the top 15 per cent of advanced courses. If there are legitimate reasons for different standards in different fields or special courses, these should be made explicit. Thus, the social good might be served by having different standards for a freshman course in physics and one in public speaking. Making the general meanings and the exceptions to them explicit is the first step in achieving uniformity of meaning.

Achieving Uniformity among Instructors.   Even when an explicit definition is achieved, instructors will still show marked variations in their application of the definition to their own class groups.   Though an agreement may have been reached to define A as "top 10 per cent of a typical freshman group," some instructors of freshmen will continue consistently to give 5 per cent of A's and others to give 25 per cent.   These remaining differences can be attacked by a continuous program of education and publicity.   Grade distributions may be prepared by each instructor and reviewed within the department.   The distributions for different departments within the institution may be assembled and reported to the faculty.   The discrepancies of individual instructors may be pointed out to them and may receive administrative review in extreme cases.   Even when this is done, however, there are likely to be a few intransigent non-conformists who will refuse to accept the institution's definition of grading symbols.   One suspects that in certain cases grading tendencies reflect rather deep-seated personality trends that are not easily overcome.

Adjusting for the Nature of the Particular Class Group.   Suppose the arbitrary and relative nature of the grading system has been recognized and a serious attempt is made to set up a system defined in terms of fractions of the total group and to use this system in a consistent and rational manner.   Then the most troublesome technical problem is to take appropriate account of the nature of a class group and of its deviation from the general reference group or groups used to define the grading categories.   When individual class groups are small or when groups are formed taking account of ability, one cannot expect each group to represent the average defining group of "typical freshmen" or the like.   Some procedure is needed to adjust for the specific nature of the group.   Several suggestions will be offered.

1. When there are several types of reference groups—e.g., underclassmen, upperclassmen, and graduate students or major students and non-major students—it may be desirable to have different definitions of the grading symbols apply to each and to make this clear.   Thus, it might be decided that an underclass population of grades should include 10 per cent A's, an upperclass group 20 per cent, and a graduate group 25 per cent.   The proportion to be expected in a mixed group would be a weighted average of the separate group percentages.   The rationale for such a differentiation would be the presumed selection of abler students at the higher levels.   Here again,

however, whether it is desirable to redefine the meaning of the symbols at successive levels is a matter of judgment to be arrived at in terms of the purposes that the symbols are to serve.

2. It will probably be desirable to let the defining population for a subject area be the total population of pupils who take work in the area. That is, chemistry grades should be assigned in terms of the general population of students taking chemistry and industrial arts grades in terms of the total group taking industrial arts. An attempt to make allowance for differences in ability between the two student populations does not seem socially desirable. It is probably more useful, and certainly more convenient, to define chemistry student S in terms of a population of chemistry students than of a population of students in general. This means that the proportion of pupils assigned a particular grade should generally remain essentially the same from subject area to subject area.

3. For large general courses handled as a single group—possibly groups of 50 or more—it will be most acceptable to use the total class group as the defining population. That is, the specified proportions in the different grading categories should be maintained fairly rigidly for the group. This will introduce less error and distortion than an attempt to make necessarily subjective allowances and corrections for differences between different groups.

4. When pupils in what is essentially a single course with common objectives and materials of instruction are broken up into separate sections for teaching, a nucleus of common testing can provide the anchor and basis for determining the number of pupils receiving each grade for each section. The common nucleus is most likely to be a common final examination, but it might include appraisals at other times, and it might conceivably be a standardized test. This common core of measurement would not control the mark received by any single student, but would control the numbers receiving each grade in each section of the course.

The way grades are adjusted by this procedure may be illustrated by a specific example. Let us assume as given:

1. A general definition of the grading symbols as follows:

$$A = \text{top 15 per cent}$$
$$B = \text{next 25 per cent}$$
$$C = \text{next 40 per cent}$$
$$D = \text{next 15 per cent}$$
$$E = \text{bottom 5 per cent}$$

2. Two class groups, receiving scores on a common final examination as follows:

Score	Section 1	Section 2	Total
120 or over	10	2	12
100–119	11	9	20
75–99	14	18	32
45–74	4	8	12
Under 45	1	3	4
Total	40	40	80

(The numerical values have been grouped and arranged to simplify computation for this numerical example.)

We see that we have 80 individuals in all. Fifteen per cent of 80 is 12, the number of A's. The data in the illustration are already grouped so that this represents the top score category. Thus, Section 1 would receive 10 A's, whereas Section 2 would receive only 2. The other groupings are also already set up to correspond to B, C, D, and E by our definition. The particular students to receive A's in either section would be selected on the basis of the total record of evaluation the instructor was using, only the number being controlled by the common examination.

A procedure much like this has been used in the elementary schools of Sweden on a nation-wide scale. Uniform achievement tests in the basic skill subjects, prepared in the Ministry of Education, are administered throughout the schools of the country. These are scored and analyzed centrally, and instructions are sent out to the separate schools telling the local authorities how many of each grade they are to give. Thus, uniform grading standards are maintained throughout the country, and one has some assurance that a certain grade in one community signifies the same level of achievement as that same grade in another community.

If a procedure such as we have described is used, it is most important that the common test tap equally the objectives and materials stressed in the different sections. The instrument should pool the ideas of all instructors and be acceptable to each. Even when this is accomplished, it may be desirable to temper somewhat the differences between groups, remembering that the common test is only a part of the total appraisal and will not correlate perfectly with it. That is, in our illustrative example, we might rule that Section 1 could have 8 to 10 grades of A; Section 2 could have 2 to 4; and so forth. Final decisions could be based on the total appraisal of individual students within each group.

5. When only a small group takes a particular course, it is probably unsafe to allocate grades mechanically, following the percentages specified for a group at that level. One way of anchoring such small groups to a common standard is to use some common evaluation instrument with groups in successive semesters and compare each new group with the accumulated evidence on groups that have gone before. The number of A's, B's, etc., may be adjusted to take account of the level of performance on the common test, a class that does exceptionally well being given an increased number of high grades and vice versa. This procedure encounters two difficulties: (1) some pupils in later groups may get advance information about the anchor test and (2) the anchor test may become inappropriate for later groups. If these difficulties can be overcome, the procedure is a promising one.

Where anchoring groups to earlier populations by a common measure seems impractical, as it would for any course in which an objective test is not an appropriate basis for evaluation, one is thrown back upon the judgment of the teacher. There is probably a kernel of accuracy in the instructor's impression that a particular class group is better than or worse than groups taught in a course in previous years, though the judgment may be as responsive to the instructor's sciatica as to the class's stupidity. So some tempering of the usual numbers at each grade level may be appropriate in such a case. However, watch must be kept to make sure that such tempering does not become habitual with the instructor in question.

A grading system in an educational institution is a deeply ingrained part of the educational culture pattern. It is usually accepted automatically and with no more critical thought than our habits of holding a knife and fork. The new teacher is not systematically instructed in grading procedures but grows into them as a child grows into the regional pronunciation of "water." It seems unfortunate that our educational evaluations should be treated in such a casual fashion. It would pay the staff of any school to go through for themselves the type of analysis that is represented in the previous paragraphs and to make explicit for each teacher definite guides as to the *statistical* meaning of different grades and the procedures for arriving at them.

SUMMARY STATEMENT

We have now completed our scrutiny of marking and reporting procedures. Clearly, a number of different issues are involved, and no simple solution appears to be at hand for any of them. This is because there are so many different purposes that the school's evaluations of the individual are designed to serve. Functions of motivation, guidance, and certification are all significant functions, but they tend to conflict with one another. The problems of marking and reporting take on quite different character at different educational levels as different purposes come to the fore and different conditions prevail.

In the elementary school, school evaluations serve primarily (1) to help motivate and guide the pupil's learnings, (2) to inform parents, so that they can work closely with the school for the child's good, and (3) to provide, for the school records, background material for understanding the child's later development. The first of these functions appears best served by the school activities themselves, together with the immediate appraisal which teacher and pupil make of them. For the second we would prefer informal and descriptive reporting to the parent, preferably in face-to-face conference. For the third, descriptive teacher appraisals can advantageously be supplemented by standardized test results. In the elementary school, the classroom teacher's contacts with his group are sufficiently extensive so that it is reasonable to expect appraisals that go beyond competence in subject matter. We believe that a formal system of numerical or letter grades makes relatively little contribution to the educational process in the elementary school.

In secondary education, other purposes take the spotlight in the school's evaluations of its pupils. Evaluations function as (1) a major element in defining future educational and vocational goals for each student and (2) evidence to be used by colleges and employers in admitting students to the goals they have chosen. At the same time with departmentalized instruction teacher-pupil contacts become less intimate. Appraisals of the pupil as a person become more difficult and less satisfactory. In this setting, the typical school may find it best to fall back on the traditional system of letter grades as a basis for appraising competence in academic skills that are important for educational progress and vocational guidance. However, cumulative records providing supplementary evidence on (1) aptitude and achievement measured by standardized tests, (2) out-of-class activities, and (3) observations of personal development are important supplements.

Whatever types of appraisal are undertaken, it is important that they be *interpreted* to pupil and to parents. Only then can they serve their guidance function. Some further aspects of this interpreting process are considered in the next chapter.

At the college level, the selective and certifying function of grades moves even more into the center of the stage. Unless comprehensive examinations or such standardized appraisals as the *Graduate Record Examination* come into more general use, grades will continue to be required in most institutions to serve these administrative functions.

If grades are to be given, they should be handled in a competent and consistent fashion. For the functions that it serves most appropriately, a grade should represent as pure a measure of competence in a field as can be prepared. It should have consistent meaning from instructor to instructor. To achieve such comparable appraisals of competence, the following steps are necessary:

1. Define the knowledges and skills that constitute competence in a field and decide what weight should be given to each.

2. Decide what types of evidence will be accepted as evidence of this competence, determine what effective weight should be given to each component, and handle the weighting of raw scores so that the desired weighting is in fact achieved.

3. Reach a negotiated agreement on the statistical meaning of the grading symbols in terms of percentiles of a defined group or groups.

4. Work out procedures for adapting the definition to small or atypical class groups.

In conclusion, a marking or reporting system should not be taken for granted. Every now and then the individual instructor or a faculty group should ask: Why do we go through this periodic agony of marks or marking? What ends are served? How might they be served better?

REFERENCES

1. Chamberlin, D., et al., *Did they succeed in college?*, New York, Harper, 1942.
2. Lindquist, E. F., *Iowa Tests of General Educational Development: Manual,* Chicago, Ill., Science Research Associates, 1951.

SUGGESTED ADDITIONAL READING

Harris, Chester W., Editor, *Encyclopedia of educational research,* 3rd ed., New York, Macmillan, 1960, pp. 783–789.

Ploghoft, Milton, The parent-teacher conference as a report of pupil progress: an overview, *Educ. admin. and supervision,* **44,** 1958, 101–105.

Smith, Eugene R., et al., *Appraising and recording student progress,* New York, Harper, 1942, Chapters 9–11.

Strang, Ruth, *How to report pupil progress,* Chicago, Science Research Associates, 1955.

Thomas, R. Murray, *Judging student progress,* rev. ed., New York, Longmans, Green, 1960, Chapters 13–15.

Traxler, Arthur E., *Techniques of guidance,* rev. ed., New York, Harper, 1957, Chapter 14.

Wrinkle, William L., *Improving marking and reporting practices in elementary and secondary schools,* New York, Rinehart, 1947.

QUESTIONS FOR DISCUSSION

1. Do you agree with the authors that every mark is a relative judgment? If not, in what cases and on what grounds do you disagree?

2. In what ways is the marking system in a school similar to a rating procedure? In what ways does it differ? What factors that limit the effectiveness of ratings also limit the effectiveness of a marking system? How could the suggestions for improving ratings given in Chapter 13 be used to improve marking procedures in a school?

3. How is the general level of ability of the class that a student is in likely to affect the marks he will get?

4. What should be the role of student self-appraisal in evaluating educational progress? What are the limits of such appraisal?

5. Try to get copies of the report cards used in one or more school systems. Examine them, and compare them with the cards obtained by other class members. What similarities and differences do you note? What shortcomings do you feel they have?

6. Talk to a school principal or superintendent and find out what changes have been made in reporting practices while he was in the school system. Why were they made? How satisfied is he with the result? What provisions are made for parent-teacher conferences? How satisfactorily have these worked out? What problems have arisen? How well does the present system of marking and reporting serve the functions listed on p. 517?

7. What problems arise when one tries to have marks on a report card take account of aptitude and effort?

8. Comment on the proposition: "A course grade is most useful when it measures as accurately as possible the pupil's mastery of the direct objectives of the course and is not messed up with any other factors."

9. For a course that you teach or plan to teach, list the types of evidence you would plan to consider in arriving at a course grade. Indicate the weight to be given to each. Why have you allocated the weights in this way?

10. You have decided to give equal weight, in a biology course, to (a) a series of quizzes, (b) a final exam, and (c) laboratory grades. A study of the score distributions shows that the quiz SD equals 10, the exam SD equals 15, and the laboratory SD equals 5. How must you weight the raw scores in order to give the desired weight to the three components of the final grade?

11. When is it appropriate to "mark on a curve"? When not? When it is, how should the fraction to get each grade be determined?

12. What steps would you propose to take to reduce differences between instructors in grading standards?

13. In college Y there are ten sections of freshman English. What steps could be taken to assure uniform grading standards, so that a student is not penalized by being in a particular section?

14. When schools are considering changing their grading system from a percentage or letter grade to some other letter system based on the ability of the individual student such as S = satisfactory; O = outstanding; N = needs improvement; and U = unsatisfactory, the following arguments against the new procedure are frequently brought up:

a. The level of achievement will be lowered because students will have no motivation to work hard.

b. It will remove competition and competition is the basis of our society.

c. When a child gets out of school, he will work for a living and earn a salary based on his competence on the job. Grades are the salaries of school children and should be given on the same basis.

d. Marks based on individual ability give a child a wrong picture of himself and the parents of the child do not know exactly where their child stands.

e. A child should learn to adjust to failure since he will experience failure many times during his lifetime. If he has never failed in school, he does not get this experience.

What are the merits of each of these arguments? What false assumptions —if any—does each make?

15. A school principal remarked to his Board of Education: "We have higher standards than Mason High. Our passing mark is 70, and theirs is only 65." What assumptions is he making in this statement? How defensible are they?

Chapter 18

▼

Measurement in Educational and Vocational Guidance

Mr. Wilson, guidance counselor at Center High School in one of the more enterprising small cities in Georgia, has a conference scheduled with Walter Kay, a tenth-grade pupil. This is the first conference. From the regular school testing program, Mr. Wilson has the following aptitude and interest test percentiles for Walter:

Differential Aptitude Tests		Kuder Preference Record, Vocational	
Verbal Reasoning	80	Scientific	62
Numerical Ability	75	Outdoor	80
Abstract Reasoning	65	Computational	46
Space Relations	80	Clerical	40
Mechanical Reasoning	80	Literary	30
Clerical Speed and Accuracy	50	Artistic	32
Language Usage: Spelling	70	Musical	45
Language Usage: Sentences	75	Persuasive	52
		Mechanical	75
		Social Service	48

Walter's course grades for the previous year gave him an academic average of 84 (or B), and placed him about 60th in a class of 200. Walter's father is a fairly successful local business man. Walter has indicated on a questionnaire that he wants to become a doctor.

What significance do these test results have for Walter's expressed vocational goal? Do they imply greater suitability of other vocational goals? How are the results and their significance to be conveyed to Walter? These are not easy questions to answer, but suitable answers to them are at the heart of counseling. We must examine them in some detail.

THE SIGNIFICANCE OF TESTS FOR A VOCATIONAL GOAL

To judge the suitability of Walter's vocational goal in the light of his test scores, we need to know what the chances are that someone with Walter's score pattern who starts out for that goal will in fact be able to reach it. This is a large order. Let us break it down, to see what is implied in it. The analysis will suggest on the one hand why the long-range forecast is such a formidable enterprise, and on the other the immediate issues with which the counselor needs to be concerned. In Walter's case we need to be able to estimate

1. The probability that he would be accepted as a student by a college.

2. The probability that he would complete a premedical program successfully, if accepted.

3. The probability that he would be accepted by a medical school if he completed premedical training.

4. The probability that he would be graduated from medical school, if accepted.

5. The probability that he would achieve minimum standards of success and satisfaction as a doctor, if he were graduated from medical school.

What sort of judgment can be made with respect to the probability that Walter will successfully get over each of these hurdles?

The first hurdle is getting into college. Since colleges are likely to pay primary attention to high-school achievement and to measures of scholastic aptitude, we should examine the evidence we have on these points. Walter stands high in the second quarter of the class in ninth-grade marks. (Our present information does not tell us what level of achievement this would represent in terms of broader norms.) A pooling of the Verbal and Numerical scores on the *DAT* comes close to representing scholastic aptitude and provides a fairly good predictor of academic achievement. On these two parts he has percentiles of 78 and 74 averaging about the 75th percentile. The aptitude tests and school achievement are in rather close agreement, and we can feel fairly secure in the picture of ability level that is provided us.

TESTS INTERPRETED IN TERMS OF EXPECTANCY

Now what about college? Walter has stated that he wants to go to the University of Georgia. What are the chances that he would be admitted?

We have chosen a Georgia college for this particular example because there is currently more information available to Georgia counselors about Georgia colleges than is true almost anywhere else in the country.   But you will see that we still have our difficulties.

The Georgia colleges use the College Entrance Examination Board *Scholastic Aptitude Test*.   At the University of Georgia, the average *SAT* Verbal score of admitted freshmen men in 1957 was 394, with a standard deviation of 90, while the Math mean was 435 with a standard deviation of 86.   The mean value for average high-school grades was 74.[2]   Walter's high-school average, at least for the ninth grade, looks quite acceptable.   We must try to translate his tenth-grade *DAT* scores into estimates of *SAT* scores in the twelfth grade. Fortunately, some data available in the *DAT* manual [1] permit us to do this, at least tentatively.   Entering Walter's scores into the prediction equation, we arrive at estimates as follows:

SAT Verbal	484
SAT Math	569

Walter appears to fall almost a full standard deviation above the mean of admitted freshmen at the University of Georgia on the aptitude measures.   Since we saw earlier that he was also above average on grades, all the evidence indicates that Walter's prospects of being admitted to the University of Georgia are very good.

If Walter changed his goal to some other college, we might have to change our forecast.   The selectivity of collegiate institutions varies widely.   Walter's record, which looks quite acceptable for the University of Georgia, would appear unsatisfactory to a very selective college with a very large group of applicants and a limited enrollment. The *CEEB* reports some colleges in which the average *SAT* Verbal score of admitted students is over 650, while there are other colleges using the test for which the average is not much above 250 on the standard score scale.   This is a difference of four full standard deviations of the original norm group.   The University of Georgia is about midway between the two extremes, and for entry here, Walter's record would look quite acceptable.   There are other colleges where it certainly wouldn't.   Thus, the problem that very often faces both counselor and student is not *whether* to plan for college, but rather *which* college or type of college to plan for.

Walter's second hurdle is doing satisfactory work in the premedical program.   We have concluded that Walter could reasonably expect to get into the University of Georgia, but how well is he likely to do after he has been admitted?   Here again, the State of Georgia provides us more information than most other places, because of an extensive study has been made of success in the different Georgia colleges in relation to *SAT* scores and high-school average.[4] Expectancy tables have been prepared for each college, based on a composite score which is the most effective combination of test scores and grades. These tables show the probability of making an average of C or better, B or better, or A during the freshman year at each composite score level.   For Walter at the University of Georgia the chances are as follows:

> C or better: 96 chances in 100
> B or better: 63 chances in 100
> A: 14 chances in 100

Once again, the counselor can tell Walter that the chances are good that he will be able to do acceptable work at the University of Georgia. No separate data are available for *completing* college, but our hunch would be that if no untoward personal or financial problems arose to interfere, Walter should be able to cope with work at the level set by that university.   Presumably the premedical program, with its science courses, is more demanding than many of the other undergraduate programs, so that Walter would find it more difficult to shine there than elsewhere, but it rather looks as though he should be able to do at least passing work.

Predicting beyond entry, into and initial success in college, Mr. Wilson's path becomes a good deal more thorny.   Walter's long-range prospects depend so much upon how successful he is in the intermediate steps that we should perhaps not even try to project our estimates beyond the freshman year of college.   But let us make the attempt.   Let us forecast that his undergraduate grade-point average will be about a C+ or B−.   This seems reasonable in the light of the expectancy for freshman grades and the somewhat more rigorous demands of a premedical program.

The third hurdle Walter faces is getting into medical school.   What is now our best projection of Walter's prospects for entry into and success in medical school?   The prospects for acceptance in medical school will depend, among other things, on Walter's undergraduate grades and his performance on the *Medical College Admissions Test*. We have made an estimate of his probable grades at the University of Georgia.   Can we now get some estimate of *MCAT* score?

Predicting performance on a set of tests that are still 6 to 8 years in the future is obviously a risky enterprise.   However, we do have some data tying the *Medical College Admissions Test* to other tests and to general population norms.[3]   A score corresponding to the 75th percentile of the general population appears to be the equivalent of roughly 415 on the *MCAT* (whose scores are expressed once again as standard scores with mean of 500, S.D. of 100). If Walter holds his own through high school and college, this is a reasonable prediction for him, but with a sizeable margin for error in the forecast.

Given this *MCAT* score and a C+ or B− college record, can Walter hope to get into medical school? The answer varies from year to year depending on the supply-demand situation. Just after World War II the answer would probably have been "no"; in 1960 it appears to be "perhaps." In 1959 about two fifths of applicants at the *MCAT* score level of 415 were admitted. In another 10 years the answer may have changed again. The answer also depends to a very great extent on *which* school. Many medical schools admit almost no one with scores this low; there are a few for whom it has been close to average for the entering class. So we would have to conclude that medical school admission is a *possibility* for Walter if his intermediate educational progress comes at least up to our predictions, and if he shows good judgment in choosing the medical schools to which to apply.

The fourth hurdle is completing medical school successfully. The proportion of students admitted to medical school who are subsequently eliminated is rather small—about 10 per cent during the first year—and a good part of the elimination is for reasons other than academic. Even at Walter's predicted *MCAT* level the nationwide elimination rate is only 15 to 18 per cent. So perhaps we should not try to predict this rather far-away event. If Walter is accepted by a school, he certainly has a good fighting chance of graduating from it.

The fifth hurdle is establishing himself as a successful doctor. Given that Walter has graduated from medical school, what are his prospects? At this point, we had better frankly admit that we don't know. Success is a tricky thing even to define, much less to predict. And there is no evidence that grades and tests available at age 15 give us any basis for forecasting it. About all we can say, from information now available to us, is that if Walter gets his M.D. his chances of making a living in medicine are as good as the next man's. If he fails, the causes probably lie outside the domain covered by our tests—or by any tests that we could give to a 15-year-old.

We have tried to show in the illustration of Walter Kay the kind of thinking a counselor must go through, either explicitly as we have done or implicitly and intuitively as is perhaps more typical, in order to arrive at a judgment as to the reasonableness of a career plan. We have tried to show the complexity, and in some spots the fragility of the chain of reasoning that is involved. The information available to permit a counselor to carry through this type of reasoning is much less than it should be. We need (1) better norming procedures and conversion tables, so that performance on one test at one grade level can be more readily translated into equivalent scores for some other test at some other grade level, (2) more and better expectancy tables to permit us to forecast later achievement from earlier indicators of ability, and (3) better ways of organizing this information for and making it available to those who will have to use it. However, even if data were much more extensive and much better organized than at present, our forecasts would still need to be quite tentative.

The need for tentativeness is shown by the expectancy values for Walter's freshman grades at one selected institution. Even if we assume that we are accurate in our prediction of his twelfth-grade *SAT* scores and his final high school average (and these predictions already contain a considerable margin of error), there is still almost 1 chance in 20 that Walter will fall below a C average, while at the same time there is 1 chance in 7 that he will be a straight-A student. Our prediction can be only in probabilities, and the range of possible outcomes is quite great.

Any predictions that try to jump two or three stages in the educational or vocational ladder are even more hazardous, since the more remote step depends so much upon the intermediate steps. This is especially true when the prediction jumps from the sheltered academic halls to the harsh world of work. School achievement and job achievement do not correspond at all closely. Prediction of job success, as we indicated more fully in Chapter 10, is a risky undertaking at very best. It would seem wise, therefore, to focus on the immediate step to be taken, and to leave future decisions somewhat fluid. Granting that present decisions must be made with an eye to future choices, we must recognize that those choices *are* in the future. They cannot be made definitely now. Choices should be made as the choice points arise, and while they should be made with an awareness of their implications for the future, a maximum of flexibility should be retained for redirecting future action.

In Walter's case, the counselor could clearly endorse a college preparatory program in school. He could support Walter's particular choice of a college as a reasonable and realistic one, and could lead Walter to expect that he would be able to handle work at that college without undue difficulty. The definitive choice of a premedical program is one that Walter does not have to make for 2 or 3 years, and application to medical school is still further in the future.   Decisions on these problems could be left for the future, with the recognition that his goal is a somewhat demanding one and that whether it will look realistic when the time comes will depend upon what Walter has achieved in the interim.

INTEREST MEASURES IN RELATION TO VOCATIONAL GOALS

So far we have paid no attention to the interest scores.   This is partly because they relate less directly to success in the academic training that is prerequisite for Walter's objective; correlations of interest scores with academic achievement in general or in specific areas are generally rather low.   In part we have avoided bringing interest into the picture because the manner in which interest patterns are related to job success and job satisfaction is far from clear.   As we indicated in Chapter 13, most of the information on interest patterns of particular occupational groups is based on persons already in the occupation.   Furthermore, it is not clear how close to the typical member of an occupation a person needs to be in order to be happy or successful in the occupation.   In many fields, such as engineering, there are wide variations in *specific jobs* within the occupation.   Some may involve much social contact work and some little; some may involve primarily outdoor work and some indoor, and so on.   Thus, there may be a place for individuals with quite different interest patterns within a single occupation.   Closeness of correspondence with the typical may be pointed out to the counselee, but we would hesitate to counsel avoidance of an occupation solely because his interest pattern departs from what is typical of the occupation.

In Walter's case, we may compare his percentiles on the *Kuder* with the average percentiles for physicians and surgeons as a group.   The comparison is shown below.

	Walter	Physicians and Surgeons
Outdoor	80	60
Mechanical	75	37
Computational	46	32
Scientific	62	79
Persuasive	52	26
Literary	30	62
Artistic	32	61
Musical	45	58
Social Service	48	60
Clerical	40	27

Clearly, there are some appreciable discrepancies—discrepancies of 30 percentile points or more. On the interest dimension (scientific) that is highest for the physicians and surgeons and therefore presumably most critical for the occupation, Walter falls 17 percentile points below the group average. However, discrepancies of this size would undoubtedly appear in many instances if we were to compare individual physicians with the average of all physicians. We cannot say how often. Thus, though Walter's *Kuder* profile does not particularly suggest the interest patterns of a doctor, we have no real basis for concluding that his interests are incompatible with that field of work. If we rank the ten interest areas in order for Walter and for the physician group and correlate the two sets of ranks, we find that the correlation is about $-.1$. Thus, Walter's order of preference is neither like nor particularly unlike that for physicians and surgeons.

We have now done about as much as we can in terms of the evidence before us to assess the realism and suitability of Walter's expressed goal. Our best judgment would indicate that the next steps toward that goal are entirely feasible ones for Walter, though the final goal may be somewhat demanding for him. His interest pattern provides neither a strong affirmation of this goal nor a denial of it. At this point, obviously, we need to get better acquainted with Walter as a person. (Often, this getting acquainted would have preceded testing, but it is assumed that in this instance the test data were gathered as part of a routine group testing program.) This getting acquainted will depend in part upon the other types of information about Walter that are already a matter of record; in part upon conference with Walter.

Let us assume that the evidence that we gather does not essentially change the picture of abilities or interests that are provided by Walter's test scores. It illuminates the pattern of Walter's motivation by bringing out a strong family commitment to a professional career for Walter and a somewhat unanalyzed but long-standing conviction on Walter's part that he wanted to "help people keep well and strong." What are we to do now?

COMMUNICATING TEST RESULTS

It would be rather generally accepted in present-day counseling that the important goals of the counseling process are that the counselee shall understand himself, accept himself, and arrive at a program of action to which he himself is committed in the light of the evidence.

If these objectives are to be achieved, the general implications of the test results must be communicated to the client. There are two keys to this statement. One is "communicated to the client"; the other is "general implications." Let us consider each of these a little further.

THE MEANING OF COMMUNICATION

What we communicate to someone else must be distinguished from what we say to him. A teacher may say to a child, "You're a dumb bunny." What she communicates is very likely: "I don't like you." The message sent and the message received are quite different in this case and in many others. Our problem, in working with a client, is not simply one of stating in an accurate and objective manner what the tests show. It is one of having the client comprehend and accept a particular picture of himself, one that may be quite a bit different from the picture he has held heretofore.

Really communicating with a client, really getting him to accept the implications of the test results and incorporate them into his picture of himself, is far from easy. This is true particularly when the change in his self-picture involves adopting a less flattering view of himself. Communicating with parents who have made firm commitments for their child's future, and who may be satisfying their own needs vicariously through their child, is often even more difficult.

There have been a number of attempts to study experimentally different ways of presenting test data. However, the findings do not point out some one procedure as particularly effective. We can at best suggest a few guiding principles.

1. Change in the self-picture should be thought of as a gradual and continuing process. Presentation of test implications may be more effective if it is a continuing process, influencing all the counselor's contacts with the client, rather than a single dramatic event.

2. Test results gain meaning and significance in relation to other life experiences. The attempt should be made to relate the test findings to other experiences in and out of school. Where test results and other experiences, i.e., of academic or work success, are congruent, they serve to reinforce and give meaning to each other. Thus, in our instance, Walter's aptitude measures and school standing are in essential agreement, and each reinforces the other as an appraisal of aptitude for college work. Where test results and other types of evidence are at variance, a search with the counselee for the reasons for the discrepancy may provide a deeper basis for self-understanding.

3. The individual should take an active role in relating the test results to himself and his plans. We have succeeded in communicating only what the client himself sees. One way of assuring and testing that communication is to have him participate in interpreting the findings. This does not mean that he can be expected to work out the technical significance of a test score. This is a job for the counselor. Rather, once the technical interpretation has been made he should participate in relating the results to his own problems or plans.

THE OBJECTIVES OF COMMUNICATION

In our communication, what we wish to convey to the client are the *general implications* of the test results. It is usually neither necessary nor particularly desirable to report to the client his exact scores or exact standing on tests. Reporting exact values may have several undesirable effects. The report is likely to convey an impression of precision not at all justified by the basic data. To tell a child's parents that his IQ is 117 or to tell an adolescent that he falls at the 78th percentile on a test conveys an atmosphere of exactness and finality quite inappropriate for our educational and psychological measuring instruments. It ignores the standard error of the score. As we have emphasized repeatedly, any test score must be thought of as identifying a fairly broad range within which the individual's true ability lies. This concept is very difficult to convey to parent or child if an exact score value is reported.

The concept of range can best be incorporated in the manner in which the test results are presented and interpreted to the client. Thus, an IQ of 107 (or one of 96) for an elementary-school child in a typical school might be reported as "about like most children in ability to do school work." An IQ of 120 in this context could be reported as "can be expected to learn school work somewhat more easily than most." One of 85 might be expressed as "will probably have more difficulty than many children in doing school tasks." These phrasings are only suggestive. The point is that our report is expressed (1) in broad and rather general terms, (2) in terms of its practical implications, and (3) somewhat tentatively.

When working with tests for which the norms are given in percentiles, we have to be particularly careful about our interpretations. This is due to the unequal units of the percentile scale. The large middle range of percentile values does not represent any very great spread in level of performance on most tests, and we must be careful not to overinterpret percentile differences occurring in this range.

Anything from the 25th to the 75th percentile should probably be thought of as "about average," and reported as such. Thus, in describing Walter's test results to him, we might say, "Your aptitude test scores show abilities on these tests somewhat better than the average boy in the tenth grade. You did about as well on one test as on another, though there is a suggestion that your clerical speed is a little below the other abilities. Your scores on tests related to college were somewhat above the average of the total group who enter the University of Georgia, but well below the average for such colleges as Harvard and Princeton. You'll have to see how you do in high school and college before you can tell much about the chances of getting into medical school. Your areas of highest interest were outdoors and mechanical." This is probably as much of an interpretation as this set of test data warrants, though other aspects of the tests might merit further discussion in relation to specific educational or vocational plans.

Related to the problem of conveying a false impression of exactness is that of overemphasizing and overvaluing the test results in the client's mind. This danger is seen perhaps most dramatically in the case of an IQ reported to a parent. In some degree most parents live vicariously through their children. Some compete through their children. They know enough about an IQ to recognize it as a mark of status. You can get ahead of Mrs. Jones next door by having a brighter child in much the same way that you can by having a more expensive car or a new fur coat. Conversely, a low IQ may be a basis for self-reproach or for rejecting the child. These are unworthy, even vicious, uses of test results. They are fostered by meager understanding of tests and by personal involvement. This type of misuse of test results is another reason why the counselor usually prefers to report test findings only in general terms.

TESTS IN THE IDENTIFICATION OF VOCATIONAL OBJECTIVES

In the case of Walter, as we have just been describing it, we had to deal with a boy who had expressed a definite educational and vocational goal. Our initial problem was to try to assess the prospects that his goal could be achieved. Clarification of Walter's plans and objectives would have to include communicating to him an estimate of the plausibility of his expressed objective. But suppose that a counselee comes in who expresses no definite objective, or suppose

Walter wishes to consider other possible objectives. What then? Let us organize our consideration of this situation around another case.

Consider this second case, that of Henry White, who is a classmate of Walter's. Henry's father works as a railroad conductor. Henry has stated that he does not know what he wants to do when he grows up. His test percentiles are as follows:

Differential Aptitude Tests		*Kuder Preference Record, Vocational*	
Verbal Reasoning	25	Scientific	46
Numerical Ability	55	Outdoor	37
Abstract Reasoning	40	Computational	45
Space Relations	55	Clerical	78
Mechanical Reasoning	60	Literary	26
Clerical Speed and Accuracy	40	Artistic	48
Language Usage: Spelling	20	Musical	81
Language Usage: Sentences	30	Persuasive	56
		Mechanical	68
		Social Service	32

In academic work, Henry is about 135th in the class of 200.

This case presents us with quite a different situation from the one we faced with Walter Kay. There our problem initially was to appraise the appropriateness of a stated objective. In Henry's case, no objective is expressed. Our problem is to see whether certain areas of educational or vocational activity appear particularly indicated by the test evidence and, if so, to help Henry to get better acquainted with these possibilities.

Henry, who is below average both on the intellectual aspects of the aptitude battery and in scholarship, does not seem a very promising candidate for college education. The probabilities are that he does not aspire to it. If he does, counseling should be directed at a thorough review of those plans in the light of the evidence on aptitude and achievement. Any education planned beyond high school should probably be in a type of institution and a type of program making rather modest intellectual demands.

Positive guidance of Henry in relation to immediate educational choices would depend to a considerable extent upon sharpening up his vocational objectives. What can we say about Henry's vocational prospects? What type of vocational objective is suitable for him in the light of his test scores? What steps should a counselor take to help Henry set up suitable and more definite vocational goals? When these steps have been taken, the resulting plan may provide guides as to the high-school program that would be desirable, e.g., clerical, vocational, prebusiness, or general.

LIMITATIONS OF APTITUDE MEASURES FOR IDENTIFYING SUITABLE VOCATIONAL GOALS

If we limit ourselves for the moment to the *DAT* subtests, we must admit that they provide only limited help in establishing a vocational goal for Henry and that what they provide is largely negative. If we exclude collegiate education, we exclude those jobs that depend upon college or professional education. We do not need to consider law, medicine, engineering, architecture, or similar professional occupations. The low verbal, spelling, and sentences scores may also steer us away from some non-collegiate jobs with a heavy linguistic loading, i.e., stenographer. However, that still leaves us perhaps 90 per cent of the world of work to choose from. Should Henry think of becoming a mechanic? A farmer? A salesman? A conductor like his father? Any of these and many others appear quite possible in the light of his aptitude profile.

Why can we offer no more specific positive guidance on the basis of Henry's abilities? Basically, four considerations enter in.

1. *Profile Not Sharply Differentiated.* In Henry's case there isn't too much difference in his different abilities. His scores on this testing range from the 20th percentile (*Spelling*) to the 60th (*Mechanical*), but in this middle percentile range the error of measurement is such that his relative standing on any pair of tests could quite possibly be reversed if he were retested with another form of the tests. Even assuming that the obtained scores are approximately correct, most of the differences are not large enough to have great practical significance. We may feel that the lower scores on the tests of verbal comprehension and language usage have some significance for vocational planning, but beyond this there is not much to say.

Many people will show test profiles of this general type. Their abilities are all at about the same level. Their test scores provide a general indication of level of ability but limited cues as to specific strengths and weaknesses. With no special strengths or weaknesses, they appear about equally likely to succeed in many different types of jobs.

2. *Lack of Unique Relationship of Ability Profile to Job Success.* Even when a person is distinctively higher on one or two abilities than on others, this need not mean that there are one or two specific jobs in which he will be uniquely successful. The boy whose specially high

point is mechanical comprehension may do well as an automotive mechanic, but he may also do well as a telephone repairman or as a farmer. The person high on numerical ability may be successful as a bookkeeper or as a surveyor. For the typical individual there are at least several superficially rather different jobs for which his ability pattern is equally suitable and many others for which his talents are adequate. In terms of their aptitude requirements, jobs come in sizable families, and one family merges gradually into the next. Fitness for different jobs is a matter of degree, and any person is about equally well suited to a number of jobs. Positive guidance can, therefore, be only in terms of broad segments of the world of work. There is no one job for which each person is best fitted.

3. *Lack of Knowledge of the Ability Requirements of Jobs.* Over and above the limitations arising out of overlap in the true ability requirements of jobs, there are limitations stemming from our own ignorance. Our knowledge of what abilities are required by what jobs is still quite limited. We are not in a position to state with confidence what abilities a high-school student should display if he is to become a successful plumber, shoe salesman, truck driver, or service-station operator. We do not know what people who have been successful and contented in these jobs were like when they entered the world of work or what they are like now. We do not know what types of people have tried to work in these fields and failed. We have a good deal of information about the abilities that are required to succeed in advanced training but only scattered information about what is required to succeed in a job.

A fair part of the information that does exist is not readily available in published form. Part of it has been done for specific private companies and has not been made public, either through specific policy or because of pressure of other activities. Part of it has been gathered by such government agencies as the U. S. Employment Service, and serves primarily the functions of the gathering agency.

4. *Techniques to Measure Certain Abilities Are Inadequate.* We have developed sound and practical tools of measurement for only part of the range of human abilities. One most impressive gap lies in the area of social skills and techniques. Abilities to understand and react sagaciously to problems involving other people appear to be important in many sales, contact, and managerial jobs. We have no tests of demonstrated validity in this area. Skill in practical problem-solving, not solving puzzles of a verbal and academic sort, is a related area in which we do not measure very well. Other important gaps also

exist. Our inability to make sound and distinctive suggestions about job possibilities stems in part from our inability to appraise important distinguishing aptitudes.

ROLE OF INTEREST MEASURES IN IDENTIFYING VOCATIONAL OBJECTIVES

So far we have not discussed the use of the interest inventory results in Henry's case. When the problem is to explore areas of work and focalize vocational objectives, the interest measures may be of as much or more value than ability measures. They should not be interpreted rigidly or taken as Gospel truth, but they do provide a starting point for discussion. Thus, the counselor could explore with Henry his apparent interest in clerical types of activities. If the test score was supported in discussions, the next step might be to provide Henry with a chance to become acquainted with possible clerical types of work in his community, either through reading or hearing about the jobs or through vacation or part-time employment.

Summarizing, in view of all the above it appears clear that guidance with relation to vocational plans will in most instances have to be couched in rather general terms. Guidance with regard to general educational level will be quite possible. Some indications of broad areas and types of jobs will often be appropriate. Beyond this, there is much free space within which interest, local opportunity, exploratory tryout, and individual idiosyncrasy may freely operate.

RESOURCES FOR JUDGING THE EDUCATIONAL AND VOCATIONAL SIGNIFICANCE OF TEST SCORES

Before he can provide constructive guidance to a client's thinking about educational or vocational plans, a counselor must have a clear picture in his own mind of the educational and vocational implications of the counselee's test scores. He must have an estimate of the probability of realizing a stated objective or a picture of objectives that are appropriate. To what sources may the counselor turn to build up his skills of evaluating test patterns in a sound and realistic manner? Where can he find help in translating a set of test scores into a prediction of probable success?

Ready-made tables showing the chances for success in any given job at different test score levels are largely non-existent at the present time. Perhaps they never can exist. For now, the counselor must be content with much more modest aids. We will consider a few of these.

REVISED MINNESOTA OCCUPATIONAL RATING SCALES

This little monograph [5] provides ratings of some 400 occupations with respect to the minimum level of (1) academic ability, (2) mechanical ability, (3) social intelligence, (4) clerical ability, (5) musical ability, (6) artistic ability, and (7) physical agility required to succeed in the occupation. Ratings are given in four levels, which are generally to be interpreted as follows:

A: above the 90th percentile of the adult population
B: 76th to 90th   "   "   "   "   "
C: 26th to 75th   "   "   "   "   "
D: 1st to 25th   "   "   "   "   "

The exception is the scales for musical and artistic ability, in which A is defined as the 97th percentile or higher, B as the 90th to 96th percentile, and C as the 26th to 90th percentile. The ratings are frankly a synthesis of judgments. However, they were the judgments of highly trained individuals whose professional careers had centered around the study of jobs and the requirements of jobs.

We might consider our two illustrative cases to see what guidance the scales can give us. First, considering Walter with his aspiration to be a doctor, we have the following picture:

	Physicians	Walter
Academic	A	B−
Mechanical	B	B−
Social	B	?
Clerical	C	C
Musical	D	?
Artistic	D	?
Physical	B	?

On the basis of this judgmental standard, we would have to question more seriously whether Walter has the academic aptitude to become a doctor. We would need information from other sources about Walter's social ability and physical agility to judge whether these also represent points of discrepancy.

Let us now suppose that Henry is considering trying to get a clerical job with the railroad that employs his father. He hopes that he might work as a ticket agent or possibly as station agent in a small town. The evidence appears in the following table:

	Station Agent	Henry
Academic	C	C
Mechanical	C	C
Social	C	?
Clerical	B	C
Musical	D	?
Artistic	C	?
Physical	C	?

We would have to judge whether the discrepancy between the evidence we have on Henry's clerical skill and the demands of the job is a sufficient basis for discouraging this particular goal. Further evidence should be sought on Henry's clerical skills.

TEST MANUALS

Some test manuals provide information on the scores of particular occupational groups. The report may include no more than the median score for specific groups. We saw such figures for the *Differential Aptitude Tests* in Table 10.3. Sometimes rather complete norms may be provided for individuals in particular occupations. Thus, the *Minnesota Vocational Test for Clerical Workers* provides percentile norms for the following groups of workers in the clerical field:

> Women: Office machine operators.
> Stenographers and typists.
> General clerical workers.
> Routine clerical workers.
>
> Men: Bank tellers.
> Accountants and bookkeepers.
> General clerical workers.
> Routine clerical workers.
> Shipping and stock clerks.

On the average, members of these occupational groups score substantially higher on this test than do workers in general. A score set at perhaps the 10th percentile of persons employed in one of these occupations might constitute a warning level in the guidance of aspiring students.

A test manual that provides extensive standards on the occupational requirements of jobs is the manual for the *General Aptitude Test Battery* (*GATB*) of the U. S. Employment Service. This manual identifies twenty "occupational aptitude patterns" and proposes minimum aptitude standards for each. Thus, Pattern 1 is defined by minimum scores of 130 * on G (general intelligence) and 130 on V (verbal ability). It includes occupations involving literary work, creative writing and translating, copy writing, and journalism. Nineteen other patterns are given, requiring different aptitude combinations and different minimum levels, and many specific jobs are assigned to each.

For many of the jobs, the evidence upon which the determination of minimum scores and the assignment of jobs to patterns is based is rather limited, and the evidence is open to some criticism on technical grounds. However, the *GATB* data available in the records at the U. S. Employment Service represent one of the major pools of data on the relation of tests to job success. It is unfortunate that this information is not more generally available to school counselors in freely distributed published sources.

DATA ON ARMY GENERAL CLASSIFICATION TEST

Information on the level of general intellectual ability of individuals in different occupations is provided by World War II *Army General Classification Test* data. The data for selected occupations are shown in Table 9.3. A much more complete table, covering many more occupations, may be found in the original journal article.[5] This table shows the general intellectual level of young men who had entered different occupations. However, it gives no indication of requirements for more specialized abilities.

FOLLOW-UP STUDIES

A few follow-up studies of men tested with an interest test or an aptitude test battery have been carried out on a scale large enough to give some picture of the sort of men that work in different occupations. Table 12.4 shows the picture for a group of veterans tested with the *Kuder Preference Record*. Table 10.6 shows part of the results from an extensive follow-up of veterans tested in the Air Force with an aptitude test battery and the study is described in some detail in that chapter. The characteristics of the people who *have* gotten into an occupation provide at least some cue to the sort of people who *can* get into that occupation.

SUMMARY STATEMENT

The process of using tests in educational and vocational counseling involves two main steps. First, the counselor must himself arrive at

---

* Standard scores with mean of 100 and S.D. of 20.

a sound interpretation of the significance of the test data. Secondly, he must communicate that interpretation to the counselee in such a way that the counselee's self-picture and plans come to correspond better with the realities of his abilities and interests.

Two somewhat different situations arise in the interpreting of test results. In one, the client expresses definite educational or vocational goals. The counselor must interpret the test results in relation to those goals. He must arrive at some judgment as to the likelihood that the goals can be attained and the probability that they will prove acceptable to the client if they are attained. The evidence by which the counselor is to reach this judgment is fragmentary and scattered. Some sources that may help him are suggested in the previous section.

In the second case, the client's goals are vague and undefined. The counselor must direct the counselee's attention to areas that look promising in terms of the test results. For most clients this type of guidance can be only in the broadest of terms because of the wide overlap in the abilities that different jobs require. Guidance as to general level of educational and vocational aspiration seems plausible, and counselees can be steered away from plans calling for abilities they lack. Positive suggestions should, however, be expressed in quite general and tentative terms.

The process of communicating test results also raises certain problems. If the test results are to be helpful, they must be presented in a way that makes it possible for the client to accept them. This is particularly difficult when the tests are less flattering than the client's previous self-picture.

Test results should usually be presented in rather general terms and with emphasis upon the interpretation and significance of the results. The interpretation should avoid overemphasis on exact test scores and should at the same time help the client to relate the tests to the plans to be made and the action to be taken.

REFERENCES

1. Bennett, George K., Harold G. Seashore, and Alexander G. Wesman, *A manual for the Differential Aptitude Tests,* 3rd Ed., New York, Psychological Corp., 1959.
2. Franz, Gretchen, Junius A. Davis, and Dolores Garcia, Prediction of grades from pre-admission indices in Georgia, *Educ. psychol. Measmt,* 18, 1958, 841–4.
3. Gee, Helen H., *Differential characteristics of student bodies: implications for the study of medical education.* Paper read at the Conference on Selection and Educational Differentiation, May 1959, Berkeley, Calif.

4. Hills, John R., Gretchen Franz, and Linda B. Emory, *Counselor's Guide to Georgia Colleges,* Atlanta, Ga., Regents of the University System of Georgia, 1959.
5. Paterson, D. G., C. d'A. Gerken, and M. E. Hahn, *Revised Minnesota occupational rating scales,* Minneapolis, Minn., University of Minnesota Press, 1953.
6. Stewart, Naomi, A.G.C.T. scores of army personnel grouped by occupations, *Occupations,* **26,** 1947, 5–41.

SUGGESTED ADDITIONAL READING

Baer, M. F., and E. C. Roeber, *Occupational information,* 2nd ed., Chicago, Science Research Associates, 1958, pp. 88–130.
Bennett, George K., Harold G. Seashore, and Alexander G. Wesman, *Counseling from profiles: a casebook for the Differential Aptitude Tests,* New York, Psychological Corp., 1951.
Berdie, Ralph F., Wilbur L. Layton, Edward O. Swanson, and Theda Hagenah, *Counseling and the use of tests,* Minneapolis, Student Counseling Bureau, University of Minnesota, 1959.
Froehlich, Clifford P., and Kenneth B. Hoyt, *Guidance testing and other student appraisal procedures for teachers and counselors,* rev. ed., Chicago, Science Research Associates, 1959, Chapters 8, 14, 15, 18, and 19.
Roe, Anne, *The psychology of occupations,* New York, Wiley, 1956, Chapters 6 and 7.
Rothney, John W. M., and Bert A. Roens, *Guidance of American youth; an experimental study,* Cambridge, Mass., Harvard University Press, 1950.
Shartle, Carroll L., *Occupational information,* 3rd ed., Englewood Cliffs, N. J., Prentice-Hall, 1959, Chapter 11.
Super, Donald E., and John O. Crites, *Appraising vocational fitness,* New York, Harper, in press.
U. S. Department of Labor, *Estimates of worker trait requirements for 4,000 jobs as defined in the Dictionary of Occupational Titles,* Washington, D. C., U. S. Government Printing Office, 1956.

QUESTIONS FOR DISCUSSION

1. If you were a counselor, how would you use expectancy tables, such as the ones for Georgia colleges described on p. 524? How should a guidance worker in high school use the data of Table 9.3?

2. How specific is the vocational guidance that can be given on the basis of scores from a battery of ability and interest tests? What other factors should be taken into account in helping a student to formulate vocational plans?

3. What obstacles to communication is a counselor likely to encounter? What steps can be taken to overcome these?

4. In reporting test results to a counselee, how specific should a vocational counselor be?

5. What sort of validity data about an aptitude test would be most useful

to a vocational counselor in giving guidance to a student? How should this information be organized and presented to the counselor for his use?

6. The son of the local banker got the following scores on the *Differential Aptitude Test Battery* and the *Kuder Preference Record* administered in the eleventh grade. What tentative plans seem suitable in the light of the test scores? How definite should these plans be at the present time? What further information should be sought?

DAT Subtest	Percentile	*Kuder* Scale	Percentile
Verbal Reasoning	95	*Scientific*	68
Numerical Ability	70	*Outdoor*	82
Abstract Reasoning	90	*Computational*	36
Space Relations	80	*Clerical*	43
Mechanical Reasoning	85	*Literary*	72
Clerical Speed and Accuracy	60	*Artistic*	45
Language Usage: Spelling	90	*Musical*	38
Language Usage: Sentences	95	*Persuasive*	67
		Mechanical	35
		Social Service	18

7. In the same eleventh grade the son of a truck driver had the following scores. What would be the objectives of counseling in his case?

DAT Subtest	Percentile	*Kuder* Scale	Percentile
Verbal Reasoning	12	*Scientific*	26
Numerical Ability	3	*Outdoor*	88
Abstract Reasoning	14	*Computational*	25
Space Relations	28	*Clerical*	58
Mechanical Reasoning	45	*Literary*	12
Clerical Speed and Accuracy	40	*Artistic*	28
Language Usage: Spelling	23	*Musical*	62
Language Usage: Sentences	8	*Persuasive*	56
		Mechanical	75
		Social Service	55

Chapter 19

Tests in the Selection
of Personnel

One major function that tests have come to serve in the United States is that of screening applicants for a training program or a job. Colleges and professional schools use standardized measures of achievement and aptitude as at least partial bases for deciding which applicants to admit. Vast numbers of civil service positions are filled on the basis of competitive examination. Industry selects men for many jobs in terms of their performance on tests of relevant abilities. All branches of the Armed Services have come to rely upon them to aid in the selection of men for entry into different types of technical schools and for assignment of men to different career fields. Such a selection program has as its objective maximizing the average level of achievement of those who are accepted for the training and the job and minimizing the occurrence of failures.

The school or employer that proposes to introduce a program of selection testing faces a number of issues. What is the best test to use, in terms of effectiveness versus cost? Should a single test be used or should it be supplemented by others? If more than one test is to be used, how should the tests be combined in order to produce the most efficient team? How should test results be combined with non-test data about the individual?

STEPS IN SETTING UP A SELECTION PROGRAM

The basic pattern of selection research is simple and straightforward. You decide what types of measures are promising as predictors of success in the training program or job with which you are concerned. You make a judgment as to what can best be accepted as an index of success in the training program or job. You buy or make the tests and administer them to a group of applicants. You get measures of success for these same applicants after they have had a period of experience in the training program or job. You determine the relationship of each predictor to the criterion measure of success. You pick the best predictor or predictors and use them to screen future applicants.

That is the basic pattern. There are, however, a number of issues that arise at each step in the proceedings. Some involve complex statistical problems that we cannot go into here. However, we shall consider the operations step by step and try to anticipate some of the recurring problems.

PICKING TRYOUT TESTS FOR SELECTION RESEARCH

How shall we decide what sorts of tests to try out as predictors of success in a given training program or job? Of course, we may have some hunches based on our familiarity with the school or job. The very fact that it is a school, for example, suggests that some type of scholastic aptitude test would be appropriate. But if we are to refine our crude original hunches, we can do it only by studying the school program or job duties. We carry out what has been called a *job analysis*. The term job analysis is a somewhat ambiguous one. It covers assorted techniques of studying jobs for one or more of a variety of purposes. The purpose may be to determine salary schedules, to improve safety procedures, to develop training programs, or to define ladders of promotion. It may also be to describe the tasks done on the job and to estimate what abilities and personal qualities are required to do those tasks well. The job analysis with which we are concerned focuses on this last type of information.

There is no special magic technique for job analysis. The analyst operates by going out and observing people working at the job, by talking to them about what they do, by examining the tools they have to use and the textbooks or instruction manuals they have to read, and by observing the conditions under which they have to work. His problem is to get a complete description of the job. From this and from his background of knowledge of human abilities, he organizes his hypotheses as to the abilities that are important for the job. These statements of job requirements are refined guesses based on scrutiny of the job.

Given a set of educated guesses as to the abilities important for a job, the next step is to translate them into actual test procedures. Often, the practical step will be to try some of the ready-made tests that appear to measure abilities much like those suggested by the job analysis. The sources suggested in Chapter 8 will identify available instruments and provide information about them.

In other cases, there may be no existing test that appears to fill the bill. It is then necessary to try to invent test tasks that will tap the functions whose importance was indicated by the job analysis. Test specifications must be prepared and tasks or items constructed. Many of the guide lines set down in Chapters 3 and 4 will apply, though tests of special aptitudes may differ quite a bit from tests of school achievement. Usually, it will be desirable to try out any new test on preliminary groups. Answers will be needed for such questions as the following:

1. Are the instructions sufficiently clear and detailed and are there enough practice items?

2. Are the time limits appropriate? If this is a speed test, are there enough materials to keep everybody busy? If the test emphasizes primarily power, are the limits long enough so everyone has a chance to try most of the items?

3. Are the separate test items satisfactory? Administration of the test to a preliminary group and analysis of the responses to each item by high- and low-scoring individuals is usually desirable as a means of eliminating items that fail to discriminate or that are too easy or too hard.

4. Does the test measure with at least moderate reliability? If reliability is very low, steps to improve it by lengthening the test or by revising and selecting items will usually be indicated.

IDENTIFYING A SUITABLE CRITERION MEASURE

If we are to evaluate a test or some other type of predictor, we must have something against which to evaluate it. When we are dealing with success in college, professional school, or some type of training program, marks in courses or grade-point average are usually ready at hand. We take them more or less for granted and use them as our criterion measure of success. This is good enough as far as it goes. We may have certain reservations about course grades as a standard of success, but the judgments they represent are at least a first approximation to the objectives of the educational program.

When our objective is to select persons for a job, as distinct from a training program, the problem of a criterion measure becomes much more troublesome. The novice in the field is likely to assume that he need only look and he will find ready at hand some suitable production record or fitness rating to tell him how good a worker each employee is. The truth of the matter is that existing records are rarely satisfactory and that better ones are hard to come by. One function of a job analysis is to explore and evaluate existing records that might serve as indices of job success and to look for other better procedures that might be substituted for them. Possible indicators of success that we may choose to use include (1) academic or training school grades, (2) proficiency tests, (3) performance records, and (4) ratings by supervisors or associates.

Academic Grades. Grade in a training program provides a fairly simple and straightforward measure that is available with little delay and is usually of satisfactory reliability. The sad thing is that a summary of evidence to date [1] indicates that there is often little correspondence between the tests that have high validity for a training criterion and those that predict success on the job itself. The tests of verbal, quantitative, and reasoning abilities that are good predictors of ability to learn are not comparably good measures of job performance. If the selection tests emphasize ability to absorb the training, they are likely to be relatively inefficient in picking persons who will later be judged to be good workers. Of course, when succcessful completion of a training program is a prerequisite for entry into the job, a certain type of administrative validity is automatically given to this type of criterion.

Job Proficiency Tests. Suitable job proficiency tests are rarely available, and the preparation of a test measuring job competence represents quite an undertaking. In some jobs, accountancy for example, many of the knowledges and skills of the job can be reduced to test tasks. In others, such as selling, a test has quite limited possibilities. Often proficiency tests will need to be performance tests or performance checks. Thus, the competence of an airplane mechanic may be evaluated with some success by having a skilled mechanic observe the person being tested as he demonstrates various key procedures in plane maintenance and repair. A proficiency test can at best measure certain job knowledges and skills; it cannot tell how effectively the individual will apply them at work on the job. It may tell how well he *can* do certain tasks, but it cannot tell how well he *will* do them.

Production Measures. The measure of job success to which one is always likely to turn first when seeking a criterion measure is some record of job output. The number of widgets produced per hour, the monthly sales of gilhickeys, or the number of defective whortlebugs per hundred seem like sound indices of the quality of a worker. In some cases, performance records can be used to advantage. However, there are many jobs for which no simple performance measure can be found. The receptionist, the bank teller, the department supervisor, the plumber, and the teacher are doing jobs in which we can hardly find any product to count or score. The product is too varied or intangible to provide us with an acceptable criterion.

Even in those jobs in which there is some product to count or score, there are many pitfalls in using the product as a criterion measure. We may consider several briefly.

1. The product may depend upon other people. Thus, during World War II attempts to use bombing records as a measure of the competence of a bombardier broke down in part because where the bomb fell was affected by the way the pilot flew the plane. Again, the sales of an insurance agent may depend upon the type and amount of supervision and help he gets from the agency manager.

2. Outside conditions may vary from person to person. The quality of equipment may be important—new tools versus old, good maintenance versus poor. Prosperity of the neighborhood may be a factor in any measure of sales volume.

3. A sample of performance may be quite unreliable. Thus, accuracy of bombing by a single student showed wide variations from day to day. A limited sample of production or sales may be similarly undependable.

4. The performance measure may represent only a limited aspect of the job. Thus, for a life-insurance salesman the dollar volume of sales may be less important than the *permanence* of the sales. There is no profit in lapsed policies. It might be possible to keep a record of the output of dictation and typing for each of a group of secretaries, but this would take no account of dependability in remembering appointments or diplomacy in answering the phone.

An actual record of performance is undoubtedly an attractive candidate as a criterion of job proficiency. But performance records need careful scrutiny in terms of such considerations as those mentioned above. If the measure holds up under scrutiny, as it sometimes will, it can be used as a standard against which predictor measures can be appraised. But if no production records are available or if existing records are unsatisfactory for one reason or another, we shall have to look elsewhere for our criterion measure.

Ratings of Job Proficiency. In actual practice, the selection research worker is often thrown back upon ratings for lack of any more satisfactory criterion measure. It is almost always possible to arrange to get some type of rating, usually by instructor or supervisor. Ratings are applicable to almost any type of job. The fact that a rater can synthesize different aspects of achievement in one judgment and can make allowances for special external factors that may have favored or handicapped the worker is in some ways an advantage. However, the limitations of ratings as evaluations of competence are many. We have discussed them in detail in Chapter 13 and need not repeat that discussion here. It will suffice to say that the reliability of criterion ratings is often low, and they are frequently biased by factors not truly related to competence. Various of the techniques of analytical check lists or forced-choice judgments have been applied in an attempt to overcome these limitations. These procedures have some promise but are quite laborious. It is surprising, but true, that in personnel research obtaining good criteria of proficiency often calls for more skill and effort than developing predictor tests.

ADMINISTERING TESTS FOR VALIDATION

Once tests have been selected for tryout and plans have been made to collect as good criterion data as circumstances permit, the tests should be administered to a group on a research basis. Ideally, tests are given to persons *before* they start on the job or training program. If the tests are given to individuals who are already on the job or who have already taken part of the training course, we cannot say how much of any relationship we find is due to actual experience in the job or training program. Thus, if we give a reading test at the end of the freshman year in college and find that those with high scholastic averages are good readers, we are never sure to what extent they did well in college because they were good readers to start with or to what extent they learned good reading skills as they worked effectively on their college courses. The motivation of applicants and of accepted students or workers may also be different, and this difference may distort the results.

It is always logically preferable to try out tests on a group that has yet to start on the job or training program. However, this procedure raises certain practical problems. Gathering data in this way is a slower process. There is always a delay of months, even years, while the persons tested are completing their training or getting well enough established in the job so that we can get a reasonable measure of their competence. Flow of new personnel into a job may be so meager that a long time is required to accumulate a sufficient sample of applicants. Reaching examinees for follow-up months or years later may be difficult. For these practical reasons, tests are sometimes tried out on groups already working in a job. But results for such a group must always be considered tentative when interpreted as evidence of the *predictive* effectiveness of the tests.

One problem that usually is serious in validating tests in a *job* con-

Table 19.1. Range Outside of Which Sample Correlation Coefficient Will Fall 50 Per Cent of Time for Samples of Different Sizes and Different Values of True Correlation

True Value of Correlation	Size of Sample				
	25	50	100	200	400
.00	−.143−+.143	−.098−+.098	−.068−+.068	−.048−+.048	−.034−+.034
.20	.058−.333	.104−.292	.133−.264	.153−.245	.167−.232
.30	.164−.425	.208−.387	.237−.362	.256−.343	.269−.330
.40	.273−.514	.315−.480	.341−.456	.359−.440	.371−.429
.50	.384−.600	.422−.570	.447−.550	.463−.536	.474−.525
.60	.500−.684	.534−.659	.555−.642	.568−.630	.578−.621

text is that of getting groups of adequate size. The accuracy with which relationships can be established depends upon the size of the sample upon which statistics are based. The precision of the correlation coefficient is illustrated in Table 19.1. Thus, if we have a sample of only 25 cases and the *true* value of the relationship in the *total population* of all cases is represented by a correlation of .20, we stand a 50-50 chance of getting a value that is either above .333 or below .058. The other entries in the table are to be interpreted in the same way.

Clearly, the larger the sample the more dependable our conclusions will be with respect to which tests to select as predictors. How large a sample do we need? This is the old question: How high is up? The only answer we can give is: The more the better. But there is probably a lower limit below which it doesn't pay to carry out statistical analysis of tests as predictors. At some point, our rational judgment based upon the nature of the tests and the nature of the job is probably more dependable than the empirical results from the small sample. We would judge that there is rarely any profit in computing predictor-criterion correlations for groups of 25 or less and that the value of analyzing groups of under 100 is often questionable. With samples as small as this, we can often put about as much trust in our judgment as in our statistics.

STATISTICAL ANALYSIS OF SELECTION TEST DATA

For the research worker analyzing several predictor tests in relation to a certain criterion of job success, the essential statistic is the correlation of each predictor with the criterion. The higher the correlation, the more effective is the predictor in identifying those who will do well on the criterion measure. We shall illustrate this point—and

also a number of other issues that arise in using predictor test data—
with a small set of actual data.

In the course of some research on electronics personnel, the decision
was made to try out test materials dealing with (1) mathematics, (2)
shop knowledge, and (3) electricity. The criterion measure in this
case was a composite of grades received in an 8-month training program. Data are analyzed here for a sample of 99 students. Some
were eliminated for academic failure before completing training, and
these were assigned grades below the lowest of those graduating. Some
of those who graduated had grades so low that they were designated
as marginal. In all, 30 cases fell in this failed or marginally satisfactory group. The correlations of the three brief tests with the academic
grades criterion were as follows:

Mathematics	.40	(20-item test)
Shop	.30	(10-item test)
Electricity	.58	(15-item test)

The numbers of unsatisfactory (failed or marginal) and satisfactory
students at each score level are shown in Table 19.2 on p. 550. To
see what these correlations mean in practical terms, let us consider two
levels of cutting score. Suppose that we are setting cutting scores to
eliminate (1) about one-third of the unsatisfactory cases and (2)
about two-thirds of the unsatisfactory cases. Considering each test,
what would be the *cost* in loss of individuals who would have become
satisfactory graduates? The results are summarized below.

	Low Cut-Off			High Cut-Off		
	Min. Score	Failures Elim.	Successes Lost	Min. Score	Failures Elim.	Successes Lost
Mathematics	9	33.3%	14.5%	14	66.7%	37.7%
Shop	5	36.7	21.7	7	73.3	56.5
Electricity	7	30.0	8.7	9	76.7	24.7

This little table shows the relationship between the validity coefficient for the test and its practical effectiveness. The difference in the
three selection tests shows up most clearly at the higher cut-off. At
this point, using the electricity test, we could screen out 76.7 per cent
of the unsuccessful group at a cost of only 24.7 per cent of our future
successes. By contrast, the shop test screens out 73.7 per cent at a
cost of 56.5 per cent. The greater efficiency of the electricity test is
clearly evident, and if we could use only one test this is the one that
we should keep.

Table 19.2.   Number of Men Receiving Satisfactory and Unsatisfactory Grades in Electronics Training at Each Score Level on Three Selection Tests

Score	Mathematics		Shop		Electricity	
	Unsatis.	Satis.	Unsatis.	Satis.	Unsatis.	Satis.
1			1	1		
2			1	2		
3	1	1	7	3		1
4	2		2	9	1	
5	4		4	11	4	3
6	1	1	7	13	4	2
7	1	4	5	12	4	2
8	1	4	2	10	10	9
9	5	1	1	6	6	11
10		4		2	1	11
11	1	3				6
12	4	5				8
13		3				6
14	1	4				6
15	3	8				4
16	1	8				
17	3	12				
18	2	9				
19		1				
20		1				
Correlation	.40		.30		.58	

Combining Tests.   When we have used several tests as predictors, a question that we often face is whether we should be content with the one best test or whether we should use more than one.   If the decision is to use more than one, we must then decide how many to use and which ones.   A full exploration of these problems leads into complexities which we cannot consider here and, indeed, brings us face to face with some unsolved statistical problems.   However, we can open up some of the main approaches to the problem.

In our illustration, the problem we face is whether to use only the electricity test or whether to give some weight to the mathematics and shop tests.   The extent to which the math and shop tests will be useful will depend upon the extent to which they are measuring abilities *different from* those measured by the electricity test.   If they are measuring essentially the same abilities as those tapped by the electricity test but not measuring them as effectively, there is no point in adding them on to our battery.   However, if they are measuring different components of our criterion, then pooling the several measures should give us more complete coverage of the essential abilities and, consequently, better prediction of the criterion.

To determine whether the predictor tests are measuring the same or different abilities, we must look at the correlations between them. These are:

Mathematics versus Shop	−.02
Mathematics versus Electricity	.37
Shop versus Electricity	.30

Thus, the electricity test shows some overlap with each of the other tests but not a very great overlap.   There is most in common between the mathematics and electricity tests.   The mathematics and shop tests are almost completely unrelated.

Is the overlap of electricity with each of the other two tests so great that they can add nothing of value to our prediction?   To answer this question, we may compute a statistic known as the *partial correlation*. The partial correlation is a measure of the relationship which remains after the effect of one or more other factors is removed.*   In this instance, it is the correlation of academic grades with math or with shop after the common influence of the electricity test score is removed from the picture.   These partial correlations are:

Math versus grades, electricity score partialed out	.25
Shop versus grades, electricity score partialed out	.16

Thus, we see that each of the other tests has some validity independent of the part held in common with the electricity test, though eliminating the part which they hold in common with the electricity test has reduced the validity of each.

The Validity of a Composite.   We must ask now how much we could gain in validity by using two tests or all three, combining them in the most advantageous way.   For this we can compute the *multiple correlation*.   The multiple correlation is the maximum prediction that

---

* The formula for partial correlation is

$$r_{12.3} = \frac{r_{12} - r_{13}r_{23}}{\sqrt{1 - r_{13}^2}\sqrt{1 - r_{23}^2}}$$

where $r_{12.3}$ is the partial correlation of variables 1 and 2, with the effect variable 3 removed.

r_{12}, r_{13}, r_{23} are the correlation of variables 1 and 2, 1 and 3, and 2 and 3, respectively.

can be obtained from an additive combination of scores on two or more tests.* In our example, the multiple correlations for combinations of two and three tests are as follows:

Electricity and Mathematics	.615
Electricity and Shop	.596
Mathematics and Shop	.500
All three tests	.634

Thus, we see that the combined tests give a somewhat higher correlation (.634) with the criterion than does the best single test (.58) if the tests are combined with the most appropriate weights.

It may be possible to get a better intuitive feeling for partial and multiple correlation (though necessarily a mathematically inexact one) from a pictorial representation. Consider the diagrams in Fig. 19.1. These are designed to portray the relationships between the criterion score (C), the electricity test (E) and the mathematics test (M). Diagrams I, II, and III show the tests taken by pairs. The fact that they overlap in what they measure (are positively correlated) is indicated by the overlapping areas. The size of the overlapping area has been made approximately proportional to the size of the correlations. Each area has been labeled with the letter or letters corresponding to the measures that it represents.

Now look at Diagram IV. This shows all three tests at once. Note that a larger area of C is covered jointly by E and M than by either of them separately. This larger area (MC + MEC + EC) corresponds to the larger *multiple correlation*. Note that the area common to M and C, but *not* to E (MC) is quite small. This corresponds to the smaller *partial correlation* between M and C. The partial correlation is considerably lower in this case because much of what M and C have in common is also measured by E. This is the part labeled MEC. The diagram shows clearly that the gain from adding a new test to a selection battery depends upon the added test measuring some *new* aspect of the criterion that is not measured by the test or tests we are already using.

Weighting Tests. Our next problem is to determine the best set of weights. These are known as *regression weights*. They are best in

* For two predictors the multiple correlation is given by the formula

$$r_{1.23} = \sqrt{1 - (1 - r_{12}^2)(1 - r_{13.2}^2)}$$

where $r_{1.23}$ indicates the multiple correlation of 1 with 2 and 3, and $r_{13.2}$ is the partial correlation of 1 and 3 with 2 held constant. The formula for more complex cases will be found in standard statistics textbooks.

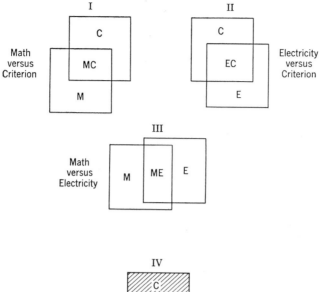

Math versus Criterion

Electricity versus Criterion

Math versus Electricity

Math, Electricity, and Criterion

Fig. 19.1.   Graphic representation of partial and multiple correlations.

the sense that they reduce to a minimum the errors in predicting the criterion score.*   For our set of three tests the regression weights are, respectively,

Mathematics	.24
Shop	.17
Electricity	.44

*With two predictor variables, the regression weights to be applied to standard scores are given by the formula

$$\beta_{12.3} = \frac{r_{12} - r_{13}r_{23}}{1 - r_{23}{}^2}$$

$$\beta_{13.2} = \frac{r_{13} - r_{12}r_{23}}{1 - r_{23}{}^2}$$

The formulas and computing procedures for three or more predictors will be found in standard statistics textbooks.

These are the weights we should use if all our tests had the same standard deviation (for example, if they were all in standard score units). However, when the tests are in raw-score units, we must take account of the standard deviation. A test with a large standard deviation already receives a heavy weight just from the variability of its scores. The relative weights to be applied to raw scores are the regression weights *divided by* the corresponding standard deviations. For our example, we have the following:

	Standard Deviation	Regression Weights	Raw-Score Weights	Integral Weights
Mathematics	4.40	.24	.055	2
Shop	2.06	.17	.083	3
Electricity	2.76	.44	.159	6

The weights in the final column of the above table are simple integers that stand in very nearly the same ratios as the raw-score weights. They are more convenient to use than the decimal weights and are as good for all practical purposes. If we wish to combine our separate tests, we can use these integers as weighting factors to be applied to the scores on the three tests. Thus, we could take 2 times the mathematics score plus 3 times the shop score plus 6 times the electricity score and prepare a composite score for each student.

We have calculated composite scores using the above multiplying factors. These composite scores were correlated with the criterion and in this instance the result checked perfectly with the predicted correlation of .634. To see what, if anything, we really gained by the pooling, we may prepare another table like Table 19.2. We have

Table 19.3. Number Passing and Failing Electronics Training at Each Composite Score Level

(2 Math + 3 Shop + 6 Electricity)

Score	Unsatisfactory	Satisfactory
50–59	2	1
60–69	5	2
70–79	6	3
80–89	8	8
90–99	7	12
100–109	2	9
110–119		11
120–129		10
130–139		7
140–149		4
150–159		2

done this in Table 19.3.   Repeating our calculations of cost and gain from two levels of cutting score, we find that we can

Eliminate 23.3% of failures at a cost of 4.3% of successes, or
"   70.0% "   "   " " "   " 20.3% "   "

Comparing this accomplishment with that for the electricity test alone, it is hard to see any difference between them.   The small difference in correlation does not show up as any clear improvement in practical effectiveness in a sample of this small size.   With a large sample, some improvement would presumably be noted.

PROBLEMS IN THE USE OF SELECTION TESTS

TWO WAYS OF USING TWO OR MORE PREDICTORS

In the last section, we showed how predictor tests could be used two or more at a time by multiplying each test score by an appropriate weight and adding them together to give a single composite score. This we shall call the method of *linear combination,* since it is based on a simple linear equation of the type $ax + by + cz$.   If we used this method mechanically, we would employ or accept for further education those individuals with the highest scores, going down the line until we had enough to meet our quota.

Another way of proceeding would be to set separate qualifying scores for our separate measures and accept only those individuals who qualified on each hurdle.   Thus, we might specify that each applicant must get at least the following scores:

Mathematics	5
Shop	3
Electricity	7

This procedure would screen out 10, or 33.3 per cent, of the failures at a cost of 8, or 11.6 per cent, of the successes.   Higher minimum scores of

Mathematics	8
Shop	4
Electricity	8

would eliminate 23, or 76.7 per cent, of the failures at the cost of 16, or 23.2 per cent, of the successes.   In this illustration, the separate cutting scores represent little or no improvement over the electricity test alone, but neither did the single composite score.

In terms of statistical theory, the use of separate cutting scores usually seems less sound than the procedure of linear combination. The one exception to this is when some minimum level of a particular trait is absolutely essential for a job, but additional amounts are not of great importance. Furthermore, the cutting scores must be determined by an essentially trial-and-error process, and once they are set they are rather inflexible. However, application of the separate minimum requirements is probably simpler for an untrained person than is computing a combined score.

The real practical advantage of separate cutting scores comes when one of the predictor tests is expensive or time-consuming to apply. Then, a simpler and more economical test may be applied to the total group and part of the group may be screened out by this economical procedure. The more costly appraisal device need be applied only to the remainder. Thus, if a written test of subject-matter knowledge and a performance test of actual classroom teaching were being used in the selection of secondary-school teachers, it would be very reasonable to use the written test as an initial screening device and to use the performance test only with those who met minimum standards on the written test.

SELECTION RATIO AND TEST EFFECTIVENESS

The minimum scores that are set for the separate tests or for the composite score in any practical testing program will depend to a considerable extent upon the law of supply and demand. When applicants are few and vacancies many, lower requirements must be set; when applicants are many and vacancies few, the selecting agency can afford to be choosy. This ratio of acceptance to application is called the *selection ratio*.

The practical value of a testing program depends as much upon the selection ratio as it does upon the validity of available tests. In the extreme case in which we can afford to reject nobody, even the most valid test is of no value as a selection device. At the other extreme, if we need take only one applicant in ten, for example, the use of even a test with rather low validity will be quite beneficial. This fact is illustrated in Fig. 19.2. If the lower selection ratio is used, in which about 15 per cent of the applicants are eliminated, a good many potential failures are accepted even for the good test, in which proportion of successes changes steeply as one goes from a low to a high score. If we can afford to use the higher of the two indicated selection ratios, the good test excludes almost all the potential failures and even the poor test improves our batting average markedly. In the numerical example that we used in the previous sections, if we had accepted only 10 out of our 99 applicants, even the shop test would have given us 9 successes, while at that same cutting score the electricity test would

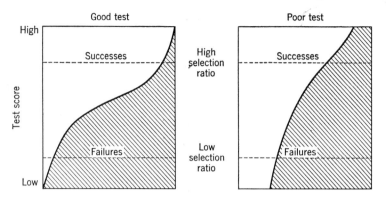

Fig. 19.2. Influence of selection ratio upon test effectiveness.

have yielded 100-per-cent successes. This compares with 70 per cent in the total group who were successful.

With a low selection ratio (few applicants accepted), a testing program gives promise of large practical gains. When the selection ratio is high (most applicants accepted), the practical gains will inevitably be much smaller.

PRESELECTION AND TEST VALIDITY

There is one factor whose influence on test validities we must mention here. The factor is a pervasive one that distorts the interpretation of tests in a good deal of personnel research. Again, the effect is a complex one that we cannot explore fully. The factor with which we are now concerned is that of preselection of the group on which we get criterion data.

In our illustrative example, suppose that a regulation had been in effect that no one with a mathematics test score below 10 would be admitted to the training program. This would have eliminated 26 of our 99 cases and among them 15 of our 30 failers. The spread of mathematics test scores within the group that remained would have been substantially less, and there would also have been less spread in grades. Under these circumstances, the correlation of test with criterion will normally be reduced. In this instance it drops from 0.40 to 0.15. Thus, if we had had a selection program in effect and had admitted only those with high math test scores, within the admitted group the math test would have appeared almost useless. Its true value would not have been changed, but the evidence available to us would not have permitted us to see that value. Those who would have failed because of math deficiency would have been cut off at the source.

We cannot indicate in this discussion the mathematical procedures to correct for preselection. In practice, these cannot always be applied anyhow, because we may not fully know the nature and extent of preselection that has been operating. We can merely give a few general guiding principles.

1. When those admitted to a job or training program have been selected on the basis of score on some test, the apparent validity of that test for those remaining will be reduced.

2. The smaller the selection ratio (i.e., the higher the cutting score), the greater will be the reduction in apparent validity.

3. Selection will also operate to reduce the validity of other tests that are correlated with the test used for screening.

4. In the correlated tests, the reduction will be in proportion to the correlation of the second test with the test used for screening. It will also be in proportion to the degree of selectivity.

If a school, military training program, or employer is installing a program of selection tests and must choose the best tests to use on the basis of validity statistics, it is important to try to appraise and allow for the effects of preselection in interpreting these statistics. A thorough discussion of both the logic and statistics of the problem has been supplied by Gulliksen.[3] For the present, it will suffice to point out the problem and warn the reader of its importance.

RATIONAL VERSUS EMPIRICAL BASES FOR WEIGHTING TESTS

In preceding sections we have outlined procedures for deciding which tests to use and how much weight to give to each, basing the decision entirely on the empirical evidence from trying out the tests. For several reasons, however, it may not be desirable to be guided entirely by the validity data. The criterion measure will usually be imperfect, i.e., incomplete or biased in some respects. The sample of cases may be rather meager. The empirical results may be distorted by the preselection effects discussed in the previous section. For these reasons, we may want to give some weight to our rational analysis of the situation as well as to the empirical evidence. Thus, in discussing selection tests for medical schools, Stalnaker says: [5]

> While I should be unwilling to discourage anyone from correlating any two variables, I am neither impressed nor concerned when a low correlation is found between scores on a test in understanding modern society and grades in laboratory work in gross anatomy. I continue

to favor selecting the men for the study of medicine who have some awareness of social sciences.

If the average grades in first-year medical school do not correlate highly with a score which may crudely be representative of intelligence, I shall not conclude that a stupid M.D. is as good as a bright one as far as diagnosis of disease in my personal family is concerned.

In this example, limitations of the criterion are recognized. The writer is expressing his belief that rational analysis is as important in defining sound selection procedures as are statistical computations.

COMBINING TEST AND NON-TEST DATA

In any program of personnel selection, consideration will usually need to be given to factors other than test scores. We have in mind such things as personal history data, educational or previous work record, and impressions or evidence gathered in a personal interview. In practice, this type of material is often used (1) without any systematic evidence of its validity and (2) in a rather haphazard and intuitive way. There is no real reason why personal data or work history items cannot be scored or rated, or why the impressions gained in an interview cannot be reduced to some quantitative estimate of probable success in the training program or value on the job. If this is done, the resulting scores can be evaluated in exactly the same way that test scores are evaluated. If they prove to have useful validity, they can be weighted in a composite score together with tests. That is, qualitative data can be first converted into quantitative terms and then pooled with other types of quantitative data. This would appear to be a sound extension of the research approach to personnel selection.

THE PLACE OF CLINICAL JUDGMENT IN SELECTION PROGRAMS

The procedures we have been proposing so far for the use of tests and even of qualitative data in personnel selection have emphasized uniform and essentially rigid procedures for pooling and evaluating the evidence on each case. This is likely to be offensive to the person who prizes his clinical judgment and would like to temper the decision in individual cases by that judgment. He is likely to feel that he can "beat the game" and make predictions that will be more accurate than those given by mechanical application of a set of regression weights.

Concrete evidence suggests that this is not generally so.[4] Where adequate empirical evidence is on hand to permit setting standard procedures for weighting and combining test results and other evidence, the mechanical combining usually gives more accurate prediction of a definite criterion than does an intuitive weighting, and persons for whom an exception is made on an intuitive basis do no better than their test scores indicated for them.

An intuitive appraisal of the individual, as by an interview, may serve a useful function as one of a team of predictors. As suggested in the previous section, this appraisal may be quantified as a rating on specific points, and the ratings may then be combined with other predictors. Again, as we indicated above, when empirical data are meager, rational and perhaps intuitive judgments may enter into original decisions as to the *weighting* of different aspects of evidence. But intuitive weighting of the evidence for each applicant seems justifiable only on the grounds of expediency and lack of any sound empirical evidence as to how different elements of information *should* be weighted.

THE OPTIMUM CUTTING SCORE

In any selection program, we face at some point the problem of deciding how selective to be. Shall we accept all but a few of the least promising applicants or shall we admit only a small group of the most promising? There are always practical limitations on how selective we *can* be, set by the number of applicants that it is possible to attract and the number of vacancies to be filled. However, there is some flexibility in the amount of recruiting done or in the speed with which vacancies are filled by the first individuals who appear as applicants.

In general, the more effort and expense we put into recruiting and testing, the higher we can set our cutting score and the more we can save in costs of training and efficiency of operation. Sometimes it may be possible to estimate the per capita cost of increasing the pool of applicants tested, on the one hand, and the per capita cost of training a new employee, on the other. Bennett and Doppelt [2] report an analysis of costs and savings for several different employee-selection projects.

With food-store checkers, for example, the cost of testing an applicant was figured to be $2.00 and the cost of training a new employee to be $300. Basing calculations on the per cent of employees at each score level rated as satisfactory, they calculate the per capita cost of obtaining a satisfactory employee. Thus, if the cutting score on the *Store Personnel Test* is set at 90, their data indicate that it is necessary to train 1.79 employees for each satisfactory one that is obtained and to test 3.89 in order to get the 1.79 to be trained. Using these figures and the costs of $300 to train and $2.00 to test, the cost per satisfactory employee becomes $544.

Similar calculations at each score level yield the data of Fig. 19.3. Thus, in so far as the costs that have been considered give a true picture of *all* costs involved, the most economical procedure here would be to set quite a high cutting score (about 110) and accept only those who fell above this score. In this particular instance, this would mean accepting only the top 10 per cent of applicants.

Such calculations as this are only partially realistic because it is almost impossible to determine either all the costs or all the gains. Thus, in our illustration we did not show the costs of recruiting a large group of applicants, and this might be substantial. At the same time, we did not show any long-term gains from having more efficient employees. The example shows the type of thinking that is involved in setting a cutting score. It is a balancing of one set of costs, tangible and intangible, against another, and setting a cutting score such that the most advantageous balance of costs and gains will be reached. However, it is rarely possible to reduce the solution to a precise matter of dollars and cents.

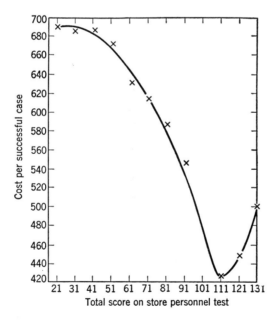

Fig. 19.3. Curve showing cost of training satisfactory female checkers in a food-store chain. (From Doppelt and Bennett.[2])

SUMMARY STATEMENT

The basic pattern of personnel selection and personnel selection research is simple. Promising predictors are identified. These are related to a suitable measure of job success. On the basis of the evidence, the most effective predictors are selected, and procedures are set up for using the evidence from them, either jointly or in succession. When future students or employees are to be selected, the relevant evidence is gathered and combined by standard procedures, and those with the highest standing or those falling above specified minimum levels are accepted. However, many specific problems arise in connection with (1) discovery of promising predictors, (2) identification of a suitable measure of success, (3) the analytical procedures for studying predictor-criterion relationships, and (4) practical routines for using the evidence from predictors. Some of these have been considered in the present chapter.

Certain general viewpoints may be expressed in closing.

1. Any type of evidence, test or non-test, quantitative or qualitative, may appropriately be used in a selection program.

2. Qualitative material should be translated into quantitative form by either a scoring or rating system.

3. The validity of any type of evidence should be tested out empirically in terms of its relationship to criteria of job success.

4. The empirical evidence on validity should not always be followed slavishly in setting up standard procedures for using and combining test data. Rational judgment should be used to temper statistical evidence, and more weight should be given to rational considerations when the empirical evidence is less satisfactory.

5. Once standard procedures have been set up, they should be used in a standard way. Subjective impressions may enter in as evidence but should not determine the way in which the evidence is applied to the individual case.

REFERENCES

1. Brown, C. W., and E. E. Ghiselli, The relationship between the predictive power of aptitude tests for trainability and for job proficiency, *J. appl. Psychol.*, **36**, 1952, 370–372.
2. Doppelt, J. E., and G. K. Bennett, Reducing the cost of training satisfactory workers by using tests, *Personnel Psychol.*, **6**, 1953, 1–8.
3. Gulliksen, H., *Theory of mental tests*, New York, Wiley, 1950.

4. Meehl, Paul E., *Clinical vs. Actuarial Prediction,* Minneapolis, Minn., University of Minnesota Press, 1954.
5. Stalnaker, J., Tests for medicine, in *Proceedings of the 1950 Invitational Conference on Testing Problems,* Princeton, N. J., Educational Testing Service, 1951.

SUGGESTED ADDITIONAL READING

Cronbach, Lee J., *Essentials of psychological testing,* 2nd ed., New York, Harper, 1960, Chapter 12.
Ghiselli, Edwin E., and Clarence W. Brown, *Personnel and industrial psychology,* 2nd ed., New York, McGraw-Hill, 1955, pp. 17–58.
Thorndike, Robert L., *Personnel selection,* New York, Wiley, 1949, Chapters 1, 2, 5–10.
Tiffin, Joseph, and Ernest T. McCormick, *Industrial psychology,* 4th ed., Englewood Cliffs, N. J., Prentice-Hall, 1958, pp. 75–109.

QUESTIONS FOR DISCUSSION

1. Think of some job you know fairly well. What measures might be used as a criterion of job success? What are the advantages and limitations of each?

2. Why is it important to have a large group of cases when studying the validity of a set of tests that have been proposed for use as predictors?

3. Why can combinations of tests predict better than a single test?

4. What advantages do you see in using two or more tests with separate cutting scores, rather than combining the predictors by a regression equation? Under what circumstances would separate cutting scores be most acceptable?

5. For a given validity coefficient, how does the selection ratio affect the value of a testing program?

6. Under what circumstances might one decide to deviate from a regression equation in weighting tests for personnel selection?

7. A test was originally tried out on an unscreened group of job applicants, and for them it was found to have a validity coefficient of .50. Then it was put into use and used to screen out 50 per cent of applicants. What would you expect to happen to the validity coefficient in the group who were accepted? Is the change real, or is it a statistical artifact?

8. What considerations limit the use of results such as those shown in Table 19.2 to determine a cutting score?

Appendix I

▼

Computation of Square Root

If facilities are available, it will be easiest to get the value of the square root by using a slide rule or a set of tables of squares and square roots. (Such tables will be found in engineering handbooks and books of tables for mathematicians and statisticians.) When no such aids are available, the following computing routine may be used.

Instructions	*Example*
1. Starting at the decimal point, break the number up into blocks of two digits each.	10.27 03
2. Look at the first block on the left. Pick the largest number whose square is equal to or less than this number.	10. $3^2 = 9$
3. Place the number from 2 to the right of the problem, and subtract the square from the block on the left.	$10.27\ 03\,|\,3$ $\quad\ \ 9$ $\quad\ \overline{\ 1}$
4. Bring down the next block of two digits.	$10.27\ 03\,|\,3$ $\quad\ \ 9$ $\quad\ \overline{1.27}$
5. Double the number on the extreme right, and place it to the left of the number in 4 above. (Leave a space on the right of the doubled value.)	$6\quad\begin{array}{l}10.27\ 03\,|\,3\\ \quad\ 9\\ \overline{1.27}\end{array}$
6. Pick the largest digit that can be put after the entry in 5 above that can be used as a multiplier of the 2-digit number and still have it less than the number resulting from 4. Put this number after the entry in 5 and also after the figure at the extreme right.	$62\quad\begin{array}{l}10.27\ 03\,|\,3.2\\ \quad\ 9\\ \overline{1.27}\end{array}$

Instructions	*Example*

7. Multiply the entry on the extreme left (62) by the digit on the extreme right (2), and put the product below the entry from 4. Subtract.

$$
\begin{array}{r|l}
 & 10.27\ 03\ \underline{|3.2} \\
 & \ \ 9 \\
\hline
62 & 1.27 \\
 & 1.24 \\
\hline
 & \ \ \ 3
\end{array}
$$

8. Bring down the next block of two digits, and repeat steps 5, 6, and 7. (Since 640 is greater than 303, it goes in zero times.)

$$
\begin{array}{r|l}
 & 10.27\ 03\ |3.20 \\
 & \ \ 9 \\
\hline
62 & 1.27 \\
 & 1.24 \\
\hline
640 & 3\ 03 \\
 & 0\ 00 \\
\hline
 & 3\ 03
\end{array}
$$

9. Bring down the next block of two digits (zeros) and repeat steps 5, 6, and 7. Repeat until the desired number of places is obtained.

$$
\begin{array}{r|l}
 & 10.27\ 03\ |3.204\ \text{Ans.} \\
 & \ \ 9 \\
\hline
62 & 1.27 \\
 & 1.24 \\
\hline
640 & 3\ 03 \\
 & 0\ 00 \\
\hline
6404 & 3\ 03\ 00 \\
 & 2\ 56\ 16 \\
\hline
 & \ \ 46\ 84
\end{array}
$$

Appendix II

▼

Calculating the Correlation Coefficient

The correlation coefficient is an index that expresses the extent to which two variables (X and Y) go together. It indicates the extent to which high X scores go with high Y scores, and vice versa. But "high" and "low" must be expressed in some uniform terms from one set of data to another if the index is to have the same meaning for different sets of data. The standard framework for expressing "high" and "low" is the mean and standard deviation of the group. If each X or Y score is expressed as being so many standard deviations above or below the group mean, the product of these X and Y *standard scores* is calculated, and the average of these products is obtained, the result is the *Pearson product-moment* correlation coefficient.

This can be expressed by the following formula:

$$r = \frac{\Sigma z_x z_y}{N}$$

where r is the correlation coefficient.

z_x and z_y are standard scores in X and Y.

N is the number of cases.

This is a *definition* of the correlation coefficient. Now we must consider the steps in computing it. Below are outlined the procedures for computing the correlation coefficient from sets of raw test scores. The procedure is illustrated with numerical data from the reading and arithmetic tests shown in Table 5.1.

Step 1. Select class intervals for both of the variables.

In our illustration, both arithmetic and reading scores are grouped by 3's.

Step 2. Prepare a two-dimensional tabulation sheet, indicating class intervals for the X variable on the top and for the Y variable on the left of the chart. Cross-section paper or special tabulating sheets can be used with advantage.

The tabulation sheet is shown in Fig. 1. The X variable is the arithmetic score and the Y variable the reading score.

Variable X (arithmetic score)

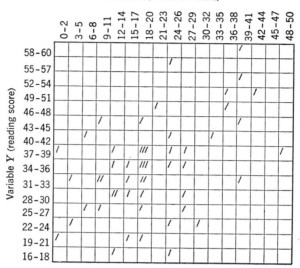

Fig. 1.

Step 3. Tally the data, entering each score as a tally mark in the cell corresponding to the X and Y score for that case. Count the number of tallies in each cell, and write in the frequencies in the upper part of the cell.

Tally marks have been entered in the tabulation sheet in Fig. 1. The frequencies are indicated in Fig. 2.

Step 4. Sum down each column and enter the totals on the bottom edge of the tabulation sheet. Sum across each row and enter on the right. These totals entered in the margin give the simple frequency distribution for X and Y, respectively.

Sums are shown in Fig. 2. The entries across the bottom are for the X (arithmetic) variable and those at the right for the Y (reading) variable.

Step 5. Consider the values entered at the right of the table in step 4. They make up a simple frequency distribution of Y scores. Following Chapter 5 (pp. 112–113), carry out the steps for calculating the standard deviation. Determine N, $\Sigma fy'$ and $\Sigma f(y')^2$.

The values for y', fy', and $f(y')^2$ are shown in the three columns just to the right of the column of frequencies in Fig. 2. For this example, $\Sigma fy' = -7$ and $\Sigma f(y')^2 = 535$. (It may be noted that the Y variable is the reading test, and that these values are identical with the ones calculated for that test in Chapter 5.)

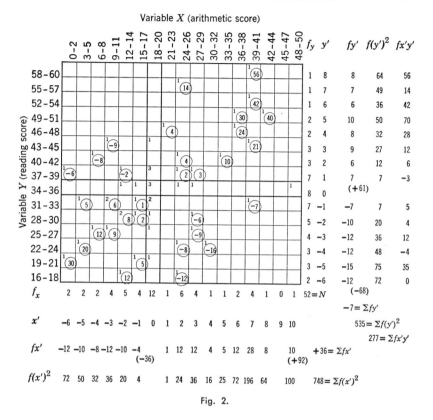

Fig. 2.

Step 6. Repeat step 5 for the frequencies of the X variable entered at the bottom of the table.

The value of $\Sigma fx'$ is $+36$; $\Sigma f(x')^2$ equals 748.

Step 7. Multiply the frequency in each cell of the two-way tabulation by the x' and the y' values for that cell. Enter this product, i.e., $fx'y'$, in the lower corner of the cell. This procedure will be easier if the column and row chosen for the arbitrary origin are enclosed in heavy rules, to show the zero point for each scale. The frequency in a cell must be multiplied by *both* the x' value for that cell and the y' value.

These entries have been circled in Fig. 2. Consider the row just above the heavy horizontal rules. Going right from the heavy vertical rules, we come to a frequency of 1 in the second cell. For this cell $f = 1$, $x' = 2$, and $y' = 1$, so the product is $1 \times 2 \times 1 = 2$. For the next cell in the row $f = 1$, $x' = 3$, and $y' = 1$, so the product is $1 \times 3 \times 1 = 3$. Notice that in the upper left and lower right quarters of the table, the products are negative, because either x' or y' is negative. Also notice that all products for cells between the heavy lines are zero.

Step 8. Sum the $fx'y'$ values for all the cells. This gives $\Sigma fx'y'$, the sum of all the products of x' and y' values.

In the example, the values have first been summed across each row, and these sums entered in the column at the far right. This column has then been summed to give $\Sigma fx'y' = 277$.

Step 9. The formula for computing the correlation coefficient is

For our example, the solution becomes:

$$r = \frac{\dfrac{\Sigma fx'y'}{N} - \left(\dfrac{\Sigma fx'}{N}\right)\left(\dfrac{\Sigma fy'}{N}\right)}{\left\{\sqrt{\dfrac{\Sigma f(x')^2}{N} - \left(\dfrac{\Sigma fx'}{N}\right)^2} \times \sqrt{\dfrac{\Sigma f(y')^2}{N} - \left(\dfrac{\Sigma fy'}{N}\right)^2}\right\}}$$

Substitute the proper values in the formula and solve. (It should be noted that the two terms in the denominator are merely the formulas for the standard deviation of X and Y, respectively.

$$r = \frac{\dfrac{277}{52} - \left(\dfrac{36}{52}\right)\left(\dfrac{-7}{52}\right)}{\sqrt{\dfrac{748}{52} - \left(\dfrac{36}{52}\right)^2}\sqrt{\dfrac{535}{52} - \left(\dfrac{-7}{52}\right)^2}}$$

$$= \frac{5.33 - (.692)(-.135)}{\{\sqrt{14.38 - (.692)^2} \times \sqrt{10.29 - (-.135)^2}\}}$$

$$= \frac{5.42}{\sqrt{13.91}\,\sqrt{10.28}}$$

$$= \frac{5.42}{11.90}$$

$$= .46$$

Appendix III

▼

Section A

GENERAL INTELLIGENCE TESTS

CALIFORNIA SHORT FORM TEST OF MENTAL MATURITY, 1957 REVISION

California Test Bureau   *Testing time:* 30–65 min.
Range: Pre-Primary (Kindergarten to grade 1); *Primary* (grades 1 to 3); *Elementary* (grades 4 to 8); *Junior High* (grades 7 to 9); *Secondary* (grades 9 to 13); *Advanced* (grades 10 to 16, adults)

Test is also available in long form. Reliability inadequately reported in manual accompanying test but technical manual gives reliability for each grade. Reliability coefficients based on a range of grades should be ignored. Test gives three scores: (1) language IQ, (2) non-language IQ, and (3) total IQ. Non-language portion of test much less reliable than language portion. Language section of test and total score correlate satisfactorily with achievement test scores although manual presents very little evidence on this point. Usefulness of the non-language score has not been demonstrated. Emphasis on the factorial nature of the test in this manual is undesirable since the special factors discussed have not been demonstrated. Diagnostic profile should be ignored since the subtests are too short to provide reliable results. Language portion of test has heavy emphasis on vocabulary.

CHICAGO NON-VERBAL EXAMINATION

Psychological Corporation   *Testing time:* 40 min.
Range: Age 7 to adults

The test is designed to measure non-verbal aspects of intelligence. It is composed of ten subtests which may be administered either with oral directions or pantomime directions. Reliability coefficients range from .80 to .93 obtained by both split-half method and retest on groups with ranges of 2 and 3 years in chronological age and 2 to 6 grades in school placement. The test will probably be useful for children with hearing difficulties or reading disabilities. It may also be useful with both children and adults who have limited use of English. Some of the pictorial material is very poorly drawn and reproduced.

COLLEGE QUALIFICATION TESTS

Psychological Corporation   *Testing time:* 80–110 min.
Range: Candidates for college entrance

A series of three ability tests: (1) V–verbal, (2) N–numerical, and (3) I–science and social science information. Tests were developed for use by college admissions officers and guidance personnel. Form B of test restricted to colleges and universities. Test yields six scores including a total score for the test. Manual provides a number of different norms by sex, type of institution, and curriculum. Validity data for different courses of study in different institutions are provided in manual and give evidence that test can be useful in the selection of students. Reliabilities are adequate, in the middle, 90's for total score and ranging from the high 70's to low 90's for the subtests. Manual is excellent.

COOPERATIVE SCHOOL AND COLLEGE ABILITY TESTS (SCAT)

Cooperative Test Division   *Testing time:* 60–75 min.
Educational Testing Service
Range: Grades 4 to 6, 6 to 8, 8 to 10, 10 to 12, and 12 to 14

SCAT yields three scores; (1) verbal, (2) quantitative, and (3) total. Test has been designed to replace *American Council on Education Psychological Examination* as a measure of the capacity of students to undertake additional schooling. Manuals and interpretive materials accompanying the tests are excellent. Reliabilities are satisfactory although those reported in the manuals may be slightly inflated because of the speed factor on some of the tests. Current data on validity are somewhat limited, but indicate the test has some promise for predicting success in school. Scores on different forms and levels have been equated to facilitate comparisons if the tests are used continuously. Forms 1C and 1D for grades 12 to 14 are restricted for use with students in college.

DAVIS-EELLS TEST OF GENERAL INTELLIGENCE OR PROBLEM SOLVING ABILITY

Harcourt, Brace and World, Inc.   *Testing time:* 70–120 min.
Range: Grades 1 to 2, and 3 to 6

This is a group intelligence test in pictorial form with no reading required—which was supposed to reduce socio-economic bias in the results. The original data report that this purpose was accomplished, but later studies done by other workers have failed to verify these results. The evidence at hand suggests that the *Davis-Eells* test has not eliminated socio-economic biases in the scores. The test correlates much lower with school achievement than do other tests of general intelligence. The test is difficult to administer and tedious to score.

HENMON-NELSON TESTS OF MENTAL ABILITY, REVISED EDITION

Houghton Mifflin Company   *Testing time:* 30–50 min.
Range: Grades 3 to 6, 6 to 9, 9 to 12, and college–freshman year through first year graduate school

The test gives only a single over-all score. The total score correlates well with other group tests of intelligence and with teachers' grades and achievement test results.   Reliability coefficients estimated by use of parallel forms of the test range from .87 to .94.   Norming procedures for the test were excellent.   The test has a very heavy emphasis on verbal abilities.

KUHLMANN-ANDERSON INTELLIGENCE TESTS, SIXTH EDITION

Personnel Press   *Testing time:* 30–45 min.
Range: Kindergarten; grades 1, 2, 3, 4, 5, and 6

A separate booklet is prepared for each grade.   Each level is identified by a letter on the test booklet, not by grade level, so that a lower level can be used in a class without the students knowing it is a lower level. Reliability is satisfactory, coefficients ranging from .88 to .95 computed for a single grade.   Validity data as given in the manual are adequate. The IQ obtained is based on the median of the mental ages on the separate subtests.   The test yields a single over-all IQ.   The test is highly verbal, although there is little actual reading.   It has many separately timed subtests, which makes administration somewhat difficult.   The subtests are not to be used for diagnosis.   This is one of the best all-around group intelligence tests for obtaining an over-all mental age.

KUHLMANN-ANDERSON INTELLIGENCE TESTS, SEVENTH EDITION

Personnel Press   *Testing time:* 35–40 min.
Range: Grades 7 to 9, and 9 to 12

A revised edition of the junior high school and senior high school tests. The revised tests yield three separate scores (1) V–verbal, (2) Q–quantitative, and (3) T–total.   All three scores can be converted to grade percentile ranks and in addition the total score can be converted to an "intelligence quotient" (deviation IQ with mean of 100 and SD of 16) for each age group.   Reliabilities of the three individual scores are high.   The difference score between V and Q does not appear to have high enough reliability to be used.   Data on concurrent validity are satisfactory but since the test was published in December 1960, no predictive validity data are available.   However it is likely that the total score of the new revision will correlate as highly with school success as did the old battery.   Like the sixth edition, this revision requires somewhat less reading than other group intelligence tests.   Re-usable test booklets and separate answer sheets are provided.

THE LORGE-THORNDIKE INTELLIGENCE TESTS

Houghton Mifflin Company   *Testing time:* 30–45 min.
Range: Kindergarten to grade 1; grades 2 to 3, 4 to 6, 7 to 9, and 10 to 12

Non-reading test through grade 3.   For grades 4 and above, separate verbal and non-verbal tests are available.   Spanish directions are available for non-verbal battery.   Reviewers in Buros' *Fifth Mental Measurements Yearbook* consider the test among the best of the group-intelligence tests. Standardization procedures and norms are outstanding.   Format of tests is very good.   Reliability coefficients estimated by use of alternate forms are high, more validity data are now available and show satisfactory correlations with the Stanford-Binet and group tests of intelligence and with achievement test scores.

OHIO STATE UNIVERSITY PSYCHOLOGICAL TEST, FORM 21

Ohio College Association   *Testing time:* No time limit
Range: Grades 9 to 16, adults

This is a power test designed primarily to predict success in college (correlations of about .60 with scholastic performance). Reliability is high. It emphasizes verbal ability. Norms are based on Ohio high-school students and freshmen in Ohio colleges. A good scholastic aptitude test at the college level.

OTIS QUICK-SCORING MENTAL ABILITY TESTS

Harcourt, Brace and World, Inc.   *Testing time:* 20–35 min.
Range: Alpha (grades 1.5 to 4); *Beta* (grades 4 to 9); *Gamma* (grades 9 to 16)

These have been among the most widely used tests in the public schools. Reliability is satisfactory. Evidence is presented that the scores have value in predicting school achievement. The tests are extremely easy to administer and score. They give a single over-all IQ. Primarily, they test verbal ability. The *Alpha* test requires no reading, but the other two levels do require reading.

PINTNER GENERAL ABILITY TESTS, NON-LANGUAGE SERIES

Harcourt, Brace and World, Inc.   *Testing time:* 50–60 min.
Range: Intermediate (grades 4 to 9)

This test requires no reading or use of language. Reliability is satisfactory. The test supplements the *Pintner* verbal series in the intermediate range. Directions are quite elaborate. The test must be hand-scored. It is useful for children with hearing or reading difficulties and is probably most useful in grades 6 and 7.

PINTNER GENERAL ABILITY TESTS: VERBAL SERIES

Harcourt, Brace and World, Inc.   *Testing time:* 45–55 min.
Range: Primary (kindergarten to grade 2); *Elementary* (grades 2.5 to 4.5); *Intermediate* (grades 4.5 to 9.5); *Advanced* (grades 9 and above)

Reliability is satisfactory. As evidence on validity, the manual reports the relationship between test scores and standardized achievement test scores, school grades, and other tests. The manual is very good. Five methods of interpreting scores are given. Each subtest is separately timed. The administration of the tests is somewhat more demanding than for other group tests.

SRA TESTS OF EDUCATIONAL ABILITY

Science Research Associates   *Testing time:* 30–55 min.
Range: Kindergarten to 2; grades 2 to 4, 4 to 6, 6 to 9, and 9 to 12

Tests are designed to provide measures of aptitude for school work and provide four scores (1) L–language, (2) R–reasoning, (3) Q–quantitative, and (4) T–total. Although the three subscores carry the same label at each grade level, it is likely that they do not represent the same kind of abilities at the different levels because the nature of the tests changes from level to level. Subtests tend to be short and to be speeded. Reliabilities of the subtests when properly computed are likely to be in the high .70's and low .80's, total score reliability is probably in the middle high .80's. Since the intercorrelations of the subtests run between .50 and .65, the differences between the scores are likely to be too unreliable to be useful. Samples on which norms are based are very limited (two school systems). Concurrent validity data presented in the technical manual indicate that the total score may have some value for immediate prediction of success in school work.

TERMAN-McNEMAR TEST OF MENTAL ABILITY

Harcourt, Brace and World, Inc. *Testing time:* 40–45 min.
Range: Grades 7 to 12

Reliability is satisfactory. The only validity data reported is the correlation between this revision and the earlier *Terman Group Intelligence Test.* The entire test is made up of verbal material involving reading, and it yields a single IQ. A well-standardized and well-constructed measure of verbal ability.

Section B

APTITUDE TEST BATTERIES

CHICAGO TESTS OF PRIMARY MENTAL ABILITIES

Science Research Associates *Testing time:* 240 min.
Range: Ages 11 to 17

The battery gives six scores (1) number, (2) verbal meaning, (3) space, (4) word fluency, (5) reasoning, and (6) memory. The battery is based on factor analysis (Thurstone's multiple factor theory). However, it is not clear that the tests are more independent than those in other aptitude batteries. Reliability data reported in the manual are actually not based on the present test but on the longer 1941 editions; therefore, the data must be discounted. Validity data are reported only for the 1941 edition. The test is a speed test rather than a power test. Norms are based only on Chicago children. Norms are not differentiated according to sex although there are marked sex differences on some tests.

DIFFERENTIAL APTITUDE TEST BATTERY

Psychological Corporation   *Testing time:* 300–330 min.
Range: Grades 8 to 12

See text, pp. 263–266, for discussion. This is a practical guidance battery for high-school use. It has an extremely full and well-organized manual. Extensive validation data are presented against educational criteria, but little against vocational criteria. Claims for validity are modest and realistic.

FLANAGAN APTITUDE CLASSIFICATON TESTS (FACT)

Science Research Associates   *Testing time:* 210–328 min.
Range: Grades 12 to 16 and above

This battery consists of nineteen tests and is essentially oriented toward vocational guidance rather than educational guidance. Each test is in a separate booklet and has a self-scoring answer sheet. Construction of test items appears to be very good. Reliability coefficients for separate tests tend to be low, but composite scores have adequate reliability. The greatest weakness in the battery is its lack of validity data to support many of the claims made in the manual and in accompanying materials. Until more validity data are available, it would probably be best to be extremely cautious in interpreting the meaning of the scores.

GENERAL APTITUDE TEST BATTERY

U. S. Employment Service   *Testing time:* 120–150 min.
Range: Grades 12 and above and adults   for group tests

See text, pp. 266–270, for discussion of this battery. It is available only for use by State Employment Offices.

GUILFORD-ZIMMERMAN APTITUDE SURVEY

Sheridan Supply Company   *Testing time:* 140–190 min.
Range: Grades 9 to 16, adults

This set of tests is based on factorial analysis of abilities. Evidence of the validity of the tests for specific occupations remains to be provided.

HOLZINGER-CROWDER UNI-FACTOR TESTS

Harcourt, Brace and World, Inc.   *Testing time:* 80–90 min.
Range: Grades 7 to 12

The nine tests in the battery yield four factor scores (1) verbal, (2) spatial, (3) numerical, and (4) reasoning. A weighted composite score is also provided as an indication of general scholastic aptitude. Equations are given for combining the factor scores in different ways to predict success in mathematics, science, social studies, and English. The manual is excellent. Alternate form reliabilities for single grades for each factor range from about .80 to .90. The verbal factor tends to be the best predictor of scholastic success in all subject areas.

MULTIPLE APTITUDE TESTS (MAT)

California Test Bureau   *Testing time:* 175–220 min.
Range: Grades 7 to 13

The battery consists of nine tests providing nine separate scores, which in turn yield scores on four basic factors. The word meaning, language usage, and arithmetic computation and reasoning tests have reliabilities in the high .80's or low .90's and are quite satisfactory; but the reliabilities for paragraph meaning, applied science and mechanics, and spatial relations tend to be only in the high .70's which makes them somewhat less useful for individual guidance. Predictive validity data for school marks are given and tend to be disappointingly low. Concurrent validity for 42 different occupational groups is given showing differences in occupational profiles on the tests; however, these were obtained for groups that were already engaged in the occupation.

Section C

READING TESTS

DAVIS READING TEST

Psychological Corporation   *Testing time:* 40–60 min.
Range: Grades 11 to 13

The test is available in four forms, each yielding two scores—one for speed and one for level of comprehension. Items on the test are well constructed and measure the subtler aspects of reading comprehension to a greater extent than do most reading tests. Materials accompanying the test are excellent, especially the materials on interpreting the meaning of each individual score and the differences between scores. Reliability, which has been determined through the use of alternate forms, is satisfactory. Evidence on statistical validity indicates that the test is valuable in predicting success in scholastic work.

DIAGNOSTIC READING TESTS: SURVEY SECTION

The Committee on Diagnostic Reading Tests   *Testing time:* 40–60 min.
New York 27, New York
Range: Kindergarten to grade 4; grades 4 to 8 and 7 to 13

The test covering kindergarten to grade 4 measures many of the same skills found in a reading readiness test, in addition to vocabulary and story reading. The tests for the upper levels measure vocabulary, rate of reading, and general comprehension. The tests have been designed for use both as survey tests (to be used alone) and as screening tests (to be used with the diagnostic tests of the same authors). Reliabilities of the survey tests are very low for use with individuals. The tests are printed on poor quality paper and are unattractive in format. The manuals are completely inadequate.

DURRELL-SULLIVAN READING CAPACITY AND ACHIEVEMENT TESTS

Harcourt, Brace and World, Inc. *Testing time:* 45 min.
Range: Primary (grades 2.5 to 4.5); *Intermediate* (grades 3 to 6)

Gives five scores (1) word meaning, (2) paragraph meaning, (3) spelling (optional), (4) written recall (optional), and (5) total. The comprehension test (word meaning and paragraph meaning) of the reading capacity section is given orally so that the examiner can obtain a measure of the pupil's capacity to understand written language. The reading achievement section is read by the pupil without help from the examiner. The fundamental assumption of these tests is that serious reading disabilities can be discovered by revealing discrepancies between the pupil's understanding of spoken language and his understanding of the printed word. Split-half reliabilities for part scores on reading capacity test for single grade groups range from .78 to .91, being somewhat higher for older children. Reliability for the reading achievement section ranges from .83 to .95. Although these reliabilities are somewhat low for individual diagnosis, the test would probably be useful to classroom teachers. Manual is fairly good.

GATES ADVANCED PRIMARY READING TESTS

Bureau of Publications *Testing time:* 40–50 min.
Teachers College, Columbia University
Range: Grades 2 (second half) to 3

These tests are part of the comprehensive series of Gates reading tests. Separate tests and scores are provided for word recognition and paragraph reading. Three equivalent forms of each test are available. Some of the paragraph-reading items can be answered by reading only the sentence giving directions for answering. Range of difficulty is adequate for measuring very superior readers but the *Gates Primary Reading Tests* probably would be better for the slower readers. Administration is easy. Reliability is satisfactory. Suggestions in manual for use of test results are very good.

GATES BASIC READING TESTS

Bureau of Publications *Testing time:* 70–80 min.
Teachers College, Columbia University
Range: Grades 3 (second half) to 8

The battery includes five tests (1) reading to appreciate general significance, (2) reading to understand precise directions, (3) reading to note details, (4) reading vocabulary, and (5) level of comprehension. There are three equivalent forms of each test. The tests may be too difficult for below-average readers in third grade and in the first half of fourth grade, and too easy for above-average readers in the seventh and eighth grades. Reliabilities of the tests are satisfactory throughout the range of grades covered. The test is easily administered. Suggestions to teachers for using test results and for remedial action are excellent.

GATES PRIMARY READING TESTS

Bureau of Publications   *Testing time:* 25–30 min.
Teachers College, Columbia University
Range: Grades 1 and 2 (first half)

The tests are of three types (1) word recognition, (2) sentence reading, and (3) paragraph reading. Each type of test comes in a separate booklet, and there are three equivalent forms of each. Raw scores can be converted to reading-grade scores, reading-age scores, and percentile scores. Reliabilities of the tests (estimated by use of alternate forms) are excellent. Format of the tests is excellent. Tests have a good range of difficulty but the advanced primary may be better for use with very superior readers in the first half of the second grade. Remedial suggestions for the teacher are very good.

GATES READING SURVEY—FORM 1

Bureau of Publications   *Testing time:* 50–60 min.
Teachers College, Columbia University
Range: Grades 3 (second half) to 10

The test yields four scores (1) speed, (2) vocabulary, (3) comprehension, (4) accuracy. The tests are easy to administer and to score if separate answer sheet edition is used but somewhat more time consuming if consumable edition is used. Use of reading age and reading grade scores is undesirable at upper levels but percentiles are provided for all grade levels. Reliabilities are satisfactory throughout the range of grades. The test would probably be most effective for use in grades 5 to 8. The manual for the test is very good for use by classroom teachers.

IOWA SILENT READING TEST: NEW EDITION, REVISED

Harcourt, Brace and World, Inc.   *Testing time:* 50–60 min.
Range: Elementary (grades 4 to 8); *Advanced* (grades 9 to 13)

There are six scores on the *Elementary Test* (1) rate and comprehension, (2) directed reading, (3) word meaning, (4) paragraph comprehension, (5) sentence meaning, and (6) location of information. The *Advanced Test* gives seven scores: (1–6) the same as the *Elementary Test,* and (7) poetry comprehension. The tests are speeded, and the reliability coefficients that are reported are spuriously high. The total score on the test gives some weight to study skills, such as use of an index, that are seldom found in a reading test. The manual is very good. The standard-score scale for the advanced tests is continuous with that for the elementary forms so that comparison from one score level to the other is possible.

KELLEY-GREENE READING COMPREHENSION TEST

Harcourt, Brace and World, Inc.   *Testing time:* 65–75 min.
Range: Grades 9 to 13

The test is designed to measure four skills in reading (1) selecting the central idea, (2) reading carefully and skimming for details, (3) generalizing and drawing inferences from what is read, and (4) remembering details. Separate scores are obtained for each of the reading skills and also for total reading comprehension. The weakest part of the test is the one devoted to remembering details. The other parts of the test are quite satisfactory. No norms are provided for college freshmen but norms for high school are good. Some concurrent validity data are reported but no data are reported on the relationship between scores on the test and success in various subject matter areas in school.

LEE-CLARK READING TEST, 1958 REVISION

California Test Bureau   *Testing time:* 20–30 min.
Range: Grade 1 (*Primer*), and grades 1 and 2 (*First Reader*)

The *Primer* test contains three parts (1) auditory stimuli, (2) visual stimuli, and (3) following directions. Each part is short, and only the total score should be used. The test appears to be too difficult for first graders unless their instruction in reading starts at the beginning of the school year. The *First Reader* test has five parts; the first three of these are the same as the three parts of the *Primer* test, and the last two are completion and inference tests. The test also appears to be too difficult for first and second graders. Reliability data and normative data are not provided for each grade for which the test has been designed to be used. Directions to students are clear and format is attractive but the manual is inadequate in respect to reliability, validity, and normative data.

NELSON-DENNY READING TEST, REVISED EDITION

Houghton Mifflin Company   *Testing time:* 35–40 min.
Range: Grades 9 to 12, college, adult

This revised test yields four scores (1) vocabulary, (2) paragraph comprehension, (3) reading rate, and (4) total. Test is easily administered and scored (particularly when self-marking answer sheets are used). Time limits are rather brief, especially for high-school students. The manual provides for conversion of raw scores to percentiles or grade-equivalent scores. However, the grade-equivalent scores are inappropriate for use with high school and college students. When a quick overview of the vocabulary knowledge and comprehension skill of high-school seniors or college students is desired, the test can be used efficiently and effectively, but the test is *not* diagnostic in any true sense.

READING COMPREHENSION: COOPERATIVE ENGLISH TEST

Cooperative Test Division   *Testing time:* 40–45 min.
Educational Testing Service
Range: Lower level (grades 9 to 12); higher level (grades 13 and 14)

The test yields four scores (1) vocabulary, (2) speed of comprehension, (3) level of comprehension, and (4) total. Speed of comprehension is a measure of rate of reading, but level of comprehension is probably less affected by speed than many comprehension measures. Reliability is satisfactory. Many studies have showed that the results of these tests correlate highly with measures of school achievement. The test undertakes to measure some of the more subtle aspects of reading comprehension such as understanding of mood and purpose. This is one of the best tests designed for high-school and college students.

TRAXLER HIGH SCHOOL READING TEST

Public School Publishing Company   *Testing time:* 50–55 min.
Range: Grades 10 to 12

This test gives five scores (1) reading rate, (2) comprehension, (3) main ideas, (4) total comprehension, and (5) total. Reliabilities are somewhat low for individual diagnosis using part scores but are adequate for group measurement. The emphasis is on comprehension.

TRAXLER SILENT READING TEST

Public School Publishing Company   *Testing time:* 50–55 min.
Range: Grades 7 to 10

Six scores are provided (1) reading rate, (2) story comprehension, (3) word meaning, (4) paragraph meaning, (5) total comprehension, and (6) total. The data on norms are inadequate. The data presented in the manual concerning validity, reliability, and equivalence of forms are insufficient. The good points are (1) comprehension is emphasized; (2) the use of sentences or phrases to test word meanings is probably a more meaningful device than use of words alone; and (3) the time allowed on each part is enough so that speed is not a factor at any of the grade levels.

Section D

ELEMENTARY-SCHOOL ACHIEVEMENT BATTERIES

CALIFORNIA ACHIEVEMENT TESTS, 1957 EDITION

California Test Bureau
Range: Lower Primary, grades 1 to 2 (90–110 min.)
   Upper Primary, grades 3 to 4 (125–145 min.)
   Elementary, grades 4 to 6 (145–165 min.)
   Junior High Level, grades 7 to 9 (180–190 min.)

These are, essentially, survey tests of reading, language, and arithmetic. Standardization procedures and norms for the revised edition are much better than were those for the 1950 edition. The tests attempt to measure a wide range of educational objectives but sampling of items is limited. The manuals have been improved markedly but they still suggest elaborate analysis of the very short subtests for diagnosis. The tests are *not* diagnostic. Reliabilities of total scores are satisfactory. The *Lower Primary* test appears to be much too difficult for grade one. At the other levels, the difficulty of the tests seem to be appropriate. The reading, language, and arithmetic tests may be bought separately or bound in a single booklet.

IOWA TESTS OF BASIC SKILLS

Houghton Mifflin Company   *Testing time:* 280–325 min.
Range: Grades 3 to 9

All the tests for all grades are bound in a single booklet and require the use of a separate answer sheet. The battery yields fifteen scores: vocabulary (one score); reading comprehension (one score); language (five scores); work-study skills (four scores); arithmetic skills (three scores); and total score. The battery emphasizes the measurement of functional skills; i.e., the general intellectual skills and abilities needed by the child if he is to make progress in school. Reliabilities of the subtests are adequate, and, of the total tests, are very high. Norms are provided for beginning, middle, and end-of-the-year testing. The manuals are excellent—particularly the ones for the teacher and for the administrator. This battery provides an excellent appraisal of significant educational outcomes.

METROPOLITAN ACHIEVEMENT TESTS, 1959 EDITION

Harcourt, Brace and World, Inc.
Range: *Primary I,* grade 1.5 to 2.5 (95–100 min.)
Primary II, grade 2 to 3.5 (105–115 min.)
Elementary, grades 3 to 4 (160–175 min.)
Intermediate, grades 5 to 6 (250–280 min.)
Advanced, grades 7 to 9 (260–290 min.)

All of the batteries measure vocabulary, reading comprehension and arithmetic skills. Word discrimination is tested in the three lowest levels, spelling begins in the *Primary II* battery and continues through the other levels. Language skills are added in the *Elementary* battery and continue through the other batteries. Language study skills, social-studies information, social-studies study skills, and science are parts of the intermediate and advanced batteries. The format of all the tests is attractive. Test content in the skills area appears to be adequate, and the test items, on the whole, are well written. Norming procedures are good. Reliabilities of total scores for all tests are adequate. The battery should continue to be useful and effective for a survey of achievement in the elementary and junior high schools.

SEQUENTIAL TESTS OF EDUCATIONAL PROGRESS (STEP)

Cooperative Test Division   *Testing time:* 450–500 min.
Educational Testing Service
Range: *Level 4,* grades 4 to 6
Level 3, grades 7 to 9
Level 2, grades 10 to 12
Level 1, grades 13 to 14

The battery is made up of seven tests (1) reading, (2) writing, (3) mathematics, (4) science, (5) social studies, (6) listening, and (7) essay. The essay test requires the student to write a composition on an assigned topic, whereas the writing test is a multiple-choice test of grammar and effectiveness of expression. Norms are presented in terms of percentile bands in order to prevent users from overestimating the precision of the scores. All tests except the essay test require 70-minute working periods. Manuals provided to help teachers interpret and use scores are very good. The tests are highly verbal (sometimes unnecessarily so) and some of the tests, particularly the essay test, are difficult to score. The score scale is not equivalent over the different levels. Reliabilities of Form A of the different tests are satisfactory, but no reliability data are provided for Form B. Normative data are not entirely adequate.

SRA ACHIEVEMENT SERIES

Science Research Associates
Range: Grades 2 to 4 (95–125 min.)
Grades 4 to 6 (355–445 min.)
Grades 6 to 9 (300–375 min.)

The battery provides for measures of vocabulary, reading comprehension, language, arithmetic, and, at the higher levels, study skills. The tests have rather high difficulty levels and are probably better suited for surveying the achievement of average or better-than-average students in each grade than for surveying the achievement of the below-average student. Reliabilities are satisfactory. The manuals and materials accompanying the test are excellent. Procedures for determining the content coverage of the test are excellent.

STANFORD ACHIEVEMENT TESTS

Harcourt, Brace and World, Inc.   *Testing time:* 80–215 min.
Range: Primary (grades 1.9 to 3.5); *Elementary* (grades 3.0 to 4.9); *Intermediate* (grades 5 to 6); *Advanced* (grades 7 to 9)

Reading, spelling, and arithmetic are included in all the batteries. Language is introduced in the elementary battery and is included in all batteries above that level. Social studies, science, and study skills are added in the intermediate and advanced batteries. The battery of tests was extensively revised in 1953. Reliabilities range from .81 to .92, based on a single grade computed by the split-half method, and compare favorably with those for other batteries. Partial batteries are available at the intermediate and advanced levels which include only the reading, language, arithmetic, and spelling tests. Separate tests are also available at these levels in arithmetic, reading, study skills, science, and social studies. The items are well constructed. The manual is excellent. One may find the content areas a little too factual in nature.

Section E

HIGH-SCHOOL ACHIEVEMENT BATTERIES

CALIFORNIA ACHIEVEMENT TESTS

California Test Bureau   *Testing time:* 160–180 min.
Range: Advanced Battery, grades 9 to 14

This is a continuation of the battery listed in Section D. The tests are probably adequate for a survey of achievement in reading, language, and arithmetic for high-school students but are not adequate for superior students above grade 12. Grade norms, which are given for this test, are inappropriate for the level for which the test is intended. Percentile norms are also given.

COOPERATIVE GENERAL ACHIEVEMENT TESTS, REVISED SERIES

Educational Testing Service   *Testing time:* 40–45 min.
Range: Grades 10 to 12 and college entrants   for each test
    Test I. Test of general proficiency in field of social studies.
    Test II. Test of general proficiency in field of natural science.
    Test III. Test of general proficiency in field of mathematics.

These tests attempt to measure, with varying degrees of success, general proficiency in each of the above fields. Each test has a section on vocabulary knowledge in its field and a second section that attempts to measure comprehension and different aspects of critical thinking. Part II of the social studies test is heavily weighted with the reading comprehension type of item. Part II of the science test is weighted in the direction of the physical sciences. Different forms of the test are not exactly comparable in the types of skills they test. The test probably has greatest value in placement of students or counseling students on their future course of study.

ESSENTIAL HIGH SCHOOL CONTENT BATTERY

Harcourt, Brace and World, Inc.   *Testing time:* 200–225 min.
Range: Grades 9 to 13

Four fields are covered in the battery: mathematics, science, social studies, and English. The items appear well constructed, the manual is very good, and the norms are very complete. The reliabilities of separate tests are somewhat low, ranging from .67 for science in grade 10 to .92 for mathematics in grade 11. These low reliabilities make the interpretation of differences between tests for individuals a somewhat hazardous procedure. This is probably the best battery available for high schools in general for measuring relatively immediate objectives of instruction. It is probably more suitable for measuring achievement in academic programs than in general or commercial programs.

THE IOWA TESTS OF EDUCATIONAL DEVELOPMENT

Science Research Associates   *Testing time:* 459–480 min.
Range: Grades 8.5 to 13.5

The battery yields ten scores: understanding of basic social concepts, general background in the natural sciences, correctness and appropriateness of expression, ability to do quantitative thinking, ability to interpret reading materials in the natural sciences, ability to interpret literary materials, general vocabulary, the subtotal of these 8 tests, and using sources of information. The manuals are very good. The test battery is designed to yield objective evidence of the degree to which concepts are understood rather than the degree to which isolated facts and operations are recalled. As a measure of certain broad aspects of the pupil's educational development, this battery is definitely superior.

SEQUENTIAL TESTS OF EDUCATIONAL PROGRESS (STEP)

Cooperative Test Division
Educational Testing Service
Range: Level 2, grades 10 to 12 (450–500 min.)
　　　　　Level 1, grades 13 to 14 (450–500 min.)

See discussion under Elementary School Batteries.

Section F

INTEREST INVENTORIES

BRAINARD OCCUPATIONAL PREFERENCE INVENTORY

Psychological Corporation   *Testing time:* 30 min.
Range: Grades 8 to 12; adults

The inventory covers six broad occupational fields (1) commercial, (2) mechanical, (3) professional, (4) esthetic, (5) scientific, and (6) personal service (for girls) or agriculture (for boys). Each occupational field is covered by twenty items which the respondent marks on a five-point scale ranging from "like very much" to "dislike very much." Data in the manual show that the instrument has moderate to low correlations with the *Kuder Preference Record—Vocational.* Scoring is simple. Evidence on validity is lacking.

KUDER PREFERENCE RECORD—OCCUPATIONAL

Science Research Associates   *Testing time:* 25–35 min.
Range: Grades 9 to 16; adults

The format and contents follow the same pattern as the *Kuder Preference Record—Vocational.* However, this form differs from the *Vocational* form in providing scores for 38 specific occupations plus a verification score. Kuder-Richardson reliabilities for the different occupational scales range from .42 to .82 with a median of .62. The long range stability of the interest scores has not been established. Validity data, especially predictive validity data, are not available. At the present time, the instrument is probably better suited for research purposes than for routine counseling and guidance work.

KUDER PREFERENCE RECORD—VOCATIONAL

Science Research Associates   *Testing time:* 30–50 min.
Range: Grade 9 and above

See discussion in text (pp. 326–328). Especially appropriate for use with high-school groups.

KUDER PREFERENCE RECORD—PERSONAL

Science Research Associates   *Testing time:* 40–45 min.
Range: Grades 9 to 16 and adults

Using the same pattern for items as the *Kuder Preference Record—Vocational,* this inventory appraises liking for five more aspects of life situations; being active in groups, being in familiar and stable situations, working with ideas, avoiding conflict, and directing others. The scores are fairly independent of each other and of those in the *Vocational* blank. The value of these scales for guidance purposes is less fully explored than that of the scales in the *Vocational* form.

OCCUPATIONAL INTEREST INVENTORY, 1956 REVISION

California Test Bureau   *Testing time:* 30–40 min.
Range: Intermediate (grades 7 to 16, adults); *Advanced* (grades 9 to 16, adults)

The inventory yields ten scores grouped in three categories (1) fields of interest (personal-social, natural, mechanical, business, the arts, the sciences), (2) types of interests (verbal, manipulative, and computational), and (3) level of interests. Normative and validity data are completely inadequate. Reliability data tend to indicate that instrument is *not* suitable for use with individuals. At the present time, it would probably be wise to consider the inventory to be an experimental instrument and not suitable for use in counseling individual students.

STRONG VOCATIONAL INTEREST BLANK FOR MEN, REVISED

Stanford University Press   *Testing time:* 40 min. (approx.)
Range: 17 years and over

See discussion in text (pp. 323–326). Particularly suitable for college groups.

STRONG VOCATIONAL INTEREST BLANK FOR WOMEN, REVISED

Stanford University Press   *Testing time:* 40 min. (approx.)
Range: 17 years and over

This inventory of 400 items is similar to the blank for men (see pp. 323–326). It yields scores for 24 occupations, chiefly at the professional level. It was developed in the same way as the *Vocational Interest Blank for Men,* but has been less thoroughly studied. The blank is particularly suitable for use with college groups.

STUDY OF VALUES, REVISED EDITION

Allport-Vernon-Lindsey   *Testing time:* 20–30 min.
Houghton Mifflin Company
Range: College students, adults

The *Study of Values* is supposed to measure the relative dominance of six basic interests or motives in personality: theoretical, economic, esthetic, social, political, and religious. The classification is based upon Sprangers *Types of Men*. The reliabilities of each of the subscales range from .73 to .90 computed by the split-half method and from .77 to .92 computed by the retest method after a 1-month interval. The inventory was standardized on a college population. The test is perhaps better suited for research purposes than for vocational guidance.

THURSTONE INTEREST SCHEDULE

Psychological Corporation   *Testing time:* 10 min.
Range: Grades 9 to 16, adults

This very brief inventory is based on choices between 100 pairs of occupations. High reliability is reported, despite the brevity of the instrument. It yields scores for 10 vocational fields: physical science, biological science, computational, business, executive, persuasive, linguistic, humanitarian, artistic, and musical. The test is based entirely on internal analysis, with no external evidence of validity. No norms are provided, each person's raw score profile being interpreted in terms of its high and low points. A quick and plausible but untested instrument for assessing occupational interests at the professional level.

Section G

ADJUSTMENT AND TEMPERAMENT INVENTORIES

ADJUSTMENT INVENTORY (BELL)

Stanford University Press   *Testing time:* 25 min.
Range: Grades 9 to 16, adults

The student and adult forms of this inventory provide an efficient means of getting self-appraisal in the areas of health, home, social, emotional, and vocational (adult form) adjustment. Scores are satisfactorily reliable and appear to discriminate extreme groups identified by experienced counselors. This inventory has been found useful to identify cases for more intensive study and to bring out leads to be explored in a counseling interview.

CALIFORNIA PSYCHOLOGICAL INVENTORY (CPI)

Consulting Psychologists Press   *Testing time:* 45–60 min.
Range: Age 13 and over

The instrument strongly resembles the *MMPI*. It contains 480 true-false items which yield eighteen scores including three control keys. Validity data are somewhat misleading. The individual profile obtained from the inventory is very elaborate and very difficult to interpret. The scales use items with value-loaded terms and tend to encourage the idea that there is one ideal personality pattern. At the present time, the *CPI* is judged to be less useful in counseling and guidance than other instruments such as the *Edwards Personal Preference Schedule* or the *Mooney Problem Check List*.

CALIFORNIA TEST OF PERSONALITY, 1953 REVISION

California Test Bureau   *Testing time:* 45–60 min.
Range: Kindergarten to grade 3; grades 4 to 8, 7 to 10, 9 to 16; adults

This is one of the few inventories that have forms for use in grades below junior high school. We have very real doubts about the validity and usefulness of any personality inventory in the elementary school. The "right" answers to the items on the test are obvious. Reliability data indicate that only the total score and its two components—social and personal—are stable enough to use. The use of the six subscores for diagnoses of the individual as suggested by the manual is *not* justified because these scores are too unreliable. Suggestions given in the manual for use of test results appear psychologically unsound. This test (as well as all other personality inventories) should not be indiscriminately administered to all students and should be used only by qualified counselors.

EDWARDS PERSONAL PREFERENCE SCHEDULE (EPPS)

Psychological Corporation   *Testing time:* 40–55 min.
Range: College level and adults

See text, p. 341. This is one of the better personality inventories in which an attempt has been made to control the social desirability values of the items. The manual is excellent. Further validation studies of the instrument are needed, but the instrument appears to have potential value in counseling and research.

GORDON PERSONAL PROFILE

Harcourt, Brace and World, Inc.   *Testing time:* 15–20 min.
Range: Grades 9 to 16, adults

A forced-choice type of inventory that yields five scores (1) ascendancy, (2) responsibility, (3) emotional stability, (4) sociability, and (5) total. The scores have satisfactory reliability and the four dimensions are relatively independent. As for most personality inventories, evidence of validity is meager and for this reason the inventory is not recommended for routine use in counseling and selection.

GUILFORD-ZIMMERMAN TEMPERAMENT SURVEY

Sheridan Supply Company   *Testing time:* 50 min.
Range: Grades 9 to 16 and adults

See text, pp. 333–351. One of the best inventories for describing aspects of normal personality. Experience is needed to determine whether the dimensions are of practical importance for personal or vocational counseling.

HESTON PERSONAL ADJUSTMENT INVENTORY

Harcourt, Brace and World, Inc.   *Testing time:* 40–50 min.
Range: Grades 9 to 16 and adults

A workmanlike inventory yielding scores for analytical thinking, sociability, home satisfaction, emotional stability, confidence, and personal relations. The last three are rather closely related. Could suitably be used as rough screening device, or provide leads for further investigation by interview.

MINNESOTA COUNSELING INVENTORY

Psychological Corporation   *Testing time:* 50 min.
Range: High-school level

The inventory yields nine scores: (1) family relationships, (2) social relationships, (3) emotional stability, (4) conformity, (5) adjustment to reality, (6) mood, (7) leadership, (8) validity, (9) questions. Reliabilities of the scales are generally satisfactory. Although nine scores are reported, some of the scores correlate with each other as high as the reliabilities of scales permit. Most of the evidence on validity is based on extreme groups and this tends to exaggerate the apparent validity.

MINNESOTA MULTIPHASIC PERSONALITY INVENTORY (MMPI)

Psychological Corporation   *Testing time:* 30–90 min.
Range: Age 16 and over

For discussion see text, pp. 337–341. This instrument is oriented towards abnormal rather than normal groups, and is designed to differentiate between them. There seems to be some doubt that it does this very effectively. It is rather lengthy to use as a screening test. However, the profile based on the separate scale scores provides a good deal of material for interpretation by the sophisticated counselor or clinical psychologist.

MOONEY PROBLEM CHECK LIST

Psychological Corporation   *Testing time:* 20–40 min.
Range: Forms for grades 7 to 9, 9 to 12, 13 to 16, and adults

These check lists provide a systematic coverage of problems often reported or judged significant at the different age levels. Though the items are grouped by areas (health and physical development; courtship, sex, and marriage; home and family; etc.) and a count can be made of items marked

in each area, emphasis is placed on using the individual responses as leads
and openings for an interview. This instrument does not claim to be a test
and the use proposed for it is the type that is probably most justifiable for
a self-report instrument.

PERSONALITY INVENTORY (BERNREUTER)

Stanford University Press   *Testing time:* 25 min.
Range: Grades 9 to 16, adults

This inventory has been widely used over the years, perhaps more widely
than its characteristics justify. It yields essentially two distinct scores—
one for neurotic tendency (introversion and submissiveness scores are
highly correlated with this) and one for self-sufficiency. Validity of the
resulting scores is questionable, but when administered with good rapport
it may be of some value in identifying cases for further study or in providing leads for an interview.

SRA JUNIOR INVENTORY

Science Research Associates   *Testing time:* 45 min.
Range: Grades 4 to 8

This is a needs and problems check list with items worded to suit children in grades four to eight. Three response boxes of different sizes are
provided for each item. The size of the box checked is supposed to indicate how strongly the respondent feels about the problem or need. The
fourth response choice, a circle, is used to indicate no problem. The use
of profiles and scores on a problems inventory is unwise, especially since
the items are made up partly of problems and partly of interests. Suggestions in the manual as to ways that test results may be used are very good.
If one ignores the profile and studies the individual items, a single student
or group of students has checked, the inventory can be useful to teachers
and other school personnel.

SRA YOUTH INVENTORY

Science Research Associates   *Testing time:* 30–40 min.
Range: Grades 7 to 12

The instrument resembles the *SRA Junior Inventory,* and the same comments apply to it.

THURSTONE TEMPERAMENT SCHEDULE

Science Research Associates   *Testing time:* 10–20 min.
Range: Grades 9 to 16 and adults

This is a brief and rather unreliable instrument yielding scores for seven
aspects of temperament: active, vigorous, impulsive, dominant, stable, so-
ciable, and reflective. Because of the relatively low reliabilities, the inventory is of doubtful value for counseling individuals, and its use should
probably be restricted to certain types of surveys and research studies.

Appendix IV

▼

Sources for Educational and Psychological Tests

Bureau of Publications
Teachers College, Columbia University
525 West 120th Street
New York 27, New York

Publishers and distributors of all levels of the *Gates Reading Tests* and of certain other educational testing materials.

California Test Bureau
5916 Hollywood Boulevard
Los Angeles 28, California

Primarily achievement and intelligence tests and interest and personality inventories for elementary and high school. Publishes the *California Achievement Tests*. Provides IBM services and technical advice on research problems. Publishes a series of Educational Bulletins (furnished free upon request) on the selection and use of tests and testing programs.

Educational Test Bureau
Educational Publishers, Inc.
720 Washington Avenue, S.E.
Minneapolis, Minnesota

Publishers of *Kuhlmann Tests of Mental Development, Minnesota Preschool Scale, Coordinated Scales of Attainment* (achievement test for elementary school), *Unit Scales of Attainment, Vineland Social Maturity Scale, Minnesota Rate of Manipulation* and *Spatial Relations Test*. Books for group guidance and developmental reading series, three reading books for retarded readers in elementary grades, and various kinds of school records.

Educational Testing Service
Cooperative Test Division
Princeton, New Jersey

Publishers of the *School and College Ability Tests, Sequential Tests of Educational Progress, Cooperative Achievement Tests* for high schools and colleges, the *Cooperative Inter-American Tests* (English and Spanish Editions), the *United States Armed Forces Institute Tests of General Educational Development*, the *College Entrance Board Examinations*, and *Graduate Record Examinations*. Sponsors two national testing programs, one for high schools and one for colleges.

Maintains an Evaluation and Advisory Service. Except for unusual requests the service is free. This service will provide assistance in selecting tests, setting up test programs, and using test results. Not limited to tests published by ETS. The company will also supply test-scoring service at cost.

Harcourt, Brace and World, Inc.
750 Third Avenue
New York 17, New York

Achievement batteries and tests for elementary and high school—best known are *Metropolitan Achievement Battery, Stanford Achievement Test;* group intelligence tests—*Otis, Pintner, Terman-McNemar; Metropolitan Readiness Test* and *Stevens Reading Readiness Test;* large number of reading tests—*Durrell-Sullivan Reading Capacity and Achievement Tests, Iowa Silent Reading Tests.* Very few personality inventories (*Heston*).

Division of Test Research and Service provides help in selecting and using tests and in interpreting test results.

Has a series of articles called *Test Service Notebook* and *Test Service Bulletins* which present briefly results secured from the use of tests, developments in the field, planning testing programs, etc.

Houghton Mifflin Company
2 Park Street
Boston 7, Massachusetts

Publishers of *Iowa Tests of Basic Skills, Lorge-Thorndike Intelligence Tests, Nelson-Denny Reading Test, Henmon-Nelson Tests of Mental Ability,* and other educational achievement, aptitude, and interest tests. Provides scoring and reporting services for *Iowa Tests of Basic Skills* and the *Lorge-Thorndike Intelligence Tests.* Also publishes *Revised Stanford-Binet Intelligence Scale* and numerous books on testing.

Psychological Corporation
304 East 45th Street
New York 17, New York

Publishers of *Differential Aptitude Tests, Wechsler-Bellevue Intelligence Scale, Wechsler Intelligence Scale for Children, Porteus Mazes, Arthur Point Scale of Performance Tests, Gesell Developmental Schedule, MMPI,* and *Mooney Problem Check List.* Distributors of *Strong Vocational Interest Blank, Rorschach, Essential High School Content Battery, Evaluation and Adjustment Series, Metropolitan Achievement Tests, Stanford Achievement Tests, Gates Reading Tests, Durrell Analysis of Reading Difficulties, Kuhlmann-Anderson Intelligence Tests, Henman-Nelson Tests of Mental Ability, Otis Mental Ability Tests,* and *Pintner General Ability Tests.*

Wide variety of clinical tests, tests for industrial uses, and group tests of aptitude and personality. Distributor and publisher of many texts in clinical, vocational, and industrial psychology. Publishes an excellent series of *Test Service Bulletins*, supplied without charge.

Composed of four divisions:

1. Test Division: handles sales of tests, advisory services available for test users, and statistical services.
2. Marketing and Social Research Division.
3. Industrial Division.
4. Professional Examinations Division: provides testing services for purposes of counseling, admission, scholarship, and personnel selection to public and private school systems, colleges, universities, professional schools, professional certification boards and other agencies. Has nationwide testing programs for evaluation of applicants to schools of nursing, practical nursing, medicine, dental hygiene, pharmacy, and veterinary medicine. Handles all test-scoring services.

Public School Publishing Company
(Bobbs-Merrill Company)
345 Calhoun Street
Cincinnati 19, Ohio

Publishes achievement tests and general intelligence tests for use in elementary, junior high, and senior high schools. Also publishes or distributes a number of books on educational topics.

Science Research Associates, Inc.
57 West Grand Avenue
Chicago 10, Illinois

Publishers of *SRA Primary Mental Abilities, Chicago Tests of Primary Mental Abilities, Army General Classification Test, Ohio State University Psychological Test, Kuder Preference Records, SRA Youth Inventories, Iowa Every-Pupil Tests, Iowa Tests of Educational Development,* various tests of vocational aptitudes and skills, *SRA Guidance Publications* (subscriptions, published monthly; subscribers receive bonus items and are entitled to the use of SRA Research Service), *Guidance Filmstrips, Occupational Information Materials,* elementary school textbooks, booklets and texts for guidance classes in high schools, reading improvement materials, and professional guidance publications.

Sheridan Supply Company
Post Office Box 837
Beverly Hills, California

Publishers of the *Guilford-Zimmerman Aptitude Survey, Creativity Tests, Guilford-Zimmerman Temperament Survey,* and other Guilford-Martin-Zimmerman tests and inventories.

C. H. Stoelting Company
424 North Homan Avenue
Chicago 24, Illinois

Motor skill and coordination tests (especially those requiring special equipment), formboard space relations tests, and general intelligence tests for high school, college, and elementary school (group and individual); clinical tests of mental deterioration, concept formation, and organic brain damage; preschool tests of intelligence and reading readiness tests; clerical aptitude and clerical skill tests; mechanical aptitude tests; Horn, Knauber, and Meier art tests; musical aptitude tests; reading and achievement tests for elementary and high schools. Handles *Cooperative Tests, Iowa Placement Examinations, Metropolitan, Stanford, Iowa Every-Pupil Tests of Basic Skills, Strong Vocational Interest Blank, Bell Adjustment Inventory, Bernreuter Personality Inventory, Vineland Social Maturity Scale, Rorschach, TAT, CAT,* and *Symonds Picture Story Test.*

Index